THE OXFORD HANDBOOK OF

HOSEA

THE OXFORD HANDBOOK OF

HOSEA

Edited by
BRAD E. KELLE

OXFORD
UNIVERSITY PRESS

Oxford University Press is a department of the University of Oxford. It furthers
the University's objective of excellence in research, scholarship, and education
by publishing worldwide. Oxford is a registered trade mark of Oxford University
Press in the UK and certain other countries.

Published in the United States of America by Oxford University Press
198 Madison Avenue, New York, NY 10016, United States of America.

© Oxford University Press 2024

All rights reserved. No part of this publication may be reproduced, stored in
a retrieval system, or transmitted, in any form or by any means, without the
prior permission in writing of Oxford University Press, or as expressly permitted
by law, by license, or under terms agreed with the appropriate reproduction
rights organization. Inquiries concerning reproduction outside the scope of the
above should be sent to the Rights Department, Oxford University Press, at the
address above.

You must not circulate this work in any other form
and you must impose this same condition on any acquirer.

CIP data is on file at the Library of Congress

ISBN 978-0-19-763959-7

DOI: 10.1093/oxfordhb/9780197639597.001.0001

Printed by Integrated Books International, United States of America

For Gomer (and the children)

Contents

Acknowledgments	xi
List of Abbreviations	xiii
List of Contributors	xvii

Introduction	1
Brad E. Kelle	

1. Does (and Should) Hosea Matter Still?	7
Carol J. Dempsey, OP	

PART I: HISTORY, TEXT, AND COMPOSITION

2. The Book of Hosea and the History of Eighth-Century BCE Israel	23
Shuichi Hasegawa	

3. Assyria and Its Image in Hosea	37
Shawn Zelig Aster	

4. Hosea the "Historical Prophet" of the Eighth Century BCE, Hosea the Remembered Prophet of Yehudite Literati, and the Book of Hosea	54
Ehud Ben Zvi and Ian D. Wilson	

5. The Book of Hosea and Israelite Religion in the Eighth Century BCE	65
Lena-Sofia Tiemeyer	

6. The Book of Hosea and the Socioeconomic Conditions of Eighth-Century BCE Israel	81
Davis Hankins	

viii CONTENTS

7. Transformation and Reinterpretation in the Composition and
Redaction of Hosea 96
SUSANNE RUDNIG-ZELT

8. The Book of Hosea and Northern/Israelian Hebrew 110
NA'AMA PAT-EL

9. Texts and Versions of the Book of Hosea 124
ERIC J. TULLY

10. Hosea in the Book of the Twelve 140
MARK LEUCHTER

PART II: KEY TEXTS: ESTABLISHED AND EMERGING PERSPECTIVES

11. Hosea 1–3, the Marriage Metaphor, and the Ties That Bind 159
AMY KALMANOFSKY

12. Hosea 5:8–6:6, Alt's Hypothesis, and New Possibilities 173
MARVIN A. SWEENEY

13. Hosea 7–8 and the Critique of Kings, Politics, and Power 185
JERRY HWANG

14. Hosea 11 and Metaphors of Identity, Relationship, and
Core Values in Contexts of Trauma 198
JENNIFER M. MATHENY

15. Hosea 12–13 and Prophetic Composition, Rhetoric,
and Recollection 211
JOHN GOLDINGAY

PART III: THEOLOGICAL AND LITERARY ELEMENTS, THEMES, AND MOTIFS

16. Metaphors in the Book of Hosea 229
MASON D. LANCASTER

17. Intertextuality and Traditions in the Book of Hosea 246
GÖRAN EIDEVALL

18.	God's Character in the Book of Hosea Bo H. Lim	261
19.	Kingship and Political Power in the Book of Hosea Heath D. Dewrell	274
20.	Sin and Punishment in the Book of Hosea Joshua N. Moon	286
21.	Repentance in the Book of Hosea Mark J. Boda	303
22.	Gender and Sexual Violence in Hosea Kirsi Cobb	317

PART IV: INTERPRETIVE THEORIES AND APPROACHES

23.	Hosea in Feminist and Womanist Interpretation Vanessa Lovelace	337
24.	Masculinity Studies and Hosea Susan E. Haddox	351
25.	Queer Theory and Hosea Jennifer J. Williams	364
26.	Postcolonialism as a Methodological Approach to Hosea Jeremiah W. Cataldo	380
27.	Prolegomena to the Ecological Interpretation of Hosea Peter Trudinger	396

PART V: RECEPTION

28.	Hosea in Rabbinic Literature Devorah Schoenfeld	411
29.	Hosea in the New Testament Steve Moyise	426
30.	Hosea in Popular Culture Emily O. Gravett	439

31. The Ghost of Hosea in African American Interpretation 452
   AARON D. DORSEY

32. Hosea in Asia-Centric Interpretation 468
   BARBARA M. LEUNG LAI

Ancient Sources Index 483
Author Index 499

Acknowledgments

At the end of the long process that a collaborative volume entails, I am grateful for the help and support I have received along the way, especially from the staff of Oxford University Press and my friend and editor Steve Wiggins. Of course my deepest debts go to the contributors for their fine work and their patience during the slow process of bringing this large project to completion. I am especially grateful for the contributors who struck out into new territory for the interpretation of Hosea, bringing to bear, in some cases for the first time in a sustained way, emerging methods and perspectives at home more comfortably with other biblical texts but that deserve a place in the conversation about Hosea. My thanks are also due to several close friends and scholars whose conversations sustained my thinking about (and work on!) this volume. Among these are especially Jenny Matheny, Mason Lancaster, Stephanie Smith Matthews, and Göran Eidevall. I am also grateful to my colleagues and students in the School of Theology and Christian Ministry at Point Loma Nazarene University, who tolerated, indulged, and encouraged my work on this volume. And as always, I appreciate the patience and support of my family, especially my now twenty-four-year-old son, Grayson, who embarked on his own new adventure of graduate school and marriage (welcome Callie!) during the life cycle of this project.

—Brad E. Kelle,
Point Loma Nazarene University,
San Diego, CA

ABBREVIATIONS

ÄAT	Ägypten und Alten Testament
AB	Anchor Bible
ABD	*Anchor Bible Dictionary*. Edited by David Noel Freedman. 6 vols. New York: Doubleday, 1992.
AJBI	*Annual of the Japanese Biblical Institute*
ANET	*Ancient Near Eastern Texts Relating to the Old Testament*. Edited by J. B. Pritchard. 3rd ed. Princeton, 1969.
AOAT	Alter Orient und Altes Testament
AOTC	Abingdon Old Testament Commentaries
Aq	Aquila
ATD	Das Alte Testamente Deutsch
BASOR	*Bulletin of the American Schools of Oriental Research*
BBR	Bulletin for Biblical Research
BDB	Brown, F., S. R. Driver, and C. A. Briggs. *A Hebrew and English Lexicon of the Old Testament*. Oxford, 1907.
BETL	Bibliotheca Ephemeridum Theologicarum Lovaniensium
BHS	*Biblia Hebraica Stuttgartensia*
BHT	Beiträge zur historischen Theologie
Bib	*Biblica*
BibInt	*Biblical Interpretation*
BIS	Biblical Interpretation Series
BJS	Brown Judaic Studies
BKAT	Biblischer Kommentar, Altes Testament
BN	*Biblische Notizen*
BRB	Bulletin for Biblical Research
BWANT	Beiträge zur Wissenschaft vom Alten (und Neuen) Testament
BZ	*Biblische Zeitschrift*
BZAW	Beihefte zur Zeitschrift für die alttestamentliche Wissenschaft
CAH	*The Cambridge Ancient History*

xiv ABBREVIATIONS

CBQ	*Catholic Biblical Quarterly*
CBQMS	Catholic Biblical Quarterly Monograph Series
CBR	*Currents in Biblical Research*
ConBOT	Coniectanea Biblica: Old Testament Series
COS	Hallo, William W., ed. *Canonical Compositions from the Biblical World.* Vol. 1 of *The Context of Scripture.* Leiden: E. J. Brill, 1997.
CTM	*Concordia Theological Monthly*
EBR	*Encyclopedia of the Bible and Its Reception*
FAT	Forschungen zum Alten Testament
FCB	Feminist Companion to the Bible
FOTL	The Forms of the Old Testament Literature
FRLANT	Forschungen zur Religion und Literatur des Alten und Neuen Testaments
GCT	Gender, Culture, Theory
GKC	*Gesenius' Hebrew Grammar.* Edited by E. Kautzsch. Translated by A. E. Cowley. 2nd. ed. Oxford, 1910.
HALOT	Koehler, L., W. Baumgartner, and J. J. Stamm, *The Hebrew and Aramaic Lexicon of the Old Testament.* Translated and edited under the supervision of M. E. J. Richardson. 4 vols. Leiden, 1994–1999.
HBM	Hebrew Bible Monographs
HBT	*Horizons in Biblical Theology*
HSM	Harvard Semitic Monographs
HTR	*Harvard Theological Review*
ICC	International Critical Commentary
IEJ	*Israel Exploration Journal*
IJST	*International Journal of Systematic Theology*
IOS	*Israel Oriental Society*
JAOS	*Journal of the American Oriental Society*
JBL	*Journal of Biblical Literature*
JNES	*Journal of Near Eastern Studies*
JNSL	*Journal of Northwest Semitic Languages*
JRS Supplement Series	Journal of Religion and Society Supplement Series
JSJ	*Journal for the Study of Judaism in the Persian, Hellenistic, and Roman Periods*
JSOT	*Journal for the Study of the Old Testament*
JSOTSup	Journal for the Study of the Old Testament Supplement Series

JTS	*Journal of Theological Studies*
KAT	Kommentar zum Alten Testament
LHBOTS	Library of Hebrew Bible/Old Testament Studies
LNTS	The Library of New Testament Studies
LXX	Septuagint
MT	Masoretic Text
NCB	New Century Bible
NICNT	New International Commentary on the New Testament
NICOT	New International Commentary on the Old Testament
NIDOTTE	*New International Dictionary of Old Testament Theology and Exegesis.* Edited by Willem A. VanGemeren. 5 vols. Grand Rapids: Zondervan, 1997.
NIGTC	New International Greek Testament Commentary
NKZ	*Neue kirchliche Zeitschrift*
NovTSup	Novum Testamentum Supplements
OBO	Orbis Biblicus et Orientalis
OBT	Overtures to Biblical Theology
OG	Old Greek
OTE	*Old Testament Essays*
OTL	Old Testament Library
OTM	Old Testament Monographs
OtSt	Oudtestamentische Studiën
ResQ	*Restoration Quarterly*
RGG	*Religion in Geschichte und Gegenwart.* Edited by Hans Dieter Betz. 4th ed. Tübingen: Mohr Siebeck, 1998-2007.
RIMA	The Royal Inscriptions of Mesopotamia, Assyrian Periods
RINAP	Royal Inscriptions of the Neo-Assyrian Period
RvwExp	*Review and Expositor*
SAA	State Archives of Assyria
SAAS	State Archives of Assyria Studies
SBAB	Stuttgarter biblische Aufsatzbände
SBLAB	SBL Academia Biblica
SBLABS	SBL Archaeology and Biblical Studies
SBLAIL	SBL Ancient Israel and Its Literature
SBLANEM	SBL Ancient Near Eastern Monographs
SBLDS	SBL Dissertation Series
SBLMS	SBL Monograph Series

SBLSymS	SBL Symposium Series
SEÅ	*Svensk exegetisk årsbok*
SEL	*Studi epigrafici e linguistici sul Vicino Oriente antico*
SJOT	*Scandinavian Journal of the Old Testament*
SNTU	*Studien zum Neuen Testament und seiner Umwelt*
StBibLit	Studies in Biblical Literature
SJT	*Scottish Journal of Theology*
TA	*Tel Aviv*
Tg	Targum
THOTC	Two Horizons Old Testament Commentary
TLZ	*Theologische Literaturzeitung*
TOTC	Tyndale Old Testament Commentaries
TRE	*Theologische Realenzylopädie*. Edited by Gerhard Krause and Gerhard Müller. Berlin: de Gruyter, 1977–.
TynBul	*Tyndale Bulletin*
UBL	Ugaritisch-biblische Literatur
UBS[5]	*The Greek New Testament*, United Bible Societies, 5th ed.
Vg	Vulgate
VT	*Vetus Testamentum*
VTSup	Supplements to Vetus Testamentum
WAW	Writings from the Ancient World
WBC	Word Biblical Commentary
WMANT	Wissenschaftliche Monographien zum Alten und Neuen Testament
WUNT	Wissenschaftliche Untersuchungen zum Neuen Testament
ZAW	*Zeitschrift für die alttestamentliche Wissenschaft*
ZTK	*Zeitschrift für die Theologie und Kirche*

CONTRIBUTORS

Shawn Zelig Aster Associate Professor in the Martin (Szusz) Department of Land of Israel Studies and Archaeology and the Zalman Shamir Bible Department at Bar-Ilan University

Mark J. Boda Professor of Old Testament at McMaster Divinity College, Hamilton, Ontario, Canada

Jeremiah W. Cataldo Professor of History in the Frederik Meijer Honors College at Grand Valley State University

Kirsi Cobb Lecturer in Biblical Studies at Cliff College and the Co-founder/Director of the Bible, Gender, and Church Research Centre

Carol J. Dempsey, OP Professor of Theology (Biblical Studies) at the University of Portland

Heath D. Dewrell Assistant Professor in the Department of Middle Eastern Studies at the University of Texas at Austin

Aaron D. Dorsey PhD Student in Hebrew Bible at Garrett Evangelical Theological Seminary

Göran Eidevall Professor of Hebrew Bible at Uppsala University, Sweden

John Goldingay Senior Professor of Old Testament at Fuller Theological Seminary

Emily O. Gravett Associate Professor of Religion and Assistant Director in the Center for Faculty Innovation at James Madison University

Susan E. Haddox Professor of Religious Studies at the University of Mount Union

Davis Hankins Associate Professor of Religious Studies at Appalachian State University

Shuichi Hasegawa Professor of Hebrew Bible at Rikkyo University

Jerry Hwang Affiliate Research Professor of Advanced Studies at Singapore Bible College

Amy Kalmanofsky Blanche and Romie Shapiro Professor of Bible and Dean of Graduate and Undergraduate Studies at Jewish Theological Seminary

Brad E. Kelle Professor of Old Testament and Hebrew and Director of the MA in Christian Ministry Program at Point Loma Nazarene University

Mason D. Lancaster Adjunct Professor of Old Testament at Point Loma Nazarene University and Pacific Theological Seminary

Mark Leuchter Professor of Hebrew Bible and Ancient Judaism at Temple University

Barbara M. Leung Lai Research Professor of Old Testament at Tyndale University

Bo H. Lim Professor of Old Testament at Seattle Pacific University

Vanessa Lovelace Associate Dean and Associate Professor of Hebrew Bible/Old Testament at Lancaster Theological Seminary

Jennifer M. Matheny Associate Professor of Christian Scriptures at Baylor University's George W. Truett Theological Seminary

Joshua N. Moon Fellows Tutor at Anselm House, Minneapolis, Minnesota

Steve Moyise Former Professor of New Testament at the University of Chichester, United Kingdom

Na'ama Pat-El Professor of Semitic Linguistics at the University of Texas at Austin

Susanne Rudnig-Zelt, apl. Professor for Old Testament and Hebrew Teacher at Christian-Albrechts-Universität Kiel

Devorah Schoenfeld Associate Professor of Theology at Loyola University Chicago

Marvin A. Sweeney Professor of Hebrew Bible at Claremont School of Theology

Lena-Sofia Tiemeyer Professor in Old Testament Exegesis, ALT School of Theology, Sweden, and Research Associate at the Department of Old Testament and Hebrew Scripture, Faculty of Theology and Religion, University of Pretoria, South Africa

Peter Trudinger Independent Scholar in Adelaide, South Australia

Eric J. Tully Professor of Old Testament and Semitic Languages and Director of the PhD (Theological Studies) at Trinity Evangelical Divinity School

Jennifer J. Williams Associate Professor of Religious Studies at Linfield University

Ian D. Wilson Associate Professor of Religious Studies at the University of Alberta, Augustana Campus

Ehud Ben Zvi Professor Emeritus of History at the University of Alberta

INTRODUCTION

BRAD E. KELLE

As I write this introduction in the early summer of 2023, the study of the book of Hosea within Hebrew Bible scholarship is undergoing something of a renaissance. Scholarship in the mid-1970s and 1980s yielded a cluster of classic and field-defining commentaries on Hosea in standard series that shaped the critical discussion for subsequent eras (and built on several commentaries that appeared in the 1960s; e.g., Mays 1969). I think here especially of Hans Walter Wolff's Hermeneia volume (1974; published originally in German in 1965), Francis I. Andersen and David Noel Freedman's work in The Anchor Bible series (1980), Jörg Jeremias's *Der Prophet Hosea* (1983), Douglas Stuart's contribution to the Word Biblical Commentary (1987), and James Limburg's commentary in the Interpretation series (1988). Beginning a decade or so later, the mid-1990s through the early 2010s saw other established series issue Hosea commentaries (e.g., Yee 1996; Macintosh 1997; Sweeney 2000; Ben Zvi 2005; Simundson 2005; Fretheim 2010; Dearman 2010). Other commentaries have appeared since that time (e.g., Green 2014; Gruber 2017; Moon 2018), and, of course, there has been a steady flow of scholarly articles and monographs on specific elements of Hosea.

Now, in the early years of the 2020s, no fewer than eight new commentaries on Hosea are in production, several of which constitute the reissuing of volumes in established series, and many of which are, happily, being written by contributors to this Handbook. I am writing the reissued commentary on Hosea for the Old Testament Library; Göran Eidevall for the reissued Anchor Bible; and Heath Dewrell for the reissued Interpretation—to name a few. The commentaries-to-be fit into a broad range of series beyond the established ones, however, and represent a variety of interpretive interests such as the feminist-critical focus of the Wisdom Commentary series (with the Hosea volume being coauthored by Cheryl A. Kirk-Duggan and Valerie Bridgeman). These in-progress commentaries will join several others that have been released just since 2020 (Routledge 2020; Hwang 2021; Goldingay 2021).

Given the burgeoning interest in the book of Hosea within current biblical scholarship, the time seemed right to consider what the study of Hosea looks like at the present moment—generally and specifically, for better or worse, with its emphases, benefits, accomplishments, oversights, and shortfalls. Indeed, that is one of the goals of this Handbook: to provide a judiciously representative snapshot of the look and feel of Hosea scholarship near the beginning of the third decade of the 2000s. But how best to provide that snapshot? Certainly, the book of Hosea presents numerous challenges that fascinate, perplex, and even trouble its readers. Alongside the (more or less) typical prophetic judgment speeches, featuring the expected course of doom and violence (mixed with some promises and hope), there are all those metaphors—most of them negative, casting imagery from family, agriculture, nature, animals, and more as symbols of a people's failure and a deity's (often harsh) response. And then there are those metaphors of marriage and children in chs. 1–3, with one-sided portrayals, salacious accusations, ominous names, threats, violence, and perhaps reconciliation. What about the rough textual terrain that raises questions about compositional growth or the connections and disconnections with larger compositions such as the Book of the Twelve? With Hosea, there is that which seems clear, but much that remains opaque and resists straightforward words of address. Interpreters must attend to long-established historical- and literary-critical perspectives that engage the book against its ancient Israelite (and ancient Near Eastern) context. Yet they surely must also pay attention to new concerns, perspectives, and questions generated by other modes of critical theory and by contemporary cultural moments and diverse readers, especially questions related to gender, violence, and sexuality. The essays in this Handbook represent many of these moves. On the whole, they testify that scholarship on Hosea seeks to encounter more than to explain, and to engage more than to exposit—for these are the things that Hosea's complexity demands.

So, again, how best to provide a snapshot of the study of the book of Hosea in our present moment? The thirty-two essays in this collection offer a diversity of persons, approaches, and conclusions that meets this goal in a way that is necessary and crucial in the current cultural and scholarly moment. A multiauthored collection can do things that a single scholarly monograph or commentary cannot. A handbook, by its very nature, is responsive to the epistemologies, convictions, and practices that might shape scholarly work on Hosea (and hopefully all biblical books) today, especially those forwarded by feminist, queer, postcolonial, and other approaches that call for a type of scholarship that endorses collaboration and decenters power.[1] I believe this Handbook (and similar volumes in this series and others) models and fosters a way of doing scholarship that seeks the just and responsible construction and engagement of knowledge— a way that moves toward diversity, cooperation, and open-endedness, while at the same time resisting (perhaps prophetically?) modes of scholarship that engage in authoritarianism, hegemony, and the monolithic erasure of other voices and perspectives.

Along these lines, then, this Handbook differs from single-authored commentaries and monographs which often use a "hegemonic summarizing approach to scholarly debate that allows little room for contestatory positions or even congenial insights in the voices of others" (Sharp 2022: 45). By contrast, here the reader will find lively scholarly exchanges among different essays on several interpretive topics for Hosea, rather than a single authoritative reading of each issue. Although the reader of this volume is the one who must place the essays and perspectives into explicit dialogue, different takes are present among the authors—sometimes explicitly so. For this reason, even if also due to the reality of a large reference work with so many different contributors, some degree of overlap exists (perhaps unavoidably) among the essays—present, at least partly, by design. One will notice, for example, that several essays touch on compositional theories and debates regarding the book of Hosea's text and origins, with several others appraising in different ways the vexed relationship of Hosea to historical realities and contexts. The instances of overlap stand as a matter of scholarly integrity: letting each contributor have her or his say. Yet I also deemed it helpful epistemologically, pedagogically, and interpretively. The end-result is a handbook that contains a polyphonic, largely unfinalized conversation about the book of Hosea.

Furthermore, this collection is able to move beyond the space limits, series conformity, and other content constraints that often bind commentaries to a narrow scope. The essays here permit engagement with a range of feminist, womanist, queer, ethnic, postcolonial, and other considerations—at least "soundings" in them—and sometimes with more than one engagement (note, for instance, the multiple essays examining gender construction and violence in Hosea). This freedom also allows room for multifaceted explorations of Hosea's reception in contexts as varied as ancient Jewish and Christian writings, African American and Asia-centric contexts, and modern popular culture's music, novels, and movies. Throughout the work, the kind of scholarship represented in the Handbook makes space for the contributors' self-consciousness and self-disclosure of their own commitments that shape interpretation. Hence, for example, one finds an essay on queer readings of Hosea that considers the experiences of modern-day sex workers and sexual violence victims for the interpretation and impact of the book's language and imagery.

With these broader characteristics and possibilities in mind, the present Handbook offers a picture of current Hosea scholarship—though not comprehensively. To do more than something representative of the state of research would be impossible. Even as a single biblical book, Hosea is too rich, with the history of its interpretation too vast, to attempt such a thing. The current volume pursues an *essential*, not exhaustive approach. Toward that end, the essays gathered here make contact with the following crucial nodes represented by the volume's five-part arrangement:

- History, Text, and Composition
- Key Texts: Established and Emerging Perspectives
- Theological and Literary Elements, Themes, and Motifs
- Interpretive Theories and Approaches
- Reception

The sections are somewhat artificial. Certainly, there is overlap—some essays in one section could easily be in another, or the same essay could, at times, fit comfortably in two different locations. Nonetheless, and while far from comprehensive, it is hoped that these nodes permit thorough and representative coverage of most, through certainly not all, of what should be included in a handbook such as this one.

This volume, like so many others these days, will likely be accessed by many readers in electronic form. Electronic formats permit certain types of metadata that print versions do not. That includes abstracts and key words for search purposes. Given these factors, I will not overview each of the essays in this introduction. There are a large number of essays, after all, and interested readers will no doubt find what they are looking for without a brief sentence or two from the editor. However, some technical matters deserve mention. Although great editorial care was taken during the review process, the reader will note some inconsistencies—a few of which, at least, are present by design. I have not, for instance, regularized all translations, whether of biblical or nonbiblical texts. Similarly, while I have attempted to note versification differences across Hebrew, Greek, and English editions of the book of Hosea, I have not done so exhaustively or consistently with regard to other biblical texts. I have not always regularized the spelling of the divine name "Yhwh," though my preference was to devocalize it. In all of these cases—and similar ones—I have often deferred to the individual preferences of the contributors. Additionally, in the case of some essays, original scripts were required; in many others, I have opted for transliteration so as to make the essays accessible to those who do not read the original languages. Again, these inconsistencies are often by design; at the least they are not naïve. I hope that whatever discomfort readers may experience upon encountering such discrepancies will pale in comparison to the insight afforded by the contributions contained herein.

I would like to conclude by offering a bit more insight into the volume's design and what I have learned in the process of editing the collection. First, with reference to design, in addition to the five nodes already mentioned above, the contributors have written their essays with attention to two guiding questions: "What does the topic/area/issue you are writing on have to do with the book of Hosea?" and "How does this topic/area/issue help readers better interpret the book of Hosea?" Answering the first question would seem the easier of the two, but the inclusion of the second—indeed the combination of the two questions together—makes, I believe, each essay of maximum benefit to readers who are not interested solely in information but also in interpretation.

Second, the editorial process has revealed several trends in the current study of the book of Hosea. Alert readers will observe these trends for themselves—they are evident, I believe, already in the Table of Contents—but the trends are especially apparent at the larger, book level, and few indeed are the readers who read reference works cover to cover. Since the editorial task requires reading (and rereading), it is worth highlighting some of the trends and themes that I noticed in editing the Handbook.

The most important trend or theme, perhaps unsurprisingly given my general comments above, is diversity. As I mentioned previously, this theme is felt on many levels and worked out in different ways throughout the collection. First, older, long-dominant ideas about historical-critical, history of religion, redactional, and compositional theories have yielded their grip on Hosea scholarship in such a way that a diversity of approaches now marks the field. Hence, questions that had previously been governed, if not constrained, by those theories may now be investigated anew and with energy. Assessments of rhetorical function, analyses of literary aspects and metaphor, considerations of gender, including masculinity, attention to violence and ecology, and so forth are all fair game—in a way that they have not been in previous generations of scholarship. So it is that readers will find plenty of discussion of traditional interpretive issues and theories concerning Hosea and newer updates to the same, and of the textual traditions themselves, which give rise to new compositional analyses; but readers will also find approaches that move in entirely different ways altogether, whether those are by attending to synchronic, literary, theoretical, or reception aspects of the text at hand.

In keeping with my previous description of the kind of scholarship represented by a handbook such as this, another way diversity is felt is in how any one particular topic or theme is engaged. So, for example, essays under "History, Text, and Composition" (Part I) run the gamut from the thorny text-critical issues of Hosea and its manuscript traditions to the nature of the social, political, and imperial world of the Iron Age and the book's vexed relationship to that world to questions concerning Hosea's compositional growth and connections to larger textual entities such as the Book of the Twelve. Similarly, "Key Texts" (Part II) features five of the central texts in the interpretation of Hosea approached by scholars who use differing methodologies and place the texts into dialogue with a diversity of perspectives including feminist criticism, compositional history, discourse analysis, and trauma theory. The topics covered under "Theological and Literary Elements, Themes, and Motifs" (Part III) range widely so as to include metaphors, intertexuality, political theory, theologies of sin and repentance, violence and sexuality studies—usually with heavy interdisciplinary engagement. So also with "Interpretive Theories and Approaches" (Part IV). Here newer theoretical approaches take center stage, with essays employing feminist, womanist, and masculinity studies, queer theory, postcolonialism, and ecological hermeneutics. On the face of it, the essays that go under the rubric "Reception" (Part V) may seem more pro forma, titled, as all but one are (and that one intentionally so), "Hosea in X." While these titles may be formulaic, here again the essays are quite diverse in representing a panoply of options when it comes to gathering, assessing, and interpreting the manifold contexts and ways the book of Hosea has been received over the centuries and now.

Finally, I would be remiss if I did not observe that the diversity of the present collection is in large measure the happy result of the diversity of the contributors themselves—again hopefully a model for what biblical scholarship can and should look like today. Readers will find here a mixture of emerging and established scholars, of differing religious background (and levels of adherence), and of different gender and ethnicity. The authors of the essays that follow come from teaching colleges to "R1" research universities; some teach only undergraduates, others teach only graduate students; some teach in confessional institutions that train students for ministry of various kinds, while others teach exclusively in secular institutions. I hope readers will not only benefit but delight in the range of persons and perspectives represented as I have.

NOTE

1. My comments on this topic are inspired by Carolyn Sharp's discussion in her recent commentary on Jer. 26-52 (Sharp 2022: 13–45).

REFERENCES

Andersen, Francis I., and David Noel Freedman. 1980. *Hosea*. AB 24. Garden City, NY: Doubleday.

Ben Zvi, Ehud. 2005. *Hosea*. FOTL 21a. Grand Rapids: Eerdmans.

Dearman, J. Andrew. 2010. *The Book of Hosea*. NICOT. Grand Rapids: Eerdmans.

Fretheim, Terence E. 2010. *Reading Hosea-Micah: A Literary and Theological Commentary*. Nashville: Abingdon.

Goldingay, John. 2021. *Hosea-Micah*. Baker Commentary on the Old Testament Prophetic Books. Grand Rapids: Baker Academic.

Green, Timothy M. 2014. *Hosea/Joel/Amos/Obadiah/Jonah/Micah: A Commentary in the Wesleyan Tradition*. New Beacon Bible Commentary. Kansas City: Beacon Hill.

Gruber, Mayer, I. 2017. *Hosea: A Textual Commentary*. LHBOTS 653. London: Bloomsbury.

Hwang, Jerry. 2021. *Hosea*. Zondervan Exegetical Commentary on the Old Testament. Grand Rapids: Zondervan Academic.

Jeremias, Jörg. 1983. *Der Prophet Hosea*. ATD 24. Neuer Göttingen Bibelwerk. Göttingen: Vandenhoeck & Ruprecht.

Limburg, James. 1988. *Hosea-Micah*. Interpretation. Atlanta: John Knox.

Macintosh, A. A. 1997. *A Critical and Exegetical Commentary on Hosea*. ICC. Edinburgh: T&T Clark.

Mays, James Luther. 1969. *Hosea*. OTL. Philadelphia: Westminster.

Moon, Joshua N. 2018. *Hosea*. Apollos Old Testament Commentary. London: Apollos. Grand Rapids: IVP Academic.

Routledge, Robin. 2020. *Hosea*. TOTC 24. Downer's Grove, IL: IVP Academic.

Sharp, Carolyn J. 2022. *Jeremiah 26–52*. International Exegetical Commentary on the Old Testament. Stuttgart: Kohlhammer.

Simundson, Daniel J. 2005. *Hosea, Joel, Amos, Obadiah, Jonah, Micah*. AOTC. Nashville: Abingdon.

Stuart, Douglas. 1987. *Hosea-Jonah*. WBC 31. Waco, TX: Word.

Sweeney, Marvin A. 2000. *The Twelve Prophets*. 2 vols. Berit Olam. Collegeville, MN: Liturgical.

Wolff, Hans Walter. 1974. *Hosea*. Hermeneia. Philadelphia: Fortress.

Yee, Gale A. 1996. "The Book of Hosea." In Leander E. Keck, ed., *The New Interpreter's Bible*. Vol. 7. 12 vols. Nashville: Abingdon.

CHAPTER 1

....

DOES (AND SHOULD) HOSEA MATTER STILL?

....

CAROL J. DEMPSEY, OP

CURRENT research on marriage indicates that marital unions, especially among heterosexual couples, are becoming less common globally. Same-sex marriages, now legal in thirty countries with more than half in western Europe, are increasing. Domestic abuse and violence against women, especially intimate partner violence and sexual violence, rank as major health problems worldwide. Numerous priests of the Roman Catholic Church continue to be convicted of pedophilia and the sexual abuse and rape of women, girls, boys, and young men. Some abusers are defrocked; other removed from active ministry; and still others sent to monasteries to repent. Few, if any, serve prison terms. Approximately one billion children worldwide, ages two to seventeen, suffer physical, sexual, and emotional violence. Child emotional abuse includes the impact of negative talk done especially by a child's parent(s) oftentimes to satisfy a parent's ego through a child or children. This type of abuse includes children in arguments and conflicts between parents, making children the battleground in marital disputes. Global political, social, and economic leaders of powerful nations and empires form alliances daily to maintain power and control in certain geographic regions and marketplaces, aimed at protecting self-interests and self-enrichment. The Christian right, especially in the United States, seems threatened by the decentering of Christianity as Islam becomes the fastest growing major religion. In response, conservative Christianity preaches a new evangelization that reinscribes a male hegemonic deity into cultures while interpreting the Bible in a fundamentalist way, and sometimes from a historical-critical perspective that not only freezes biblical meanings in the past but also condemns other religious expressions, thereby thwarting interreligious dialogue.

These and many other global realities raise questions for today's readers of Hosea: What have these situations to do with the book of Hosea, and why should interpreters of the Bible continue to be interested in the book? The answers are simple: in one form or another, all of these realities connect to the fibers of this rich book classified as one of the Twelve Minor Prophets, and everyone needs to read and interpret Hosea in the context of all these realities. For connections to be made between biblical texts and the contemporary world and for discovering the impact that both have on each other, the book of Hosea needs to be approached in new ways. Readers grounded in their social locations can create (biblical) meanings that address today's realities.[1] The business of interpreting Hosea cannot continue as usual with its disconnect from the present-day world if this book is to remain significant for the twenty-first century and have an impact on it.

In light of past and present work on Hosea, this essay suggests new strategies for reading the book in a global context. The first section demonstrates why the book of Hosea has mattered by showcasing the interests and work of scholars who have explored Hosea from the worlds behind and of the text. What is it about this book that has piqued scholarly and readerly interest for decades? The second section then asks whether the book of Hosea should still matter to readers today, and whether it is deserving of continued study by scholars. The third section responds by considering why the book of Hosea needs to matter still, and why scholars need to move beyond text fetishism if the book is to have a significant impact on the world today. A conclusion summarizes the key points and presents two strategies for interpreting Hosea in dynamic ways for the twenty-first century. In writing this essay, I acknowledge appreciatively a selection of the notable scholarly work done on the book of Hosea, but I am also cognizant of how some of this work perpetuates discrimination, marginalization, gender injustice, male hegemony, and imperial power with little attention to attitudes and structures that are systemically violent, oppressive, exclusionary, binary, and nontransformative.

1.1. Why the Book of Hosea Has Mattered

The book of Hosea has consistently piqued the interest, engaged the critical thought, and sparked the imagination of scholars past and present. An unstable Hebrew text feeds the linguistic appetite of Bible translators and text critics forever trying to determine "original" meanings. Hypothesis after hypothesis speculates about authorship, authorial intention, dating, final editor, even its fit within and contribution to the Book of the Twelve. Detailed analyses unpack the book's rich poetic rhetoric to ascertain how metaphors, images, similes, chiasmic and parallel structures not only function in texts but also help to illuminate "the meaning" of various passages and the overall book. Said differently, the worlds behind the text and of the text provide scholars with bountiful avenues for exploration resulting in a plethora of commentaries, articles, essays, bibliographic entries, and even a handbook such as this one. The sheer quantity of work done on the book of Hosea indicates its long-standing significance to scholars, especially to those engaged in translation theory and historical and literary criticism.

Historical-critical scholars with expertise in translation theory and focused on the world behind the text view the book as ambiguous and obscure because, in many places, the Hebrew text is corrupt. In other words, it makes no sense. Three possible reasons exist for such ambiguity, obscurity, and corruptness. Either the text may have only been preserved in fragments, or it may represent the last of a now-lost northern Israelite dialect spoken during the time when the book was written, or perhaps biblical writers intentionally chose certain words and phrases that explicitly and implicitly have multiple meanings to allow for complexity and flexibility of texts.

To provide an understandable English translation, translators are frequently left with little choice except to emend the text as they strive to establish the "original meaning" of words and verses. This process of emendation, however, involves much guesswork among translators, resulting in many different English translations of the same word or verse. For example, Ehud Ben Zvi (2003) offers an annotated translation with attention to both the historical interpretation of the book and its interpretation within Judaism. Stephen L. Cook (2006) provides another annotated translation that focuses on the book's historical, literary, and theological dimensions. Hans Walter Wolff (1974) uses ancient Semitic and classical languages such as Canaanite, Akkadian, Syriac, Greek, and Latin to provide his own translation of the Masoretic Text (MT) of Hosea. More recently, J. Andrew Dearman, a contributor to *The Common English Study Bible* (2013), tries to make the book of Hosea accessible to all types of readers, especially those possessing little or no knowledge of Hebrew and with a minimal understanding of biblical-world terms and phrases. Thus, biblical scholars working on either emending, annotating, or translating into English the Hebrew text of Hosea find the book intriguing because it is so unstable, therefore offering many translation possibilities. Note, however, that most of the translations produced thus far are from white, western, Eurocentric, Global North, male scholars, with their own biases in translation.

When taking into account any Bible translation, especially the translation of Hosea, the assertions of feminist biblical scholar, Susanne Scholz, need consideration. Scholz (2017: 180) articulates three hermeneutical principles:

> The first hermeneutical principle posits that all sacred texts, including the Bible, are inherently flexible, elastic, and ambiguous. The second hermeneutical principle affirms that every translation is an interpretation. The third hermeneutical principle maintains that readers, grounded in social locations, create (biblical) meanings.

Not only are all translations interpretations, but so are biblical and classical dictionaries that define Hebrew, Syriac, Akkadian, Coptic, Greek, and Latin words. This reality raises an important question: Is it possible to translate Hosea in such a way that the "original meaning" of the text comes to light? Given the condition of the text, its many emendations, and Scholz's three hermeneutical principles, the notion of establishing an "original" text is highly unlikely. Yet, scholars interested in translation theory continue with their translation work, adding new nuances to the book of Hosea along with text-critical notes to substantiate their translation choices.

Other historical-critical scholars fascinated with the world behind the text find Hosea well-suited for their historical interests. Philip J. King (1988), employing an archaeological lens, uses the material culture of the Iron Age II (1000–586 BCE) recovered through archaeology to discuss such topics as practices of warfare, altars and high places, cult images, agricultural metaphors, fortifications, and cities. He dates the book to the eighth century BCE. Questions about whether Hosea was an actual historical person, whether he wrote most of the book, and when the book was written intrigue scholars engaged in historical studies. Using a traditional historical-critical approach and reading Hosea through this lens, Wolff (1974) argues that Hosea was a historical figure and did write portions of the text. Like King, he also places Hosea in an eighth-century BCE setting. Others, however, date the book to the Persian period (e.g., Bos 2013; Trotter 2001). Ben Zvi (2005) posits that an elite community living in Jerusalem during the fifth century BCE wrote Hosea as a book that was read and reread in postmonarchic times. Susanne Rudnig-Zelt (2006) considers the redaction history of Hosea and argues that the book reached completion in the Hellenistic period. Presently, authorship, dating, and author intentionality remain unknown, allowing scholars to continue with their research and create hypotheses based on their analyses.

For scholars reconstructing Israel's history, the book of Hosea offers a rich and descriptive storyline about the final years of King Jeroboam II and the superpowers Assyria and Egypt who were Israel's primary eighth-century BCE enemies. According to the prophet's proclamations, the Northern Kingdom of Israel grew weak because the king and many other political, social, and religious leaders forgot the egalitarianism of the Sinai covenant, worshipped gods other than Israel's God, and ignored the marginalized and vulnerable in their societies. This theo-geo-socio-political situation provides opportunities to pursue a broad range of ethical, cultural, and theological questions related to Israel's history and to delve more deeply into it, even as some scholars insist that the Hebrew Bible cannot be used as a source for history.

Another area of historical criticism relates to the translation issues noted above—namely, the study of ancient versions of Hosea. Work in this area has attracted many scholars and yielded significant findings. For example, Lawrence A. Sinclair (1980) examines the MT of Hosea in relation to the Peshitta, the Septuagint, a Qumran fragment, and other texts found in the region of the Dead Sea. Based on his research, he argues that the fragment Hosea 4QXII(d) was written in a mixed/semicursive hand that dates back to the early first century BCE. Sinclair also makes the case that evidence exists to support a dual tradition for Hosea—specifically, Palestinian (Qumran and the MT) and Egyptian (the Septuagint). Mayer I. Gruber's (2017) textual commentary employs the insights of behavioral sciences to uncover lost and forgotten meanings of metaphors, similes, idioms, and allusions in Hosea.

In sum, whether creating a fresh translation, examining recently discovered archaeological material, or studying pieced-together fragments on fragile parchments, the book of Hosea has been and remains a source of great interest for biblical historical critics grappling with the world behind the text. But Hosea is about more than past happenings and events recorded as if history were unfolding before the eyes of the book's readers.

Hosea is poetry, and the text's poetics likewise have captured and fed the imagination of biblical scholars working from the perspective of the world of the text and using the tools of literary criticism to examine rhetoric and interpret passages.

Imagery, metaphors, chiasms, parallelism, similes, the use of multiple voices, divine proclamations, genre, word play, inclusios, and a whole host of other literary forms and techniques constitute the fabric of the book of Hosea whose poetics lure biblical literary scholars into wondering about how all of these elements function in Hosea and contribute to the book's coherence and "meaning." Several scholars working in literary criticism find the book's poetics scintillating, and their research makes notable contributions. Lenart de Past Regt (2000) focuses on the grammatical shifts of person in Hosea. He concludes that these shifts are a structuring device for the entire book. Captivated by Hosea's images and metaphors, Emmanuel O. Nwaoru (1999) analyzes the book's marriage imagery (Yhwh as husband, Israel as a wife of whoredom, the land as a harlot) and parent-child metaphors. He concludes that the biblical nation Israel is not devoid of tradition and culture. Assuming the prophet to be a historical figure, Nwaoru concludes further that Hosea chose these images specifically so that he could make his own religious and spiritual mark. In trying to ascertain the genre of the book, Gerald Paul Morris (1996) draws on the thought and work of philosophers, literary writers and poets, and other biblical scholars working in the area of literary studies to investigate whether the book could be classified as poetry. He concludes that Hosea was a poet who wrote a sustained lyric poem that discloses who God is. Other scholars investigate the book's imagery, metaphors, and similes, noting how these elements work conceptually, how the historicizing of images is illusive, how Yhwh is often portrayed as an enemy, and what impact inclusios have on the book's audience. Laurie J. Bratten (2003) specifically considers the land and suggests that this theme serves to unite the Book of the Twelve into one single unit.

Overall, Hosea interpreters working from the perspective of the worlds behind, of, or in the text are never without plenty of source material to hypothesize how the poetry of Hosea contributes to the understanding of the book as a whole, and how the book fits within and contributes to the unity of the Book of the Twelve. All of these scholars, whether delving into translations, text criticism, or the historical and literary dimensions of Hosea, find this book to have significant value, worthy of ongoing research, and suitable for continued discussion. Even though the scholarly discourse presented in this section adds to the body of knowledge about this book, those who use historical and literary criticism all read with the grain of the text as they try to ascertain its "meaning." None of them reads against the grain, and none of their work reflects Scholz's third hermeneutical principle. By contrast, scholars working from the world in front of the text and using contemporary hermeneutical approaches to deconstruct texts are able to create new biblical meanings, thereby making the reading of Hosea even more lively and in tune with the present-day world. Using these perspectives, I now turn to the question of why the book of Hosea continues to be significant and deserves ongoing study and readership.

1.2. Should the Book of Hosea Still Matter?

Historical-critical and literary scholars studying the book of Hosea continue to make notable contributions. These contributions, however, give rise to an important question: Should the book of Hosea still matter, especially in the twenty-first century? I offer four points in response. First, the book of Hosea is a sociopolitical, cultural, and theological document shaped by different political, social, economic, and theological perspectives. As a cultural document, it came into existence through a cultural process. Culture is embedded in the Bible, and the Bible is embedded in culture. Widely accepted among biblical scholars today is the idea that males wrote and edited the Hebrew Bible, including the book of Hosea, and both were originally for an upper-class, male audience and readership.

Second, the images, symbols, language, and metaphors found in the Hebrew Bible in general and Hosea emerge from a hierarchical, patriarchal, hegemonic, militaristic, ethnocentric, gendered, racist, nationalist, and heteronormative culture. These kinds of textual expressions often sustained this culture. Esther Fuchs (2016: 16) notes that the Bible "is not merely authored, edited, transmitted, and canonized by men, but . . . it also endorses and promotes a patriarchal ideology." Furthermore, a feminist approach to the Bible "does not see the Bible merely as a product of male-centered culture, but as one of the texts that actively created this culture, having disrupted and replaced previous cultures in which women were regarded as deities, as potential leaders, as equals" (p. 16). These comments also pertain to the book of Hosea as a text within the Bible. The book of Hosea, then, is a deeply cultural text.

Third, the book of Hosea is not only a text *of* cultures but also a text *in* cultures, and people in diverse social locations throughout the globe receive this biblical book in different ways. People of different faith persuasions, denominations, traditions, and of none at all hear passages from Hosea in different ways. In today's global world, new approaches to reading the book challenge a masked, supposedly objective, nineteenth-century historical-critical approach to biblical interpretation and its focus on authorship, dating, and authorial intent as determining "the meaning" of the text through the world behind the text and the history of that world. No interpretation is objective because interpreters bring their own cultural biases to the reading process. Readers give meanings to texts; the text has no meaning of its own; and diverse readers from different social locations with various hermeneutical lenses hear texts in various ways, adding to the plurality of understanding and meaning-making, as well as the richness of conversation that Hosea evokes.

Fourth, since culture shapes one's interpretation, a dialogue exists between culture and the book of Hosea. Because of a growing evangelical fundamentalism on the one hand and a growing secularism on the other hand, Hosea can continue to be an influential text particularly for generations of people today who either take the Bible literally and follow it religiously or have no religious tradition "and live disconnected from religious institutions" (Scholz 2017: 21). Within the context of various faith traditions and denominations, Hosea is interpreted by some readers as if it were literally "the Word of God." To New Testament scholar Sandra Schneiders (1999), the "Word of God" is first and foremost a linguistic and metaphorical expression and does not imply that the Bible and its divine discourse should be taken literally. Often when readers read the book of Hosea through the lens of their various faith traditions and belief systems, they do so through their own cultural and religious biases. The way various faith traditions have interpreted Hosea, and who gets centered in the reading of various passages and interpretations, has sometimes led to the forms of oppression known today.

In sum, the book of Hosea is embedded in cultures past and present, and cultural attitudes and mindsets continue to shape readerly perceptions today. On the one hand, how the book of Hosea is heard and interpreted can give readers a vision of justice for the disenfranchised, marginalized, and those who suffer any form of violence and abuse in our world today. On the other hand, the book can preserve, inscribe, and reinforce certain attitudes, mindsets, actions, and practices that are oppressive and unjust. These often go without critique. Because they are not only part of the book of Hosea's fabric and but also part of the Bible as a whole, a "holy book" which people of various faith traditions or no faith tradition read, study, pray with, and use for spiritual nourishment, these elements of oppression become reinscribed in people's imaginations, thoughts, and lives and serve to legitimate oppression and injustice today. To address this situation, some scholars have begun to read against the grain and with the margins. They use a variety of hermeneutical approaches such as feminist studies, gender studies, ecological studies, empire studies, masculinities studies, decolonial and postcolonial studies, queer studies, and womanist studies to interpret texts, casting light on power, sexual violence, hegemony, erasure, and inscription of multiple forms of discrimination and other expressions of oppression.

Among the many scholars who address such issues as gender, sexuality, and power in the book of Hosea are Mayer I. Gruber (1995), Alice Keefe (2001), Marie-Theres Wacker (2012), Susanne Scholz (2010), and Gale A. Yee (2012). They use a feminist approach. Gruber examines the key problem behind the book's ethics of sexuality, noting that the confusing of physical intimacy with true intimacy lays the groundwork for infidelity. Keefe reorients the conventional and dominant reading of Hosea, offers a critique of the text and the culture that shaped it, and addresses the interrelatedness of the female body, the fertile land, and the community of Israel. Wacker explores the image of Gomer, the imagination of power and the power of imagination, the problem of priests and patriarchs in relation to power and privilege, and the image of the womb as a tomb and as a place of life. In dealing with the "God as mother" metaphor in Hos. 11, Wacker (2012: 381–82) challenges traditional interpretations that present God as a compassionate parent. After critiquing the thought of Helen Schüngel-Straumann (1986), who revived the gynocentric speech about God, she concludes that "the text does not present YHWH unalloyed in a feminine-motherly form; rather, it shows a divine figure with the two dimensions of anger, ready to destroy, and compassion." She sees the "asymmetry of the contrast between 'warrior' and 'mother' " as a "warning against constructing a gender ontology that has women to be motherly and men more anger-prone by nature" (p. 382). To Wacker, the God as mother metaphor is not one that speaks solely of divine care and compassion. Stuart Macwilliam (2011) also moves beyond binary, gendered divisions to read Hos. 11 from a queer perspective. In his queer reading, the inscription of God has both genders and thus escapes the roles of either mother or violent husband.

Other feminists also dealing with the metaphorical language for God focus on Hos. 1–3 and the extended marriage metaphor to bring to light Yhwh as an abusive husband, underscoring how the violent depiction justifies violence against women. Scholz's (2010) interpretation of Hos. 2:4–25 (Eng. 2:2–23), however, takes the husband imagery to new depths. Scholz asserts that "feminist interpreters define Hosea 2 as a prime text for imagery of sexual violence in the Hebrew Bible" and that "in their view, it is not a description of an actual event between the prophet and his wife, Gomer, but an important metaphor that also appears elsewhere in the prophetic literature" (p. 97). Like many other scholars analyzing this poem, to Scholz the extended metaphor presents God as the husband and Israel as the wife. She interprets the text as a poem that "describes the interior dialogue of a husband who dreams of acting out his rage over the sexual independence of his wife" (p. 93). Scholz notes that the wife has left her husband. Because he can no longer control her, he fantasizes the extreme rage that he will do to her and also dreams of taking her back as if nothing ever happened. She observes that "the androcentric neurosis in 2:4–25 deals with the husbandly fear come true" (p. 99). Scholz then points out how this poem "reinforces androcentrism" and "exploits the idea that monogamy parallels monolatry" (p. 98). She explains that the husband's behavior is "typical of sexually violent and controlling men" (p. 94). Creating a new meaning for Hos. 2:4–25 by analyzing it from the perspective of the world in front of the text while also carefully engaging the text, Scholz moves from the text to contemporary marital difficulties. This move allows the text to be heard in a new and dynamic way.

Another feminist reading of Hos. 1–3 comes from Gale Yee (2003). She considers the marital metaphor as a strategy to criticize the male leaders of Israel. To Yee, "feminizing men in a marital relation with a male God reinscribes into the text the ideological and social links among women, subordination, shame, and sin" (p. 98). Finally, in another work on Hosea, Yee (2012) focuses on class conflicts and ecological struggles over land. She sees this situation intertwined with social attitudes about gender and sexuality and argues that both dimensions have a bearing on the book's overall theological message.

Scholars employing a masculinist approach to the book of Hosea examine the genre of male hegemony. Among the scholars working in this area are John Goldingay and Susan E. Haddox. Goldingay (1995) explores how dominant, oppressive male characteristics appear in Hos. 1–3 as attributes of the prophet and Yhwh. He observes that the notion of "grace" in the book is constructed from a male perspective. In his interpretation of Hos. 11, he notes the pain and compassion of the deity and challenges males to redefine themselves in the likeness of this deity, thereby redefining their understanding of masculinity. Arguing that the audience of the book of Hosea is primarily male elites who have a strong masculine social persona, Haddox (2011) views the book as an attack on the elite males' masculinity. She also explores male and female imagery and discusses the implications that female imagery has for masculinity. She notes that the imagery in the book reinforces the masculinity of the deity while undermining the masculinity of the prophet and the prophet's audience.

A recent engagement with ecological studies in biblical scholarship, spearheaded by the work of Norman Habel, has also impacted Hosea studies. Braaten (2001, 2022) argues that the book of Hosea omits the important story of God's relationship with the land. Braaten, reading from the perspective of the Earth, brings to life Earth's story and the struggles Earth faces to make its voice heard through the victimized land. He argues that the Earth Community is more than the Northern Kingdom or the Holy Land, and he invites readers to reflect on the world's contemporary environmental crisis and human sin. Also using an ecological approach, Melissa Tubbs Loya (2008) considers the suffering of the Earth in Hosea. She focuses on the Earth's mourning, languishing, and perishing, along with all of Earth's inhabitants. Loya makes the case that the suffering is a consequence of Israel's breach of moral order, which she then links to the suffering of the Earth in today's environmental crisis.

In commenting on Hos. 4:3, and recognizing the ecological trauma of Earth, Anne Elvey (2021: 570) argues that "Earth's mourning signals the interrelationship of people, land, law, and G-d, and the Earth impacts of failures in this relationship, even the failure inherent in the violence of sacrifice that underwrites the land-law-people-divine relationship. Earth and humans in partnership cry out against these failures." Reading with the grain of the text, Elvey demonstrates how Hosea can be a resource for global transformation.

The preceding sampling of hermeneutical approaches, used to interpret Hosea from the world in front of the text, demonstrates that the book can be interpreted in new ways. By interrogating the text, scholars bring to light how oppressive cultural elements are inscribed in Hosea, in scholarly interpretations, and in contemporary contexts. They show us how inscriptions and interpretations legitimate pernicious, androcentric, hegemonic, heteronormative masculinity embodied by the character of the deity and the prophet. They also bring to light spousal abuse, domestic violence done against women and children, sexual violence, and negative male depictions and narrations of women embedded in texts. They show readers how elements of inscription normalize patriarchy, patriarchal heteronormative marriage, and even an androtheistic, colonizing relationship of a monotheistic religion. Specifically, when the male God and the male prophet speak, the masses, inclusive of men, must listen and obey or else serious, and even lethal, repercussions will occur. Readers see how power, privilege, authority, and voice rest with the male—whether a male deity, a male prophet, or other male religious or political leaders. Thus, scholars interrogating the book of Hosea and its interpretations expose critical cultural issues of power, control, sexism, discrimination, colonization, gender, hegemony, and a whole host of other systemic and structural oppressions that continue to affect people's lives, as well as their social, political, and religious beliefs, even how they understand and imagine the Divine. As a literary work, the book of Hosea plays a role along these lines in art and music. Its interpretation by artists, however, often inscribes a negative image of Gomer. Hence, a negative image of women is further inscribed into contemporary culture (see Sawyer 2021).

Thus, depending on how people read and interpret the content of Hosea, the book can affect, adversely or positively, cultures and peoples today, especially those religious communities that view the text as "prophetic" and authoritative for prayer, study, preaching, and a blueprint for living a "faithful" and "holy" life. It is high time to put an end to the weaponization of the Bible and the book of Hosea in support of hegemony that keeps those on the margins marginalized, the disenfranchised colonized, and the "other" othered. So, should the book of Hosea still matter? Yes. But why does Hosea need to matter still?

1.3. WHY THE BOOK OF HOSEA NEEDS TO MATTER STILL

Scholars studying the book of Hosea have produced and continue to produce commentaries, essays, articles, and bibliographies. The sheer volume of work is too expansive to list and too numerous to count. This biblical text has mattered to scholars and readers and needs to matter still for two reasons.

First, authoritarianism is on the rise. Governments and their dictators, officials, oligarchs, biotechnofeudal lords, and other power-grabbing, colonizing, and greedy economic, political, social, and religious leaders, along with the media outlets that they own, are all asserting more and more power over people. By controlling economic, healthcare, educational, religious, political, and social institutions, those with power who want to colonize the masses are consciously chipping away at people's freedoms and gaining control over how people think and live their lives. Coupled with this global rise of authoritarianism is religious evangelical fundamentalism within Judaism, Islam, Christianity, Hinduism, and Buddhism, and types of biblical literalism. For example, the Christian right within the United States is becoming increasingly more powerful within the judicial and legislative branches of government and among some political parties and their followers. Because of the rise of authoritarianism, evangelical fundamentalism, and biblical literalism as three intersecting forces operative in the world today, the interpretation of the book of Hosea matters still. Biblical scholars need to become interpreters of conscience, shifting from the historical, poetic, and text-fetished fascination and preoccupation with the worlds behind and of the text to the world in front of the text. To this end, the globalized world and the book of Hosea present scholars with a challenge: If the work of today's scholars is to have any far-reaching credibility and be a resource for transformative global justice, then it must address the abuse of power, colonization, sexism, gender discrimination, hegemony, and violence embedded in the book of Hosea and its reception history. All of these inscribed cultural elements embedded in the text can lead to systemic oppression. If these things are not addressed, then oppressive elements will continue to be repeatedly and systemically inscribed, legitimated, normalized, and rewarded in present-day cultures, institutions, and belief systems. The book of Hosea, then, needs to matter still because the world is aching for justice. Studies on Hosea can make a positive contribution to begin to quell this ache if scholars shift their lenses and approaches to produce interpretations in touch with the elements noted above. Such studies will also help to decenter evangelical fundamentalism and biblical literalism.

Second, New Testament and Christian spirituality scholar Sandra Schneiders (2001) argues that the most crucial question for the twenty-first century is the "God question." One of the central characters in the book of Hosea is the deity. In an increasingly literal world, how people perceive, understand, and talk about the deity can affect how they understand their lives and roles in society and how they live on the planet with the rest of creation. Hosea offers readers and scholars the opportunity to interrogate their assumptions about God, the portrait of the deity, and the rhetoric of empire associated with the deity in the text. In other words, Hosea presents opportunities to decolonize the Divine (see Schüssler Fiorenza 2007).

Do these reasons, and the scholarly work already done, go far enough for Hosea to find continued interest among global readers today? Do further steps need to be taken to make the book matter still today in more profound ways? I do not believe that the scholarly work done already goes far enough for global readers to maintain interest in the book today. And at least two further steps need to be taken to make Hosea matter still in more profound ways.

1.4. Conclusion: Two Strategies for Reading and Interpreting Hosea Dynamically

This essay has showcased various efforts of scholars past and present who have taken the book of Hosea as a work that matters. I have suggested that the most interesting and effective works consider the world in front of the text in hermeneutical fashion. These studies deal with the many forms of interlocking oppression inscribed into the text. All of the work done thus far makes clear this point: the book of Hosea still matters.

For the book of Hosea to have continued credibility and interest among readers today, however, biblical scholars need to take two further steps. These steps consist of embracing two new strategies for doing continued work on Hosea. The first strategy involves a paradigm shift. Renowned New Testament scholar Elisabeth Schüssler Fiorenza calls for a new paradigm for doing biblical interpretation—namely, the rhetorical-emancipatory paradigm. According to Schüssler Fiorenza (2007: 254), this approach understands the bible and biblical interpretation as a site of struggle over authority, values, and meaning. Since the socio-historical location of rhetoric is the public polis, the rhetorical-emancipatory paradigm shift seeks to situate biblical scholarship in such a way that its public character and political responsibility become an integral part of its contemporary readings and historical reconstructions. It insists on an ethical radical democratic imperative that compels biblical scholarship to contribute to the advent of a society and religion that are free from all forms of kyriarchal inequity and oppression.

The interpretation of the book of Hosea now becomes an ethical endeavor meant to effect public life. Said differently, this radical-democratic approach "examines the structures of globalized inequalities and injustices in the social, political, economic realms of human societies and relates them to the reading of biblical texts" (Scholz 2017: 25). The present world, then, as well as the examination of one's presuppositions and social location, becomes the starting point for reading and interpreting Hosea, not the biblical text itself. For example, an interrogation into the global prevalence of spousal abuse and domestic violence examined through sociopsychological lenses and global intercultural perspectives would shape any discussion of Hos. 1–3.

A second strategy is for all biblical scholars to broaden their interpretive horizon. Going forward, the lenses through which scholars translate, read, and interpret Hosea, and assess its history of scholarship, will have to be increasingly interdisciplinary, transdisciplinary, multihermeneutical, multicultural, inclusive of voices from the Global North and the Global South, especially those on the margins, and representative of both Western and Eastern thought. Said differently, biblical scholars will have to do their work in the context of conversations and studies occurring in interreligious dialogue, science, psychology, comparative spirituality, political science, popular culture, contemporary linguistics, and always in the context of present-day social, political, cultural, and religious global realities. A model for this type of work is *The Oxford Handbook of Feminist Approaches to the Hebrew Bible* (Scholz 2021). This volume explores the impact of globalization on feminist biblical studies, the impact of neoliberalism on feminist biblical interpretation, the impact of (digital) media cultures on feminist biblical exegesis, and the emergence of intersectional feminist readings, which include interreligious readings of various texts.

To date, no work like Scholz's *Handbook* exists for the book of Hosea. Furthermore, much work waits to be done if the book is to be "prophetic" in the midst of present-day, twenty-first-century global and cultural contexts and realities. Perhaps this volume on Hosea will advance that goal, offering readers new insights and understandings that can lead to justice and social transformation. This is my hope.

NOTE

1. This statement is adapted from one of Susanne Scholz's (2017: 180) three hermeneutical principles—namely, "that readers, grounded in social locations, create (biblical) meanings."

References

Baumann, Gerlinde. 2003. *Love and Violence: Marriage as a Metaphor for the Relationship between YHWH and Israel in the Prophetic Books*. Trans. Linda M. Maloney. Collegeville, MN: Liturgical.

Ben Zvi, Ehud. 2003. "Hosea." In Adele Berlin and Mark Brettler, eds., *The Jewish Study Bible*. Oxford and New York: Oxford University Press, 1143–65.

Ben Zvi, Ehud. 2005. *Hosea*. FOTL 21A/1. Grand Rapids: Eerdmans.Bos, James M. 2013. *Reconstructing the Date and Provenance of the Book of Hosea: The Case for Persian-Period Yehud*. LHBOTS 580. London; New York; T&T Clark.

Braaten, Laurie J. 2001. "Earth Community in Hosea 2." In Norman C. Habel, ed., *The Earth Story in the Psalms and the Prophets*. The Earth Bible 4. Sheffield: Sheffield Academic, 185–203.

Braaten, Laurie J. 2003. "God Sows: Hosea's Land Theme in the Book of the Twelve." In Paul L. Redditt and Aaron Schart, eds., *Thematic Threads in the Book of the Twelve*. BZAW 325. Berlin; New York: de Gruyter, 104–32.

Braaten, Laurie J. 2022. "God's Good Land: The Agrarian Perspective of the Book of the Twelve." In Hilary Marlow and Mark Harris, eds., *The Oxford Handbook of the Bible and Ecology*. New York: Oxford University Press, 148–65.Cook, Stephen L. 2006. "Hosea." In Harry W. Attridge et al., eds., *The Harper Collins Study Bible*. New York: HarperCollins, 1193–208.

Dearman, J. Andrew. 2013. "Hosea." In Joel B. Green et al., eds., *The CEB Study Bible*. Nashville: Abingdon, 1425–43.

Dempsey, Carol. 2013. *Amos, Hosea, Micah, Nahum, Zephaniah, Habakkuk*. Collegeville, MN: Liturgical.

Elvey, Anne. 2021. "A Multidimensional Approach in Feminist Ecological Biblical Studies." In Susanne Scholz, ed., *The Oxford Handbook of Feminist Approaches to the Hebrew Bible*. New York: Oxford University Press, 555–573.

Fuchs, Esther. 2016. *Feminist Theory and the Bible: Interrogating the Sources*. Feminist Studies and Sacred Texts. Lanham; Boulder; New York; London: Lexington Books.

Goldingay, John. 1995. "Hosea 1–3, Genesis 1–4, and Masculinist Interpretation," *HBT* 17: 37–44.

Gruber, Mayer I. 1995. "Marital Fidelity and Intimacy: A View from Hosea 4." In Athalya Brenner, ed., *A Feminist Companion to the Latter Prophets*. FCB 8. Sheffield: Sheffield Academic, 169–79.

Gruber, Mayer I. 2017. *Hosea: A Textual Commentary*. LHBOTS 653. London; New York: Bloomsbury.Habel, Norman, and Peter Trudinger, eds. 2008. *Exploring Ecological Hermeneutics*. SBL Symposium Series 46. Atlanta: SBL.

Haddox, Susan E. 2011. *Metaphor and Masculinity in Hosea*. Studies in Biblical Literature 141. New York: Peter Lang.

Hornsby, Teresa J. 1999. "Israel Has Become a Worthless Thing: Rereading Gomer in Hosea 1–3," *JSOT* 82: 115–28.

Keefe, Alice. 2001. *A Woman's Body and the Social Body in Hosea*. JSOTSup 338. GCT 10. Sheffield: Sheffield Academic.

King, Philip J. 1988. *Amos, Hosea, Micah: An Archaeological Commentary*. Philadelphia: Westminster.

Loya, Melissa Tubbs. 2008. "Therefore the Earth Mourns: The Grievance of Earth in Hosea 4:1–3." In Norman C. Habel and Peter L. Trudinger, eds., *Exploring Ecological Hermeneutics*. The Earth Bible 4. Atlanta: SBL, 53–62.

Macwilliam, Stuart. 2011. *Queer Theory and the Prophetic Marriage Metaphor in the Hebrew Bible*. Sheffield: Equinox.

Morris, Gerald Paul. 1996. *Prophecy, Poetry, and Hosea*. Sheffield: Sheffield Academic.

Nwaoru, Emmanuel O. 1999. *Imagery in the Prophecy of Hosea*. Wiesbaden: Harrassowitz.

O'Brien, Julia. 2008. *Challenging Prophetic Metaphor: Theology and Ideology in the Prophets*. Louisville: Westminster John Knox.

O'Brien, Julia M., ed. 2021. *The Oxford Handbook of the Minor Prophets*. New York: Oxford University Press.

Regt, Lenart de Past. 2000. "A Genre Feature in Biblical Prophecy and the Translator: Person Shift in Hosea." In Johannes Moor and H. R. Rooy, eds., *Past, Present, Future: The Deuteronomistic History and the Prophets*. OtSt 44. Leiden; Boston; Cologne: Brill, 230–50.

Rudnig-Zelt, Susanne. 2006. *Hosea-Studien: Redakionskitische Untersuchungen zur Genese de Hoseabuches*. Göttingen: Vandenhoeck & Ruprecht.

Sawyer, John A. 2021. "The Twelve Minor Prophets in Art and Music." In Julia O'Brien, ed., *The Oxford Handbook of the Minor Prophets*. New York: Oxford University Press, 279–95.

Schneiders, Sandra. 1999. *The Revelatory Text*. 2nd ed. Collegeville: Liturgical.

Schneiders, Sandra M. 2001. "God Is the Question and God Is the Answer." In Mary Hembrow Snyder, ed., *Spiritual Questions for the Twenty-First Century: Essays in Honor of Joan D. Chittister*. Maryknoll, NY: Orbis, 68–71.

Scholz, Susanne. 2010. *Sacred Witness: Rape in the Hebrew Bible*. Minneapolis: Fortress.Scholz, Susanne. 2017. *The Bible as Political Artifact: On the Feminist Study of the Hebrew Bible*. Minneapolis: Fortress.

Scholz, Susanne, ed. 2021. *The Oxford Handbook of Feminist Approaches to the Hebrew Bible*. New York: Oxford University Press.Schüngel-Straumann, Helen. 1986. "Gott als Mutter in Hos 11," *Theologische Quartalschrift*: 119–34.

Schüssler Fiorenza, Elisabeth. 2007. *The Power of the Word: Scripture and the Rhetoric of Empire*. Minneapolis: Fortress.

Sherwood, Yvonne. 1995. "Boxing Gomer: Controlling the Deviant Women in Hosea 1–3." In Athalya Brenner, ed., *A Feminist Companion to the Latter Prophets*. FCB 8. Sheffield: Sheffield Academic Press, 101–25.

Sherwood, Yvonne. 1996. *The Prostitute and the Prophet: Hosea's Marriage in Literary-Theological Perspective*. JSOTSup 12. Sheffield: Sheffield Academic Press.

Sinclair, Lawrence A. 1980. "A Qumran Biblical Fragment: Hosea 4QII[d] (Hosea 1:7–2:5)," *BASOR* 239: 61–65.

Trotter, James M. 2001. *Reading Hosea in Achaemenid Yehud*. JSOTSup 328. London: Sheffield Academic.

Wacker, Marie-Theres. 2012. "Hosea: The God-Identified Man and the Woman/Women of Israel." In Luise Schrottroff and Marie-Theres Wacker, eds., *Feminist Biblical Interpretation*. Grand Rapids: Eerdmans, 371–85.

Wolff, Hans Walter. 1974. *Hosea*. Hermeneia. Philadelphia: Fortress.

Yee, Gale A. 2003. *Poor Banished Children of Eve: Woman as Evil in the Hebrew Bible*. Minneapolis: Fortress.

Yee, Gale A. 2012. "Hosea." In Carol A. Newsom, Sharon H. Ringe, and Jacqueline E. Lapsley, eds., *Women's Bible Commentary*. Rev. and updated ed. Louisville: Westminster John Knox, 299–308.

PART I

HISTORY, TEXT, AND COMPOSITION

CHAPTER 2

THE BOOK OF HOSEA AND THE HISTORY OF EIGHTH-CENTURY BCE ISRAEL

SHUICHI HASEGAWA

2.1. INTRODUCTION

ACCORDING to the superscription in Hos. 1:1, the prophet Hosea acted in the early eighth century BCE during the reigns of Uzziah, Jotham, Ahaz, and Hezekiah of Judah, the period equivalent to the reign of Jeroboam II (r. 788/787–748 BCE) of Israel. On the other hand, scholars identify the historical background of some passages in the book of Hosea in the period after the reign of Jeroboam II, but the chronological extent of Hosea's activities is debated (see Wolff 1974; Andersen and Freedman 1980; Davies 1992; Macintosh 1997). Hosea's prophecies were also subject to alterations in the course of transmission before they were collected in writing; and even thereafter, the book of Hosea was redacted multiple times before it was shaped into the present text that we now possess. Since traces of such redactions are not always obvious, it is hard to go back to the original Hosea's prophecies, even if they were dated to the eighth century BCE.

With this limitation in mind, I first sketch the history of the Northern Kingdom of Israel that emerges from biblical and extrabiblical sources from the late ninth to the eighth century BCE until its demise. The Kingdom of Israel saw a period of political turmoil in the latter half of the eighth century BCE. Understanding the sociopolitical history of the Kingdom of Israel during this period illuminates the milieu in which the historical Hosea may have acted, even though it may not help to discern the original Hosea's prophecies. Second, I explore the relationship between the relevant passages in the book of Hosea and the history of the Northern Kingdom, and discuss whether it is possible to associate them with specific historical situations.

2.2. Israelite History in the Ninth and Eighth Centuries BCE

2.2.1. The Rise of Jehu and Assyria (the Late Ninth Century BCE)

Jeroboam II was the fourth king of the Jehu dynasty. Jehu (r. 841–814 BCE),[1] the founder of the dynasty, is one of the six kings of Israel mentioned in the Assyrian royal inscriptions. The Black Obelisk of Shalmaneser III (r. 858–824 BCE) records Jehu's tribute to this Assyrian monarch with a relief depicting the Israelite delegation.[2] Four more inscriptions of Shalmaneser also mention Jehu's tribute (see Hasegawa 2012). This incident occurred in 841 BCE and was a major turning point in the history of the Kingdom of Israel. Other inscriptions of Shalmaneser rank King Ahab (r. 874–853) of Israel in the top three powers among the coalition of different kingdoms and groups that attempted to halt the Assyrian army in northern Syria in 853 BCE, twelve years before Jehu's tribute.[3]

With Jehu's subjugation, the Kingdom of Israel became a client state of Assyria. Israel's pro-Assyrian policy probably continued throughout Jehu's dynasty until the mid-eighth century BCE, except for a few decades of possible intermittence caused by the dominance of Aram-Damascus in the region, as described below.

According to 2 Kgs. 8:28–10:27, Jehu killed King Joram of Israel, annihilated the descendants of Ahab, usurped the throne, and swept the Baal cult from the kingdom. One of the major arenas of Jehu's coup was in the Jezreel Valley, where Jehu killed King Joram at Naboth's property (9:21–26) and Queen Jezebel in the city of Jezreel (9:30–37). Then Jehu requested the elders in Samaria to send the heads of the princes of Ahab's dynasty to Jezreel (10:1–12). This series of events, if historical, should have happened sometime between 845 and 841 BCE—that is, between the last mention of the anti-Assyrian coalition including Israel and Jehu's tribute in Shalmaneser's inscriptions. The Tel Dan Inscription, dating to the late ninth century BCE, commonly ascribed to Hazael of Damascus, also offers information on Israel–Damascus relations during this period. Yet, the author of the inscription boasted of the murder of the kings of Israel and Judah, creating discrepancy between the information in Kings and the inscription.

2.2.2. The Aramean Hegemony (the Late Ninth and Early Eighth Centuries BCE)

The Assyrian domination of the Levant did not last long. Shalmaneser III conducted military campaigns to this region in 838–837 BCE, and in 829 BCE (to Unqi) (Hasegawa 2012). After the last campaign, Assyria suffered from internal revolts that prevented the

Assyrian monarchs from launching military campaigns to this region. Hazael of Aram-Damascus took power in the region during the last years of Shalmaneser III and the reign of his son Šamšī-Adad V (r. 823–811 BCE).[4] Hazael and his son Bar-Hadad had a significant political impact on the Levant, including the Kingdom of Israel (2 Kgs. 10:32–33). Archaeological excavations at Tell eṣ-Ṣāfī in the Shephelah, commonly identified as biblical Gath, have revealed a surrounding moat along with a trace of massive destruction layer dating to the late ninth or the beginning of the eighth century BCE, probably reflecting Hazael's siege of the city and its conquest (2 Kgs. 12:18; Maeir 2003; Hasegawa 2012: 74, 78). Destruction layers from other sites in the southern Levant in this period may also attest to Hazael's military attacks (Hasegawa 2012). Two Aramaic inscriptions, and possibly another, calling Hazael "our lord" have been discovered in different places, all dating perhaps to the late ninth century BCE. If this monarch can be identified as Hazael of Damascus, these inscriptions may also demonstrate Hazael's sovereignty over the region during this period (see Kelle 2002: 646–51). The Zakkur Inscription describes Bar-Hadad as the leader of a coalition of Syrian kingdoms besieging Hadrach, the city of Zakkur, king of Luʿash and Hamath. The siege took place either in the late ninth or the beginning of the eighth century BCE. This inscription demonstrates Bar-Hadad's leading status among the kingdoms in Syria in the period. The absence of Israel in the coalition may suggest that it had already been set free from the yoke of Damascus by the time of the siege of Hadrach.

2.2.3. The Rise of Israel under Joash (the Early Eighth Century BCE)

The tide changed in the last decade of the ninth century BCE under Adad-nērārī III (r. 810–783 BCE), the successor of Šamšī-Adad V. The Eponym Chronicles[5] indicate that this Assyrian king conducted military campaigns toward the west in 805, 803, and possibly also in 802 BCE, more than twenty years after Shalmaneser III's last campaign to this region in 829 BCE.[6] Adad-nērārī mentions in his inscriptions his campaign to Damascus and the subjugation of its ruler Mariʾ, identified most probably with Bar-Hadad son of Hazael, who paid a large amount of tribute to him (see Hasegawa 2012). This event took place plausibly in 796 BCE.[7] Aram-Damascus consequently lost its hegemony over the region.

Adad-nērārī's inscription also records the tribute of Joash (r. 799/798–784 BCE), grandson of Jehu, together with those of the Phoenician rulers. This event may also be dated to 796 BCE, the same year when Assyria subjugated Damascus (see Hasegawa 2012). By the tribute payment, Joash, at that time presumably soon after his enthronement, expressed his pro-Assyrian policy. The description of Joash's victory over the Arameans in 2 Kgs. 13:25, as well as the legendary narrative of the siege of Samaria by the Arameans and the subsequent delivery in 2 Kgs. 6:8–7:20, can be understood against the historical background in which Assyria marched against Damascus and conquered it in 796 BCE. The fall of Damascus as a leading power created a vacuum and subsequent turmoil among the kingdoms that were formerly subjugated by Damascus. Due to the weakness of Damascus, Judah could extend its power even into the Arabah (2 Kgs. 14:7). Against this background, Joash of Israel fought with Amaziah of Judah at Beth-Shemesh (2 Kgs. 14:8–14). Joash won the battle, besieged Jerusalem, and took booty and hostages from Judah, which now became a vassal to Israel.

No toponyms in the Levant appear in the event entries of the Eponym Chronicles between 795 and 776 BCE. Yet, Assyria maintained its dominance in the west through its powerful official Šamši-ilu, the *turtānu* (field marshal), whose seat was in Til-Barsip (Tell Aḥmar) on the Euphrates in northern Syria. His leading role and power in this region are well attested in his inscriptions. According to one of his inscriptions, Šamši-ilu played the role of arbitrator in a border dispute among the kingdoms in the region (see Hasegawa 2012). He fell from power probably after 752 BCE, the last year his name appears as *turtānu* in the Eponym Chronicles.

2.2.4. The Prosperity of Israel under Jeroboam II and the End of Jehu's Dynasty (the Early to Mid-Eighth Century BCE)

The Eponym Chronicles register "to Damascus" as the destination of the Assyrian monarch's military campaign in the entry for 773 BCE in the last year of Shalmaneser IV (r. 782–773 BCE), who succeeded Adad-nērārī. The campaign to Damascus was probably led by Šamši-ilu, who erected an inscription concerning this event, together with the name and genealogy of Shalmaneser, his suzerain.

Considering the Assyrian dominance over the Levant in the early eighth century BCE discussed above, Israel's expansion of influence both northward and southward mentioned in Kings (2 Kgs. 13:12, 25; 14:11–15, 25) can be best explained by collaboration between Assyria represented by Šamši-ilu in west, and Israel under Jehu's dynasty that had been loyal to Assyria (see Lipiński 1991; Halpern 2001; Kelle 2002; Hasegawa 2012). The wine lists discovered at Fort Shalmaneser in Nimurd dating to the early eighth century BCE mention Samarians (*Samerināya*), attesting Samarians' presence in Nimrud, the capital of Assyria at that time. This piece of evidence may also corroborate the view that Israel and Assyria collaborated at that time, although the role of the Samarians in Nimrud is not clear.

Hebrew inscriptions mentioning "Yhwh of Samaria" in Phoenician script were discovered at Kuntillet ʿAjrud in southern Sinai, on a trade route connecting Elat and the Mediterranean (Darb el-Ghaza) (see Meshel 2012). The inscriptions are dated to the late ninth or the early eighth century BCE, possibly to the reign of Jeroboam II. Personal names in the inscriptions contain a theophoric element spelled with -יו (-*yw*) typical to names in the Northern Kingdom, rather than -יהו (-*yhw*) more common in Judah.

Moreover, petrographic analysis of small vessels indicates their origin in northern Israel (Gunneweg et al. 1985; Goren 1995). Whatever the function of the site, the inscriptions and pottery indicate the presence of Israelites, probably with Phoenicians, as well as their possible peaceful relationship with the Philistines who lived on the outskirts of the route (Lemaire 1984; Na'aman 1995).

Sixty-six Hebrew inscriptions were discovered from Samaria (Reisner 1924). They are commonly called "the Samaria Ostraca" and dated to the reign of Jeroboam II, providing information concerning the delivery of oil and wine. Although the function of the ostraca is disputed, they demonstrate an organized tax-collecting system in the early eighth century BCE—a possible witness of the centralized administrative system adopted by the royal court at Samaria.

According to the biblical texts, Jeroboam II expanded the territories of Israel (2 Kgs. 14:25). The eighth century BCE falls within the Iron Age IIB, an archaeological periodization of the southern Levant encompassing ca. 800–700 BCE. Archaeological excavations of the related sites have not offered unequivocal evidence of the Israelite expansion in this period, but they have revealed traces of prosperity in the Iron Age IIB. For example, luxury objects such as ivories and well-constructed buildings at Tel Hazor (Stratum VI) in the Upper Galilee date to this period (Yadin 1975; Hasegawa 2012). The largest dwelling structures in the Iron Age discovered in Stratum P-7 at Tel Beth-Shean in the Beth-Shean Valley also date to the eighth century BCE (Mazar 2006). A massive fortification and new buildings found in Stratum III at Tel Rehov located also in the Beth-Shean Valley may date to this period, too (Mazar 1999; Hasegawa 2012). An impressively large public building complex dated to the eighth century BCE, and identified as stables by the excavators, was found in Stratum H-3 in Area L at Tel Megiddo in the west Jezreel Valley. Should these be stables, they may indicate that the Northern Kingdom was engaged in horse trade in that period (Cantrell and Finkelstein 2006; Hasegawa 2012). A well-planned city in Stratum XII at Tel Yoqne'am at the foot of Carmel Range, where the Jezreel Valley abuts from east, can be dated to this period (Ben-Tor et al. 2005; Hasegawa 2012). Stratum VIId at Tell el-Far'ah (North), located to the east of the Samarian mountains and commonly identified as ancient Tirzah, reflects the prosperity of the site with well-constructed houses, larger than those of the preceding strata (Chambon 1984). Strata VII–VI at Tel Gezer, located on the northern boundary of the Shephelah, reflects the prosperous period of the site with a strong fortification (Finkelstein 1994). On the other hand, excavations at Samaria, the capital of Israel in the eighth century BCE, do not show explicit evidence for its prosperity during the period. This is probably due both to the later intensive building activities on the site and to the Assyrians' looting of prestigious objects (Barnett 1982; Hasegawa 2012).

Jehu's dynasty reigned over Israel for about ninety years—the longest dynasty in the history of the kingdom. Zechariah (r. 748–747 BCE), the last monarch of the dynasty, was killed by Shallum son of Jabesh possibly in 747 BCE, who subsequently took the throne (2 Kgs. 15:10, 13).

2.2.5. The Last Days of the Northern Kingdom (the Late Eighth Century BCE)

After one month, Shallum (r. 747 BCE) was murdered by Menahem (r. 747–738 BCE) son of Gadi, who likewise usurped the throne (2 Kgs. 15:14). Considering Assyria's influence on the political arena in the Levant during the late ninth and the early eighth century BCE, this political turbulence may have been triggered by the wane of Assyria in the mid-eighth century BCE due mainly to the rise and expansion of Urartu in the north under Argishti I and Sarduri II (Hasegawa 2012). Menahem's tribute payment to Tiglath-Pileser III (r. 744–727 BCE), dated to 738 BCE, is recorded both in 2 Kgs. 15:19–20 and in Tiglath-pileser's inscriptions.[8] After ascending the throne, this Assyrian monarch resumed Assyria's expansion policy, launched military campaigns to the north and the west, and annexed the territories of the conquered kingdoms. The annexed regions were then transformed into provinces, the populations were deported and resettled, and the culture and demographic structure of the entire ancient Near East underwent radical change (see Tadmor and Yamada 2011).

Pekahiah (r. 738–737 BCE) son of Menahem was killed by Pekah (r. 737–731/730 BCE) probably in 737 BCE, who subsequently took the throne of the Northern Kingdom (2 Kgs. 15:25). Pekah adopted an anti-Assyrian policy alongside some other kingdoms in the Levant. Second Kings 16:5 describes the so-called Syro-Ephraimite war, a siege of Jerusalem under Ahaz by the coalition of Rezin of Aram-Damascus and Pekah (cf. 2 Kgs. 15:37; Isa. 7; 8:1–10, 23; 17:1–3). The coalition withdrew because of the impending campaign of Tiglath-pileser against Damascus in 733 BCE. As a result of this campaign, Damascus fell and was annexed to Assyria. Tiglath-pileser's invasion of Israel, annexation of the Gilead and the Galilee, and deportation of its population during Pekah's reign (2 Kgs. 15:29) happened in the same year, all of which appear in Tiglath-pileser's inscriptions.[9] Assyrian inscriptions also refer to the revolt against Pekah in 732 BCE and the ensuing enthronement of Hoshea (r. 731/730–723/722 BCE) by Tiglath-pileser.[10] Second Kings 15:30 describes this event somewhat differently, in which Hoshea himself took the throne through a coup d'état.

In 722 BCE, Hoshea, who ruled only Samaria and its surrounding region, revolted against Assyria. This triggered the conquest of Samaria by Shalmaneser V (r. 726–722 BCE) and the mass deportation of its inhabitants to Assyria under Sargon II (r. 721–705 BCE) in the following years (see Hasegawa et al. 2019).

The above discussion indicates that the history of Israel in the eighth century BCE was considerably influenced by its relationship with Assyria. The Twenty-Second Dynasty of Egypt was not strong enough to rival Assyria's presence in the southern Levant. When Assyria gained power, Israel had to choose either to become its client kingdom or to fight against it by forming a coalition with other small kingdoms in the region, expecting military support from Egypt. The latter choice under Hoshea eventually led Israel to its catastrophic end.

2.3. HISTORICAL BACKGROUND OF HOSEA'S PROPHECIES

Many interpreters have assumed that some passages in the book of Hosea reflect specific economic-political situations in the history of the Northern Kingdom of Israel. For example, the economic prosperity under Jeroboam II, enabling its bountiful sacrifices and debauched rituals, may stand behind some prophetic indictments (e.g., 2:4–15 [Eng. 2:2–13]; 4:7–14; 12:9 [Eng. 12:8]; see Macintosh 1997). I will consider seven passages often associated with specific historical situations and examine whether each of them reflects the distinct events outlined above or should be interpreted otherwise.

2.3.1. Hosea 1:2–5

This passage refers to "the blood of Jezreel" for which Yhwh will punish "the house of Jehu." Readers who know the story about Jehu's murders of the Omride descendants in the Jezreel Valley may easily associate the passage with the events described in Kings (2 Kgs. 9:14–36; 10:7, 11, 14). The reason for the termination of Jehu's dynasty is specifically "the blood of Jezreel" and not "the sin of Jeroboam" for which Kings blames most of the northern kings, including those of Jehu's dynasty (2 Kgs. 10:31; 13:2, 11; 14:24; 15:9). This might also corroborate the view that the passage alludes to Jehu's murders of the Omride descendants narrated in Kings. Yet, the possibility should not be excluded that the "blood of Jezreel" alludes to events on which we have no information. Furthermore, we do not possess any clue to determine whether this passage harkens back to what really happened in the course of history or merely refers to the story in Kings, which could be historical or ahistorical (cf. the Tel Dan Inscription).

Hosea 1:2 mentions the Jezreel Valley as the place where Yhwh will "break the bow of Israel." This passage may imply a future military defeat of Israel, to which 2:2 (Eng. 1:11) refers as "the day of Jezreel." But we can identify the implied battle neither in biblical texts nor in any other historical sources. The report of Shallum's coup against Zechariah, the last king of Jehu's dynasty, in 2 Kgs. 15:10 does not mention any battle. If we accept the emendation of the MT and read the location of the murder ("before the people": קבל עם in MT) as Ibleam (יבלעם) preserved in the Antiochene text (LXX^L),[11] the event took place at the southern edge of the Jezreel Valley, where King Ahaziah of Judah was shot by Jehu's command (2 Kgs. 9:27; Cogan and Tadmor 1988; Hasegawa 2006). Even so, it is still difficult to take the one-sided shot as the battle implied in Hos. 2:2. The verb שבר *qal* is used also in Jer. 49:35, where Yhwh announces the desolation of Elam, and the same verb in the *piel* is used in Pss. 46:10 and 76:4, in which breaking of the bow has a symbolic meaning for ending war (cf. Ps. 37:15). It is thus difficult to determine whether the reference is to a historical battle or only a metaphor of the ultimate fall of the kingdom.

Another question concerning the passage is whether it concerns the end of Jehu's dynasty or that of the kingdom of Israel as a whole. If 1:4bβ "I will put an end to the kingdom of the house of Israel" is a later expansion, the prophecy originally announced only the end of the rule of Jehu's dynasty. In that case, the ascription of Hosea's activities to the reign of Jeroboam II in the superscription relies on the original information in this passage. At any rate, the passage may refer to a decisive battle that took place in the Jezreel Valley in the eighth century BCE, but we have no sources to specify which battle.

2.3.2. Hosea 5:8–14

The section describes an enemy's impending attack and the subsequent destruction of Ephraim. Verse 8 mentions three toponyms, Gibeah, Ramah, and Bethaven, each of which is related to a sound (horn, trumpet, and battle cry) associated with war. Some scholars have suggested the historical background of the passage is an event during the Syro-Ephraimite War, either the Judahite counterattack against the Northern Kingdom, or Tiglath-pileser's invasion of the Benjamite territory (cf. Alt 1964; Wolff 1974; Macintosh 1997; Na'aman 2015). Considering the critical attitude toward Judah in v. 10, a Judahite attack on Benjamite territory makes sense. Even so, the figurative language of the passage and the limited information on the Syro-Ephraimite War offer no solid conclusions (cf. Andersen and Freedman 1980).

2.3.3. Hosea 6:7–9

The passage describes how the Israelites do evil at certain places and mentions "blood." Some scholars regard the setting of this passage as the same as Hos. 5:8–14, namely, the Syro-Ephraimite War (Wolff 1974; Na'aman 2021). Others seek the historical background in a coup that began in Gilead and continued westward to Samaria, especially Pekah's rebellion, based on the description in 2 Kgs. 15:25 that reports Pekah's conspiracy with fifty Gileadites against Shallum (Alt 1964; Macintosh 1997). Verse 7 states that the Israelites "transgressed (עברו) the covenant like Adam (כאדם MT)," but such a tradition is not found in any biblical text. Adam and the verb עבר are used in Josh. 3:16, where the people "passed (עברו)" the Jordan westward when the water of the river stood "at Adam (באדם; *ketiv*)." The text of Hos. 6:7 could accordingly be emended as "at Adam (באדם)." Adam as a toponym appears only in these two verses in the Hebrew Bible, and there is no reason to see the Israelites' crossing of the Jordan at Adam as an evil action. We have therefore no clues to identify the cited event.

In v. 8, Gilead is associated with "evildoers (פעלי און)," an expression frequently used in Psalms (Pss. 5:6; 6:9; 14:4; 28:3; 36:13; 53:5; 64:3; 92:8, 10; 94:4, 16; 101:8; 141:4, 9; Isa. 31:2; Job 34:8, 22). However, the nature of the evil in these psalms is too generalized to fit with any specific event. The mention of evildoers of Gilead does not necessarily have to do with Pekah's conspiracy with the Gileadites. For example, Judg. 12:1–6 describes an intertribal dissension between the Gileadites and the Ephraimites, causing a battle and subsequent murders of the Ephraimites— an episode atrocious enough to invoke the image of the Gileadites' evildoings.

2.3.4. Hosea 7:3–7

This passage, by using metaphors, seems to describe how the Israelite officials rebelled and killed their king. Some scholars seek the historical background of this passage in the murder of a king of Israel, either Zechariah, Pekahiah, or Pekah (cf. Andersen and Freedman 1980; Macintosh 1997; Nissinen 2019; Wolff 1974; Na'aman 2015). The book of Kings depicts a series of regicides at Samaria's royal court during the late eighth century BCE (2 Kgs. 15:10, 14, 25, 30). However, the highly figurative language of the passage does not warrant any of these associations. Since v. 7 refers to kings in the plural, and v. 2 states that Yhwh remembers "all their wickedness," it is also possible that the passage refers not to the murder of a specific king, but to the repeated regicides in the last decades of the Northern Kingdom.

2.3.5. Hosea 8

This chapter warns Israel of a punishment for their sins. In vv. 5–6, the "calf of Samaria" (v. 6) is sentenced for destruction. First Kings 12:28–32 states that Jeroboam I made two golden calves and set one at Dan and the other at Bethel, but none at Samaria (cf. Hos. 10:5–6). Because of the singularity of the calf in this passage, some hold that the chapter reflects the historical reality after Tiglath-pileser III captured Dan and carried off the calf in 733 BCE (Wolff 1974). In that case, however, the passage should mention the calf of Bethel and not Samaria. The existence of a calf representing the presence of the national god Yhwh in the temple in Samaria (v. 1), the capital of the Northern Kingdom, is not surprising, although no biblical texts preserve such memory. Samaria here may alternatively represent the entire Northern Kingdom.

Verse 9 may imply Israel's tribute payment to Assyria for protection. However, such an action often appears in the history of the Northern Kingdom described in Kings (2 Kgs. 15:10–11; 17:3) and Assyrian royal inscriptions (Jehu, Joash, Menahem, and Hoshea), which makes it difficult to associate the passage with any specific event. The verse may refer to the habitual action of the Israelite monarchs after Jehu.

2.3.6. Hosea 10

Using agricultural metaphors, this chapter depicts an exigent punishment upon Israel. Some scholars locate the chapter between Tiglath-pileser III's invasion of Israel in 733 BCE and the fall of Samaria in 722 BCE during Hoshea's reign (Wolff 1974; Macintosh 1997).

Verse 5 states that the heifers (עגלות; MT, Vul) or the calf (LXX) at Bethaven will be carried off to Assyria. Like the pejorative term "his idolatrous priests (כמריו)" in the same verse, Bethaven ("the house of wickedness") should be regarded as a derogative term for Bethel ("the house of god"), and the heifers as the representation of the gods of the falling nation. Assyria indeed carried off the idols of conquered people. Tiglath-pileser III left in his palace a relief depicting a scene in which his soldiers are carrying four statues of divinities, perhaps from a town in Syria that this Assyrian monarch conquered (BM 118931) (Barnett and Falkner 1962). Sargon II, the conqueror of Samaria, boasted of carrying off the "gods" of the Israelites as booty.[12] If golden heifers/calves really stood at Bethel, they were probably taken away to Assyria when the land was conquered. Even if the author of the passage could guess the number of the calves based on the information in 2 Kgs. 15:29 that reports Tiglath-pileser's capture of the upper Galilee including Dan, it is inconceivable that the author would invent such a historical setting in the reign of Hoshea if the passage were not original. As noted above, the heifers at Bethaven are plural in the MT in contrast to the description in Kings. If the plurality is original, this may mean that the author used the term as the equivalent of "idols," denunciating the cult of the Northern Kingdom as polytheistic.[13]

Verses 14–15 harken back to Shalman's atrocious destruction of Beth-Arbel as an example for how Bethel will be destroyed when Israel falls. Shalman, mentioned only here, has been identified either as Shalmaneser of Assyria or as Salamanu of Moab, mentioned as a tributary in Tiglath-pileser III's inscriptions.[14] If Shalman is the name of an Assyrian king, either Shalmaneser III or Shalmaneser V could be the candidate (Astour 1971). If Hosea mentions this destruction in the time of Jeroboam II, Shalmaneser III is the most plausible candidate, but some scholars see the verse as secondary (see Astour 1971). Scholars often identify Beth-Arbel with Arbela, a site close to modern Irbid in Jordan.[15] However, destruction of Arbela is recorded neither in the Hebrew Bible nor in extant extrabiblical sources. It is equally possible that the readers in the eighth century BCE were familiar with this incident of which no information remains in extant historical sources (Na'aman 2015). If the event was not historical, the author may have created these two proper nouns based on the names of Shalmaneser (2 Kgs. 17:3) and Bethel, but it is hard to explain why he would have.[16]

2.3.7. Hosea 11:8

In this verse, Admah and Zeboiim are mentioned as examples of complete destruction and abandonment. These two cities, the exact locations of which are unknown, appear together with Sodom and Gomorrah in Gen. 10:19; 14:2, 8; and Deut. 29:22. Unlike Sodom and Gomorrah, the destructions of these two are not narrated in Gen. 18:16–19:29. Yet, Gen. 19:29 states that God destroyed the "cities of the plain," the expression possibly meant to include cities nearby such as Admah and Zeboiim. If so, why would the author cite these two cities instead of Sodom and Gomorrah (see Macintosh 1997: 462–63)? It seems best to explain that the author draws on another tradition which the biblical text does not preserve (Na'aman 2015).

2.3.8. Summary

The genre and nature of the book of Hosea prevent the identification of concrete historical settings for each passage. Many of the passages lack information on who did/does what, when, and where. The use of figurative expressions blurs the contents and hinders the association of the passages with specific historical events. In addition, since the current book is the result of *Fortschreibung* through centuries, it contains textual accretions from later periods. Even if the situation depicted in the text appears to fit the assumed sociohistorical circumstances of a period, we should not readily draw conclusions on the historical reliability of the passage. For the same reason, the use of the details of the text for historical reconstruction raises considerable methodological difficulties.

2.4. CONCLUSION

Available historical sources, such as the book of 2 Kings, extrabiblical texts, and archaeological data, suggest that the fate of the Northern Kingdom in the eighth century BCE was considerably influenced by its relationship with the Assyrian Empire, the dominant power in the ancient Near East at the time. Since we possess only a handful of sources relating to the history of the eighth century BCE, we should not a priori dismiss anything that could possibly serve as historical source, including the book of Hosea. Yet, at the same time, naïve use of the book on the assumption that it reflects the historical situation of the eighth century BCE must be avoided due to its genre and nature. Arguments to determine specific historical settings for passages are sometimes based on such an assumption, which may cause either arbitrary interpretation or even emendation of the text. Search for the historical background of a passage must consider the results of textual and redactional analyses.

The available historical data leads us, consciously or unconsciously, to associate texts with that data. We must not forget, however, that a large part of the dataset for the eighth century BCE is the biblical text. When examining the historical background of a passage in the book of Hosea, several principles should apply. When the situation depicted in a passage seems to suit specific historical circumstances, we should ask ourselves how we know such circumstances. If our historical knowledge is based only on biblical texts, we should recall that the author of a passage could also make use of it. If ambiguous expressions in a passage hinder the identification of specific historical events, we should consider whether it is because the primary readers who were familiar with the events might have understood without details, or that the author did not wish to specify the events, perhaps for his own safety. To speak without specific details might have been how the prophet in the eighth century BCE prophesied, or how the later author projected his realities onto the text to leave the text open to different interpretations in different historical contexts. If the historical information in a passage differs from what we know from other biblical texts, we should ask ourselves if the author might have had another tradition at his disposal. To determine which is authentic between the two is sometimes quite difficult. Interpreters should also note that the text of Hosea was considerably revised from the Jerusalemite view in the time of the rivalry between Jerusalem and Samaria during the Achaemenid and Hellenistic periods. Thus, for example, the idolatrous sins of the northern people do not necessarily reflect the reality of Israel in the eighth century BCE, but perhaps the author's image of the "heathen" sibling of his time.

In sum, some passages in the book of Hosea may indeed reflect the historical circumstances in the eighth century. However, due to the book's genre and nature, the historical information is not easy to mine. We should scrutinize the historical value of each passage and use the information for the investigation of the history of the Northern Kingdom only with great caution.

Notes

1. For the chronology of the kings of and after Jehu's dynasty, see Hasegawa 2012.
2. Whether the person kneeling to the Assyrian monarch in the relief is to be identified as Jehu cannot be determined.
3. The Kurkh Monolith inscription; Col. ii 91–92 (Grayson 1996).
4. The Eponym Chronicles record consecutive revolts in 826–820 BCE. Šamši-Adad V conducted campaigns in other directions in the following years (819–810 BCE). See Millard 1994.
5. The Eponym Chronicles register the name of the eponym and his title annually, as well as the major event that occurred during the same year. See Millard 1994.
6. The event entry for 802 BCE records "to the sea (ana tâmtim)," which is possibly identified as the Mediterranean. For this identification, see Hasegawa 2012.
7. The Eponym Chronicles record "to Manṣuate" in this year, which is likely to be identified as a city in northern Syria.
8. Tiglath-pileser III 14, 10; 27, 3; 32, 2; 35; Col. iii, 5 (Tadmor and Yamada 2011).
9. Tiglath-pileser III 22, 1′–11′; 22, 1′–8′a (Tadmor and Yamada 2011); see also Tadmor 1994; Naʾaman 1995.
10. Tiglath-pileser III 42, 15′b–19′a; 44, 17′–18′; 49, 9–11 (Tadmor and Yamada 2011).
11. Or "in Bileam (בבלעם)." For the toponym Bileam in this region, see 2 Chr. 6:55.
12. Sargon II 74; Col. iv 31–32 (Frame 2020). Esarhaddon also states something similar in his inscriptions (Esarhaddon 1; Col. iv 71–72; Leichty 2011).
13. Naʾaman (2015) construes the plurality of the heifers differently; one is the old calf that was already carried away to Assyria and the other is the newly manufactured one.
14. Tiglath-pileser III 47; Rev. 10′; Tadmor and Yamada 2011.

15. In the LXX, Beth-Arbel is written as οἴκου Ιεροβααλ, meaning "house of Jerubaal." Jerubaal is another name of Gideon (Judg. 7:1). It seems the LXX reflects later interpretation of the otherwise unknown toponym Beth-Arbel.

16. Beth-Arabel (בית ארבאל = בית אל (Bethel) + ארב ("to ambush").

REFERENCES

Alt, Albrecht. 1964. "Hosea 5,8–6,6: Ein Krieg und seine Folgen in prophetischer Beleuchtung." In *Kleine Schriften zur Geschichte des Volkes Israel*, vol. 2, 3rd ed. Munich: C. H. Beck, 163–87. (originally published in *NKZ* 30 [1919]: 567–68).

Andersen, Francis I., and David Noel Freedman. 1980. *Hosea*. AB 24. New York: Doubleday.

Astour, Michael C. 1971. "841 B.C.: The First Assyrian Invasion of Israel." *JAOS* 91: 383–89.

Barnett, Richard D. 1982. "Urartu." In *CAH*², 3/1. Cambridge: Cambridge University Press, 314–27.

Barnett, Richard D., and Margarete Falkner. 1962. *The Sculptures of Ashur-nasir-apli II (883–859 B.C), Tiglath-pilesar (745–727 B.C), Esarhaddon (681–669 B.C) from the Central and South-West Palaces at Nimrud*. London: British Museum.

Becking, Bob. 1992. *The Fall of Samaria: An Historical and Archaeological Study*. SHANE 2. Leiden: Brill.

Ben-Tor, Amnon, Anabel Zarzecki-Peleg, and Shulamit Cohen-Anidjar. 2005. *Yoqne'am II: The Iron Age and the Persian Period; Final Report of the Archaeological Excavations (1977–1988)*. Jerusalem: Israel Exploration Society.

Ben-Zvi, Ehud. 2005. *Hosea*. FOTL 21A. Grand Rapids, MI: Eerdmans.

Cantrell, Deborah O., and Israel Finkelstein. 2006. "A Kingdom for a Horse: The Megiddo Stables and Eighth Century Israel." In Israel Finkelstein, David Ussishkin, and Baruch Halpern, eds., *Megiddo IV: 1998–2002 Seasons*. Tel Aviv: Emery and Claire Yass Publications in Archaeology, 643–65.

Chambon, Alain. 1984. *Tell el-Far'ah I: L'âge du fer*. Paris: A.D.P.F.

Cogan, Mordechai, and Hayim Tadmor. 1988. *II Kings*. AB 11. New York: Doubleday.

Davies, Graham I. 1992. *Hosea*. NCB. London: Marshall Pickering.

Finkelstein, Israel. 1994. "Penelope's Shroud Unravelled: Iron Age Date of Gezer's Outer Wall." *TA* 22: 213–39.

Frame, Grant. 2020. *The Royal Inscriptions of Sargon II, King of Assyria (721–705 BC)*. RINAP 2. University Park, PA: Eisenbrauns.

Goren, Yuval. 1995. "Petrographic Analysis of Horvat Teiman (Kuntillet 'Ajrud)." *TA* 22: 206–7.

Grayson, Albert Kirk. 1991. "Assyria: Tiglath-pileser III to Sargon II (744–705 B.C.)." In *CAH*², 3/2. Cambridge: Cambridge University Press, 71–102.

Grayson, Albert Kirk. 1996. *Assyrian Rulers of the Early First Millennium BC, II (858–745 BC)*. RIMA 3. Toronto: University of Toronto Press.

Gunneweg, Jan, Isadore Perlman, and Zeev Meshel. 1985. "The Origin of the Pottery of Kuntillet 'Ajrud." *IEJ* 35: 270–83.

Halpern, Baruch. 2001. "The Taking of Nothing: 2 Kings 14.25, Amos 6:14 and the Geography of the Deuteronomistic History." In David M. Golomb, ed., *"Working with No Data": Semitic and Egyptian Studies Presented to Thomas O. Lambdin*. Winona Lake, IN: Eisenbrauns, 119–39.

Hasegawa, Shuichi. 2006. "Historical Reality vs. Theological Message: Deuteronomist's Insertions in 2 Kgs 9:27–28." *AJBI* 32: 5–14.

Hasegawa, Shuichi. 2012. *Aram and Israel during the Jehuite Dynasty*. BZAW 434. Berlin: De Gruyter.Hasegawa, Shuichi, Christoph Levin, and Karen Radner, eds. 2019. *The Last Days of the Kingdom of Israel*. BZAW 511. Berlin: De Gruyter.

Irvine, Stuart A. 1990. *Isaiah, Ahaz, and the Syro-Ephraimitic Crisis*. SBLDS 123. Atlanta: Scholars.

Jeremias, Jörg. 1983. *Der Prophet Hosea*. ATD 24/1. Göttingen: Vandenhoeck & Ruprecht.

Kelle, Brad. 2002. "What's in a Name? Neo-Assyrian Designations for the Northern Kingdom and Their Implications for Israelite History and Biblical Interpretation." *JBL* 121: 639–66.

Leichty, Erle. 2011. *The Royal Inscriptions of Esarhaddon, King of Assyria (680–669BC)*. RINAP 4. Winona Lake, IN: Eisenbrauns.

Lemaire, André. 1984. "Date et origine des inscriptions hébraïques et phéniciennes de Kuntillet 'Ajrud." *SEL* 1: 131–43.

Lipiński, Édouard. 1991. "Jéroboam II et la Syrie." In Daniele Garrone and Felice Israel, eds., *Storia e tradizioni di Israele: Scritti in onore di J. Alberto Soggin*. Bresica: Paideia, 171–76.

Macintosh, Andrew Alexander. 1997. *A Critical and Exegetical Commentary on Hosea*. ICC. Edinburgh: T&T Clark.

Maeir, Aren. 2003. "Notes and News: Tell eṣ-Ṣâfi/Gath, 1996–2002." *IEJ* 53: 237–46.

Mazar, Amihai. 1999. "The 1997–1998 Excavations at Tel Rehov: Preliminary Report." *IEJ* 49: 1–42.

Mazar, Amihai. 2006. *Excavations at Tel Beth-Shean 1989–1996. Vol. 1: From the Late Bronze Age IIB to the Medieval Period*. Jerusalem: Israel Exploration Society.Meshel, Ze'ev. 2012. *Kuntillet 'Ajrud (Ḥorvat Teman): An Iron Age II Religious Site on the Judah-Sinai Border*. Jerusalem: Israel Exploration Society.

Millard, Alan R. 1994. *The Eponyms of the Assyrian Empire 910–612 BC*. SAAS 2. Helsinki: The Neo-Assyrian Text Corpus Project.

Na'aman, Nadav. 1993. "Azariah of Judah and Jeroboam II of Israel." *VT* 43: 227–34.Na'aman, Nadav. 1995. "Tiglath-pileser III's Campaign against Tyre and Israel (734–732 B.C.E.)." *TA* 22: 268–78.

Na'aman, Nadav. 2015. "The Book of Hosea as a Source for the Last Days of the Kingdom of Israel." *BN* 59: 232–56.

Na'aman, Nadav. 2021. "Harsh Criticism on Pekah's Rebellion in the Book of Hosea." *BN* 188: 43–49.

Nissinen, Martti H. 2019. "The Book of Hosea and the Last Days of the Northern Kingdom: The Methodological Problem." In Shuichi Hasegawa, Christoph Levin, and Karen Radner, eds., *The Last Days of the Kingdom of Israel*. BZAW 511. Berlin: De Gruyter, 369–82.

Reisner, George Andrew. 1924. *Harvard Excavations at Samaria, 1908–1910*. Cambridge, MA: Harvard University Press.

Tadmor, Hayim. 1994. *The Inscriptions of Tiglath-pileser III King of Assyria*. Jerusalem: Israel Academy of Sciences and Humanities.

Tadmor, Hayim, and Shigeo Yamada. 2011. *The Royal Inscriptions of Tiglath-pileser III (744–727 BC), and Shalmaneser V (726–722 BC), Kings of Assyria*. RINAP 1. Winona Lake, IN: Eisenbrauns.

Wolff, Hans Walter. 1974. *Hosea*. Hermeneia. Philadelphia, PA: Fortress.

Yadin, Yigael. 1975. *Hazor: The Recovery of the Great Citadel of the Bible*. London: Weidenfeld and Nicolson.

CHAPTER 3

....

ASSYRIA AND ITS IMAGE
IN HOSEA

....

SHAWN ZELIG ASTER

THE overwhelming majority of the book of Hosea was composed in the Assyrian period, more specifically the period between the middle of the eighth century BCE, when Assyria began to conquer the eastern coast of the Mediterranean, and 720 BCE, when Sargon II exiled the inhabitants of Samaria. In this essay, I will argue for specific connections between passages in Hosea and Assyrian practices, and between these passages and Israelite reactions to Assyrian practices. I will show how these passages rely on Assyrian practices, and argue that this reliance strongly suggests that they were composed during the period when these practices were known and relevant. I will also expose how Hosea encourages Israel to react to Assyrian imperialism and explore how these reactions fit anthropological discussions of conquered societies' reactions to empires. To explore both the connections to the Assyrian period and the (recommended and actual) reactions of the Israelites to Assyrian imperialism, I will focus on three texts: Hos. 5:11–6:3; 7:1–3; and 14:2–5 (Eng. 14:1–4).

Dating Hosea to the Assyrian period is hardly a novel position. The superscription of the book (1:1) dates it to this period (see discussion in Dearman 2010: 21–28). Scholars such as Mays (1969: 3–5) and Andersen and Freedman (1980: 37) date the prophecies of Hosea to the middle of the eighth century. More specifically, they argue that the prophecies began sometime late in the reign of Jeroboam II (whose reign ended about 749 BCE) and ended before the exile of Samaria in about 720 BCE. But in contrast to scholarship on Isaiah (e.g., Machinist 1983 and 2016; Aster 2017 and references there), which has explored how Assyriology might inform our reading of Isa. 1–39, little attention has been dedicated to the ways in which our knowledge of Assyrian practice and rhetoric sheds light on Hosea. The purpose of this essay is to consider how we can better understand Hosea in the light of the reactions to Assyrian imperialism.

First, however, the very idea that much of Hosea is a product of the eighth century must be defended. The strongest argument in favor of the traditional eighth-century dating is encapsulated in Day's statement (2010: 202): "So much that we find in Hosea is inconsistent with a post-exilic origin, but makes eminently good sense against a pre-722 BCE background." Day was reacting to the views of Ben Zvi (2005) and others who argued that not only was Hosea edited in the postexilic period but also many of the passages contained in the book were composed after the exile. Ben Zvi argued that the mentions of Assyria and Egypt in Hos. 4–14 were almost fictive "constructions of the past" (2006: 14). More recently, Bos (2013) has argued that the political views expressed in Hosea could not belong to the Assyrian period. In what follows, I will develop Day's statement with reference to specific passages. I will demonstrate that the specific mentions of Assyria in Hos. 4–14 correspond to what we know from the textual record of Assyrian practices and Israelite reactions in the mid-eighth century, in the period preceding the exile of c. 720 BCE. But before this, I will present a brief synopsis of the background of the relations between Israel and Assyria in the period preceding the prophecies of Hosea.

3.1. HISTORICAL BACKGROUND

The Northern Kingdom of Israel had direct but intermittent contact with the Assyrian empire from the time of Ahab onward (see Kelle 2005). The following paragraphs review this contact, and also explain the background for Hosea's determination that this contact was injurious to Israel.

Contact began no later than 853 BCE, when Ahab joined with other kings of the eastern Mediterranean in an attempt to prevent the Assyrian king Shalmaneser III from advancing Assyrian exploitation of the region (Rainey and Notley 2005: 199–211). Assyria fought against this coalition for a dozen years, until dynastic changes in both Israel and Damascus caused realignments in the alliances of both of these kingdoms around 841 BCE.

In that year, Jehu, the newly installed king of Israel who had risen to power with Aramean support, submitted to Assyria and paid tribute. In the same year, Hazael, who was both Jehu's patron and the newly installed king of Aram-Damascus, suffered a serious but temporary set-back in the battle against Assyria. (On Jehu's submission and Hazael's defeat, see Cogan 2008: 22–31; on the Aramean support of Jehu, see Schniedewind 1996.)

Assyria's last gambit to the Levant for the next thirty years took place in 838 BCE, when Assyria again defeated Hazael (as narrated in the Black Obelisk; Cogan 2008: 22). Shortly afterward, Assyria entered a period of weakness, which was exploited by Hazael of Damascus to become the hegemon of the Levant and to extract wealth throughout Syro-Palestine, harming both Israel and Judah (2 Kgs. 12:18–19; 13:1–9; Rainey and Notley 2005: 206–7; Kleiman 2016). Hazael's hegemony lasted for nearly forty years, until Adad-nērārī III of Assyria demoted him (or his successor) sometime between 805 and 796 BCE (2 Kgs. 13:5; Rainey and Notley 2005: 214–15; Cogan 2008: 33–41).

In 796 BCE, under the leadership of Jehu's grandson Joash, Israel again paid tribute to Assyria, as detailed in the Tell a-Rimah stele (Cogan 2008: 39–41). Following the payment of this tribute and Damascus's loss of hegemony, Israel began to control trade routes throughout the region in the period of Jeroboam son of Joash. This control is detailed in 2 Kgs. 14:25, which describes Jeroboam as ruling "from Lebo of Hamath till the sea of the plain."

However, Jeroboam's control of the region did not come cheaply. Assyria was still a powerful kingdom. When Adad-nērārī III took the throne in 810 BCE, Assyria's period of weakness came to an end and was replaced by a period in which Assyria tried to control regional hegemony and reap rewards. (For a discussion of Assyrian policy in this period, see Siddall 2013.) During the reigns of Adad-nērārī III (810–783) and his sons and successors (Shalmaneser IV, 782–773 BCE; Ashur-Dan III, 772–755, and Ashur-nirāri V, 754–745), Assyria allowed other rulers to rise in the Levant, as long as they paid tribute to Assyria.

The last kings of the Jehu dynasty, who ruled Israel during this period, cooperated in implementing this Assyrian policy. They repeatedly paid tribute during this period, both in 796 under Joash (as noted above), and again under his son Jeroboam on several occasions in the period 791–779, as can be learned from the Nimrud wine lists (Aster 2016). Therefore, Jeroboam's achievement of hegemony "from Lebo of Hamath till the sea of the plain" (2 Kgs. 14:25) was partly the result of payment of tribute to Assyria. For the Israelite elite who benefited from this hegemony, the payment was the "cost of doing business"; the Assyrians might have regarded it as a symbolic recognition of Assyrian power. In either case, the "increased prosperity with an influx of luxury goods as a result of Israel's control of trade routes," which characterized Jeroboam's rule, came at a cost: payment to Assyria (Rainey and Notley 2005: 217).

This payment forms the background of many of Hosea's prophecies. Years before Hosea prophesied, the elite in the kingdom of Israel had developed the tendency to transfer some of the kingdom's resources to Assyria and, as a result of this, to benefit from lucrative trade opportunities. These trading opportunities brought wealth to the elite. This wealth was not distributed equally among the majority of Israel's population, who were engaged primarily in subsistence agriculture. In particular, those who lived in the Samarian hill country, far from any trade routes, were unlikely to benefit from this wealth. Furthermore, the payments to Assyria made by the king were not necessarily extracted only from those benefiting from the trading opportunities. The resulting economic and social inequities form the background of much of Hosea's portrayal of Assyria.

The attitude of Israel's trading elite toward Assyria is hardly unique in the history of how local elites react to imperial domination. Anthropologists have noted how empires co-opt local elites in order to exploit existing revenue-collection systems and hierarchies, without the need to develop anew such systems in client states. Simultaneously, local elites bolstered their powerful position through reliance on the empire's power (Sinopoli 1994: 164). In this case, the elite were able to exploit trade thanks to Assyrian support. As in the systems studied by Sinopoli, the symbiotic-beneficial relationship between the local elite and the empire resulted in the exclusion of the nonelite strata in the population of the client state of Israel from wealth and power. Hosea rails against this process of co-optation, bolstering, and exclusion.

Hosea focuses specifically on the enticements Assyria offered to elites whose kingdoms paid tribute, and thereby became (at least from the perspective of Assyria) client states. Assyrian inscriptions clearly emphasized that those who entered such vassal relationships had something to gain from Assyria, such as political backing of the local leaders or alliances against enemies (Parpola and Watanabe 1988: xvi). Assyria promoted the idea that those who entered into such arrangements stood to gain. Against this argument, Hosea waxes most prolix, arguing repeatedly that alliances with Assyria do not provide Israel with any true benefit.

3.2. HOSEA 5:11–6:3

The passage opens in 5:11 by declaring that Ephraim has been despoiled and continues in 5:12 by describing Ephraim as affected by rot. Hosea 5:13–6:1 presents Ephraim's reaction to these problems:

> (13) Ephraim became aware of his sickness, and Judah of his sore. Ephraim went to Assur and sent envoys to the great king. But he cannot cure you and he cannot heal from you the sore. (14) For I am like a lion to Ephraim and a lion cub to the house of Judah. I, even I, will take prey and go, I will carry off with no one to rescue. (15) I will go and return to My place until they recognize their guilt and seek My face, for in their distress they will seek Me. (6:1) [The Israelites say the following:] "Let us go and return to Yhwh. Although He tore, He will heal us; He hit, He will bind us up."

The "rot" and "sickness" in 5:12–13 symbolize military weakness, and the instability and lack of political power of the Israelite king. These are precisely the problems that Assyrian propaganda claimed would be addressed through an alliance with Assyria (Parpola and Watanabe 1988: xvi; Dearman 2010: 186). Hosea 5:13b describes how "Ephraim," a term consistently used in Hosea to refer to the elite of the Northern Kingdom, sent emissaries to Assyria. The phrase מלך ירב in this verse is a Hebrew translation of the Akkadian title *šarru rabbu* (Paul 1986: 199). The clear goal of this embassy is to seek Assyrian support for the king, strengthening his kingdom. But in 5:13b, Hosea argues that the Assyrian king is unable to "heal" Israel, a metaphor for solving these problems.

In vv. 14 and 15, Yhwh is presented using leonine imagery. This imagery places him in clear contrast to the Assyrian king, who not only compared himself to a brave lion, but was also depicted, in his royal seal, as fighting and subduing a lion in an act of bravery.[1] This depiction was widely circulated throughout the Near East from the ninth to the seventh centuries, and was perhaps the most well-known example of Assyrian royal art (Millard 1965; Herbordt 1992: 134–36). The motif of the Assyrian king subduing a lion was surely known in eighth-century Israel. Coming immediately after a verse in which the Assyrian king is referred to by a Hebrew version of his Akkadian title, the leonine imagery intentionally engages the royal Assyrian reference: the lion is the rival of the Assyrian king, whom the Assyrian king subdues, thereby showing his supremacy (Weissert 1997). Here, Yhwh is portrayed as that rival, but one who is not subdued by the Assyrian king.

The actions of Yhwh in these verses dovetail with the imagery and further contrast with the Assyrian king. While the Assyrian king *cannot* heal Israel in 5:13, in 5:14–15 Yhwh *will not* rescue Israel. He takes prey and goes back to his "place." The Assyrian king is *approached* by Israelite emissaries; Yhwh *waits* for the Israelite emissaries and is unwilling to act until they, in their distress, come seeking. Yhwh is portrayed here as a sovereign, an alternative to the Assyrian king. If the Israelite emissaries decide to seek Yhwh, and accept Yhwh's conditions, then Yhwh will solve Israel's problems.

But like Assyria's help, Yhwh's help does not come cheaply. For the Israelites to benefit from this help, they must "recognize their guilt and seek My face," thereby accepting Yhwh's sovereignty. The action of recognizing guilt and seeking the sovereign's face is itself taken from the political vocabulary of Assyrian royal inscriptions. It encapsulates the expectation of a client state which rebelled and then decided to pay the tribute to avoid Assyrian military retribution. Consider the actions of an unidentified rebellious state narrated in the annals of Tiglath-pileser III (Tadmor 1994: 176, 282; Tadmor and Yamada 2011: 125–27):

> ḫīṭišunu amḫurma, massunu ú-bal-[li-it],

A literal translation of this line might be:

> "I faced their sin, I healed their land."

The meaning, of course, is:

> "I accepted [a plea to forgive] their rebellion, and I spared their land."[2]

As we see here, the guilty party is responsible for recognizing its guilt and beseeching the sovereign, much as Israel is portrayed as doing in Hos. 5:15. Like the rebellious states in the Assyrian inscriptions, the Israelites recognize that they had previously acknowledged Yhwh as their sovereign, as they say in 6:1: "Let us return to Yhwh."

The Israelites then express their expectations of being helped by Yhwh in 6:1: "Although he tore, he will heal us, although he hit, he will bind us up." The actions of healing here also reference Assyrian imagery. As seen in the short passage from Tiglath-pileser III above, Assyrian inscriptions use the verb "healing" to describe a sovereign forgiving and pardoning a rebellious vassal (see Berkovitz and Aster 2018 for examples, and Barré 1978 on Hos. 6:2). Hosea is aware of the Assyrian usage and formulates this passage so that 5:13 refers to the failure of the Assyrian king to heal Israel, and 6:1 refers to Yhwh's willingness to do so. In both 6:1 and the Assyrian royal inscriptions, "healing" is a metaphor expressing reacceptance of a client after a period of rebellion. Its use in Hos. 6:1 is a clear reference to the language of Assyrian imperialism known from the Assyrian inscriptions.[3]

In this passage, the Israelites long for divine pardon, recognizing (in 6:1) that this pardon is forthcoming from Yhwh in a way that it is not from the Assyrian king (in 5:13). By using the sickness metaphor, Hosea sharpens the contrast between Yhwh and the Assyrian king. The latter (according to 5:13) will neither solve political problems nor pardon. The former (according to 6:1) will grant pardon. Yhwh, who caused the political problems in the first place, as 5:11 implies, will grant the pardon. Yhwh is the real power and threat. Yhwh causes the problem and can also heal Israel.

Together, Hosea references a series of Assyrian images: the rebellious vassal, the lion-like king, the term מלך ירב, and healing-as-forgiveness. But he consistently does so in a way that expresses contrast between Yhwh and the Assyrian king. Yhwh is able to punish, forgive, and heal; the Assyrian king is unable to solve Israel's problems. The passage is fundamentally subversive. It uses Assyrian imagery while arguing against the utility of submission to Assyria. In this way, Hosea emphasizes the futility of vassalage to Assyria.

3.3. Hosea 7:1–7

Hosea 5:13– 6:1 describes how valueless alliances with Assyria are for Israel, and views "Israel" as a collective whole. The interesting but difficult passage in 7:1–7 also uses the verb רפא, "to heal." While it does not explicitly mention Assyria, it refers to Israel's servitude to a king and officers (7:3), who appear to be those of Assyria. The passage highlights the property crimes of Israel's elite. It explores social rifts that develop from the servitude to Assyria, whose anthropological basis I explored in the introduction.

The passage begins in 6:11b, "When I return the return of my people," and continues:

> (1) In my pardoning Israel, the disloyalty of Ephraim will be revealed, and (so too) the evil deeds of Samaria, for they act treacherously: the thief would come and the band would take property in the street. (2) They would not say in their heart "I (Yhwh) remember all their evil." Now their deeds surround them, and are before My face. (3) In their wickedness they would make the king glad, by their treachery—the officers.

The רפא, or pardoning of Israel, is here the occasion for the revelation of Israel's property crimes. The question of the link between the healing (רפא) of Israel and the revelation of its property crimes has long perplexed interpreters. Dearman (2010: 200) understands the verse as a failed attempt at divine pardon: Yhwh cannot forgive the people because of their sins. In his view, the revelation of sins interferes with the release from punishment.[4] This interpretation is difficult: iniquities may be of such magnitude as to prevent pardon, but what role does their revelation play?

I suggest that we understand רפא here as referring to Yhwh's pardon of Israel, a pardon that follows Israel's return, which is mentioned in 6:11b. The sequence of Israel's return to Yhwh followed by pardon (expressed by רפא) is found in Hos. 6:1, and also in 14:2–5 (Eng. 14:1–4). Hosea 6:11b–7:1 should be understood as another example of this sequence. The return of Israel in 6:11b refers to Israel returning to recognize Yhwh as its sovereign, abandoning Assyria. Yhwh then pardons Israel, as mentioned in 7:1.

Once that pardon is effective, Israel's vassal relationship with Assyria is effectively over. Already in 5:13–6:1, Hosea sees Israel's relationship with Yhwh and its recognition of Assyrian sovereignty as mutually exclusive. With the end of Israel's vassalage to Assyria comes an accounting: "Ephraim's disloyalty is revealed." The full cost of Israel's servitude to Assyria, which ultimately benefited the Israelite political leadership at the expense of the populace, is only made clear when that servitude ends, to be replaced by loyalty to Yhwh.

Then and only then does Yhwh reveal Ephraim's deceit and property crimes (7:1). These crimes included thieves coming and bands stealing property in the open, acts that clearly benefit the king and his officers (7:3). As I argued (Aster and Berkovitz 2018: 165–66), these iniquities are best understood within a political matrix: the property seizures benefit the political leadership. The simplest explanation of this imagery is that the king and his officers seize property of less highly ranked citizens for their own benefit. They used these for tribute payments to Assyria. By paying Assyria, they strengthened their own status as elites. The king and officers referenced in 7:3 may be those of Israel or of Assyria, although the context suggests that they are Israelite. But it matters little which they are, because the benefit was accrued by both, who acted in league. The Israelite king paid the Assyrian one, while the latter bolstered the status of the former.

The term כחש (7:3), here translated "treachery," should be discussed in this context. In Hosea, the term refers to oath repudiation, and is used in that sense in Hos. 4:2. In 12:1–2 (Eng. 11:12–12:1), כחש and כזב refer to Israel's pursuit of client relationships with Assyria and Egypt; these relationships repudiate Israel's prior covenant relationship with Yhwh and therefore constituting oath breaking and lying. In 7:3 too, כחש refers to Israel's relationship with Assyria, which is implicitly a repudiation of its previous oath of loyalty to Yhwh.

I now return to the question of "revealing" the sin of Ephraim (7:1). This revelation of sin takes place after Israel ends its subservience to Assyria and returns to acknowledge the sovereignty of Yhwh. As long as Israel acknowledged Assyrian sovereignty, both ideologically and by payment, the full extent of Assyrian resource extraction was "swept under the rug." Only when the servitude to Assyria is over, and when Israel finally returns to Yhwh, is the extent of the payments made clear (7:1). And only then is Ephraim reminded that Yhwh was aware the whole time of Ephraim's actions, noting them and watching (7:1–2). The description of Yhwh as watching and waiting is reminiscent of the imagery in 5:15. It is consistent with a wider tendency in Hosea for Yhwh to demand that Israel take the first step in returning (as in 6:1 and 14:2–5 [Eng. 14:1–4]).

Hosea 7:1–3 continues concepts found in 5:11–6:3 in other ways, too. In 5:11–6:3, Hosea contrasts Yhwh's pardon with that extended by the Assyrian king. The former results in a beneficial covenantal relationship, the latter in resource extraction, which does not benefit Israel. Hosea 5:11–6:3 emphasizes the lack of utility of this relationship, while 7:1–3 emphasizes the economic costs, borne disproportionately by those not part of the elite.

Hosea 7:1–3 is widely recognized as part of a larger unit, extending to 7:7. Hosea 7:4–7 expatiates on the actions of the elite.

> (4) They are all adulterers, like an oven burning without a baker. He refrains from awakening them to knead the dough until it rises. (5) On the day of our king, the officers begin to become warmed up from wine. He also pulls his hand together with the scoffers. (6) For their hearts are bringing near like an oven while they wait.[5] All night their baker sleeps so that in the morning, the oven is burning with a fiery flame. (7) They have all become heated up like an oven and they devour their judges. All their kings fall. None among them call to Me.

The main image in these verses is that of the oven (vv. 4, 6, 7). Dearman (2010: 201) interprets this as a reference to "the heat of political intrigue." There is certainly a great deal of political intrigue here, but there is also a clear explanation of the image in 7:4, where the burning oven is presented as a metaphor related to adultery. The metaphor is not an unusual one: sexual desire is described as warming the body (1 Kgs. 1:1–2). Similarly, other intense passions, such as the desire for revenge, are described as "heating the heart" (Deut. 19:6). Therefore, the sexual excitement that leads to adultery could easily be compared to an oven burning out of control. Both 7:4 and 7:6 describe how the oven is burning intensely because the baker is failing to tend to the fire.

Hosea speaks extensively about adultery (4:10–15; 5:3; 6:10), and has a somewhat innovative understanding of the term. In 4:10–15, he makes clear that not only "your daughters" are guilty of adultery but also the male Israelites who become drunk (4:11) and then consort with prostitutes (4:14). As Gruber (2017: 226) noted, 4:14 is a "profound and timeless castigation of men who cheat on their wives." In that passage, the adulterous men take advantage of a religious festival to have extramarital sex (Gruber 2017: 222). In 7:4–7, the opportunity for adultery is presented by "the day of our king" (4:5). We know two things about this day: one is that it is characterized by drinking, and the second is that it is characterized by adultery.

These two characteristics of the "day of our king" strongly suggest that the day referenced is the annual gathering of representatives of different kingdoms in Assyria to pay tribute to the Assyrian king. First, concerning the drinking. Based on the Nimrud wine lists and other administrative documents, Fales (1994: 367–69) describes this gathering as an annual feast, at which court personnel, army officers, and royal administrators, along with dozens of emissaries from client states, received allocations totaling over one-thousand liters of wine. The feast coincided with the annual gathering of emissaries from client states, who were required to travel to Assyria and present tribute. Representatives of the Israelite kings, who were themselves high-ranking officials, certainly traveled to this annual gathering throughout the first half of the eighth century and remitted tribute (Aster 2016). This annual presentation of loyalty to Assyria could certainly be called by Hosea, in a mocking way, "the day of our king," and surely involved wine drinking.

The second characteristic, adultery (a term Hosea uses also to refer to males engaging in extramarital sex), is easy to understand in this context. Male emissaries, traveling away from their homes and wives, having their passions inflamed by a wine-feast, would probably find it challenging to remain celibate. (See Dorsey 1991: 43 for evidence from Mesopotamia for inns catering to travelers and providing female prostitutes for men; see also literature cited in Gruber 2017: 373 n. 12.) This annual gathering, therefore, seems to be the simplest understanding of Hosea's "day of our king" (7:5) at which royal officials of Israel traveled to Assyria, drank, became "heated" (to use a euphemism), and committed adultery.

This understanding of 7:4–7 suggests a clear and continuous argument in Hos. 7:1–10. Verses 1–3, as discussed, refer to the economic and social consequences of Israel's subservience to Assyria. Verses 4–7 refer to the travel to Assyria for the mandatory annual gathering, and castigate the release of passions at that event. Verse 7b describes how despite Israel's annual payment of loyalty, "they devour their judges. All their kings fall." Here, Dearman's interpretation of the passage as referring to political intrigue holds true. In this verse, "the end results of political intrigue and forced regime changes are summarized" (Dearman 2010: 205). Forced regime changes in Israel were directly connected to the annual gathering of emissaries, for it was by means of the tribute paid at this gathering that Israelite kings maintained their position. This was particularly true for two pro-Assyrian kings, Menahem and Hoshea.

Despite the presentation of tribute, "all their kings fall" (7:7b). Here, Hosea resumes the theme seen above in 5:11–6:3: Israelite submission to Assyria will not result in strengthening the kingdom or solving its political problems. Instead, Israelite submission will result in weakening and failure of kings. Indeed, Menahem's downfall was directly connected to the rise of an anti-Assyrian rival, and Hoshea's dependence on Assyria certainly weakened the kingdom.

The subsequent verses (7:8–10) continue the theme expressed in 7:1–7:7 of the failure of Israel's subservience to Assyria. The prophet castigates Israel in 7:10 for not doing as it ought: "Nevertheless, they have not returned to Yhwh their God, nor have they sought Him out." Here, too, Hosea contrasts the sending of Israelite emissaries to Assyria ("mixed among the nations") with Israel's return to Yhwh.[6]

In the next section, I explore other passages that describe the journey of the tribute-bearing emissaries to Assyria and to Egypt.

3.4. Tribute-Bearers' Journey: Hosea 9:1–3 and 12:1–2 (Eng. 11:12–12:1)

In discussing this journey, I begin with 9:1–3, where the criticism of these emissaries is most intense. (This passage is part of a unit comprising 9:1–9, whose thematic connection to 7:8 is noted by Dearman 2010: 235.)

> (1) Do not rejoice Israel, as other nations exult, for you have turned away from your God. You have been loyal to harlot's wages at every threshing-floor. (2) Neither threshing-floor nor winepress will shepherd them, and the new wine will act treacherously to her. (3) They will not dwell in the land of Yhwh, and so Ephraim will go back to Egypt, and they will eat impurity in Assyria.

As Gruber (2017: 371) notes, 9:2 refers to crop failure, with both the grain and grape crops failing to provide the expected yield. Therefore, Israel must not rejoice at harvest as other nations do (9:1). This crop failure is a divine punishment, visited on Israel for its disloyalty to Yhwh and for going after prostitutes (9:1). In response to Israel's economic problems, the Israelite elite sent emissaries to Egypt, and formed alliances with Assyria (9:3).

Many commentators understand 9:3 as referring to exile from the land of Yhwh (Mays 1969: 127; Dearman 2010: 238). I believe this is incorrect for two reasons. First, exile is not the direct result of crop failure. If Israelites had to leave their land because of poor crop yields, more proximate places of refuge than Assyria were at their disposal (as in Ruth 1:1 and Jer. 40:11–12). Second, Egypt and Assyria are paired numerous times in the book of Hosea, including 7:11, 11:5, and 12:2 (Eng. 12:1). In each of these cases, the reference is to Israel's alliances with Egypt or with Assyria, by which the elite of the kingdom seek to bolster their position. Egypt and Assyria are generally not mentioned as exile destinations. (Hosea 10:6, which Gruber [2017: 375] understands as an exile destination, also refers to bringing tribute to Assyria.)

Hosea 9:3 elaborates on the reasons for Israel experiencing crop failure. As discussed in 9:1, there are two reasons for this punishment. One is the harlotry, and the second is the turning away from Yhwh. In Hosea, turning away from Yhwh refers to acknowledging a foreign power such as Assyria as sovereign. In this passage, as in many others, Hosea castigates Israel for sending emissaries to Egypt and to Assyria, in order to bring tribute and form alliances. The sending of emissaries to Egypt is expressed as "returning to Egypt," evoking the Exodus and the curse-formula we know from Deut. 28:68. The sending of emissaries to Assyria is expressed by describing the eating of impurity in Assyria. This is not because of the idea that "any food, no matter how kosher it may be, if consumed outside the land of Israel is *ipso facto* unclean" (Gruber 2017: 374), but because the verse references the banquets celebrated in Assyria on the occasion of the visit of the tribute-bearing emissaries. We have already seen Fales's (1994) discussion of wine consumption at these affairs. Earlier, Postgate noted that the tribute-bearers were fed at the state's expense, and given gifts in order to encourage those who actually made the journey to undertake it again (Postgate 1974: 127–28). "They will eat impurity in Assyria" (9:3) refers to tribute-bearing emissaries from Israel attending these banquets, and 9:3 as a whole refers to the journeys made to Egypt and to Assyria in order to conclude alliances. Since these alliances represent turning away from Yhwh, Israel is to be punished for them. The failed crops described in 9:2 are the punishment both for the harlotry described in 9:1 and for the disloyalty to Yhwh described in 9:3.

The subsequent verses (9:4–6) are often understood as presenting the loss of temple-sacrifice as a consequence of exile (Mays 1969: 127; Dearman 2010: 241). However, I would suggest that they function somewhat differently. Hosea 9:4–6 nowhere references the loss of the temple itself or its destruction, but only the fact that Israelites will not celebrate festivals in the temple, or come into the house of God. These verses serve as a counterpoint to 9:1–3. In 9:1–3, the Israelites are blamed for acknowledging either Assyrian or Egyptian sovereignty by forming alliances with these powers. In 9:4–9, by contrast, the prophet highlights how the Israelites will not acknowledge Yhwh's sovereignty by visiting the temple and sacrificing in it on the festivals. The key to understanding the connection between 9:1–3 and 9:4–6 is recognizing that sacrificing on festivals is a way of acknowledging Yhwh as sovereign of the land, as indicated in Exod. 34:23. Hosea 9:1–6 contrasts the actions of Israelites traveling to bring tribute to Egypt and Assyria, thereby creating client relationships with those powers and recognizing their sovereignty, with the ideal but absent action of Israelites recognizing the sovereignty of Yhwh by celebrating his festivals in the temple. Thus, 9:5: "What shall you do on the appointed day, on the day of the festival of Yhwh?"

Another passage describing the experience of the tribute-bearing emissaries is Hos. 12:1–2 (Eng. 11:12–12:1). Like 7:1–3, it explicitly links the client relationship with theft.

> (1) Ephraim has surrounded Me with treachery, and the House of Israel has done so with deceit, while Judah is still ruled by God and loyal to the holy ones. (2) Ephraim shepherds the wind and runs after the east wind. All day, he does much lying and stealing. They make a covenant with Assyria and oil is brought to Egypt.

Hosea 12:2b describes covenants with Assyria and with Egypt (here following Heintz 2001).[7] But 12:1–2 contains several comments on these covenants. First, 12:1 describes these covenants as "treachery" (כחש). We have seen above, in 7:3, that Hosea considers the act of making an alliance with Assyria "treachery" because it involves repudiating an earlier covenant with Yhwh. Second, the covenant is useless and pointless, like "chasing after the east wind" (12:2). We have seen in 5:13–6:1 that Hosea considers the Assyrians incapable of solving Israel's political problems by making alliances with Israel. And third, 12:2 connects frequent robbery with treaties with Egypt and Assyria. We have seen earlier that 7:1–3 condemns the Israelite elite for robbing less-fortunate Israelites of their property in order to cement the client relationship with Assyria, a relationship that ultimately benefits only the Israelite elite. Hosea 12:1–2, therefore, castigates those who

3.5. HOSEA 14:2–9 (ENG. 14:1–8)

Hosea 14:2–9 (Eng. 14:1–8) functions as the summary of the book. One of the most beautiful passages in Hosea, it extracts lessons from Israel's experience with Assyria, lessons that outlive that experience.

> (2) Return, O Israel, to Yhwh your God, for you have failed through your disloyalty. (3) Take words with you, and return to Yhwh. Say to Him: "You will forgive all disloyalty[8] and take good, and we will pay [for the] cows [we owe] with our lips. (4) Assyria will not save us! We will not ride on horses! Nor will we any longer say 'our god' to the work of our hands! For through You will an orphan be loved."[9] (5) [God says:] "I will pardon their rebellion; I will be loyal to them without payment, for my anger has abated from being against them. (6) I shall be like dew for Israel; they shall flower like the lily, and strike roots like [trees of] Lebanon." (7) His shoots will extend, and his vigour will be like that of an olive tree, and his fragrance like that of Lebanon. (8) Those who dwell in his shade will return and keep the grain alive and flower like the grape-vine; his mention is like that of the wine of Lebanon.

The passage begins by calling on Israel to return to Yhwh, echoing the return language of 6:11b, בשובי שבות עמי. It goes on to state, "You have failed through your disloyalty," arguing that the experience of disloyalty to Yhwh and of vassalage to Assyria has itself been a failure. In v. 3, Israel is called upon to engage in a new type of transactional relationship, different from that which governs its tribute to Assyria. Commercial terms such as "תשא", "קח" and "נשלמה" are used, but these are placed within a larger framework: Israel need only declare its loyalty to God. Whereas in relation to Assyria, Israel needed to actually engage in payment, in relation to Yhwh, Israel need only declare its loyalty. In v. 4, Israel repudiates its relationships with Assyria and with Egypt, and accepts that lacking a political patron, it has achieved "orphan status." In v. 4, Israel expects Yhwh to accept it as vassal and Yhwh then declares, in v. 5, that he will pardon Israel, freely. The client relationship with Assyria, centered on resource extraction, has ended, and Israel now has an old/new sovereign, Yhwh, who does not require tribute, but only recognition of his sovereignty.

Verses 6–8 each end with the mention of "Lebanon," and highlight the lush fauna of Lebanon. Each verse contains a different metaphor about the fauna of Lebanon: rootedness (v. 6); fragrance (v. 7); and flowering (v. 8). The emphasis on Lebanon seems connected to the use the Assyrians made of the Lebanon coast, which served in the time of Tiglath-pileser III as a point of control for Assyria of all of the southern Levant (Aster f.c.). The use of these metaphors underscores the contrast between Yhwh's and Assyria's sovereignty. While the Assyrians capitalized on Lebanon as a commercial hub, and their relationship with Israel consisted of resource extraction, Yhwh's will reinstate Lebanon's status as a place of lush flora. Hosea here contrasts the husbanding of nature, an act of Yhwh, with commercial enterprise, an act of Assyria.

3.6. CONCLUSION

From all of the passages cited above, a clear picture emerges of Assyrian practices and of their effect on the Israelite polity. Assyria was bent on extracting resources from Israel, as it did from its other client states, and used the annual visit of the emissaries as a means of co-opting the local elites to support this policy of resource extraction. It offered these elites the benefit of the annual banquet and gathering in return for their support. But Assyrian support exacerbated social cleavages in Israel, and did not strengthen the polity as a whole.

Assyrian support was valuable to such kings as Menahem and Hoshea, who owed their rule to Assyrian support. But Hosea the prophet emphasized the social effects of onerous tribute payments. These created a clear divide between the Israelite elites and the Assyrians on the one hand, and the rest of the people on the other. The former extracted resources, and the latter provided them. Benefits accrued only to the elite who cooperated with Assyria, and the resource extraction was considered by others, including the prophet, as equivalent to theft. These social ills can be remedied, in the prophet's view, by repudiating the alliance with Assyria and resuming Israel's ancient alliance with Yhwh.

It is exceedingly difficult to view the portrayal of Assyria in Hosea as merely a fictive representation of the past and thus to place these passages in the Persian period. Yehud, in the Persian period, was a Persian province, not a client state. Resources were therefore extracted directly, and the local elites were not as closely tied to resource extraction as were those of the Assyrian-era client kingdom of Israel. The alternative of allying with Egypt instead of Assyria, which recurs in Hos. 7:11; 9:3; 10:6; 11:5; and 12:2 (Eng. 12:1), simply did not exist in the Persian period. Most importantly, the contrast between recognizing Yhwh's sovereignty or that of Assyria was irrelevant in the Persian period, when Yehud's residents had no option other than to live under Persian sovereignty.

Hosea is fundamentally a reflection on history, and to understand it fully, historical background is needed. The contrast between the ancient alliance with Yhwh and subservience to Assyria is a theological concept, but Hosea connects it to a social context: alliance with Assyria means that the Israelite elite have been co-opted and rob the nonelite Israelites. I have identified examples of Hosea bemoaning this co-optation. When Hosea references an ideal historical period, one that can serve as a contrast to the reality he describes, he evokes the Exodus and wilderness-wandering periods, as in 2:16–22 (Eng. 2:14–20) and in 11:1–6. These represent the idyllic phase to which Israel must return. While recognizing the high degree of idealization in this description, we must also acknowledge its connection to historical reality. "Early Israel," i.e., the earliest settlement of Israelites (in the Iron I) in the region that would become the kingdom of Israel, was characterized by a high degree of egalitarian social structure, and society was structured largely on the basis of extended families (Faust 2006.) Iron I Israel shows little evidence for administration and resource extraction or for social stratification, in contrast to Iron II-B Israel. In comparing the material culture from the twelfth-eleventh to the eighth centuries BCE in the highlands of Samaria, it is impossible to ignore the increasing evidence for social stratification shown by the development of different types of dwellings and the concomitant evidence for resource extraction (Faust 2012). In Hos. 2:16–22 (Eng. 2:14–20) and 11:1–6, the prophet calls on Israel to revert to the premonarchic period's egalitarian ethos. In his view, this premonarchic period was one of an exemplary bond of loyalty between Yhwh and Israel.

This perspective raises the question of the intervening period, after the Israelite monarchy was established, but before Joash made Israel into a client-state of Assyria. How does Hosea view this period? History recognizes that social stratification in Iron II Israel was not solely the result of subservience to Assyria: by the mid-ninth century BCE, at least fifty years before Joash's submission, buildings such as the Jezreel enclosure and the Samaria acropolis attest to an elite. How did Hosea view this period of Israelite history, in which an elite had developed, but Israel was not yet an Assyrian client?

Hosea 1–3 address this period before Joash, with particular emphasis on Jehu's revolt. They reference divine vengeance on the House of Jehu (1:4) and see Jezreel, the site of Jehu's revolt, as a site for punishment (1:5), destruction (2:2 [Eng. 1:11]), and future exhibition of Yhwh's mercy (2:24 [Eng. 2:22]). Gruber (2017) cites scholars who view these chapters as the work of an earlier prophet, who lived in the period around Jehu's revolt. But there is good reason to see these chapters as part of Hosea's long-term historical reflection. In these, he makes no mention of Assyria, but he does establish theological principles that carry over into the historical commentary on the Assyrian period in Hos. 4–14. These include the insistence on Yhwh as Israel's only covenant patron: only Yhwh is Israel's protector, to whom Israel owes loyalty (2:19–22 [Eng. 2:17–20]). As we find in 11:1–6, the rivals for Israel's loyalty are both the Baals and other political forces. These other political forces are referenced in 2:7 and 14 (Eng. 2:5 and 12) as those who give Israel material benefits after whom Israel "runs" (2:9 [Eng. 2:7]), while the Baals are referenced in 2:10 and 19 (Eng. 2:8 and 17).

While the theological principles of Hos. 1–3 carry over into chs. 4–14, the social commentary of 4–14 differs profoundly from that in 1–3. Hosea 1–3 make no mention of an Israelite elite, or of the "Ephraim" group so frequently mentioned in chs. 4–14. It would appear that Hosea's antagonism to the elite is specifically linked to their alliance with Assyria, an alliance Hosea sees as victimizing the nonelite Israelites. In simpler terms, elites are fine, as long as they do not make common cause with the enemy of the nonelites against the weaker group.

Hosea's view of Assyria is grounded in the economic and social impact of empire on Israel. Theologically, empire is dangerous because it presents an alternative patron for Israel, whom Israel recognizes as owner of the land and defender of Israel's hold on the land. But far more insidious, for Hosea, are the practical ways in which the Assyrian empire impacted Israel. Assyria co-opted local elites into assisting in resource extraction, and thus corroded the social cohesion that tied together the different strata of Israelite society. In response to this corrosion, Hosea offers the healing power of loyalty to God. This healing power is not simply a metaphor: it is also an expression of a hope for social change. If Israelite elites end their loyalty to Assyria, they will instead see themselves as part of an Israelite whole. They will cease resource extraction, and the pitting of different classes of Israelite society one against another will end.

Notes

1. Examples of comparisons to a lion include Frame 2021: 65, line 420, in Sargon's eighth campaign; Leichty 2011: 2, col. ii' line 1'. Both these examples and several others use leonine imagery in describing the king's bravery in conquering rebellious lands. References to depictions of the king fighting a lion appear below in this essay.
2. A further example of such behavior appears in the annals of Esarhaddon, in narrating the actions of the rebellious state of Shubria, whose emissaries "sent a message for the preservation of their lives" (g 2011: Esarhaddon text 33, Tablet 1, obv ii 7).
3. It is likely that the use of "sickness" and "sore" in 5:13 reflect the use of "healing" as a metaphor for forgiveness.
4. Dearman (2010: 200) translates: "(6:11b) When I would turn the fortunes of my people, (7:1) when I would heal Ephraim, then the iniquity of Ephraim is revealed, and the evil deeds of Samaria. They indeed deal falsely: the thief enters in and a band marauds in the street." Similarly, Macintosh (1997: 253) understands the passage as an attack on the "faulty reasoning of Ephraim," "the supposition that YHWH does not see or pay attention to faulty deeds." While this explains 7:2, it fails to elucidate the use of ונגלה in 7:1 or its connection with רפא.
5. "Bringing near" for קרבו follows the medieval commentator R. Isaiah di Trani (in Cohen et al. 2012).
6. For more on 7:8–10, see Gruber 2017: 322 and Paul 1968.
7. Following Heintz (2001), "oil is brought" does not refer to shipping oil to Egypt but to vassal oaths.
8. For the syntax of the phrase כל תשא עון, see Sweeney 2000: 138, who argues that כל modifies עון.
9. ירחם reflects Aramaic רחם as well as Akkadian *rēmu*. The reference to remission of punishment together with רחם in Hos. 14:4–5 has an interesting parallel in Esarhaddon's *Gottesbrief*, in which the king of Šubria forsakes his rebellion and seeks to resume vassalage to Esarhaddon, asking *rēmu rišanimma, puṭur ennitti*, usually translated as "grant me mercy, remove my punishment" (Leichty 2011, Esarhaddon 33, Tablet 2, obv., col. i, line 24).

References

Andersen, F. I., and D. N. Freedman. 1980. *Hosea: A New Translation with Introduction and Commentary*. AB. Garden City: Doubleday.Aster, S. Z. 2012. "The Function of the City of Jezreel and the Symbolism of Jezreel in Hosea 1–2." *JNES* 71: 31–46.

Aster, S. Z. 2016. "Israelite Embassies to Assyria in the First Half of the Eighth Century." *Bib* 97: 175–98.

Aster, S. Z. 2017. *Reflections of Empire in Isaiah 1–39: Responses to Assyrian Ideology*. Ancient Near East Monographs 19. Atlanta: SBL Press.

Aster, S. Z. Forthcoming. "Assyrian 'Control Points' in the Domination of the Southern Levant in the Reign of Tiglath-Pileser III." *Aula Orientalis*.

Aster, S. Z., and Berkovitz, A. J. 2018. "Akkadian *Bullutu* and Hebrew רפא: Pardon and Loyalty in Hosea and in Neo-Assyrian Political Texts." *Hebrew Studies* 59: 149–71.

Barré, M. L. 1978. "New Light on the Interpretation of Hosea 6:2." *VT* 28: 131–35.

Ben-Zvi, E. 2005. *Hosea*. FOTL 21A. Grand Rapids: Eerdmans.

Bos, J. M. 2013. *Reconsidering the Date and Provenance of the Book of Hosea: The Case for Persian-Period Yehud*. LHBOTS. London: Bloomsbury T&T Clark.

Cogan, M. 2008. *The Raging Torrent: Historical Inscriptions from Assyria and Babylonia Relating to Ancient Israel*. Jerusalem: Carta.

Cohen, M., et al. 2012. *Mikra'ot Gedolot Haketer: Sefer Trei Asar* (Heb.). Ramat-Gan: Bar-Ilan.

Day, J. 2010. "Hosea and the Baal Cult." In J. Day, ed., *Prophecy and Prophets in Ancient Israel: Proceedings of the Oxford Old Testament Seminar*. LHBOTS 531. London: T&T Clark, 202–24.

Dearman, J. A. 2010. *The Book of Hosea*. NICOT. Grand Rapids: Eerdmans.

Dorsey, D. A. 1991. *The Roads and Highways of Ancient Israel*. Baltimore: Johns Hopkins.

Emmerson, G. I. 1984. *Hosea: An Israelite Prophet in Judean Perspective*. JSOTSup 28. Sheffield: Sheffield Academic Press.

Fales, F. M. 1994. "A Fresh Look at the Nimrud Wine Lists." In L. Milano, ed., *Drinking in Ancient Societies: History and Culture of Drinks in the Ancient Near East—Papers of a Symposium Held in Rome May 17–19, 1990*. History of the Ancient Near East Studies 6. Padova: Sargon, 361–80.

Faust, A. 2006. *Israel's Ethnogenesis: Settlement, Interaction, Expansion and Resistance: Approaches to Anthropological Archaeology*. London: Equinox.

Faust, A. 2012. *The Archaeology of Israelite Society in Iron Age II*. Winona Lake, IN: Eisenbrauns.

Frame, G., ed. 2021. *The Royal Inscriptions of Sargon II, King of Assyria (721–705 BC)*. RINAP 2. University Park: Eisenbrauns.

Gruber, M. I. 2017. *Hosea: A Textual Commentary*. LHBOTS 653. London: Bloomsbury.

Heintz, J.-G. 2001. "Osée XII 2B á la lumiere d'un vase d'alabâtre de l'époque de Salmanasar III et le rituel d'alliance assyrien: Une hypothèse de lecture." *VT* 60: 466–80.

Herbordt, S. 1992. *Neuassyrische Glyptik des 8.-7. Jh. V. Chr.* SAA 1. Helsinki: Neo-Assyrian Text Corpus Project.

Kelle, B. E. 2005. "What's in a Name? Neo-Assyrian Designations for the Northern Kingdom and Their Implications for Israelite History and Biblical Interpretation." *JBL* 121: 639–66.

Kleiman, A. 2016. "The Damascene Subjugation of the Southern Levant as a Gradual Process (ca 842–800 BCE)." In O. Sergi, M. Oeming, and I. J. de Hulster, eds., *In Search of Aram and Israel: Politics, Culture, Identity*. Oriental Religions in Antiquity 20. Berlin: Mohr Siebeck, 57–78.

Leichty, E., ed. 2011. *The Royal Inscriptions of Esarhaddon, King of Assyria (680–669 BC)*. RINAP 4. Winona Lake: Eisenbrauns.

Levine, B. A. 2005. "Assyrian Ideology and Israelite Monotheism." *Iraq* 67: 411–27.

Machinist, P. 1983. "Assyria and Its Image in the First Isaiah." *JAOS* 103: 719–37.

Machinist, P. 2016. "'Ah Assyria . . . (Isaiah 10:5ff)': Isaiah's Assyrian Polemic Revisited." In G. Bartoloni and M. Giovanna Biga, eds., in collaboration with A. Bramanti, *Not Only History: Proceedings of the Conference Held in Honor of Mario Liverani, Sapienza, Universita di Roma, Dipartimento di Scienze dell'Antichità, 20–21 April 2009.* Winona Lake, IN: Eisenbrauns, 183–218.Macintosh, A. A. 1997. *A Critical and Exegetical Commentary on Hosea.* ICC. Edinburgh: T&T Clark.

Mays, J. L. 1969. *Hosea.* OTL. London: SCM.

Millard, A. 1965. "The Assyrian Royal Seal Type Again." *Iraq* 27: 12–16.

Parpola, S., and K. Watanabe. 1988. *Neo-Assyrian Treaties and Loyalty Oaths.* SAA 2. Helsinki: Helsinki University Press.

Paul, S. M. 1968. "The Image of the Oven and the Cake in Hosea 7:4–10." *VT* 18: 114–20.

Paul, S. M. 1986. "Hosea 8:8–10 and Ancient Near Eastern Royal Epithets." In S. Japhet, ed., *Studies in Bible.* Scripta Hierosolymitana 31. Jerusalem: Magnes, 193–204.

Postgate, J. N. 1974. *Taxation and Conscription in the Assyrian Empire.* Studia Pohl Series Maior 3. Rome: Biblical Institute Press.

Rainey, A. F., and S. Notley. 2005. *The Sacred Bridge: Carta's Atlas of the Biblical World.* Jerusalem: Carta.

Schniedewind, W. M. 1996. "Tel Dan Stele: New Light on Aramaic and Jehu's Revolt." *BASOR* 302: 75–90.

Siddall, L. R. 2013. *The Reign of Adad-nērārī III: An Historical and Ideological Analysis of an Assyrian King and His Times.* Leiden: Brill.

Sinopoli, C. M. 1994. "The Archaeology of Empires." *Annual Review of Anthropology* 23: 159–80.

Sweeney, M. A. 2000. *The Twelve Prophets.* Berit Olam. Collegeville MN: Liturgical.

Tadmor, H. 1994. *The Inscriptions of Tiglath-pileser III King of Assyria.* Jerusalem: Israel Academy of Sciences and Humanities.

Tadmor, H., and S. Yamada. 2011. *The Royal Inscriptions of Tiglath-pileser III (744–727) and Shalmaneser V (726–722) Kings of Assyria.* RINAP 1. Winona Lake, IN: Eisenbrauns.

Weissert, E. 1997. "Royal Hunt and Royal Triumph in a Prism Fragment of Ashurnasirpal." In S. Parpola and R. McCray Whiting, eds., *Assyria 1995: Proceedings of the Tenth Anniversary Symposium of the Neo-Assyrian Text Corpus Project, Helsinki, September 7–11, 1995.* Helsinki: Neo-Assyrian Text Corpus Project, 339–58.

CHAPTER 4

HOSEA THE "HISTORICAL PROPHET" OF THE EIGHTH CENTURY BCE, HOSEA THE REMEMBERED PROPHET OF YEHUDITE LITERATI, AND THE BOOK OF HOSEA

EHUD BEN ZVI AND IAN D. WILSON

4.1. INTRODUCING THE ISSUE

THERE are at least two distinct historical approaches to studying the prophets that feature in the prophetic books of the Hebrew Bible. The main goal of the first approach is to reconstruct the "historical" prophets, and especially the "classical" prophets from Israel and Judah's monarchic era. The second approach focuses on the prophetic figures as they are represented in Yehudite prophetic texts, and on the memories that would be associated with them within the earliest communities that read prophetic books as such. That is, the second approach focuses on "remembered" prophets (see, e.g., Ben Zvi 2021).

The majority of scholars have followed the first approach (for surveys, see Kelle 2014, 2010, 2009). This is to a large extent anticipated. Already in ancient times the focus was on the individual "historical" prophets, not on the prophetic books, even if what was known about the prophets was derived from those books.[1] Moreover, it is certainly easy to understand why widely divergent groups across time and space have focused on the far more memorable "historical" prophets than on the books as texts, their bookish authors, and the limited target readerships that imagined their prophets of memory and imagination when reading these books.[2]

These "historical" prophets have served well as sites of memory for ages. They were often lionized, and remembering them performed strong rhetorical roles in various societies and groups within societies (for different examples, see Geiger 1865: 47–54; Houston n.d.; Thompson n.d.). Just as important, attempting to recover these "historical" prophets meant attempting to recover memorable social worlds in which the prophet/speaker addressed his audience: worlds populated by local and foreign kings, courts, and empires, suffused with trappings of human power (and its eventual undoing). In these worlds, the "historical" prophets were heroic and powerful characters, even if their calls to their contemporaries went mainly unheeded. In other words, these worlds were tragic but intoxicating in their grandeur. They were also far removed from the world of a few literati with no political power in a remote place in a large empire, writing and reading books among themselves in Persian (or Neo-Babylonian) times.[3]

Against this background, in recent decades a significant group of scholars has focused on these "remembered" prophets. They have focused on the multivocal, complex prophetic characters as they appear in the prophetic books, the sociohistorical context of these prophets of imagination and memory, the roles that they performed for the community that conjured them, and the issues and questions that emerge when this approach is taken.[4]

In contemporary research, the two approaches outlined here have sometimes been characterized as "prophecy as a social phenomenon" and "prophecy as a literary construct." The former is associated with the project of reconstructing historical Hoseas, Amoses, Isaiahs, and so on, and the latter with a focus on the prophets that populate the world of the prophetic books. The logic behind this classification is that each approach construes a different category of prophecy. The former is said to be more attuned to prophecy and prophetic activity as usually understood across different societies throughout the ancient Near East; the latter represents an imaginary construct of prophecy encoded in the relevant books that existed among the Yehudite literati who produced and consumed these books and which was deeply intertwined with their socially shared memories about their past (Kelle 2014).

We will return to these matters in the last section of this essay. Already at this point, though, it is crucial to emphasize that this latter concept of prophecy is surely a social and historical product, and thus no less a social and historical phenomenon than what we know about prophetic activity and writing from other ancient Near Eastern contexts. The prophetic books emerged as such, with their prophetic personages and with their implied concept of prophecy, because of historically and socially contingent conditions in Yehud. They too are social phenomena worthy of historical investigation.

Conversely, one should note that the "historical" Hoseas and the like emerge out of literary texts. They emerge out of a particular mode of reading—namely, reading the prophetic book as a textual resource for the reconstruction of the "real" world and the "real" prophet who lived in it.[5] This is so because "real" prophets relate and must relate to social institutions, and speak about contemporary issues that are relevant to their audience. To persuade their audience, they must use a rhetorical approach appropriate to the addressees' situation, knowledge, and general social world.[6] All that said, the basic (and really only) source for all these historical reconstructions is certainly a literary product—i.e., the relevant prophetic books and a particular mode of reading them. To read the books in this way, with these particular goals in mind, involves bracketing out or altering basic information about the past that is communicated by the books themselves as well as putting aside basic assumptions shared by the ancient readers and writers of the literature.[7]

4.2. WHAT DIFFERENCE DO THESE TWO APPROACHES MAKE? ILLUSTRATIVE CASES IN HOSEA

Differences in basic approaches to a text imply not only differences in the research questions that are raised and the methods used to address them but also, very often, differences in the data that scholars observe when reading the text.[8] For instance, does Hos. 1–2 (or 1–3) provide evidence for the life of an eighth-century BCE prophet whose (prophetic) actions were known to a contemporaneous audience? Scholars who focus on Hosea as a character in a prophetic book and as a site of memory associated with a prophet of old would tend to respond with a clear "no." But this is not necessarily the case for those scholars who reconstruct a "historical" prophet. They "see" the prophet as actually performing what would be—in that historical context—"strange" actions, serving to embody the people's (and their polity's) future fate. For these scholars, these actions would have been drastic acts meant to attract attention to the said fate and the reasons for it. Such scholars, and many earlier interpreters over the ages, tend thus to develop their image of the "historical" prophet by discussing the (reconstructed) prophet's human perspective. They, for instance, tend to comment on the toll that these actions may have taken on him, and thus also the impact of this prophetic work on the prophet's life.[9] Some of these scholars would then consider either the toll to be too much or the actions to be too difficult to associate with a "true" prophet of Yhwh, and therefore they tend to reconfigure the actions of their "historical" Hosea or "historical" Gomer or both to account for the discrepancies between the prophet of the book and how they imagine prophets and understand prophetic activity from that particular historical era.[10] Even those who are hesitant to take a biographical approach to Hosea may still attempt to reconfigure the events reported in the book, to understand them as an indirect reference to cultic and social practices in eighth-century Israel.

Already at this point, we stress that critical scholars[11] who propose these historical, eighth-century Hoseas (and Gomers) do not base them on the book of Hosea as we know it or on any of its known ancient versions, but on what they propose to be an original, eighth-century text of Hos. 1–3 (or a text that is at least somewhat close in time to that context). The reason is simple: some of the statements in Hos. 1–3 seem unlikely to have been uttered by a northern prophet at that time (e.g., Hos. 2:1–3, 16–25

[Eng. 1:10–2:1; 14–23]; and 3:5—all of which have been proposed as products of later redactors). In other words, most critical scholars who reconstruct a historical, eighth-century northern Israelite Hosea argue explicitly or implicitly that such a prophet is inconsistent with the Hosea that is apparent in the book of Hosea.

Scholars who focus on Hosea as a character in the world created by the book, or on Hosea as a site of memory visited by the literati of Yehud who construed their past by reading this book and similar ones, obviously do not need to reconstruct a supposedly older, "original" text that would more faithfully report the words of a "historical," eighth-century prophet. Instead of turning their attention to reconstructing the life of the prophet or his preaching in the eighth century, scholars who focus on Hosea as a character—on Hosea as memory—attend to how the Hosea of the book and the book itself fit within their cultural and social context, and on what the prophet and the book would contribute to that context. They may pay attention, for example, to the book's (in)famous marital metaphor in the context of social constructions of hierarchical systems, and to the role of metaphors in not only shaping such constructions but also conceptually interlinking them (see Ben Zvi 2022).[12] They may also draw attention to the book's lack of any substantial interest in the (internal) life of Hosea (and Gomer), which is consistent with similar systemic tendencies in the twelve prophetic books (Hosea–Malachi).[13] Or they may stress that, on the whole, the book of Hosea and its message do not differ significantly in genre and style from those books associated with "southern" prophets. Like all prophetic books of the Hebrew Bible, Hosea communicates to its readers a generic metanarrative about Israel and the people's relationship with Yhwh: (1) Yhwh chose Israel long ago, becoming its patron deity; (2) Israel, the client, broke its obligations toward the deity; (3) Yhwh punished Israel, causing its political, social, and religious institutions to fall—but the deity did not completely destroy the people on account of the original patron–client relationship; and finally (4) because of this patronage, Yhwh will eventually restore the relationship to its ideal and proper form. Moreover, like many other prophetic books, Hosea evokes and shapes memories of future utopian worlds. It promotes, for instance, a future in which an elevated Davidide plays a central role in some passages (e.g., Hos. 3:5; cf. Isa. 9:5–7; 11:1–9). But in other literary units within the same book, it is saliently devoid of any reference to a future Davidide, elevated or not (e.g., Hos. 2:18–22 [Eng. 2:16–20]; 14:6–9 [Eng. 14:5–8][14]; cf. Isa. 40–66; Jer. 50:4–5, 19–20; Obad.; Zeph. 3). It thus presents a horizon of possible futures for its readers—some centered on a future, utopian Davidic king and some clearly not—just as other prophetic books do, and as was common in the discourse of the time.

Consider also the book's "northern" disposition. Given the many texts about Ephraim, Assyria, and Egypt in Hos. 4–14, Hosea's apparent association with the Northern Kingdom, and especially that so little is known from any textual sources about society and culture in northern Israel, it is expected that scholars with historical interests in the Northern Kingdom in the eighth century BCE would focus their attention on the book of Hosea, whose eponymous character is the only northern prophet of the Hebrew Bible's prophetic literature. Of course, scholars disagree on the details of historical reconstruction, but the tendency and the allure of the approach is clear (see Wolff 1974; Macintosh 1997; Na'aman 2015; Nissinen 2018; Leuchter 2021).[15]

How would scholars who focus on the prophets as characters that populate the prophetic books, and on the prophetic books as such, approach these issues? These scholars note that, in the book of Hosea, there is a consistent vagueness about the particular contexts in which the putative prophetic speeches were uttered and prophetic actions were carried out. The book asks its intended readers to remember Hosea's words, and thus Yhwh's words associated with Hosea, but it never tells them about the circumstances in which they were uttered in the world portrayed in the book. Where did the character Hosea talk? To whom precisely did he speak, within the world of the book, imagined and vicariously experienced by its readers?

Even when seemingly specific past events are mentioned, readers can experience only a very blurred "historical" picture. For instance, when they read, "the roar of war shall rise against your people, and all your fortresses shall be devastated just as Shalman devastated Beth Arbel on the day of battle" (Hos. 10:14), readers face a text that remains open in terms of geography, time, and particular protagonists. Surely, a blurred "historical" past encouraged not only multiple readings and imaginations, but also at least some level of potential transtemporality, which facilitated the book's continuing ability to communicate to readers living centuries after its time, and in very different worlds than that portrayed in the book itself. Even more importantly, the book of Hosea, along with most of the other prophetic books, communicated to readers that matters such as who is Shalman, where is Beth Arbel, and where and when precisely did Hosea say this or that are not really worth remembering, or even addressing. Instead, the book emphasizes that what readers should remember is the book's godly message, presented as relevant to all who read it with (proper) understanding in any historical circumstances (14:10). The book states clearly that this should be the focus of attention for readers, and what they should remember through their reading (Ben Zvi 2019).

The same scholars would likely notice that this preference in Hosea, and in the other relevant prophetic books, served rhetorical purposes. The book, however, lacks some basic elements of traditional rhetoric—namely, that of a particular author communicating a text to a particular audience at a particular time/setting for a particular purpose. This traditional rhetorical stance might be apparent if one focuses solely on the world populated by the character Hosea as portrayed in the book. But this is not the case when one considers the book's implied author (as shaped by the literati reading the book) as the communicator, the readers themselves (i.e., the implied audience), the world in which those readers lived (i.e., their particular sociohistorical setting), and the evident interests of the readers and the implied author—or one may say, the purposeful role of reading the book of Hosea as part of a collection of authoritative texts about past prophets.

This approach also draws attention to the fact that the book shapes an image of a prophet who purportedly addresses the north, yet his ideological positioning is southern. Already in the superscription (1:1), the book situates the prophet's message during the reign of the northern king Jeroboam II, and yet it also situates that message during the reigns of the southern kings Uzziah, Jotham, Ahaz, and Hezekiah. This chronological statement is peculiar in that the northern timeline appears to be incomplete, and in that the Judean kings are mentioned first; but it is fitting for the prophet presented in the book, given his peculiar positioning between (putative) northern concerns and southern ideals. Moreover, both the character Hosea in the book and the Yhwh who interacts with him, as well as the implied author of the book and the target readership who construed this author, are all too aware of how the book's implied narrative about the fall of Israel is strongly intertwined with the story of Judah and Jerusalem. In fact, in the larger context of prophetic literature, which was part of the literati's reading repertoire and which would certainly inform their understanding of Hosea, the book provides a kind of prelude to the basic story about Judah and Jerusalem's downfall.[16] The story of the Northern Kingdom, in this larger context, would shape memories of other prophetic warnings to Judah (e.g., Zech. 1:2–6a), but this message came from outside Judah, creating an underlying sense that even northern prophets cared about the Southern Kingdom (cf. 2 Chr. 21:12–15). Even more importantly, the northern Hosea of the book (and his Yhwh) indict and proclaim the fall of both monarchies, but in doing so they clearly prefer the Davidic line (Hos. 3:5).[17] In all these matters, the book and its two main characters (the northern prophet and the deity) advance the ideological world of postmonarchic Yehud which was so familiar to the literati from their readings of other prophetic texts. From a rhetorical perspective, this point is made even more poignant by the prophet's northern location (see Ben Zvi 2015).

4.3. What Is at Stake in All This?

For contemporary readers interested in the role of the Bible's prophets in current imagination and theological thought, perhaps what is at stake is clear. Take, for instance, Jeremiah Cataldo's (2022) recently published article, "Did the Prophets Teach Us to Protest?" The rhetorical impact of Cataldo's argument will be strongly undermined by a focus on scribes living centuries after the political and social context of monarchic Israel—scribes who, through their texts, imagined a world in which a prophetic character proclaimed his words—rather than on the "heroic," "historical" prophet Hosea and his preaching to contemporaries in the eighth century BCE.[18]

In terms of historical research, however, what else might be at stake? First, a focus on searching for the "historical" prophet who lived in the Northern Kingdom comes with a price. It often involves bracketing out the main messages of the book of Hosea and removing from consideration numerous sections of the book. It also actively shuts down the voice of the prophet inhabiting the world that is portrayed in the book and who would be remembered by its readers in antiquity. The reconstructed "historical" Hoseas—both book and character—end up looking very different from the textual source with which scholars begin, and that source is the only extant, attested historical evidence available in the first place. See, for instance, the above-mentioned preference for blurred historical references, which is an important feature of the book. Surely, scholars might try to explain away this feature by claiming that the historical prophet did not have to provide precise information to his audience because the audience was well aware of the realities to which the prophet referred (Na'aman 2015: 254). But whether this argument is correct or not, the historical prophet reconstructed in this manner is, at times, drastically different from the prophet that inhabits the world of the book of Hosea, and that ancient readers would socially remember through their interactions with the book. Scholars searching for a "historical" Hosea, therefore, have to alter the book and character of the prophet to accomplish their goal. To do so, at times they even have to alter basic constructions of time as they are presented in the book. For example, Na'aman's (2015) "historical" prophet preached during the reign of Hoshea, certainly not during the time of Jeroboam II. This timeline is not accidental, but a necessary requirement for his argument to hold, yet it explicitly contradicts what the book states.

In other words, these historians do not address the book of Hosea as an object of study in itself, which is a substantial price to pay. Instead, their mode of reading Hosea is to reconstruct hypothetical, earlier versions of the text—versions that would be centuries older than the book itself—to glean footprints of the prophet and information about the social and cultural institutions of his time and place. Their assumption is that these footprints somehow survived complex and very substantive redactional processes, which would have occurred alongside drastic political, social, and cultural changes. Surely, some such footprints may have survived in the present form(s) of the book, and thus the approach is worthwhile, at least in principle. But the problem is how to identify these footprints, and if they are found, how to assess whether they are actually faithful representations of a historical Hosea (see, e.g., Nissinen 2018).[19]

The high level of uncertainty in relation to any precise reconstructions of the prophetic books' redactional histories raises substantial concerns (Ben Zvi 2016: 6–36). Additionally, while it is true that historians should look for all possible sources about the "historical" Hosea and his time, questions and concerns of historical methodology still apply. Historians should be cautious—even skeptical—with their sources, and especially with reconstructed sources. There is, too, the pesky matter of what historians should do with single sources. Historians in other fields of study have tended to reject uncorroborated, single-text evidence in their work (see Tucker 2004: 259; Zammito 2014). Yet much of the historical work in Hebrew Bible studies is based on single-source evidence, often out of necessity.

That said, historians who focus on Hosea as he would be imagined and remembered by literati who read the book of Hosea in Yehud also pay a hefty price. There are almost no additional textual resources for the study of the Northern Kingdom's culture and society in the tumultuous period leading to its collapse. So, drawing attention away from reconstructions of Hosea the eighth-century prophet (and other "historical" prophets) diminishes the capacity to make historical claims about eighth-century Israel. Further, any shift away from Hosea the "historical" prophet to a focus on prophetic characters as they are represented in prophetic books lessens the historians' ability to draw on anthropological studies of prophecy and divination in the late Iron Age Levant and ancient Near East more broadly. Thus, scholars who consistently take this approach have to accept that, from their viewpoint, very little (if anything) can be known about the historical Hosea of the eighth century, and that their studies will not contribute much (or anything) to our knowledge of the actual Northern Kingdom, its social structures, and its cultural institutions and authoritative texts. They also have to accept that their Hosea will never look like a typical ancient Near East prophet. Finally, they have to accept that their Hosea is unlikely to relate well to the Hosea socially remembered by most nonacademic readers of the book, or to the Hosea referenced by contemporary theologians and social activists (of any kind). Their reward is, of course, a better understanding of the world of ideas, memory, and imagination of the literati of the early Second Temple Period.

Most scholars situate themselves on a spectrum between these two different approaches to Hosea. This essay cannot deal with the multiple attestations of positions along the spectrum, but we have drawn attention to the methodological gap between the two poles, the different types of Hoseas that each brings forward, and what is at stake in these matters. Finally, although we have clear personal positions on these issues, it is worth stressing that both general approaches discussed here are necessary and complementary in the study of Hosea. Each one carries its own limitations and costs. Each one addresses different questions, focuses on different periods and polities, and reads the book differently. By necessity, each must reach different conclusions. This methodological diversity only enriches all those interested in Hosea and the book that bears his name.

NOTES

1. See, e.g., Sirach 48–49, in which the prophets (not the books) are praised. In other words, the role of the prophetic book was seen as bringing to life a memory of a great prophet of old. There are, of course, crucial differences between contemporary, critical reconstructions of the "historical" prophets and how the book of Sirach (and other ancient texts) understands the prophets as figures of the past. But the focus on the prophets themselves is apparent in both contexts.
2. It is easy to understand why "[t]oday in North America many people name their children Isaiah, Jeremiah, or even Amos or Micah, but not 'the redactor of the Book of the Four' or 'the Deuteronomist' or 'the group of literati who shaped the Prophetic Book Collection'" (Ben Zvi 2021: 9).
3. Even today, works dealing with Judah/Israel during the period between the so-called Syro-Ephraimite war and the Babylonian conquest of Jerusalem (about 150 years) vastly outnumber those works focused on the Persian period of Yehud and Samaria (about 200 years). This has been true since antiquity, even though the main textual corpus that informed Second Temple Judaism and its eventual successors emerged in the latter period.

4. For an illustrative view of the range of approaches, questions, and issues raised within this scholarly trend, see, e.g., Carroll 1989; Davies 1996; Floyd 2006; Ben Zvi 2009a, 2009b; Weeks 2009; Nissinen 2017: 144–67; Wilson 2017: 182–222. On Hosea, see, e.g., Ben Zvi 2005, 2015; Bos 2012; Nissinen 2018.

5. Of course, as anticipated, there are many researchers who combine in various ways these two basic approaches, and many reconstruct not only the original, "real" prophets, but also the many "real" redactors who contributed to the eventual emergence of the texts we have. On these matters, see, e.g., Kelle 2014; and cf. Nissinen 2018.

6. Of course, even among scholars who follow this basic approach, there are notable differences that regrettably cannot be addressed here. Compare, e.g., Hayes 1988 and Hayes and Irvine 1988 with Na'aman 2015.

7. Thus, among many scholars, there is a need to prioritize proposed forerunners of the prophetic books that suit better their interests in reconstructing the relevant "historical" prophet. On this issue and on the use of the prophetic books in light of general approaches to history and theory in history as a contemporary discipline, see more below.

8. The data that scholars "see" in a text is not an absolute, universal, self-existing object, but requires a seer and a seer's perspective and world of knowledge. Moreover, data is observed only as part of a pattern, an ecosystem in which multiple data are entangled in various ways.

9. Their impact on Gomer's life or on their children has rarely been the focus of attention. There has been a shift on these matters in recent years, however.

10. This chapter is not the place to discuss this interpretive approach at length. The approach has been attested in multiple ways for centuries. See, e.g., Wolff 1974: 13–17; Davies 1992: 105–9; Macintosh 1997: 117–19 (notice that Macintosh titled this section of his commentary "Historical Conclusions"). For a survey of this type of reconstruction of various historical Hoseas and Gomers through the ages, see Sherwood 2009: 19–82. On these matters generally, and for a critique of the "biographic" approach, see Kelle 2009.

11. Unlike precritical interpreters. See Sherwood 2009.

12. For more on the marital metaphor and on the possibilities of interpreting gender in the book, see Graybill 2016: 49–69.

13. The only character in the book that is allowed to express strong emotions is Yhwh. On the issue in general, see Rossi 2021.

14. See Ben Zvi 2005: 307–8. Note that the Targum felt it necessary to add an explicit note about a messianic king in 14:8 [Eng. 14:7], so as to resolve the situation.

15. On Assyria and Egypt in the book, see Zimran 2021, and the works cited therein.

16. Although the book does not mention the city of Jerusalem directly, its readers in antiquity would certainly have had the city on their minds. The reference to King David (3:5), the many references to Judah, and the criticisms of Samaria as home of the northern monarchy would all serve as opportunities to reflect on how Hosea's message related to Jerusalem, its monarchy and people, and the eventual Babylonian conquest.

17. On the issue of David and Davidic kingship in prophetic literature, see chs. 4–5 in Wilson 2017. On kingship in Hosea especially, see Machinist 2005; Wilson 2017: 194–98, 218–19.

18. Of course, part of the issue is the modern tendency, apparent now for centuries, to strongly prefer "historical" events over "fictional" worlds, but these matters go beyond the scope of this essay.

19. On history and method in Hebrew Bible studies generally, see Wilson 2018.

References

Ben Zvi, Ehud. 2005. *Hosea*. FOTL 21A/1. Grand Rapids: Eerdmans.

Ben Zvi, Ehud. 2008. "Reading Hosea and Imagining YHWH." *Horizons in Biblical Theology* 30: 43–57.

Ben Zvi, Ehud. 2009a. "The Concept of Prophetic Books and Its Historical Setting." In Diana V. Edelman and Ehud Ben Zvi, eds., *The Production of Prophecy: Constructing Prophecy and Prophets in Yehud*. London: Equinox, 73–95.

Ben Zvi, Ehud. 2009b. "Towards an Integrative Study of the Production of Authoritative Books in Ancient Israel." In Diana V. Edelman and Ehud Ben Zvi, eds., *The Production of Prophecy: Constructing Prophecy and Prophets in Yehud*. London: Equinox, 15–28.

Ben Zvi, Ehud. 2015. "Remembering Hosea: The Prophet Hosea as a Site of Memory in Persian Period Yehud." In Ehud Ben Zvi, Claudia V. Camp, David M. Gunn, and Aaron W. Hughes, eds., *Poets, Prophets, and Texts in Play: Studies in Biblical Poetry and Prophecy in Honour of Francis Landy*. LHBOTS 597. London: Bloomsbury, 37–57.

Ben Zvi, Ehud. 2016. "Remembering Twelve Prophetic Characters from the Past." In Elena Di Pede and Donatella Scaiola, eds., *The Book of the Twelve: One Book or Many?* FAT II. Tübingen: Mohr Siebeck, 6–36.

Ben Zvi, Ehud. 2019. "Balancing Shades of 'Historical,' 'Historically-Blurred' and 'Trans-Historical' Contexts and Temporal Contingency in Late Persian/Early Hellenistic Yehudite Memories of YHWH's Words and Prophets of Old in the Prophetic Book Collection and Its Subcollections." In Guido Benzi, Elena Di Pede, and Donatella Scaiola, eds., *Profeti Maggiori e Minori a confronto: Major and Minor Prophets Compared*. Rome: Libreria Ateneo Salesiano, 37–54.Ben Zvi, Ehud. 2021. "From 'Historical' Prophets to Prophetic Books." In Julia M. O'Brien, ed., *The Oxford Handbook of the Minor Prophets*. Oxford: Oxford University Press, 5–16.Ben Zvi, Ehud. 2022. "The Marital Metaphor of YHWH and Israel in Ancient Israel with a Focus on Its Occurrence in Hosea 1–3." In Emmanuel Pfoh, ed., *Patronage in Ancient Palestine and in the Hebrew Bible: A Reader*. Sheffield: Sheffield Phoenix, 384–422.Bos, James M. 2012. *Reconsidering the Date and Provenance of the Book of Hosea: The Case for Persian-Period Yehud*. LHBOTS 580. London: Bloomsbury.

Carroll, Robert P. 1989. "Prophecy and Society." in R. E. Clements, ed., *The World of Ancient Israel*. Cambridge: Cambridge University Press, 203–25.

Cataldo, Jeremiah. 2022. "Did the Prophets Teach Us to Protest?" *Religions* 13, no. 6: 16. https://doi.org/10.3390/rel13060487.

Davies, Graham I. 1992. *Hosea*. New Century Commentary. Grand Rapids: Eerdmans.

Davies, Philip R. 1996. "The Audiences of Prophetic Scrolls: Some Suggestions." In Stephen Breck Reid, ed., *Prophets and Paradigms: Essays in Honor of Gene M. Tucker*. JSOTSup 229. Sheffield: Sheffield Academic Press, 48–62.

Floyd, Michael H. 2006. "The Production of Prophetic Books in the Early Second Temple Period." In Michael H. Floyd and Robert D. Haak, eds., *Prophets, Prophecy, and Prophetic Texts in Second Temple Judaism*. LHBOTS 427. London: T&T Clark, 276–97.

Geiger, Abraham. 1865. *Judaism and Its History*. Translated by Maurice Mayer. New York: M. Thalmessinger & Co.

Graybill, Rhiannon. 2016. *Are We Not Men? Unstable Masculinity in the Hebrew Prophets*. New York: Oxford University Press.

Hayes, John H. 1988. *Amos, The Eighth-Century Prophet: His Times and His Preaching*. Nashville: Abingdon.

Hayes, John H., and Stuart A. Irvine. 1988. *Isaiah, The Eighth-Century Prophet: His Times and His Preaching*. Nashville: Abingdon.

Houston, Walter J. n.d. "Social Justice and the Prophets." n.p. (cited June 19, 2022). Online: https://www.bibleodyssey.org/passages/related-articles/social-justice-and-the-prophets/.

Kelle, Brad E. 2009. "Hosea 1–3 in Twentieth-Century Scholarship." *CBR* 7, no. 2: 179–216.

Kelle, Brad E. 2010. "Hosea 4–14 in Twentieth-Century Scholarship." *CBR* 8, no. 3: 314–75.

Kelle, Brad E. 2014. "The Phenomenon of Israelite Prophecy in Contemporary Scholarship." *CBR* 12, no. 3: 275–320.

Leuchter, Mark. 2021. "Hosea 6:5 and the Decalogue." *VT* 71: 76–88.

Machinist, Peter. 2005. "Hosea and the Ambiguity of Kingship in Ancient Israel." In John T. Strong and Steven S. Tuell, eds., *Constituting the Community: Studies on the Polity of Ancient Israel in Honor of S. Dean McBride, Jr.* Winona Lake, IN: Eisenbrauns, 153–81.

Macintosh, A. A. 1997. *Hosea*. ICC. Edinburgh: T&T Clark.

Na'aman, Nadav. 2015. "The Book of Hosea as a Source for the Last Days of the Kingdom of Israel." *BZ* 59: 232–56.

Nissinen, Martti. 2017. *Ancient Prophecy: Near Eastern, Biblical, and Greek Perspectives*. Oxford: Oxford University Press.

Nissinen, Martti. 2018. "The Book of Hosea and the Last Days of the Northern Kingdom: The Methodological Problem." In Shuichi Hasegawa, Christoph Levin, and Karen Radner, eds., *The Last Days of the Kingdom of Israel*. BZAW 511. Berlin: De Gruyter, 369–82.

Rossi, Benedetta. 2021. "Do the Prophets Have a Private Life? Women as Literary and Redactional Tools." In L. Juliana Claassens and Irmtraud Fischer, with the assistance of F. O. Olejede, eds., *Prophecy and Gender in the Hebrew Bible*. Atlanta: SBL Press, 293–314.

Sherwood, Yvonne. 2009. *The Prostitute and the Prophet: Reading Hosea in the Late Twentieth Century*. JSOTSup212. Sheffield: Sheffield Academic Press.

Thomas, Samuel. n.d. "Let Justice Roll Down Like Waters (Amos 5–6)." (cited June 19, 2022). Online: https://www.bibleodyssey.org/passages/main-articles/let-justice-roll-down-like-waters-amos-5--6/.

Tucker, Aviezer. 2004. *Our Knowledge of the Past: A Philosophy of Historiography*. Cambridge: Cambridge University Press.

Weeks, Stuart. 2009. "Jeremiah as a Prophetic Book." In Hans M. Barstad and Reinhard G. Kratz, eds., *Prophecy in the Book of Jeremiah*. BZAW388. Berlin: De Gruyter, 265–74.Wilson, Ian D. 2017. *Kingship and Memory in Ancient Judah*. New York: Oxford University Press.

Wilson, Ian D. 2018. *History and the Hebrew Bible: Culture, Narrative, and Memory*. Leiden: Brill.

Wolff, Hans Walter. 1974. *Hosea*. Hermeneia. Philadelphia: Fortress.

Zammito, John H. 2014. Review of *Our Knowledge of the Past: A Philosophy of Historiography* by Aviezer Tucker. *Notre Dame Philosophical Reviews*: n.p. Online: http://ndpr.nd.edu/news/our-knowledge-of-the-past-a-philosophy-of-historiography/

Zimran, Yisca. 2021. "The Prevalence and Purpose of the 'Assyria-Egypt' Motif in the Book of Hosea." *JSOT* 46, no. 1: 3–23.

CHAPTER 5

THE BOOK OF HOSEA AND ISRAELITE RELIGION IN THE EIGHTH CENTURY BCE

LENA-SOFIA TIEMEYER

5.1. INTRODUCTION

THIS essay explores the religious polemic in the book of Hosea, with a focus on its use of the Hebrew terms *baal/baalim* and *el*. Questions include: Are these names or titles? What deities do they represent? What can Hosea's polemic against them tell us about the religion of the Northern Kingdom of Israel in the eighth century BCE?

5.2. SOURCES FOR ISRAELITE RELIGION IN THE EIGHTH CENTURY BCE

Three main types of sources shed light upon the religion of ancient Israel in the eighth century BCE: (1) nonwritten archaeological artifacts (altars, temples, votive vessels, etc.); (2) ancient Near Eastern texts (including epigraphic material); and (3) biblical texts. Each set comes with benefits and constraints.

At one end of the scale, the nonwritten artifacts are primary sources, which open authentic, although somewhat haphazard, windows into life in the eighth century. They can tell us about religious practices, such as where people worshipped and what they sacrificed. The focus is on what the ancient Israelites did rather than in whom they believed.

At the other end of the scale, the biblical texts tell us not only what people did but also in whom they believed. Yet, given their heavily curated nature, their insights and historical value need to be carefully appraised. First, biblical texts are difficult to date. The book of Hosea is a case in point. Although a significant part of the book may stem from a historical prophet named Hosea who was active in the Northern Kingdom of Israel in the eighth century BCE, its final form is most likely a product of postmonarchic Yehud. Its final, Judahite redaction, in turn, has probably contributed to the anti-Israelite bias of the book. Second, the scribal character of books like Hosea suggests that the viewpoints are not representative of the entire people. Rather, the opinions probably reflect the male, upper-class intelligentsia (i.e., a fraction of the population). Third, the polemical character of books like Hosea means that the opponents in the text are not likely to be depicted objectively.

Ancient Near Eastern texts, including epigraphic material, fall somewhere in the middle of the spectrum. On the one hand, presuming that the texts are found in established archaeological excavations, they can offer datable glimpses into the reality of ancient Israel. Further, as they are written, they can tell us about what their authors thought. On the other hand, ancient Near Eastern texts may be as polemical, biased, and nonrepresentative as biblical texts. An inscription may represent a small segment of the society, although not necessarily the one represented by the biblical material. Likewise, its aim may be to convince an opponent of the writer's point of view, although, again, not automatically the same point of view as advocated by the biblical texts.

Due care needs to be taken when seeking to establish the religious practices and beliefs of eighth-century Israel from the available sources.

5.3. Israelites, Canaanites, and Objects of Worship

To assess the religion of eighth-century Israel, interpreters need to address the ethnic identity of its inhabitants. Many biblical texts differentiate between the Canaanites (i.e., the original inhabitants of the land) and the Israelites, who originated in Ur in Mesopotamia and reached peoplehood during their four-hundred-year sojourn as slaves in Egypt. When the latter invaded Canaan, they sought, but failed, to eradicate the original inhabitants, with the result that the Israelites shared the land with the indigenous Canaanites. This picture, found in Genesis to Judges, is an ideological construct, and modern archaeology has cast doubts on its broad brushstrokes. It is nowadays considered settled in scholarly circles that the Israelites came into existence as an independent ethnic identity in the land of Israel. Gradually, the people that later came to identify as "Israel" emerged as a separate entity and broke with its own "Canaanite" past. What later came to be identified as "Canaanite" was, in fact, nothing other than Israel's own early heritage (Smith 1990: 7).

Likewise, what later came to be labeled as "Canaanite religion" may be nothing else but Israel's own early religion. This religion included a set of deities, among them El ("the deity") and Baal ("Lord"). These deities, mentioned in many biblical books, are also known from extrabiblical material, most significantly from the Ugarit Baal Cycle. The depictions of Yhwh in the Hebrew Bible resemble those of these two deities.

5.3.1. El: The Evidence from the Baal Cycle and the Hebrew Bible

The patriarchal narratives not only preserve but also transform many of the traditions about El. The name El (אל) denotes Israel's God in multiple psalms. Further, many of the names of God in Genesis, such as El Shaddai (17:1; 35:11; 49:25), El Elyon (14:18–24), and El Bethel (31:13) are indebted to Canaanite traditions. Finally, many depictions of Yhwh, among them the image of him sitting enthroned amid the divine council (e.g., Ps. 29), are reminiscent of the depictions of El in the Baal Cycle (KTU 1.1 IV, lines 2–4 [Smith 1994: 131]; cf. Smith 2003: 135, 141–42).

The onomastic evidence testifies further to the Israelite connection to El. Many Israelite names, both in the biblical and the epigraphical texts, contain a theophoric element. In his now classical study, Tigay demonstrated that, according to the epigraphic material, a form of the name Yhwh was by far the most popular theophoric element (557 examples), with "El" far behind (77 examples). In contrast, a mere six names contain "Baal" (Tigay 1986: 12–13). These statistics suggest that most people worshipped Yhwh, and many either worshipped El or identified Yhwh with El.

The biblical material confirms the identification of Yhwh with El. According to Exod. 3:14–16 and 6:1–3, Yhwh revealed himself gradually. He was known as El Shaddai to the patriarchs, but later generations recognized that he had been Yhwh all along. Historically speaking, however, it is difficult to determine whether Yhwh was a title of El or a son of El (see Dijkstra 2001: 101–2), or if Yhwh was secondarily identified with El (see Smith 2003: 140–41). The fact that the name "Israel" has the theophoric element -el (rather than Yhwh) suggests that Israel originally called its deity "El" (Dijkstra 2001: 105). Further, Deut. 32:8–9 indicates that, at one point, Yhwh was considered one of El's sons, as does the description in Ps. 82:1–2 of how Elohim stands in the congregation of El among the *elohim* to judge (אלהים נצב בעדת־אל בקרב אלהים ישפט). Alternatively, El, understood as the deity of what later became the kingdom of Israel, at one point merged with Yhwh, understood as the deity of the southern regions (e.g., Seir, Edom, Teman, Sinai) (Smith 2003: 140–45).

5.3.2. Baal: The Evidence from the Baal Cycle and the Hebrew Bible

Like the word *el*, the word *baal* (בעל) has a wide semantic range. Its nominal form means "lord," which may refer to a woman's husband (e.g., Gen. 20:3) or designate a deity's supremacy. It may also serve as the personal name of the Canaanite god Baal-Hadad. The depictions of Yhwh in the Hebrew Bible owe much to the Ugaritic descriptions of Baal-Hadad. For example, the Baal Cycle KTU 1.2 IV envisages Baal-Hadad as riding on the clouds, imagery that appears for Yhwh and others in Deut. 33:26; 2 Sam. 22:11 // Pss. 18:10; 68:32–35; 104:3; and Isa. 19:1; 66:15. This imagery is extended to include images of Yhwh riding in a storm chariot (e.g., Hab. 3:8, 15) (Smith 1990: 80–82; Day 2002: 91–127; Anderson 2015: 86–93). This affinity is natural. As Hubler highlights, if the Israelites understood Yhwh to be and do what the surrounding people believed Baal-Hadad to be and do, it would have been appropriate to reuse and adapt the qualities and characteristics of one deity for the other (Hubler 2020: 614; cf. Yee 2001: 351).

According to Judges and 1 Samuel, the people of Israel worshipped Baal alongside Yhwh. Judges like Gideon and Samuel sought to quench the cult of Baal (Judg. 6:25–32; 1 Sam. 7:3–4), albeit with limited success (see further Anderson 2015: 60–61). Likewise, the book of Kings informs us that the worship of Baal (and Asherah/Astarte) continued throughout the monarchic period (e.g., 1 Kgs. 18:19). Taken at face value, these texts testify to a situation where most people in the land of Israel worshipped not only Yhwh but also other deities. At the same time, the biblical records suggest that Yhwh was Israel's main deity. Even King Ahab (living in the ninth century BCE), who is depicted as having built a temple to Baal (1 Kgs. 16:32), nonetheless named his children Ahaziah (1 Kgs. 22:40), Jehoram (2 Kgs. 1:17; 8:25), and Athaliah (2 Kgs. 8:18, 25; 11:1)—names with the theophoric element of Yhwh (Levin 2014: 219–20). Thus, "the official Omride religion was not the kind of anti-Yahweh Baalism described in the Elijah cycle" (Anderson 2015: 106). Further, 2 Kgs. 10:28 makes the bold claim that Jehu (r. 841–814 BCE) eradicated Baal worship from Israel. Although this claim may be an example of hyperbole, on par with what is found in the Neo-Assyrian inscriptions (King 2017), it nonetheless implies that, by the eighth century BCE, Baal was not worshipped in Israel.[1] Pointing in the same direction, there is little evidence of Baal worship in the other prophetic texts from the eighth century BCE (e.g., the earliest strands of Isaiah, Amos, and Micah) (Keefe 1995: 78; Kelle 2005: 138–39, 141).

The onomastic evidence paints a related picture (cf. Tigay above). Beginning with the Hebrew Bible, only a handful of names use the theophoric element *baal*, and these names are limited to Gideon (Jerubaʿal) and members of Saul's (Ishbaʿal and Meribbaʿal) and David's (Beʿalyada, Beʿalyah, Baal-Hanan) extended households. As nothing in 1–2 Samuel suggests that these men worship Yhwh and Baal in tandem, it is preferable to treat the theophoric element *baal* as an acceptable title for Yhwh (i.e., "lord," cf. David's son Adonijah) (Dearman 1993: 187–90; Levin 2014: 204–8, 218–19; Anderson 2015: 75; Hubler 2020: 613–14).[2] The onomastic evidence from inscriptions and ostraca further enhances the impression that most people in Israel and Judah worshipped Yhwh. According to the available material from eighth-century Samaria, 49% of names have Yhwh as the theophoric element and 27% have Baal, while the corresponding evidence from Judah does not attest to a single name with Baal. Instead, most names contain the theophoric element, Yhwh. The epigraphic evidence points to exclusive Yahwism by the eighth century, a picture that blatantly contradicts the impression from the

Deuteronomistic History and the prophetic literature (Levin 2014: 221; cf. Kelle 2005: 144–48).

Taken together, a compromise emerges whereby most people worshipped Yhwh as the national deity of Israel and Judah and where many treated the term *baal* as a title ("lord") that was applicable to Yhwh. At the same time, few people, with the obvious exception of the authors of the prophetic books, upheld a rigorous practice of monolatry (cf. Dijkstra 2001: 124).

5.4. BAAL IN HOSEA

The book of Hosea, which is set "in the days of Uzziah, Jotham, Ahaz, and Hezekiah, kings of Judah, and in the days of Jeroboam [II], the son of Jehoash, king of Israel" (1:1), purportedly offers a scathing polemic against Baal and El. This polemic aims to propagate the cult of Yhwh (cf. Anderson 2015: 43). Yet, the above-mentioned claim in 2 Kgs. 10–11 that Baal worship had come to an end in Israel during the reign of Jehu, more than fifty years earlier, raises the question of which of the two descriptions, that in 2 Kings or that in Hosea, best reflects the situation in eighth-century Israel.

The word בעל (*baal*) appears seven times in Hosea: 2:8, 13, 16, 17 (Heb. 2:10, 15, 18, 19); 9:10; 11:2; and 13:1. In three of these cases, the term appears in the plural בעלים (*baalim*) (2:13, 17 [Heb. 2:15, 19]; 11:2). Yet, it is unclear who is meant when Hosea uses the term.[3] The term may denote:

1. A variety of local, Canaanite deities—this view was advocated by many scholars at the beginning of the twentieth century (see the overview in Dearman 2001: 9–10).
2. The specific deity named Baal, the epithet of the Canaanite storm god Hadad, who is mentioned in the Ugaritic Baal Cycle, composed between 1400 and 1200 BCE. The plural form denotes local manifestations of that same deity (e.g., Day 2002: 68; Chung 2010: 170).
3. The lordship of Yhwh, whom Israel, at least according to the prophet, worships wrongly. According to this view, there is little difference between the singular and the plural form (e.g., Jeremias 1983: 20, 49). A version of this view will be advocated here.

Hosea's polemic can further be understood in three main ways:

1. Hosea's target audience is misled by a case of mistaken identity: they think that Baal is responsible for the events around them, while the prophet knows that it is Yhwh. The people must therefore learn to differentiate between the two and worship only Yhwh (e.g., Chalmers 2006: 612; Chung 2010: 122–23, 135, 166–67, 179).
2. The audience believes that Yhwh and Baal are the same and that when they worship Baal, they worship Yhwh, albeit under a different name. In response, Hosea

makes the (monotheistic) claim that there is no other Lord (*baal*) than Yhwh (e.g., Day 2002: 73).

3. The audience sincerely worships Yhwh and sees nothing unorthodox about referring to him as Baal. Hosea disagrees (e.g., Hubler 2020).

Evaluating these options in light of the discussion above, there are few indications of a rampant Baal cult in eighth-century Israel. At the same time, there is onomastic evidence of the use of Baal as a name for Yhwh, for example in the name of David's servant Be'alyah (1) (בעליה Chr. 12:5), which literally means "Yhwh is Baal / Lord" (see Dearman 1993: 190–91). I agree with Hubler, who regards the polemic in Hosea to be a matter of conflicting Israelite identities: What is the name of Israel's deity and where should this deity be worshipped (Hubler 2020: 611–12)? Given the scarce evidence of Baal worship in eighth-century Israel, a few scholars have argued Hosea's use of the term *baal* has political rather than religious connotations. Yee, for example, identifies the lovers of Hos. 2 with "profitable foreign entanglements" upon which Israel depended economically (Yee 2001: 377). Likewise, Keefe highlights that Hos. 4–14 repeatedly attacks Israel's cult because it serves as a symbol for Israel's corrupt royal administration. In her view, Hosea's polemic targets the disintegration of Israel's identity and social structures (Keefe 1995: 88–92). More recently, Kelle has also argued that *baal* in Hosea represents foreign alliances rather than foreign deities. In particular, in his view, the polemic of Hos. 2 targets Israel's role in the Syro-Ephraimite war (734–732 BCE) (Kelle 2005: 152–66, 181–200). Yet, although sexual and marital metaphors sometimes have political connotations (e.g., Ezek. 16 and 23) and many passages in Hosea criticize Israel's political alliances, especially with Assyria and Egypt (e.g., 5:11; 7:11; 8:9; 12:1 [Heb. 12:2]), a religious, rather than a political, context of the references to Baal(s) in Hos. 2 is more likely (Dearman 2010: 251).

5.4.1. Israel's Perceived Misunderstanding (Hosea 2)

Hosea 2 contains four of the seven references to Baal(s) in the book, twice in the singular (vv. 8, 16 [Heb. vv. 10, 18]) and twice in the plural (vv. 13, 17 [Heb. vv. 15, 19]). This chapter continues, yet also expands, the marital and sexual metaphors in ch. 1, where the metaphors GOD AS HUSBAND and ISRAEL AS WIFE are used to denote Israel's relationship with Yhwh. Through these metaphors, Hosea threatens that Yhwh will punish the people of Israel because of their unfaithfulness. This message is systemic to the entire book of Hosea, as evidenced by Hos. 1:2, which, coming directly after the heading in 1:1, serves as a second heading:

When Yhwh first spoke to Hosea,
Yhwh said to Hosea: "Go, get yourself a wife of whoredom and children of whoredom; for the land will surely commit whoredom rather than following YHWH."

The first singular reference occurs in verse 8bβ (Heb. v. 10bβ). The speaker in the text (Yhwh) seeks to clarify an apparent misunderstanding. In his view, the woman fails to grasp reality. She believes that her lovers (here understood as other deities) satisfy her needs (bread, water, wool, flax, and oil) (v. 5 [Heb. v. 7]), yet the truth is that it is Yhwh who gives her not only grain, wine, and oil (v. 8a), but also silver and gold (v. 8bα). The first three products belong in the realms of agricultural fertility and the cult (Garton 2020: 545–46). Yhwh, rather than her lovers, sends rain to water the earth (cf. vv. 21–23 [Heb. vv. 23–25]; 4:3; cf. Hag. 1:10–11). In contrast, the latter two commodities recall Exod. 32:1–4 and the golden calf. Verse 8bβ, "they made to the baal" (עשׂו לבעל), is unclear, in part due to the introduction of a third-person masculine plural verb which presumably refers to Israel (i.e., the entity behind the metaphoric woman). If this reading is correct, Yhwh gave the woman precious metals, which she then spent on "the baal." The definite article, as indicated by the *patach* under the preposition *lamed* (cf. also the LXX, τῇ Βααλ) suggests that the term *baal* here is not the personal name of a deity but a title, i.e., "the lord" (Dearman 2010: 350). Taken together with the reference to silver and gold, the text probably refers to the physical depiction of the deity (an idol).

The speaker continues in v. 13 (Heb. v. 15) by describing the woman's misguided acts. The plural term *baalim* occurs in the context of "days of the *baalim*." On those days, the woman, decked with earrings and jewels, brought offerings to them, while she forgot Yhwh. The textual evidence again suggests that the *baalim* are deities, yet here they are contrasted, rather than equated, with Yhwh. In v. 16 (Heb. v. 18), the divine speaker proclaims that in the future the woman will call him "[her] man" (אישׁי) rather than "[her] Baal" (בעלי). The integral word-pun is difficult to render in English. As mentioned above, the Hebrew word בעל means both "husband" and "lord." Given the word play, the most likely interpretation would be, "You shall call me 'my man' but you shall no longer call me 'my husband.'" There are at least two ways of understanding this statement. According to most scholars, Hosea claims that Israel has until now treated Yhwh as a Hebrew manifestation of the Canaanite Baal (e.g., Andersen and Freedman 1980: 278–79). Yet, it makes more sense to interpret the verse as an inner-Yahwistic polemic. From the woman's perspective, there is nothing wrong with calling Yhwh "her Baal" (Hubler 2020: 615). Yet, Hosea insists that she should call him "her man" for two interconnected reasons. First, in contrast to the surrounding deities, Yhwh does not have a spouse. Second, as emphasized by the sexual and marital metaphors throughout Hosea, Israel is his true wife, joined with him through the covenant. By insisting on the more neutral name "man" rather than "husband/lord," Hosea thus invites Israel into a more mutual partnership than what is found between a deity and their people in the surrounding cultures (Hubler 2020: 619–21; cf. Jeremias 1983: 49; *contra* Yee 2001: 380). Verse 17 (Heb. v. 19) complicates the matter by proclaiming that Yhwh will remove the names of the *baalim* from her mouth so that they shall be mentioned no more. This verse, in contrast to v. 16, again points to and polemicizes against multiple deities (cf. Dearman 2010: 350).

Looking at the whole of Hos. 2, a pattern emerges. When the term *baal* appears in the singular, he is equated with Yhwh and emphasizes his lordship. Yet Israel must learn to call him Yhwh. In contrast, the plural term *baalim* never stands for Yhwh but refers to a heterogeneous group of unspecified deities that are contrasted with him (cf. Jer. 2:23 and 9:14).

5.4.2. Israel's Memory of the Time in the Wilderness (Hosea 9:10; 11:2)

While Hos. 2 addressed the prophet's contemporaries in Israel, Hos. 9:10 and 11:2 use the term *baal* to speak in retrospect about Israel's time in the wilderness. Hosea 9:10 mentions a place called Baal-peor, where, according to Hosea, Israel "dedicated themselves to *the* shame" (וינזרו לבשת) and thus became "detestable things" (שקוצים) "like those that they love" (כאהבם). This verse does not specify whom the Israelites worshipped, merely that their act was shameful and detestable. Yet, the specific term בשת, here in the definite form as indicated by the *patach* under the *lamed*, may be a veiled reference to Baal, as suggested by the common practice in the Deuteronomistic History of replacing the theophoric element *baal* in a name with *boshet* (see, e.g., Jonathan's son Mephibosheth [מפיבשת, 2 Sam. 4:4; 9:12] // Merib-baal [מריב בעל, 1 Chr. 8:34; 9:40]) (Day 2002: 81–83; cf. Anderson 2015: 81–82).

The name Baal-peor recalls predominantly the incident in Num. 25, where the men of Israel had sexual relationships with the women of Moab (v. 1) and sacrificed to their gods (v. 2), with the result that Yhwh became angry (v. 3) and commanded Moses to kill the people's leaders (v. 4). Moses obeyed, and the judges/Phinehas carried out the killings (vv. 5–8). Gradually, however, Baal-peor came to be associated with idolatry rather than sexual immorality (Deut. 4:3; Josh. 22:17; Ps. 106:28). Even so, apart from the name Baal-peor, nothing in these later texts confirms that this idolatry involved worship of Baal. Even so, given the strong associations with idolatry, Num. 25:1–5 probably forms the backdrop of Hos. 9:10 (see Beale 2008: 105–6). Yet, lacking shared vocabulary, it is not a matter of a direct allusion. Rather, the incident at Baal-peor likely constituted an agreed, cultic memory, wherein sexual acts were conflated with Baal worship (Ben Zvi 2005: 201). Thus, by the eighth century BCE, the name Baal-peor evoked a mixture of sexual immorality and idol worship. Alternatively, Num. 25:1–5 originated in the same context as Hos. 9, in which the worship of foreign deities and marriage to foreign women were two sides of the same coin (Levine 2000: 292–95).

Hosea 11:2b likewise recalls Israel's journey in the wilderness. This verse speaks of how the Israelites sacrificed to the *baalim* (v. 2bα, לבעלים יזבחו) and lit fires to the idols (v. 2bβ, ולפסלים יקטרון) rather than heeding Yhwh's call. As in Hos. 2:17, the *baalim* and Yhwh are contrasted with one another.

In sum, Hos. 9:10 and 11:2, as well as 13:1 (using the perfect from נשא, see below), do not talk about any form of religious activity that is contemporary with Hosea; rather they offer a retrospective glance at Israel's past behavior during the time in the wilderness

(Kelle 2005: 159–63). As such, they shed only limited light upon the religious practices of eighth-century Israel.

5.5. A Matter of Calves

Hosea 8:5–6 (עגל) and 13:1–2 (עגלים) refer to calves, either in the singular or plural. In these verses, the speaker accuses Israel of effectively abandoning Yhwh when they began to worship the calves in Bethel and Dan. As in Hos. 2, however, the addressees may have considered their worship to be entirely orthodox because, from their perspective, the calves represented Yhwh. Or, phrased differently, although the bovine imagery may originally have represented a different deity, by the time of Hosea, it was fully associated with Yhwh. The question remains, though, whether the underlying imagery is primarily related to El or Baal. A case can be made for both deities.

5.5.1. The Case for El

The term *el* (אל) has, like the above-mentioned term *baal*, two meanings. El is the generic Semitic word for "deity," and is often best translated as "god." As such, it does not denote a particular god, but can be applied to anyone (Yhwh, Hadad, Marduk, etc.). The Hebrew term אלהים is a derived form of the same word, which can either be translated as "God," or understood as a plural form, "gods." It is employed regularly in poetic literature to refer to Yhwh in Psalms (e.g., 5:5; 7:12; 18:3, 33, 48; 103:25), Isa. 40–55 (e.g., 40:18; 43:12; 45:14, 22; 46:9), and Job (e.g., 37:1–5). In this context, Exod. 6:3 is important, as it explicitly equates El Shaddai with Yhwh. At the same time, *el* is also the specific name, El, of the highest deity in the Canaanite pantheon.

5.5.1.1. *El, the Bull, the Exodus, and Jeroboam*

Both El and Yhwh are represented by bovine imagery, either by a bull (Heb. שׁור or אביר) or a calf (Heb. עגל). In the Baal Cycle, El is often described as "Bull El" (*ṯr'il*) (KTU 1.1 V, line 22; cf. Smith 1994: 117; Smith 2003: 135). Genesis 49:24 and Isa. 1:24 use "the bull of Jacob" (אביר יעקב) as an epithet for Yhwh.

The bull imagery comes to the forefront in 1 Kgs. 12 and Exod. 32. First Kings 12:28–30 narrates how Jeroboam erects two calves of gold (עגלי זהב) in Bethel and Dan to discourage the Israelites from traveling to Jerusalem to worship. Pointing to the calves, Jeroboam tells Israel that "this is your God (הנה אלהיך), who brought you out of the land of Egypt" (v. 28). This account should most likely be viewed as an example of Yahwism, albeit in a place (i.e., not Jerusalem) that later, Judahite traditions were to condemn (Anderson 2015: 107–8, 111–15). By contrast, Wyatt (1992) has argued, unconvincingly in my view, that rather than being an example of Yahwistic politics (worship Yhwh

74 LENA-SOFIA TIEMEYER

here rather than in Jerusalem), Jeroboam is seeking to lead the people of Israel back to its roots and to reinstate the original cult of El.

Jeroboam's words resemble Exod. 32:1–4. This text narrates how Aaron makes a golden calf (ויעשהו עגל מסכה), whereupon the people proclaim (ויאמרו) that it represents the gods (אלה אלהיך) who brought them out of Egypt (v. 4). This statement is ambiguous. It may mean that the calf was understood as a visual image of Yhwh. Alternatively, it may suggest that the earliest Exodus traditions associated Israel's liberation out of Egypt with El rather than with Yhwh. Numbers 23:22, for instance, states unequivocally that El brought the people out of Egypt, as does Num. 24:8 (Smith 2003: 147).

5.5.1.2. *Hosea and the Calves (Hosea 8:5–6; 11:1–2, 9; 12:10 [Eng. 12:11])*

Hosea interacts with both traditions. Hosea 8:6 refers in an unambiguous fashion to the calves in Samaria that Jeroboam set up (cf. 8:14aα, which talks about Israel forgetting its maker and building temples). Even so, in 8:13aβ, Hosea later pushes the responsibility for the break between Israel and Yhwh upon the latter: the people are sacrificing at the altar (presumably dedicated to Yhwh), yet Yhwh does not want the offerings. Hosea 10:5 likewise refers to the calves in Bethel, although this verse calls the place Beth Aven, i.e., "the house of iniquity" (see further below).

Hosea also refers to the Exodus traditions. Chapters 11–13 repeatedly seek to correct Israel's understanding of Yhwh's role in Israel's liberation from Egypt. In 11:1a, Yhwh declares that he was the one who called them out of Egypt, yet rather than adhering to him, the people turned to the *baalim* (11:2). Likewise, in 12:9 (Heb. 12:10), Yhwh declares that he, and no one else, was with them from their time in Egypt. Hosea 13:4 testifies to the same insistence that Yhwh alone is responsible for the people's liberation from Egypt. Hosea's Exodus-related polemic is part of Hosea's larger criticism of the fusion of Yhwh with El, whereby Yhwh gradually had "absorbed" and "inherited" the legacy of El (Chalmers 2006: 613–14). For Hosea, this equating of Yhwh with El was unacceptable. He sought to convince Israel that any act that was attributed to El was actually carried out by Yhwh. Other texts in Hosea tackle the issue of Yhwh's assimilation with El differently. In 11:9, for example, the speaker states explicitly that "I am El" (כי אל אנכי). In other words, Yhwh is the real El (Chalmers 2006: 621–23).

5.5.1.3. *Hosea and Bethel (Hosea 12:3–5 [Heb. 12:4–6])*

Hosea 12:3–5 (Heb. 12:4–6) is one of the most curious texts in Hosea. Verses 3–4 narrate how Jacob wrestled with an angel, whom he met at Bethel. In v. 4b (Heb. v. 5b), Bethel is mentioned explicitly: "[At] Bethel, he will find him, and there he will talk with him." Earlier, the MT of 10:15a refers to Bethel as a place that has committed many sins ("great wickedness," רעת רעתכם). Verses 3–4 appear to conflate the traditions preserved in Gen. 28:11–19; 32:22–32; and 35:1–15. In Gen. 28, Jacob dreams of a ladder going up to heaven and receives a promise from God of offspring. As he wakes up, he recognizes God's presence and accordingly names the place "Bethel" ("the house of El"). Later, in Gen. 32, Jacob has another nighttime encounter with God, this time at the Jabbok, where he wrestles with a man. He subsequently calls the place Penuel ("the face of El"). Even later, in Gen. 35, God commands Jacob to go to Bethel, settle there, and build an altar to commemorate the events of Gen. 28.

The references to Bethel in Hos. 10:5, 15, and 12:3–4 (Heb. 12:4–5) suggest that the place had a particular significance for Hosea. McKenzie, among others, argues that 12:3–4 is a quotation, or possibly a parody, of a liturgy that was carried out in Bethel in the eighth century BCE. In support of this claim, McKenzie maintains that the notoriously difficult phrase וישר אל־מלאך ויכל in v. 4aα (Heb. v. 5aα) originally spoke of "El" (אל) while "angel" (מלאך) is a later, explaining gloss. The removal of the word "angel" results in a text where Jacob wrestled with El, which, in turn, constitutes a wordplay on the name Isra-El (וישר אל) (McKenzie 1986: 313–14, 319–20). Thus, just as in the case of the Exodus (above), Hosea strives to clarify the identity of Jacob's opponent: it is not El, which his contemporary Israelites claim, but Yhwh, as v. 5 immediately explicates (והי אלהי הצבאות הי זכרו) (Chalmers 2006: 629–30). This emendation is supported by the statement in 11:12–12:1 (Heb. 12:1–2), where Israel "lies" and Judah "strays" (deriving the verb רד from רוד = "to roam") with El (ויהודה עד רד עם־אל) and is faithful to "the holy ones" (ועם־קדושים נאמן). Assuming a correspondence between the respective behavior of Judah and Israel here,[4] Hosea condemns the worship of El and its holy attendants (Coote 1971: 390–92).

5.5.1.4. *Hosea and Gilgal (Hosea 4:15; 9:15; and 12:11 [Heb. 12:12])*

Alongside Bethel, the name Gilgal is significant in Hosea. In contrast to Bethel, Gilgal plays no role in the patriarchal narratives but instead gains prominence in the traditions preserved in Joshua and 1 Samuel. In Josh. 4:19–5:12, for example, Gilgal is remembered as the place where Israel crossed over the Jordan river into the promised land. In 1 Samuel, the place is associated with the tribe of Benjamin in general and King Saul in particular. In 1 Sam. 7, Gilgal, along with Mizpah and Bethel, is the place where Samuel judges the people. Later, in 1 Sam. 11, it is the place where Saul is proclaimed king in a ceremony accompanied by sacrifices (11:15). Even later, in 1 Sam. 15, Gilgal is where Samuel declares God's rejection of Saul as king. Finally, in 2 Kgs. 2, Gilgal, together with Bethel, is associated with Elijah and Elisha. In short, Gilgal and Bethel are significant in the history of the Northern Kingdom of Israel in both the political and cultic realms.

The book of Hosea mentions Gilgal several times and always with negative connotations. It is referred to in 9:15aα as a place where Israel did "evil," and Yhwh accordingly began to "hate them." It is, however, unclear to what specific evil this verse refers. The term can mean a range of things, including idolatry, yet the reference to "all the princes who are rebelling" later in the same verse suggests social and political rather than religious transgressions. In contrast, the reference to Gilgal in 12:11 (Heb. v. 12) probably refers to cultic activity. First, Gilgal is called a place of "iniquity" (און). Elsewhere in Hosea, Beth Aven (בית און) is another name for Bethel, as indicated by its association with the calves in Hos. 10:5 (see above). The same is probably also true in 4:15, where Beth Aven is mentioned together with Gilgal, and in 5:8, where it appears alongside Gibeah and Ramah. The connection between Bethel and

Gilgal is strengthened by the rather opaque statement in v. 11aβ, which states that Israel sacrificed bulls there (בגלגל שורים זבחו). Although there is no evidence elsewhere that Jeroboam (or anyone else) erected a statue in Gilgal, Hosea clearly associates both places with the cult of bulls.

5.5.2. The Case for Baal (Hosea 13:1–2)

Despite the strong evidence in favor of identifying the calves in Hosea and the underlying traditions in 1 Kings and Exodus with El, an equally strong case can be made for associating them with Baal. Looking at the ancient Near Eastern material, textual evidence suggests that not only El but also Baal was associated with a bull. As Smith (1990: 82–85) argues, many of the references to El in the Baal Cycle belong to Baal.

In Hosea, the identification of bovine imagery with Baal draws support predominantly from 13:1–2. The speaker in v. 1 claims that, in the past, Ephraim "was exalted in Israel." At that time, Ephraim "incurred guilt with the *baal* and died" (ויאשם בבעל וימת). As in 2:8 (Heb. 2:10), the *patach* under the preposition *beth* indicates a definite article. Taken together with v. 2, which speaks about idols made of silver (cf. 2:8 [Heb. 2:10]), the text probably refers to a specific depiction of Baal. The juxtaposition of vv. 1–2 further implies a link between, on the one hand, the worship of the *baal* and, on the other hand, the worship of calves and the making of idols. Taken together, the speaker makes the threefold claim that making images is sinful, images are human-made and thus not divine, and the whole endeavor is ill-conceived. The references to calves in Hosea are probably part of the religious-political anti-Israel and pro-Judahite discourse: Israel should not worship in the temple in Samaria that Jeroboam built, but instead join the people of Judah and worship in the temple in Jerusalem. Thus, although it is impossible to distinguish between religion and politics in this matter, it is likely that Hosea's polemic here has less to do with idolatry and more to do with geopolitical power. Expressed differently, orthodoxy may here be a matter of where you worship, not whom you worship.

5.6. Rejection of Cultic Paraphernalia

We have noted Hosea's disdain for the worship of Yhwh in the visible form of a bull, even though the people of Israel may have considered this type of cultic expression to be not only acceptable but also integral to Yhwh's cult. There are a few indications that Hosea also rejects other cultic practices that may have been considered orthodox among his audience.

In Hos. 3:4, the speaker threatens Israel that they will have to live for a long time without their customary cultic paraphernalia: sacrifice (זבח), cultic pillar (מצבה), ephod (אפוד), and teraphim (ותרפים). Nothing in this verse points to these items being associated with cultic practices outside the worship of Yhwh. Rather, in line with 1 Samuel (ephod [14:18, 37; 21:9–10; 23:4], teraphim [19:13–17]), these items filled a function within the official cult of Yhwh (see Tiemeyer 2023). Furthermore, neither Exod. 24:4 nor Josh. 4:1–9 condemn cultic pillars. At the same time, other passages in Hosea speak against many of these same items. Hosea 10:1–2, for example, predicts how he (presumably Yhwh) will break Israel's cultic pillars (v. 2bβ, ישדד מצבותם). Further, Hos. 4:12 mentions derisively that Israel seeks counsel from "their wood" (בעצו), which presumably means a human-made idol (cf. the idol fabrication passage in Isa. 44:9–17), and "their rod" (ומקלו). Although the term מקל is never used to denote the ephod, it is possible to interpret the reference here as an oblique reference to that object. In sum, Hos. 4:12 and 10:1–2 suggest that Hosea rejects cultic practices that Israel considered to be orthodox parts of the cult of Yhwh.

5.7. Excursus: Cultic Prostitution?

A few texts in Hosea speak of prostitution. Hosea 4:12–14, for example, speaks of how Israel's daughters are whores (v. 13b) and how Israel's men have sex with whores and הקדשות, a word that seems to denote some form of female attendants at the temple precinct (v. 14). It has long been discussed whether these passages refer to cultic sex/cultic prostitution—a debate involving the following questions:

1. Are they part of the extended sexual and marital metaphors that pervade the entire book, where worship of anyone other than Yhwh is described in terms of "whoring"? In other words, are the people described in these three verses, men and women alike, worshipping other deities than Yhwh?
2. Do they refer to regular prostitution or "sexual orgies" (e.g., Chung 2010: 155–61, 165)?
3. Do they refer to so-called cultic prostitution, i.e., "the sale of a person's body for sexual purposes where some (if not all) of the money or goods received for this transaction belongs to a deity" (Budin 2008: 3)?

Although I do not doubt that prostitution took place in ancient Israel (e.g., Gen. 38:15–19), the concomitant references to sacrifices, temples, and high places in the Hoseanic passage under consideration speak against that option. If prostitution per se were condemned, the text would have looked differently. There is also precious little evidence of cultic prostitution elsewhere in the Hebrew Bible. If it had existed, I would have expected texts which deal with the resulting pregnancies of these rituals and the social status of the multiple children born as a result (Hos. 5:7 is unlikely to address that issue). The absence thereof suggests that cultic prostitution did not exist. I agree with Budin, who argues that Hos. 4:12–14 should be understood metaphorically: the men and women of Israel are accused of worshipping other deities than Yhwh (Budin 2008: 37–38). At the same time, as Moughtin-Mumby highlights, the juxtaposition of whores and הקדשות, which she translates as "holy women," is slanderous toward the women serving in a cultic capacity (Moughtin-Mumby 2008: 72–75; cf. Yee 2001: 355).

5.8. CONCLUSION: SEEKING YHWH

Throughout this essay, I have contended that Hosea and the people of Israel speak at cross purposes. The prophet accuses the people of worshipping other deities, while the people maintain that they are worshipping Yhwh. This communicative failure appears at regular intervals. In ch. 2, Hosea's polemic against Israel turns out to be a matter of using the right name for Yhwh in order to represent the true nature of their covenant relationship. Rather than calling Yhwh "Lord" (*baal*), Israel should use the correct, personal name. At 8:5–6 and 13:1–2, as well as 9:10 and 11:2, Hosea strives to make Israel reevaluate their understanding of history. They must learn that the God of their ancestors, who interacted with the patriarchs and later led them out of Egypt, should be called by his specific name Yhwh, even though other traditions may have named him simply "God" (El). Other passages support the claim that the people of Israel are worshipping Yhwh, albeit not in the way that Hosea deems fitting. In 5:6, for example, Hosea acknowledges that the people are seeking Yhwh. Likewise, 6:6 suggests that the Israelites are making offerings to Yhwh, even though their sacrifices are rejected, predominantly due to their noncultic crimes against their neighbors (vv. 6–11). Hosea 6:1–3 paints a similar picture, where the plural speakers refer to their desire to return to Yhwh. The same is also true, finally, for 8:2, where the people call out to God and claim to know him. In both cases, however, God spurns their endeavors.

Ultimately, the book of Hosea, together with relevant biblical and nonbiblical sources, tells us much about the religion in eighth-century Israel. Yhwh was its prime deity and most people worshipped him, although not necessarily under that name and not necessarily in monolatrous ways. The debate between Hosea and the people is not about rampant idolatry. Instead, it concerns their divergent understandings of religious orthodoxy.

Notes

1. In contrast, 2 Kgs. 21:3 claims that worship of Baal continued in Judah, as do Jer. 7:9; 11:13, 17; 19:5; 23:13, 27; 32:29, 35.
2. It is important to distinguish between history and narrative. I am only arguing that the biblical material never depicts Gideon, Saul, Jonathan, and David as worshipping anyone but Yhwh.
3. I am using the term "Hosea" as a shorthand to denote the speaker in the book. This use should not be confused with a claim of Hoseanic authorship of the book.
4. For a noncontrasting reading, among English Bible translations, see NIV. For a contrasting reading, see the Authorized Version.

References

Andersen, Francis, and David Noel Freedman. 1980. *Hosea: A New Translation with Introduction and Commentary.* AB 24. Garden City, NJ: Doubleday.

Anderson, James S. 2015. *Monotheism and Yahweh's Appropriation of Baal.* LHBOTS 617. London: Bloomsbury T & T Clark.

Beale, Gregory K. 2008. *We Become What We Worship: A Biblical Theology of Idolatry.* Downers Grove, IL: Intervarsity Press.

Ben Zvi, Ehud. 2005. *Hosea.* FOTL 21A/1. Grand Rapids, MI: Eerdmans.

Budin, Stephanie. 2008. *The Myth of Sacred Prostitution in Antiquity.* Cambridge: Cambridge University Press.

Chalmers, R. Scott. 2006. "Who Is the Real El? A Reconstruction of the Prophet's Polemic in Hosea 12:5a." *CBQ* 68: 611–30.

Chung, Youn Ho. 2010. *The Sin of the Calf: The Rise of the Bible's Negative Attitude towards the Golden Calf.* LHBOTS 523. London: T&T Clark International.

Coote, Robert B. 1971. "Hosea xii." *VT* 21: 389–402.

Day, John. 2002. *Yahweh and the Gods and Goddesses of Canaan.* JSOTSup 265. Sheffield: Sheffield Academic Press.

Dearman, J. Andrew. 1993. "Baal in Israel: The Contribution of Some Place Names and Personal Names to an Understanding of Early Israelite Religion." In M. Patrick Graham, William P. Brown, Jeffrey K. Kuan, eds., *History and Interpretation: Essays in Honour of John H. Hayes.* JSOTSup 173. Sheffield: Sheffield Academic Press, 173–91.

Dearman, J. Andrew. 2001. "Interpreting the Religious Polemics against Baal and the Baalim in the Book of Hosea." *OTE* 14: 9–25.

Dearman, J. Andrew. 2010. *The Book of Hosea.* NICOT. Grand Rapids, MI: Eerdmans.

Dijkstra, Meindert. 2001. "El, the God of Israel—Israel, the People of YHWH: On the Origins of Ancient Israelite Yahwism." In Bob Becking, ed., *Only One God? Monotheism in Ancient Israel and the Veneration of the Goddess Asherah.* Biblical Seminar 77. London: Sheffield Academic Press, 81–126.

Garton, Roy E. 2020. "First Fruits Rites in the Book of the Twelve." In Lena-Sofia Tiemeyer and Jakob Wöhrle, eds., *The Book of the Twelve: Composition, Reception, and Interpretation*. VTSup 184. Leiden: Brill, 532–53.

Hubler, Caitlin. 2020. "No Longer Will You Call Me 'My Ba'al': Hosea's Polemic and the Semantics of 'Ba'al' in 8th century B.C.E. Israel." *JSOT* 44: 610–23.

Jeremias, Jörg. 1983. *Der Prophet Hosea*. ATD 24/1. Göttingen: Vandenhoeck & Ruprecht.

Keefe, Alice A. 1995. "Female Body, the Body Politic and the Land: A Sociopolitical Reading of Hosea 1–2." In Athalya Brenner, ed., *A Feminist Companion to the Latter Prophets*. Sheffield: Sheffield Academic Press, 70–100.

Kelle, Brad E. 2005. *Hosea 2: Metaphor and Rhetoric in Historical Perspective*. SBLAB 20. Atlanta, GA: SBL.

King, Andrew M. 2017. "Did Jehu Destroy Baal from Israel? A Contextual Reading of Jehu's Revolt." *BBR* 27.3: 309–32.

Levin, Yigal. 2014. "Baal Worship in Early Israel: An Onomastic View in Light of the 'Eshbaal' Inscription from Khirbet Qeiyafa." *Maarav* 21.1–2: 203–22.

Levine, Baruch A. 2000. *Numbers 21–36*. AB 4A. Garden City, NJ: Doubleday.

McKenzie, Steven L. 1986. "The Jacob Tradition in Hosea xxii 4–5." *VT* 36: 312–22.

Moughtin-Mumby, Sharon. 2008. *Sexual and Marital Metaphors in Hosea, Jeremiah, Isaiah, and Ezekiel*. OTM. Oxford: Oxford University Press.

Smith, Mark S. 1990. *The Early History of God: Yahweh and the Other Deities in Ancient Israel*. San Francisco, CA: Harper San Francisco.

Smith, Mark S. 1994. *The Ugaritic Baal Cycle, Volume I: Introduction with Text, Translation and Commentary of KTU 1.1.–1.2*. VTSup 55. Leiden: Brill.

Smith, Mark S. 2003. *The Origins of Biblical Monotheism: Israel's Polytheistic Background and the Ugaritic Texts*. Oxford: Oxford University Press.

Tiemeyer, Lena-Sofia. 2023. "The Power of Revelation in 1–2 Samuel." In Mark G. Brett and Rachelle Gilmour, eds., *Political Theologies in the Hebrew Bible*. Journal of Ancient Judaism Supplement Series 35. Paderborn: Brill, 227–41.

Tigay, Jeffrey H. 1986. *You Shall Have No Other Gods: Israelite Religion in the Light of Hebrew Inscriptions*. Harvard Semitic Studies. Atlanta: Scholars Press.

Wyatt, Nicolas. 1992. "Of Calves and Kings: The Canaanite Dimension in the Religion of Israel." *SJOT* 6: 68–91.

Yee, Gale A. 2001. "'She Is Not My Wife and I Am Not Her Husband': A Materialist Analysis of Hosea 1–2." *BibInt* 9: 345–83.

CHAPTER 6

THE BOOK OF HOSEA AND THE SOCIOECONOMIC CONDITIONS OF EIGHTH-CENTURY BCE ISRAEL

DAVIS HANKINS

6.1. INTRODUCTION

THE editorial superscription at the beginning of the book of Hosea identifies Hosea as a prophet who received "the word of the LORD" during the reigns of four kings of the Southern Kingdom of Judah, Uzziah, Jotham, Ahaz, and Hezekiah, and during the reign of Jeroboam II of the Northern Kingdom of Israel. Jeroboam II's reign ended around 747 BCE, but the other kings mentioned suggest that Hosea may have been active until the time of Hezekiah (727/715–698/687 BCE). Scholars generally agree that the materials associated with Hosea were preserved and transmitted to future generations by Judahite scribes after Israel's destruction in 722 BCE, and that these scribes were likely responsible for adding at least some material to the book, such as some of the references to Judah (e.g., 1:7; 3:5; 6:11; 11:12 [Heb. 12:1]). Still, much of the material in the book makes sense against the background of the complex conditions that led to Assyria's destruction of Israel and its capital city of Samaria. At the same time, the book is a literary work that does not provide unmediated access to any historical figure, and this book, like all prophetic books, underwent long periods of redaction and recomposition in subsequent times and places. While this essay therefore tries to avoid making connections between the late eighth-century BCE and texts that scholars conclude for good reasons to be later additions to the book, scholars disagree widely about such questions and, generally speaking, much is regularly taken for granted in dating these texts.

This essay begins by sketching the historical circumstances that existed in Israel in the years leading to its destruction, based largely on material evidence. Then I propose a sociohistorical framework in response to the archaeological data as well as literary sources from the time, even as some parts of Hosea—and the book as such—are undoubtedly products of later periods. Next, I consider some geopolitical dynamics that plagued the state of Israel in its final decades. Finally, after speaking generally about Hosea's religious criticisms of Israel, the essay concludes with a brief discussion of the household metaphor with which the book begins.

Historical developments in southwest Asia in the late-eighth century BCE, which led on one hand to major upheavals and even the ultimate destruction of the kingdom of Israel, also had larger, world historical consequences. "Developing from a small core area in what is today northern Iraq, the Neo-Assyrian empire (tenth–seventh centuries BCE) was the first large empire of the ancient world, and . . . it initiated what is sometimes called the 'Age of Empires', i.e., a sequence of empires that ruled the Near East (and beyond) in tight succession until the twentieth century" (Faust 2021: 1). While the seeds from which the Neo-Assyrian empire grew were planted in preceding centuries, Hosea's prophetic career roughly coincided with its expansion and establishment as the dominant superpower with territorial claims over much of southwest Asia. More specifically, the size of Assyria's sphere of influence more than doubled during the decades of rapid expansion from c. 745–725 BCE.

While the idea of an "Age of Empires" has some value, it also risks obscuring important differences between distinct empires, periods, and even within a particular empire at any specific moment. Despite the impression one might get from two-dimensional maps showing the territorial extent of, for example, the Neo-Assyrian empire (but also ancient states like Israel), the actual control and influence of the empire was not homogeneous; instead, it changed over time, and in some times and places could be quite minimal. Before detailing some of the evidence for how life in Israel changed during these dramatic decades, in no small part because of Assyrian colonial ambitions within a complex environment of geopolitical machinations, the next section focuses primarily on domestic conditions in Israel at this time.

6.2. DOMESTIC LIFE IN EIGHTH-CENTURY BCE ISRAEL

In the eighth century BCE, the royal administration of the Northern Kingdom achieved the height of its wealth and control before rapidly falling into turmoil and ultimately being overthrown.[1] Israel was always bigger and wealthier than its southern neighbor Judah. Israel was better resourced with more rain and arable fertile land, had a larger population, and was more integrated into trade networks. Only in the eighth century did Israel solidify its position as a peer state with neighboring Aram (Syria), whose capital was in Damascus, and which had been an oppressive and destructive menace to Israel in the preceding century (see Miller and Hayes 2006: 327–47). With its capital in

SOCIOECONOMIC CONDITIONS OF EIGHTH-CENTURY BCE ISRAEL   83

Samaria, Israel (re)gained control of areas previously ceded to Aram such that it eventually administered, in addition to the region around the capital that was also known as Samaria, territories south as far as Bethel, as well as some lands in Judah, north to the Galilee, Gilead in the Transjordan, and all the way to Dan in the modern Golan heights (see 2 Kgs. 14:25). Israel controlled all major roadways in the area, was densely settled in many areas, and was connected to the coast and maritime trade primarily through the Phoenician city of Tyre. In the final decades of the century, however, the state faced trouble on several fronts and rapidly declined. Many interpreters suggest that several of Hosea's descriptions of Israel's chaotic conditions reflect the kingdom's final years (e.g., 5:8–15; 7:1–13; 8:1–4; 9:15–17; 10:13–15; 13:9–11). Moreover, while Ephraim is sometimes used synonymously for the kingdom of Israel, it could also refer to a more restricted region surrounding Samaria, and so Hosea's preference for this term may reflect and emphasize his expectation or awareness of Israel's diminishing size and control, among other connotations.[2]

Archaeological evidence from excavations and surveys indicates that the state apparatus increased its control over agricultural production in the eighth century. Approximately sixty potsherds found in excavations at Samaria bear inscriptions that record the distributed flow of agricultural products to royal officials in the capital (see Premnath 2003: 60–62). Known as ostraca, these inscribed potsherds were found in what was likely a royal storehouse. According to Miller and Hayes (2006: 336), "Typical are ostraca numbers 4 and 19, which bear the following inscriptions: 'In the ninth year, from Kozah to Gaddiyau, jar of old wine. In the tenth year, from Yazith, to Ahinoam, jar of fine oil.' These were obviously records concerning dispatches of wine and oil, possibly tax records of some sort, or records of wine and oil shipments from royal estates to Samaria." Furthermore, these references to "old" or vintage wine as well as "fine" or washed oil appear to indicate high-quality, luxury products of labor-intensive processes that were reserved for elite consumption. According to Chaney (2017: 126), "washed oil" likely refers to "a superior grade of olive oil extracted by water from crushed olives without the use of presses. Subsequent processing of the pulp and the use of presses introduced impurities into the oil and reduced its quality. Since only a small fraction of the total output of oil could be produced by this method of 'washing,' Samaria's ruling elite are shown to have had luxurious tastes" (see also van der Veen 2003: 405–27; cf. King and Stager 2001: 96). The production of luxury food items for regular consumption—rather than, say, a festival or special occasion—indicates the existence of a ruling elite within a society stratified by class divisions (see Boer 2015: 62, n. 22).

Other artifacts found in archaeological excavations further support this picture of Israelite society as stratified and oriented toward the benefit of an elite class through the extraction of surplus resources from the laboring peasantry. For example, hundreds of ivory fragments, some inlaid with stone and glass, were uncovered in Samaria, most in the area of the royal palace, which 1 Kgs. 22:39 calls "the ivory house" (cf. Amos 6:4) (see Younker 2017: 375–76). Such *preciosities* were attainable only through foreign trade and importation, which raises questions about what might have been offered in exchange for them. In several passages, Hosea appears to allude to the state's increased prosperity, luxury goods, metals, heightened trade, building projects, and more. For example, "Israel is a luxuriant vine that yields its fruit. The more his fruit increased the more altars he built; as his country improved, he improved his pillars . . . now they must bear their guilt. The LORD will break down their altars, and destroy their pillars" (10:1–2). In 8:14, Hosea accuses Israel of building palaces and forgetting their maker, and he accuses Judah of fortifying cities and constructing strongholds that, he promises, are doomed to be destroyed. Several passages in Hosea also mention objects fashioned from precious metals that Israel used in practices of veneration, such as "silver and gold that they used for Baal" (2:8 [Heb. 2:10]; cf. 8:4; 13:2). In this passage, Hosea uses the metaphor of adultery to criticize the ruling male elite of Samaria of infidelity to Yhwh, their true husband, by expressing devotion to rival authorities. A few verses later, Hosea continues, "I will punish her . . . for when . . . she decked herself with her ring and jewelry, and went after her lovers, and forgot me, says the LORD" (2:13 [Heb. 2:15]). While some of these references are to actions in the past, and here the description occurs in the context of the adultery metaphor and so may not be referring to actual luxury items of jewelry, the references to luxury goods in Hosea are nevertheless consistently negative and critical. Finally, in 12:1 (Heb. 12:2), Hosea refers to oil as a commodity traded with or paid in tribute to Egypt.

Abundant evidence indicates that economic activities in Israel (and Judah) were increasingly organized around the production of surpluses of cash crops such as wine, oil, and grain over the course of the eighth century. Archaeologists have identified numerous facilities used to process grapes and olives for the production of wine and oil, as well as storage towers, grain pits, and more. One strategy for increasing surpluses produced and thus available for extraction by a ruling class is regional specialization. For example, the steep slopes of the hill country or the coastal zones were favorable places to plant vines and grow olive trees; grains are easier to raise in fertile valleys and other flat zones; and more arid areas are well suited for husbandry, herding, and grazing. Some degree of regional specialization is expected in any place, of course, but doing it successfully and at scale requires significant centralized control and coordination for collection, distribution, protection, and storage, to which the Samaria Ostraca and other evidence attest.

The proliferating installations for manufacturing wine and oil also indicate technological standardization and innovations, which is a second means for increasing the productive capacities of land and labor. For example, the beam press that increased output and improved efficiencies in the production of olive oil was adopted at a widespread scale only in the eighth century (Chaney 2017: 127). The pottery record also shifts from locally produced, varying types of mostly small wares, to "mass-produced, limited variety forms ideal for more efficient transport and distribution of goods" (Pioske 2015: 90; cf. Premnath 2003: 66–67). Moreover, production facilities for oil and wine appear in the eighth century in otherwise perennially under- or uninhabited marginal areas, such as the ecological fringe of western Samaria. In his survey of the area, Dar (1986:

147–90) discusses numerous new settlements in the eighth century, with many on virgin sites that appear to have been constructed according to similar layouts, suggesting some degree of central planning. This then is a third means for increasing the production of surpluses—namely, by introducing productive, economic activities in novel areas. Incentives and/or pressures to work in previously unproductive areas can be exceedingly difficult to apply successfully because such lands tend to present various hardships and/or produce smaller yields, which of course is typically why they are otherwise unworked. Aside from other contributing factors, successfully introducing such efforts often requires a relatively high degree of population density. It is typically only when people lack possibilities for migration that they can be pressed into working such difficult, marginal environs. Demographic estimations are notoriously problematic, but scholars generally agree that the kingdom of Israel "was the most densely populated settled region in the entire Levant," and that its population peaked just prior to the Assyrian military campaigns of the late eighth century (Finkelstein and Silberman 2001: 208; see also Broshi and Finkelstein 1992: 47–60; Faust 2012: 3; Chaney 2017: 126–27, 140, 245–46; Premnath 2003: 70–72).[3]

While population density is a significant, enabling factor for controlling agricultural production, collection, distribution, and consumption, other mechanisms are often employed in conjunction with a dense population to curtail the control of laboring peasants over their economic activities. So, for example, legal and debt instruments may be used to transfer control over the means of production from laborers to nonproducing landowners in processes that lead to growing estates, or latifundialization. Although Hosea does not directly describe such processes, in several passages these issues appear to hover in the background. For example, in 7:1, Hosea criticizes corruption, false dealings, and theft. In 12:7–9 (Heb. 12:8–10), Hosea condemns rich merchants for enriching themselves through false balances and oppression. In 5:10, Hosea also accuses the rulers in Judah of what sounds like an illegal seizure of land: "The princes of Judah have become like those who remove the landmark; on them I will pour out my wrath like water." Although the full meaning of this verse may ultimately elude us, laws prohibiting and teachings against the moving of boundary stones in many texts indicate that such a practice could lead to the dispossession of some from their lands (e.g., Deut. 19:14; 27:17; Prov. 22:28; 23:10). Plus, criticisms of similar-sounding practices appear in other passages from eighth-century prophetic texts (e.g., Isa. 5:8; Mic. 2:2). In addition, the mere presence of a boundary stone can also indicate the existence of a ruling class trying to control the land at some remove from the laborers who worked it, since clear boundary markers are often unneeded in agrarian village life (see Knight 2011: 147, 205–7). This passage may thus indicate both the existence of an urban elite extending their control over new regions of productive land and the undermining of laboring peasants' capacities to allocate shares of land and determine their agricultural practices (see Premnath 2003: 107–8).

6.3. A Sociohistorical Framework

From the evidence surveyed in the preceding section, among other considerations, several scholars in recent decades have concluded that the political and economic background for understanding the eighth-century prophets, including Hosea, involves considerable tension and conflict between two competing, native regimes of economic production and social reproduction. Most of the population lived as peasant laborers, which was always the case in the ancient, preindustrial world. But while some were able to organize their lives and productive activities according to subsistence strategies aimed at sustaining small communities over time through optimal allocation of resources, the lives and productive activities of others were increasingly controlled by centralized and mostly urban elites who were interested in maximizing the production of surpluses capable of, at a minimum, (1) sustaining an elite urban class with diminished participation in productive, agricultural labor, e.g., the king and royal court, priests, scribes, and artists or craftspeople; (2) supplying native elites with resources that could be exchanged and traded for luxury items, metals, military materiel, and the like; and (3) meeting the demands of foreign, imperial tribute quotas.

Marvin Chaney (2017: 129), for example, tends to speak of this fundamental antagonism as a conflict between a society aimed at sufficiency versus one that is driven to maximize efficiencies. Thus he emphasizes various negative consequences that practices aimed at maximal efficiency present in contrast to agrarian communities oriented around sustainable reproduction. From one (limited) angle and for a (limited) time, such large-scale regional specialization may increase the production of surpluses, but it also undermines various practices that spread and reduce risk, maintain the health and vitality of the soil, and foster diversity and creativity in laboring activities. In a region prone to threats from (1) drought, earthquakes, and other natural disasters; (2) "more or less routine difficulties of all Middle Eastern agriculture— seasonal aridity and . . . extreme variation in rainfall, wind patterns, and solar radiation even within small areas" (Davis 2009: 108); and (3) more directly human disruptions, e.g., from raiding bandits and marauding armies (see Hos. 7:1), regional specialization heightens vulnerabilities and eliminates risk-reducing and sustainability-oriented practices such as poly-cropping, fallow periods, crop rotations, and more. Thus, for example, periodically planting legumes in a field that previously produced cereals enriches the soil with nitrogen that the cereals deplete on top of supplying the peasant community with protein from vegetal products (legumes also require very little water to grow and capture a lot of carbon dioxide from the atmosphere).

D. L. Premnath (2003: 72) provides a similar analysis of these socioeconomic realities within which prophets like Hosea lived, although he tends to speak of the conflict between a subsistence and a market economy. In a discussion of Amos and Hosea as "agrarian prophets," Ellen Davis (2009: 122) similarly writes, "This sudden outburst of rural prophecy, apparently unprecedented in the depth and range of its vision and replete with language and images that evoke the experience of farmers, seems to have been prompted by a large-scale transformation of both the land and the rural economy. . . . The old subsistence economy, as it had been practiced in semiautonomous villages cooperating within regional networks, was supplanted by intensified and specialized agriculture. The new system was designed to maximize production."[4] Gale Yee (2003: 83–84) similarly refers to "two conflicting systems of land tenure," which she describes as "the familial mode of production" that came under threat from "the tributary mode of production." Yee's use of the term "tributary" nicely captures the flow of goods from laboring peasants to native and nonnative or imperial elites. Roland Boer (2015: 1) also contributes some helpful nuance to this overall sociohistorical framework. On one hand, he emphasizes the ongoing nature of this conflict. As in the above quotation from Davis, scholars sometimes describe this conflict as a transformation whereby one socioeconomic regime supplants another. However, the subsistence-survival regime of allocation never disappeared; it remained present and in conflict with the regimes of extraction. On the other hand, Boer also adds nuance by identifying multiple types of regimes that existed and at times competed with each other. Thus the conflict is not simply between two discrete and competing socioeconomic regimes. Nonetheless, the multiple regimes that Boer identifies remain fundamentally conflicted between what he distinguishes as "regimes of allocation" versus various forms of "regimes of extraction" (p. 1). Regardless of one's preferred terms—e.g., sufficiency versus efficiency, familial versus tributary, allocation or permanence versus extraction—many scholars agree that this overall sociohistorical framework makes the best sense of the material and textual evidence associated with eighth-century Palestine.

6.4. Geopolitical Dynamics

Around 745 BCE, the Neo-Assyrian empire forcefully reasserted its presence in the region under the leadership of Tiglath-pileser III (known in some biblical texts as Pul) in a series of military campaigns. After Jeroboam II's death in 746 BCE, Israel under king Menahem (745–738 BCE) began again to pay heavy tribute to the north Mesopotamian empire, which, according to 2 Kgs. 15:19–20, Menahem extracted by taxing the wealthy—whose wealth was of course initially produced by and extracted from laboring peasants. This payment is corroborated by an Assyrian inscription: "The Iran Stele (ca. 737 BCE; Fragment 1, Column IIIA) provides a list of western kings who paid tribute to Tiglath-Pileser III. This list includes 'Menahem of Samaria'" (Younker 2017: 386). While many details remain unclear, there emerged in Israel and across the region a desire and will among some in the ruling elite (and surely others as well) to resist violently Assyrian control and demands for tribute. Pekah, a prorevolutionary ruler, usurps the throne in Israel in 737 BCE by murdering Menahem's son and heir. Pekah joins a coalition with neighboring administrations, including the Syrian king Rezin who reigned in Damascus, initiating a resistance strategy that had some success in the previous century.[5] Judah refuses to join this coalition, which leads to some violent clashes between these neighboring armies (see 2 Kgs. 16:5–9; Isa. 7:1–2). Assyria responds with a devastating campaign of retaliation in 733 BCE, but stops short of sacking the capital Samaria, perhaps in part because Hoshea ben Elah kills Pekah and takes the throne, reigning from 733 to 724 BCE. According to another Assyrian inscription of Tiglath-pileser III, "The house of Omri . . . overthrew their king Pekah, and I placed Hoshea as king over them. I received 10 talents of gold, 1000 talents of silver, as their tribute and brought them to Assyria" (*ANET* 284). Assyria converts territories to the north and east of Israel, such as Gilead, Dor, and Megiddo, into imperial provinces (see 2 Kgs. 15:29). Hoshea, however, eventually also revolts against Assyria, which gives the new Assyrian king Shalmaneser V cause to invade Israel again around 724 BCE. Shalmaneser apparently dies during the siege of Samaria, but Sargon II completes the conquest of the capital and the overthrow of the state administration of Israel. What remained of Israel's territories became provinces of the Assyrian empire, ruled by Assyrian-appointed governors. Many Israelites were killed in the fighting, as well as in the forced deportations by which Assyria transplanted some of the population, including especially king Hoshea and other elites, to areas closer to the center of the empire (2 Kgs. 15:30; 17:1–6). In addition to deportations and destruction, Sargon claims also to have restored and repopulated Samaria with "people of lands conquered by my two hands" (*COS* 2:295–96). The population in lands administered by Judah suddenly spikes and Jerusalem expands dramatically at this time, in part because many Israelites apparently also migrated south.

We have no information about what happened to the prophet Hosea during and after the destruction in 722 BCE. But the book alludes to that destruction, sometimes sees a future beyond it, and even explicitly refers to Assyria in various passages. One clear allusion to Israel's destruction is in 13:9–11, and another, along with an indication of a future beyond the destruction, can be found in 3:4–5, which is likely a later addition given the reference to the Davidic king. In 5:13, Hosea ridicules the nation's political rulers for pursuing aid from Assyria: "When Ephraim saw his sickness, and Judah his wound, then Ephraim went to Assyria. . . . But [Assyria] is not able to cure you or heal your wound." The surrounding verses (5:8–15), according to many, allude to the conflicts between Israel and Judah in the Syro-Ephraimite war. Whereas Judah turned to Assyria for aid against the anti-Assyrian coalition of Israel with Syria (perhaps the referent for Israel going after vanity or filth in v. 11), v. 13 may allude to Hoshea's efforts to appease Assyria following Pekah's defeat and death once the Assyrians defeated the alliance. Instead of aid however, Israel and Judah will experience Yhwh's wrath as a punishing lion, presumably in the form of Assyria's ravaging conquests. In 8:9, Hosea similarly ridicules the people: "For they have gone up to Assyria, a wild ass wandering alone; Ephraim has bargained for lovers." The prophet then reports the result: "They shall soon writhe under the burden of kings and princes" (8:10; cf. 7:11–12). In 10:5–6, Hosea describes the priests' lamentation over the loss of valuable objects used in worship to the insatiable plundering of the Assyrian empire. Then in vv. 7–8, Hosea anticipates that such destruction will only worsen as "Samaria's king shall perish" and places of worship "shall be destroyed."

In 11:10–11, Hosea presses the lion imagery toward a contrasting end to assert that, after being punished with exile to Egypt and Assyria (11:5), Yhwh will again roar like a lion and "his children shall come trembling from the west. They shall come trembling like birds from Egypt, and like doves from the land of Assyria; and I will return them to their homes, says the LORD." In 12:1 (Heb. 12:2), Hosea criticizes Israel again for pursuing international political and economic relations that lead to deceit and violence at home: "they multiply falsehood and violence; they make a treaty with Assyria, and oil is carried to Egypt." Finally, the book includes another explicit reference to Assyria in 14:3 (Heb. 14:4) as the prophet instructs the people to confess: "Assyria shall not save us; we will not ride upon horses; we will say no more, 'Our God,' to the work of our hands. In you the orphan finds mercy." Thus the book concludes with the prophet calling Israel to repent and restore their relationship with Yhwh by turning away from the plunderous foreign empire abroad, from their own military machinery at home (i.e., horses), and from the religious objects and ideas that legitimated such violence. Orphaned from such deceitful promises of security, perhaps also from their divine parent, Hosea promises that they will then receive Yhwh's mercy.

6.5. Hosea's Religious Criticisms and Metaphors

The book of Hosea is highly critical of religious beliefs and practices in Israel, which Hosea denigrates by repeatedly but not exclusively deploying metaphors of sexual immorality (e.g., 4:10–19; 5:3–4; 7:4; 9:1). Many questions and problems pervade scholars' understandings of (1) what the people described in these texts were actually thinking and doing; (2) why these beliefs and practices were offensive to Hosea; and (3) what Hosea imagined the people could do that would be an acceptable alternative. Part of the difficulties derive from Hosea's unparalleled propensity to layer metaphors upon metaphors, sliding from one image to another, often without explanation, description, transition, or propositions (see Sharp 2010). Yet problems also derive from the role played by interpreters' presuppositions and understandings of Hosea's sociohistorical world. These distinct sources of problems may be linked insofar as a reader's recourse to prevailing conceptions may occur more frequently and with less friction when struggling with excessive poetic imagery and allusion.

Traditional biblical scholarship held the general idea that Israel emerged as a distinct people alongside non-Israelites in the land of Canaan as a consequence of Israel's covenantal faith in Yhwh as the true God in contrast to ongoing Canaanite beliefs in rival gods, especially the storm and fertility deity, Baal. Canaanite religion was understood to be based on natural cycles of generation and corruption and motivated by the desire to ensure the resurgence of nature's life-giving powers of regeneration, which were heavily influenced by divine agency. Thus, Canaanite religion was one of many "fertility religions," enthralled by ideas of copulating deities who could be influenced by, among other things, ritualized sexual acts that ensured the fertility of humans, agriculture, other animals, and so on. Hosea's polemics against Israel, especially the priestly and royal elites, for adultery, promiscuity, prostitution, fornication, and so on, were thus symbolic of Israel's idolatry, worship of gods other than Yhwh, adoption of non-Israelite religious practices, among other forms of apostasy, and to the neglect of their covenantal moral and religious obligations to Yhwh.

Recent work has highlighted numerous problems with this picture, including explanations for why these ideas arose and persisted for so long despite a lack of good evidence, as well as why and how they have now been subjected to much critical scrutiny.[6] Briefly, this narrative was shaped by a larger trend diagnosed decades ago by Edward Said as *Orientalism*, with its nefarious intersection of misogyny, racism, colonialism, androcentrism, Eurocentrism, and more. This particular example of an Orientalist narrative was also rooted in several mistaken understandings: (1) of Israel's origins as an ethnically distinct, non-Canaanite group, when the evidence indicates instead that early Israel emerged out of indigenous Canaanite peoples; (2) of Israel's theology as monotheistic in contrast to native polytheisms, when it is more accurately described as pantheon reduction characteristic of others across the region, with explicitly monotheistic claims developing only gradually and belatedly, long after Hosea's time; and (3) of Hosea's polemical monolatry as representative of orthodox Yahwism, whereas it now appears to have been a development intended to combat official and popular religious beliefs and practices that, while primarily devoted to the dynastic and main national deity Yhwh, also recognized and integrated the veneration of other deities such as Asherah, and perhaps Baal.[7]

An alternative framework for understanding the context and content of Hosea's prophecy is readily available from the above discussion of the changing historical circumstances that reshaped Israel's political economy in the eighth century BCE. As Chaney (2017: 178) writes, in concert with Keefe, Yee, and others mentioned above, "'promiscuity' in the book of Hosea is primarily a figure for dynamics in the political economy of Israel, most particularly for the dynamics of agricultural intensification. To the extent that 'religious' institutions and practices come within the purview of that figure they involve the sacral legitimation of agricultural intensification, its architects, and short-term beneficiaries." This is not to say that the allusiveness, play, ambiguity, and polyvalence in Hosea's metaphors—and particularly in the metaphorical speech about sexuality, promiscuity, marriage, parentage, family, etc.—can be neatly resolved by the idea of agricultural intensification, but rather that these features of Hosea's prophetic poetry should be elucidated by the sociohistorical context of Israel in the late eighth century.[8] Davis (2009: 132) similarly writes, "Hosea's trope of fornication refers not simply to apostasy but to the whole religio-political system of state-controlled agriculture and international trade, run by an urban-based elite and endorsed by priests and prophets at the central shrines. Venality and greed are reconfigured as rampant sexual impropriety."

6.6. Hosea's Household Metaphor

I want to conclude with some brief remarks on the most well-known part of the book, chs. 1–3. Hosea begins with rather lewd details that are ostensibly about the prophet and his wife, Gomer, and their three children. The story is shocking because of how Yhwh describes the prophet's wife and children in the divine command: "Go, take for yourself a wife of whoredom and have children of whoredom" (1:2). The story initially sounds biographical, yet at the very outset the text states that the personal details are intended to symbolize problems in the nation's relationship with Yhwh and the land: "for the land commits great whoredom by forsaking the LORD" (1:2). Although enigmatic, accusing the land of fornicating may be a metaphorical way of criticizing agricultural practices that Hosea deems unfaithful. The agricultural connotations and symbolism are carried further still by the children's names. Yhwh instructs Gomer and Hosea to name their first child Jezreel, which literally means "God sows" (1:4), but has numerous other significant associations (see Yee 2003: 101–3). The names of their second and third children signify the parent's rejection of the children—"Name her Lo-ruhamah" (1:6; "unpitied"); "Name him Lo-ammi" (1:8; "Not-my-people")—even as they also carry the potential for reversal into Ruhamah ("Pitied") and Ammi ("My-people"; see 2:1 [Heb. 2:3]).

Chapter 2 develops the household metaphor further but does not refer to the prophet's family. Instead, Yhwh speaks as the male head of household who has been betrayed and shamed by the people Israel as his promiscuous wife and by his unfaithful children. Yhwh reports Israel's lecherous determination: "I will go after my lovers; they give me my bread and my water, my wool and my flax, my oil and my drink" (2:5 [Heb. 2:7]). Yhwh speaks metaphorically about Israel's licentious desire for sexual satisfaction in order to criticize their religious infidelities, yet the long list of staples and commodities emphatically indicates that these religious infidelities are primarily driven by and take the form of economic activities. In Hos. 2:8 (Heb. 2:10), Yhwh claims to be the true source of the primary agricultural and trade commodities listed in 2:5 (Heb. 2:7), which Yhwh threatens to withdraw from Israel as punishment (2:9, 12 [Heb. 2:11, 14]). While many modern readers have been trained to think about religion, politics, economics, and sexuality as more or less distinct from each other, Hosea blends them together seamlessly in ways that reveal their inseparability and that are rooted in historical connections among these areas in ancient Israel. For example, priests and religious sanctuaries were deeply involved in agricultural production, allocation, and extraction (see Yee 2003: 89–92). Also, political alliances were sealed with treaties that included religious oaths and describe the parties united by the covenant as in love, as in Hos. 8:9.[9] Hosea also refers to Israel's illicit lovers as *baal(s)*, which later in the book refers to Israel's veneration of the storm and fertility god Baal in previous generations (see 9:10; 11:2; 13:1). But the term can also mean husband and can have a more political meaning of ally or overlord, which fits best with Hosea's use of the term in ch. 2. As Kelle (2005: 165) writes, Hosea's use of the term *baal* in ch. 2 "makes the subtle theological statement that the present generation's political misconduct with allies is the theological equivalent of the past generation's religious misconduct with Baal. . . . Through the use of this term, Hosea offers a powerful critique that denies the compartmentalization of political and religious life and elevates the ruling house's inappropriate political alliances to the level of a breach in the exclusive relationship with Yahweh." If we add economics to Kelle's point, the ties that bind the past to the present and religion to politics are only strengthened (cf. the story of Naboth's vineyard in 1 Kgs. 21). According to Yee (2003: 94), "For Hosea, the cult in eighth-century Israel embodied a mode of production that was unjust and intolerable: an agricultural intensification, tied to a profitable foreign market and an aggressive foreign hegemony that insistently imposed its will on Israelite internal affairs; and corrupt Israelite institutions of kingship, prophecy, and priesthood that oversaw this agribusiness, funneling profits to their own social sectors, and furthering the exploitation of the peasant classes."

The chapter dramatically turns in 2:14–23 (Heb. 2:16–25) as Yhwh promises to remarry Israel through a covenant with all creation. This covenant will lead to military disarmament, which Hosea again places in the context of the land ("I will abolish the bow, the sword, and war from the land," v. 18), as well as the flourishing of the human and nonhuman environment, which Hosea also once again conceptualizes in terms of agriculture and the food economy ("the earth shall answer the grain, the wine, and the oil, and they shall answer Jezreel; and I will sow her for myself in the land," 2:21–23). These interconnected domains are all evoked by another emphatic list of terms that Hosea uses to describe this promised future state of blessing: "in safety," "in righteousness," "in justice," "in steadfast love," "in mercy," and "in faithfulness" (2:18–20 [Heb. 2:20–22]). The totality of these terms is summed up as a matter of knowing Yhwh: "and you shall know the LORD" (2:20 [Heb. 2:22]). Chapter 3 then offers a few sparse, biographical details that are similar to yet intriguingly distinct from those in ch. 1.

As throughout the book, Hos. 1–3 evokes and leaves unsynthesized multiple intersecting and overlapping semantic domains, including agricultural production, religious veneration, political alliances, parentage, sexuality, marriage, and procreation. Yet the land and agricultural activities as the primary means of production are unmistakably prominent, as are Hosea's criticisms of Israel's rulers for their political alliances. The collective political and economic dynamics that are one subject of these chapters are more directly relevant to this essay than the many fascinating ambiguities and uncertainties that they raise, especially regarding the prophet's personal life. While a reader's attention may be captured initially by the salacious sexual details about the prophet's private life, on closer consideration Hos. 1–3 actually offers sparse references to anything overtly sexual and instead focuses primarily on matters concerned with Israel's political economy. This is not to deny or downplay the book's concerns with sexual matters, but rather to say that the book extends what it conceptualizes as sexual far beyond the usual range.

Hosea uses the marriage metaphor primarily to criticize Israel's male aristocracy, to expose their exploitative and oppressive policies and practices that threatened human and nonhuman flourishing; to undermine their toxic ideals of masculinity as elite, urban warriors and rulers; and to push them to (re)turn to relationships of covenant, care, justice, and solidarity with Yhwh, one another, and nonhuman creation. And yet, as feminist readers have repeatedly shown, Hosea's marriage metaphor is dangerous for numerous reasons, not least because it "reinforces patriarchal social structures, silences the woman's voice, legitimates violence against her, and identifies women with sin and evil" (Keefe 2014: 827). Readers must be mindful of these dangers, even as these dangers do not undermine the fact that the primary targets of Hosea's subversive text are the oppressive policies, exploitative practices, and unjust powers and privileges of Israel's ruling male elite. Moreover, Hosea's criticisms of injustice and hope for a more just and sustainable future may also enable readers to subject the patriarchy and misogyny that undergirds the book's conceptions of marriage and sexuality to the same sphere of injustices that the book otherwise condemns and hopes to escape.

Notes

1. One could also argue that Israel peaked under the Omride dynasty in the mid-ninth century BCE after the capital was moved to Samaria and before the troubles with Syria. See, e.g., Dearman 1988: 139–42.
2. See Kelle 2002. For other connotations, see Davis 2009: 134–35.
3. The macrosociological work of Lenski (1984) demonstrates the powerful role played by population—on par with technology—in determining the shape of different types of human societies.
4. While discussing more recent agricultural practices as reiterations of this earlier conflict, Davis distinguishes "an economics of permanence . . . in contrast to industrial agriculture's economics of extraction and total consumption" (2009: 108).
5. The Qarqar coalition, named like the Qarqar Stele of Shalmaneser III after the town on the Orontes river, had some success in 853 BCE at repelling Assyrian efforts to control trade routes in Syria-Palestine. See Tadmor 1975: 36–48.
6. See especially, Keefe 2001. My discussion is heavily influenced by Keefe as well as similar interpretations that either largely follow or generally agree with her position, especially in works cited above by Yee, Chaney, Davis, and others.
7. Evidence for the worship of Asherah alongside Yhwh appears in contemporaneous inscriptions from Kuntillet 'Ajrud and Khirbet el-Qôm, and is strongly suggested by countless female figurines found primarily in domestic contexts from the eighth and seventh centuries (see Yee 2003: 87). Associations between Asherah and sacred poles, the tree of life, and other wooden symbols suggest to some that Hos. 4:12 likely alludes to her veneration in Israel. The worship of Baal, however, is not attested so directly. Apart from a few passages in Hosea (e.g., 2:8, 13, 17 [Heb. 2:10, 15, 19]; 13:1–2), and the memory of Baal worship under the Omrides during the previous century (1 Kgs. 17–2 Kgs. 10), the only potential indications from material evidence are found in the Samarian Ostraca that preserve Israelite names with the theophoric element Baal. Since Baal can also mean lord, master, or husband, however, these do not necessarily attest to veneration of the deity Baal. Furthermore, no other eighth-century prophets indicate that the worship of Baal was an issue or a reality at the time.

8. On metaphor in Hosea, see the beautiful essay by Landy (2001). For a more comprehensive treatment of metaphor, although a more limited treatment of Hosea, see Kelle 2005. See also the essay by Lancaster in this volume.
9. On the lovers as political allies in Hos. 2 specifically, see Kelle 2005: 119–22.

REFERENCES

Boer, Roland. 2015. *The Sacred Economy of Ancient Israel*. Library of Ancient Israel. Louisville: Westminster John Knox.

Broshi, Magen, and Israel Finkelstein. 1992. "The Population of Palestine in Iron Age II." *BASOR* 287: 47–60.

Chaney, Marvin L. 2017. *Peasants, Prophets, and Political Economy: The Hebrew Bible and Social Analysis*. Eugene, OR.: Cascade.

Dar, Shimon. 1986. *Landscape and Pattern: An Archaeological Survey of Samaria 800 B.C.E.– 636 C.E.* British Archeological Report 308. Oxford: British Archaeological Report.

Davis, Ellen F. 2009. *Scripture, Culture, and Agriculture: An Agrarian Reading of the Bible*. Cambridge: Cambridge University Press.

Dearman, John Andrew. 1988. *Property Rights in the Eighth-Century Prophets: The Conflict and Its Background*. SBLDS 106. Atlanta: Society of Biblical Literature.

Farver, Zev I., and Jacob L. Wright, eds. 2018. *Archaeology and History of Eighth-Century Judah*. SBL Ancient Near East Monographs. Atlanta: Society of Biblical Literature.

Faust, Avraham. 2012. *The Archaeology of Israelite Society in Iron Age II*. Winona Lake, IN: Eisenbrauns.

Faust, Avraham. 2021. *The Neo-Assyrian Empire in the Southwest: Imperial Domination and Its Consequences*. New York: Oxford University Press.

Finkelstein, Israel, and Neil Asher Silberman. 2001. *The Bible Unearthed: Archaeology's New Vision of Ancient Israel and the Origin of Its Sacred Texts*. New York: Free Press.

Keefe, Alice A. 2001. *Woman's Body and the Social Body in Hosea*. JSOTSup 338. New York: Sheffield Academic.

Keefe, Alice A. 2014. "Hosea." In Gale A. Yee, Hugh R. Page Jr., and Matthew J. M. Coomber, eds., *Fortress Commentary on the Bible: The Old Testament and Apocrypha*. Minneapolis: Fortress, 823–35.Kelle, Brad. E. 2002. "What's in a Name? Neo-Assyrian Designations for the Northern Kingdom and Their Implications for Israelite History and Biblical Interpretation." *JBL* 121: 639–66.

Kelle, Brad E. 2005. *Hosea 2: Metaphor and Rhetoric in Historical Perspective*. SBLAB 20. Leiden: Brill.

King, Philip J., and Lawrence Stager. 2001. *Life in Biblical Israel*. Library of Ancient Israel. Louisville: Westminster John Knox.

Knight, Douglas A. 2011. *Law, Power, and Justice in Ancient Israel*. Library of Ancient Israel. Louisville: Westminster John Knox.

Landy, Francis. 2001. "In the Wilderness of Speech: Problems of Metaphor in Hosea." In *Beauty and the Enigma: And Other Essays on the Hebrew Bible*. JSOTSup 312. Sheffield: Sheffield Academic, 273–97.

Lenski, Gerhard E. 1984. *Power and Privilege: A Theory of Social Stratification*. Chapel Hill and London: University of North Carolina Press.

Miller, J. Maxwell, and John H. Hayes. 2006. *A History of Ancient Israel and Judah*. 2nd ed. Louisville: Westminster John Knox.

Pioske, Daniel D. 2015. *David's Jerusalem: Between Memory and History*. New York and London: Routledge.

Premnath, D. N. 2003. *Eighth Century Prophets: A Social Analysis*. St. Louis: Chalice.

Sharp, Carolyn J. 2010. "Hewn by the Prophet: An Analysis of Violence and Sexual Transgression in Hosea with Reference to the Homiletical Aesthetic of Jeremiah Wright." In Chris Franke and Julia M. O'Brien, eds., *Aesthetics of Violence in the Prophets*. LHBOTS 517. New York: T&T Clark, 50–71.

Sherwood, Yvonne. 1996. *The Prostitute and the Prophet: Reading Hosea in the Late Twentieth Century*. London: T&T Clark.

Tadmor, Hayim. 1975. "Assyria and the West: The Ninth Century and Its Aftermath." In Hans Goedicke and J. J. M. Roberts, eds., *Unity and Diversity: Essays in the History, Literature, and Religion of the Ancient Near East*. Baltimore: Johns Hopkins University Press, 36–48.

van der Veen, Marijke. 2003. "When Is Food a Luxury?" *World Archaeology* 43, no. 3: 405–27.

Weems, Renita J. 1995. *Battered Love: Marriage, Sex, and Violence in the Hebrew Prophets*. OBT. Minneapolis: Fortress.

Yee, Gale A. 2003. *Poor Banished Children of Eve: Woman as Evil in the Hebrew Bible*. Minneapolis: Fortress.

Younker, Randall W. 2017. "Israel: The Prosperous Northern Kingdom." In Jennie Ebeling et al., eds., *The Old Testament in Archaeology and History*. Waco: Baylor University Press, 363–89.

CHAPTER 7

TRANSFORMATION AND REINTERPRETATION IN THE COMPOSITION AND REDACTION OF HOSEA

SUSANNE RUDNIG-ZELT

7.1. THE PROBLEMS OF THE BOOK OF HOSEA

THE difficulty of the book of Hosea has been notorious throughout the history of the book's exegesis. Most texts lack even the basic structure of beginning, middle, and ending. So Hos. 1 has two beginnings (vv. 1 and 2), and it is not clear if the chapter ends with 1:9 or 2:3 (Eng. 2:1). But at least Hos. 1 has a clear subject matter. The children of Hosea with Gomer, the woman of whoredom (1:2), represent the ultimate end of the relationship between Yhwh and Israel, which will be reversed (2:1–3 [Eng. 1:10–2:1]), unless that is a later addition.

Most texts in the book of Hosea, especially in chs. 4–14 cannot be summarized in a similar manner. It is impossible to sum up the message of a chapter like Hos. 6, which begins with people ardently expressing their wish to return to Yhwh (6:1–3). The reader would expect Yhwh's warm answer to this wish. Yet what follows is a debate about Israel's and Ephraim's lack of grace (חסד), an issue that did not matter in 6:1–3. The debate about grace is interrupted by a saying about prophets as Yhwh's weapon (6:5a), yet the judgments of one male person "comes forth like light" (6:5b). Then the text turns into a series of accusations of transgressing the covenant (6:7), doing evil (6:8), lurking like robbers and murdering (6:9), and whoredom (6:10). It is not clear what keeps this series together, which continues seamlessly into the following chapters.

Some verses in the book are still more unclear and hardly understandable at all. We have already seen the contradiction in 6:5. But what should one make of a verse like

7:5: "Day of our king—they have weakened princes—heat/fury from wine—he gives his hand to mockers" (see Wolff 1990: 236; Jeremias 1983: 90; Rudnig-Zelt 2006: 212; Vielhauer 2007: 86; contra Macintosh 1997: 259–61; Schütte 2016: 37–38)? This verse and the main bulk of Hos. 4–14 resemble a patchwork of thoughts and phrases that waver from one subject to another without any overall logic. What keeps these chapters loosely together are recurrent themes connected with keywords (Vielhauer 2007: 3). So הלך ("to walk to/after") is used throughout especially chs. 5–7 and also in ch. 2 to express the people's misdirected loyalty toward political allies (5:13; 7:11b) or other gods (2:7, 15 [Eng. 2:5, 13]) or as its general attitude (5:11b).[1] But the word can also stand for the desire to return to Yhwh (2:9 [Eng. 2:7]; 6:1–3), which may be in vain (5:6). Yhwh uses this word to declare that he is as dangerous as a lion for the guilty people (5:14) and to announce his withdrawal (5:15). The author of Hos. 11:10 may try to pull the threads together (cf. esp. 5:14 and 6:1–3): the people walk after the roaring lion Yhwh. Because of the contradictions between these verses and the different understandings of misdirected loyalty, most of them probably were not written by the same person. Rather, these texts should be understood as variations on the theme of disloyalty, repentance, and punishment. The key word הלך is used again and again to add new ideas and to correct the already extant text. Yet some of these texts share a common interest. Hosea 5:12–14 seems to look back on the history of the Northern and Southern Kingdoms during which both kingdoms preferred foreign allies to Yhwh and misunderstood him.[2] According to 5:15, Yhwh will withdraw after such a history of failure, and 6:1–3 expects a fresh approach to Yhwh following this history. So in the book of Hosea, we encounter layers of text that were likely written by multiple authors with different opinions yet are still united by their general perspective and interest (Nissinen 1991: 341; Wacker 1996: 224; Rudnig-Zelt 2006: 44).

Only Hos. 1–3 contains narratives (chs. 1, 3) and a speech (2:4–25 [Eng. 2:2–23]) that have at least a discernable subject matter—the story of a marriage, its offspring (or not, cf. 3:3), and its crisis (or not, cf. ch. 1). That is why Jörg Jeremias and Wolfgang Schütte have reconstructed a different history of growth for these chapters. Jeremias finds here separate collections of Hosea's words (2:4–25*) and narratives by himself (ch. 3*) or one of his followers (ch. 1*). Yet in the opinion of most contemporary exegetes, chs. 1–3 were connected with a version of chs. 4–14 from the beginning.

If one looks at the book of Hosea without any presuppositions, one would not think that such texts were written by one author or deliver the sayings of a single prophet. One would rather guess that the book was composed as a kind of rolling corpus through a long history of adding small bits and pieces. Marie-Theres Wacker (1996: 329) describes it thus: "The development of Hosea cannot be reduced to a straight-line scheme. Rather it is an ongoing discussion" (author's translation). Nonetheless, the book has been understood as a recording of the sayings of the prophet Hosea at least until the last quarter of the twentieth century (e.g., Wolff 1990), because since antiquity prophetic books usually have been read as an echo of the lives and deeds of the prophets whose names they bear. But is this kind of reception really based on the text of the prophetic books (Schöpflin 2002: 5–10; de Bos 2013: 1–7)?[3]

Some prophetic books support this kind of biographic reading, especially Jeremiah and Ezekiel.[4] In these books, the speeches and words are often linked with the prophet's life and the history through which he lived. This can be achieved by telling stories about the prophet delivering the word of Yhwh and the reaction of his audience (e.g., Jer. 1; 13; 26; Ezek. 1–3; 4; 12), or through formulas like "The word of Yhwh came to me" (e.g., Jer. 2:1; 16:1; Ezek. 7:1; 12:1) sometimes accompanied by a date (e.g., Jer. 25:1; Ezek. 8:1; Hag. 2:20; Zech. 7:1). A description of the situation (e.g., Jer. 21:1; 24:1) may also make sure that the sayings or speeches were transmitted by Yhwh to a certain prophet at a particular moment of history. But there are also prophetic books where such a reading is not so deeply rooted. Here the prophet is absent from large parts of the book without any explanation. In the book of Isaiah, the prophet Isaiah has his last appearance in 39:8, where King Hezekiah accepts his word. It is a decision of the reader to identify the first-person singular formulation in Isa. 40:6 (especially according to the LXX) as the prophet Isaiah. In the book of Amos, there is the superscription (1:1), the report of the prophet's visions (chs. 7–9), and one story about the prophet (7:10–17). In the rest of the book, the prophet is not mentioned. Several other books in the Twelve have the prophet's name only in the superscription (Joel, Obadiah, Micah, Nahum, Habakkuk, and Zephaniah). It is not self-evident that the sayings in those books go back to a prophet who does not seem to matter in the main corpus of the book.

The book of Hosea resembles the book of Amos. The prophet Hosea appears in the superscription (1:1) and in the first sentence of the following story (1:2).[5] He is the main character of the story about his marriage to Gomer, the woman of whoredom (1:2), and their three children, whose names express Yhwh's decision to make an end of Israel and the reversal of that decision. This story as it stands now ends in 2:3 (Eng. 2:1). The remainder of the book does not mention the prophet's name. He might be the first-person narrator of 3:1–4, but that is a matter of interpretation. The woman in 2:4–25 and 3:1–4 can be identified with Gomer—or not. The first three chapters deal with wives, their husbands, and their children, but it is by no means clear that they are all identical, let alone that all three chapters describe the family life of the historical prophet (on proposals for an identification of the woman, see Wacker 1996: 120–24, 244–45). Though the prophet Hosea may still be present in ch. 3, he is not mentioned in chs. 4–14, and neither is any other family member from chs. 1–3. The characteristic formulas of prophetic books like "And the word of Yhwh came to me" are also almost completely missing (cf. only 11:11). So strictly speaking, Hos. 4–14 are hardly transmitted as prophetic words, let alone as the words of the prophet Hosea ben Beeri. Like Isaiah and Amos, the prophet Hosea disappears from his own book. To read Hos. 4–14 as a collection of Hosea's sayings means to take over a way of reading suggested in Jeremiah and Ezekiel (so also Nissinen 1991: 39–41, 347). Even if other prophetic books require different strategies of reading, one has to explain why the formulas linking the text with a prophetic persona and with history do not appear in Hosea.

7.2. The Prophet and His First Editors (Jörg Jeremias)

Jörg Jeremias (1983) has offered the most influential exegesis of Hosea in the last quarter of the twentieth century.[6] The difficulty of the words and the lack of introductory and final formulas in chs. 4–14 are Jeremias's starting points to explain how these chapters were put together.

According to Jeremias, the major part of chs. 4–14 goes back to the followers and pupils of Hosea who wrote down his words after the fall of the Northern Kingdom in 722 BCE. Most of the prophetic words Hosea's pupils as first editors collected were uttered more than ten years earlier during conflicts among Israel, Aram, Judah, and Assyria commonly called the Syro-Ephraimite war. But the pupils did not write down the words verbatim.[7] Rather, they added key texts such as 5:12–14 with their interpretation. Readers then had to read the often obscure words of Hosea in 5:8–11 and 5:15–6:6 in the light of 5:12–14. There are no formulas at the beginning or end of Hosea's words to make sure that the readers read on until this explanation. The editors integrated Hosea's words into their text, and even shortened them, because the words of Hosea function only as examples for the editors' theological message. Since a lot of Hosea's words were preserved as sketches or fragments, it is understandable that they make a somewhat difficult reading. And it is impossible to reconstruct them. So compared to the exegesis of Jeremias's predecessors, the prophet loses importance. He is no longer responsible for the book's theological profile.

Although Jeremias cannot reconstruct the prophet's words, he is convinced that this profile in the end goes back to Hosea's preaching. Jeremias (1986: 586–87) sees the prophet as a passionate critic of the Northern Kingdom, its policies, and its leading groups. Yet the question remains whether such a precise picture of the historical Hosea can be gleaned from such an obscure corpus as chs. 4–14. Does not Jeremias understand Hos. 4–14 in the light of other stories about other prophets (e.g., 1 Kgs. 18:22; 2 Kgs. 22; Jer. 26; Ezek. 8), which describe a prophet fearlessly attacking the faults of kings, other leaders of the community, or the community itself? Ancient Near Eastern parallels from the eighth century BCE show a different kind of prophetic activity, and so it will not come as a surprise that others are more reluctant to draw such a picture of a preexilic prophet (see below).

For Jeremias, Hos. 4–14 can be mainly explained through the dynamic between the prophet and his first editors (1983: 24). There are only a few later additions to the version of the book the prophet's pupils produced. Some later verses explain the book to Judean readers or add related aspects and keywords from other prophetic books (e.g., 4:10; 5:5bβ; 6:10f; 8:1b, 14; see Jeremias 1986: 592 for a complete list). But can Jeremias really explain the difficulty of the text in this way? The importance of key texts like 5:12–14 is plausible. The significance of these texts goes undisputed in recent research, yet they

7.3. THE PROPHET, HIS FIRST EDITORS, AND HIS REDACTORS (GALE A. YEE, ROMAN VIELHAUER)

Secondary additions, which were not put in place by the first collectors, were of minor importance for Jeremias. This is clearly different with Gale A. Yee, who was one of the first exegetes to attribute more text to redactors working after the prophet's pupils. According to Yee, the history of the book starts with original prophetic words (e.g., 2:4aαb, 7b, 12; [Eng. 2:2–3, 5b, 10]; 4:4*[without 5 ,[וכהן], 12bα, 18[the last two words]–19a; 7:1[without the first two words]–3, 5–9; 13:15–14:1; Yee 1987: 122–23, 262–64, 282–85) and a first collector, who mainly put the basic layer of Hos. 1 in front of the book (1987: 307–8). Then there was a first redactor (R1), who was close to the theologians writing a first version of the Deuteronomistic History. Like the deuteronomists, he was a Judean, and also like them, he was very much concerned with the purity of the cult. While the prophet had condemned alliances with foreign powers, R1 emphasized cultic abuses and called them "harlotry." From this redactor came 2:10a–11, 13–15a (Eng. 2:8a–9; 11–13a); 4:4, 6; 5:6–7; 6:6, as well as the first retrospective of Israel's history in 9:10 (pp. 308–9). Yee, who follows F. M. Cross on the growth of the Deuteronomistic History, dates R1 in the time of Josiah, and thinks Deuteronomistic influence remained strong in the book of Hosea. The last redactor (R2), who worked after 587 BCE, also had a Deuteronomistic background. He gave the book its present structure by adding the superscription (1:1) and the final verse (14:10 [Eng. 14:9]). He wrote chs. 3, 11, and the bulk of 14. There were few, if any, positive perspectives in earlier stages of Hosea, but R2 introduced into the book a journey of repentance and return to Yhwh (e.g., 2:8–9, 16–17 [Eng. 2:6–8, 14–15]; 5:15–6:3; 14:2–9 [Eng. 14:1–8]; see Yee 1987: 309–13).

Yee clearly understood that later redactors added more to Hosea than a few explanations and actualizations. R1 and R2 brought new theological concepts to the book. So it is no surprise that Yee was one of the first exegetes who turned around the relative chronology of Hosea and the deuteronomists. In her opinion, the deuteronomists were no longer influenced by the book of Hosea, but vice versa. This was a minority position before Yee (cf. Day 1909/10), but today many exegetes follow her (e.g., Nissinen 1991: 156–211; Wacker 1996: 223–24; Vielhauer 2007: 228; de Bos 2013: 130–63).

Roman Vielhauer also ascribes important theological concepts to later redactors, but he finds far more of them than Yee (for the following, see mainly Vielhauer 2007: 225–29). He basically agrees with Jeremias that the prophet's words were only transmitted in a shortened way as part of the first editor's composition (see also Kratz 1997: 19).

Yet he finds far fewer of them. According to Vielhauer, only 5:8–11*, 6:7–9, 7:5–6, and 7:8b–9 preserve prophetic words. These words do not necessarily go back to a prophet Hosea ben Beeri. They may have been uttered from the perspective of the Northern or Southern Kingdom, though Vielhauer prefers a northern perspective because of מלכנו ("our king") in 7:5–6. In Vielhauer's view, these sayings do not differ much from ancient Near Eastern prophecy. The words criticize abuses in the wake of a coming disaster in the hope that Yhwh as the god of the kingdom and its dynasty will preserve both. These abuses are not seen as a sin against Yhwh, nor is the anticipated catastrophe his punishment. So Vielhauer does not present a Jeremiah-like or Ezekiel-like figure as the historical prophet, Hosea. But is it really sure that the oldest texts in Hosea stem from a prophet at all? Here a comparison with ancient Near Eastern prophecy might help (see below).

Jeremias's key text (5:12–14) was only added in the third version of the growing book according to Vielhauer. In Vielhauer's perspective, the first written version of the book was much shorter and consisted of 5:1–2 and 6:7-7:12*. Yet the authors of this version deeply changed the meaning of the transmitted words. Now the abuses were condemned as sins against Yhwh, who punished them with the downfall of the Northern Kingdom in 722 BCE.[8] If Yhwh can annihilate a kingdom and a dynasty, which were considered his property, he becomes independent of them both. The scribes behind this first version of the book of Hosea were northerners who had to flee to Judah following the Assyrian invasion. So the book had to be adapted to its new southern context. This was done during between 720–701 BCE. Hosea 5:8–14 and 8:7–10 were added to demonstrate that the foreign policy both in Israel and in Judah was wrong. Both their guilt and the threat of Yhwh's punishment united the two (one extant, one not) kingdoms as one people of Yhwh, Israel.

The next layer of the book added a profound criticism of Israel's cult. This is the beginning of chs. 4, 8, and 9 (4:1–2, 4–10*, 11–14; 5:6–7; 5:15–6:6*; 7:13–16; 8:1–3*, 11–12; 9:3–4a, 6, 7–9). The scribes separated Yhwh from the cult practiced in Israel, since this cult could not preserve both kingdoms. The god really worshipped in the cult will later be called Baal (cf. Kratz 1997: 21–23). The growing book now consisted of Hos. 4:1–9:9*. After Yhwh was no longer considered the god worshipped in Israel's cult, the first layer of Hos. 2 could join the book (2:4a, 7b, 12 [Eng. 2:2a, 5b, 10]). This is the kernel of Hos. 1–3, and it declares the divorce of the country's soil embodied by a woman and Yhwh as its god. The motive of the ruined marriage did not enter the book as a memory from the life of the historical prophet, but as a relic of Canaanite religion (Vielhauer 2007: 152). However, the evidence for such a relic is scarce and doubtful (Kató 2019: 65–68). And if no such Canaanite background existed, Hos. 2 is better explained as a variation on texts like Hos. 1 or Ezek. 16.

Deuteronomistic Theology had a significant impact on the growing book of Hosea, beginning with the first secondary layer of Hos. 2 (2:4b–5, 10a, 11, 15 [Eng. 2:2b–5, 8a, 9, 13]), which also left traces in Hos. 4–9 (4:12b, 16–19; 5:3–4; 6:10b; 7:4; 9:1–2, 5). According to Vielhauer, only in this layer is the woman in Hos. 2* identified with Israel. Deuteronomistic influence can be found in the first version of Hos. 10 (10:1–2, 5–6a* together with 8:4b–6*), as well. Other late texts in Hosea also show Deuteronomistic influences, e.g., the retrospectives of Israel's history (9:10–17; 10:9–15). The two biographies of Hosea (chs. 1 and 3) belong to these late additions and so do not allow any conclusions on the life of the historical prophet. Hosea 3 criticizes Deuteronomistic Theology by emphasizing Yhwh's unconditional love for the people. Hosea 3 thus anticipates 2:1–3 (Eng. 1:10–2:1), which is part of a bigger layer of oracles of salvation (2:16–25* [Eng. 2:14–23]; 11:7–11*; 14:2–10* [Eng. 14:1–9]). These late oracles stem from different hands and give the book its structure (Vielhauer 2007: 225–29).

Vielhauer concedes more influence of later, especially Deuteronomistic, texts in the book of Hosea and so strengthens impulses present elsewhere in the discussion (Yee 1987; Nissinen 1991; Wacker 1996; Pfeiffer 1999). He is right to explain the obscurity of the book through a very complex history of development. Yet maybe some of his many layers belong together and are better understood as manifold additions sharing one general perspective. For example, at least some of the texts offering retrospectives of Israel's history (e.g., 9:10–17) could be seen together with texts like 5:12–14, which do just the same (cf. below). Vielhauer correctly sees that the book does not go back to a prophet like Jeremiah or Ezekiel as presented in their respective books. But the question remains whether the origins of the book really have to do with prophetic words. And would preexilic prophetic collections really turn upside down the foundations of Israel's religion? By comparison, de Jong (2007: 311–12) stresses that even critical prophets in the ancient Near East worked within the existing political and theological framework. De Bos has underscored that literacy in preexilic Israel was restricted to the royal administration, and he finds it difficult to believe that within this administration texts were produced or preserved that put their very foundation upside down. He cannot find any ancient Near Eastern analogies for a production of literature like prophetic books within the royal administration (de Bos 2013: 5–16, 35–39). So Vielhauer's reconstruction of the early stages of Hosea might prove anachronistic.

7.4. Words Transmitted and Transformed (Martti Nissinen, Marie-Theres Wacker, Susanne Rudnig-Zelt)

Vielhauer shows a tendency not to find a typical prophet at the origins of the book of Hosea. This tendency is even stronger with Nissinen and in my own work. Nissinen (1991) presented the first hypothesis about the book of Hosea that did not start with a kind of prophetic word that one would expect from texts like 1 Kgs. 18:22, Jer. 7:26, or Ezek. 8 (for the following, see Nissinen 1991: 134–37, 336–47). Rather, Nissinen considered prophetic laments about Samaria's downfall in 722 BCE as the oldest texts. These texts stand in Hos. 4 and 11 (4:1a, 2b[including כי and בארץ from v.1bβ]–3aα;

THE COMPOSITION AND REDACTION OF HOSEA   103

11:1, 3a, 4aα, 4b, 5a).[9] It is impossible to say whether these prophetic laments go back to Hosea ben Beeri. The first redaction of the book was still concerned with grief over the destructions of 722. It used the older prophetic laments for public mourning rituals and added the imperatives in 4:1a; 5:1, 8; 8:1; and 9:1, retrospectives on Israel's history like 9:10 and 10:1, and other texts like 5:15–6:3 and 7:8–9. This version of Hosea consisted of chs. 4–11*, beginning with the imperative in 4:1a and ending with יהוה נאם in 11:11.

In the next stage, Deuteronomistic Theology of the covenant influenced the growing book. Texts were added in early postexilic times that focused on a criticism of priests (e.g., 4:1b–2a, 4, 6b; 6:4–7; 8:1b, 4; 11:2, 3b; 12:1–3 [Eng. 11:12–12:2]). The typically Deuteronomistic criticism of any cult outside of Jerusalem was also important. Now probably a basic layer of Hos. 1–3 joined the book, as can be seen from the characteristic key word 2:4) ריב [Eng. 2:2]; 4:1b; 12:3 [Eng. 12:2]). So for Nissinen, as for Yee and Vielhauer, Hos. 2 is the most important text of chs. 1–3. But criticism and lawsuit (ריב) did not have the last word. In a third and final layer according to Nissinen, oracles of salvation found their place in the book (e.g., 1:7; 2:1–3, 16–25 [Eng. 1:10–2:1; 2:14–23]; 3:1–5; 14:2–9 [Eng. 14:1–8]).

Marie There-Wacker (1996) sees the succession of criticism and promise the other way around. She presents a thorough analysis of Hos. 1–3 under several perspectives (synchronic, diachronic, feminist, and the history of religion). She is an exegete who takes the book's difficulties and ambiguities seriously and so formulates her results only tentatively.

Wacker does not reconstruct the origins of the book. But through her analysis of Hos. 1–3, she suggests interesting layers of the whole book. The author of Hos. 3, who was under Deuteronomistic and later influences, also reworked an older collection that already contained a version of Hos. 1–2. He was busy in chs. 4–14 as well, adding the critique of cultic images in 13:2–3 and the basic layer of 6:7–7:2, which quotes older texts in 6:8, 9a and 7:1b. This basic layer in Hos. 6:7ff was already under the influence of the book of Jeremiah. Most important, Wacker concludes this layer of Hosea does not address the former Northern Kingdom, but postexilic Samaria. So the polemic against the north in Hosea can be explained in a very convincing way, which takes the late influences on the book into account (Wacker 1996: 228–43 and already Emmerson 1984: 159–60). The version of Hos. 1–2 that was reworked by the author of ch. 3 once belonged to a book that announced the salvation of the former Northern Kingdom and thus resembled Deutero-Isaiah. Wacker dates this earlier book in the early postexilic time. Parts of Hos. 4–14 belonged to it, and Wacker reconstructs the end of this earlier book in 11:8–9, 13:12–14, and 14:5–9* (Eng. 14:4–8): although Ephraim is unable to return to Yhwh (13:12–13), he will redeem it (pp. 243–53). So Wacker claims that a positive perspective was not a late addition to the book (contra Nissinen and Vielhauer). Yet did this perspective exist without judgment? At least some of the texts that can be read in a positive way (e.g., 6:1–3; 13:14a) now stand in a context of accusations.

In my own analysis (Rudnig-Zelt 2006), the key text of Hos. 5:12–14 belongs to even later stages of the book than Vielhauer thought. I approach the beginnings of the book of Hosea through an analysis of 6:9, 7:7–3, and 7:8–12. Only the passages which do not fit into the present context are traces of older collections—e.g., a baker (7:4) and a burned cake (7:8b), which appear in a context that suggests a happening at court (7:3, 5aα, 7; see Rudnig-Zelt 2006: 261–78 for the following). The burned cake in 7:8b is one of the oldest texts in the book. In the beginning, there was a small series of similes comparing Ephraim or its king to something worthless like a burned cake (7:8b), a palm tree with dry roots and without fruit (9:13a*,16aβ), a broken twig floating on water (10:7), a dry reed (13:15abα; Jeremias 1983: 160; contra Macintosh 1997: 550–51), or a silly dove (7:11a). These earliest words do not speak about Yhwh. Neither do they talk about sin and punishment. Rather, somebody mocks the woeful state of the Northern Kingdom from a secular perspective. A comparison with Neo-Assyrian prophecy shows that this lack of a theological perspective makes it highly unlikely that we are dealing with prophetic words here. Vielhauer followed the right path when he thought it possible that the oldest texts of Hosea could come from the Southern Kingdom. One can actually feel a distance from the Northern Kingdom in these similes. They resemble Isa. 28:1–3* in their scornful attitude toward the north and in their usage of the name "Ephraim." So the oldest texts in Hosea probably show the same Judean perspective (Becker 1997: 227–28; Rudnig-Zelt 2006: 240–43). Their authors were not prophets, but officials from the Judean court, who watched the downfall of their rival with glee—and with some discomfort. Implicitly, these similes warn Judah not to imitate the anti-Assyrian activities of the last king of Israel, Hosea ben Elah.

Until exilic times, these similes were preserved and commented upon by Judean court officials and their descendants. This group started to look for a cause for Ephraim's downfall and was not sympathetic. As they saw it, the Northern Kingdom was destroyed because of the silliness of its king and politicians. So they personified Ephraim as a stupid old man (7:4b, 5b) who allows foreigners to exploit him. Taking a clue from the burned cake in 7:8b, they introduced the silly baker (7:4*; Rudnig-Zelt 2006: 219–23) who wastes the fuel for his oven. After 587 BCE, those authors started to use "Israel" for both former kingdoms, but their mood did not soften when their own kingdom came into view. In 7:10a, they condemned the haughtiness and pride of both kingdoms.

With the introduction of Hos. 5:1* ("Harken this, priests, and listen, royal house, since the judgment concerns you, because you have been a trap for Mizpah and a net spread on Tabor!"; Rudnig-Zelt 2006: 108–11), this thoroughly profane collection was turned into the speech of a nameless prophet. Now we find the social criticism typical of prophetic books in the Hebrew Bible, but with a special focus. Not all leading groups are addressed, but mostly the priests. The prophets are not attacked, but appear as the victims of the vicious priests (9:8) (see also Schütte 2008: 182–89). So the whole layer could be called "*priesterkritische Texte.*" Hosea 5:1* does not clearly attack people from the north or from the south. Hosea 5:10a, which also belongs to this version of the book, makes sure that the south is not excluded.

This version of Hosea grew slowly. Its most important later components were the beginnings of Hos. 4 (4:4b, 7–8, 10a, 13a, 14a), turning the prophetic speech against the priests and the court into a legal dispute addressing the priests. In Hos. 5–7, originally 6:4b, 9 followed 5:1* (Rudnig-Zelt 2006: 135–46) before 5:10a was added. The verses

THE COMPOSITION AND REDACTION OF HOSEA   105

6:10a and 7:2, 3, 4aα, 5a, 7aβ, 7b also belong to this layer, and there were other additions (9:8; 10, 3b, 4a). With the addition of a basic layer of Hos. 1 (vv. 1, 2b–4, 6 together with 4:1abα, 2a), the former anonymous prophetic text was attributed to the prophet Hosea ben Beeri. The prophetic speech or lawsuit was turned into a prophetic book according to the model of Jeremiah and Ezekiel. The new superscription in 1:1 contains quotations from the superscriptions of other prophetic books, which explains why the kings mentioned here do not fit the words transmitted in the book (Isa. 1:1; Amos 1:1). Hosea 1:1 also resembles a type of superscription characteristic of the Book of the Twelve (cf. Joel 1:1; Mic. 1:1; Zeph. 1:1; Rudnig-Zelt 2006: 100, 104–8). Through the addition of Hos. 1*, this version of the book became a part of the collection of the Twelve.

Even apart from the superscription, Hos. 1* is brimming with influences from other texts, e.g., narratives about the life of a prophet illustrating his message (e.g., Isa. 8:1–4; Jer. 16; Ezek. 24). There are also Deuteronomistic influences. So it is impossible to draw any conclusions about the life of a historical Hosea ben Beeri. Like Jonah ben Amittai (2 Kgs. 14:25; Jon. 1:1), he might have been prominent as a prophet before an originally anonymous book was connected with him.[10] Hosea 1* looks back on the history of the Northern Kingdom, but addresses north and south as readers. This focus on both kingdoms becomes stronger in the next layer, along with an interest in their past history. Hosea 2:4–25 (Eng. 2:2–23) successively joins the book together with many texts in chs. 4–14, like 5:12–14. All these texts agree that at some point in history both north and south have left their god Yhwh. There are tendencies to find this point earlier and earlier in history, on the way from the desert to the land (9:10) or even with the trickster Jacob in his mother's womb (12:4 [Eng. 12:3]). About the future of the fallen Israel there is inconsistency within the layer. Some texts suggest that the relationship between Israel and Yhwh is finished (1:8–9; 2:12–15 [Eng. 2:10–14]; 9:15; cf. 5:15). Later members of this school take such texts as threats from Yhwh. In their opinion, the people will understand its faults and return to its god (2:8–9 [Eng. 2:6–7]; 6:1–3; 12:5–6 [Eng. 12:4–5]; 14:2–4 [Eng. 14:1–3]). At the end of their development, texts like 5:12–6:3 describe a full circle from neglect of Yhwh and his punishment to repentance and return. This whole group of texts can be called "*Abfall-Umkehr-Texte*" (cf. Yee's R2 for a similar position and de Bos 2013: 102–29). It is important to note that the "*Abfall-Umkehr-Texte*" do not form a homogeneous group. They were slowly added by different theologians as a kind of rolling corpus within one redactional layer. What kept all these authors together was their common worldview, maybe as members of one theological school. I would call this kind of layer, "*Konglomeratschicht*" (Rudnig-Zelt 2006: 44).

In the last period of the composition of Hosea, the controversies became even more intense. They centered around the Samaritan community that slowly developed in the former Northern Kingdom after its end in 722 BCE (cf. de Bos 2013: 74–75, 98–101). In the background of these controversies likely stood the so-called Samaritan Schism, the final separation of Jerusalem and Samaria in Hellenistic times. The "*Abfall-Umkehr-Texte*" had emphasized that north and south turned away from their god and back again together. A group of younger texts stressed that the north (i.e., the [proto-] Samaritan community) was guilty alone (the so-called *junge Samariapolemik*). That is why they placed 5:3 before 5:12–6:3 to make sure that the following texts concern only the north. Others disagreed. They expected Yhwh's judgment against north and south together (e.g., 6:11a) or even thought that Yhwh remained attached to the north (the basic layer of Hos. 11 in 11:1*, 3a, 4aα, 8a). With all the polemic already present in the book, they could only do so by relying on Yhwh's unconditional mercy and grace. This theological focus challenged some of their contemporaries, and they also added their opinion to the book. They did not deny Yhwh's mercy toward the north, but they thought that the north did not even notice Yhwh's love toward them. So they wrote 11:3b into ch. 11 and added 1:2a and 3:1–4, as well as 7:13–16. Again, they could not convince everybody. There was still hope for Samaria, and that was uttered in texts like 3:5 and 14:5 (Eng. 14:4). For their authors, an Israel without Samaria just was not complete, and there had to be a way to bring it back (so de Bos 2013: 102–29).

7.5. GENERAL TENDENCIES IN RESEARCH ON THE COMPOSITION OF HOSEA

In the last fifty years of research on Hosea, it has become clear that the question of the relationship of the book and the prophet is deeply vexed. The comparison of the oldest texts of Hosea with ancient Near Eastern parallels has been very important for this reappraisal (a development that started with Nissinen 1991). Today, most exegetes would not find a verbatim recording of the sayings of Hosea ben Beeri in the book. Rather, they would describe the beginnings of the book as an anonymous collection (e.g., Nissinen 1991: 346). For some, at least, if this collection contained prophetic sayings, they did not look like the prophetic words one would expect from other biblical books like Jeremiah or Ezekiel, but lamented the fall of Samaria in 722 BCE (Nissinen) or expected that Yhwh as the national god would save his people (Vielhauer). Some would even doubt that the beginnings of the book have to do with a prophet at all. As I have suggested, perhaps the book started with the mockery of Judean court officials about their northern rival kingdom, Israel.

The vexation in research concerning the relationship between the book and the prophet reflects a thorough shift of perspective. For Jeremias (1986: 593–94), the prophet Hosea exerted deep influences on other biblical books like Jeremiah or groups of redactors like the Deuteronomists. Now, many scholars see the relationship of Hosea, the Deuteronomists, and Jeremiah the other way around. Some see Jeremiah's influence on Hosea. At least one deuteronomistic or deuteronomistically influenced redaction is often suggested (Yee 1987; Nissinen 1991; Vielhauer 2007). Such a deuteronomistic redaction can be very important for connecting Hosea with the Book of the Twelve. My own work sees the deuteronomistically influenced basic layer of Hos. 1 joining Hosea with the growth of the Book of the Twelve. Such an approach is even more important for exegetes like Wöhrle (2006: 229–44, 461–63), for whom a deuteronomistic redaction is responsible for connecting Hosea, Amos, Micah, and Zephaniah as a nucleus of the later Twelve collection, the so-called *Vier-Prophetenbuch*.

If one concedes exilic and postexilic influences on the book of Hosea, two more shifts of perspective follow. First, these texts probably stem from Judah, and not from the Northern Kingdom as it has been assumed. So we have an outside view of the north in (at least) most texts in Hosea. Second, it is not plausible then that a text from exilic and postexilic times mainly criticizes the Northern Kingdom in its final years. So the critical, mocking, and sometimes hostile attitude toward Samaria and Ephraim has nothing to do with the kingdom that was conquered in 722 BCE, but with its successors, the Samaritans and their forbears (so Wacker 1996).

Both Yee and Nissinen reconstructed several redactional layers in Hosea. Considering the difficulty of the book, it has to be asked whether there had really been such systematic redactions. One may take as a warning that redactions have multiplied with Vielhauer, and there are still not enough to explain the complexity of the book. It might be a better approach to give more consideration to a slow growth of the book as a kind of rolling corpus. Redactional layers are not homogeneous texts, but rather express diverse and even contrary perspectives. If one allows for diversity within one redactional layer, the number of layers can be reduced without simplifying the book's complexity (so Rudnig-Zelt 2006). The scribes responsible for this kind of *Konglomeratschicht* may have accepted their opponents by not erasing their words. The resulting book certainly is not an easy reading experience, yet it has stood the test of time. And in their acceptance of difference and debate, these scribes might even set an example for the world today.

NOTES

1. The similarity with the Deuteronomistic use of הלך is obvious. For a long time, the prophet Hosea has been considered a predecessor of the Deuteronomists (e.g., Weinfeld 1972: 364; Emmerson 1984: 160–64; Jeremias 1986: 594). But this slowly changed after the middle of the twentieth century. A certain distance between the historical prophet and the Deuteronomists started to open up with Wolff. For him, not the prophet himself, but his pupils and followers were the predecessors of the Deuteronomists (Wolff 1990: xxxvi).

2. Hosea 5:12–14 emphasizes that Ephraim and Judah act just the same way, and thus mentions both. Judah does not appear in v.13aβ, but considering the line of thought in the unit it should be added (Rudnig-Zelt 2006: 158).

3. For reasons of scope, exegetes considering the book of Hosea as a work by one author, be it the historical prophet, a later scribe, or a scribal community, will not be treated in this essay, though I will occasionally refer to their results.

4. The same kind of biographic framework can be found in Haggai and Zechariah (Hag. 1:3; 2:20; Zech. 4:8; 6:9; 7:1). So it was probably typical of prophetic books whose hero was shown as a witness of the fall of Jerusalem and/or its reconstruction. Even if such a framework exists, it is not always historically accurate and might be the result of a later theological interpretation (e.g., on Jeremiah and Ezekiel, see Pohlmann 1989: 115–92; 1992: 137–204; Levin 1985: 153–56; Schmid 2008: 128–32).

5. The two superscriptions (1:1 and 1:2a) are full of problems. Only one Northern King, Jeroboam II, occurs next to three Judean ones. That does not match a prophet who is believed to be a northerner himself. Additionally, the reign of all these kings taken together might lead to the conclusion that Hosea was active for eighty or ninety years, which is hardly plausible, though Schütte (2008: 25) seems to accept this.
6. For the history of research before Jeremias, see Rudnig-Zelt 2006: 15–34.
7. Here Jeremias differs from Wolff (1990), who argues that formulas are missing from chs. 4–14 because Hosea's pupils recorded his public appearances word by word (so-called *Auftrittsskizzen*). The sudden shift of subject matter has to do with the prophet reacting to comments from his audience or turning toward other listeners. Still earlier, the difficulty of the words and the shifts of their subject matter were explained by the character of the prophet. He was seen as a passionate person who found it impossible to stick to one subject as he himself felt the woe he had to foretell (e.g., Keil 1873). The approach of Wolff has been renewed by Schütte (2008: 192–96) with an important modification. Schütte compares the first written version of Hosea in 4:4; 11:11; 12:1–14:1 to the Greek poetry of Alkaios (sixth century BCE). Both were used in a circle of insiders and thus could use unclear allusions or pronouns like "they" that were not explained. But neither with Alkaios nor with Hosea was there one quasi-canonical written version. Even after the texts had been written down, they were still performed orally and changed in these performances.
8. Zehetgruber (2020) criticizes the deeply engrained talk of judgment or punishment in the exegesis of Hosea. She emphasizes that the book must be rather read in the light of a connection between the people's deeds and their consequences coming back to them. Considering the growth of Hosea, Zehetgruber mainly agrees with Vielhauer.
9. Nissinen has sometimes emended the texts in translation (see 1991: 86–90, 233–35).
10. The figure of Balaam also shows that quite different texts like Num. 22–24 and the inscription from Tell Dēr ʿAllah could be attributed to one prophetic character.

REFERENCES

Becker, Uwe. 1997. *Jesaja: Von der Botschaft zum Buch*. FRLANT 178. Göttingen: Vandenhoeck & Ruprecht.

Bos, James M. de. 2013. *Reconsidering the Date and Provenance of the Book of Hosea: The Case for Persian-Period Yehud*. LHBOTS 580. New York: Bloomsbury.

Day, Edward. 1909/10. "Is the Book of Hosea Exilic?" *American Journal of Semitic Languages* 26: 105–32.

Emmerson, Grace I. 1984. *Hosea: An Israelite Prophet in Judean Perspective*. JSOTSup 28. Sheffield: JSOT Press.Jeremias, Jörg. 1983. *Der Prophet Hosea*. ATD 24/1. Göttingen: Vandenhoeck & Ruprecht.

Jeremias, Jörg. 1986. "Hosea/Hoseabuch." *TRE* 15: 586–98.

Jeremias, Jörg. 1996. "Hosea 4–7: Beobachtungen zur Komposition des Buches Hosea." In Jörg Jeremias, ed., *Hosea und Amos: Studien zu den Anfängen des Dodekaprophetons*. FAT 13. Tübingen: Mohr Siebeck, 55–66.

Jong, Matthijs J. de. 2007. *Isaiah among the Ancient Near Eastern Prophets: A Comparative Study of the Earliest Stages of the Isaiah Tradition and the Neo-Assyrian Prophecies*. VTSup 117. Leiden; Boston: Brill.

Kató, Szabolcs-Ferencz. 2019. *Jhwh: der Wettergott Hoseas? Der "ursprüngliche" Charakter Jhwhs ausgehend vom Hoseabuch*. WMANT 158. Göttingen: Vandenhoeck & Ruprecht.

Keil, Carl Friedrich. 1873. *Biblischer Commentar über die zwölf kleinen Propheten*. Biblischer Commentar über das Alte Testament 3/4. 2nd ed. Leipzig: Dörffling und Franke.

Kratz, Reinhard Gregor.1997. "Erkenntnis Gottes im Hoseabuch." *ZTK* 94: 1–24.

Levin, Christoph. 1985. *Die Verheißung des neuen Bundes in ihrem theologiegeschichtlichen Zusammenhang ausgelegt*. FRLANT 137. Göttingen: Vandenhoeck & Ruprecht.

Macintosh, A. A. 1997. *Hosea: A Critical and Exegetical Commentary*. ICC. Edinburgh: T&T Clark.

Nissinen, Martti. 1991. *Prophetie, Redaktion und Fortschreibung im Hoseabuch: Studien zum Werdegang eines Prophetenbuches im Lichte von Hos 4 und 11*. AOAT 231. Kevelar: Butzon and Bercker; Neukirchen-Vluyn: Neukirchener.

Pfeiffer, Henrik. 1999. *Das Heiligtum von Bethel im Spiegel des Hoseabuches*. FRLANT 183. Göttingen: Vandenhoeck & Ruprecht.

Pohlmann, Karl-Friedrich. 1989. *Die Ferne Gottes—Studien zum Jeremiabuch: Beiträge zu den "Konfessionen" im Jeremiabuch und ein Versuch zur Frage nach den Anfängen der Jeremiatradition*. BZAW 179. Berlin; New York: de Gruyter.

Pohlmann, Karl-Friedrich. 1992. *Ezechielstudien: Zur Redaktionsgeschichte des Buches und zur Frage nach den ältesten Texten*. BZAW 202. Berlin; New York: de Gruyter.

Pohlmann, Karl-Friedrich. 2008. *Ezechiel: Der Stand der theologischen Diskussion*. Darmstadt: Wissenschaftliche Buchgesellschaft.Rudnig-Zelt, Susanne. 2006. *Hoseastudien: Redaktionskritische Untersuchungen zur Genese des Hoseabuches*. FRLANT 213. Göttingen: Vandenhoeck & Ruprecht.

Schmid, Konrad. 2008. *Literaturgeschichte des Alten Testaments: Eine Einführung*. Darmstadt: Wissenschaftliche Buchgesellschaft.

Schöpflin, Karin. 2002. *Theologie als Biographie im Ezechielbuch: Ein Beitrag zur Konzeption alttestamentlicher Prophetie*. FAT 36. Tübingen: Mohr Siebeck.

Schütte, Wolfgang. 2008. *"Säet euch Gerechtigkeit!" Adressaten und Anliegen der Hoseaschrift*. BWANT 179. Stuttgart: Kohlhammer.

Schütte, Wolfgang. 2016. *Israels Exil in Juda: Untersuchungen zur Entstehung der Schriftprophetie*. OBO 279. Fribourg: Academic Press; Göttingen: Vandenhoeck & Ruprecht.Vielhauer, Roman. 2007. *Das Werden des Buches Hosea: Eine redaktionsgeschichtliche Untersuchung*. BZAW 349. Berlin/New York: de Gruyter.

Wacker, Marie-Theres. 1996. *Figurationen des Weiblichen im Hosea-Buch*. Herders Biblische Studien 8. Freiburg: Herder.

Weinfeld, Moshe. 1972. *Deuteronomy and the Deuteronomistic School*. Oxford: Clarendon.

Wöhrle, Jakob. 2006. *Die frühen Sammlungen des Zwölfprophetenbuches: Entstehung und Komposition*. BZAW 360. Berlin; New York: de Gruyter.

Wolff, Hans Walter. 1990. *Dodekapropheton 1: Hosea*. BKAT XIV/1. 4th ed. Neukirchen-Vluyn: Neukirchener.

Yee, Gale A. 1987. *Composition and Tradition in the Book of Hosea: A Redaction Critical Investigation*. SBLDS 102. Atlanta: Scholars.

Zehetgruber, Katrin. 2020. *Zuwendung und Abwendung: Studien zur Reziprozität des JHWH/Israel-Verhältnisses im Hoseabuch*. WMANT 159. Göttingen: Vandenhoeck & Ruprecht.

CHAPTER 8

THE BOOK OF HOSEA AND NORTHERN/ ISRAELIAN HEBREW

NA'AMA PAT-EL

8.1. INTRODUCTION

THE book of Hosea is the only book in the Hebrew Bible whose purported author is presented as a resident of the northern monarchy. It is also the only book to explicitly engage with internal northern politics and social problems as its primary theme. The language of Hosea is notoriously difficult and replete with *hapax legomena* and lexemes whose semantics deviates from their typical use elsewhere (Andersen and Freedman 1980: 66; Seow 1992: 292). While early scholars suggested the text might be corrupt, later scholars, starting with Nyberg (1935), attributed the linguistic peculiarities of Hosea to an unfamiliar dialect which was spoken by residents of the northern monarchy, so-called Israelian Hebrew,[1] which is different from the Judean dialect used in contemporary books of the Hebrew Bible, better known to scholars today as Classical Biblical Hebrew (CBH).

The nature of Israelian culture, its literature, and language are a matter of a heated scholarly debate. Since Hosea may have been written by an inhabitant of the Northern Kingdom, the language of the book is central to the assumption that Israelian Hebrew is attested and recoverable. Early works found support for this claim primarily in the lexicon (e.g., Harper 1905: 202–3), while later works pointed also to peculiar morphology and syntax (e.g., Rendsburg 2003). Although given its assumed provenance, Hosea should be considered the most distilled example of the northern dialect, to date there is only one book-length work dedicated to its linguistic profile (Kuhnigk 1974), and even so, that work does not offer a coherent grammatical profile of either Israelian Hebrew or Hosea. Another work (Yoo 1999) is an unpublished dissertation; however, it does not offer new information or analysis and only gathers what had been sporadically published prior to 1999. Despite the lack of robust extrabiblical evidence for a northern dialect, and the problems with identifying model northern texts in the Hebrew Bible, the assumption that northern Hebrew is an attested reality is prevalent among biblical scholars (Kelle 2010: 319).

The literature dealing with the linguistic profile of Hosea straddles two major debates in biblical philology, which are often conflated: linguistic dating and dialectology. In this essay, I will not comment on linguistic dating, but will review much of the evidence for Israelian dialectal features in Hosea and offer an analysis.

8.2. ISRAELIAN HEBREW AND ITS IDENTIFICATION

While the Bible is primarily engaged with the story of Judah's history, it has been acknowledged that at least some of the narratives represent the point of view of its northern neighbor, Israel (Rendsburg 1992; Fleming 2012). These texts include primarily Hosea, the Elisha-Elijah narratives, and the Song of Deborah (Judg. 5). A number of scholars hypothesized that the north had a distinct literary tradition, which is reflected especially in the premonarchic history of the tribes after the conquest (Rabin 1981: 120; Fleming 2012: xxx). Whether these texts represent a separate *linguistic* tradition is less obvious. In the literature dealing with these questions, "Israelian Hebrew" refers to the dialect of the northern monarchy, which is assumed to be reflected in northern compositions.

Since the northern monarchy is located in close proximity to several northern groups—namely, the Phoenicians, Arameans, and the city of Ugarit—scholars hypothesized that influence of the relevant languages is likely to be found in suspected northern texts (Kuhnigk 1974: 1; Rendsburg 1992: 68). Such influence may include literary devices, which will not be treated here. The only source of confirmed northern Hebrew compositions is epigraphic and includes primarily the Samaria Ostraca (eighth century BCE), which are roughly contemporary with Hosea, and the Kuntillet 'Ajrud inscriptions (ninth century BCE).[2] The epigraphic record from the north is meager, but these documents are the only genuine material written by inhabitants of the region at our disposal and are therefore key in the attempt to reconstruct the grammar of Israelian Hebrew.

The Samaria Ostraca contain a number of possible northern features. The primary linguistic features assumed to be indicative of the northern dialect are (1) the contraction of the diphthongs *aw and *ay (Sam 5 יֵן yên "wine" for BH יַיִן yayin); (2) a different feminine ending on the word for "year" (Sam 1 שַׁת šatt <*šan-t "year" for BH שָׁנָה <*šan-at) (Rabin 1981: 121–22; Garr 2004: 94); and (3) reduction of intervocalic /h/, which is found primarily in theophoric names (KAjr 9 עבדיו, KAjr 10 שמעיו, KAjr 19A 2 אמריו, Sam 38 ידעיו, Sam 50 אריו, etc.) (Dobbs-Allsopp et al. 2005: 283). Another possible feature is the relative marker שֶׁ rather than אֲשֶׁר (Williams 1976: §129;

Rendsburg 2003: 12). This marker is attested twice in Judg. 5; the Samaria Ostraca, however, use אֲשֶׁר consistently. The relative marker שׁ is not attested in Hosea. (See Fredericks 1996: 17–18 for arguments against its identification as a northern feature.) In other aspects, epigraphic texts from the north are not substantially different from southern epigraphic texts or from biblical monarchic texts. The Hebrew Bible, however, offers much longer texts of possible northern origin, which may potentially contain many more northern features, and so, ironically and circularly, it is the biblical text to which scholars turn in order to substantiate the existence of Israelian Hebrew in the biblical text.

Initial studies of Israelian Hebrew in the Hebrew Bible did not follow a coherent methodology and primarily provided lists of arbitrary features (Andersen 1976: 575). However, in a number of publications in the 1990s, Gary Rendsburg adapted Avi Hurvitz's method of identifying late features to isolate and identify Israelian features in Biblical Hebrew. Rendsburg's adapted method was accepted in principle by other scholars (Schniedewind and Sivan 1997). Hurvitz (1968) proposed several criteria in order to empirically substantiate a late date: (1) demonstrating a distribution of a feature solely or primarily in books assumed to be late; (2) establishing an opposition of a suspected late feature with another, early feature with the same function or semantic range; and (3) providing extrabiblical corroboration to serve as a historical peg. The final and crucial part is the requirement that (4) multiple such features accumulate in a single text in order to confidently determine that it is late. Rendsburg made a number of modifications in his attempt to adjust the methodology for the synchronic study of Hebrew dialectology: (1) demonstrating that a suspected dialectal feature is found in northern texts, primarily Hosea and the Elisha-Elijah narratives in 2 Kings; (2) establishing an opposition between features in Israelian and Judahite texts, whose distribution could be explained as dialectal; and (3) providing evidence that the feature is found in extrabiblical sources neighboring with the Northern Kingdom, primarily Phoenician, Aramaic, and Moabite. The extrabiblical sources are used not as historical pegs, but as possible sources of feature transference through contact between speaker populations.

Criterion (1) is often found to be invalidated when features appear in both Judahite and Israelite texts. In such cases, Rendsburg uses the category of style- or addressee-switching. Features treated under this category are said to add a foreign color to the narrative, whether it is northern or not. In other words, any feature that appears in a biblical narrative can be northern if it is either spoken by, or to, any foreigner, or is used in the context of a northern story (e.g., Rendsburg 2006). Examples are all the biblical stories about Aram or Arameans (e.g., involving Laban or his daughters), prophecies about any foreign entity (e.g. Isa. 21), and narratives about a foreign character (e.g., Balaam in Num. 22). When suspected northern features appear in nonnorthern texts, the assumption is that these texts are non-Judahite (Rendsburg 1992: 69). Furthermore, since even the most Israelite texts are written primarily in CBH, Rendsburg assumes the existence of a diglossic state, whereby written texts are composed in a formal dialect, while speakers use a colloquial dialect that is only apparent textually in specific episodes

(Rendsburg 1990). This methodology has yielded a long list of features in a variety of linguistic categories (Rendsburg 2003).

Criterion (3) helps identify similar features in texts of nations neighboring with Israel. Since the languages of these nations are genealogically closely related to Hebrew, similarity between their linguistic features is expected from a historical linguistics perspective. But in many cases, such similarity is taken to indicate not a genealogical relation, but rather contact and feature borrowing. This approach favors synchrony and dismisses other, often more plausible, explanations.

Hosea is an ideal ground to test this methodology and the Israelian hypothesis more generally. In what follows, I will review some of the linguistic evidence supporting an Israelite origin for the text of Hosea and evaluate its merit. I respond here to published arguments in favor of the Israelian hypothesis; my comments do not negate the possibility that there are, in fact, Israelian features in the text of Hosea that have not been identified thus far.

8.3. A Selection of Israelian Features in Hosea

Per proponents of the Israelian hypothesis, Israelian features in Hosea are phonological, morphological, semantic, and lexical. Suspected Israelian lexemes belong in two separate categories: *hapax legomena* (marked with HL in this essay) and known lexemes with a specialized meaning. There is no consensus as to which features belong here. The most expansive list of linguistic features is found in Rendsburg (2003),[3] but shorter lists were collated by others (e.g., Kuhnigk 1974; Rabin 1981; Morag 1984):

- Phonological features: sound shift $*ḏ > ʕ$, which occurs only with the root רעה; sound shift $ô > û$, which occurs only in the verb יְסוּרוּ (7:4).
- Morphological features: fs demonstrative זוֹ (7:16); nominal fs ending in -*at* (e.g., 7:5 חֲמָת); III-weak Inf construct חֲבֵי (6:9); the negative particle בַּל (7:2); and tG form תִּרְגַּלְתִּי (11:3).
- Lexical features:
  - Nouns: אָהַב (9:10), אֲהָבִים (8:9), HL אֶתְנָה (2:14 [Eng. 2:12]), אַרְמוֹן (8:14), HL הַבְהָב (8:13), הֵיכָל (8:14), חוֹחַ (9:6), HL חֶלְיָה (2:15 [Eng. 2:13]),[4] חֵלֶק (5:7), HL מָגֵן (4:18),[5] שַׁחֲטָה (13:1), רֶתֶת (6:8), קִרְיָה (8:8), HL עַלְוָה (10:9),[7] מְשׁוּבָה (11:7),[6] מַמְלָכוּת (1:4), (5:2).
  - Verbal roots:[8] בקק (10:1),[9] HL גהה (5:13), גוּר in hitpolel (7:14), לבט (4:14), נכר (10:11), שׁדד (4:14), פרד (7:1), פעל (9:4), ערב in Hiphil (2:11[Eng. 2:9]), נצל (3:2), שׁוה (10:1),[10] שׁוּר (13:7),[11] תנה (8:9, 10).[12]

The discussion below will cover grammatical features and a sample of the lexical features, and supply a very brief review of the literature.

Sound shift *ḏ > ʕ: This sound shift, known also in Official Aramaic, allegedly occurs only in one root, PS *rḏy: יִרְעֵם (9:2) and 12:2) רֹעֶה [Eng. 12:1]), if this root means "desire" (Heb. רצה; cf. Aram. רעא). This was first suggested for Hosea by Rudolph (1966: 171–72). The sound change was described as a widespread feature of Israelian Hebrew (Rendsburg 1990: 19). However, except for this root, Hosea consistently represents PS *ḏ as Hebrew ṣ (צ); e.g., אֶרֶץ (1:2; cf. Aram. ארע), עֵץ (4:12; cf. Aram. אע), צֹאן (5:6; cf. Aram. ען). Some commentators see no issue with the Hebrew root רעה "to pasture" in this context (e.g., Andersen and Freedman [1980: 603] read "shepherds [v]"). Sound changes are regular and should affect any phoneme in their domain, which is not the case with this assumed sound change.

Sound shift ô > û: this sound change, attested in Phoenician (Fox 1996: 40–41), is found in only one form in Hosea: יְסוּרוּ (7:14). The reality of this feature depends on the identification of the root. Rendsburg (2003) suggests that it is derived from the root סרר, not סור, and should therefore be vocalized as יָסֹרוּ (<*yasurru) in CBH. Even if we accept that the root is geminate, not hollow, the Phoenician sound change is not relevant for this form. In Phoenician *u > ü, while *aw > o > u, but the sound change ô > û assumes the process in Israelian Hebrew to be *u > o > u. The Phoenician sound change should have also affected forms such as הוֹשַׁעְתִּים (1:7), יוֹם (2:23 [Eng. 2:21]), or הוֹרַתָם (2:7 [Eng. 2:5]), but it has not. Some scholars suggest that the meaning of סור is appropriate in Hos. 7:14 (e.g., Andersen and Freedman 1980: 475–76). Tully (2018: 176) suggests emending the vocalization to יָסוֹרוּ.

The fs demonstrative זוֹ (7:16) is a demonstrative pronoun, which is also spelled with a final he (זֹה; 2 Kgs. 6:19). Nyberg (1935; see also Rabin 1981: 124) assumed that it functions in Hosea as a relative marker, a function that is known elsewhere in Biblical Hebrew (e.g., Allegro 1955). Others consider it a demonstrative pronoun, an Israelian equivalent of the Judahite זֹאת (Yoo 1999: 96; Rendsburg 2003: 13).[13] This demonstrative, however, also occurs in nonnorthern texts (Judg. 18:4; 2 Sam. 11:25; 1 Kgs. 14:5) and in post-Biblical Hebrew (Eccl. 2:2, 24; 5:15; MishH Nid. 4:7). Based on its wide distribution, Fredericks (1996: 16–17) concludes that this demonstrative is more likely to be a vernacular feature with no specific dialectal association.

Nominal fs ending in -at (7:5 חֲמַת): while fs Hebrew nouns show a consistent *-at > ā change, some related regional languages, like Moabite and Phoenician, retain the original *-at ending, e.g., mʔt "hundred" (cf. Hebrew מֵאָה). Dahood (1952: 46–47) and Rendsburg (1991: 89–90) suggest that the fs absolute -at (or -ot) ending on Hebrew nouns is, therefore, a northern feature. However, I have argued that most of these nouns are in construct, not absolute, and therefore the termination -at is expected (Pat-El 2017: 20–21). This is certainly the case for Hos. 7:5 חֲמַת מִיָּיִן "anger on account of wine," referring to alcohol-infused unruly behavior. Such a construction, not just with feminine singular nouns, is attested throughout the Hebrew Bible (e.g., Ps. 53:1) and is not restricted to northern texts. (See discussion and examples in Pat-El and Treiger 2008.)\

III-weak Inf construct (חֲכֵּי 6:9): Typically, III-weak infinitives construct terminate in -t (cf. נְסֹת Exod. 20:20; גְלוֹת Lev. 6:18). In Hosea, there are two infinitives without the expected -*t*: אֵלֹה and חֲכֵי (perhaps also שְׁתִי in 10:10, although this is less likely). Such forms are superficially more similar to Aramaic infinitives (e.g., Old Aramaic לחזיה Sf I A: 13) than to the Canaanite type (cf. Phoen. לבנת Kartepe A II 11).[14] However, similar forms are found in nonnorthern contexts as well (e.g., שְׁתוֹ Isa. 22:13, רְאֹה Gen. 48:11). There is a simple explanation for this: functional overlap between the infinitive absolute and construct is attested already in CBH, which leads to some morphological confusion (Fassberg 2007). Even in Hosea, an unexpected infinitive absolute אָלוֹת (10:4) occurs instead of אֵלֹה.

Negative particle בַּל (7:2; 9:16Q): This negation is attested also in Ugaritic (*bl nmlk* KTU 1.6.i.48) and Phoenician (בל פעל KAI 24.2:3). Of the sixty-nine occurrences of this negation in the Hebrew Bible, only thirty are in what Rendsburg (2003) considers northern texts; in other words, most of the attestations of this feature are not in northern texts. Given the distribution of this negative particle in Hebrew and in Semitic more broadly, there is no reason to assume it is limited to just one dialect of Hebrew.

tG instead of the typical Gt form: The peculiar form תִּרְגַּלְתִּי (11:3) was analyzed by Hutton and Marzouk (2012) as a tG, namely the corresponding T stem of G, with an unusual prefix -*t*. Most tG forms have been reanalyzed as tD in Hebrew after the loss of the productive tG and its replacement by the N stem. Hutton and Marzouk (2012: 36) suggest that a tG lacking an epenthetic syllable (*hit-*) is an isogloss between Israelian and Judahite Hebrew dialects. They argue that the lack of epenthesis is due to the environment of the form—namely, after a pronoun ending with a vowel—which allows a consonant cluster in the following word. Hutton (2012) identified an additional tG form without an epenthetic syllable in Jeremiah (וּתְפוֹצוֹתִיכֶם Jer. 25:34). Both forms, however, represent the type of sandhi one expects to find in speaking, not in a standard prophetic text. Jeremiah is identified as a Benjaminite prophet (Jer. 1:1), which leads Hutton (2012) and Rendsburg (2003: 7) to assume that the Benjaminite dialect is a border dialect between Israelian and Judahite, although there has been no study to substantiate this claim. Furthermore, Jeremiah lived a century and a half after the fall of Samaria.[15]

מַמְלְכוּת (1:4) "kingdom": Yoo (1999: 38–40) concludes that both the noun and the derivational suffix -*ût* are northern. This particular noun, however, is attested in Josh. 13:12, 2 Sam. 16:3, and Jer. 26:1, texts which are not claimed to be Israelian. Furthermore, the suffix -*ût* is attested in all periods of Hebrew, although it becomes more frequent in Late Biblical Hebrew.[16]

אֶתְנָה (2:14 [Eng. 2:12]) / אֶתְנַן (9:1) "wages, payment": Both lexemes occur in the context of payment or gift. The first, a *hapax legomenon*, is a gift to a prostitute by her lovers, and the second, which is not unique to Hosea, also likely indicates a fee for sexual favors (Andersen and Freedman 1980: 523). The etymology of these words is unclear. Proposals range from *ntn* "give" (*HALOT*) to *tny* "repeat" (~Aram *tny*) to "hire" (*BDB*). The root *ntn* is semantically more likely (cf. *mattān* "gift"), but the nouns do not show the expected gemination of *taw*. Morag (1984: 503) harmonizes by arguing that these nouns originally referred to a repeated action (e.g., repeatedly complementing a lover), which developed to mean "a gift to a loved one" and finally "a gift to a prostitute." In any case, אֶתְנַן is a pan-Hebrew word and אֶתְנָה is a *hapax* and so impossible to place specifically.

הֵיכָל (8:14) "palace": Rendsburg (1990: 48) and Yoo (1999: 106) argue that the meaning "palace" (rather than "temple") appears only in northern contexts and is likely the Israelian equivalent of the Judean בֵּית הַמֶּלֶךְ. Ugaritic and Aramaic alleged equivalents provide support for the northern identification. Schniedewind and Sivan (1997: 314–15), however, have noted that term בֵּית הַמֶּלֶךְ also occurs in Hos. 5:1. The meaning "palace," on the other hand, is also attested in nonnorthern contexts (e.g., 2 Kgs. 20:18 in a story about Hezekiah). The noun is known to be a *wanderwort*, which spread from Sumerian to the rest of the Near East and is not confined to a particular area; it is also attested in Ethiopic and Arabic.

אַרְמוֹן (8:14) "palace": This word occurs multiple times in Isaiah[17] and Jeremiah. This lexeme is equivalent to הֵיכָל, which is also claimed to belong to the Israelian dialect (see above). It does not appear in any of the Semitic languages typically used to substantiate a northern origin, like Aramaic and Phoenician. Speiser (1924) notes the Akkadian *rimītu* "dwelling" (< *rmy*) as a possible cognate. As the forms in Hebrew and Akkadian are not identical morphologically, but rely on the same cognate root, it is likely the lexeme is original in both languages. The distribution does not support a dialectal feature, as it is attested in Isa. 23:13; Jer. 6:15; Amos 2:15 (about Jerusalem).

Verbal root תנה (8:9, 10) "repeat, tell": The root *tny* allegedly reflects a *θ > t* sound change, while typically in Hebrew the reflex of this proto- Semitic consonant is *š* (שׁנה). The same sound change is attested in Official Aramaic, much later than the suspected date of Hosea's composition (Rabin 1981: 120; Pat-El 2017: 19). The hypothesis that Israelian Hebrew reflects *θ > t* is quite common in the literature about Israelian Hebrew; however, as Bloch (2008) conclusively shows, there is no evidence to support either a retention of *θ* in the northern Cisjordan or a merger of *θ* and *t*. Andersen and Freedman (1980: 505) assume a different root, a secondary form from *ntn*, meaning "hire." A similar root can perhaps account for the forms אֶתְנָה and אֶתְנַן above.

Verbal root לבט (4:14) "throw down": the root occurs only three times in the MT, always in N, once in Hosea and twice in Proverbs,[18] as well as in QH (1QHa 10:21, 12:8). The root has a cognate in Arabic and Akkadian. Morag (1984: 504–5) suggests that a Syriac cognate meaning "to incite" may explain the semantics of the verb in Hosea. Yoo (1999: 61) relies on the biblical distribution, as well as on the Syriac cognate, to argue that the root is Israelian. But this conclusion ignores the occurrence in the Qumran Hodayot scroll (10:21; 12:8), which is indicative that the root is native to Judean Hebrew. Given the distribution of the root, there is no objective reason to assume that it is a dialectal isogloss.

Verbal root פרד (4:14) "separate": this is the only occurrence of the root in D, although it occurs in Dt four times (Pss. 22:15; 92:10; Job 4:11; 41:9). Yoo (1999: 60–61), based on Wieder (1965: 163–64), connects this verb to Ugaritic *brd*, which Wieder renders "to offer." The connection to Ugaritic, Yoo argues, marks it as Israelian. In fact, the verb means "to separate" in Ugaritic (*DUL* 233), and is attested also in Akkadian, Aramaic, Arabic, and Ethiopic. In other words, it has a common Semitic provenance. The fact that it is attested in Dt in Job and in Judean Psalms is indicative that it was common in Judean Hebrew and not a specific Israelian isogloss.

THE BOOK OF HOSEA AND NORTHERN/ISRAELIAN HEBREW   117

Verbal root פעל (7:1) "to do": Yoo (1999: 87) suggests that the use of the root instead of the more common עשׂה is a northern feature; however, the root is also used in early poetry (Exod. 15:17; Deut. 32:27) and Psalms (Ps. 7:14), a distribution that does not support a dialectal identification. The existence of two roots with the same meaning in a single dialect/language is not atypical. The root פעל is found in Phoenician, Ugaritic, and Deir 'Allā, but also in Aramaic (alongside עבד) and Arabic, and is therefore common West Semitic.[19]

8.4. ANALYSIS

Most scholars accept the possibility that there were a number of Hebrew dialects in premonarchic and monarchic Israel. Given the linguistic diversity in the ancient Levant, a reality of several Hebrew dialects is plausible. But the hypothesis that the Hebrew Bible in general, and Hosea in particular, reflect this linguistic reality has little evidence to support it. The epigraphic record from the north contains a number of possible northern features. However, none of the features identified as Israelian in this corpus is attested in Hosea: there is not a single case of diphthong collapse;[20] the word for "year" does not occur in the book;[21] and there are no theophoric names with a final יו (< יהו) component. It has been suggested that the relative marker in the north was שׁ (Garr 2004: 233; Rendsburg 1990: 115); however, the only relative marker used in Hosea is אֲשֶׁר (e.g., 2:2, 14, 15 [Eng. 1:11; 2:12, 13]). The lack of clear Israelian features in Hosea, the only self-proclaimed northern book in the Hebrew Bible, is a critical problem, which may explain the dearth of linguistic work on the language of the book from proponents of the Israelian hypothesis. Indeed, there are more studies of the northern features in Ecclesiastes than in Hosea. Even Kuhnigk (1974) was not able to establish that Hosea contains more northern features than any other biblical composition (Andersen 1976). Levin (2009), whose dissertation treated the language of the book, lists a number of unique features in Hosea,[22] but concludes that they cannot be tied specifically to a northern, or other, dialect.

Scholars who reject the assumption that Hosea was written in an Israelian dialect do so for two reasons: either they date the text to the Persian period (e.g., Ben Zvi 2005; Bos 2013)[23] or argue that while the text is early, it shows no concrete, unambiguous dialectal features (e.g., Andersen 1976). Bos's case for an early Persian period date relies primarily on literary and historical considerations, not on the book's language; in fact, the linguistic case against a monarchic date is completely reliant on the denial of linguistic dating as a viable methodology (Bos 2013: 16–17). Bos's dismissal of the possibility of an Israelite dialect is more substantial. He argues that Rendsburg's methodology fails because there is not enough data to establish which features are Israelian and which Judahite. He notes that most of the alleged northern features which Rendsburg and others have used are either absent or rare in Biblical Hebrew, which include, for example, diphthong collapse and the feminine morpheme *-t (שׁת) for "year." In other words, the basis to make an informed evaluation of the dialect is lacking.

Other scholars deny Rendsburg's assertion that the number of Israelian features in the Hebrew Bible generally and in Hosea specifically is decisive. Andersen and Freedman note that "[t]he supposition that Hosea is written in a distinctive dialect of Hebrew has not been confirmed" (1980: 67). Rabin, who is fairly sympathetic to the possibility of a northern stratum in Hosea, comments "I was not able to prove that even one of Hosea's unique words is northern" (1981: 126). Morag (1984: 509–10), in a thorough study of multiple difficult features in Hosea, concludes that there is no grammatical difference between the language of Hosea and Judahite Hebrew; the lexicon shows some peculiar features, but none of them are related to Aramaic. The only lexical item that can be associated with northern texts is the verb 10 ,8:9) תנה), which occurs twice in Hosea and twice in Judges in stories about the north (Judg. 5:11; 11:40). Similarly, Macintosh (1997: liv–lvi) notes that there are no obvious indications of a northern dialect in Hosea (compared, for example, to the Samaria Ostraca) and points to the vocabulary as the only place where dialectal features are located. Schniedewind and Sivan (1997: 337), who studied the alleged northern Elijah-Elisha cycle, argue that "[g]iven the similarity of the northern prophetic books such as Hosea and Amos to SBH . . . and the limited evidence for Northern Hebrew in the Elijah-Elisha narratives studied here, there is still little evidence for significant differences in the *literary dialects* of Samaria and Jerusalem" (my emphasis). Tully (2018: 15) notes that the Israelian hypothesis "is ultimately speculation without substantive support." Other scholars do not reject the possibility of an Israelite dialect, but rather the possibility that such a dialect is attested in the Hebrew Bible (e.g., Fredericks 1996; Fleming 2012; Pat-El 2017).[24]

With the absence of physical and political borders, dialects and cultural expression were not confined to a political entity. The material culture of both monarchies (e.g., architecture and pottery patterns) is very similar, but is distinct from neighboring people (Faust 2017). Furthermore, the orthography of Hebrew inscriptions across the Hebrew-speaking areas shows synchronic consistency, while it varies in some details from other national and regional scripts, such as Aramaic and Phoenician (Rollston 2006). Rollston (p. 67) has argued that this likely reflects a standardized scribal education. If the region is homogeneous in terms of the material culture and epigraphy, does that mean that it was also homogeneous linguistically? Of course not. But it is unlikely that two traditions with starkly different linguistic profiles would be found in our extant texts. Given the evidence, it is more likely that there was one standard, overshadowing any linguistic differences, at least in the formal written texts.

8.5. A Note on Methodology

Many scholars do not question the validity of the methodology used to identify Israelian features, but rather the specifics of its application (e.g., Schniedewind and Sivan 1999: 306). It is, therefore, crucial to note the flaws of this methodology.

THE BOOK OF HOSEA AND NORTHERN/ISRAELIAN HEBREW   119

Dialects are linguistically defined by isoglosses, i.e., meaningful and systematic differences between dialects (e.g., 3fs perfect in Hebrew *hāləkā* versus Phoenician *hlkt*). For the most part, scholars have not systematically identified isoglosses, but rather hypothesized that some words are Israelian without making a claim about what is the Judahite isogloss. Several of these words and verbal roots are *hapax legomena* (e.g., אֶתְנָה and חֶלְיָה), whose meaning and origin are unclear.

Since many occurrences of alleged Israelian features also appear in non-Israelian contexts, supporters of the Israelian hypothesis invoke the poorly defined concept of switching—namely, a literary device to mark the speech of an individual as foreign (Kaufman 1988).[25] Signs of this device are the use of rare words and synonyms, and it is used at key junctures in the narrative, but also may appear in isolation (Bompiani 2016: 52). Although the term was initially used for foreign speech, Rendsburg (1996) expanded it to refer to stories in foreign lands, stories in Canaan with a foreign character, or when a speaker of Hebrew addresses foreigners. The key problem with this term is that it does not help to identify dialectal features. Even if we could identify non-Judahite features using it, these may be Moabite or Phoenician or some other regional language, not necessarily Israelian. In order to identify specifically Israelian features in a text, we would need a textual record of Israelian Hebrew to compare it to, a record we do not have.[26] Thus, even the most careful and judicious use of switching cannot produce a sample of Israelian Hebrew features, if we do not know the grammar and lexicon of this dialect.

A later Judean editing is another explanation to the lack of significant linguistic difference between Hosea and other prophetic books of his time. Acknowledging that Hosea shows none of the typical features one expects from a northern composition, Yoo (1999: 178–79) suggests that the Northern Kingdom used the same literary standard as the south. But this, of course, means that northern texts will be indistinguishable from southern texts.

The reason many scholars accept that Hosea is written in a northern dialect is a result of a wide consensus that the book was composed by a northerner before the fall of Samaria in 722 BCE. That date was, however, recently questioned. Dewrell (2016) notes that beyond Hos. 1:1, which dates the beginning of Hosea's career to around 750 BCE, Hosea's author does not name any individual and provides few details to place the book in a defined northern geography and pre-Samaritan exile timeframe. He identifies one of the obscure names in the book, מֶלֶךְ יָרֵב, with the Assyrian king Sennacherib, who ruled from 705– 681 BCE, contra Mcintosh (1997: 209) and others, who connected the title to the Assyrian *šarru rabû*, "the mighty king." This identification, if correct, places the book two decades after the exile of Israel. Dewrell (2021) provides additional evidence for the later date from the description of Egypt in the book. He identifies the reference to Egypt's involvement in the region, and dates it not to King Hoshea's reign as it is usually understood, but rather to Sennacherib's siege of Jerusalem in 701 (2 Kgs. 19:9). Dewrell's analysis that the book was written decades after the fall of Samaria, if correct, may explain why the book is written in the standard language of the Southern Kingdom.

8.6. Conclusion

Despite the fact that the author of Hosea presents himself as a northern prophet and despite the relatively high number of *hapax legomena* in the book, there is very little evidence, if any, that the language of the book is significantly different than the standard CBH associated with the southern monarchy. While many scholars still assume that the book reflects an Israelian dialect, those who carefully studied its language (e.g. Morag, Rabin, Andersen and Freedman, and others) all concluded that there is no reason to assume it was written in a dialect different than that of other contemporary compositions. My analysis confirms this conclusion.

At this point, and until further evidence comes to light, we should assume that the existence of a separate dialect, or dialects, in the north, is historically likely, but the linguistic evidence for it in our attested records is lacking.

Notes

1. The name "Israelian Hebrew" was coined by Ginsburg (1982) and picked up by Rendsburg (1991: 88).
2. Another possible text is the Gezer calendar. There is no doubt that the text was found in the south, but since its orthography represents contracted diphthongs, some scholars suggest that it is northern (Ahituv 2008: 252), or even possibly Phoenician (Pardee 2013).
3. The features from Hosea in Rendsburg (2003) are taken from Yoo (1999), though not all the features treated in the latter were included in the former.
4. A related חֲלִי is attested in Prov. 25:12 and Song. 7:2.
5. Rendsburg (2003) connects this noun to the root מגן but given the dagesh in the *nun* (מָגִנֶּיהָ) it is likely derived from the root גנן.
6. The root occurs multiple times in the Hebrew Bible, but Morag (1984: 507) suggests that its meaning here is unique and equivalent to the later religious term תְּשׁוּבָה.
7. This form is likely a misspelling of עֻלָה, which occurs in the Hebrew Bible dozens of times.
8. The following roots will not be discussed because they are not unique to Hosea and occur in nonnorthern compositions:11:8) מגן) also occurs in Gen. 14:20, which takes place in the south (per the story, the future site of Jerusalem), נכר (Deut. 2:6; Job 6:27; 40:30), 2:11) נצל [Eng. 2:9]) also occurs in Gen. 31:9 in the speech of Jacob, not an Aramaic protagonist, פעל 7:1)) appears dozens of times in texts that are not northern or foreign.
9. This root typically means "to empty" (Isa. 24:1; Jer. 51:2), but in Hosea it seems to mean the opposite, "to be abundant" (Morag 1984).
10. This root occurs multiple times in the Hebrew Bible, but Rendsburg (2003) suggests only here does it occur with a specialized meaning "to produce."
11. The root occurs multiple times in the Hebrew Bible, but Rendsburg (2003) suggests that in Hosea it has a specialized meaning "to jump."
12. Rendsburg (2003) distinguishes between the verb in Hosea and תנה in Judg. 5:11. Other scholars (e.g., Morag 1984: 503) treat both together.

THE BOOK OF HOSEA AND NORTHERN/ISRAELIAN HEBREW   121

13. Dahood (1952: 44) suggested that it is a result of Phoenician influence. Since the standard Hebrew demonstrative זֹאת is also attested in Moabite and Early Aramaic (Tel Fekheriye), it is more likely to be a shared feature of Aramaeo-Canaanite (Pat-El and Wilson-Wright 2018: 790–91).

14. Garr (2004: 141) suggests that the difference between III-weak G infinitives in Canaanite and Aramaic is a diagnostic feature between the two.

15. If the identification of the village Anata (عناتا) with biblical Anatot (ענתות) is accurate, then Jeremiah lived about four kilometers northeast of the Old City of Jerusalem, itself a Benjaminite city (Josh. 18:28), and the political and cultural center of the southern kingdom.

16. For example, אַלְמָנוּת (CBH Gen. 38:13; LBH Isa. 54:4), מַלְכוּת (CBH Num. 24:7; LBH Esth. 1:2), קוֹמְמִיּוּת (CBH Lev. 26:13).

17. Yoo (1999: 107) claims that most of the occurrences in Isaiah are addressed to foreign nations and are therefore cases of style-switching.

18. Yoo and other proponents of Israelian Hebrew assume that Proverbs is an Israelian composition, a position that is ahistorical (Pat-El 2017: 13–15).

19. Rainey (2007: 71–73) claims that the root פעל is not native to Hebrew, despite being attested in the earliest strata of the language, and was borrowed from Phoenician. See Hackett and Pat-El (2010: 182–83) for a detailed refutation of this claim.

20. The lexeme יַיִן "wine," which is spelled with only one *yod* in the Samaria Ostraca, is attested three times in Hosea in the absolute with two *yods* (4:11; 7:5; 9:4). Even in the single attestation of the construct, יֵין (14:8 [Eng. 14:7]), it is spelled with two *yods*, as we find elsewhere in the Hebrew Bible, including in Amos 2:8.

21. None of the suspected Israelian texts in the Hebrew Bible uses a form different than Judean שָׁנָה.

22. Use of reduplication (נַאֲפוּפֶיהָ 1:2, זְנוּנִים 2:4 [Eng. 2:2], הַבְהֲבַי 8:13 etc.), preference for the C stem (הִזְנוּ 4:10, הִתְנוּ 8:9 etc.), feminine nouns where masculine are expected (זִבְחוֹתָם 4:19 vs. זֶבַח), the use of בַּל (7:2) etc.

23. In scholarship predating Hurvitz's work, the suggestion that the book is postexilic did not also mean that it is non-Israelian (e.g., Harper 1905: 204).

24. Young (1997) correctly notes that variation is not necessarily a sign of dialects, since Judahite Hebrew may show variation, too.

25. Kaufman's (1988) discussion specifically refers to switching as a signal of Trans-Jordanian speakers, not northern Hebrew.

26. Hays (2019: 170–71), who, while recognizing the problems with switching, is sympathetic to it and finds it valuable, notes that "we would not want to try to extract a grammar of Israelian Hebrew from these scattered examples."

REFERENCES

Aḥituv, S. 2008. *Echoes from the Past: Hebrew and Cognate Inscriptions from the Biblical Period.* Jerusalem: Carta.

Allegro, J. M. 1955. "Uses of the Semitic Demonstrative Element *z* in Hebrew." *VT* 5: 309–12.

Andersen, F. I. 1976. "Review of *Nordwestsemitische Studien zum Hoseabuch.*" *Bib* 57: 573–75.

Andersen, F. I., and D. N. Freedman. 1980. *Hosea.* New York: AB. Doubleday.

Ben Zvi, E. 2005. *Hosea.* FOTL. Grand Rapids: Eerdmans.

Bloch, Y. 2008. "On Some Alleged Developments of the Proto-Semitic Phoneme /ṭ/ in Iron Age Canaanite Dialects." *Journal of Semitic Studies* 53.1: 1–28.

Bompiani, B. 2016. "Style Switching in the Speech of Transjordanians." *Hebrew Studies* 57: 51–71.

Bos, J. M. 2013. *Reconsidering the Date and Provenance of the Book of Hosea: The Case for Persian-Period Yehud*. LHBOTS 580. New York: T&T Clark Bloomsbury.

Dahood, M. J. 1952. "Canaanite-Phoenician Influence in Qoheleth." *Bib* 33: 30–52.

Dewrell, H. D. 2016. "Yareb, Shalman, and the Date of the Book of Hosea." *CBQ* 78/3: 413–29.

Dewrell, H. D. 2021. "Depictions of Egypt in the Book of Hosea and Their Implications for Dating the Book." *VT* 71: 503–30.

Dobbs-Allsopp, F. W., J. J. M. Roberts, C. L. Seow, and R. E. Whitaker., eds. 2005. *Hebrew Inscriptions: Texts from the Biblical Period of the Monarchy with Concordance*. New Haven: Yale University Press.

Fassberg, S. E. 2007. "The Overlap in Use between the Infinitive Construct and the Infinitive Absolute in Biblical Hebrew [Hebrew]." In Moshe Bar Asher, Dalit Rom-Shiloni, Emmanuel Tov, and Nili Wazana, eds., *Shai le-Sara Japhet: Studies in the Bible, Its Exegesis and Its Language*. Jerusalem: Bialik Institute, 427–32.

Faust, A. 2017. "An All-Israelite Identity: Historical Reality or Biblical Myth." In Justin Lev-Tov, Paula Hesse, and Allan Gilbert, eds., *The Wide Lens in Archaeology: Honoring Brian Hesse's Contributions to Anthropological Archaeology*. Columbus, GA: Lockwood, 169–90.

Fleming, D. E. 2012. *The Legacy of Israel in Judah's Bible: History, Politics, and the Reinscribing of Tradition*. Cambridge: Cambridge University Press.

Fox, J. 1996. "A Sequence of Vowel Shifts in Phoenician and Other Languages." *JNES* 55: 37–48.

Fredericks, D. C. 1996. "A North Israelite Dialect in the Hebrew Bible? Questions of Methodology." *Hebrew Studies* 37.1: 7–20.

Garr, W. R. 2004. *Dialect Geography of Syria-Palestine 1000–586 B.C.E.* Winona Lake, IN: Eisenbrauns.

Ginsberg, H. L. 1982. *The Israelian Heritage of Judaism*. New York: Jewish Theological Seminary.

Gordon, C. H. 1955. "North Israelite Influence on Postexilic Hebrew." *IEJ* 5.2: 85–88.

Hackett, J. A., and N. Pat-El. 2010. "On Canaanite and Historical Linguistics: A Rejoinder to Anson Rainey." *Maarav* 17.2: 173–88.

Harper, W. R. 1905. *A Critical and Exegetical Commentary on Amos and Hosea*. ICC 21. Edinburg: T&T Clark.

Hays, C. B. 2019. *The Origins of Isaiah 24–27: Josiah's Festival Scroll for the Fall of Assyria*. Cambridge: Cambridge University Press.

Hurvitz, A. 1968. "The Chronological Significance of 'Aramaisms' in Biblical Hebrew." *IEJ* 18: 234–40.

Hutton, J. M. 2012. "A Morphosyntactic Explanation of *təpôṣôtîkem* (Jer. 25:34)." In R. Hasselbach and N. Pat-El, eds. *Language and Nature: Papers Presented to John Huehnergard on the Occasion of His 60th Birthday*. Chicago: The Oriental Institute, 151–69.

Hutton, J. M., and S. Marzouk. 2012. "The Morphology of the tG-Stem in Hebrew and *Tirgaltî* in Hos 11: 3." *Journal of Hebrew Scriptures* 12: 1–42.

Kaufman, S. A. 1988. "The Classification of the Northwest Semitic Dialects of the Biblical Period and Some Implications Thereof." In M. Bar-Asher, ed., *Proceedings of the Ninth World Congress of Jewish Studies, Jerusalem, August 4–12, 1985*. Jerusalem: World Union of Jewish Studies, 41–57.

Kelle, B. E. 2010. "Hosea 4—14 in Twentieth-Century Scholarship." *CBR* 8.3: 314–75.

Kuhnigk, W. 1974. *Nordwestsemitische Studien zum Hoseabuch*. Rome: Biblical Institute Press.

Levin, A. 2009. *Hosea and the North Israelite Traditions: The Distinctive Use of Myth and Language in the Book of Hosea*. PhD diss., University of Toronto.

Macintosh, A. A. 1997. *Hosea*. ICC. Edinburgh: T&T Clark.

Morag, S. 1984. "On Semantic and Lexical Features in the Language of Hosea." [Hebrew] *Tarbitz* 53.4: 489–511.

Nyberg, H. S. 1935. *Studien zum Hoseabuche: Zugleich ein Beitrag zur Klärung des Problems der alttestamentlichen Textkritik*. Uppsala: Uppsala Universitets Arsskrift.

Pardee, D. 2013. "A Brief Case for Phoenician as the Language of the 'Gezer Calendar.'" In R. Holmstedt and A. Schade, eds., *The Phoenician Language: Studies in Writing and Linguistics*. Winona Lake, IN: Eisenbrauns, 226–46.

Pat-El, N. 2017. "Israelian Hebrew: A Re-Evaluation." *VT* 67: 1–37.

Pat-El, N., and A. Treiger. 2008. "On Adnominalization of Prepositional Phrases and Adverbs in Semitic." *Zeitschrift der deutschen morgenländischen Gesellschaft* 158.2: 265–83.

Pat-El, N., and A. Wilson-Wright. 2018. "Features of Aramaeo-Canaanite." *JAOS* 138: 781–806.

Rabin, H. 1981. "The Language of Amos and Hosea [Hebrew]." In B"Z Lurya, ed., *Studies in the Minor Prophets*. Jerusalem: Kiryat Sefer, 117–36.

Rainey, A. F. 2007. "Redefining Hebrew: A Transjordanian Language." *Maarav* 14.2: 1–15.

Rendsburg, G. A. 1990. *Linguistic Evidence for the Northern Origin of Selected Psalms*. SBLMS 43. Atlanta: Scholars.

Rendsburg, G. A. 1991. "The Strata of Biblical Hebrew." *Journal of Northwest Semitic Languages* 17: 81–99.

Rendsburg, G. A. 1992. "Morphological Evidence for Regional Dialects in Ancient Hebrew." In Walter R. Bodine, ed., *Linguistics and Biblical Hebrew*. Winona Lake, IN: Eisenbrauns, 65–88.

Rendsburg, G. A. 1996. "Linguistic Variation and the 'Foreign' Factor in the Hebrew Bible." *IOS* 25: 177–90.

Rendsburg, G. A. 2003. "A Comprehensive Guide to Israelian Hebrew: Grammar and Lexicon." *Orient* 38: 5–35.

Rendsburg, G. A. 2006. "Israelian Hebrew in the Song of Songs." In S. E. Fassberg and A. Hurvitz, eds., *Biblical Hebrew in Its Northwest Semitic Setting*. Winona Lake, IN: Eisenbrauns, 315–23.

Rollston, C. A. 2006. "Scribal Education in Ancient Israel: The Old Hebrew Epigraphic Evidence." *BASOR* 344.1: 47–74.

Rudolph, W. 1966. *Hosea*. Gütersloh: G. Mohn.

Schniedewind, W. M., and D. Sivan. 1997. "The Elijah-Elisha Narratives: A Test Case for the Northern Dialect of Hebrew." *Jewish Quarterly Review* 87: 303–37.

Seow, C. L. 1992. "Book of Hosea." *ABD* 3: 291–97.

Speiser, E. 1924. "The Etymology of ארמון." *Jewish Quarterly Review* 14: 329.

Tully, E. J. 2018. *Hosea: A Handbook on the Hebrew Text*. Waco: Baylor University Press.

Wieder, A. A. 1965. "Ugaritic-Hebrew Lexicographical Notes." *JBL* 84.2: 160–64.

Williams, R. J. 1976. *Hebrew Syntax: An Outline*. Toronto: University of Toronto Press.

Yoo, Y. J. 1999. *Israelian Hebrew in the Book of Hosea*. PhD diss., Cornell University.

Young, I. 1997. "Evidence of Diversity in Pre-exilic Judahite Hebrew." *Hebrew Studies* 38.1: 7–20.

CHAPTER 9

TEXTS AND VERSIONS OF THE BOOK OF HOSEA

ERIC J. TULLY

THE book of Hosea has a long-standing reputation for the difficulty posed by its Hebrew text. Strange syntax, uncertain roots, unusual repetition, and other problems frustrate our attempts to understand the basic linguistic sense of utterances before we can move to exegesis, interpretation, and significance. The Masoretic Text (MT), with all its linguistic challenges, is our most important textual witness to Hosea, because the book was originally composed in Hebrew. The texts from the Judean Desert, while very fragmentary, give us additional Hebrew readings, while the ancient translated versions such as the Greek Septuagint (G), Aramaic Targums (T), Syriac Peshitta (S), and Latin Vulgate (V) add more variables. On the one hand, these translations provide us with additional insight into the meaning of the Hebrew either by witnessing to textual variants or by indicating how the respective translator resolved the linguistic problems. On the other hand, when translators make texts available to new audiences, they inevitably introduce more changes to clarify and simplify the text or to highlight a particular interpretive perspective.[1] This essay surveys the main textual witnesses to Hosea and the distinctive character of each. An overall understanding of this evidence is an important basis for using these witnesses in textual criticism, as well as giving insight into ancient exegesis of the book—both of which assist us in our own interpretive efforts today.

9.1. MASORETIC TEXT

The MT is the only complete Hebrew manuscript tradition for the book of Hosea. Although the Hebrew text in the Second Temple period existed in diverse forms, at least outside of Jerusalem, the Hebrew text antecedent to the MT became the sole, authorized standard within Judaism and was eventually transmitted meticulously by the Masoretes. The major MT codices which contain Hosea are the Aleppo Codex (MT[A], 925 CE), the

Leningrad Codex (MT^L, 1008 CE), and the Cairo Codex (MT^C, 11th century). The best, scholarly printed edition of the MT, based on the Leningrad Codex, is *The Twelve Minor Prophets: Biblia Hebraica Quinta*, edited by Gelston and Schenker (2010).[2]

As mentioned above, the Hebrew text of Hosea contains many obscurities and anomalies. Patterson, writing in 1891, states, "These peculiarities may be stated summarily as follows: brief and unconnected sentences; frequent neglect of gender, person and number; intermingling of similes and metaphors; scanty use of particles; feeble parallelism; rare words; peculiar constructions; inversions; anacolutha and corruption of text" (1891: 192). David Noel Freedman, frustrated by the challenges in Hosea, wrote that his commentary with Frank Andersen (1980) was a "monumental failure," adding, "Needless to say, we don't blame ourselves; the fault lies with the book. Most scholars would agree that there is something wrong with it" (Freedman 1979).

Early scholars explained the problems in the Hebrew text as corruptions from transmission. If so, the corruptions must have occurred at a very early stage because the difficulties were evidently present in the *Vorlagen* of the versions. Harper (1905: clxxiii) writes, "The text of Hosea . . . is one of the most corrupt in the OT, the number of passages which almost defy interpretation being extremely large. . . . Hosea's reputation for obscurity is due in large measure to the corrupt form in which the text of his message has reached us. Similarly, Neef (1986: 195) writes, "The text of Hosea is in some verses so badly preserved that the original meaning can hardly be determined with absolute certainty" (my translation). Scholars who attribute the difficulties to corruption or poor preservation have often sought to correct the text through emendation (Fresch 2016: 591).

Other scholars have argued that the obscurities arose from the provenance of the book, i.e., the prophet's northern Hebrew dialect (see Yoo 1999: 1–33). Schniedewind (2013: 75) identifies the following texts as those reflecting "Israelian Hebrew": 1 Kgs. 17–2 Kgs. 18; Gen. 49; Deut. 32–33; Judg. 5; Ecclesiastes; Song of Songs; Hosea; Amos; and some psalms and proverbs. This is the majority position in recent scholarship.

However, despite the extensive scholarship on the issue, there are reasons to question the proposal that the textual difficulties are due to northern dialect. First, the evidence is very limited. For example, after a thorough investigation of spelling variations in the Hebrew Bible, Barr (1989: 201) concludes that while there certainly were regional dialects, he has "seen no constant features that run across books or sources of (say) probable North Israelite origin and distinguish them clearly from Judean sources" (see also Bos 2013: 16–21). Second, the question remains whether the list of problems quoted from Patterson above (1891: 192; e.g. "brief and unconnected sentences, frequent neglect of gender . . . intermingling of similes and metaphors . . . feeble parallelism," etc.) is likely dialectical. We typically think of dialect in terms of features such as vocalization, morphemes, and lexicon. In many cases in Hosea, we can make sense of all of the morphemes and lexemes individually, but their meaning is obscure when combined in a clause. Third, if these utterances did reflect a northern dialect, should we expect them to be difficult? We might recognize isoglosses in obvious northern texts such as the Samaria Ostraca or in texts that claim to be northern, such as the book of Amos, or

9.2. TEXTS FROM THE JUDEAN DESERT

It is difficult to conceive of a more significant discovery for the text and versions of the Hebrew Bible than the manuscripts from the Judean Desert, including what are commonly called the Dead Sea Scrolls. Prior to the discovery of the scrolls, it was impossible to know with certainty the accuracy of the MT codices from the Middle Ages (answer: they were translated very carefully), to what extent the differences in the versions such as G were due to translator interference as opposed to the Hebrew *Vorlage* (answer: both were responsible), and the extent of textual variation apart from the Hebrew text that is antecedent to the MT (answer: there was textual pluriformity).

The primary depository of biblical texts was discovered in Cave 4, including all of the books of the Hebrew Bible except for Esther. Tov (2002: 150) writes, "It is significant that virtually all the so-called canonical books were represented in this cave, which probably implies that an effort was made to store in that cave among other things all the books which were considered authoritative at that stage." We have a number of extant manuscripts that contain parts of the Book of the Twelve, but not the book of Hosea, likely because that part has been lost from them. These include 4QXII[a] (parts of Zechariah, Malachi, and Jonah), 4QXII[b] (parts of Zephaniah and Haggai), 4QII[e] (parts of Haggai and Zechariah), and 4QXII[f] (only Jonah). Nahal Hever, or 8HevXIIgr, is a manuscript in Greek that contains Jonah to Zechariah. Murabba'at, or MurXII, is a leather scroll that contains most of Joel 2:20–Zech. 1:4.

Three biblical manuscripts contain parts of Hosea, though they are highly fragmentary.[3] The first is 4QXII[c], which comes from the first half of the first century BCE (Fuller 2000: 555). There are 52 fragments containing 397 partial or complete words, including Hos. 2:13–15 (Eng. 2:11–13); 3:2–4; 4:1–5:1; 7:12–13; 13:3–10; and 13:15–14:6 (Eng. 14:5). Fuller (2016: 602) considers this manuscript to be "nonaligned," meaning that it does not primarily agree with G or MT. The reading of Hos. 13:4 contains a significant plus that agrees with G against the MT:

Hosea 13:4

MT: "But I am Yhwh your God."

4QXII[c]: "But I am Yhwh your God **who forms heaven and makes the earth, whose hands created all the host of heaven. And I did not reveal them to you to go after them.**"

G: "But I am the Lord your **God who makes heaven firm and creates earth, whose hands created all the host of heaven. And I did not reveal them to you to follow after them.**"

Fuller views the plus as original, which was lost in the MT due to parablepsis (2016: 602). By contrast, Kim (2018: 47) argues that the longer reading is a theological expansion, warning against worship of the host of heaven which was relevant in later times. The presence of the longer reading in 4QXII^c indicates that it was present in the Hebrew tradition and not only G.

A second manuscript, 4QXII^d, comes from the middle of the first century BCE. It likely contained all the books of the Twelve with Hosea at the beginning. On the whole, it is closer to the MT (Fuller 2000: 556; see also Sinclair 1980: 61–65). For Hosea, we have extant only two adjoining manuscripts containing 1:6–2:5 (Eng. 2:3) (Brooke 2006: 23).

A third manuscript, 4QXII^g, comes from the last third of the first century BCE. It is poorly preserved in 249 fragments, with over 130 of them as yet unidentified, containing 876 partial or complete words (Fuller 2016: 603). For Hosea, we have 2:1–5 (Eng. 1:10–2:3), 14–19 (Eng. 2:12–17), 22–4:1; 4:10–11, 13–14; 6:3–4, 8–7:1; 7:12–13; 7:13–8:1; 9:1–4; 9:9–10:14; 11:2–5; 11:6–13:1, 6–8, 11–13; and 14:9–10 (Eng. 14:8–9). Scholars debate whether this manuscript is closer to the Hebrew text behind the MT (Fuller 2000: 556) or nonaligned (Brooke 2006: 25).

The *Editio princeps* of these biblical manuscripts is Ulrich et al. (1997). Another helpful edition is Ulrich (2013). In summary, the biblical manuscripts containing Hosea were created over the course of approximately 150 years, from the middle of the second century to the end of the first century BCE. A variety of text forms were collected together, with some agreeing mostly with the Hebrew text antecedent to the MT, others agreeing with the Hebrew text behind G, and others nonaligned. Some of the manuscripts are so fragmentary and incomplete that it is impossible to identify the relationship (Fuller 2016: 601). The manuscripts have no evidence of verse division (Tov 2002: 144). In Hosea, the variants vis-à-vis the MT are quite minor, including plus or minus conjunctions, different number in nouns, and so forth. The exception is the long plus in Hos. 13:4 discussed above.

9.3. THE GREEK SEPTUAGINT

Our earliest extant manuscript of G-Hosea is the Washington Papyrus (third century CE), which is fragmentary and incomplete for Hosea (Dines 2015: 438). Codex Sinaiticus (fourth century CE) is one of our most important codices for G, but it lacks Hosea. Codex Vaticanus (fourth century CE) is reliable for the Book of the Twelve.[4] Codex Alexandrinus (fifth century CE) is characterized by expansions and harmonizations. The essential scholarly edition of G-Hosea is Ziegler (1984). For a recent English translation, see Pietersma and Wright (2007).[5]

The Septuagint of the Torah was translated in Egypt in the middle of the second century BCE (Glenny 2016: 616–17). Distinctive vocabulary and cultural references suggest an Egyptian provenance for the Torah and some books (Tov 1993: 113), while other books were produced in Palestine (Tov 2022: 217). Dines (2015: 441) believes that references to architecture and certain agricultural practices may allow us to be more specific and locate the translation in Alexandria. The Koine Greek language of the translation is fused with semitic interference, such as maintaining the Hebrew word order of the *Vorlage* (Dines 2015: 441).

Although we often talk about *a* Septuagint, G is not a single translation with a unified approach, but "a collection of translations with different types of translation technique in evidence" (Theocharous 2012: 12). Therefore, when we examine the translation character of various books in the Hebrew Bible, we must do so on a case-by-case basis. The translator of Hosea may have had a very different translation philosophy, theological perspective, willingness to adapt the text, and so on, than another translator of a different book such as Amos. However, if a translator worked on more than one book, then analysis of all of those books could be combined and correlated. In the case of Hosea, scholars have debated whether one translator produced the Greek translation for all twelve books in the Book of the Twelve.

A number of scholars made the original argument that the Book of the Twelve was translated by one individual (see Thackeray 1903: 398–411). Kaminka (1928: 10) suggests that perhaps a small group of translators, who knew each other, could explain the great number of translation solutions shared within the Twelve, and the equal number of translations distinct from other books. He acknowledges that possibility that a single author is responsible for the whole. Ziegler (1971: 42) admits that there are inconsistencies in the Book of the Twelve, but that "one cannot speak of a second translator." However, there has been dissent. For example, Harrison (1988: 55) argues that these studies "suffer from a combination of generality, over limitation and unreflective methodology" and have assumed unity "too easily." According to Harrison (59), if Ziegler is able to overlook the inconsistency in the Book of the Twelve, then by that logic the entire Septuagint might have one translator. He writes, "To say that a given translation unit is consistently inconsistent is to construct a no-lose situation; one can marshal both consistent and inconsistent usage patterns in an attempt to demonstrate a relationship between what might be genuinely disparate translation units" (63). More recently, scholars have returned to a defense of the one-translator position (see Muraoka 1989; 2002; Tov 2019: 129–31). Glenny (2016: 381) summarizes and concludes, "Since it is generally assumed that one translator, or group of translators, was responsible for the [Twelve Minor Prophets], the results of the study of different parts of the collection have relevance for each individual book and for the collection as a whole."

In terms of the character of the translation, it is difficult to characterize G of the Book of the Twelve (and therefore G-Hosea) as either "literal" or "free." The translation is mainly quantitative, maintains Hebrew word order, and uses stereotyped lexical equivalents. However, the translator also shows "flexibility," adding words for clarity and harmonizing with other passages (Dines 2015: 440, 443–44).

As noted above, the translator of G apparently faced many of the same difficulties in the Hebrew text that confront us. Sometimes he translated what he thought the word meant even when the resulting translation is nonsensical:

TEXTS AND VERSIONS OF THE BOOK OF HOSEA   129

Hosea 13:3
MT: "like chaff [that] swirls from a threshing floor and like smoke from **a window**."
G: "like dust that blows from a threshing floor and like smoke from **locusts**."

Sometimes, when an entire verse and its context is unclear, the translator resorts to a wooden, word-for-word rendering that makes no sense in combination.

Hosea 12:12
MT: "Since Gilead **was wicked, surely they have become** deceitful. In Gilgal they have sacrificed **bulls**; furthermore their altars are also like **heaps of stones beside the furrow** of the field" (Tully 2018: 288).
G: "If Galaad **does not exist, then the rulers** offering sacrifices in Galgal **were false, and their altars like mounds on the dry land** of the field."

The Hebrew is difficult to understand in context, but the translator of G has arguably made things worse by apparently focusing on individual constituents at the expense of meaning of the whole.

When faced with a difficult text, it is not always certain whether an easier reading in G is due to a (better?) textual variant in the Hebrew tradition, or whether the translator has simply made the best sense possible. For example, in 5:2, the Hebrew is quite challenging:

Hosea 5:2
MT: "**And the rebels have intensified the slaughter**, but I am **fetters for all of them**" (Tully 2018: 110).
G: "... **which those who hunt game have set**. But I am **your instructor**."

In G, verse 2 begins with a relative clause headed by *diktuon* ("net") in 5:1. Thus, 5:1b–2a forms one sentence. Patterson (1891: 211) writes that here the MT is "so peculiar that one is inclined to look with favor on the versions of the LXX and Peshitta, which carry the figure of the preceding verse. But it is very difficult to determine what was the basis of these readings." It seems likely that the hunting imagery in G and S has arisen from polygenesis since, beyond this similarity, the two versions have several significant differences (Tully 2015: 107).

G sometimes makes more intrusive changes for euphemistic, ideological, or theological reasons. In 5:12 in the MT, Yhwh uses the metaphor of "moth" and "rot" in self-description. G decodes the first metaphor and changes the second, apparently to soften the imagery as applied to the deity:

Hosea 5:12
MT: "And I am like a **moth** to Ephraim and like **rot** to the house of Judah."
G: "And I am like **confusion** to Ephraim and like a **goad** to the house of Judah."

There has also been some debate whether one can detect increased messianism in G. Van der Woude (1974: 510) argues that there are "definite deviations" from the Hebrew that point to messianic hope, and gives Hos. 8:10 as an example:

Hosea 8: 10
MT: "king and princes will writhe because of the **tribute** (*masa'*)."
G: "from **anointing** (reading *mashakh*?) kings and princes."

However, Lust (2004: 10) disagrees that G augments messianic expectation, arguing that one cannot overlook many passages in which we might expect messianic expectation but it is not present. "One cannot say that the LXX as a whole displays a messianic exegesis" when, in some cases, G actually weakens the potential sense (12). For example, Hos. 11:1, which is quoted in Matt. 2:15 in reference to Jesus, is translated in G with a plural "sons," obscuring a potential connection (Dines 2015: 448).

Hosea 11:1
MT: "out of Egypt I called **my son**."
G: "out of Egypt I called **his** [i.e., Israel's] **children**."

Having examined the translator's overall approach and specific techniques, scholars conclude that the Hebrew *Vorlage* of G was very similar to the MT in the Book of the Twelve (Dines 2015: 17, 308; Palmer 2004: 176; Theocharous 2012: 9–11). Overall, G does not contain many significant actual textual variants in the Book of the Twelve—and therefore, Hosea. The lengthy plus in Hos. 13:4, mentioned above in connection with 4QXII^c, is an exception (Utzschneider 2009: 1166).

In summary, G supplemented, improved, smoothed, and interpreted its Hebrew *Vorlage* without significant shifts in meaning (Neef 1986: 217). The translator(s) considered the text of Hosea to be the word of God both for the original audience of the Hebrew text and for those meant to benefit from the translation (Glenny 2013: 21).

9.4. THE ARAMAIC TARGUM

The word "Targum" can refer to any translation of the Bible, but it is especially used for translations into Aramaic, which had replaced Hebrew as the *lingua franca* of the Jews in the centuries before and after the turn of the era (Cathcart and Gordon 1989: ix). Targums were created—likely in pre-Christian times—primarily for use in synagogue worship. They reflected a tension: on the one hand, rabbis were concerned not to allow the Targums to replace the authority of scripture. They were read alongside the Hebrew text and as a companion to it. On the other hand, "targum offered a useful means of imposing a certain reading on Scripture, without resorting to the drastic expedient of altering the text of the original" (Alexander 2004: 239).

Our earliest witness to the Targum of the Book of the Twelve is Codex Reuchlinianus (1105 CE) (see de Lagarde 1872). Targum Jonathan contains the Latter Prophets and thus the book of Hosea. The scholarly printed edition is Sperber (2004). For an English translation and commentary, see Cathcart and Gordon (1989).

The date of the Targums is uncertain. Some references seem to reflect a date pre-70 CE but others reflect a date post-70 CE. For example, the translation of Nah. 1:9 mentions "two afflictions," which may refer to the twin Babylonian and Roman destructions of Jerusalem and the temple (Cathcart and Gordon 1989: 17). The "preponderance of evidence points to the period after [70 CE] as that when significant work of composition of Tg. Prophets was carried out" (18). All the Targums are composite and developed over time, making dating difficult (Flesher and Chilton 2011: 161).

T was translated from a text very similar to the proto-MT. Tov (1993: 11) writes, "The texts belonging to the Masoretic group [i.e., Targum, Peshitta, and Vulgate] differ slightly from each other, and are not consistent internally with regard to their spelling. It is not known whether they derive from one common ancestor, but the amount of differentiation between members of the group is remarkably low for texts written in the Second Temple Period." As is well known, the Targums are characterized by extensive expansion. Therefore, it is often difficult to reconstruct the Hebrew *Vorlage* with precision. However, one should not conclude that the translators of T translated recklessly and liberally. Rather, they operated according to fixed rules. When the translator added material, he worked to minimize the disruption to the flow of the text (Flesher and Chilton 2011: 40).

As stated above, the translator of T had two primary aims. First, as in all translation, the aim was to make the Hebrew text linguistically accessible to Aramaic speakers. The translator used stock words and phrases that were known to the implied readers. One of the purposes of literary expansion was to increase the clarity of the text. Like G, T decodes metaphors, even when the intended sense is obvious:

Hosea 2:1 (Eng. 1:10)
MT: "And the number of the Israelites shall be like the sand of the sea."
T: "And the number of the Israelites shall be **numerous** like the sand of the sea."

A second aim of the translator goes beyond linguistic rendering to guide the reader toward an authoritative (rabbinic) interpretation. The first example of this in Hosea is the prophet's central sign-act: his marriage. Apparently deciding that it would be morally and theologically problematic for God to instruct the prophet to marry a promiscuous woman, the translator removes the sexual imagery and replaces it with a more literal sense:

Hosea 1:2
MT: "Go, take for yourself a wife of whoredom and children of whoredom."
T: "Go (and) **speak a prophecy against the inhabitants of the idolatrous city**" (Cathcart and Gordon 1989: 29).

In the MT, the meaning of the sign-act is easy enough to discern, and it is also explained along the way, first as applied to the nation of Israel in ch. 2 and then more explicitly in ch. 3.

Similarly, T-Hosea attempts to protect God's transcendence and reputation by avoiding expressions that are too mundane. One strategy for this is the use of the word "Memra," which represents God's agent or intermediary. For example:

Hosea 1:7
MT: "But I will have mercy on the house of Judah, and I will save them by Yhwh their God."
T: "But I will have mercy on the house of Judah, and I will save them by **the Memra** of the Lord their God."

Rather than Yhwh profaning himself by being a direct instrument of the deliverance of humans, it is the Memra who stands in and creates a "buffer." The translator also uses other intermediaries such as "Shekinah" (the manifestation of God's glory) in Hos. 5:6 or even the "fear" of Yhwh:

Hosea 14:2 (Eng. 14:1)
MT: "Return, Israel, to Yhwh your God."
T: "Return, Israel, to **the fear** of Yhwh your God."

A final illustration from Hosea shows how the translator attempts to avoid possible theological misconceptions:

Hosea 4:6
MT: "You forgot the law of your God; I will also **forget** your children."
T: "And because you have forgotten the law of your God, I will also **reject** your children."

T cannot take the chance that the reader will attribute weakness and forgetfulness to God, so it goes directly to (the translator's interpretation of) the intended sense.

9.5. THE SYRIAC PESHITTA

The name "Peshitta" means "simple"—a straightforward translation of the Hebrew Bible and the Greek New Testament into Syriac, a late dialect of Aramaic. Our best complete manuscript is MS 7a1 from the seventh century CE. Another manuscript, MS 9a1, has significant, older readings for Hos. 1:1–14:6 (Eng. 14:5) (van der Kooij 2016: 631). Overall, manuscript evidence is quite limited (Gelston 1988: 82). The best scholarly edition of S-Hosea is Gelston (ed.), *Dodekapropheton, Daniel and Bel and the Dragon*, in the series,

"The Old Testament in Syriac According to the Peshitta Version" (1980). This is primarily based on MS 7a1 with an apparatus and readings from other manuscripts as well. Another important edition is David (2010), which is vocalized and contains an introduction. For the Mosul text and a contemporary, careful English translation, see Walter et al. (2012).

The date of the Peshitta is uncertain. Gelston (1987: 195) places it in the middle or late first century CE while most scholars date it to the late second century CE (see Weitzman 1999: 248–58). It was produced in Edessa, northern Mesopotamia, a cosmopolitan city on trade routes with a mix of Greeks, Persians, Jews, and other ethnic and religious groups. These culturally diverse inhabitants and visitors worked and lived together in a multilingual environment (Tully 2015: 26). The Peshitta has elements which indicate a Jewish and a Christian provenance. A Jewish background is suggested by the Hebrew *Vorlage* (similar to the MT), as well as translations that reflect Jewish exegetical traditions, sometimes also seen in Aramaic Targums. However, a Christian context is suggested by some apparent influence from G, as well as its transmission within the Christian church. Weitzman (1999: 258–59) has made a convincing argument that the version was created by Jewish converts to Christianity, thus explaining these apparently conflicting features.

Studies have consistently shown that S comes from a Hebrew *Vorlage* very close to proto-MT but with some contact with G. Gelston (1987: 118) writes, "It is hard to avoid the conclusion that the Hebrew *Vorlage* of the Peshitta was very nearly identical with MT, though it seems probable that the translation was made at a date when some variant readings were still in circulation." I have argued elsewhere that "the translator had at least two choices [of source text]: a Hebrew version and a Greek version. It is possible that an early Aramaic targum was available to him, but there is no evidence of it. That he had a choice is noteworthy, for it shows that his selection of the Hebrew as his primary source was purposeful. He or his authorities evidently viewed the Hebrew as having a higher status and thought that a translation of Scripture should be based upon it" (Tully 2015: 326). When the MT has a Ketiv/Qere reading, S tends to follow the Qere. It is common for S to presuppose a different vocalization from that of the MT, since the translator was working from an unpointed Hebrew manuscript.

As in the case of G, it is interesting to observe how S reacts and solves difficult Hebrew verses or clauses in Hosea. The translator has a number of different strategies. Sometimes, S abdicates and translates the Hebrew text as is, without any attempt to make better sense of it:

Hosea 13:2

MT: "They say to them, 'Those who sacrifice a person kiss calves.'"

S: "And they were saying to them, 'The ones who sacrifice people and kiss the calf.'"

S's translation here has a few differences from the MT (plural "people" and singular "calf"), but otherwise it is just as obscure as the Hebrew.

Another strategy is to omit difficult elements:

Hosea 4:18
MT: "[When] **their drink has ended** they prostitute abundantly; they love the dishonor of **her** shamelessness."
S: "All of them commit prostitution and they love shame and false religion."

S has a number of minuses, including "their drink has ended," the infinitive absolute (*hazneh*), the uncertain word *hebu*, and the third feminine singular suffix on "her shamelessness" (Tully 2015: 103–4). The verse is now more general and speaks to overall spiritual degeneracy. The most obscure elements of the Hebrew are no longer present.

At other times, the translator may infer the meaning from the context (see 9:7) or look at the versions for some help (see 7:16; 11:6). In a particularly difficult verse, S might have multiple points of contact with G at the focal point of the problem, but then returns in the following verse to the Hebrew *Vorlage* without any continuing similarities to G (Tully 2015: 272).

Sometimes S will make more intrusive shifts that affect the interpretation of the text:

Hosea 3:4
MT: "For the Israelites will live many days without a king and without a prince and without sacrifice and without a pillar and without an Ephod or Teraphim."
S: "Because the Israelites will live many days without a king and without a prince and without sacrifice and without an **altar** and without an ephod garment and **placing incense**."

In the context, Yhwh is judging the people by temporarily removing the means of Israel's relationship with the deity. However, although it makes sense to remove "sacrifice," how is it a punishment to remove "pillar" and "Teraphim" since those were illegitimate or at least morally ambiguous in Israel's history? The translation in S resolves this problem by shifting those items which had previously been connected to idolatry to items which were unambiguously orthodox.

S does contain some true textual variants distinct from the MT. One indicator of this may be when S, G, and T all agree against the MT. While that agreement might in some cases be due to polygenesis or direct influence, in other cases the confluence indicates a variant that the witnesses have preserved. One example is found in Hos. 11:3:

Hosea 11:3
MT: "And I taught Ephraim; **he** took them on **his** arms."
S: "And I led Ephraim and I took them on **my** arms."
G: And I bound Ephraim's feet; I took him on **my** arm."
T: "I, by an angel, sent before me; I led on a good path; as for Israel, I carried them as on arms."

TEXTS AND VERSIONS OF THE BOOK OF HOSEA   135

S, G, and T all have a first-person subject of *laqaḥ* (if that is the root of the MT's *qaḥam*) and a first-person possessive pronoun "my arm(s)." However, they are all different in minor details such as singular or plural object pronouns and singular or plural "arm"/ "arms." Because of these minor differences, it seems this is a case of a different *Vorlage* rather than coincidental translator behavior or direct dependence between them.

9.6. THE LATIN VULGATE

The name "Vulgate" means "common one." Although the Western church already had Latin translations (*Vetus Latina*) in the first centuries CE, there was a need for a single authoritative Latin version in the common language. Eusebius Hieronymus, whom we usually know by the name Jerome, realized that this version needed to be translated from the Hebrew text (Brotzman and Tully 2016: 86). He began translating this new version in 391 CE and completed the Latter Prophets in 393 CE (Graves 2016: 645). (For a critical edition of the Vulgate, see Weber et al. 2007).

The Vulgate of Hosea is of limited text-critical value. Graves (2016: 649) writes that Jerome's Hebrew *Vorlage* "is so close to MT . . . throughout that it may be considered as if it were an early text in this family." Therefore, when V deviates from the MT, especially when it agrees with another version, this potentially indicates a true textual variant. In Hosea, we find an example in Hos. 2:16 (Eng. 2:14) (Graves 2016: 650).

Hosea 2:16 (Eng. 2:14)
MT: "**you** will call me 'my husband' and **you** will no longer call me 'My Baal.'"
V: "**she** will call me 'my husband' and **she** will no longer call me 'Baalim.'"
G: "**she** will call me 'my husband' and **she** will no longer call me 'Baali.'"

However, while this does reflect a textual variant, it is not ultimately significant. In the MT, the preceding and following context refers to Israel (the referent of the image) in the third-person singular, but in 2:16 Yhwh suddenly addresses her directly with "you." The versions are more consistent in referring to Israel in the third-person throughout.

In terms of translation approach, Jerome has some consistent patterns. He sometimes divides clauses and sentences differently than the (later) masoretic accents indicate in the MT, and there are "innumerable omissions and additions of *waw*" (Kedar-Kopfstein 1974: 76). Some readings in V presume a different vocalization than the MT (see Hos. 14:6 [Eng. 14:5]). Like other translations, he simplifies and clarifies. For example:

Hosea 2:11 (Eng. 2:9)
MT: "and my flax **to cover** her nakedness."
V: "and my flax **which covered** her nakedness."

ERIC J. TULLY

This is a subtle shift, but the change from a purpose clause to a relative clause clarifies the intent of the syntax. In addition, it has the effect of placing the event in the past which is more consistent with the context. Sometimes, Jerome makes subtle shifts that reflect his own exegesis:

Hosea 11:4
MT: "With cords of **man** I was drawing them—with ropes of love."
V: "With ropes of **Adam** I will draw them—with bonds of love."

The MT's reading probably means something like "humane" but Jerome takes *'adam* as a proper name.

9.7. CONCLUSION

The examples and previous scholarship presented in this essay indicate that the Hebrew text of Hosea—in the MT and texts from the Judean Desert, as well as the reconstructed *Vorlage* of the versions—is fairly consistent across the extant textual witnesses. None of the versions have many significant variants. The translated versions, including G, are working from Hebrew *Vorlagen* similar to the Hebrew text behind the MT. This means that those translators also faced many of the obscurities and difficulties in the text that we encounter today. Although they had the opportunity to "fix" the text in a dramatic fashion, for the most part they translated their Hebrew texts faithfully and passed on many of those difficulties to their readers.

NOTES

1. For more on translator interference and its effect on using translations for textual criticism, see Tully 2014, 2020.
2. For a brief overview of the development of the Biblia Hebraica series as well as other important printed editions of the MT, see Brotzman and Tully 2016.
3. There are also a few fragments of the book of Hosea in a commentary (or *Pesher*) found at Qumran; see Allegro 1968.
4. For a commentary on Hosea in Vaticanus, see Glenny 2013.
5. For a German translation see Utzschneider 2009. For French, see Bons et al. 2002.

REFERENCES

Alexander, Philip S. 2004. "Jewish Aramaic Translations of Hebrew Scriptures." In Martin Jan Mulder and Harry Sysling, eds., *Mikra: Text, Translation, Reading and Interpretation of the Hebrew Bible in Ancient Judaism and Early Christianity*. Peabody, MA: Hendrickson, 217–53.

Allegro, John M. 1968. *Qumran Cave 4: I*. Discoveries in the Judaean Desert V. Oxford: Clarendon.

Andersen, Francis I., and David Noel Freedman. 1980. *Hosea*. AB. New York: Doubleday.

Barr, James. 1989. *The Variable Spellings of the Hebrew Bible*. The Schweich Lectures of the British Academy. Oxford: Oxford University Press.

Bons, Eberhard, Jan Joosten, Stephan Kessler, Philippe Le Moigne, Takamitsu Muraoka, Marguerite Harl, Gilles Dorival, Olivier Munnich, and Cecile Dogniez. 2002. *La Bible d'Alexandrie, Les Douze Prophetes, Osee*. Paris: Ed. du Cerf.

Bos, James M. 2013. *Reconsidering the Date and Provenance of the Book of Hosea: The Case for Persian-Period Yehud*. LHBOTS 580. New York: Bloomsbury.

Brooke, George J. 2006. "The Twelve Minor Prophets and the Dead Sea Scrolls." In Andre Lemaire, ed., *Congress Volume Leiden 2004*. Leiden: Brill, 19–43.

Brotzman, Ellis R., and Eric J. Tully. 2016. *Old Testament Textual Criticism: A Practical Introduction*. 2nd ed. Grand Rapids: Baker Academic.

Cathcart, Kevin J., and Robert P. Gordon. 1989. *The Targum of the Minor Prophets*. Aramaic Bible. Wilmington, Delaware: Michael Glazier.

David, Clemens Joseph. 2010. *The Syriac Bible According to the Mosul Edition*. Piscataway, NJ: Gorgias.

Dines, Jennifer M. 2015. "The Minor Prophets." In James K. Aitken, ed., *T and T Clark Companion to the Septuagint*. London: Bloomsbury T&T Clark, 438–55.

Flesher, Paul V. M., and Bruce Chilton. 2011. *The Targums: A Critical Introduction*. Boston: Brill.

Freedman, David Noel. 1979. "Problems of Textual Criticism in the Book of Hosea." In Wendy Doniger O'Flaherty, ed., *Critical Study of Sacred Texts*. Berkeley: Graduate Theological Union, 55–76.

Fresch, Christopher J. 2016. "9.1 Minor Prophets: Textual History of the Minor Prophets; Witnesses to the Minor Prophets; Hebrew Witnesses." In Armin Lange and Emanuel Tov, eds., *Textual History of the Bible, Vol. 1: The Hebrew Bible, Part 1b; Pentateuch, Former and Latter Prophets*. Leiden: Brill, 598–601.

Fuller, Russell E. 2000. "Minor Prophets." In Lawrence H. Schiffman and James C. VanderKam, eds., *Encyclopedia of the Dead Sea Scrolls*. New York: Oxford University Press, 554–57.

Fuller, Russell. 2016. "9.2 Minor Prophets: Ancient Hebrew Texts; Masoretic Texts and Ancient Texts Close to MT." In Armin Lange and Emanuel Tov, eds., *Textual History of the Bible, Vol. 1: The Hebrew Bible, Part 1b; Pentateuch, Former and Latter Prophets*. Leiden: Brill, 606–10.

Gelston, Anthony. 1980. *The Old Testament in Syriac/ Pt. 3, Fasc. 4, Dodekapropheton-Daniel-Bel-Draco*. Leiden: Brill.

Gelston, Anthony. 1987. *The Peshitta of the Twelve Prophets*. Oxford: Clarendon Press.

Gelston, Anthony. 1988. "Some Readings in the Peshitta of the Dodekapropheton." In Peter B. Dirksen and Martin J. Mulder, eds., *The Peshitta: Its Early Text and History; Papers Read at the Peshitta Symposium, Leiden, Aug 1985*. Leiden: Brill, 81–98.

Gelston, A., and Adrian Schenker. 2010. *The Twelve Minor Prophets*. Biblia Hebraica Quinta (BHQ) 13. Stuttgart: Deutsche Bibelgesellschaft.

Glenny, W. Edward. 2013. *Hosea: A Commentary Based on Hosea in Codex Vaticanus*. Boston: Brill.

Glenny, W. Edward. 2016. "9.3 Minor Prophets: Septuagint." In Armin Lange and Emanuel Tov, eds., *Textual History of the Bible, Vol. 1: The Hebrew Bible, Part 1b; Pentateuch, Former and Latter Prophets*. Leiden: Brill, 614–23.Graves, Michael. 2016. "6–9.1.7 Latter Prophets: Primary Translations; Vulgate." In Armin Lange and Emanuel Tov, eds., *Textual History of* the Bible, Vol. 1: The Hebrew Bible, Part 1b; Pentateuch, Former and Latter Prophets. Leiden: Brill, 645–52.

Harper, William Rainey. 1905. A Critical and Exegetical Commentary on Amos and Hosea. ICC. Edinburgh: T&T Clark.

Harrison, C. Robert, Jr. 1988. "The Unity of the Minor Prophets in the LXX: A Reexamination of the Question." Bulletin of the International Organization for Septuagint and Cognate Studies 21: 55–72.

Kaminka, Armand. 1928. Studien zur Septuaginta: an der Hand der Zwölf Kleinen prophetenbücher. Schriften der Gesellschaft zur Förderung der Wissenschaft des Judentums 33. Frankfurt: J. Kauffmann.

Kedar-Kopfstein, Benjamin. 1974. "Textual Gleanings from the Vulgate to Hosea." Jewish Quarterly Review 65: 73–97.

Kim, Sungjin. 2018. "Is the Masoretic Text Still a Reliable Primary Text for the Book of Hosea?" BBR 28, no. 1: 34–64.

Lagard, Paul de. 1872. Prophetae Chaldaice. Lipsiae: B.G. Teubneri.

Lust, J. 2004. Messianism and the Septuagint: Collected Essays. Edited by K. Hauspie. BETL 178. Leuven: Leuven University Press.

Muraoka, Takamitsu. 1989. "In Defence of the Unity of the Septuagint Minor Prophets." Annual of the Japanese Biblical Institute 15: 25–36.

Neef, Heinz-Dieter. 1986. "Der Septuaginta-Text Und Der Masoreten-Text Des Hoseabuches Im Vergleich." Bib 67, no. 2: 195–220.

Palmer, James K. 2004. "'Not Made with Tracing Paper': Studies in the Septuagint of Zechariah." PhD diss., University of Cambridge.

Patterson, Gaylard H. 1891. "The Septuagint Text of Hosea Compared with the Massoretic Text." Hebraica 7, no. 3: 190–221.

Pietersma, Albert, and Benjamin G. Wright. 2007. A New English Translation of the Septuagint. New York: Oxford University Press.

Schniedewind, William. 2013. A Social History of Hebrew: Its Origins through the Rabbinic Period. New Haven, CT: Yale University Press.

Sinclair, Lawrence A. 1980. "A Qumran Biblical Fragment: Hosea 4QXIId (Hosea 1:7–2:5)." BASOR 239: 61–65.

Sperber, Alexander, ed. 2004. The Bible in Aramaic. Leiden: Brill.

Thackeray, H. St J. 1903. "The Greek Translators of the Prophetical Books." JTS 4: 398–411.

Theocharous, Myrto. 2012. Lexical Dependence and Intertextual Allusion in the Septuagint of the Twelve Prophets: Studies in Hosea, Amos, and Micah. LHBOTS 570. New York: T&T Clark.

Tov, Emanuel. 1993. "Some Reflections on the Hebrew Texts from Which the Septuagint Was Translated," JNSL 19: 107–22.

Tov, Emanuel. 2002. "The Biblical Texts from the Judaean Desert: An Overview and Analysis of the Published Texts." In Edward D. Herbert and Emanuel Tov, eds., The Bible as Book: The Hebrew Bible and the Judaean Desert Discoveries. London: British Library, 139–66.

Tov, Emanuel. 2019. "The Textual Value of the Septuagint Version of the Minor Prophets." In Cécile Dogniez and Philippe Le Moigne, eds., Les Douze Prophètes dans la LXX: Protocoles et procédures dans la traduction grecque; Stylistique, poétique et histoire. VTSup180. Leiden: Brill, 129–47.Tov, Emanuel. 2022. Textual Criticism of the Hebrew Bible. 4th ed. Minneapolis: Fortress.

Tully, Eric J. 2014. "Translation Universals and Polygenesis: Implications for Textual Criticism." The Bible Translator 65, no. 3: 292–307.

Tully, Eric J. 2015. *The Translation and Translator of the Peshitta of Hosea*. Leiden: Brill.

Tully, Eric. J. 2018. *Hosea: A Handbook on the Hebrew Text*. Waco, TX: Baylor University Press.

Tully, Eric J. 2020. "A Model for Distinguishing between Textual Variants and Translation Shifts in Old Testament Textual Criticism." *SJOT* 34, no. 2: 245–66.Ulrich, Eugene Charles, ed. 2013. *The Biblical Qumran Scrolls: Transcriptions and Textual Variants. Volume 2: Isaiah-Twelve Minor Prophets*. Leiden: Brill.

Ulrich, Eugene, Frank Moore Cross, Russell E. Fuller, Judith E. Sanderson, Patrick W. Skehan, Emanuel Tov, Catherine M. Murphy, and Curt Niccum. 1997. *Qumran Cave 4: X*. Discoveries in the Judaean Desert XV. Oxford: Clarendon.

Utzschneider, Helmut. 2009. "Dodekapropheten: Das Zwoelfprophetenbuch." In Wolfgang Kraus and Martin Karrer, eds., *Septuaginta Deutsch*. Stuttgart: Deutsche Bibelgesellschaft, 1165–1229.

Van der Kooij, Arie. 2016. "9.1.4 Minor Prophets: Primary Translations; Peshitta." In Armin Lange and Emanuel Tov, eds., *Textual History of the Bible, Vol. 1: The Hebrew Bible, Part 1b; Pentateuch, Former and Latter Prophets*. Leiden: Brill, 630–37.

Walter, Donald M., Gillian Greenberg, George Anton Kiraz, and Joseph Bali. 2012. *The Book of the Twelve Prophets According to the Syriac Peshitta Version with English Translation*. The Syriac Peshitta Bible with English Translation. Piscataway, NJ: Gorgias.

Weber, Robert, et al., eds. 2007. *Biblia Sacra: Iuxta Vulgatam Versionem*. Ed. altera emendata. Stuttgart: Deutsche Bibelgesellschaft.

Weitzman, Michael. 1999. *The Syriac Version of the Old Testament*. Cambridge: Cambridge University.

Woude, A. S. van der. 1974. "Messianic Ideas in Later Judaism." In Gerhard Kittle and Gerhard Friedrich, eds., *Theological Dictionary of the New Testament*. Grand Rapids: Eerdmans, 509–10.

Yoo, Yoon Jong. 1999. "Israelian Hebrew in the Book of Hosea." PhD diss., Cornell University.

Ziegler, Joseph. 1971. "Die Einheit Der Septuaginta Zum Zwölfprophetenbuch." In *Sylloge: Gesammelte Aufsätze Zur Septuaginta*. Gottingen: Vandenhoeck & Ruprecht, 29–42.

Ziegler, Joseph. 1984. *Duodecim Prophetae*. 3. durchgesehene Aufl. Septuaginta: Vetus Testamentum Graecum 13. Göttingen: Vandenhoeck & Ruprecht.

CHAPTER 10

HOSEA IN THE BOOK OF THE TWELVE

MARK LEUCHTER

10.1. INTRODUCTION

THE book of Hosea's position in the Book of the Twelve (BT) has drawn tremendous scholarly attention not only in terms of the relationship between the former and the other prophetic books in the latter. The origin of the book's various groups of oracles, the role of the cult and mythological traditions found within it, and the degree to which its contents may be traced to an historical prophet living in the last days of the northern monarchy are common foci of inquiry and examination. But the ways in which all of these issues were understood by the book's earliest tradents were affected by the role it plays in the BT, a work produced by scribes of the late Persian period (c. 350–330 BCE) that attests to ancient suppositions regarding the sources inherited by the redactors as much as to the ancient memories of prophets and prophecy sustained by their audiences. As I will discuss further below, the BT was constructed to affirm the ongoing vitality of prophecy at a time when claims of authoritative revelation had been subsumed within the ritual system of the Jerusalem temple under Persian imperialism. That the book of Hosea provides the opening canto to this literary enterprise speaks to the place of the Hosea tradition as a cornerstone of prophetic thought in relation to ritual cultures set against the background of foreign empires down to the late Persian period—the time in which the redactors of the BT set about their work.

Before going further, a few words are in order regarding some working assumptions about both the BT and the book of Hosea itself. In light of research over the last two decades, it has become clear that the BT grew in various stages (see below), though scholars remain remarkably divided on redaction-critical approaches to the material. Legion are the proposals that attempt to reduce this or that prophetic book in the BT to an original stratum consisting of no more than a small handful of verses, with countless subsequent redactional accretions responsible for major thematic motifs characterizing most of the oracular material therein. In some cases—and to some degree overall—these proposals shed useful light on the process of literary development from source/sources to finished product. However, the models that identify the groundwork for a given prophetic book as little more than half-thoughts or brief comments do not adequately account for advances in the study of orality and literacy, ancient Near Eastern scribal culture of the mid-first millennium BCE, anthropological models for institutional textuality, or the sociological conventions of literary preservation.

These considerations indicate that the oracles within the various books of the BT need not (always) be fragmented into minute discrete strata characterized by distinct lemmas deriving from different redactional hands. The recognition of recurring themes may indicate a consequent scribal incursion into earlier material, but such a conclusion must be supported by other indications of secondary interpolations. And even so, secondary interpolation does not necessarily point to a dramatic gulf in compositional setting. Material recited, performed, and transmitted within the same close circle of tradents can evolve quickly and dramatically, especially when considered against the background of an active cultic setting where variegated liturgical traditions countenance each other (Dalit Rom-Shiloni [2014] and Lena-Sofia Tiemeyer [2018] have provided evidence for this in the books of Jeremiah and Zechariah, respectively.) In brief, there are clear indications that the prophetic materials arranged in the BT have crosslisted lemmas stitched into them and show signs of redactional growth before their collection into a single comprehensive work, but the impulse to view the "original" layers of prophetic material as only very brief lexical formulae on which the bulk of oracular material was later built is problematic. It prioritizes redactional-critical theories over social-scientific, sociolinguistic, and philological evidence that suggests more likely alternatives for conceiving of the growth of this material before its redaction into the BT.

10.2. DATING THE ORACLES OF HOSEA AND THE TITULAR PROPHET IN ORAL LORE

The foregoing carries implications for approaches to the book of Hosea. Arguments placing the work primarily in a postmonarchic setting rely too heavily on models for Israelite literacy/textuality that are several decades old and which do not account for more contemporary research into state formation and text production in Near Eastern antiquity (for an overview, see Richele 2016). Moreover, proposals that the majority of the book's contents derive from Judahite scribal creativity do not recognize the distinctive northern concepts that permeate throughout the various levels of the book and bind them together (Levin 2009). Some of these passages may well be older than others, but subsequent additions or expansions carrying a similar linguistic and mythological profile speak to their origination within a limited group of writers closely connected to the older material in one way or another. There are also anthropological dimensions to the oracles throughout the book that align well with the character of Hosea presented therein as a northerner deeply concerned with ritual, sacrifice, wisdom, instruction, law, and prophetic methods of revelatory disclosure.

The oracles overall assume an insider's perspective on the northern cult rather than a retrospective projection from a Jerusalemite scribe living well after the fall of the Northern Kingdom. As Stephen Cook (2004: 231–66) has discussed, this points to a substantial amount of material within the book originating in some manner with a prophet named Hosea who possessed priestly, indeed, Levite heritage, and who lived while an active northern cult still operated. A variety of texts from the late monarchic period appears to show familiarity with Hosea both as a figure of legend and as the namesake of a written oracular tradition (see below). As several scholars note, the formation of an eighth- to seventh-century BCE book of Amos (from a collection of that prophet's earlier oracles) appears to follow precedent set by an extant textual collection of Hosea's oracles (Schart 1998; Jeremias 2020: 118–19). The Levite prophet Jeremiah engages both textual and oral traditions connected to Hosea in the last decade of the seventh century (see below), and the well-known overlaps between the oracles assigned to Hosea and the Deuteronomistic literature suggest an extant interaction between the Hosea tradition and scribal groups in Judah who studied and developed the memory of earlier prophets and the texts associated with them (see especially Yee 2001: 350–57).

The redactors of the BT thus inherited a variety of traditions regarding not only the book of Hosea but also the prophetic figure associated with it, and it is important to distinguish between the two. The place of material texts within a larger network of literary concepts and oral lore has been the subject of much research over the last decade. Emerging from this is an awareness that literary works carrying the names of specific legendary characters do so in different ways, pointing to a more diverse collection of evolving traditions surrounding those figures as conceptual topoi that exist beyond the limits of material texts (Vayntrub 2019; Mroczek 2016; see also Perdue 2007). While this is most evident in the Jewish literature of the Hellenistic period and later, evidence for this phenomenon can be traced to the Persian period, which saw the redaction of the BT (Leuchter 2022) and, indeed, even to earlier eras.

A text containing the words or an account of the deeds of a particular figure is only one indication of the role of that figure in a society's literary culture spanning scholarly, sapiential, ritual, and mythological contexts. It is clear from the foregoing that even before the end of the monarchic period, Hosea's renown was not limited solely to the literary work bearing his name or containing oracles assigned to him. But throughout the Persian period, when the Jerusalem temple became the central institution for the preservation of textual and ritual traditions for Jews residing in Yehud, it is likely that the priestly groups therein laid claim to the oral traditions connected to this prophet and his written oracles (Carr 2011: 6). The formulations and reformulations of who Hosea was and the meaning of his oracles must have become a hallmark of the scholarly/scribal culture of the Jerusalem temple faculty by the time the redactors of the BT constructed their work.

The position of Hosea within that work and the implicit relationship between Hosea's oracles and those that follow may point in some way to the oral lore surrounding Hosea as a prophet and the way the oracles assigned to him were understood and read. By creating a sequence initiated by the book of Hosea, the redactors of the BT present all the prophets who follow him as metaphorical disciples reading his oracles and carrying forward his teachings. To return to a matter mentioned above, the relationship between Amos and Hosea in this sequence is instructive. Though Amos's activity is chronologically earlier than that of Hosea (Amos 1:1–2; cf. Hos. 1:1), Hosea's discourses on covenant, law, ritual, ethics, and myth serve as a symbolic curriculum that Amos's oracles go on to further engage on the literary level. When Amos makes his brief references to the exodus, they appear as expositions of Hosea's more detailed discussions of that motif; when he repudiates the rituals at Bethel, those repudiations function as developments of Hosea's. This literary relationship between Amos and Hosea points to a cultural memory of how Hosea's Ephraimite oracles were encountered and digested among Judahite audiences following the fall of the north, and in a way that may have affected how other prophetic oracles were textualized and read.

Since Hosea is the only Ephraimite prophet in the entirety of the BT, the presentation of the ensuing prophets as students/disciples who take their cues from his oracles is suggestive of the degree to which Hosea's prophetic legacy left an impact on the development of identity within Judah in the late-eighth through seventh centuries BCE. This was a time when Israelite and Judahite identities were in flux, as lineage structures, economies, language differences, theologies, rituals, and myths from diverse northern and southern populations intermingled as Jerusalem and its environs accommodated not only to the flow of refugees from the north but to the urbanization of rural populations under Hezekiah's reign. It was during this period that literary compositions and collections emerged to address these and other issues (Finkelstein and Silberman 2006; Halpern 1991: 79–81), the zenith of which was the composition of Deuteronomy (c. 622) as a comprehensive socioethnic charter (Crouch 2014; see also Rainey 2021: 150–51 on anxiety regarding ethnicity in Deuteronomistic rhetoric).

Deuteronomy's extensive reliance on Hosea is a potent indication of how highly regarded the prophet was during this period, even beyond the texts assigned to him. Even if oral traditions regarding figures known from textual works become more prominent in later periods, the phenomenon has earlier roots fleetingly attested within monarchic-era works, and this included the memory of Hosea in traditions surrounding his oracles. The odd story of the prophet and the man of God from Judah in 1 Kgs. 13 and its call-back in 2 Kgs. 23:17–18 are connected to Hosea and Amos (Barrick 2002: 220–21), possibly reflecting the way these oracular collections were already understood in relation to each other in the seventh century BCE. Further evidence is found in Jer. 3:1:

> A saying (*l'emor*): If a man puts away his wife, and she goes from him, and become another man's, may he return unto her again? Will not that land be greatly polluted? "But you have played the harlot with many lovers; and would you yet return to Me?" says Yhwh.

In this famous verse, Jeremiah refers in near-explicit terms to the discourses in Hos. 1–3 regarding Israel as Yhwh's wayward spouse (using the metaphor of Hosea's own marital issues as a point of departure), and two features stand out. The first is that Jeremiah specifies that this was not solely a matter of textuality but part of an oral tradition ("*l'emor*", from the root *'amar* ["say"] rather than a formulation of *katab* ["write"]), revealing that Hosea's oracles were discussed and even debated. The likelihood of the latter is reinforced by the second feature of Jeremiah's reference, which is that Jeremiah goes on to disagree with Hosea's teachings (Jeremias 1994: 33–36). The ensuing verses in Jer. 3 clarify that Yhwh will not take Israel back and that earlier conceptual models such as Hosea's can no longer apply. But disagreement does not mean dismissal: the vitality of Hosea's oracles and memory in the Deuteronomistic tradition (to which Jeremiah was strongly connected) set notable parameters for making sense of changes in historical and social conditions. The persistence of such a tradition regarding Hosea down into the late Persian period—also a time of changing social conditions (with various Jewish groups struggling to define the boundaries of their identity)—accounts for its position as the opening strophe of the BT.

10.3. A Tentative Proposal for the Growth of the Book of the Twelve and the Function of Hosea

Some of the ancient rabbinic sources made the case that the formation of the BT took place so that the smaller, independent prophetic books it now contains would not be lost or forgotten (Baba Bathra 14b). Yet the Rabbis also preserved diverse traditions about the growth of the work that align better with the results of the last few decades of contemporary scholarship. Since the 1990s, redaction-critical approaches to the development of the BT have yielded countless models for the emergence of the work, some of which contend against each other. Nevertheless, these scholars have made clear that the origin of the work cannot simply be viewed as the collection/compilation of twelve once-independent prophetic books. There are notable antecedent collections, some of which stretch far back in time well before the Persian period. A late eighth-century BCE collection of prophetic literature (perhaps inspired in part by the extant curricular dimensions of the Hosea tradition) probably emerged during the reign of Hezekiah that included Amos, Hosea, Micah and Isaiah (Halpern 1991: 79–80). Others have argued for an exilic "book of four" consisting of Hosea, Amos, Micah, and Zephaniah (Nogalski 1993: 278–80; Wöhrle 2006: 51–284), and both Boda (2016: 30–31) and Curtis (2012: 194–96) have argued for the existence of a Haggai-Zechariah-Malachi scroll developing after the mid-fifth century (so also Leuchter 2022: 11–13).

The BT thus grew out of existing literary units, and it is important to bear in mind the scholarly character of these works as part of a slow but certain shift from prophecy as a primarily performance-oriented phenomenon to one rooted in the materiality of texts (van der Toorn 2007: 206–21). Ezra-Nehemiah bears witness to the persistence of prophetic oral performances (Neh. 6:7, 14), but also discredits them in favor of literary monuments to prophecy and revelation more generally. This concept appears elsewhere in Chronicles. Both Ezra-Nehemiah and Chronicles are products of the late Persian period and thus rough contemporaries of the BT, and both highlight the role of Levites in handling and reciting the contents of prophetic texts (van der Toorn 2007: 79–80, 89–90). These works thus reflect overlapping concepts of ancient Jewish literary sociology and processes of reading, study, and teaching from the perspective of priestly figures adjacent to the center of ritual power held by Aaronide priests in the Persian period.

Such a situation sheds light on the role Hosea occupies within the BT. While the book may have already occupied an initial position in an earlier, antecedent collection (a "book of four;" a preexisting Hosea-Amos scroll, etc.), the redactors of the BT could easily have moved it to a different location. The BT is clearly a more elaborate and intricate work than these proposed antecedent collections, and must be viewed as a new and unique prophetic text in its own right. That the redactors retained the book of Hosea as the first prophetic book in their work speaks to the agenda-setting position it held in their eyes not only as an introduction to the idea of written prophecy as scribal/scholarly works but also as a symbolic statement regarding their own sacral authority. Sarah Milstein's discussion of scribal revision through introduction (Milstein 2016) clarifies the significance of Hosea occupying the first position in the work of these scribes, identifying their own priorities.

The disdain for priesthood and power influenced by foreign imperialism, the interest in wisdom (Van Leeuwen 1993) and liturgy, and the intertwining of prophecy with the medium of material textuality in Hosea's oracles identify these as the concerns of the redactors of the larger work. These concepts are taken up by the subsequent titular prophets vis-à-vis their oracular testimony, which positions them as symbolic disciples of Hosea as the originator of these themes. The use of the book of Hosea thus makes Hosea a literary character within the BT, whose words create conceptual cornerstones for the entire work. Even if the redactors believed that Amos historically predated Hosea, the choice to open the BT with the latter points to their prioritizing of theme over chronology and possibly challenging extant understandings regarding the historical significance of prophecy and its place in ancient Jewish life.

10.4. Hosea as a Levite within the Book of the Twelve

The character of Hosea appears as a Levite within his own book and thus becomes a stand-in for the Levite redactors of the BT more generally. Already in the 1950s, Wolff observed that the contents and style of Hosea's oracles had significant points of contact with the depiction of Levites in various places within the Hebrew Bible (Wolff 1956). Wolff's proposal was reinforced by Cook's (2004: 231–366) thorough study, which brought social-scientific approaches to the evaluation of the linguistic, sociolinguistic, and rhetorical dimensions of the oracles in Hosea. Cook demonstrated that Hosea's oracles drew from a deep tradition of Levite discourse with origins in the prestate period, where Levites rather than kings held sway over Israel's major cultic institutions, and revealed that Hosea's critiques of monarchic institutions matched precisely the ideology of someone steeped in a priestly identity and tradition that was marginalized from a position of cultic power.

Hosea's Levite pedigree also explains why the entire book of Hosea is saturated with the mythology of the Baal Cycle attested at Ugarit. Though this mythology is found in various iterations throughout the Hebrew Bible, the way it plays out in the book of Hosea evidences a specifically northern-Ephraimite understanding of its terms (Levin 2009). Whether the texts in question derive from the historical Hosea or a circle of disciples that carried forward his tradition, the book presents an extended discourse on Israel struggling on one hand against Death and, on the other, as Yhwh's offspring dedicated exclusively to his service. This also reflects an old Levitical perspective: before heredity determined their status, the Levite caste in the prestate period was formed through children being devoted to priestly service at local sanctuaries, especially those connected to the Mushite priesthood (i.e., priestly orders who claimed Moses as their ancestral founder) where myths of the cosmic battle with Death were cultivated (Leuchter 2017: 79–80). The interplay with the Baal mythology in Hosea possesses the same angle of vision, projecting it over the entirety of the Israelite population as a defining covenantal trait that was lacking within the northern state cult.

That the redactors of the BT were aware of this Levitical aspect of the book of Hosea is highlighted by the features of the larger work that point to their own Levite heritage. As Nogalski (2009: 40–46) has noted, the prophetic oracles within the BT are punctuated by blocks of liturgical material that speak to the priestly orientation of the work's principal shapers. That this priestly orientation is specifically Levite—and not Aaronide—is evident through both the larger rhetorical context in which these liturgical blocks appear and the sociological setting for the collection of sources within the BT itself. Regarding the former: the BT is primarily an assortment of prophetic critiques of power emanating from monarchs, foreign empires, and cultic officials serving their interests—hardly a work that would come from Aaronide priests whose own power derived from their support of a Persian ruler and their place within an imperial superstructure. Regarding the latter: the collection of these prophetic texts and their retextualization onto a single, discrete scroll (van der Toorn 2007: 252–53) reveals an attempt to reframe their relationship to each other in contradistinction to a status quo tradition involving their usage.[1] In light of Nogalski's observation that the BT draws blocks of material from the cult into its chapters, it is likely that the very creation of the BT was a way to reframe prophetic literature independent of the cult.

Whatever position prophetic texts had within the ritual system of the Jerusalem temple, the BT provides a space where they can be encountered in a specifically literary and scholarly setting beyond ritual functionality. This aligns well with indications in other Persian-period (and subsequent ancient) sources that apart from their duties and obligations within the Aaronide-led temple cult, Levites preserved textual traditions of reading, teaching, and exegesis that were not strictly defined by temple ritual. The presentation of Levites in the (late Persian-period) book of Chronicles provides important insight into this by further emphasizing that this Levitical tradition was distinctively prophetic in orientation (Schniedewind 1995). In light of the Chronicler's depiction of Levites, we may see the BT as a literary monument to the connection between Levite identity in the Persian period and the legacy of Israelite and Judahite prophecy from earlier eras. If the Levites functioned prophetically through their recitations and performances of prophetic texts in temple ritual, so too then would the collation, study, and teaching of those texts carry a prophetic imprimatur.

This possibility makes the position of Hosea within the BT all the more relevant. I have previously discussed that Hosea contributes to a Levitical framework in tandem with the book of Malachi (Leuchter 2014). Debate continues regarding the origin and dating of the book of Malachi, and whether or not it existed as a discrete prophetic book before the creation of the BT. But virtually all scholars recognize that the oracles within Malachi originated sometime in the Persian period (most likely the fifth century BCE) and are heavily inflected with Levitical language. Malachi thus provides something of an "answer" to the Levitical language in Hosea that opens the work, signaling that prophecy functions within a crucible of Levite authority distinct from the role of prophets or Levites within the ritual system of the Jerusalem court. It has been observed often that this results in a "history of prophecy" from the eighth to fifth centuries BCE within the BT, but this common view should be adjusted, or at least qualified. Because Hosea's oracles are so given to appeals to the more distant (prestate) past, the BT is better viewed not as a history of eighth- to fifth-century prophecy but rather as a discourse on how prophets from those centuries thought about and remembered Israel's distant past before the rise of foreign imperialism and even before the rise of native kings. Surrounding the work with Hosea and Malachi shows how Levites of the Persian period were trustees of a tradition of sacral remembering already taken up by Hosea before the fall of the north.

10.5. HOSEA, MOSES, AND PROPHECY IN THE BOOK OF THE TWELVE

Related to Hosea's position as an archetypal Levite is his position within the BT as the archetypal prophet like Moses. The redactors of the BT shaped the work to make mention of Moses three times (including Mic. 6:4 and Mal. 3:22), beginning with Hosea's famous reference in Hos. 12:13 (Heb. 12:14):

By *a prophet* Yhwh brought Israel out of Egypt, and by *a prophet* was he preserved.

There is widespread consensus that though Moses is not mentioned by name here, the verse has Moses specifically in mind with its invocation of the exodus tradition and the pivotal role of prophets as caretakers or trustees of Israelite peoplehood. For a Levite active in the north like Hosea, only Moses—who was so strongly woven into the northern state's exodus mythology—could be intended. But this is not reason enough for the avoidance of Moses's name. The reference reflects a deliberate and even strategic choice to do so, and this must be weighed against what we can say about religion in the northern state cult in Hosea's own day.

Moses in Hos. 12:13 (Heb. 12:14) is not identified by name because more significant to Hosea is the social typology represented by Moses. Hosea's language reveals that among the Levite circles in which he traveled, Moses's sacrality was understood in distinctively prophetic terms. This is not entirely surprising, since prophecy and priestly function had long overlapped. The early traditions about Samuel presuppose this connection (cf. 1 Sam. 3:1), and the overlap continued well into later eras (Schaper 2005: 334). By referring to Moses by typology rather than by name, Hosea emphasizes that Moses established a sacral category that prophets after him continued to occupy. If the contents of the oracle units in Hos. 4—11 are any indication, such prophets were trustees of cultic and covenantal knowledge that had lost its place in official cult spaces (at least in Hosea's purview). The later Deuteronomistic tradition, which also emphasized the problem of public disengagement from cultic and covenantal knowledge, relies on Hosea's language here in conceiving of the office of "Prophet-Like-Moses" (Deut. 15:15–18), a role that Jeremiah would go on to claim in nearly explicit terms (Jer. 1:9; 15:1). But the choice to use this language already points to concepts that Hosea inherits rather than invents. The appeal to a Mosaic typology in Hos. 12:13 (Heb. 12:14) affirms that this typology had an enduring and living lineage, one that presumably would continue in the social world of the intended audience of the verse.

The cultivation of this idea in Hos. 12:13 (Heb. 12:14) requires that we consider the more proximate literary setting in which it appears—one that highlights liturgical aspects of the northern state cult, especially at Bethel. In this state sanctuary, according to ch. 12, ancestral rites and traditions (especially about Jacob) were observed and reinforced, something that Amos's earlier oracles appear to affirm as well (Amos 2:8). But ancestral rites were networked early on in the formation of the northern state cult in the days of Jeroboam I, who was also remembered for disenfranchising Levites from cultic posts (Cook 2011) within his realm and for associating himself—and his cult iconography—with the exodus and the memory of Moses. Much scholarly attention has been devoted to this dimension of Jeroboam's reign, with many observing that Jeroboam makes himself a sort of Moses Redivivus alongside the functionality of the exodus as a charter myth for the northern state and its cult (van der Toorn 1996: 287–315; Albertz 1994: 141–43).[2] Though subsequent northern monarchs came from different dynasties, the mythological association of the office of the king with the figure of Moses persisted throughout the life span of the northern state. Hosea's claim that it is prophets like him who bear the trans-generational mantle of Moses constitutes a rejection of the royal northern tradition that associated Moses with the office of the monarch (Leuchter 2018). Dismantling this royal claim also involved the drawing of attention to old myths of agrarian ethnogenesis, ancestry, and Yhwh's position as the people's actual (divine) ancestor/kinsman (already attested in the premonarchic Song of the Sea [Exod. 15:13]).

Though the redactors of the BT lived long after Hosea's day, they likely retained at least some awareness of the aforementioned ideas in his oracles regarding Moses, the northern state, and mythologies of political and ethnic identity. Curricular memory within scribal groups has a long duration (Carr 2011: 4–6), and the institution of new trends or methods does not obviate or obscure older ideas but provides new frameworks for preserving and engaging them. The scribal trends of the Persian period tilted overall toward antiquarianism and the connection of the ancient to the contemporary. As participants in this imperial culture of letters and memory, the redactors of the BT turned to the events and figures from Israelite antiquity for the purpose of reframing their here-and-now—something that the oracles of Hosea do repeatedly throughout the book for (primarily) monarchic-era audiences.

The brief but potent reference to Moses in Hos. 12:13 (Heb. 12:14) sets the tone for a larger work meant to direct the reader back not only to the legends surrounding Moses in hoary antiquity but to the way Moses's memory was taken up as a rhetorical point countering claims of power and royal hierarchies by prophets in the past. Because the first book in the BT invokes the typology of Mosaic prophecy, all of the subsequent prophetic books become examples of an enduring tradition of Mosaic prophecy—this, at a time when the Aaronide priests had attempted to subordinate the entire history of prophecy through ending the Pentateuch with the statement that no prophet like Moses had arisen since his death (Deut. 34:10–12). The BT argues emphatically that this was not the case, as Hosea and the other prophets in the work evidence the ongoing vitality of Moses's prophetic office even beyond the lifespan of Moses himself.

Hosea's function within the BT places it alongside not only the Pentateuch but also the earlier Deuteronomistic History as a scribal meditation on the legacy of Moses. Though the component parts of the Deuteronomistic History were reaggregated into different literary works by the end of the Persian period (Römer and Brettler 2000), Persian-period scribes retained knowledge of its earlier theological and intellectual function, the role of Moses's *torah* as the foundational covenantal concept running through its chapters, and the function of prophetic works like Hosea as prooftexts of its rhetoric and ideology. Weinfeld's classic study of the Deuteronomistic tradition included a discussion of its dependence on Hosea's oracles (Weinfeld 1972: 366–70). Weinfeld argued that the architects of the Deuteronomistic tradition were not Levites; subsequent research has indicated otherwise (Geoghegan 2006; Leuchter 2017: 155–88) and thus Deuteronomistic thought is best viewed as a repository of Levite ideas revolving around the legacy of Moses. The redactors of the BT tilt in this direction by positioning Hosea as the inaugural voice in their work, packaging Mosaic typology into the blueprint for prophetic functionality. They thereby occupy a similar position to the Levite scribes of the Deuteronomistic tradition, inheriting this Mosaic tradition in written form (Deut. 31:22–30).

10.6. The Book of Hosea, the Book of the Twelve, and the Mythic Role of Material Texts

The formation of a book of Hosea already in the late monarchic period—and its subsequent development well into the post–monarchic era—means that there was a well–established view of the collection of Hosea's oracles not only as a material text used for teaching and scribal enculturation but as an iconic text with extra–literary qualities. As James Watts (2013) has discussed, texts in Jewish antiquity were used as objects of ritual display, containing numinous power simply through occupying material space within ceremonial settings and thus conferring authority to those who possessed such texts. The Pentateuch is the outstanding example of this phenomenon, but we encounter considerable evidence of this even before the Pentateuch's emergence (c. 450 BCE). We find already in Deut. 27 the directive to write Yhwh's law as a public display through which the entire people are to cross in a ritual fashion, and Jer. 36:21–25 presupposes that the material form of a text is what carried its potential to affect history.

The late eighth century BCE was a pivotal moment in conventionalizing the material collection of prophetic oracles as iconic texts. The incursion of Assyrian imperialism into the north brought with it an emphasis on written texts as symbols of world–ordering power through the construction of monumental inscriptions. The fall of the Northern Kingdom in 721 BCE and the ensuing crises in Judah during the reign of Hezekiah created an increased need for new symbols of stability and control that material texts could provide. Especially for Judahite audiences who had witnessed the fall of the north, the book of Hosea would easily occupy such a position as the lens through which that event could be understood. If Schart (1998) is correct that the book of Hosea influenced the development of the book of Amos, then Amos becomes the first literary work to affirm this role for Hosea's oracles. Read together, Amos becomes a Judahite taking rhetorical cues from the written text of Hosea.

But the recognition of the power of iconic material texts is already evident within the book of Hosea even before we can speak of the scribal collection of the late eighth-century BCE oracles attributed to him. Hosea 6:5 refers to the prominence of Neo-Assyrian display inscriptions in the northern landscape and, more significantly, formulates an Israelite response to or repudiation of these monumental texts. Following a proposal by Shalom Spiegel (1934: 136–39), the MT of Hos. 6:5 should be reconstructed as such:

> Upon rock (*'al keph*) have I hewn (*hatzavti*) [them],
> Through prophets (*be-nebi'im*) I communicated (*higgadetim*) [them]
> As words of my mouth (*b'imrei pi*) my statutes (*mišpatai*)
> Went forth as the light (*ke'or yotzei*)

In this reconstruction, Yhwh speaks through writing, and it is prophets who convey this speech through their written oracles. A statement such as this does not decommission the dimensions of oral performance that had long characterized prophetic phenomena in ancient Israel and Judah, but it introduces the idea that prophetic words revealed by Yhwh retain their power when committed to a material, textual form. This, the verse suggests, is the form of Israelite divine revelation that could stand against the cultural impressions left by Neo-Assyrian inscriptions, creating associations with written prophecy, law, scribal prestige, and political/spatial power and authority (Leuchter 2021).

The emphasis on material texts in conversation with (or as a challenge to) imperial parallels also characterized the very creation of the BT. Throughout the Persian period, the materiality of texts had served as physical icons of royal power, symbolizing and even grounding the cosmic order within the geographic spaces and administrative structures of the empire. Chief among these was the famous Behistun Inscription containing the narrative of the founding of the Achaemenid dynasty under Darius I (521 BCE). Subsequent royal inscriptions served similar purposes as material icons of imperial power, and there is evidence that Jewish scribes in Jerusalem were well versed in the particulars of these public literary monuments (Whitters 2017; Strawn 2008; Mitchell 2014). But iconic texts in the Persian period were not restricted to royal inscriptions housed or displayed in administrative edifices. The reproduction and compilation of pre-Persian Akkadian mantic texts (such as Babylonian and Assyrian prophetic oracles) became hallmarks of scribal training that situated scribes within the ranks of the cultural and imperial elites (van der Toorn 2007: 98–99).

The formation of the Book of the Twelve aligns with these realities insofar as it too is a cataloging of prophetic texts affirming the scribal power of its authors to access and orchestrate these elite texts, but this is no mere matter of cultural mimesis or elite emulation of imperial power structures. The closing frame of the BT contains Mal. 3:16–18, which identifies the book of Malachi (or possibly a Haggai-Malachi collection) as a *sefer zikkaron*—often translated as "book of remembrance," it may also be read as a "book of notices," a parallel to Aramaic scribal works that collected texts and drew attention to specific features worthy of note within them (Mitchell 2017: 141). Such notice books were not simply curricular texts but symbols of scribal elitism, works that highlighted the power of scribes to both collect important literary works and to determine how their contents should be encountered. They were also archival in nature, modeled on the imperial archive structures where the deed and doings of the Achaemenid rulers were recorded and consulted for authoritative policy. By ending the BT with Malachi, the redactors identify it as the *sefer zikkaron* in question, but by beginning it with the book of Hosea, they project Hosea's internal repudiations and critiques onto the remainder of its contents. Such repudiations and critiques thus become the basis for Jewish authenticity in the face of competing systems of identity.

Hosea's opening critique therefore transforms the *sefer zikkaron* lemma in Mal. 3:16–18 into something else: a challenge to the very empire whose linguistic technologies it deploys. The original ethos of Hos. 6:5 as a challenge to the hegemony of Neo-Assyrian textual monuments is repurposed here to apply to the tradition of Achaemenid monumental inscriptions that had become part of common scribal enculturation throughout the empire. The equation of Persian and Assyrian imperialism was not uncommon. Ezra 4:2 and Neh. 9:32 seem to invoke Assyrian emperors in the course of narratives set decidedly in Persian contexts, and the later book of Daniel implies that all foreign imperialism, from Assyria down to Persia and beyond, contribute to the same structural edifice (ch. 2). This surely had to do with the Achaemenid penchant for embracing Neo-Assyrian aesthetics in the production of imperial reliefs (Root 1979). The application of an anti-Assyrian oracle in Hos. 6:5 to a literary project taking place in the late Persian period fits a setting where Persian convention was understood as an expression of imperial conventions begun under Assyria. The production of the BT as a *sefer zikkaron* thus pushes back against those conventions even as it abides by them, manifesting in material form precisely what Hos. 6:5 lays out in conceptual terms.

The mythic implications of this maneuver are far-reaching. Persian-period text-building was conceived as an extension of the imperial myth narrated in the Behistun Inscription, where the copying and circulation of the inscription through the mechanism of the scribal chancery (DB §70) actualized its terms and maintained both imperial and cosmic order. All imperial text production—from the ritualistic to the administrative—reinforced this concept, symbolizing the presence and power of the empire over against forces of chaos and corruption. The hypertextuality of Persian administration is explained by the view of material texts as holding decidedly cosmic functions. The materiality of the BT functions in this manner, but in a way that reaffirms Yhwh's hegemony within Jewish spaces over against the potential threats emanating from foreign horizons. Just as Persian imperial inscriptions in the wake of the Behistun Inscription presented subsequent emperors and their deeds in the likeness of Darius (Root 1979: 309–10), the BT presents the prophets within it as successors of each other following in the footsteps of Hosea and the prestate (and thus preimperial) ideas he championed. A new myth of prophecy emerges from the very materiality of this work: the scribes who created it revealed anew the written words of these prophets and the covenantal terms initiated long before even Hosea's time. The BT served as a "book of notices," putting those too trusting of the imperial status quo on notice that Yhwh's voice was embodied in these material prophetic texts that criticized past power structures.

Notes

1. Most researchers working on the formation of the Book of the Twelve, however, would date the creation of the aforementioned single scroll to a mid-to-late fourth-century BCE setting rather than van der Toorn's proposed mid-third-century setting. See the essays in Albertz et al. 2012 for an overview.

2. Much of the northern state's exodus ideology is refracted through a political allergy to Davidic kingship; see Oblath 2000; Callender 1998: 76–80.

REFERENCES

Albertz, Rainer. 1994. *A History of Israelite Religion in the Old Testament Period: From the Beginnings to the End of the Monarchy*. Louisville: Westminster John Knox.

Albertz, Rainer, et al. 2012. *Perspectives on the Formation of the Book of the Twelve*. BZAW 433. Berlin: de Gruyter.

Barrick, W. Boyd. 2002. *The King and the Cemeteries*. VTSup 88. Leiden: Brill.

Boda, Mark J. 2016. *The Book of Zechariah*. NICOT. Grand Rapids: Eerdmans.

Callender, Dexter. 1998. "Servants of God(s) and Servants of Kings in Israel and the Ancient Near East." *Semeia* 83/84: 67–83.

Carr, David M. 2011. *The Formation of the Hebrew Bible: A New Reconstruction*. Oxford: Oxford University Press.

Cook, Stephen L. 2004. *The Social Roots of Biblical Yahwism*. SBL Studies in Biblical Literature 8. Atlanta: SBL.

Cook, Stephen L. 2011. "Those Stubborn Levites: Overcoming Levitical Disenfranchisement." In Jeremy M. Hutton and Mark Leuchter, eds., *Levites and Priests in Biblical History and Tradition*. SBLAIL 9. Atlanta: SBL, 155–70.

Crouch, Carly L. 2014. *The Making of Israel: Cultural Diversity in the Southern Levant and the Formation of Ethnic Identity in Deuteronomy*. VTSup 162. Leiden: Brill.

Curtis, Byron. 2012. "The Mas´ot Triptych and the Date of Zechariah 9–14: Issues in the Latter Formation of the Book of the Twelve." In Rainer Albertz, James D. Nogalski, Jacob Wöhrle, eds., *Perspectives on the Formation of the Book of the Twelve: Methodological Foundations, Redactional Processes, and Historical Insights*. BZAW 433. Berlin: de Gruyter, 194–96.

Finkelstein, Israel, and Neal Asher Silberman. 2006. "Temple and Dynasty: Hezekiah, the Remaking of Judah and the Rise of the Pan-Israelite Ideology." *JSOT* 30.3: 259–85.

Geoghegan, Jeffrey. 2006. *The Time, Place and Purpose of the Deuteronomistic History: The Evidence of "Until This Day."* BJS 347. Providence: Brown University.

Halpern, Baruch. 1991. "Jerusalem and the Lineages in the Seventh Century B.C.E.: Kinship and the Rise of Individual Moral Liability." In Baruch Halpern and Deborah W. Hobson, eds., *Law and Ideology in Monarchic Israel*. JSOTSup 124. Sheffield: JSOT Press, 11–107.

Jeremias, Jorg. 1994. "The Hosea Tradition and the Book of Jeremiah." *OTE* 7: 7–20.

Jeremias, Jorg. 2020. "Hosea in the Book of the Twelve." In Lena-Sofia Tiemeyer and Jakob Wöhrle, eds., *The Book of the Twelve: Composition, Redaction, and Reception*. VTSup 184. Leiden: Brill, 111–23.

Leuchter, Mark. 2014. "Another Look at the Hosea/Malachi Framework in the Twelve." *VT* 64: 249–65.

Leuchter, Mark. 2017. *The Levites and the Boundaries of Israelite Identity*. Oxford: Oxford University Press.

Leuchter, Mark. 2018. "The Royal Background of Deut 18,15–18." *ZAW* 130: 364–83.

Leuchter, Mark. 2021. "Hosea 6:5 and the Decalogue." *VT* 71: 76–88.

Leuchter, Mark. 2022. "The Name 'Berechiah' in Sach 1." *ZAW* 134: 55–67.

Levin, Adina. 2009. "Hosea and North Israelite Tradition." PhD dissertation, University of Toronto.

Milstein, Sara J. 2016. *Tracking the Master Scribe: Revision through Introduction in Biblical and Mesopotamian Literature.* Oxford: Oxford University Press.

Mitchell, Christine R. 2014. "A Note on the Creation Formula in Zechariah 12:1–8, Isaiah 42:5–6, and Old Persian Inscriptions." *JBL* 133: 305–8.

Mitchell, Christine R. 2017. "Berlin Papyrus P. 13447 and the Library of the Yehudite Colony at Elephantine." *JNES* 76: 139–47.

Mroczek, Eva. 2016. *The Literary Imagination in Jewish Antiquity.* Oxford: Oxford University Press.

Nogalski, James D. 1993. *Literary Precursors to the Book of the Twelve.* BZAW 217. Berlin: de Gruyter.

Nogalski, James D. 2009. "One Book of Twelve Books? The Nature of the Redaction Work and Implications of the Cultic Source Material in the Book of the Twelve." In Thomas C. Römer, ed., *Two Sides of a Coin: Juxtaposing Views on Interpreting the Book of the Twelve/the Twelve Prophetic Books.* Piscataway, NJ: Gorgias, 11–46.

Oblath, Michael. 2000. "Of Prophets and Kings: Whence the Exodus?" *JSOT* 87: 23–42.

Perdue, Leo G. 2007. "Baruch among the Sages." In John Goldingay, ed., *Uprooting and Planting: Essays on Jeremiah for Leslie Allen.* LHBOTS 459. New York: T&T Clark, 260–90.

Rainey, Brian. 2021. "Ethics and Ethnicity in the Deuteronomistic History." In Carly L. Crouch, ed., *The Cambridge Companion to the Hebrew Bible and Ethics.* Cambridge: Cambridge University Press, 147–62.

Richele, Matthieu. 2016. "Elusive Scrolls: Could Any Hebrew Literature Have Been Written Prior to the Eighth Century B.C.E.?" *VT* 66: 556–94.

Romer, Thomas C., and Marc Brettler. 2000. "Deuteronomy 34 and the Case for a Persian Hexateuch." *JBL* 119: 401–19.

Rom-Shiloni, Dalit. 2014. "'How can you say, "I am not defiled . . ."?' (Jeremiah 2:20–25): Allusions to Priestly Legal Traditions in the Poetry of Jeremiah." *JBL* 133: 757–75.

Root, Margaret Cool. 1979. *The King and Kingship in Achaemenid Art: Essays on the Creation of an Iconography of Empire.* Acta Iranica 19. Leiden: Brill.

Schaper, Joachim. 2005. "Exilic and Post-Exilic Prophecy and the Orality/Literacy Problem." *VT* 55: 324–42.

Schart, Aaron. 1998. *Die Entstehung des Zwölfprophetenbuchs: Neubearbeitungen von Amos im Rahmen schriftenübergreifender Redaktionsprozesse.* BZAW 260. Berlin: de Gruyter.

Schniedewind, William M. 1995. *Word of God in Transition: From Prophet to Exegete in the Second Temple Period.* JSOTSup 197. Sheffield: Sheffield Academic Press.

Spiegel, Shalom. 1934. "A Prophetic Attestation of the Decalogue: Hosea 6:5 with Some Observations on Psalm 15 and 24." *HTR* 27: 105–44.

Strawn, Brent. 2008. "A World Under Control: Isaiah 60 and the Apadana Reliefs from Persepolis." In Jon L. Berquist, ed., *Approaching Yehud: New Approaches to the Study of the Persian Period.* Leiden: Brill, 85–116.

Tiemeyer, Lena-Sofia. 2018. *Zechariah's Vision Report and Its Earliest Interpreters: A Redaction-Critical Study of Zechariah 1–8.* LHBOTS 626. London: T&T Clark.

Van der Toorn, Karel. 1996. *Family Religion in Babylonia, Syria and Israel.* Leiden: Brill.

Van der Toorn, Karel. 2007. *Scribal Culture and the Making of the Hebrew Bible.* Cambridge, MA: Harvard University Press.

Van Leeuwen, Raymond. 1993. "Scribal Wisdom and Theodicy in the Book of the Twelve." In Leo G. Perdue, Bernard Brandon Scott, William Johnston Wiseman, eds., *In Search of Wisdom: Essays in Memory of John G. Gammie.* Louisville: Westminster John Knox, 34–48.

Vayntrub, Jacqueline. 2019. "Before Authorship: Solomon and Prov. 1:1." *BibInt* 26: 182–206.

Yee, Gale A. 2001. "She Is Not My Wife and I Am Not Her Husband: A Materialist Analysis of Hosea 1–2." *BibInt* 9: 345–83.

Watts, James W. 2013. "Scripturalization and the Aaronide Dynasties." *Journal of Hebrew Scriptures* 13.6: 1–15.

Weinfeld, Moshe. 1972. *Deuteronomy and the Deuteronomic School*. Oxford: Clarendon.

Whitters, Mark. 2017. "The Persianized Liturgy of Nehemiah 8:1–8." *JBL* 136: 63–84.

Wöhrle, Jackob. 2006. *Die frühen Sammlungen des Zwölfprophetenbuches: Entstehung und Komposition*. BZAW 360. Berlin: de Gruyter.

Wolff, Hans Walter. 1956. "Hoseas geisteige Heimat." *TLZ* 81: 83–94.

PART II

KEY TEXTS
Established and Emerging Perspectives

CHAPTER 11

HOSEA 1–3, THE MARRIAGE METAPHOR, AND THE TIES THAT BIND

AMY KALMANOFSKY

VERY rarely in biblical scholarship do critical ideas take root and become accepted "fact" for generations of scholars. Perhaps the best example is the acceptance of the documentary hypothesis by biblical scholars who, since its introduction in the nineteenth century, perceive the Pentateuch to be a composite and redacted work, although they debate the identification and dates of its original texts. For feminist biblical scholars, the identification and interpretation of the marriage metaphor in the prophetic texts of the Hebrew Bible is a similarly rooted idea. Although earlier readers of the Bible recognized the metaphor, twentieth-century feminist scholars offered a perspective on God's marriage to Israel that has become, if not universally accepted, certainly impossible to ignore.

Disparate prophetic texts that detail God's courtship of and marriage to Israel comprise the marriage metaphor.[1] When analyzing the marriage metaphor, scholars often weave together the unique details each prophet provides into a coherent narrative that chronicles the stages and nature of Israel's relationship with God. In the first stage, God falls in love with and marries Israel. These are the blissful "days of her youth" (ימי נעוריה Hos. 2:17 [Eng. 2:15]), when Israel expressed gratitude to God, her husband, and manifested a "youthful love" (חסד נעוריך Jer. 2:2) of God. In the next most-detailed stage of the metaphor, the marriage disintegrates after Israel commits adultery and God responds violently. In this stage, Israel's crimes and punishments are extensively set forth. Once Israel has been punished for her misdeeds, the final stage describes the reconciliation of God and Israel and God's recommitment to their marriage.

The metaphor's focus on Israel's sexual improprieties and the disintegration of the marriage suggests that the prophets employed the metaphor to account for, or to prevent, a rupture in God and Israel's relationship that is manifest in ancient Israel's social, religious, or political reality. Precisely how the rupture is manifest in ancient Israel's reality is not made explicit by the metaphor or the prophet who employs it. Within the realm of the metaphor, Israel's crimes are clear. Israel abandons God to pursue delusion (Jer. 2:5) and lovers who she mistakenly thinks will provide her with grain, wine, and oil (Hos. 2:10 [Eng. 2:8]; Ezek. 16:18–19). Equally clear in the metaphorical realm is that Israel's crimes bring brutal punishment, as Ezek. 23:9–10 illustrates:

> Therefore, I delivered her into the hands of her lovers, into the hands of the Assyrians whom she lusted after. They uncovered her nakedness and took her sons and daughters. They slew her with the sword and she became a legend among women because of the punishment done to her.[2]

Feminist biblical scholars have addressed the salaciousness[3] and violence of the marriage metaphor, as well as its gendered assumptions, thereby transforming the way critical and lay readers engage with the marriage metaphor. Among the first feminist Bible scholars to study the metaphor, Renita J. Weems (1995: 105–6) notes how the metaphor's gendered assumptions reflect, substantiate, and perpetuate hierarchical social assumptions and violent behaviors:

> For ancient audiences, the metaphor connoted power and authority, and its promises of reconciliation and grace were secondary themes. It ties love and intimacy to aggression, power, domination, and authority; and it makes women's bodies and sexuality the object of male abuse and control.

For Linda Day (2000), the promises of reconciliation and grace are not secondary themes in the metaphor, as they are for Weems, but rather are essential features of the metaphor and its violence. Day chillingly observes how the stages of God's marriage to Israel, including the reconciliatory stage, mirror the stages evident in an abusive marriage. For Day, God's love, or to be more precise, the promise of God's love, traps Israel into a vicious cycle of abuse, thereby providing a biblical paradigm for domestic violence that extends well beyond its intended ancient audience.[4] Following Day, the marriage metaphor should be viewed as a threat that intertwines love with violence. Within the parameters of the metaphor, God's love is conditional. Israel's behavior easily could trigger another cycle of violence.

Scholars such as Weems and Day pose significant challenges for all who encounter the marriage metaphor and especially for scholars who continue to work closely with it. Just as the documentary hypothesis has been almost universally accepted by biblical scholars, critical analysis of the marriage metaphor has been similarly accepted. Although there remains disagreement around the origin and intended rhetorical impact of the metaphor, as will be evident in my discussion of the metaphor in the context of Hosea, scholars now broadly accept and address the development of the metaphor across prophetic texts and recognize the difficulties the metaphor poses for contemporary readers.[5] For feminist scholars, the challenge is now two-fold. They must address two essential questions: What remains to be said about this metaphor? And, given the critique that has been offered and accepted by so many, is it possible to view the marriage metaphor as a literary device that does more than justify gendered violence and perpetuate a cycle of abuse?

I consider these questions in my analysis of the marriage metaphor in Hos. 1–3. I begin by addressing the unique and shared features of the marriage metaphor in Hosea that have captured critical attention and then suggest ways for further engagement with the metaphor that is both fruitful and essential. It remains important for biblical scholars to address the rhetorical power of metaphor, and that the marriage metaphor provides a rich opportunity to do so. There are also new ways to approach this metaphor that will provide fresh insights, particularly those related to the role the prophet plays within the metaphor and how the construction and performance of the prophet's masculinity shapes the metaphor. These insights not only deepen our understanding of the marriage metaphor but also provide ways to see the metaphor as doing more than justifying gendered violence and perpetuating a cycle of abuse. The marriage metaphor depicted in Hos. 1–3 compromises the husband as well as the wife, and offers both an opportunity for transformation that enables them to move beyond the cycle of abuse.

11.1. BEGINNING THE METAPHOR

Scholars consider the eighth-century prophet Hosea the first prophet to introduce the marriage metaphor.[6] When God first addresses Hosea, God commands the prophet in Hos. 1:2:

> Yhwh said to Hosea: Take for yourself a wife of promiscuity and children of promiscuity, for the land strays from following Yhwh.

This verse drops like a bomb into biblical literature, introducing the marriage metaphor and making its vehicle and tenor abundantly clear.[7] The prophet is to God as the prophet's wife, named Gomer daughter of Diblaim, is to Israel—both the land and its people.[8] Despite this clarity, God's first words to the prophet raise many questions. There is no scholarly consensus on what "a wife of promiscuity" means nor to whom "the children of promiscuity" refer.[9] Some suggest that God commands Hosea to marry a prostitute; others suggest that Hosea marries a sexually promiscuous woman who is not a professional prostitute.[10] The children of promiscuity may refer to children born out of wedlock that are brought into the marriage or they may refer to the children yet to be born who will be fathered by the woman's lovers.

The confusion that opens Hosea continues throughout the book, frustrating its commentators. As Yvonne Sherwood (1996: 11) observes, there "is only one consensus on the book of Hosea . . . that this is a disturbing, fragmented, outrageous and notoriously problematic text." The marriage metaphor emerges from the first three chapters of the book relatively whole, but there remain textual questions that vex scholars, especially concerning the poetic and narrative cohesion of chs. 1–3. Hosea 2:1–3 describes a redeemed Israel and appears out of place amid the oracles of doom that surround it.[11] Hosea 3 seems repetitive. In this passage, the prophet is commanded again to marry a woman, only this time the woman is referred to as an adulteress (מנאפת), prompting scholars to question if she is the same woman referred to in ch. 1 (see Routledge 2018: 29). In this essay, I am not interested in addressing these textual issues. Instead, I address the broad contours of the metaphor presented in Hos. 1–3, focusing my attention on chs. 1–2, in which the stages of the marriage metaphor are manifest fully.

The crime, punishment, and reconciliation stages of the marriage metaphor are developed in Hos. 1–2, as they are in the other major marriage metaphor texts found in Jeremiah and Ezekiel. God accuses Gomer-Israel of pursuing lovers who she thinks provide her with basic provisions and luxuries (Hos. 2:7 [Eng. 2:5]). Along with ingratitude and infidelity, Gomer-Israel is also guilty of idolatry, as Hos. 2:10 [Eng. 2:8] conveys:

> She did not know that I gave to her grain, wine and oil. I increased her silver and gold which she used for Baal.[12]

In response to these misdeeds, God threatens to punish Gomer-Israel by stripping her naked, transforming her into a parched desert, and killing her with thirst (Hos. 2:5 [Eng. 2:3]).[13] Once the punishment is administered and God's anger is spent, God entices Israel into the wilderness and recommits to her with a new covenant, promising to marry her in righteousness, justice, love, and mercy forever (Hos. 2:16–22 [Eng. 2:14–20]).

Missing from Hosea's depiction of the marriage metaphor is the initial courtship between God and Israel or between Hosea and Gomer.[14] Hosea only hints at the courtship by describing "the days of her youth" [ימי נעוריה] in 2:17 (Eng. 2:15), which suggests an initial, tender, and loving period that existed between God and Israel and, by extension, between Hosea and Gomer. Despite this hint of a honeymoon period, the feature of the marriage metaphor that is most unique to Hosea is God's initial command that the prophet marry a woman with a history.[15] Identifying her as a promiscuous woman, whether this indicates a tendency toward or a history of promiscuity, God commands Hosea to marry a marked woman. In Hosea's depiction of the marriage metaphor, Gomer-Israel is not like the devoted, loving, youthful, and sanctified bride of Jer. 2:2. Nor is she like the abandoned and helpless infant that God cares for and falls in love with in Ezek. 16:1–13. Instead, Gomer is anything but innocent. She is, as Joshua Moon (2015: 341) observes, either "one who *will be* unfaithful to Hosea, or some form of retrospective is employed, re-framing the command after she *has been* unfaithful."[16] Either way, Gomer-Israel is destined to disappoint her husband.[17]

Hosea's marriage to Gomer introduces the marriage metaphor and grounds it within the prophet's life. Although the marital status of other biblical prophets does intersect with their prophecy, no other prophet enacts God's marriage to Israel as Hosea does.[18] The intersection of the prophet's life with the birth of the metaphor raises questions about the metaphor's origin. Although some scholars suggest that the metaphor reflects Hosea's actual marriage and personal history,[19] most posit that the prophet constructs the metaphor in response to an external social or religious reality.[20] When viewed as a constructed response, and not as reflecting a personal reality, scholars then must consider the form the metaphor takes and its intended impact.

Feminist biblical scholars Alice A. Keefe and Gale A. Yee understand the marriage metaphor in Hosea to be primarily a response to social and political realities of eighth-century Israel.[21] Keefe (2001: 12) asserts that Hosea's metaphor grows out of an "atmosphere of crisis in eighth-century Israel concerning matters of community identity, socioeconomic practice, sacral meaning and corporate survival" which "was precipitated by the erosion of indigenous structures of community life under the pressure of a rising market-based economy revolving around interregional trade, land consolidation and cash cropping." According to Keefe, the crisis develops from the "transition from a subsistence agrarian economy to a trade-based market economy," which "typically results in increasing wealth for a shrinking number of landowners, and an increasing poverty for the dispossessed peasantry" (p. 28). Yee (2003: 83) also considers the eighth century to be a period of social upheaval in which Israel transitions from a "native-tributary mode of production" to a "foreign-tributary mode of production." In order to pay its tribute to then ruling Assyria, Israel increased its production of the "highly exportable and lucrative cash crops" of oil, wine, and grain, placing an enormous burden on the peasant class and creating a rift between the peasants and the elite (p. 84).[22]

Both Keefe and Yee understand the marriage metaphor to be situated within ancient Israel's gendered social and religious norms and directed to a primarily male audience. For Keefe (2001: 199), Hosea crafts a metaphor directed toward "a class of powerful men aligned with the interests of the monarchical state, whose mercantile dealings threatened to precipitate the dissolution of a traditional way of life in Israel, and whose 'deadly games' of power politics would in time bring the nation to total destruction." Similarly, Yee (2003: 98) observes how Hosea "aims his accusations primarily at a male audience," and how the marriage metaphor "effectively *feminizes this male ruling hierarchy* by depicting its members collectively in the graphic image of a promiscuous wife." For Keefe and Yee, the marriage metaphor is primarily a powerful rhetorical tool that reflects a patriarchal society with an embedded gender hierarchy that privileges men and uses female imagery to condemn and shame elite men.

In spite of the example of these two scholars, the fact that the marriage metaphor relies on patriarchal assumptions, depicts violence, and, even worse, may perpetuate these assumptions and their violence, makes it difficult for many feminist biblical scholars to continue to engage with, let alone find positive meaning in, the metaphor. One potentially positive feature of the metaphor noted by scholars is the intimacy between God and Israel it communicates. For example, Hos. 2:16 (Eng. 2:14) describes how God will entice Israel into the wilderness and speak tenderly toward her, after which, as Hos. 2:18 (Eng. 2:16) relates, Israel will no longer refer to God as "my master [בעלי]," but rather will use the seemingly more loving address of "my husband [אישי].[23]" Even the passages that convey God's anger toward Israel indicate God's love for Israel and, like the passages of reconciliation, communicate an intimacy, albeit a violent one. These passages reveal how God cares enough about Israel to be hurt by and angry with Israel.[24] Recognizing the unique intimacy inherent in the marriage metaphor, Weems (1989: 99) observes that the metaphor "enables the reader to recognize the more passionate and compassionate side of YHWH" and suggests that Hosea employed this metaphor to advocate "for a relationship between YHWH and people built not simply on absolute obedience and loyalty, but intimacy and (mutual) love."

The God of the marriage metaphor is passionate, vulnerable, and ultimately merciful. Arguably, the effectiveness of the metaphor can be attributed to how decisively it condemns the wife/Israel and communicates beyond a doubt that God is justifiably angry, and that punishment is warranted.[25] Adultery is a capital offense in biblical law (Lev. 20:10; Deut. 22:25–27). Therefore, it is an act of compassion for God not to kill Israel, let alone to reconcile with her.[26] For feminist biblical scholars, this compassion is a mixed bag. God may be compassionate, but God also has the power to be compassionate (see Weems 1995: 72). Similarly, recognizing God's ultimate power as conveyed by the metaphor, Yee (2003: 107) asserts that Hosea employs the marriage metaphor to emphasize how the "very existence and continuance of the Israelite nation is dependent solely on YHWH." Readers may choose to emphasize God's compassion over God's abuse, but both are evident in the marriage metaphor and arguably are codependent in the metaphor's context (Day 2000: 224–27). The measure of God's compassion toward Israel must be viewed in relation to the measure of God's violence toward Israel.

11.2. MOVING FORWARD WITH THE METAPHOR

Undoubtedly, feminist biblical scholarship has illuminated the marriage metaphor and offered an insightful critique that is difficult to encounter and to counter. It is difficult for scholars to continue to engage with the violence depicted by the metaphor and to offer new ways to interpret it. Despite these difficulties, Rhiannon Graybill (2021: 2) urges scholars to continue to work with them, arguing "that the frameworks we use to talk about sexual violence in the Bible are exhausted, dated, and even unfeminist" and that we need new models for reading and theorizing about them. Graybill encourages interpreters of biblical texts that depict sexual violence to resist "paranoid readings" that "demand strong theories and eschew ambiguities of all sorts" (23), instead advocating for "unhappy" readings that do not fetishize the voice of the female victim in these texts and that are not focused on saving women (145). These readings do not inject fixed meaning into a text nor do they demand resolution (151). Most importantly, unhappy readings are not sympathetic readings that speak on behalf of or in place of the victims of the violence (121).

The feminist critique of the marriage metaphor could be an example of a paranoid reading of texts depicting sexual violence. The critique certainly offers a strong theory of how to understand these texts that is sympathetic to the female victim and that may be more concerned with identifying and curtailing a pattern of gendered violence than it is in explicating an ancient text. In other words, feminist biblical scholars who analyze the marriage metaphor, like Weems and Day, indeed may be trying to save women.[27] I have been deeply informed by these scholars and convinced by their critique, but I feel the weight of Graybill's challenge to find new ways of reading and understanding the marriage metaphor that could illuminate new dimensions of it, as well as of the feminist critique.[28] I contend that there is value in continuing to work with the marriage metaphor texts in general, and that there is more to be said about each one of them. In the context of this essay, my focus remains on Hos. 1–3.

The marriage metaphor is among the clearest, most developed examples of biblical metaphor. Because it appears in different prophetic texts with different features, it provides scholars with an opportunity to discuss the development of a literary trope within different social, political, and personal contexts. The textual and contextual insights gained from considering the unique and shared features of each of the marriage metaphor texts are tremendous. Hosea 1–3 provides a window into the political, social, and religious realities of eighth-century Israel and may even provide a window into the personal life of one prophet. Studying the particularities of each prophet's depiction of the metaphor will only yield more insights into their social-historical and religious realities. Yet, more important in my view, is the attention paid by scholars, particularly feminist biblical scholars, to the power of metaphor to shape thought effectively. This work remains vital to understanding the religious imagination in general, but certainly as it is expressed in the Hebrew Bible.

Weems's study of the marriage metaphor (1995: 115) insists that readers and scholars do not dismiss the marriage metaphor as "only a metaphor," but that they take seriously the power of this metaphor, like all metaphors, to influence "our thinking about what is true, real, or possible." Weems, along with other scholars, recognizes how metaphors powerfully communicate and preserve ideology. For Yee (2003: 81), the marriage metaphor "becomes an extraordinarily effective vehicle to communicate to and reinforce in the prophets' hearers the contours and demands of God's covenant with Israel." Similarly, Ehud Ben Zvi (2004: 369) notes how the texts that comprise the marriage metaphor "shape an ideological discourse marked by anxiety about the ability of the woman/Israel to keep her/its vows in the present, and therefore, both reflect an emphasis and emphasize the importance of the education/socialization of Israel."[29] He further observes how the metaphor works to continuously educate and socialize those who reread its texts and situate themselves within its imagery (p. 373).

It remains important to address the relationship between metaphor and ideology, and that the marriage metaphor offers a rich opportunity to do so by providing a window into an ancient ideology that remarkably remains relevant. Feminist biblical scholarship has provided great insights into the ideology of the marriage metaphor, but there is more work to be done on individual texts and on the metaphor at large. As figurative language, metaphors are imprecise and invite interpretation. Metaphors are not intended to be fully explicated and understood, but rather are meant to express a range of meanings that evolve over time. Sherwood is right that Hosea is a disturbing, fragmented, outrageous, and problematic text—particularly Hos. 1–3—and that is why it remains an essential text for analyzing the marriage metaphor, ripe for continuous interpretation and discovery.

One particular avenue worth exploring more is the role Hosea the prophet plays in the construction of the metaphor and how the metaphor identifies the prophet with God. As I noted, God's command that Hosea marry a promiscuous woman may be the most unique feature of the marriage metaphor as depicted in Hosea. Perhaps this command reflects the prophet's personal life. But more interesting is the degree to which the prophet identifies with God. It is remarkable to speak for God, as all prophets do. It is even more remarkable to act like God. Other prophets engage in similar sign acts, in which they physically enact their prophecy. Jeremiah smashes a pot to illustrate Israel's destruction (Jer. 19), and places a yoke around his neck to symbolize the impending conquest of Judah by Babylon (Jer. 27). Ezekiel lies on his side for days that correspond to the years of exile and eats bread baked on dung to reflect the impurities of exile (Ezek. 4). Unlike his prophetic counterparts who communicate God's message through these acts, Hosea is the only one to assume God's identity.

This conflation of the prophet with Yhwh demands more critical attention, especially the maleness of both Hosea and Yhwh in the text. Susan E. Haddox (2011) examines the relationship between metaphor and masculinity in Hosea. Like Yee and Keefe, Haddox assumes that "Hosea's intended audience was predominantly composed of elite males" (32). Given this, understanding masculinity, particularly the audience's masculinity, is essential for understanding the construction of and intended rhetorical impact of the marriage metaphor.[30] Yet understanding the portrayal of the deity's masculinity is equally as important to assessing the construction of the metaphor and its intended impact.

Haddox (2011: 67) identifies three areas of concern expressed by metaphors with female imagery in Hosea, all of which align with important components of masculinity in the ancient world: provisioning, fidelity, and reproduction. Gomer-Israel's infidelity, her children of promiscuity,[31] and her ingratitude challenge Hosea's and God's masculinity and suggest to Haddox that masculinity was a "more fragile construct than femininity," and therefore required "more vigilance and effort to maintain it" (2011: 88). Haddox concludes that the rhetoric of masculinity in Hosea "serves to manipulate the positions of YHWH and the audience in social space" by reinforcing Yhwh's position as "the most masculine being" and by subordinating the audience to YHWH (160).

The fragility Haddox perceives in the construction of masculinity in Hosea is noteworthy and worth further exploration. Amplifying the fragility in the construction of all genders is one way to counter the victim-centered, strong-theoried, paranoid reading of the marriage metaphor that has dominated feminist biblical discourse and could invite the messier unhappy readings that Graybill encourages.[32] Although perceiving God's and Hosea's gender fragility risks presenting them as victims of their promiscuous wives, an interpretation I would not be eager to endorse, it also presents them both as flawed figures. God's and Hosea's masculinity has been compromised. Perhaps they were too weak to protect their masculinity, or they did not value it enough to do so. Either way, there are grounds to critique them, and by doing so, to demonstrate the strength of their wives.

Offering this kind of critique of Hos. 1–3, Teresa J. Hornsby (1999: 116) argues that "the active metaphor in this section is one of a prosperous and independent prostitute who is doggedly pursued by an obsessive and dangerous individual who will go to any length to possess her." Hornsby describes God as "a man obsessed with possessing the strong, independent, wealthy Israel," and Gomer-Israel as "the sovereign woman who thrives through the adoration of all others" (p. 125). This interpretation refreshingly inverts the gendered power dynamic that is the bedrock of most feminist biblical interpretation of the marriage metaphor. In Hornsby's reading, "the operative metaphor in Hosea 1–3 is not one of an abusive husband chasing after his adulterous wife but one of a jealous client of a prostitute who desires to possess an autonomous, strong woman" (124).

Another way of challenging the strong theory that the marriage metaphor depicts and enforces a cycle of abuse is to take the text at face value and to acknowledge the transformation it records. Certainly there are editing seams evident in Hos. 1–3. The message of hope conveyed in Hos. 2:1–3 (Eng. 1:10–11; 2:1) is out of place and may be a later editorial addition. The prophecy of reconciliation in Hos. 2:16–25 (Eng. 2:14–23) abruptly follows the expression of God's violent threats of Israel's brutal punishment. Hosea 3 brings the prophet and his wife back to the beginning by repeating the command to marry a promiscuous woman. All this textual instability injects other kinds of instability into the reconciliation between God and Israel. Hopeful promises may not be kept. God's love may remain conditional, and the cycle of love and violence could repeat.

And yet, surrounded by imagery that suggests a moment of national and cosmic recreation,[33] God promises to betroth Israel in justice, love, and mercy *forever*. Granted this passage is aspirational, promising a reconciliation that has yet to happen, it is not presented as a conditional reconciliation. Instead, the reconciliation is meant to be eternal (לעולם).[34] Given this, it is possible, if not preferable, to understand the reconciliation between God and Israel to be a moment of transformation that will endure, encapsulated by how they will come to refer to each other. Marriage, which formalizes a relationship and marks a shift in status, provides an effective metaphorical vehicle to communicate this transformation. It certainly comes at a cost to the subordinate party, as the feminist critique has shown, but that critique should not preclude recognizing the fundamental and lasting transformation that both God and Israel ultimately undergo.

Once transformed, Israel will call God "my husband (אישי)" and God will call Israel "my people (עמי [Eng. 2:16, 23])." With these new names, each redefines themselves in relation to the other and claims the other. There will also be a new covenant, witnessed by the heavens and earth, that marks a new, as opposed to renewed, relationship between God and Israel. There may be a pattern to their relationship. As they did once before, God and Israel meet in the wilderness to formalize their relationship. But there is not, as the text presents it, a cycle to their relationship. Rather, God betroths Israel in enduring faith (באמונה), thereby promising to abide by the just, loving, and merciful terms of their new relationship.[35]

11.3. Conclusions

The book of Hosea opens with the marriage metaphor, testifying to its significance and effectiveness as a rhetorical tool that impacts its audience and that captures the nature of the relationship between God and Israel—its emotional content and hierarchical structure. The fact that the metaphor takes root in Hosea, evolves in other prophetic books, and remains a focus of contemporary scholarship indicates its staying power. The ties that bind readers to the marriage metaphor have remained strong over centuries. Feminist biblical criticism has changed the ways readers encounter and understand the texts that comprise the marriage metaphor, sensitizing readers to their violent imagery and helping readers to contextualize the imagery and understand its rhetorical impact. Feminist biblical scholars have provided such a convincing critique that it becomes difficult to engage with these problematic texts and to discover new meaning in them.

Scholars should continue to work with the marriage metaphor texts by exploring several avenues that provide new insights into the metaphor at large, as well into the specific expression of the metaphor in Hosea. There is more work to be done on the rhetorical power of metaphor to communicate and shape ideology in general and more consideration to be paid to how the construction of masculinity rhetorically and ideologically shapes the marriage metaphor in the Bible. Hosea 1–3 provides an excellent opportunity to do both, given the metaphor's full expression in this passage and the unusual intersection between the metaphor and the prophet's life. More attention should also be paid to the language of transformation within the marriage metaphor related to both God and Israel, which is evident in Hos. 1–3. Exploring these avenues will reveal dimensions of the marriage metaphor typically overlooked, or even denied, by the feminist critique that may interest, or even resonate with, a new generation of readers.

Notes

1. Gerlinde Baumann (2003: 41) writes: "Prophetic marriage imagery can be found in the following texts: Isa 1:21; 50:1; 54:1–6; 57:6–13; 62:4–5; Jer 2:1–3, 13; 4:1–31; 13:20–27; Lam 1:1–22; Ezekiel 16 and 23; Hos 2:1–23 [MT 2:4–25]; 9:1; Mic 1:6–7; Nah 3:4–7; Mal 2:10–16. In addition there are some texts that do not use the corresponding vocabulary and do not explicitly address or mention the 'woman,' but that clearly have the prophetic marriage imagery as background: for example, Isa 49:15–23; 51:17–52:2; Jeremiah 30–31; Mic 1:4; Zeph 3:14–17, and other."
2. All translations are my own.
3. Feminist biblical scholars debate whether to consider the sexually explicit passages of the marriage metaphor to be pornographic. See Setel 1985; van Dijk-Hemmes 1993. See also my distinction between pornographic and obscene nudity in Kalmanofsky 2015: 61–62.
4. Day (2000: 229) writes: "As the abused woman believes that the next time her man will not beat her if she changes her behavior to what she hopes will please him, likewise (so the myth

goes) if the Israelite people repent, that is, change their behavior, then the next time YHWH will not physically punish them, by sending them out of the land into exile in Babylon."

5. Addressing specifically the marriage metaphor in Hosea, Willem Boshoff (2002: 38) concludes: "Very much can be learnt about Hosea and how his message can be received today, by listening to the voices of female scholars. One of the most obvious lessons is that they do not speak with one voice, and that many are simply not feministic. However, those who approach the book from an ideological critical feministic angle are particularly aware of and sensitive to the contemporary communication of the book."

6. Baumann (2003: 85) observes: "There is much in favor of seeing Hosea 1–3 as the 'primal text' of the prophetic marriage imagery."

7. On tenor and vehicle, see Day 2008: 222.

8. Given the significance of names in Hosea, evident in the names of Hosea's children, scholars assume that Gomer's name is equally significant, although there is disagreement about its meaning. In his commentary, James Luther Mays (1969: 26–27) writes: "'Gomer' appears to be the short form of a theophoric name formed with the verb *gmr*; see Gemariah (Jer. 29.3). ... Diblaim is not found in the OT as a personal name, but it is not likely to be corruption of the place-name Diblathaim (Num. 33.46; Jer. 48.22) which would be unexpected in the expression 'daughter of-' ... Diblaim is more likely an intentional corruption of the personal name *Debalyām*, a theophoric which contains the name of the Canaanite deity Yam."

9. Hans Walter Wolff (1974: 13) writes: "What kind of woman is meant by 'wife of whoredom' (אשת זנונים)? It cannot simply mean a soliciting prostitute— which would have to read אשה זונה; nor is it an intensive form of זונה. As a plural abstract זנונים refers to a personal quality, not an activity." Wolff further comments: "To elucidate this abbreviated manner of speaking a second verb is required, such as '... and she will give birth to....' The 'children of whoredom' born to the 'wife of whoredom,' according to our interpretation, were not necessarily born before the marriage and by no means were they born outside of marriage" (15).

10. Robin Routledge (2018: 33) asserts: "In my view, the most likely interpretation is that Hosea married a woman (Gomer) who was not a prostitute at the time, but who may have had promiscuous tendencies, which became apparent only later in their relationship."

11. For a discussion of the rhetorical units that comprise Hos. 1–3 see Kelle 2005: 8–13.

12. In Jer. 2:20–29 God accuses Israel and Judah of pursing lovers and engaging in idolatry. Like Hos. 2:10, Ezek. 16:15–22 accuses Israel of infidelity, ingratitude, and idolatry. As Gale A. Yee (2003: 86) observes, eighth-century Israelite religion had "a strong heritage in the Canaanite religion itself" and "included the worship of several other deities in addition to YHWH." Yee labels Hosea's theological position "polemical monolatry," which "venerated one deity without denying the existence or activity of other deities, but was intolerant or critical of them."

13. Similar punishments can be found in Jer. 13:22, 26 and Ezek. 16:35–37, 39; 23:22–29. Stripping the woman is a common punishment in Hosea, Jeremiah, and Ezekiel, leading some commentators to suggest that stripping was a punishment for adultery in the ancient world. For example, commenting on Ezek. 16:39, Moshe Greenberg (1983: 287) writes: "The angry threat of Hosea 2:5 ... presumably reflects more closely what happened to such a woman: her husband (or males of the family) inflicted the punishment symbolizing the withdrawal of all her husband's goods and gifts from her." I offer a poetic understanding of stripping as a motif that communicates shame and vulnerability in Kalmanofsky 2015: 49–62.

14. See Jer. 2:1–3; Ezek. 16:8–13.

15. Joshua Moon (2015: 335–36) asserts: "Hosea's marriages stand head and shoulders above the remainder of the book as the best-known, most oft-cited and perhaps most important material of Hosea. . . . But the graphic suggestions, the uniqueness of the command, and the prominence in the book have led to a tireless scrutiny of the marriage scenes."

16. For Moon, the marriage metaphor in Hosea communicates shame and disgrace—Israel's shameful behavior and God's disgrace at being in relationship with Israel; he writes: "Yahweh commands Hosea to act in a way that would bring public shame, and so demonstrate Yahweh's status of disgrace in being bound to Israel" (2015: 342).

17. The identification of Gomer with Israel raises an essential theological question, as Ehud Ben Zvi (2004: 382) observes: "Whereas Hosea was commanded to marry Gomer, YHWH was not ordered to marry, as it were, Israel. An important ideological question hovering over texts such as Hosea 1–3 and over the self-understanding of the community of readers is why would YHWH have knowingly chosen a bride such as Israel/Gomer?"

18. In Jer. 16:2, God commands Jeremiah not to marry or have children to spare the prophet the sorrow that will befall those who do. In Ezek. 24:15–17, God commands the prophet not to mourn the death of his wife as an example to Israel who must stoically accept their fate. For a discussion about the impact of Jeremiah and Ezekiel's marital status on their prophecy, see Carvalho 2013: 237–67.

19. So Routledge 2018: 33; Mays 1969: 23.

20. For an overview on approaches to understanding the origin of the metaphor, see Anderson 2021: 1–20.

21. Although Keefe and Yee recognize a "religious" component to the metaphor, neither views the metaphor as exclusively, or essentially, critiquing the religious practices of ancient Israel. Keefe (2001: 195) writes: "Hosea's image of the woman Israel chasing after her lovers or baalim does not involve a conflict between fertility religion and orthodox Yahwism, but rather, the legitimacy of Israel's international 'liaisons,' an issue which the prophet addresses elsewhere more directly (Hos. 5.13; 7.8–9, 11; 12.1)." Similarly, Yee (2003: 96) asserts: "Hosea's polemical monolatry—his insistence on the worship of one God YHWH—marginalized women's popular religion, particularly in its devotion to Asherah. Nevertheless, condemnation of women's popular religion was not the determinative factor in the formation of his adulterous-wife metaphor."

22. Yee writes: "The tribute Israel paid to Assyria in the consecutive stages of their relations exacted a considerable price for the elite (cf. 2 Kgs 15:20), who passed the burden on to an already hard-hit peasantry. Thus the political struggles the Israelite elite faced in their own subordination to more powerful ancient Near Eastern countries affected the way they imposed an aggressive hegemony over their own countrymen and women. Hosea labels Israel's contradictory and oppressive foreign and domestic policies with a sexual trope, 'promiscuity'" (2003: 85).

23. Although not referring to God as "my master" certainly indicates that Israel no longer worships Baal and therefore is no longer guilty of apostasy, the transition from "master" to "husband" also may communicate a renewed and less hierarchical intimacy between God and Israel, as Wolff (1974: 49) comments: "The change of address from one to the other should be understood in terms of the metaphor of marriage Hosea uses. 'My husband' (אישי) is apparently an endearing expression; it addresses the husband as one who belongs to and who even enjoys a deep personal relationship with the 'wife' (אישי). On the other hand, the address 'my lord,' 'my Baal' (בעלי) emphasizes the legal position of the husband as lord and 'owner' of the wife."

24. As Jer. 2:5, 17–18 make explicit, God feels abandoned and hurt by Israel. Even though Gomer-Israel behaves true to form, she clearly abandons her first husband when pursuing her lovers, causing insult (Hos. 2:10 [Eng. 2:8]).

25. As Weems (1995: 29) writes: "The metaphor of the promiscuous wife expected its audience to share the values and attitudes of Hebrew society—the belief in a wife's exclusive sexual devotion to her husband, her failure to do so constituting shame on her part that brought dishonor upon her husband and warranted retaliation."

26. The biblical laws related to divorce found in Deut. 24:1–4 prohibit a husband from remarrying a former wife who had remarried after the divorce. The language of Hos. 2:9 (Eng. 2:7), in which Gomer-Israel expresses the desire to return to her first husband, echoes the prohibition in Deut. 24:4. According to biblical law, after having been with many lovers, Israel should not be allowed to return to her first husband.

27. Weems (1995: 115–16) concludes: "Not only does the image of the promiscuous wife have the potential to reinforce violence against women. It also has the potential to exclude whole segments of the population from hearing and responding to the biblical message.... On these grounds alone, metaphors require our constant vigilance."

28. Like Graybill, I appreciate textual and interpretive ambiguity and advocate for what I label "equivocal readings" of biblical texts that recognize textual ambiguities and interpretive biases in my forthcoming book (Kalmanofsky 2022).

29. Ben Zvi (2004: 366–67) notes how metaphors "work by creating discursive conceptual domains," and that "the husband-wife metaphor serves the rhetorical purpose of using particular but central attributes of the *ideological* image of a human marriage that was shared by the male authorship and the primary and intended male readership as building blocks for their imagining of the relationship between Israel and its deity in their present, as well as in their constructed past, and anticipated, hopeful future."

30. Haddox (2011: 32) writes: "Because the implied audience is male, examining the nature of masculinity portrayed in the text provides insight into its rhetoric."

31. Haddox (2011: 71) observes: "In Hosea, the presence of children vouches for the virility of the husband, but the possibility that they are not his threatens this element of his masculinity."

32. I address the fragility of gender construction in Kalmanofsky 2017 and 2020.

33. The new covenant made in the wilderness evokes Israel's initial covenant and suggests a national re-creation. The mention of the creatures of the land, sea, and sky and the heaven and earth evoke Gen. 1 and suggests a cosmic re-creation.

34. Wolff (1974: 52) comments: "'Forever' is legal terminology for a lifelong, final unalterable commitment."

35. Wolff (1974: 53) notes: "אמונה is given particular emphasis as the last word in the series. It summarily underlines the truly divine constancy and dependability of that intimate, living community that has been established."

References

Anderson, Bradford A. 2021. "Family Dynamics, Fertility Cults, and Feminist Critiques: The Reception of Hosea 1–3 through the Centuries." *Religions* 12: 1–20.

Baumann, Gerlinde. 2003. *Love and Violence: Marriage as Metaphor for the Relationship between YHWH and Israel in the Prophetic Books*. Collegeville: Liturgical Press.

Ben Zvi, Ehud. 2004. "Observations on the Marital Metaphor of YHWH and Israel in Its Ancient Israelite Context: General Considerations and Particular Images in Hosea 1.2." *JSOT* 28, no. 3: 363–84.

Boshoff, Willem. 2002. "The Female Imagery in the Book of Hosea: Considering the Marriage Metaphor in Hosea 1–2 by Listening to Female Voices." *OTW* 15, no. 1: 23–41.

Carvalho, Corrine L. 2013. "Sex and the Single Prophet: Marital Status and Gender in Jeremiah and Ezekiel." In Jonathan Stökl and Corrine L. Carvalho, eds., *Prophets Male and Female: Gender and Prophecy in the Hebrew Bible, the Eastern Mediterranean, and the Ancient Near East.* Atlanta: Society of Biblical Literature, 237–67.

Day, Linda. 2000. "Rhetoric and Domestic Violence in Ezekiel 16." *BibInt* 8, no. 3: 205–30.

Day, Peggy L. 2008. "Yahweh's Broken Marriages as Metaphoric Vehicle in the Hebrew Bible Prophets." In Martti Nissinen and Risto Uro, eds., *Sacred Marriages: The Divine-Human Sexual Metaphor from Sumer to Early Christianity.* State College: Penn State University Press, 219–41.

Graybill, Rhiannon. 2021. *Texts after Terror: Rape, Sexual Violence and the Hebrew Bible.* Oxford: Oxford University Press.

Greenberg, Moshe. 1983. *Ezekiel 1–20.* AB 22. Garden City: Doubleday.

Haddox, Susan E. 2011. *Metaphor and Masculinity in Hosea.* Studies in Biblical Literature 141. New York: Peter Lang.

Hornsby, Teresa J. 1999. "'Israel Has Become a Worthless Thing': Re-Reading Gomer in Hosea 1–3." *JSOT* 82: 115–28.

Kalmanofsky, Amy. 2015. "Bare Naked: A Gender Analysis of the Naked Body in Jeremiah 13." In Else K. Holt and Carolyn J. Sharp, eds. *Jeremiah Invented: Constructions and Deconstructions of Jeremiah.* London, New Delhi, New York, Sydney: Bloomsbury T&T Clark, 49–62.

Kalmanofsky, Amy. 2017. *Gender-Play in the Hebrew Bible: The Ways the Bible Challenges Its Gender Norms.* London and New York: Routledge.

Kalmanofsky, Amy. 2023. "Ezekiel and Gender." In Corrine Carvalho, ed., *The Oxford Handbook of the Book of Ezekiel.* Oxford: Oxford University Press, 402–17.

Kalmanofsky, Amy. 2022. *The Power of Equivocation: Complex Readers and Readings of the Hebrew Bible.* Minneapolis: Fortress.

Keefe, Alice A. 2001. *Woman's Body and the Social Body in Hosea.* Sheffield: Sheffield Academic.

Kelle, Brad E. 2005. *Hosea 2: Metaphor and Rhetoric in Historical Perspective.* SBLAB 20. Atlanta: Society of Biblical Literature.

Mays, James Luther. 1969. *Hosea.* OTL. Philadelphia: Westminster Press.

Moon, Joshua. 2015. "Honor and Shame in Hosea's Marriages." *JSOT* 39, no. 3: 335–51.

Routledge, Robin. 2018. "Hosea's Marriage Reconsidered." *Tyndale Bulletin* 69, no. 1: 25–42.

Setel, T. Drora. 1985. "Prophets and Pornography: Female Sexual Imagery in Hosea." In Letty M. Russell, ed. *Feminist Interpretation of the Bible.* Philadelphia: Westminster, 86–95.

Sherwood, Yvonne. 1996. *The Prostitute and the Prophet: Reading Hosea in the Late Twentieth Century.* London and New York: T&T Continuum.

van Dijk-Hemmes, Fokkelien. 1993. "The Metaphorization of Woman in Prophetic Speech: An Analysis of Ezekiel XXIII." *VT* 43: 162–70.

Weems, Renita J. 1989. "Gomer: Victim of Violence or Victim of Metaphor." *Semeia* 47: 87–104.

Weems, Renita J. 1995. *Battered Love: Marriage, Sex, and Violence in the Hebrew Prophets.* Minneapolis: Fortress.

Wolff, Hans Walter. 1974. *Hosea.* Trans. Gary Stansell. Philadelphia: Fortress.

Yee, Gale A. 2003. *Poor Banished Children of Eve: Woman as Evil in the Hebrew Bible.* Minneapolis: Fortress.

CHAPTER 12

HOSEA 5:8–6:6, ALT'S HYPOTHESIS, AND NEW POSSIBILITIES

MARVIN A. SWEENEY

12.1. INTRODUCTION

ALBRECHT Alt's seminal paper, "Hosea 5,8–6,6: Ein Krieg und seine Folgen in prophetischer Beleuchtung" (English translation, "Hosea 5:8–6:6: A War and Its Consequences in Prophetic Elucidation"), originally published in 1919, stands as one of the foundational studies of modern historical scholarship on the book of Hosea. Alt argues that Hos. 5:8–6:6 portrays a Judean attack against northern Israel that accompanies the Assyrian assault against Israel called for by King Ahaz ben Jotham of Judah in the aftermath of the Syro-Ephraimitic attack against Jerusalem and Judah in 733 BCE. Alt characterizes the Judean attack as a "land grab" in which Judah attempted to annex Benjaminite and Ephraimite land in retaliation for the 734 BCE attempt by the Syro-Ephraimitic coalition, led by King Pekah of Israel and King Rezin of Aram, to remove Ahaz from the Davidic throne, replace him with a figure named ben Tabeel, and thereby bring Judah into the anti-Assyrian coalition.

Due to Assyria's intervention and Judah's own assault against Benjamin and southern Ephraim, the Syro-Ephraimitic coalition collapsed. The Assyrians destroyed Damascus and stripped northern Israel of its holdings in the Transjordan, the Galilee, and the coastal plain, leaving the north in possession only of its territory in the hill country of Ephraim and Manasseh, now largely identified with the northern portions of the West Bank. Because both King Ahaz of Judah and Pekah's successor, King Hoshea of Israel, turned to Assyria, Hosea condemned both northern Israel and southern Judah for infidelity to Yhwh in that they would have turned to foreign gods of the nations in the context of their alliances with Assyria.

Most historical interpreters of Hosea (e.g., Mays, Wolff, Andersen and Freedman, Macintosh, Davies, Dearman, and Gruber) largely follow Alt's hypothesis in their own work.[1] But there are several major problems in Alt's interpretation, most notably the absence of any documented evidence concerning a Judean attack against Benjamin and southern Ephraim during the Syro-Ephraimitic War and the fact that the book of Hosea raises sustained objections against the alliance between Israel and Assyria initiated by King Jehu of Israel, the founder of the ruling House of Jehu, that continued throughout the reigns of his descendants on the throne. Indeed, Pekah's alliance with Aram represented an attempt to withdraw from alliance with Assyria in order to return to a state of confrontation with Assyria, much like the policy of the House of Omri when it was previously allied with Aram in the late ninth century BCE. The Assyrian invasion of 734 and afterward destroyed Aram and crushed Israelite resistance. Hosea himself was apparently forced to flee to Judah for safety in the aftermath of the war, presumably because he had become persona non grata in northern Israel.

This essay, therefore, reexamines Alt's hypothesis in an attempt to address the problems here named and offer a revised understanding of Hosea's condemnation of Israel and Judah. It begins with a close examination of Alt's treatment of Hos. 5:8–6:6; it reexamines Hosea's condemnation of Israel's and Judah's alliance with Assyria (and Egypt); and it constructs a revised model for understanding Hos. 5:8–6:6 and Hosea's views concerning King Pekah of Israel and his alliance with King Rezin of Aram. I conclude that Alt's hypothesis does not fully account for the evidence presented in the book and in ancient Assyrian records. Hosea supported Pekah's attempt to withdraw Israel from its alliance with Assyria and to reestablish relations with Aram. But with the failure of the Syro-Ephraimitic alliance, northern Israel was forced to submit to Assyria under a new king, and Judah was forced to accept increased tribute because Assyria saved Ahaz, Jerusalem, and Judah from the Syro-Ephraimitic threat. In the end, Hosea fled northern Israel to take refuge in southern Judah, where he would have continued his efforts to call for opposition against alliance with the Assyrian empire.

12.2. The Alt Hypothesis

Alt published his study of Hos. 5:8–6:6 in 1919 at a time when biblical scholars were accustomed to studying texts, particularly prophetic compositions, as relatively short and self-contained texts that arose as written renditions of originally oracular speeches. Consequently, scholars of the time did not always give full attention to the literary contexts in which the texts now appear, particularly because they judged so much of the prophetic literature to be the product of later redactional work that often differed in viewpoint from the so-called authentic words of the prophets.

Alt's analysis begins with Hos. 5:8–9, which in his opinion constitutes a self-standing unit. He observes the calls to sound the shofar and trumpets in Gibeah, Ramah, and Beth Aven, which he identifies as Beth El. The purpose of this act is to sound the alarm in Benjamin and Ephraim among the tribes of Israel of an attack that comes from the south, Judah, and proceeds north as indicated by the location of the three sites named in the text. Alt identifies Gibeah with Tell el-Ful, which is located about three miles north of Jerusalem (Arnold 1992a). Ramah, identified with the site of er-Ram, is located about five miles north of Jerusalem (Arnold 1992b). And Beth Aven (Beth El), identified with the modern village of Beitin, is located some sixteen kilometers or ten miles north of Jerusalem (Killebrew 2011). Altogether, the sites as noted by Alt point to the route that an invader from Jerusalem and Judah would take to advance north into the tribal territory of Benjamin and the southern region of Ephraim. On this basis, Alt argues that Hos. 5:8–9 presupposes a Judean attack against northern Israel during the Syro-Ephraimitic War of 734–732 BCE, when northern Israel and Aram allied together to form an anti-Assyrian coalition (Alt 1919: 164–70). Although this coalition attracted a number of allies in western Asia, southern Judah refused to join the coalition, which prompted Israel and Aram to attack Judah with the goal of removing the Davidic monarch, Ahaz ben Jotham, from the throne and replacing him with a man known only as ben Tabeel, as indicated in Isa. 7:1–9 and 2 Kgs. 16. Ben Tabeel is apparently from the ancestors of the Tobiad clan in the Transjordan, which was then ruled by Israel, although the Arameans had strong influence there. Such a shift in the Judean monarchy would have brought Judah into the Syro-Ephraimic coalition. But Ahaz appealed to Tiglath-Pileser III, king of Assyria, for assistance. When the Assyrian army attacked, first Damascus and later northern Israel, in 733 BCE, Alt posits that Judah must have joined in the attack from the south in retaliation for the initial Syro-Ephraimitic invasion of Judah.

Alt then turns to Hos. 5:10, which accuses the rulers of Judah of attempting to shift the boundaries of Judah and Israel, thereby provoking the wrath of Yhwh (Alt 1919: 170–74). He speculates here that verses 8–10 constitute a single unit. His analysis supports his claim of a Judean invasion of the north, but it quickly turns to consideration of the social dimensions of the time with an argument that the Judean latifundia of the region sought to expand their holdings by means of a land grab in which Judah sought to annex Israelite territory in Benjamin and Ephraim. His argument is based especially on Isa. 5:8 and Mic. 2:2, which portray the attempts of ancient landowners in Israel and Judah to displace peasant farmers from their ancestral plots of farmland. Alt's view is hampered by the fact that he does not recognize the full dimensions of Judah's relationship with Israel and Israel's relationship with Assyria. Judah during the late ninth through late eighth centuries BCE was a vassal of northern Israel from the reign of the House of Omri and throughout the reign of the House of Jehu. Judah would therefore have paid tribute to Israel as indicated by the economic problems in Judah that motivate much of the critique of Israel by the Judean prophet, Amos (esp. Amos 7–9; see Sweeney 2000: 1:189–276). But northern Israel was a vassal of Assyria, beginning in the reign of Jehu and continuing throughout the reign of the House of Jehu (see below). If Israel did not pay its tribute to Assyria, it would suffer attack from Assyria. Likewise, if Judah did not pay its tribute to Israel, Israel would not be able to pay its tribute to Assyria and would therefore attack Judah to ensure payment of the required amount.

176   MARVIN A. SWEENEY

Alt's analysis of Hos. 5:11 begins with his assertion that it constitutes a self-standing speech, but this speech turns to the consequences for Israel of the Syro-Ephraimitic War (Alt 1919: 174–77). He maintains that this verse is preoccupied with the major political problem of the time, viz., the Assyrian question. Alt argues that Israel has pursued a policy of false politics, and the result has been that the country has stunned itself and incurred guilt by running after its enemies throughout its history. He maintains that Israel has been played by the Assyrians, who had taken the northern and eastern provinces of the Galilee and the Transjordan, and enabled Judah to take territory in the south, leaving Israel as a weakened rump state that had lost control of much of its territory outside of the northern Israelite hill country. In Alt's judgment, Hosea held Judah to blame for the outcome of the war since Assyria was not of the Syro-Palestinian state system.

Alt's treatment of Hos. 5:12–14 begins with his assertion that this is another self-contained unit that is concerned with Israel's past (Alt 1919: 177–82). He argues that Israel had recognized the error of any attempt to ally with Aram as well as its historical relationship with Judah, and that both repaired to Assyria to submit to Tiglath-Pileser III and end their hostilities. He points to the past history of the relationship between Israel and Assyria in 2 Kgs. 15:19–20, which portrays the tribute to Pul, a nickname for Tiglath-Pileser III, paid by King Menahem ben Gadi of Israel, who ruled Israel prior to the Syro-Ephraimitic War. Menahem had assassinated King Shallum ben Jabesh, who in turn had assassinated King Zechariah ben Jeroboam, the last king of the House of Jehu, apparently in a bid to break the alliance with Assyria that had stood throughout the reign of the House of Jehu. By paying tribute to Tiglath-Pileser III, Menahem restored that alliance and protected his kingdom against any repercussions that the assassination of Zechariah might have caused. But Menahem's submission to Assyria set the course for the coming catastrophic outcome of the Syro-Ephraimitic War in which King Pekah ben Remaliah assassinated Menahem's son, Pekahiah, and allied with King Rezin of Aram to revolt against the Assyrian empire. The outcome, of course, was the Assyrian invasion of 733 BCE, accompanied in Alt's view by the Judean invasion of Benjamin and southern Ephraim, and the consequences suffered by both Israel and Judah as a result.

Alt's treatment of Hos. 5:8–6:6 includes an extensive textual reconstruction of proposed readings that serve his interpretation of a Judean attack against Benjamin and southern Ephraim (see Alt 1919: 164–65). For example, he proposes reading *haḥărîdû* (sic, read: *haḥărîdû*) *binyāmîn* as "setz Benjamin in Schrecken" ("be terrified Benjamin!") in place of the MT, *'aḥăreykā binyāmîn* ("[we are] behind you, Benjamin"). Macintosh (1997: 193–225) offers a detailed critique of Alt's textual emendations.

Finally, Alt's treatment of Hos. 5:15–6:6 recognizes that unlike the previous pericopes, this unit is not so clearly self-standing (Alt 1919: 182–87). Nevertheless, Alt sees in this lengthier passage signs of hope on the part of the prophet that Israel and Judah would recognize the serious error that both of them made in turning to Assyria, in the case of Israel by King Hosea's submission to Assyria and in the case of Judah by King Ahaz's submission. But there was no positive outcome as both Israel and Judah were forced to suffer the consequences of submission to the Assyrian empire. Israel would ultimately be destroyed by Assyria in 724–721 BCE due to the revolt carried out during the reign of King Hoshea, and Judah would be severely decimated in 701 BCE during the reign of King Hezekiah ben Ahaz.

12.3. PROBLEMS AND POSSIBILITIES

Although Alt's hypothesis has been foundational to the historical study of Hosea to the present time, there are problems with his hypothesis that require attention and rethinking (see esp. Macintosh 1997: 193–235; Sweeney 2000: 1:1–144; Gruber 2017: 259–303).

The first major issue is the complete lack of any evidence for Alt's proposal that Judah attacked the tribal territories of Benjamin and southern Ephraim during the Syro-Ephraimitic War. There is no record of such an attack in biblical sources, other than the inferences in the present text of Hos. 5:8–6:6, nor is there any reference to such an attack in the inscriptions of Tiglath-Pileser III of Assyria (see Tadmor 1994; Luckenbill 1989: 269–96, sec. 761–827; Pritchard 1969a: 282–84). There is documentation of the tribute paid by King Menahem ben Gadi of Israel in 2 Kgs. 15:19–20, and there is likewise documentation of the "bribe" (Heb. *šōḥad*) paid by King Ahaz ben Jotham of Judah to Tiglath-Pileser III to deliver him from the Syro-Ephraimitic invasion in 2 Kgs. 16:5–9 (cf. 2 Chr. 28:16–21). The submission of King Hoshea ben Elah of Israel to King Shalmaneser V of Assyria and his subsequent revolt against Assyria appear in 2 Kgs. 17:1–6. Tiglath-Pileser III records Ahaz as one of his tributaries under the name Yehoahaz of Judah (Akkadian, ^{m}*Ia-ú-ha-zi* ^{kur}*Ia-ú-da-a + a*) in the Summary Inscriptions of Calah 7:r.11′ (Tadmor 1994: 170–71). He states that either he or they (the Israelites) killed Pekah (Akkadian, ⸢^{m}⸣*Pa-qa-ha šarra-*⸢*šú*⸣), their king (of the Land of Bit Humria, i.e., Israel), and that he installed Hoshea (Akkadian, ⸢^{m}⸣*A-ú-si-'i*) as their new king in the Summary Inscription of Calah 4:17′. He further states that he spared Samaria because they had overthrown Pekah, their king (Akkadian, *[*^{m}*Pa-qa]-*⸢*ha*⸣ ⸢*šarra*⸣-*šú-nu*) in the Summary Inscription of Calah 13:18′ (Tadmor 1994: 140–41, 202–203; see also Luckenbill 1989: sec. 816).

Although a Judean attack against southern Israel is possible during this time, a number of additional factors mitigate against such a move on the part of Judah, particularly as reconstructed by Alt. There are problems with the identification of the site of Gibeah mentioned in Hos. 5:8. Alt had identified the city with the site of Tell el-Ful, which most interpreters still accept, but there is also considerable support for an identification with the modern village of Jeba, located about two miles to the east of Ramah/er-Ram (see Arnold 1990: 107–24; cf. Gruber 2017: 259–303). Arnold argues that there are no remains dating to the eighth century BCE at Tell el-Ful, and that the site of Jeba offers a more acceptable identification for the site of Gibeah. If Gibeah is indeed identified with Jeba, it disrupts Alt's assertion that the references to Gibeah, Ramah, and Beth-Aven offer a south-to-north route for his postulated Judean attack against southern Israel. The placement of Gibeah at Jeba presents a triangular pattern for the location of the cities with Gibeah to the east, Ramah to the west, and Beth Aven to the north between them. Such locations would suggest a very different pattern of attack that would begin with the area around Jericho in the Jordan Valley, move up the Wadis Perat and Mikhmas north of present-day Kefar Adummim to strike Gibeah/Jeba first, move west to Ramah/Ram second, and finally, move north to Beth Aven/Beth El/Beitin. Such an attack would not come from Judah. The path would more likely indicate an Assyrian move from the Transjordan toward Jericho, up the wadis to the Benjaminite heartland, and then on to Beth El in southern Ephraim, a sanctuary site where potential booty would be located. It would also allow Tiglath-Pileser III to bypass Samaria and proceed west into the coastal plain, where he could attack Gaza as he claims.

The documentation of Tiglath-Pileser III's attack against Israel in 733–732 BCE includes a siege against Damascus in the annals of Tiglath-Pileser III (Annals 23:1'–17'); a campaign in Gilead to the east of the Sea of Galilee in 2 Kgs. 15:29 and 1 Chr. 5:6, 26, with an indirect reference in the Calnah Summaries 13:17'–18'; campaigns to the Galilee and the conquest of the territory of Naphtali in 2 Kgs. 15:29, Annals 18:3'–7' and 24:3'–11', and Calnah Summaries 4:15'–17' and 9:r9; the capture of Damascus and the death of Rezin in 2 Kgs. 16:9; and the annexation of the wide land of Bit Haza'ili (i.e., Aram) in Calnah Summaries 4:5'–8' and 9:r3–4.[2] This documentation suggests that Tiglath-Pileser III's route of attack would have been through the Transjordan, insofar as he discusses his campaigns in Gilead and the upper Galilee. Since he tends to use Gilead as a name for the Transjordan, it is possible that he moved south along the Jordan River to the vicinity of Jericho, which is approximately where the Mesha Inscription locates King Mesha's concurrent northern advance into Israelite Transjordanian territory.[3] This proposal is just as hypothetical as Alt's, but it points to the uncertainty concerning Alt's projected route of invasion from Judah and his proposal that Judah engaged in a land grab against northern Israel during the Syro-Ephraimitic War. It provides a plausible model for Tiglath-Pileser III's advance into Benjamin and southern Ephraim from the Jordan Valley.

During the history of Judah's relationship with northern Israel, there was no serious attempt on the part of Judah to attack northern Israel until the reign of King Josiah ben Amon of Judah in 2 Kgs. 22:1–23:30, approximately a century following the destruction of northern Israel by Assyria in 722–721 BCE.[4] When northern Israel revolted from Judah at the outset of the reign of King Rehoboam ben Solomon, Rehoboam wanted to invade northern Israel to put down the revolt, but Shemaiah, the Man of G-d, talked him out of it (1 Kgs. 12:21–24). Rehoboam was left to set up defensive positions to protect Judah against invasion by Israel (2 Chr. 11:1–12). Following the assassination of Ahaziah ben Jehoram by Jehu, Ahaziah's Mother, Athaliah bat Omri,[5] a northern Israelite princess, assassinated most of the royal House of David, except for her grandson, Joash, who was hidden by his aunt, Jehosheba, and the high priest, Jehoiada. According to 2 Kgs. 11:1–20, Athaliah ruled Judah for six or seven years, until she was assassinated in a coup d'état orchestrated by Jehoiada, which enabled Jehoash to become king. During the reign of King Jehoash ben Jehoahaz of Israel, 2 Kgs. 14 recounts how King Amaziah ben Jehoash of Judah attempted to revolt against Israel, which apparently functioned as a suzerain over Judah at the time. But there was no attempt by Amaziah to attack Israel. Rather, Jehoash first attempted to talk Amaziah out of what would prove to be a rash move, and then defeated him in battle at Beth Shemesh along the Philistine-Judean border. Jehoash then marched against Jerusalem, broke down a portion of its wall, and left Amaziah to be assassinated at Lachish by his own people, who apparently lost confidence in his leadership. Perhaps Hezekiah ben Ahaz had designs on reestablishing Davidic rule over the territory of the former kingdom of Israel, but his 701 BCE revolt against Assyria failed miserably, and he never had the chance to carry out any such plan.

A second major problem is Alt's assertion that King Hoshea ben Elah's submission to Tiglath-Pileser III is the basis for Hosea to condemn northern Israel for its relationship with Assyria and its foreign gods. Alt is certainly aware of the earlier submission to Assyria by King Menahem ben Gadi as documented in 2 Kgs. 15:19–20, but he does not appear to be aware of earlier indications of northern Israel's submission to Assyria as documented in Assyrian sources. The first is the Black Obelisk of Shalmaneser III.[6] The Black Obelisk depicts various triumphs of Shalmaneser III, including the submission of King Jehu ben Jehoshaphat ben Nimshi to him. Jehu was an officer in the Israelite army in battle against the Arameans at Ramoth Gilead. With things going poorly in the war against Aram (i.e., King Ahab ben Omri was killed according to 1 Kgs. 22 and his son, King Jehoram (Joram) ben Ahab, was severely wounded according to 2 Kgs. 8:28–29), Jehu assassinated Joram, the Judean king Ahaziah, and the Israelite queen mother Jezebel, and established a new dynasty, the House of Jehu, that would produce five Israelite kings. But when the Arameans invaded Israel and forced its submission, Jehu apparently turned to the Assyrian king, Shalmaneser III, to gain relief from the Arameans. The Black Obelisk pictures Jehu bowing at the feet of Shalmaneser III, and the inscription indicates that he received tribute from Jehu, identified as "the son of Omri" in typical Assyrian fashion. By submitting to Assyria, Jehu would have gained some relief from Aram insofar as the threat of Assyrian invasion would have forced Aram to station more troops along its northern borders with Assyria, leaving fewer troops to harass Israel.

It is necessary to consider here the historical reality of Aram's war with Israel.[7] Some interpreters argue that the Bible's account is fictitious or based on a different historical scenario, due in part to the inscription of Shalmaneser III concerning his 853 BCE attempt to cross the Euphrates River to attack Aram (see McKenzie 1991: 88–93; 2018). He maintains that the Aramean coalition was led by Hadadezer (i.e., ben Hadad in the Bible), and that King Ahab of Israel was part of the coalition. The alliance between Israel and Aram portrayed here renders the assertion of a war between Aram and Israel impossible in the view of these scholars. But one must consider the circumstances. Shalmaneser III asserts that Ahab brought 2,000 chariots and 10,000 foot soldiers to the battle, and that Hadadezer brought 1,200 chariots, 1,200 cavalry, and 20,000 foot soldiers. Other allies brought lesser numbers of troops and equipment.[8] Shalmaneser III claims a great victory over these forces, but he is never able to advance into Aram, which indicates that he was stopped. With the victory of the Aramean coalition, including Ahab, these scholars argue that there is no cause for war between Aram and Israel. But such a view overlooks the costs of alliance with Aram and war with Assyria for Israel. Ahab reportedly brought the greatest number of chariots in the coalition. Chariots were a very powerful and technologically advanced offensive weapon in ancient Near Eastern warfare, and their loss entails great cost in expensive equipment, well-trained soldiers who man the chariots, and well-trained horses that pull the chariots. Given their numbers, Ahab's chariots would have led the charge against Shalmaneser's forces and suffered heavy casualties in doing so. Insofar as Shalmaneser III repeatedly crossed the Euphrates to attack Aram during his reign, Ahab would have to consider what his alliance cost him, and at some point must have made the decision to withdraw from his alliance with Aram. This is what provoked the Aramean attack against Ahab and Israel as narrated in the Bible. First Kings 22 portrays the battle at Ramot Gilead, where Ahab was killed in battle—and later his son, Jehoram, was wounded. Ramot Gilead is the gateway to the Israelite Transjordan, and the Arameans would have concentrated their attack at Ramot Gilead in a bid to force Ahab and Israel back into its anti-Assyrian coalition. When the war did not go well for Israel, Jehu led a coup d'état against the House of Omri, overthrew the dynasty and established himself as king. He then endured further war against Aram, which advanced through the Jezreel and into the coastal plain to force Israel's—and Judah's—submission (2 Kgs. 10:32–34; 12:18–20; 13:1–8). Israel's subjugation to Aram then prompted Jehu's turn to Shalmaneser III for assistance against Aram.

A further indication of Israel's relationship with Assyria appears in the Tell el-Rimah Inscription of the Assyrian king, Adad-Nirari III, who lists Jehu's grandson, King Jehoash ben Jehoahaz, among his tributaries (Page 1968). Jehoash would have remained a vassal of Assyria to continue to protect his country against Aramean invasion. Alt would not have known about the Tell el-Rimah inscription, as it was only published in 1968. With both Jehu and Jehoash identified as tributaries to Assyria, it appears that Israel had a longer relationship with Assyria than Alt realized.

Although Alt notes the tribute paid by Menahem ben Gadi to Tiglath-Pileser III, he does not appear to recognize the full dimensions of this payment (see Sweeney 2007). King Zechariah ben Jeroboam, the fifth monarch of the House of Jehu, was assassinated by Shallum ben Jabesh according to 2 Kgs. 15:8–12. But Shallum ruled only one month before he was assassinated by Menahem, an officer in the Israelite army, who promptly submitted to Assyria. The biblical account does not identify the reasons for these assassinations, but it appears that there was a question of foreign policy at stake, viz., should Israel ally with Assyria, as was the policy of the House of Jehu, or should Israel ally with Aram, as was the former policy of the House of Omri? It appears that Shallum assassinated Zechariah in order to shift Israel's alliance from Assyria to Aram, and that Menahem assassinated Shallum to restore Israel's relations with Assyria. Menahem ruled for the rest of his life, but his son, Pekahiah ben Menahem, was assassinated by Pekah ben Remaliah, who was accompanied by fifty men from Gilead in the Transjordan, according to 2 Kgs. 15:23–26. Pekah promptly shifted Israel's alliance from Assyria back to Aram and allied with King Rezin of Damascus to prepare for revolt against Assyria. Pekah was assassinated by Hoshea ben Elah, who submitted once again to Tiglath-Pileser III, who in turn invaded the region to restore his own rule over his revolting

12.4. A New Interpretation

I now return to Hos. 5:8–6:6 for a reexamination and interpretation (see Sweeney 2000: 1:59–73).

As noted above, there is no documented assault by Judah against the southern regions of Israel, including the tribal territory of Benjamin and the southern portion of Ephraim. The recognition that Gibeah is to identified with the site of Jeba (rather than Tell el-Ful) suggests that Hos. 5:8–6:6 understands the assault, whether real or anticipated, to have come from the Jordan Valley rather than from Judah. Assyria would be the power that launched the assault against Israel, not Judah. This scenario would be consistent with Hosea's viewpoint that Yhwh will punish Israel, and that Assyria serves as the agent of Yhwh's punishment. Judah does not serve as a divine agent, but suffers punishment itself, also at the hands of Assyria.

Additionally, the fact outlined above that Israel's relationship with Assyria began much earlier than Alt imagined (i.e., when Jehu of Israel submitted to Shalmaneser III in the mid-ninth century) may shed light on several texts in Hosea. The initial narrative in ch. 1 uses Hosea's failing marriage with Gomer as a paradigm for the troubled relationship between Yhwh and Israel (see Sweeney 2000: 1:10–40). Yhwh commands Hosea to marry Gomer, allegedly an unfaithful wife, and to have children with her, each one of which is symbolically named to represent dimensions of Jehu's pro-Assyrian foreign policy and its consequences for Israel. The first child is a son to be named Jezreel, after the site of Jehu's revolt where he assassinated King Jehoram ben Ahab of Israel, King Ahaziah ben Joram (and Athaliah bat Omri) of Judah, and Jezebel bat Ittobaal, the Gebirah (or queen mother) of the House of Omri. The second child, a daughter, is to be named Lo-Ruhamah, "Not Pitied," which signifies Yhwh's lack of mercy for Israel under the rule of the House of Jehu. The third child, a son, is to be named Lo-Ammi, "Not My People," which signifies the disruption of the relationship between Yhwh and Israel under the rule of the House of Jehu. The alliance between Israel and Assyria continued throughout the Jehu dynasty, as indicated by the submission of King Jehoash ben Jehoahaz, the grandson of Jehu, to Adad-Nirari III, King of Assyria, and the success of Jehoash in thwarting the Aramean threat against Israel, apparently with Assyrian support. This enabled his son, King Jeroboam ben Jehoash of Israel, to enjoy a peaceful and prosperous reign, devoid of threat by the Arameans. Insofar as the Assyrians would have expected Israel to serve their ambitions to extend their rule into Egypt, Israel would have been required to facilitate trade in olive oil between Assyria and Egypt, as noted in Hos. 12:1–2, and to pay a heavy tribute to Assyria to ensure continued Assyrian support.

Hosea appeals to past tradition, especially concerning Israel's hold over the Transjordan and the role played by Egypt as Israel's oppressor, through citations of an early pentateuchal tradition in ch. 12 (see Sweeney 2000: 1:117–30). Although some scholars view these references as later additions that were concerned to establish a relationship between the prophetic book of Hosea and the Pentateuch (Wöhrle 2006; 2008), the citation of the proto-pentateuchal narratives in Hos. 12 is key to Hosea's argument against alliance with Assyria. Hosea 12:3–7 (Eng. 12:2–6) illustrates Jacob's (Israel's) contentious nature by recounting the struggles between Jacob, the eponymous ancestor of northern Israel, and both his brother (Esau) and an angel of G-d, both of whom were tied to the Transjordan (Gen. 25–35). The passage also cites Jacob's vision at Beth El (Gen. 28:10–22), eventually the major sanctuary of the Northern Kingdom, which secured his relationship with Yhwh in the hill country of Ephraim. Hosea 12:8–12 (Eng. 12:7–11) recounts Ephraim's attempts to gain power through trade with Assyria and Egypt, but reminds readers that Yhwh had redeemed Israel from Egypt according to the proto-pentateuchal narrative, that Yhwh spoke to Israel through the prophets, and that the boundaries in the allegedly worthless Transjordanian territory of Gilead had been marked by heaps of stone (Gen. 31, esp. vv. 43–50). Such heaps of stone function as boundary markers, as indicated by Jacob's resolution of his boundaries with Laban, and therefore Israel's close relationship with Aram. The passage reminds readers that Jacob traveled to Aram to find a wife (Gen. 28–29), that Yhwh brought Israel up from Egyptian bondage by means of a prophet (Moses), and that Ephraim had offended Yhwh. Israel had rebelled against Moses and Yhwh in the wilderness (Exod. 16–18; 32–34; Num. 11–25). Israel of Hosea's day had ignored this past experience, allying with Assyria and Egypt rather than with Aram, from which Israel's ancestors came. These citations of Israel's proto-pentateuchal tradition serve as a basis to argue that Israel should be aligned with Aram, not with Assyria and Egypt. Hosea is opposed to the House of Jehu and its policy of submission to Assyria. He may have supported Shallum's assassination of Zechariah ben Jeroboam, and he would have certainly have supported Pekah's move to ally with Rezin of Aram in an effort to break free from its alliance with Assyria (contra Kelle 2005).

The superscription of the book of Hosea, which places the prophet in the reigns of King Jeroboam ben Joash of Israel (786–746 BCE) and Uzziah (783–742 BCE), Jotham (742–735 BCE), Ahaz (735–715 BCE), and Hezekiah (715–687/686 BCE), kings of Judah, may also bear upon Hos. 5:8–6:6 (see Sweeney 2000: 1:8–10). Interpreters have wondered why the dates of the Israelite and Judean kings do not fully overlap and why reigns of later Judean kings might be mentioned at all. The reason may lie in the failure of Pekah's attempt to revolt against Assyria and the consequences for Hosea as a supporter of Pekah's pro-Aramean policy. When the Syro-Ephraimitic coalition attacked Jerusalem in 734 BCE, Ahaz appealed to Assyria for assistance. When Tiglath-Pileser III invaded in 733–732 BCE, he destroyed Damascus and decisively defeated Israel, stripping Israel of its territories in the Transjordan, the Galilee, and the coastal plain, and replacing Pekah with Hoshea as the new King of Israel. As a supporter of Pekah's alliance and revolt, Hosea would have continued to resist Israel's alliance with Assyria, perhaps continuing to call for revolt against Assyria. But when that revolt came in 724 BCE, King Hoshea was removed from power and exiled to Assyria, and the Assyrian assault against Samaria and the kingdom of Israel at large proceeded. Hosea the prophet would not have been a welcome presence in northern Israel, and he likely fled to Judah to escape retribution, if he had not already done so earlier under Menahem or Pekahiah. Ahaz would have been dissatisfied with Assyria for imposing greater tribute on Judah for saving his life, and that dissatisfaction continued under Ahaz's son, Hezekiah, who ultimately engineered a revolt against Assyria in 705 BCE. Hosea would have found at least some degree of support in Judah, where he could have continued his condemnation of alliance with Assyria, this time on the part of Judah, for the rest of his life.

Hosea's calls for reconciliation with his allegedly wayward wife would have symbolized his called-for reconciliation by Israel with Yhwh. Such reconciliation would have entailed Israel's rejection of its foreign lovers (i.e., Assyria and Egypt), and its return to Yhwh, its husband, as represented in the marriage metaphor of Yhwh, the groom, and Israel, the wayward bride.

NOTES

1. Mays 1969: 85–98; Wolff 1974: 103–30; Andersen and Freedman 1980: 399–431; Davies 1992: 145–93; Dearman 2010: 140–55. Cf. Macintosh 1997: 193–235; Gruber 2017: 259–303, who also have reservations concerning Alt's thesis.
2. For a summary of Tiglath-Pileser III's campaign against Israel and its textual documentation, see Tadmor 1994: 279–82.
3. For discussion of the Mesha Inscription, see the studies published in Dearman 1989, esp. Dearman 1989: 155–210. For a convenient translation of the Mesha Inscription, see Pritchard 1969a: 320–21.
4. For critical discussion of texts from 1–2 Kings, see Sweeney 2007; Klein 2006, 2012.
5. Athaliah is identified as the daughter of King Omri in 2 Kgs. 8:26, but she is also identified as the daughter of Ahab in 2 Kgs. 8:16.
6. For photos, see Pritchard 1969b: 351, 355; for the inscriptions on the Black Obelisk, see Prichard 1969a: 277–80.
7. For full discussion, see Younger 2016: 564–654.
8. See Pritchard 1969a: 278–79; Sweeney 2007: 237–40; Luckenbill 1989: 1:610–11.

REFERENCES

Alt, Albrecht. 1919. "Hosea 5,8–6,6. Ein Krieg und seine Folgen in prophetischerBeleuchtung." *Neue kirchliche Zeitschrift* 30: 537–68. Republished in *Kleine Schriften zur Geschichte des Volkes Israel. Zweiter Band*. 3rd ed. München: C. H. Beck, 3rd edition, 1964, 163–87.

Andersen, Francis I., and David Noel Freedman. 1980. *Hosea*. AB 24. Garden City, NY: Doubleday.

Arnold, Patrick M. 1990. *Gibeah: The Search for a Biblical City*. JSOTSup 79. Sheffield: Sheffield Academic Press.

Arnold, Patrick M. 1992a. "Gibeah." *ABD* 2: 1007–9.

Arnold, Patrick M. 1992b. "Ramah." *ABD* 5: 613–14.

Davies, G. I. 1992. *Hosea*. NCB. London: Marshall Pickering. Grand Rapids, MI: Eerdmans.

Dearman, J. Andrew, ed. 1989. *Studies in the Mesha Inscription and Moab*. Atlanta: Scholars.

Dearman, J. Andrew. 2010. *Hosea*. NICOT. Grand Rapids, MI: Eerdmans.Gruber, Mayer I. 2017. *Hosea: A Textual Commentary*. LHBOTS 653. London and New York: T&T Clark Bloomsbury.

Kelle, Brad E. 2005. *Hosea 2: Metaphor and Rhetoric in Historical Perspective*. SBLAB 20. Atlanta: SBL Press.

Killebrew, Ann E. 2011. "Bethel (North of Jerusalem)." *EBR* 3: 967–68.

Klein, Ralph W. 2006. *1 Chronicles*. Hermeneia. Minneapolis: Fortress.

Klein, Ralph W. 2012. *2 Chronicles*. Hermeneia. Minneapolis: Fortress.

Luckenbill, David Daniel. 1989. *Ancient Records of Assyria and Babylonia. Part One*. London: History and Mysteries of Man, reprint of the original edition, Chicago: University of Chicago, 1926.

Macintosh, A. A. 1997. *Hosea*. ICC. Edinburgh: T&T Clark.

Mays, James L. 1969. *Hosea: A Commentary*. OTL. Philadelphia: Westminster.

McKenzie, Steven L. 1991. *The Trouble with Kings: The Composition of the Book of Kings in the Deuteronomistic History*. VTSup 42. Leiden: Brill.

McKenzie, Steven L. 2018. *1 Kings 16–2 Kings 16*. International Exegetical Commentary on the Old Testament. Stuttgart: Kohlhammer.

Page, Stephanie. 1968. "A Stela of Adad-Nirari III and Nergal-ereš from Tell al-Rimah." *Iraq* 30: 139–53.

Pritchard, James B. 1969a. *Ancient Near Eastern Texts Relating to the Old Testament*. Princeton: Princeton University Press.

Pritchard, James B. 1969b. *The Ancient Near East in Pictures*. Princeton: Princeton University Press.

Sweeney, Marvin A. 2000. *The Twelve Prophets*. Berit Olam. Collegeville, MN: Liturgical.

Sweeney, Marvin A. 2007. *1–2 Kings: A Commentary*. OTL. Louisville: Westminster John Knox.Tadmor, Hayim. 1994. *The Inscriptions of Tiglath Pileser III, King of Assyria*. Jerusalem: Israel Academy of Sciences and Humanities.

Wöhrle, Jakob. 2006. *Die frühen Sammlungen des Zwölfprophetenbuchs. Enstehung und Komposition*. BZAW 360. Berlin and New York: Walter de Gruyter.

Wöhrle, Jakob. 2008. *Der Abschluss des Zwölfprophetenbuches. Buchübergreifende Redaktionsprozesses in den späten Sammlungen*. BZAW 389. Berlin and New York: Walter de Gruyter.Wolff, Hans Walter. 1974. *Hosea*. Hermeneia. Philadelphia: Fortress.

Younger, K. Lawson, Jr. 2016. *A Political History of the Arameans: From Their Origins to the End of Their Polities*. SBLABS 13. Atlanta: SBL Press.

CHAPTER 13

HOSEA 7–8 AND THE CRITIQUE OF KINGS, POLITICS, AND POWER

JERRY HWANG

HOSEA 7–8 contains one of the more potent but overlooked statements of political theology in the Hebrew Bible. This passage provides a concise and integrated commentary on domestic intrigue, international diplomacy, leadership, salvation history, economics, religion, and cult. In scholarship, however, it has been common to view these spheres of Israel's life as being mutually exclusive in ancient Israel. A standard introduction to the Hebrew Bible prophetic books expresses a frequently voiced contrast between the two main prophets who ministered to the kingdom of Samaria in the eighth century BCE: "Amos inveighs against *social and economic practices* in the northern kingdom, whereas Hosea focuses on *religious and political misdeeds*" (Petersen 2002: 10, emphasis added). When compartmentalization of this sort meets the reality that most biblical scholarship originates in the modern liberal democracies of North America and western Europe, it becomes instinctive to interpret Hos. 7–8's critique of sacral kings and power politics in one's own secularized image. Anachronism results when political theologians or biblical scholars neglect Max Weber's warning that "no prophet was a champion of 'democratic' ideals . . . no prophet announced any sort of religious 'natural law,' even less a right to revolution or self-help of the masses suppressed by the mighty. Anything of the sort would undoubtedly have appeared to them as the very pinnacle of godlessness" (Weber 1952: 278).

Besides the risk of cultural revisionism, any study of Hos. 7–8 is also complicated by how historical reconstruction and literary criticism of this passage have been entwined in scholarship to an unusual degree. There is an abundance of atypical imagery in these chapters which lends an opaqueness despite their references to Israel's foundational narratives in the exodus (7:11; 8:13), revelation of the Torah (8:1), and golden calf/calves (8:5–6). This combination of strangeness and familiarity has made Hos. 7–8 fertile ground for tradition critics to excavate its prehistory as a text. In this regard, the superscription to the book (1:1) clearly places Hosea alongside the other three prophets who criticized kings of Israel and Judah in the latter eighth century BCE (cf. Isa. 1:1; Amos 1:1; Mic. 1:1) and whose prophetic books were edited together (Freedman 1987). At the same time, chs. 7–8 do not name specific persons or events that would allow the oracles to be dated precisely. The passage's references to the empires of Egypt and Assyria (7:11, 16; 8:13) are also general enough to fit the circumstances of multiple periods.

This confluence of factors suggests a threefold procedure for recovering and harnessing Hos. 7–8 as a force for political theology. First, I will draw on historical studies of the eighth century BCE to establish the factors at work in the ancient Near East which underlie Hosea's trenchant critique of power. Second, I will examine the complex literary world of Hos. 7–8, drawing attention to the unusual use of metaphor and simile. Third, I will join these historical and literary threads to trace a distinctive *theopolitics* (borrowing Martin Buber's coinage to be explored below) which bridges the vast divide between the eighth century BCE and the modern day. Hosea's combination of creativity, misdirection, and boldness in confronting toxic leaders and their enablers still demands a hearing today.

13.1. The Historical Background of Hosea 7–8

The circumstances in which Amos and Hosea prophesied to the Northern Kingdom of Samaria during the eighth century BCE are well established by a broad range of evidence (see Richter 2014). Earlier in the eighth century BCE, the kingdoms of Israel and Judah had enjoyed a time of stability during the reigns of Jeroboam II (793/792–753 BCE) in the north and Uzziah (792/791–740/739 BCE) in the south. Their long tenure as kings coincided with periods of relative peace between the two Israelite kingdoms as well as weakness in the Assyrian Empire. Jeroboam II (not to be confused with the Jeroboam described in 1 Kgs. 12, who had led the northern tribes out of Solomon's kingdom and established the golden-calf cults at Dan and Bethel) managed to recover Samaria's territory that the Arameans had taken during the ninth century BCE (2 Kgs. 14:25, 28). Additionally, the capital of the Northern Kingdom engaged in a robust trade in oil and wine. This wealth can be seen in the Samarian ostraca records of transactions involving these agricultural goods which were evidently imported from the countryside for the elite. The prophet Hosea also links the Northern Kingdom's production of "my flax, my oil, and my drink" (2:5, 8 [Heb. 2:7, 10]) with trading partners who sought these agricultural goods (12:1 [Heb. 12:2]). In addition, the olive oil mentioned in Hosea (2:5, 8, 22 [Heb. 2:7, 10, 24]) was native to Canaan but not the rest of the ancient Near East, while the opposite was true for the precious metals that Israel needed for making images (8:4; 13:2). The prophecy of Amos rounds out this picture of the Northern Kingdom by exposing how these agricultural goods were stockpiled (probably through the cult) for gratuitous consumption by the rich at the expense of the poor (e.g., Amos 2:8; 4:1; 5:11; 6:6).

Similarly in the Southern Kingdom of Judah, the strengthening of central government and participation in international trade continued along the lines started by David and Solomon (cf. 2 Sam. 24:9; 1 Kgs. 4:7, 27–28; 10:26; 2 Chr. 2:17–18). Archaeological finds show that the urban population also swelled around this time, particularly in Jerusalem, accelerating the transfer of human and financial capital from Judah's countryside to its cities (Albertz 1994: 159–60). The prophets Isaiah and Micah confronted the related problem of political, economic, and religious leaders conspiring to annex ancestral plots of land into larger plantations. In this exploitative process known as *latifundialization* (see Premnath 2003: 20–24), the consolidation of agriculture in the hands of landowners left those who worked the land as tenant farmers at best and debt slaves at worst, clinging to life on the familial plots that the Torah had assigned inviolably to Israelite clans (cf. Lev. 25:1–46).

The transition from subsistence agriculture to commodity-based agronomics heightened the vulnerability of the average Israelite in dangerous ways. The former kind of farming involved planting an assortment of crops that could tide over a family during lean years in a manner that the latter's focus on a single cash crop never would. Any lean harvest of that commodity would send farmers further into debt toward their creditors. Eighth-century prophets such as Hosea exposed how the latter controlled the land and its production to begin with, while also conspiring with other leaders in a vicious cycle that impoverished Israelite farmers even further.

13.1.1. The Synergy of Power Politics in Hosea 7–8

The interwoven nature of this crisis across politics, economics, and religion underlies the brief but pregnant references in Hos. 7–8 to the "calf/calves of Samaria" and "Baal." As a prelude to these chapters, Hos. 2 had already linked the figure of Baal with the international market in which Canaan's agricultural commodities were exchanged for precious metals and luxury goods (2:8 [Heb. 2:10]). Several of the Samarian ostraca mention transactions with Israelite individuals whose names contain "Baal," strengthening the connection between economic activity and a personal deity along the lines of Baal-Hadad, the fertility god native to Canaan who was indelibly associated with rain and agriculture (Chung 2010: 122).

Since the formal cult of Baal-Hadad the storm god had been extinguished violently in the Northern Kingdom by King Jehu a century before (cf. 2 Kgs. 10:18–28), it appears that informal veneration of "Baal(s)" continued in Hosea's time through various domestic vices such as the high places (4:13; 10:8), cultic use of sacred pillars (3:4; 10:1–2), divining rods (4:12), and calf images (8:5–6; 10:5; 13:2) (Jeremias 1994: 441–62). And since some form of "Baal" was invoked by the leaders who controlled the commodity trade that brought in precious metals (2:16; cf. v. 5 [Heb. 2:18; cf. v. 7]), it appears that agricultural offerings were collected at the Northern Kingdom's golden-calf sanctuaries for use in procuring more gold and silver on the international market. Apostasy thus had a self-perpetuating character in which the domestic industry of making images and the international trade that procured raw materials for images reinforced each other (see Hwang 2014). Already in the opening verses of Hosea, there is an unexpected combination of "a wife of whoredom," "children of whoredom," and "a land that commits great whoredom" (1:2), which reflects a certain synergy of literal immorality at cultic sites (4:13–14) and immorality with "lovers" (2:10, 12, 13 [Heb. 2:12, 14, 15]) who were Samaria's idols as well as trading partners. In myriad ways, then, harlotry with "Baal(s)" became a socioreligious cipher to join economic and political sins on the international scene with the "calf/calves of Samaria" across these same realms on the domestic scene (Perdue and Carter 2015: 184).

Not every aspect in this reconstruction of Israel's apostasy can be explicitly confirmed by the evidence available, but its plausibility finds support in the literary analysis of Hos. 7–8 that follows. A minicommentary on these chapters, as well as on literary criticism's proposals to smooth its roughness, reveals Hosea's holistic arguments against the abuse of power. The oracles of this eighth-century prophet move fluidly across topics that modern people (biblical scholars among them) would usually classify as the discrete categories of politics, economics, and religion.

13.2. LITERARY ANALYSIS AND LITERARY CRITICISM OF HOSEA 7–8

Hosea 7–8 stands at the junction of two larger sections in 5:8–7:16 and 8:1–9:9, which address both foreign and domestic aspects of political theology. Following an exposé of Israel's sins in international diplomacy (5:8–15) and failure to repent from them (6:1–11a), Hosea's oracles in these chapters start to intersperse domestic and foreign matters in a manner that becomes difficult to untangle. The passage begins with Israel rejecting Yhwh's latest offer of restoration (6:11b–7:1b), choosing instead to engage in various kinds of intrigue, both foreign (7:1c–7) and domestic (7:8–12). Even after Yhwh's pronouncement of woe and another indictment for rebellion against his ways (7:13–16), Israel remains unwilling to stop perpetuating the sin-clusters of king and cult (8:4–8a), as well as politics and religion (8:8–14).[1] In short, the usual distinction between sacred and secular realms does not readily apply in these oracles.

In scholarly discussions, however, each section within these oracles is typically viewed as an independent literary unit which is assigned its own *Sitz im Leben* ("life-setting") in Israel on the basis of vocabulary, content, or style. The influential Hosea commentary by Hans Walter Wolff is representative of such a form-critical approach, even as Wolff concedes that his usual methods falter in chs. 7–8 due to the absence of redactional markers to demarcate one saying from another. Wolff thus hints at a more integrative approach by tracing how terminology and themes recur across the adjacent literary genres within Hos. 7–8. His form-critical instincts ultimately lead him to regard the variegated content in these chapters as different reactions to the same *Sitz im Leben*, namely, the aftermath of Tiglath-Pileser III's attack against the Syro-Ephraimite coalition in 733 BCE (Wolff 1974: 110–12).

But once a single event is seen to spawn a variety of interrelated reactions in multiple life-settings (e.g., cultic, political, economic, military), the necessity of historical criticism's signature assumption—that only one idea or perspective can be attributed in a given period to a single speaker, author, or source, and even then restricted to short sayings or literary units—becomes questionable at best. Particularly for the book of Hosea, these criteria have been prominent in the tendency to regard negative and positive assessments of kingship as contradictory and thus belonging to different historical periods and/or scribal schools in ancient Israel. However, the interplay of various leadership themes in Hos. 7–8 captures the holistic political theology of the entire book.

Hosea 7 starts by confronting abuses of power in general rather than the power politics of specific rulers. The opening references to "the corruption of Ephraim" (7:1), "the evil deeds of Samaria" (7:1), and "wickedness" (7:2) contain three of the Hebrew Bible's broadest terms for sin, with the most pronounced expression of such "wickedness" (7:3) occurring through a *coup d'état* in the Israelite royal court. Hosea repeatedly describes this insurrection as a form of "heat" (7:4, 5) that is "like an oven" (7:4, 6, 7). Like the danger and secrecy of the coup itself, Hosea's metaphorical use of the Mediterranean "[bread] oven" (Heb. *tannûr*, cognate to the Central/South Asian *tan[d]oor*) is ingenious for exposing the scalding motives of the conspirators who are hiding inside.

Much debate has concerned whether the oven-metaphor in Hos. 7:3–7 is portraying a rebellion by a specific Israelite king or against him (with diverse proposals for redactions or emendations adduced in support of one view or the other) (e.g., Yee 1985: 179). In either case, the assumption is that this passage is part of Hosea's larger polemic against Israelite kingship in general or its particular form in the northern monarchy, which lacked the Davidic promises (cf. 3:5; 13:9–11). But at face value, Hos. 7:3–7 strings together several baking images to condemn the machinations of "*all of them* [who] are hot like an oven, and *they* devour their rulers" (7:7a–b). It is mainly the people who are under censure for the figurative heat of their "adultery" (7:4), as expressed also through the fiery schemes of their leaders (7:5–6).

In mutually reinforcing ways, then, the sins of "all of them" (i.e., the people) and "their rulers" (i.e., the leaders, not necessarily just kings) work together without being reducible to either immorality or politics, or to only one group of evildoers or the other (see Eidevall 1996: 109). In addition, sin's spread is mainly from the people to their leaders rather than in the opposite direction, much like Hosea's earlier rebuke of the people for polluting their leaders through various kinds of immorality (4:1–5:7) (Crüsemann 1978: 90). Hosea asserts that the flaw with Israel's leaders lies not so much with particular kings or even kingship as an institution, but the fact that "*all their kings* have fallen; *none of them* calls upon me" (7:7c–d) (Machinist 2005: 163; cf. Gelston 1974: 95). The stubborn pattern of self-reliance in both Israel's people and leaders has been the main problem with the Israelite monarchy, as well as its populist opponents, from the very beginning.

Kitchen metaphors form a bridge from domestic intrigue (7:3–7) to international intrigue (7:8–12) (Nwaoru 2004: 219). The Northern Kingdom is no longer the baker and oven who are in control (cf. 7:4, 6–7), but a contaminated dough that is first "mixed with the nations" (7:8a) and then burned on the grill as "a flatbread not turned over" (7:8b). Comically, the autonomous verbal subject has been demoted to the helpless verbal object. To highlight these themes of Ephraim's futility and unattractiveness, the passage then shifts from culinary to creational word-pictures of senile old age (7:9) and a stupid dove that flies toward its predators instead of away from them (7:11a–b). The verdict that "they call to Egypt, they go to Assyria" (7:11c–d; cf. 8:9, 13) summarizes this section about unwise alliances by warning that flirting with stronger powers will always hurt the people of Yhwh more than help them. Moreover, the fact that suzerain-vassal agreements in the ancient Near East invoked multiple deities as witnesses meant that any entanglement with empire was irreducibly political, religious, and military in nature. The real power for Israel to reckon with is not an empire, but the all-powerful God who thwarts the journeys of the fickle people in seeking lesser powers. Yhwh thus vows in an extension of the previous simile with birds: "As they go, I will cast my net over them; I will bring them down like birds of the air" (7:12a–c). The result is that their "allies" will witness the shameful demise of Israel as well (7:12d) (Kruger 1992).

Hosea 7 concludes with a woe oracle (7:13–16) that expands on the folly of Israel's self-reliance, but in less metaphorical language. Continuing the address to the entire people as "they," Yhwh laments their unwillingness to turn away from destructive paths (7:13a–c). His declaration that "I would redeem (פדה) them, but they speak lies against me" (7:13c–d) is especially poignant for Yhwh's offer to "redeem" (פדה) Israel in a new exodus from imperial bondage (cf. Deut. 7:8; 9:26). Israel's rejection of such a promise in favor of the Faustian bargain of seeking assistance from Egypt (and/or Assyria; cf. 7:11; 11:5) will backfire as exile rather than refuge "in the land of Egypt" (7:16). On this note, the "return to Egypt" motif in Hosea often strikes a typological contrast between suffering at the hands of empire (whether before the exodus or after exile) and carefree weakness in a vulnerable place which Yhwh nonetheless watches over (such as life in the land or wilderness) (Gottwald 2007: 133–36).

Hosea 8 heralds the onset of Israel's self-inflicted crisis in the form of an unnamed threat.[2] The sound of the ram's horn and the sight of an eagle's arrival in Samaria (8:1a–b) appears at first to signal the arrival of the Assyrian army. Much like Hos. 7, Israel has become its own worst enemy by antagonizing Yhwh as its true protector. The sovereign God of Israel laments that his people "have broken my covenant and transgressed my law" (8:1c–d), a reference to the Torah that came through Moses following the exodus. In response, however, Israel dares to reach further back into salvation history and claim to "know" Yhwh's self-revelation in Egypt—"My God, we of Israel know you!" (8:2; cf. Hos. 12:9; 13:4). This is a clear allusion to the "recognition formula" of Exod. 4–14 (e.g., Exod. 5:2; 6:7; 7:5; 14:4).

The final word on the exodus comes in Yhwh's retort that he does "not know" the leaders of the people: "They have set up kings, but not by me; they have appointed princes, but I did not know" (8:4a–b). Such a pointed statement echoes the "recognition formula" but turns it upside-down by joining it to Israel's later request for kings during the time of Samuel. While scholars often focus on the redactional links and relative dating between Yhwh's verdict against kings in Hosea (cf. also 13:9–11) and the Deuteronom(ist)ic passages about kingship (1 Sam. 8:11–18; e.g., Bos 2013: 48–53), of greater significance for my purposes is the holistic politics of Hos. 8:1–6: the northern kings are guilty of the economic practice of acquiring precious metals for idol-making (8:4) and the religious sin of using the Canaanite fertility symbol of a calf to replace the Creator (8:5–6), thereby reaping the military result of enemies consuming the land's produce (8:7–8a). The multifaceted political sins of Israel generate unexpected consequences in the acts of sowing and reaping.

Following this sin-cluster of king and cult (8:4–8a), the polemic of Yhwh moves to the related sin-cluster of politics and religion. The previous section's mention of "strangers" coming to "devour/swallow" Israel's grain (v. 7) becomes a larger discourse about Israel being "swallowed" (8:8a) in its suffering "among the nations as a useless vessel" (8:8b–c). Far from being an innocent victim, Israel has chosen this self-destructive path for itself. The people of Yhwh are renamed "Ephraim" ("double-fertility") in this section to enable a series of wordplays that mock their futile attempts at control: (1) "Ephraim" (אֶפְרַיִם) is the promiscuous "donkey" (פֶּרֶא) who "went up to Assyria/Asshur" (8:9a–b), and (2) "double-fertility" has sought to "multiply" (רבה) sinful altars and offerings as part of regarding the "multitude" (רֹב) of Yhwh's laws as "strange/foreign" (8:12; זָר). Yet what is truly unusual, according to Yhwh, is the necessity that "strangers" (8:7; זָרִים) come to devour Israel. Oddness lies not only in Israel's pursuit of unreliable "lovers/allies" (8:9c; cf. ch. 2),[3] but in the even greater absurdity of Israel paying them instead of receiving payment as a regular prostitute would (8:9c–10a). As noted above, the concepts of adultery and harlotry are used in Hosea to denote various kinds of apostasy against Yhwh in a manner that cuts across economics, religion, and politics.

In the final section of Hos. 8, religious and military issues continue to reinforce each other in wordplays. Israel's earlier attempt to "multiply" illicit altars (8:11) is paralleled by Judah's desire to "multiply" (רבה) fortified cities (8:14). The desire to "eat" (אכל) the sinful sacrifices offered on these altars (8:13) will meet Yhwh's response in the punishing fire that will "eat/consume" (אכל) the symbols of royal pride in both kingdoms (8:14). Besides these Hebrew verbs which outline cause-and-effect relationships in parallel spheres, the repeated use of the particle כִּי (six times in Hos. 8:6–11) underscores both the literary unity of ch. 8 and the sinful synergies in Israel among economics, religion, and politics (Gnuse 1982: 83–92).

Such a holistic outlook on life was not limited to ancient Israel. In the eighth century BCE, it would have been impossible to escape the prevailing ideology of "Assyrianism," which also claimed to govern all of life in the ancient Near East by exalting Assyria's "great king" (Hos. 5:13) in the name of Ashur, the patron deity (whose name was conveniently also that of his empire and capital city). In response to Assyrianism, eighth-century prophets like Hosea made the striking claim that Yhwh was both the national god of Israel and a universal deity who could even deploy other nations (whether their gods, armies, or both) against his own people when he chooses. This assertion would

13.3. Hosea 7–8 in the Ancient and Modern Worlds

An initial step in exploring the modern political implications of Hos. 7–8 is to marvel that a contrarian book such as Hosea exists at all. Any text from the ancient Near East that achieved canonical status, like Hosea's prophecy, would have been the product of royal scribes whose literary output was dictated by the kings sponsoring their work. Then and now, in other words, state-sponsored media that criticizes the state tends to be a category fallacy (cf. Bos 2013: 37). For the Assyrian empire in particular, the bloviating tone of its propaganda (which lies constantly in the background of Hosea) has been humorously critiqued by Baruch Halpern (2001: 126):

> In Assyrian royal inscriptions, then, the torching of a grain field is the conquest of a whole territory beyond it. A looting raid becomes a claim of perpetual sovereignty. But this does not mean that campaigns can be confected. The technique is that of putting extreme spin on real events. Interpreting such literature demands only a simple rule, *the Tiglath-Pileser principle*. The question is, what is the minimum the king might have done to lay claim to the achievements he publishes? . . . *Each small mark of prestige becomes the evidence for grand triumph*.

For these reasons, the Neo-Assyrian kings were not unlike Nazi Germany over two millennia later for how both of these regimes combined the traits of hypersensitivity to criticism, dissemination of "fake news," and overwhelming military power.

Similarly in Egypt at the time of Hosea, the analogue to the "Tiglath-Pileser Principle" in Assyria was at work through the "Piye Principle." In a victory stela, Piye the Cushite claimed that he became the ruler of Egypt because the gods had chosen him: "Hear what I did, exceeding the ancestors, I the king, image of god, Living likeness of Atum! Who left the womb marked as ruler, Feared by those greater than he! His father knew, his mother perceived, He would be ruler from the egg, The good gods, beloved of gods, The Son of Re, who acts with his arms, Piye beloved of Amun" (Hallo and Younger 2003: 42–43). The victory stela of Piye is one of the least propagandistic documents from ancient Egypt, since he goes on to record both victories and setbacks in his quest to unite Upper and Lower Egypt under his rule. But as with Tiglath-Pileser, a revisionist slant is unmistakable in Piye's insistence that he is the likeness of a god who possesses accomplishments that are "exceeding the ancestors." Here is a textbook example of the motif of divine abandonment—the rise of an ancient Near Eastern king or empire in place of another explained by asserting the new regime as a change in the ruler whom the gods had chosen.

The divine exceptionalism that Israel receives throughout Hos. 7–8 is altogether different from the "Tiglath-Pileser Principle" and "Piye Principle." This passage begins not with the human king's assertion of divine approval upon him (as in the Assyrian annals and Piye's stela), but with the divine king's disapproval toward all his human vassals. Their attempts to compartmentalize or otherwise minimize their wickedness are pointless since Yhwh perceives sin in every form and setting: "I remember all their wickedness. Now their deeds surround them; they are before my face" (Hos. 7:2). Hosea 7 has inverted the exceptionalism of its cultural counterparts: rather than elevating the deity's "beloved" ruler above regular human limitations, all people in Israel are placed under the same holistic standard that encompasses all of life, shows no favoritism toward those in authority, and looks unfavorably on those who rationalize their behavior in the name of deity.

Hosea 8 also overturns the cultural expectation that kings erect outsized symbols to honor their national god (cf. 2 Chr. 36:23; Ezra 1:2–4). Instead of rewarding grandiosity, Yhwh proclaims the opposite through his prophet: "Israel has forgotten his maker and built palaces; Judah has fortified many towns. But I will send fire upon their cities that will consume their fortresses" (Hos. 8:14). The familiar theme of divine abandonment has become a present accusation against the occupants of the deity's own land rather than a retrospective account by the land's new occupants of how their deity was greater than that of their predecessors or had chosen them instead (e.g., Assyria's self-understanding expressed in 2 Kgs. 19:19–25; see Cogan 1974). Hosea's commitment to truth-telling at his people's expense stands out against a backdrop of ancient Near Eastern imperialism.

Due to the prophetic challenge to power, the Jewish philosopher Martin Buber highlighted the need to expand the typical category of "politics" to reflect the holism of the biblical worldview. He observed that the Latter Prophets exhibit "a special kind of politics, *theopolitics*, which is concerned to establish a certain people in a certain historical situation under the divine sovereignty, so that his people is brought nearer to the fulfilment of its task, to become the beginning of the kingdom of God" (Buber 1949: 135, emphasis added). The nature of the political enterprise is irreducibly theological, and not just in ancient Israel. Much of the modern West has forgotten its Greco-Roman heritage, which regarded politics, when rightly understood, as virtually synonymous with ethics and religion (Pecknold 2010: 2–7). Hosea 7–8 epitomizes a similarly wide-ranging vision whereby "in ancient Israel there was no clear separation between religion, morals, law and politics; all were parts of one comprehensive system of norms" (Falk 1994: 49). Yhwh is sovereign over the entire order of creation and empires, against all appearances, even as his own people and land are shrinking. This results in a national identity for Israel which defies the usual categories of power politics, while also drawing the line between friends and enemies in unexpected places (Walzer 2012: 100). Israel's theopolitics of trusting Yhwh thus involves a remarkable combination of unrelenting holism in life and the embrace of weakness rather than strength.

To summarize, Hosea mounts a pointed corrective to abuses of power in every sphere and across every age. Since claiming authority for oneself cuts across political, economic, and religious lines, Hos. 7–8 provides a creative and inspiring model for how to expose sinful synergies of power across spheres that would otherwise remain hidden. This passage's brilliant satire of Baal(s), the calf-cult, and the interconnections between domestic idol-making and foreign trade exemplifies a kind of resistance literature. Divine election could never justify the predation that it usually became elsewhere. Instead, being appointed by God is grounds for a harsher judgment, especially when religion works together with economics and politics in the service of enriching oneself.

Whistleblowing became institutionalized in Israel when the voice of prophets at the margins rose above those of leaders and institutions in the center. Yet, as Max Weber (1952) hinted, the antiestablishment posture of a prophet like Hosea is rather different from the ideals of a free press, individual rights, and democratic activism that modern people might assume to be at work. Given such a reality of cultural distance, how can we implement Richard Bauckham's sage guidance that, "while the law and the prophets cannot be *instructions* for our political life, they can be *instructive* for our political life" (2011: 6, emphasis original)?

The way forward requires a brief detour to revisit the Enlightenment's conception of the "separation of powers," which has exercised a largely unseen influence in Western political theology and Hebrew Bible scholarship. Particularly in its Anglo-American forms, the antiroyalism of thinkers such as John Locke, John Milton, and Thomas Jefferson has regarded the concept of sacral kingship (also known as "the divine right of kings") as merely a disguise for religiously legitimated autocracy. Since Christian monarchies in Europe often looked to the Hebrew Bible for models of kingship (e.g., the christening of the boy-king Edward VI in 1547 CE as a "new Josiah" for the English Reformation), the post-Christendom West has usually theorized the ideal relationship between state and religion as a secular-sacred divide. Economics and politics lie on the secular side as public, modern, and practical matters, while religion is consigned to the sacred realm as that which is private, primitive, and otherworldly.

The so-called secularization thesis has become an axiom in how the West conceives its own identity (Demerath 2003: 1). Tellingly, however, many sociologists of religion who once advocated the thesis are now its biggest opponents (Woodberry 2012; Berger 1999). Modernity witnessed the privatization and weakening of traditional religion overall, but the corollary that human cultures would progress toward the secular did not follow. Economics and politics entered the vacuum left by religion and were themselves (re)sacralized using quasi-religious language and concepts. Economic growth and the political policies that support it have become a de facto religion in the modern world for how they shape national identity and demand exclusive loyalty, even to the point of requiring military intervention.[4]

Although sociologists have come to see that the transition from religion to secularity is greatly overstated, biblical scholars still tend to regard the evolution of leadership offices in the Hebrew Bible as a transfer of authority from "sacred" religious functionaries in Israel's early history to the "secular" political-military-economic leaders of later eras. Space precludes analysis here, but the most prominent example is the view that the

Torah moves from a near-absolute authority figure with divine approval (like Moses) to a secularized distribution of powers among judge, prophet, priest, sage, and other leaders (e.g., Lohfink 1993). And when this idea of a "Mosaic Constitution" (Hammill 2012) is projected onto the era of classical prophecy in Israel, the result is that Hos. 7–8, and similar critiques of sacral kingship, are distorted by the post-Christian West into a mirror image of its own secularism, just as Max Weber warned against.

By contrast, separation of powers in ancient Israel could never entail a secularization of powers. The latter not only excludes the possibility of sacral kings on earth but also leaves no room for the divine king to display his sovereignty and relationality from heaven toward a covenant people. Hosea 7–8 does not merely concern a present world order within a limited area called "politics," but the Israelites' everyday theology of Yahwism in which "defeats" of every kind are always stronger than Assyrianism's "victories." In this way, Hos. 7–8 offers an arresting portrayal of the God of Israel whose actions transcend the retribution principle. This moral law of the cosmos is part of "a common theology of the ancient Near East" in which virtue is rewarded with blessing and vice with curse (Smith 1952). But rather than equating suffering and weakness with sin, retribution in Yahwism is the work of an impassioned Creator who is as agitated by the people's stubbornness as eager for them to return. Yhwh's thundering words, "For they sow the wind, and they shall reap the whirlwind" (Hos. 8:7), echo the key metaphor for retribution in eastern religions (both ancient and modern), but with an intensely personal and this-worldly focus that differs from the impersonal notion of karma and its focus on the afterlife (as in Buddhism and Hinduism).

Distinctively in Yahwism, then, God leads the way in the protest politics of challenging human authority. The dictum of imperialism that "might makes right" is placed on notice by a deity whose weakness is paradoxically stronger than all forms of human strength. The result is a distinctive emphasis in Hos. 7–8 (and the Hebrew Bible at large) on leadership, whether political or otherwise, as the domain of those who are least likely to lead (Morgenstern 2009: 5–6). In a postmodern age when people still often feel that "religion poisons everything" (Hitchens 2008), a passage like Hos. 7–8 offers the surprise that religion—rightly and holistically understood—is actually the answer.

Notes

1. For details on these divisions, see corresponding sections of Hwang 2021.
2. Cf. the cultic *Sitz im Leben* proposed by Emmerson 1975: 700–710.
3. On the "lovers/allies" multivalency in Hosea, see Kelle 2005.
4. For an application of the Hebrew Bible to this nexus of factors, see Barrett 2009.

References

Albertz, Rainer. 1994. *A History of Israelite Religion in the Old Testament Period: Volume I: From the Beginnings to the End of the Monarchy*. OTL. Louisville: Westminster John Knox.

Barrett, Rob. 2009. *Disloyalty and Destruction: Religion and Politics in Deuteronomy and the Modern World.* LHBOTS 511. New York: T&T Clark.

Bauckham, Richard. 2011. *The Bible in Politics: How to Read the Bible Politically.* 2nd ed. Louisville: Westminster John Knox.

Berger, Peter L. 1999. "The De-Secularization of the World: A Global Overview." In *The De-Secularization of the World: Resurgent Religion and Global Politics.* Edited by by Peter L. Berger. Grand Rapids: Eerdmans, 1–18.

Bos, James M. 2013. *Reconsidering the Date and Provenance of the Book of Hosea: The Case for Persian-Period Yehud.* LHBOTS 580. New York: Bloomsbury T&T Clark.

Buber, Martin. 1949. *The Prophetic Faith.* New York: Harper and Row.

Chung, Youn Ho. 2010. *The Sin of the Calf: The Rise of the Bible's Negative Attitude toward the Golden Calf.* LHBOTS 523. New York: T&T Clark.

Cogan, Mordechai. 1974. *Imperialism and Religion: Assyria, Judah, and Israel in the Eighth and Seventh Centuries B.C.E.* SBLMS 19. Missoula, MT: Scholars Press.

Crüsemann, Frank. 1978. *Der Widerstand gegen das Königtum: Die antiköniglichen Texte des Alten Testamentes und der Kampf um den frühen israelitischen Staat.* Wissenschaftliche Monographien zum Alten und Neuen Testament 49. Neukirchen-Vluyn: Neukirchener Verlag.

Demerath, N. J. 2003. *Crossing the Gods: World Religions and Worldly Politics.* New Brunswick, NJ: Rutgers University Press.

Eidevall, Göran. 1996. *Grapes in the Desert: Metaphors, Models and Themes in Hosea 4–14.* Coniectanea Biblica: Old Testament Series 43. Stockholm: Almqvist & Wiksell.

Emmerson, Grace I. 1975. "The Structure and Meaning of Hosea 8:1–3." *VT* 25: 700–10.

Falk, Ze'ev W. 1994. "Religion and State in Ancient Israel." In Henning Reventlow, Yair Hoffman, and Benjamin Uffenheimer, eds., *Politics and Theopolitics in the Bible and Postbiblical Literature.* JSOTSup 171. Sheffield: JSOT Press, 49–54.

Freedman, David Noel. 1987. "Headings in the Books of the Eighth-Century Prophets." *Andrews University Seminary Studies* 25: 9–26.

Gelston, Anthony. 1974. "Kingship in the Book of Hosea." In James Barr, ed., *Language and Meaning: Studies in Hebrew Language and Biblical Exegesis; Papers Read at the Joint British-Dutch Old Testament Conference Held at London, 1973.* Leiden: Brill, 71–85.

Gnuse, Robert K. 1982. "Calf, Cult, and King: The Unity of Hosea 8:1–13." *BZ* 26: 83–92.

Gottwald, Norman K. 2007. *All the Kingdoms of the Earth: Israelite Prophecy and International Relations in the Ancient Near East.* Minneapolis: Fortress.

Hallo, William W., and K. Lawson Younger, eds. 2003. "The Victory Stela of King Piye (Piankhy) (2.7)." In *The Context of Scripture, II: Monumental Inscriptions from the Biblical World.* Leiden: Brill, 42–43.

Halpern, Baruch. 2001. *David's Secret Demons: Messiah, Murderer, Traitor, King.* Grand Rapids, MI: Eerdmans.

Hammill, Graham L. 2012. *The Mosaic Constitution: Political Theology and Imagination from Machiavelli to Milton.* Chicago: University of Chicago Press.

Hitchens, Christopher. 2008. *God Is Not Great: How Religion Poisons Everything.* London: Atlantic.

Hwang, Jerry. 2014. "The Unholy Trio of Money, Sex, and Power in Israel's 8th-Century BCE Prophets." *Jian Dao* 41: 181–204.

Hwang, Jerry. 2021. *Hosea: God's Reconciliation with His Estranged Household.* Zondervan Exegetical Commentary on the Old Testament. Grand Rapids, MI:

Zondervan Academic.Jeremias, Jörg. 1994. "Der Begriff 'Baal' im Hoseabuch und seine Wirkungsgeschichte." In Walter Dietrich and Martin A. Klopfenstein, eds., *Ein Gott Allein? JHWH-Verehrung und biblischer Monotheismus im Kontext der israelitischen und altorientalischen Religionsgeschichte.* OBO 139. Göttingen: Vandenhoeck & Ruprecht, 441–62.

Jeremias, Jörg. 1996. "The Interrelationship between Amos and Hosea." In James W. Watts and Paul R. House, eds., *Forming Prophetic Literature: Essays on Isaiah and the Twelve in Honor of John D. W. Watts.* JSOTSup 235. Sheffield: Sheffield Academic Press, 171–86.

Kelle, Brad E. 2005. *Hosea 2: Metaphor and Rhetoric in Historical Perspective.* SBLAB 20. Atlanta: Society of Biblical Literature.

Kruger, Paul A. 1992. "The Divine Net in Hosea 7,12." *Ephemerides Theologicae Lovanienses* 68: 132–36.

Lohfink, Norbert. 1993. "Distribution of the Functions of Power: The Laws concerning Public Offices in Deuteronomy 16:18–18:22." In Duane L. Christensen, ed. *A Song of Power and the Power of Song: Essays on the Book of Deuteronomy.* Sources for Biblical and Theological Study 3. Winona Lake, IN: Eisenbrauns, 336–52.

Machinist, Peter. 2005. "Hosea and the Ambiguity of Kingship in Ancient Israel." In John T. Strong and Steven Shawn Tuell, eds., *Constituting the Community: Studies on the Polity of Ancient Israel in Honor of S. Dean McBride, Jr.* Winona Lake, IN: Eisenbrauns, 153–81.

Morgenstern, Mira. 2009. *Conceiving a Nation: The Development of Political Discourse in the Hebrew Bible.* University Park: Pennsylvania State University Press.

Nwaoru, Emmanuel O. 2004. "The Role of Images in the Literary Structure of Hosea VII 8–VIII 14." *VT* 54: 216–22.

Pecknold, C. C. 2010. *Christianity and Politics: A Brief Guide to the History.* Cascade Companions 12. Eugene, OR: Cascade.

Perdue, Leo G., and Warren Carter. 2015. *Israel and Empire: A Postcolonial History of Israel and Early Judaism.* London: Bloomsbury.

Petersen, David L. 2002. *The Prophetic Literature: An Introduction.* Louisville, KY: Westminster John Knox.

Premnath, D. N. 2003. *Eighth Century Prophets: A Social Analysis.* St. Louis, MO: Chalice.

Richter, Sandra. 2014. "Eighth-Century Issues: The World of Jeroboam II, the Fall of Samaria, and the Reign of Hezekiah." In Bill T. Arnold and Richard S. Hess, eds., *Ancient Israel's History: An Introduction to Issues and Sources.* Grand Rapids, MI: Baker Academic, 319–49.

Smith, Morton. 1952. "The Common Theology of the Ancient Near East." *JBL* 71: 135–47.

Walzer, Michael. 2012. *In God's Shadow: Politics in the Hebrew Bible.* New Haven: Yale University Press.

Weber, Max. *Ancient Judaism.* 1952. Trans. Hans H. Gerth and Don Martindale. London: George Allen & Unwin Ltd.

Wolff, Hans Walter. 1974. *Hosea.* Translated by Gary Stansell. Hermeneia. Minneapolis: Fortress.

Woodberry, Robert D. 2012. "The Missionary Roots of Liberal Democracy." *American Political Science Review* 106, no. 2 (May): 244–74.

Yee, Gale A. 1985. *Composition and Tradition in the Book of Hosea.* SBLDS 102. Atlanta: Scholars.

CHAPTER 14

HOSEA 11 AND METAPHORS OF IDENTITY, RELATIONSHIP, AND CORE VALUES IN CONTEXTS OF TRAUMA

JENNIFER M. MATHENY

14.1. INTRODUCTION

HOSEA 11 stands as the concluding section of the book's second block of material (chs. 1–3; 4–11; 12–14 [Eng. 11:12–14:8]) and dramatically shifts the metaphor of Yhwh's relationship with Israel from the husband/wife metaphor appearing in chs. 1–3 to an intimate parent/child metaphor. Hosea 11 refashions the gripping rhetoric from the dynamic of husband/wife to a broader democratized familial entity of Israel, coupled with animal imagery and gendered imagery. The poetry and muddle of metaphors is "dense, intense, closely packed, involved, and complex" (Goldingay 2021: 35). Oppression, liberation, calling, and identity formation characterize the exodus story with which Hos. 11 begins (Landy 2011). Domains of human, land, and animal all serve to entice Israel to return (*šûb*) and to maintain relationship with Yhwh, even when their future is threatened by the growing Neo-Assyrian empire.

The theological-political backdrop of the Neo-Assyrian empire in eighth century BCE is apparent, as the chapter mentions Assyria by name twice (11:5; 11:11). There is significant attention to the interplay of "religious obedience, social and moral behavior, and the welfare of the land" (Marlow 2013: 201). Pressure to retain an identity as Yhwh's covenant people meets the social, economic, and religious realities of the day. Political subversion imagery is rich through Hosea's oracles and metaphors. Likewise, in ch. 11, the interplay of specific terms such as Egypt and Assyria, coupled with the parental and animal imagery, constitutes possible theological and political rhetoric alluding to the

Assyrian goddess Ishtar as hidden polemics to call Israel back to their covenant fidelity and identity as Yhwh's people.

14.2. Metaphors of Relationship, Identity, and Core Values

The language of metaphor is rich and complex in Hos. 11, embodying rhetorical provocation through intense positive and negative emotions that extend from love (11:1) to anger (11:9). The relational language of parenting roots Israel's story through exodus allusions. Hwang (2021: 263) discuss the complexities in detailing a coherent outline of Hos. 11 as it generally traces a brief geographical movement (from Egypt to exile) and to some degree a chronological development "from past (11:1–4) to near future (11:5–6) and eschatological future (11:10–11), with rhetorical questions and their answers (vv. 8–9) that signal the turning point between these horizons." Following Morris (1996), Hwang (p. 56) views Hos. 11 more as a "lyrical plot" that is "nonlinear" and "subordinates time and geography" with a focus on themes such as "estrangement, judgment, and reconciliation." This nonlinear movement suggests an understanding of the chapter that highlights the interplay of political, religious, and relational rhetoric through metaphor, demonstrating reversals of estrangement and death from Hos. 9 to homecoming and hope in Hos. 11 (Landy 2011).

Hosea 11:1–2

1 When Israel was a youth,
   I loved him,
   and from Egypt, I called my son.

2 Then called to them,
   then they went away from them,
   to the Baals they sacrificed,
   to the idols they burned incense.[1]

The image of the "young boy" (*na'ar*) being "called" (*qara*) by Yhwh narrows to the more intimate familial term "son" (*ben*) in the second stanza. The verb "call" serves as an invitation to follow and "to name," and "when God summons Israel from Egypt, God also names Israel as an adopted son" (Yee 1996: 277). In Exod. 4:22–23, Yhwh instructs Moses to tell Pharaoh that Israel is Yhwh's son and to release Israel so they may worship Yhwh. Israel is no longer under the thumb of Egypt but is struggling to "grow up" into a people that trusts and worships Yhwh. Hosea 11:1–3 centers on the corporate Israel (Ephraim) imagined as a youth summoned by a parent. Israel's apostasy then comes into focus as v.

2 describes turning away from Yhwh to sacrifice to the Baals and offer incense to images. In Exod. 4:22–23, Yhwh desires to release Israel from the oppression of Egypt for worship, and here, under the threat of the Neo-Assyrian empire, Israel continues to struggle with faithful worship to Yhwh. Israel's struggle to be faithful in the worship of Yhwh is nothing new, as references to Egypt also evoke memories of the golden calf incident in Exod. 32 (Sweeney 2000).

The precise meaning of Baal(s) is unclear throughout Hosea. Keefe (2001: 197) demonstrates that Baals and lovers are connected metaphors and reveal Israel's unfaithfulness. They are a source of judgment against Israel's unfaithfulness. Disloyalty, whether religious or political, indicates that Israel is not living into its identity as Yhwh's chosen people (see Exod. 19). Hosea 11:2 then may encompass a broader theopolitical concern beyond the worship of a particular deity such as the Canaanite fertility god/storm god (Kelle 2005; Nogalski 2011). The term *ba'al* was a common designation widely attested throughout the ancient world, and its meaning extended from the specific Canaanite god or local gods (e.g., Baal-Hadad; Baal-Shamem) to references to "husband" and "landowner" to a particular royal designation of a king (Baal of Tyre). Sweeney (2000: 138) views Baal in Hos. 11:2 as a possible reference to the "Assyrian King." In connection with the preceding verse, Israel's calling and identity is compromised through its entanglements with these Baals, whatever their precise form.

Hosea 11:3–4

3 Yet it was I who taught Ephraim to walk;
I took them by the arms
but they did not know that I healed them.

4 With bonds of humanity I drew them,
with cords of love.
I was for them as those
who remove the yoke from their cheeks.
Then I bent down to them and I fed them.

Feminist biblical scholarship has attended to the possibilities of the gendered imagery in these verses, especially the possible maternal metaphor for Yhwh (Keefe 2001; Sherwood 1996; Yee 1996; Wacker 2012). Nogalski (2011: 156) emphasizes the relational metaphor of God as father: "Hosea 11:1 begins a soliloquy where YHWH expresses—as nowhere else in the Old Testament—the pathos of a father's love over a wayward child . . . the portrayal of God as 'father' is unusual in the Old Testament." Landy (2011: 159) notes the "lack of a maternal counterpart" in Hos. 11, seeing a connection between the husband in Hos. 2 and the imagery in Hos. 11. However, building on the research of Schüngel-Straumann (1995), Wacker (2012: 380–81) argues that the "core metaphor" of Hos. 11 is maternal, with activities of feeding, nursing, lifting up, and even the term "womb" (*rehem*) later in vv. 8–9 deriving from "compassion" (*niḥûmîm*) rather than "repentance." Sweeney (2000) highlights possible maternal imagery concerning cords and birthing pangs. Yee (1996: 279) emphasizes that neither "mother" nor "father" is explicitly used to describe Yhwh in Hos. 11. Some feminist biblical scholars see a possible rejection of overtly masculine identification when Yhwh later declares, "For I am God (*'ēl*) and not a man (*'îs*)" (see Schüngel-Straumann 1995). Yee (1996: 279) argues that this reading contains questionable exegesis, and she connects the self-declaration of Yhwh with the notion that Yhwh is unlike humanity in general. Therefore, Yhwh will respond with love to maintain the relationship, unlike humanity, which neglects loyalty and reveals no knowledge of God (see Hos. 4:1). In any case, the relational metaphor of the loved yet unfaithful spouse in Hos. 1–3 shifts into one of renewed intimacy and the breadth of record of relationship, harkening back to Egypt.

In the tender scene in 11:3–4, Israel's failings are noticed, yet Yhwh is love expressed with the continued pursuit of a parent (possibly a mother) teaching and guiding. The Hebrew term for "taught to walk" (*tirgaltî*) is rare in form and derives from the noun for "foot" (*regel*). The idea demonstrates the care of Yhwh with Ephraim, to "make steady" by taking Ephraim by the arm (LXX) or in the arms (MT) (Landy 2011; Hwang 2021). Examples of Yhwh's care for Ephraim will move tenderly from the feet, to the arms, to the cheek (*lehî*) (11:4). Here is an example of how metaphors and movement through complex images, along with Hebrew parallelism and intertextuality with key linguistic features, abound throughout the chapter. The movement of Yhwh reaching down to assist Israel in these formative moments parallels with their healing (*rapa*), a healing performed by Yhwh but whose source is not known (or acknowledged?) by Israel (v. 3b). Marlow (2013: 198) notes the irony of Israel's lack of knowledge given Yhwh's past actions cited in v. 1, an irony Marlow links to a cuneiform tablet of Ishtar that expresses the goddess's disapproval over the deficiency of offerings and lack of gratitude:

> Word of Ištar of Arbela to Esarhaddon, King of Assyria. . . . Did I not gather your foes and adversaries like butterflies? What have [yo]u in turn given to me? The [fo]od for the banquet is no[t there], as if there were no temple at all! . . . Verily see to it that there is a bowl of one seah of food and a pitcher of one seah of best beer! (quoted in Marlow 2013: 198)

Israel's disregard for Yhwh and lack of understanding are even greater than what angered Ishtar concerning the king of Assyria. At least the Assyrian king knows where to worship, unlike Israel, who do not know their healer and offer sacrifices to the Baals and incense to idols.

Verse 4 further enhances the multifaceted relational image that describes the manner of leading by evoking the concept of the adopted son being guided gently with "bonds (*hebel*) of humanity (*adam*)," and "cords (*abot*) of love (*ahăbâ*)." Ben Zvi (2005: 234) suggests that in combination with maternal imagery, the bond/rope of humanity could mean a lighter cord indicating "human ropes," while others have suggested heavier ropes that would pertain to an animal. Some view the animal construction as an intertextual correlation between Ephraim and the obstinate heifer in Hos. 4:16 and the trained heifer in Hos. 10:11. This possible interplay of metaphors for Israel as child and animal is one of restraint and care, a relationship between "parenthood and animal husbandry" (Hwang 2021: 266).

Maternal imagery may come back into focus with the second half of v. 4, which some translations render as Yhwh lifting an infant to the cheek to feed it (Mays 1969: 150; Wolff 1974: 191). In keeping with the possible maternal imagery for Yhwh, Schüngel-Straumann (1995: 202) translates cheek as "breast." This shift is not exegetically sound and an unlikely translation because the consonants of these two terms are entirely different. The MT has "yoke" (*ōl*), suggesting "yoke on their jaws/cheeks" (Eidevall 1996; Moon 2018: 275). Some interpreters continue the metaphor of a parent-child and propose that "yoke" (*ōl*) should be "infant" (*'ul*). Routledge (2020: 151) deems the emendation "minor," with "both interpretations possible," and it is "reasonable to see this as a continuation of the parent-child metaphor." One of the difficulties is understanding the placement of the yoke on the cheek or jaws. Yokes are normally placed over the back of the animal. Even so, the reference to cords leading an animal maintains the possible connection with the heifer figure from Hos. 10. Hwang (2021: 266) mediates the discussion by suggesting "harness" as a possible translation. Metaphors play with images and communicate values through creative language. Hence, another possibility is that an idea (rather than specific word choice) of communicating a "release from restraint" is intended by the metaphor. The cords, bonds, and yoke are no longer required to keep the animal moving in the desired direction. Metaphors can intentionally and creatively amalgamate ideas to engage the imagination in innovative ways in order to expose core values (see discussion of ACT below).

The imagery across 11:3–4 may include hidden polemics with the Assyrian goddess Ishtar. Assyrian prophecies depict Ishtar in a motherly relationship of nurturing to the king (Parpola 1997; Landy 2011)[2]:

> I am Ištar of [Arbela]! . . . I am your great midwife, I am your excellent wet nurse. For endless days and everlasting years I have established your throne under the great heavens. (quoted in Marlow 2013: 197)

Strategic relational images and metaphors like these anchor Hos. 11 within the broader theological and political context of Neo-Assyrian imperialism (Schüngel-Straumann 1995; Ben Zvi 2005). The parental goddess figure raises the semidivine king. Another Assyrian prophetic oracle interchanges animal and human metaphors to describe the relationship, similar to Hos. 11: "The Goddess declares: 'I am your father and mother, I raised you between my wings'" (Parpola 1997: xxxvi). The interplay of heifer/animal and child images is widely attested in the larger collection of ancient Near Eastern prophecies.

In Hos. 11, however, the child nurtured by the deity is democratized to all of Israel as Yhwh's chosen people. As designated in Exod. 19:3–6, Israel's unique role provides a contextual connection to the paternal imagery of being raised and appointed by a deity as a "treasured possession" (*segullah*), established as a "kingdom of priests," and carried on eagles' wings. Just as the Assyrian mother-child imagery for Ishtar and the king served to legitimize the king's rule, so Hos. 11 uses similar imagery to remind Israel of its identity as a holy nation. Rather than strictly dichotomizing Hosea's use of either female/mother or male/father imagery for Yhwh (and similarly, human or animal), the connection to Ishtar as parent may allow for both/and with regard to Yhwh. Such motifs could be one way Hosea reimagines Israel's function and role within the complex theological and political landscape of the eighth century.

Hosea 11:5–9

5 He will not return to the land of Egypt,
and Assyria, he is king;
for they refuse to turn.

6 So a sword will move about in their cities;
It consumes their plans

7 because my people are determined on turning away from me.
To the god above they will call together, but he will not raise them up.

8 How can I give you up, Ephraim?
How can I surrender you, Israel?
How can I give you over like Admah, appoint you like Zeboiim?
My heart is overthrown within me.
My compassion is strengthened.

9 I will not perform my burning anger;
I will not return to destroy Ephraim.
Because I am God and I am not a human,
in your midst, holy.
Therefore, I will not disembark in wrath.

Hosea 11:5 recalls the exodus story with the reference of Egypt. Translation difficulties abound (e.g., is the opening statement positive or negative?), but the overall sense is that Israel's disloyalty to Yhwh will result in the foreign rule and domination of Assyria, perhaps in exile in Egypt. Israel's apostasy has brought on a powerful oppressor as consequence or perhaps punishment (Routledge 2020: 152; Hwang 2021: 267). Israel behaves like Assyria is their true political and religious alliance: "Assyria is its king" (Landy 2011: 162). Even so, Yhwh continues to call Israel to return and restore relationship. Note the wordplay of the same Hebrew term to mean "turn" and "return" (*šûb*) (Hos. 11:5[2x], 7, 9).

In these portrayals, Israel struggles as it did in the wilderness, and Yhwh continues to reimage the parent/child dynamic metaphor. Deuteronomy 1:26–33 addresses Israel's rebellious ways in the wilderness, and Yhwh's response is similar to Hos. 11, with the recollection of Egypt and paternal care:

The Lord your God, who goes before you, is the one who will fight for you, just as he did for you in Egypt before your very eyes and in the wilderness, where you saw how the Lord your God carried you, just as one carries a child, all the way that you traveled until you reached this place. But in spite of this, you have no trust in the Lord your God, who goes before you on the way to seek out a place for you to camp, in fire by night, and in the cloud by day, to show you the route you should take. (Deut. 1:30–33 NRSVue)

The deuteronomic parental images and actions (carrying, lifting) and lexical terms (Egypt, return/turn, child, carrying/lifting) are reimagined in Hos. 11. Israel's disobedience runs throughout the chapter and is matched by Yhwh's parental care and consistent love. The verbs used with Yhwh indicate relational care: love (11:1), calling (11:1), teaching (11:3), leading (11:4), lifting (11:4), and bending down (11:4). Israel is indicted for not listening (11:2), apostasy (11:2), turning away (11:7), and not knowing (11:3). Nonetheless, in Hos. 11:8–9, the anger of Yhwh becomes a response of compassion and even inner turmoil because of Yhwh's love for Israel. Yhwh's heart moves to compassion. The verb *hāpak* in v. 8 means "turn, subvert, overthrow." In the niphal form, it carries the sense of something turning on itself. The deep pathos of this term is apparent through the connection with the violent images of the overthrow and judgment of Admah and Zeboiim, two cities destroyed alongside Sodom and Gomorrah (see Gen. 14:2; Deut. 29:23; cf. Gen. 19:21–28). Note also the wordplay in v. 9 with return (*šûb*). Israel will not return to Yhwh, yet Yhwh will not return to destroy Ephraim. The main object turning in this section is the heart of Yhwh.

> Hosea 11:10–11
> 10 They will follow the Lord;
> he will roar like a lion.
> When he roars,
> his children will come fluttering from the west.
>
> 11 They will flutter like a bird from Egypt,
> like a dove from the land of Assyria.
> Then I will settle them in their houses
> —an utterance of Yhwh.

Verses 10–11 use animal imagery to depict Yhwh as a lion and Israel as a bird and a dove. The leonine image is positive in Hos. 11:10. Strawn (2005: 194) notes that lions and gods/goddesses are often correlated, especially "frequently associated with female deities," and "nowhere is this frequency more apparent than in the case of Ishtar who is often portrayed as standing on a lion." Ishtar's prevalence as an Assyrian "parent" deity of kings and representation with a lion might underlie the gendered metaphors at play in Hos. 11. Ishtar "was the major Mesopotamian goddess of (sexual) love and war, not to mention rain, fertility, and the morning/evening star" (Strawn 2005: 194).

Fluttering (*ḥārēd*) is often translated as "trembling" (Landy 2011: 166; Hwang 2021: 272; Sweeney 2000: 139). Out of its thirty-nine uses in the Hebrew Bible, there is a range of meaning from fear to a heartbeat. The use of this verb in Exod. 19:16 carries the sense of fear and awe, as Moses led Israel before Yhwh at Mt. Sinai. The term can also indicate a startling moment that does not lead to fear, such as Boaz awakening with surprise at midnight to find Ruth at his feet (Ruth 3:8). In Job 37:1, *ḥārēd* carries the sense of "the non-linear motion of the heart" (Swanson 1997). The sense of "startling" may possibly indicate, similar to its use in Ruth 3:8, that the roar of the lion "startles" Israel into a flurry of activity. In Hos. 7:11–12, Israel is compared to a foolish dove, senseless, literally "without heart, calling to Egypt and going to Assyria." There is an image of Israel fluttering about in a confused, unrepentant state and without wisdom or fear of Yhwh. Here in Hos. 11:10, the immediate response is a true return (*šûb*), a migration home. The return is "from the west" or "from the sea." In connection to the exodus imagery throughout Hos. 11, this homecoming harkens back to their birth/adoption story, "through the sea" (Exod. 14). Landy (2011: 167) remarks on the "from the west" as the representation of "effortless travel" with large quantities of fowl. In this semantic range, fluttering may serve as a possible translation, similar to the heartbeat in Job, corresponding to the movement of a bird's wings (see also Sweeney 2000: 139). Unlike the animals being led by cords, the bird imagery describes a free creature without restraint, one that turns toward Yhwh when called. The yoke has been lifted, and they choose willingly to return at the sound of the lion's roar.

14.3. Interdisciplinary Engagement with Trauma, Emotion, and Metaphor in Hosea 11

Social scientific approaches, such as psychological hermeneutics, can continue the interpretive efforts and offer beneficial voices within the landscape of contemporary perspectives and future trajectories in study of Hos. 11. Two specific areas that may contribute here are trauma studies and the therapeutic approach known as acceptance and commitment therapy (ACT). Both approaches pay attention to individual and communal experiences of suffering. These approaches have value for reading Hos. 11 in terms of both ancient and contemporary contexts.

Trauma studies have opened new horizons in understanding how the function of rhetoric in Hosea (along with other texts such as Genesis, Jeremiah, and Samuel) enables the communal processing of trauma, a process that includes didactic retelling and meaning-making (for examples within biblical studies, see O'Connor 2011; Garber 2015; Boase and Frechette 2016). Insights from trauma or survival literature reveal the importance of the process and techniques communities and individuals appropriate to handle trauma in the wake of the events (Caruth 1995). Trauma studies provide a frame to consider persons, experiences (personal and communal), and ongoing impact within the literature (e.g., observing characters, dialogue, metaphors, experiences, literary modes), as well as possible effects and implications to modern-day readers.

As noted above, Hos. 11 deals with key issues of Israel's identity and relationship with Yhwh during the ascending power of the Neo-Assyrian empire in the eighth century BCE. The realities of the communal trauma expressed in that setting appear in Hosea's use of relational and gendered metaphors such as a parent, nursing mother, animals, and emotions. These complex images center on relationship and restoration, with literary techniques such as wordplay with repentance (*šûb*) and key identity reminders of Israel's story through the recollection of Egypt. To process the current trauma, previous retelling of past traumatic events (such as the exodus) help form and inform the current theological and political threats that may cause disruption and disorder of identity, core values, and previous covenant commitments. Trauma theory is helpful in highlighting how Hos. 11 serves as a link to Israel's identity and beliefs through symbols that can be digested in the wake of loss, fear, and suffering.

Trauma studies reveal that during and after traumatic events, communities and individuals often process through symbols, metaphors, and ideological frameworks because the actual event is still too close to process directly. Using an illustration from Jeremiah, O'Connor (2011: x) expounds on how poetry and symbol can help a community process pain and suffering "without overwhelming their victims anew." Hosea 11 funds hope through intimate relational imagery and metaphor in the shadow of the Neo-Assyrian empire. Israel (Ephraim) is portrayed as a community that is still loved by Yhwh, even through covenant failings and brokenness. The text serves as subversive literature, navigating Neo-Assyrian political-theological ideology through the gendered metaphors and references to political entities such as Egypt. Egypt serves as a powerful reminder of the exodus story and Yhwh's faithfulness, even amid Israel's unfaithfulness. Ben Zvi notes that Hosea's political rhetoric incorporates the past and a future hope with intentionality. This creative narrative act in the identity-forming Israel-Egypt contrast is a feature of trauma literature:

> Hosea's silence on Aram—along with his multiple references to the dyad Assyria–Egypt and the construction of their lands as spaces for Exile and its counterpart, a future, utopian Return (e.g., Hos 9:3; 11:5, 11)—was consonant with and strengthened a core Yehudite narrative about the place of Exile and the overcoming of Exile, in a way that both included Northern Israel (see Assyria as a place of Exile) and undermined its separate existence. (Ben Zvi, Camp, Gunn, and Hughes 2015: 50)

Hosea 11 does this work of inviting construction and reconstruction of key identity-forming narratives, especially through relational imagery, emotive language, and key political entities on the horizon, as literature composed under the "imperial gaze" (Smith-Christopher 2011: 260).

Acceptance and commitment therapy (ACT) has emerged as an interdisciplinary dialogue partner for biblical studies that offers a helpful framework for the strong emotions that appear throughout Hos. 11 (Matheny and Hale 2023).[3] ACT postulates that emotions alert us to what is important in our lives and can reflect an individual's and community's core values. Jeremiah provides an example of strong emotion. The prophet expresses rage, and this rage is encouraged to be expressed by Yhwh (see Jer. 6). "Through the lens of ACT, anger is understood as a reflection of a person's desire to protect an important boundary and as a tool that can help them fight for something that they value" (Matheny and Hale 2023: 237). Jeremiah illustrates how anger/rage is associated with core values. Strong emotion, especially anger, can be misunderstood as solely negative in modern contexts. "ACT focuses on the function of different internal experiences (e.g., thoughts, emotions) and behaviours, asking only if the experience serves to move toward the person engaging more fully in valued living. The goal of ACT is never to rid people of negative emotions or thoughts but to change the relationship with them such that people are able to live lives that are rich and meaning-filled even in the presence of difficulty" (Matheny and Hale 2023: 238). ACT is helpful in that it reveals the importance of strong emotions as identifiers of core values. In ACT, metaphor and embodied practices help express trauma along with these core values.[4] "Values are understood as one's 'heart's deepest desires for how you want to behave—how you want to treat yourself, others, and the world around you'" (Matheny and Hale 2023: 240, quoting Harris 2019: 213). For Jeremiah, rage is connected to covenant obligations—core values for Yhwh and Jeremiah. The purpose for the anger in Jeremiah (4:4; 6:11; 7:20; 10:25; 18:20; 21:5; 21:12; 25:15; 30:23; 32:31–32, 37) is a reflection of covenant values—namely, covenant faithfulness and justice for the oppressed and marginalized.

Hosea 11 also contains a wide range of divine emotion from love (11:1) to a struggle of an upheaval and churning of the divine heart (11:8) to anger (11:9). Metaphors shift and change throughout the text (parent, heifer/infant, goddess). ACT illuminates how to see the pathos of Yhwh as going beyond expressing a relationship to communicating core values. Nogalski (2011: 156) views relationship as central in Hos. 11, but sees the positive emotion of divine love in v. 1 as parental relationality in the parent/son metaphor, while the anger in v. 9 removes the relational closeness and Yhwh becomes "more distant . . . as Holy One . . . not a tender father" (161). Yee views the emotion of compassion as a key relational turning point for Yhwh in v. 9. Even though, as a rebellious "son," Israel deserves death, the "bonding" and "compassion" Yhwh has for Israel prevents Yhwh from acting on this anger in a destructive fashion and "transcends legal institutions" (Yee 1996: 278). Verse 9 also reveals that Yhwh's heart is in a state of upheaval. On a strictly relational level, this has been understood as indecisiveness or even Yhwh acting "too human." However, ACT adds a key interpretive layer in connecting the divine emotions to core values. Hwang (2021: 27) cautions that emotions are a "limiting" human attribute, warning to "be cautious about speaking too readily about YHWH as changing his mind or vacillating between anger and compassion." But ACT enables a reading that connects strong emotive elements and metaphors to core covenant values. Yhwh values covenant faithfulness and is committed to Israel. Strong emotive language, rather than being understood as placing human limitations on a Holy God, communicates Yhwh's values in creative, embodied ways. This can be particularly helpful with more difficult texts that detail abusive relational metaphors (e.g., Hos. 2:4–25 [Eng. 2:2–23]; Jer. 13) where the metaphor signifies pain, breach of relationship, attempting to communicate deep relational pain within an ancient context, along with core values for covenant faithfulness.

The image of the "trembling" bird in 11:11 also takes on new possibilities of meaning through the lens of ACT. The common translation of Israel's return at the sound of the lion's roar is depicted as a frightened "trembling" bird. Strawn (2005: 63–64) notes that the bird illustration here seems "awkward," and many scholars see this as a later addition due to the change of person (Yhwh in third person) and the positive image of a lion mixed with the fear and trembling of Israel's approach as birds. Through the lens of ACT, attending to Yhwh's core values throughout Hos. 11 signals a more hopeful image of the bird in flight. If the leonine imagery is positive, then the bird may also serve as a positive image, as a creature that is "fluttering" home and choosing Yhwh. The movement of images in Hos. 11 reveals a deity who loves Israel and desires for Israel to willfully follow. This core value of Israel choosing Yhwh over the Baals, without yoke or force, reveals a demonstration of faithful love returned to Yhwh. Therefore, through the ACT lens, emotions communicate core values through the metaphors. This adds nuance to the possible reading of Hos. 11:8–9. Attending to Yhwh's core values, the bird imagery is one of a chosen return, and in advancing the migration image farther, a response to the roar that is natural and free, perhaps even free from dread. Yhwh values Israel's knowing (*yada*) and returning (*šûb*) to covenant faithfulness.

Even so, trembling with fear could also be part of the nuance of this image. In wisdom texts, to fear Yhwh is the beginning and the end (Prov. 9:10; Job 28:28; Eccl. 12:13–14), encompassing Israel's identity as image bearers, knowledge of God, covenant faithfulness, and love of Yhwh and neighbor. Rather than a restrictive use of fear as dread or panic, a more holistic proposal that connects to core values denotes a broader semantic range of fear and its biblical significance. Thinking through the ACT lens opens possibilities that difficult emotions and complex metaphors actually center on Yhwh's core values.

In any case, approaching Hos. 11 through psychological frameworks can broaden interpretive possibilities in understanding the complex environment and thought world of an ancient community such as Israel, a community in pain and processing traumatic experiences. Trauma studies and the specific therapeutic approach of ACT open new horizons of possibilities by focusing on the relationship of suffering, pain, and loss to core values, and the use of metaphors to communicate and process trauma.

NOTES

1. Unless otherwise noted, all translations are the author's.
2. Parpola (1997: xxxvi) writes, "Most commonly, the king is portrayed as a baby suckled, comforted, tended, carried, reared and protected by the Goddess . . . and appears as his

mother . . . as midwife . . . and tenderly calls him 'my calf' or 'my king' while she fiercely attacks his enemies."

3. Pronounced "act." Matheny and Hale (2023: 238) explain, "Originally developed in the late 1980s by Dr. Steven C. Hayes, ACT is a 'third wave' cognitive behavioural therapy. Like other iterations of cognitive behavioural therapy ACT rests on the foundational understanding that human experience, thought and action are intertwined. Unlike other forms of psychotherapy, ACT does not divide behaviours or thoughts or emotions into discrete 'good' and 'bad' categories" (see also Stoddard and Afar 2014).

4. Matheny and Hale (2023: 239) write, "the 'passengers on a bus' metaphor can provide a way for people to understand the concept of allowing difficult emotions or thoughts to be present while still making choices about their outward behaviour; sometimes thoughts and emotions can fill one's head, clamoring for attention (some of them very loud, smelly and obnoxious), but the goal is for the bus driver to continue driving the route in a safe way, respectful of all the passengers s/he carries." The "bus metaphor" acknowledges all passengers, all emotions and experiences, and provides a way forward that integrates all of life and experiences, both positive and negative, giving tools for assisting clients to drive according to their core values. See Hayes, Strosahl, and Wilson 1999: 157–58. This is a helpful corrective to dangerous triumphalist theology or toxic positivity. ACT creates room to embrace all of what makes us human, acknowledges pain, and honors negative emotions, especially as appropriate responses to trauma.

REFERENCES

Ben Zvi, Ehud. 2005. *Hosea*. FOTL 21A/1. Grand Rapids: Eerdmans.

Ben Zvi, Ehud, Claudia V. Camp, David M. Gunn, Aaron W. Hughes, eds. 2015. *Poets, Prophets, and Texts in Play: Studies in Biblical Poetry and Prophecy*. LHBOTS 597. London: T&T Clark.

Boase, Elizabeth, and Christopher G. Frechette, eds. 2016. *Bible through the Lens of Trauma*. Semeia Studies. Atlanta: SBL.

Caruth, Cathy. 1995. *Unclaimed Experience: Trauma, Narrative, and History*. Baltimore: John Hopkins University Press.

Eidevall, Göran. 1996. *Grapes in the Desert: Metaphors, Models, and Themes in Hosea 4–14*. ConBOT 43. Stockholm: Almqvist and Wiksell.

Garber, David G. 2015. "Trauma Theory and Biblical Studies." *CBR* 14, no. 1: 24–44.

Goldingay, John. 2020. "Hosea 4 and 11, and the Structure of Hosea." *TynBul* 71: 181–90.

Goldingay, John. 2021. *Hosea—Micah*. Baker Commentary on the Old Testament. Grand Rapids: Baker.

Hayes, S. C., K. Strosahl, and K. G. Wilson. 1999. *Acceptance and Commitment Therapy: An Experiential Approach to Behavior Change*. New York: Guilford.

Harris, Russ. 2019. *ACT Made Simple: An Easy-to-Read Primer on Acceptance and Commitment Therapy*. Oakland, CA: New Harbinger.

Hwang, Jerry. 2021. *Hosea*. Zondervan Exegetical Commentary on the Old Testament. Grand Rapids: Zondervan Academic.

Keefe, Alice A. 2001. *Woman's Body and the Social Body in Hosea*. GCT 10; JSOTSup 338. Sheffield: Sheffield Academic.

Kelle, Brad. 2005. *Hosea 2: Metaphor and Rhetoric in Historical Perspective*. SBLAB 20. Atlanta: SBL.

Landy, Francis. 2011. *Hosea*. Readings: A New Bible Commentary. 2nd ed. Sheffield: Sheffield Phoenix.

Marlow, Hilary. 2013. "Ecology, Theology, Society: Physical, Religious, and Social Disjuncture in Biblical and Neo-Assyrian Prophetic Texts." In Robert P. Gordon and Hans M. Barstad, eds., *"Thus Speaks Ishtar of Arbela": Prophecy in Israel, Assyria, and Egypt in the Neo-Assyrian Period*. Winona Lake, IN: Eisenbrauns, 187–202.

Matheny, Jennifer, and Amy E. Hale. 2023. "The Raging Prophet: Acceptance Commitment Therapy (ACT) as a Pathway Forward through Pain." In Heather A. McKay and Pieter van der Zwan, eds., *When Psychology Meets the Bible*. Bible in the Modern World 83. Sheffield Centre for Interdisciplinary Biblical Studies Monographs 6. Sheffield: Sheffield Phoenix, 236–56.

Mays, James Luther. 1969. *Hosea*. OTL. London: SCM.

Moon, Joshua. 2018. *Hosea*. AOTC 21. London: Apollos; Downer's Grove, IL: IVP Academic.

Morris, Gerald. 1996. *Prophecy, Poetry, and Hosea*. JSOTSup 219. Sheffield: Sheffield Academic.

Nogalski, James. 2011. *The Book of the Twelve:Hosea-Jonah*. Smyth & Helwys Bible Commentary. Macon, GA: Smyth & Helwys.

O'Connor, Kathleen. 2011. *Jeremiah: Pain and Promise*. Minneapolis: Fortress.

Parpola, Simo. 1997. *Assyrian Prophecies*. SAA 9. Helsinki: Helsinki University Press.

Routledge, Robin. 2020. *Hosea*. TOTC 24. Downer's Grove, IL: IVP Academic.

Schüngel–Straumann, Helen. 1995. "God as Mother in Hosea 11." In Athalya Brenner, ed., *A Feminist Companion to the Latter Prophets*. FCB 8. Sheffield: Sheffield Academic, 194–218.

Sherwood, Yvonne. 1996. *The Prostitute and the Prophet: Reading Hosea in the Late Twentieth Century*. London and New York: T&T Continuum.

Smith-Christopher, Daniel L. 2011. "Reading War and Trauma: Suggestions toward a Social-Psychological Exegesis of Exile and War in Biblical Texts." In Brad E. Kelle, Frank Ritchel Ames, and Jacob L. Wright, eds., *Interpreting Exile: Displacement and Deportation in Biblical and Modern Contexts*. SBLAIL 10. Atlanta: SBL, 253–74.

Stoddard, Jill A., and Niloofar Afar. 2014. *The Big Book of ACT Metaphors: A Practitioner's Guide to Experiential Exercises and Metaphors in Acceptance and Commitment Therapy*. Oakland, CA: New Harbinger.

Strawn, Brent A. 2005. *What Is Stronger Than a Lion? Leonine Image and Metaphor in the Hebrew Bible and the Ancient Near East*. OBO 212. Göttingen: Vandenhoeck & Ruprecht.

Swanson, James. 1997. *Dictionary of Biblical Languages with Semantic Domains: Hebrew (Old Testament)*. Oak Harbor: Logos Research Systems Inc.

Sweeney, Marvin A. 2000. *The Twelve Prophets*. Vol. 1. Berit Olam. Collegeville, MN: Liturgical.

Wacker, Marie-Theres. 2012. "Hosea: The God-Identified Man and the Woman (Women) Israel." In Louise Shotroff and Marie-Theres Wacker, eds., *Feminist Biblical Interpretation: A Compendium of Critical Commentary on the Books of the Bible and Related Literature*. Grand Rapids: Eerdmans, 371–385.

Wolff, Hans Walter. 1974. *Hosea*. Hermeneia. Philadelphia: Fortress.

Yee, Gale A. 1996. "The Book of Hosea: Introduction, Commentary, and Reflections." In L. E. Keck et al., eds., *The New Interpreter's Bible Volume 7*. Nashville: Abingdon, 195–297.

CHAPTER 15

HOSEA 12–13 AND PROPHETIC COMPOSITION, RHETORIC, AND RECOLLECTION

JOHN GOLDINGAY

HOSEA 12–13 fits the typical profile of Hebrew Bible (First Testament) prophecy, while also having distinctive characteristics. It is typical of the prophets, especially in the monarchic period, that:

- On Yhwh's behalf, they critique Israel for its faithlessness.
- They threaten Israel with trouble to come from Yhwh.
- They aim thus to turn Israel from its faithlessness.
- They deliver their messages orally in poetic missives of a few lines.
- They use all manner of rhetorical devices to seek to achieve their aim.
- To this end, they also appeal to Israel's awareness of Yhwh's past involvement with the people.
- They or their curators put their messages into writing and string them into longer units.
- In doing so, they adapt them for later application.
- Their messages commended themselves to Israel in such a way that they became part of Israel's scriptures.

It is a Wittgensteinian "family resemblances" profile: that is, not every prophet needs to manifest every feature in order to count as belonging to the family, and individual members of the family have their personal characteristics. Hosea 12–13 has all the features and also manifests some distinctiveness in its embodiment of them, in particular in the number and variety of its allusions to the stories of Israel's ancestors and of

Israel itself, which play a significant role in the chapters. The two chapters thus combine a number of characteristics in a way that gives them a distinctive profile:

- They are a piece of rhetoric, in the sense that their aim is to change the thinking and the life of people who read them, and they use language and argument to that end.
- Their language and argument takes poetic form, with features one would then expect such as rhythm, parallelism, paronomasia, and unusual word order.
- They use metaphor, which can enable readers to see things and thus itself has a rhetorical purpose: it is designed to change people's way of seeing.
- Paradoxically they also seek to achieve their aim by being allusive, bivalent, and ambiguous, rather than transparent in meaning.
- In seeking to change their readers' thinking, they appeal to their inherited memory of their ancestors' lives and actions, while likely tweaking their version of that memory.
- In making this appeal, they interact with existent formulations of that memory, semifixed in writing or in the way the story is told.

The allusiveness and ambiguity of the chapters is understood in varying ways by the Septuagint, the Vulgate, the Targum, Aquila, Symmachus, and Theodotion, among others. While these variations might indicate that translators were working with different forms of the text than the one represented by the MT, and thus with potentially more ancient ones, it is at least as likely they were wrestling to make sense of a text that is not so different from the MT but is more allusive and difficult than, say, Amos. In light of its difficulties, Hosea's text has also been the subject of many modern suggestions for revision. In general, it seems wiser and more productive to work with the MT with its challenges and allusiveness, "not because the MT is sacrosanct, but because we cannot pretend to know better" (Andersen and Freedman 1980: 628). In this essay, I thus make little reference to ancient or modern alternative versions of the text. Additionally, I assume that the process of curating Hosea's messages will have meant that the book now includes words that did not derive from Hosea himself. I work here with the version of the text that issued from this process, and when I use expressions such as "Hosea says," I do not at every point necessarily imply a reference to Hosea in person as opposed to the Hosea scroll that we now have.

15.1. COMPOSITION

The material in Hos. 12–13 will have begun life as messages of a few lines delivered in a location such as the Samaria city square or the Beth-El sanctuary, or sent as missives to the palace. The chapters we have are a compilation of such messages. I take the first unit, for instance, to be a compilation from at least three short messages, so that there is no original link between 12:1–3, 4–5, and 6–7 (Eng. 11:12–12:2, 3–4, and 5–6), and something similar is true throughout the chapters. The logic in the resultant arrangement of prophetic scrolls is sometimes clear but sometimes not—at least, interpreters sometimes agree on it and sometimes do not. As is the case with Proverbs, I hypothesize that the curators of Hosea's messages could sometimes see ways to link sayings, but were sometimes left with messages that evaded arrangement, which they therefore simply juxtaposed to other messages and left as postscripts to them. In Hos. 12–13, the opening verses, 12:1–7 (Eng. 11:12–12:6), provide a clue to the arrangement of the chapters; or, to put it another way, I imagine readers of the scroll reading Hos. 12–13 in light of those opening verses. Admittedly, this is to oversimply the interpretive process, because there is commonly a two-way interpretive relationship between the introduction to a document and the material that follows it. Thus the body of Hos. 12–13 draws attention to and clarifies those opening verses, even while those verses introduce what follows.

There is no warrant before the time of the medieval chapter divisions associated with Stephen Langton for seeing Hos. 12 and 13 as two units (cf. Gruber 2017: 522), and neither does the material in the chapters suggest any such warrant. Consideration of the interaction between the opening verses and what follows rather generates the proposition that Hos. 12–13 consists of a series of five substantially parallel units, assembled from originally briefer messages. The units characteristically comprise critique of Israel, threat of consequences to follow, and recollection of moments from the history of Israel and of its ancestors that encourage reflection on the critiques and threats and an appropriate response. It seems quite an oversimplification to say that "the main intention of the text [Heb. 12:1–14:9] is to communicate hope to the readers" (Ben Zvi 2005: 243), but neither does Hosea wish his readers to think that their situation is hopeless.

In the outline and discussion of the five units that follows, I mostly leave questions about rhetoric and recollection for the later sections in this essay, and I presuppose conclusions about many other aspects of the chapters' exegesis that are discussed in the commentaries listed in the bibliography.

15.1.1. 12:1–7 (Eng. 11:12–12:6)

Critique:

12:1 [11:12]Ephraim has surrounded me with deceit,
Israel's household with fraud.
And Judah, he is still wandering with God,
with holy ones being truthful.
2 [1]Ephraim is shepherding a wind,
pursuing an east wind all day long.
Falsehood and destruction he makes plentiful,
a pledge with Assyria they solemnize,
and oil to Egypt is carried.

Threat:

3 [2]So Yhwh: a confrontation with Judah,
and attending to Jacob in accordance with his practices;
in keeping with his deeds he will give back to him.

Recollection:	4 [3]In the womb he grasped at his brother,
	and in his manhood he exerted himself with God.
	5 [4]He exerted himself towards an envoy and won;
	he cried and sought grace with him.
	At Beth-El he finds him,
	and there he speaks with us.
Exhortation:	6 [5]So Yhwh [is] the God of Armies,
	Yhwh [is] his invocation.
	7 [6]So you, through your God you are to go back;
	commitment in the exercise of authority, keep it,
	and hope in your God continually.

First Testament poets sometimes provide readers with hints regarding the beginning and end of units (tricola are a marker in these chapters, as this unit illustrates), but they often leave readers to work things out. Here, the MT is surely right to see 11:11 as the end of a subsection, at least, and thus to put a setumah there. The version of the medieval chapter divisions that appears in printed Hebrew Bibles (BHS, NJPS, BHQ) is thus right to begin a new chapter at 12:1 (Eng. 11:12), not at a verse later, like other English translations.

This opening unit begins with a critique of Ephraim that leads into a threat. While the first Judah line could be a later adaptation of the message, it is harder to peel off the second Judah reference. I take 12:1–3 (Eng. 11:12–12:2) as an original two-part indictment and threat. The critique moves from the metaphorical (Ephraim has surrounded Yhwh like a hostile army), the unspecific (deceit, fraud), the ambiguous (wandering, with holy ones being truthful), the metaphorical and also bivalent (shepherding a wind, pursuing an east wind, falsehood, destruction), eventually to the straightforward and explicit (shepherding wind is spelled out in terms of making commitments to Assyria and Egypt) (see Na'aman 2015: 236–38).

Yhwh therefore has "a confrontation with Judah": it is a verbless sentence, a common feature of Hebrew and specifically of Hebrew poetry. Being verbless need not issue in ambiguity, and English translations routinely render such sentences as present-tense statements. Here, the verbless construction continues in the parallel colon, which combines it with the convention whereby an infinitive can take the place of a finite verb. But then the unexpected third colon has a finite verb, a yiqtol form. I infer that v. 3 (Eng. v. 2) refers to the argument Yhwh has now with Judah and Jacob about their faithlessness, which will issue in retribution.

In light of preceding chapters and of what will come in the rest of Hos. 12–13, the recollection of Jacob's story in vv. 4–5 (Eng. vv. 3–4) is not a surprise, but the subsequent exhortation stands out because there will be no more exhortation in chs. 12–13. This one will in due course be complemented by the substantial exhortation comprising 14:2–4 (Eng. 14:1–3), which faces both ways: it brings chs. 12–13 to a conclusion, resolving the possible suspense raised by the shortfall in the intervening units, and also introduces the conclusion to the Hosea scroll as a whole. Three times Hosea explicitly urges Ephraim to turn back to Yhwh (10:12; 12:7 [Eng. 12:6]; 14:2–4 [Eng. 14:1–3]), "but everything in between is *implicitly* deployed to that same end" (Lancaster 2021: 419). To put it another way, the rhetorical aim of 12:1–7 (Eng. 11:12–12:6) remains implicit until the last verse, where the bidding (a yiqtol), "you are to go back," and the two imperatives, "keep" and "hope," make unequivocal the aim of what precedes. They take the passage from the metaphorical and implicit to the straightforward and explicit.

15.1.2. 12:8–14 (Eng. 12:7–13)

Critique:
8 [7]Phoenicia: fraudulent balances in his hand,
    likes extorting.
9 [8]Ephraim has said, "Yes, I have gotten rich,
    I have found wealth for me.
All my labors: people will not find for me
    waywardness that is an offence."

Threat:
10 [9]But I [am] Yhwh your God
    since the country of Egypt.
Again I will have you live in tents
    as in the days of assembly.
11 [10]I will speak to the prophets,
    (and I have made vision plentiful),
    and by the hand of the prophets I will represent things.
12 [11]If Gilead [is] trouble,
    yes, they have become empty.
At the Gilgal they have sacrificed bulls;
    their altars, too:
    like rock piles on the open country's furrows.

Recollection:
13 [12]So Jacob fled to the open country of Aram,
    and Israel served for a wife,
    for a wife he acted as a keeper.
14 [13]But by a prophet Yhwh brought up
    Israel from Egypt,
    and by a prophet it was kept.

The nature of 12:8–9 (Eng. 12:7–8) as critique is eventually clear, though it might not be immediately so. Hosea here plays the same game as he does in 4:1–3 and as Amos does in Amos 1:3–3:2, where they sound as if they are indicting the nations but they are softening up their hearers for an indictment of the hearers themselves (Goldingay 2021: 73–88; 2020: 181–90). The unit actually begins with an exclamation about Phoenicia, but the word for Phoenicia (*kəna'an*, Canaan) can also denote a trader, the role for which Phoenicia was known. Subsequent phrases in vv. 8–9 (Eng. vv. 7–8) indicate this to be the significance here (cf. Tg). Ephraimites would surely enjoy hearing their prophet critique the great northwestern trading power for its dishonesty, though the sharp-minded

216 JOHN GOLDINGAY

might not be surprised when it transpires that really Ephraim itself is the dishonest trader to whom the exclamation refers. In the preceding verses, the prophet has indicted Ephraim for deceit, fraud, and falsehood. "Fraud" was also Isaac's accusation against Jacob in Gen. 27:35, while Jacob with some ironic bullishness could claim to be free of any "offense" in Gen. 31:36. Ephraim cannot make that claim, though Hosea has Ephraim implying, "My prosperity proves I am not a wrongdoer!" (cf. Macintosh 1997: 497).

In the middle section, the alternating between yiqtol, weqatal, qatal, and yiqtol forms has generated almost every possible combination of future, present, and past translations of the verbs and the noun clauses. But the semantically and rhetorically redundant pronoun "I" before the surprising qatal verb ("and I have made vision plentiful") signals a circumstantial clause (see GKC 142d) paralleling in its time reference the preceding allusion to "Egypt" and the "days of assembly."[1] The verse as a whole, then, continues the declaration of intent begun in v. 10 (Eng. v. 9). In v. 12 (Eng. v. 11), "Gilead" and "trouble" suggest an allusion to the coup to which Hosea has already referred (6:8–9; 2 Kgs. 15:25) (Na'aman 2021). The verse's opaqueness likely illustrates how some ambiguity in these chapters reflects our lacking information available to Hosea's original audience. But Hosea is also trading on the ambiguity of the word "trouble" (ʾāwen), which can denote both wrongdoing and its consequences (the word may have already lurked in v. 4 [Eng. v. 3] with this implication). The allusiveness may also link with the upcoming reference to Jacob's sojourn in Aram and thus with events in Gilead on the way home from there (Gen. 31). The context of the threat in vv. 10–11 (Eng. vv. 9–10) then suggests that the noun clauses in v. 12 (Eng. v. 11) can point to trouble and destruction that will follow on Gilead's becoming "empty," worthless, false (see Exod. 20:7) and on Gilgal's being the location of sacrifices that were also empty—sacrifices offered on the occasion of the coup, or originally on the occasion of kingmaking (1 Sam. 11:15), or simply on regular festival occasions (Hos. 4:15). The altars will end up as merely heaps of rocks.

15.1.3. 12:15 (Eng. 12:14)–13:5

Critique: 12:15 [14] Ephraim has provoked to multiple bitterness,
his bloodshed he will let rest on him,
and his reviling he will bring back to him—the Lord will.
13:1 When Ephraim spoke with quivering,
when he lifted up [his voice] in Israel,
He incurred guilt through the Master, and died,
2 but now they continue to offend.
They have made themselves a cast image,
from their silver, in accordance with their discernment, an idol.
Manufacture by craftworkers, all of it,
they are saying of them.
People who sacrifice a human being,
they kiss bullocks.
Threat: 3 Therefore they will be like morning cloud,

PROPHETIC COMPOSITION, RHETORIC, AND RECOLLECTION   217

or like the dew going early.
Like chaff that is whirled from a threshing floor,
or like smoke from a vent.

Recollection: [4]But I: Yhwh your God,
from the country of Egypt.
A God apart from me you do not acknowledge,
and a deliverer, there is none except me.
[5]I was the one who acknowledged you in the wilderness,
in a country of much drought.

Critique dominates the first section, though the opening line anticipates the threat that follows as the second section. While it would be natural to relate 12:15 (Eng. 12:14) to the coup referred to in 12:12 (Eng. 12:11), it is more natural to relate 13:1 to the origin of the Ephraimite nation (the meaning of the word translated "quivering" is quite uncertain). Ephraim's origins, with its encouraging of worship that was too redolent of worship of the Master (*habbaʿal*), sentenced it to death, and led to its being counted dead or effectively dead.[2] "Ephraim continues in the way of sin like zombies, the walking dead" (Mays 1969: 172).

15.1.4. 13:6–11

Critique: [6]When they pastured, they were full;
they were full, and their inner being lifted up;
therefore they put me out of mind.

Threat: [7]So I have become to them like a lion,
like a leopard by the road I will keep watch.
[8]I will meet them like a bear bereaved,
and I will rip the casing of their heart.
I will devour them there like a lion,
a creature of the open country that will tear them apart.
[9]Your devastation, Israel,
because in me [is] your help.

Recollection: [10]Where is your king, then,
so that he may deliver you in all your towns,
Or your leaders, of whom you said,
"Give me a king and officials."
[11]I give you a king in my anger,
I get him in my wrath.

The threat of devastation contrasts with 11:9.[3]

15.1.5. 13:12–14:1 (Eng. 13:12–16)

Critique:
^{12}Ephraim's waywardness is bound up,
  its offense hidden away.

Threat:
^{13}The pains of a woman birthing, they will come to him;
  he [will be] not a wise son.
Because [at] the time he will not stand firm,
  at [the time for] the breaking out of children.
^{14}From the hand of Sheol I will save them,
  from death I will restore them?
Where is your great epidemic, Death,
  where is your destruction, Sheol?
Relenting will hide from my eyes,
  ^{15}because he—among brothers he acts the wild donkey.
An east wind, a supernatural wind, will come,
  going up from the wilderness,
And his fountain will be shamed,
  his spring will dry up.
It—it will plunder the storehouse,
  every valuable object.
$^{14:1 [13:16]}$Samaria will make restitution,
  because it has defied its God.
By the sword they will fall,
  their babies will be dashed down,
his pregnant women will be torn apart.

An account of Ephraim's wrongdoing is securely on record against the time when its penalty will be exacted. The subsequent threat is in part a puzzle. Whereas the bulk of 13:13–14:1 (Eng. 13:16) comprises warnings ("Hosea's last and harshest announcement of Israel's end," Mays 1969: 179), Hosea 13:14a looks more like a promise. I assume the usual way of resolving the difficulty, by treating v. 14a as an unmarked question (see the survey of possibilities in Ben Zvi 2005: 274–75). The subsequent cola about epidemic and destruction either underscore the promise or respond to the question; the last colon in v. 14, with its denial of relenting, more directly answers the question and is hard to fit with a promise. Its denial of relenting (*nōḥam*) contrasts with the declaration about relenting in 11:8 (*niḥûmâ*) (Landy 2011: 194), but 13:15–14:1 (Eng. 13:15–16) provides its rationale.

The unit includes no recollection, but exhortation follows in 14:2–4 (Eng. 14:1–3). A regular assumption in the Latter Prophets is that Israel has to decide how to respond to Yhwh's critique and threats, and its response will determine whether it experiences Yhwh as "life-giver" or "death-dealer" (Yee 1996). The effect of the continual switching between the two portraits of Yhwh in Hosea is "to destabilize Israel, to maintain the ambiguity of Israel's *actual* future among the various *possible* futures presented in the book. It is to communicate that Israel's future is indeterminate, and which future will obtain depends ostensibly on Israel's choice of actions" (Lancaster 2021: 421, italics original). The unmarked question is a real question, not a rhetorical one.

15.2. RHETORIC: AMBIGUITY AND PARONOMASIA

While I envision Hosea proclaiming his messages to an Ephraimite public in the city square or the sanctuary courtyard, or sending them to the king and his staff, the intellectually challenging form of his communication suggests that he aimed in particular to get it home to the people whom Proverbs would call the (supposedly) wise (cf. Hos. 14:10 [Eng. 14:9])—the opinion-formers, the influencers, the people with power, the people who would argue out what should be Ephraimite religious and political policy, the people equivalent in Jesus's ministry to the Pharisees, the Sadducees, and the scribes. Hosea and other First Testament poets, such as the theologians whose work features in Proverbs, sometimes use words and compose sentences of straightforward and unequivocal meaning, sometimes use words and compose sentences that seem ambiguous but whose meaning can eventually be divined, and sometimes use words and compose sentences that are systematically ambiguous and stimulate readers' reflection. And sometimes they use words with homonyms or they juxtapose similar words in a way that can also stimulate reflection. One cannot establish that poets or their original audiences were aware of paronomasia or ambiguity, or that the distinction between apparent and irresolvable ambiguity was real for poet and original audience rather than being one we need because we lack clarifiers that they would have had. But paronomasia, ambiguity, and allusiveness are regular features of poetry, and it seems plausible to assume that they are inherent in First Testament poetry. When an element in a prophecy seems capable of more than one meaning, then, it is a mistake to assume that we have to decide which understanding the author intended.

Hosea 12–13 begins with a metaphor ("you have surrounded me"), then adds another ("Ephraim is shepherding a wind, pursuing an east wind"). Surrounding someone need not be a hostile action, but it often is, and here the surrounding involves "deceit" and "fraud," later "falsehood." Surrounding suggests encompassing, enclosing, circumscribing—the action of an adversary seeking to overwhelm a victim, in this case by duplicity and treachery. Ephraim goes through the motions of commitment to Yhwh, but they are only motions. Ironically, the subsequent metaphors indicate that Ephraim is also deceiving itself, in that it is trying to do the impossible—to shepherd or pursue wind (pursuing takes shepherding further, and the reference to the fierce "east wind" off the desert takes "wind" further). Hosea extends the irony in a fashion of which Proverbs, again, is especially fond. Ephraim is (unconsciously) seeking to deceive Yhwh, but it is actually deceiving itself. It is seeking to achieve something positive for itself by way of safety or deliverance, which it hopes to make abundant, but it is actually guaranteeing that its own "destruction" will abound. Hosea's words are not polyvalent in the sense of being open to multiple interpretations according to the readers' insight (except in the sense that they might be polyvalent on the basis of some theories of language and meaning). They are bivalent in the sense that a double meaning is inherent in them.

Hosea's words are open to a further double reading. Ephraim is engaged in fraud and falsehood with Yhwh. Does Hosea imply that Ephraim also engaged in fraud and falsehood in its relationships with Aram and/or Assyria and/or Egypt? In explicitly referring to the two imperial powers, Hosea speaks straightforwardly and explicitly, as well as metaphorically and theologically, though his words illustrate how statements that may have been unequivocal for his listeners are less clear to us. Ephraim's falsehood lies in the solemnizing of pledges on different occasions with Assyria and Egypt, pledges that would be encouraged by gifts of oil, sealed by anointing with oil, or paid for in forms such as oil. Hosea's parallelism works by separating what could be a prose sentence into two cola, dividing between them what would be the elements in the prose sentence. Ephraim is not false just once, perhaps by oversight; it makes falsehood plentiful (and also makes destruction plentiful). Although the description of the falsehood is down-to-earth in its reference to specific political alliances, it intensifies the critique of the falsehood because solemnizing a pledge (*kārat bərît*) with anyone other than Yhwh is exactly what Israel should not be doing (Deut. 7:2).

Hosea's words are bivalent or multivalent in yet a third way. Hosea's critique of Ephraim in 12:1–2 (Eng. 11:12–12:1) is clear. But in its midst lies an ambiguous line about Judah that could be read as complimentary or critical. Hosea might compliment Judah to underscore his critique of Ephraim (or a curator might incorporate a compliment to Judah), though elsewhere Hosea includes a number of critical remarks about Judah, and a compliment here would be unique. The translation above preserves some of the line's ambiguity. Its two verbs could be participles or qatal forms, though this makes little difference. The preposition "with" ('*im*) can be positive or negative; Hosea will shortly refer to a pledge "with" Assyria and a confrontation "with" Judah (12:2–3 [Eng. 12:1–2]). "Wandering" (*rûd*) could be positive, negative, or neutral; the verb occurs elsewhere in the First Testament only a handful of times (Gen. 27:40; Jer. 2:31; perhaps Ps. 55:3 [Eng. 55:2]), and its meaning is uncertain to us, though it might have been clear to Hosea's readers. Further, it is sufficiently akin to more familiar verbs (*rādâ* "rule," see Aq; *yārad* "descend," see, e.g., Vg) to confuse people or provide alternatives to a critical reading of the statement (see, e.g., Tg, NRSV). In the context in Hosea, it can be no coincidence that the reference to wandering constitutes a first link with the Jacob and Esau story in Genesis: Isaac had destined Esau to be a wanderer, whose life would thus contrast with Jacob's (Gen. 27:40). It is therefore a neat, snide description to apply either to Ephraim or to Judah, who are drifting away from Yhwh.

In the parallel colon about Judah, the idea of "holy ones" (*qədôšîm*) being "truthful" would raise no problems, but it is odd that "truthful" is singular. Might *qədôšîm* refer to Yhwh, the word being formally plural yet singular in its reference (like *'ĕlōhîm*)? But there are no parallels for that usage; more likely the colon refers to Judah being truthful toward holy ones other than Yhwh, to other supernatural beings. Positively, this could signify truthfulness in Judah's relationship with Yhwh's staff as well as with Yhwh himself, truthfulness with the holy ones who "surround" Yhwh as his servants along with his own "truthfulness" (Ps. 89:8–9 [Eng. 89:7–8])—whereas Ephraim has "surrounded" Yhwh with deceit. On the other hand, as part of a critique, the colon would signify Judah's wrongful truthfulness toward supernatural beings who are Yhwh's rivals. Most of these aspects that are ambiguous for us would have been ambiguous for Hosea's audience, who would have needed to think fiercely about the words even while they assimilated Hosea's straightforward critique of them and his pointing out the trouble they were bringing on themselves and the scandalous implications of their political and religious policies.

In 12:8–14 (Eng. 12:7–13), the critique section begins with the multivalent *kəna'an* (Canaan/Phoenicia/merchant) and goes on to finding wealth (*'ôn*) "for me" and to people not finding waywardness (*'āwōn*) "for me." Hosea again implies that Ephraim is deceiving itself. The similarity in the words for wealth and waywardness implies a closer association of the two than Ephraim acknowledges. Further, the word for wealth was also the word for manliness or vigor in v. 4 (Eng. v. 3). So Ephraim's ancestor Jacob reached manliness or vigor, and Ephraim might also be prepared to claim it. But once again, for Ephraim the juxtaposition implies something that Ephraim half-acknowledges by its use of words—that in its case manliness or vigor is akin to waywardness.

A fruitful bivalence then opens the threat section in 12:8–14 (Eng. 12:7–13). It drives people to think about what Yhwh intends to do. The first thing is to have them "live in tents as in the days of assembly." Is this good news or bad news? Might the threat suggest living in tents in the manner of a festival, but imply an irony, with negative implications (Rudolph 1966: 234)? If Yhwh speaks to the "prophets," will this mean an encouraging message or a critical and threatening one? Prophets were means of slaughter in 6:5. Prophetic "vision" in the past has heralded both blessing and trouble. To "represent" things could likewise go either way. And which verb is it that closes the verse, anyway? *Dāmâ* I (piel) indeed means "represent." But every other occurrence of *dāmâ* in Hosea has been *dāmâ* II (qal or niphal; 4:5, 6; 10:7, 15, five of the verb's fourteen occurrences), which means "destroy" (so NRSV here). The threat then closes with the opaque references to trouble and devastation that issue from people having become "empty" or fake (*šāw'*) as they sacrificed bulls (*šəwārîm*), which will issue in "the Gilgal" becoming mere rock piles (*gallîm*).

In 13:6–11, Yhwh's threat to keep watch (*'āšûr*) is a threat to be Assyria (*'aššûr*; cf. LXX). But the ambiguity lies in the word *'ĕhî*. In v. 10, LXX, Vg, and Tg take it as an alternative to *'ê* and *'ayyē*, as a word meaning "where" (see Rudolph 1966: 236). But in v. 7 *wā'ĕhî* on Yhwh's lips means "and I was"; *'ĕhî* is the apocopated form of Yhwh's *'ehyeh*, "I am" (1:9; also Gen. 26:3, to Isaac; 31:3, to Jacob; Exod. 3:12, 14; 4:12, 15, to Moses).[4] Could it be that "*'ĕhî*, as "I am," vanishes into *'ĕhî* as "where" (Landy 2011: 194; see also Gruber 2017: 540–44)? Does Yahweh challenge Ephraim simultaneously to face the question, "Where is your king now?" and his own assertion, "I am your king" (cf. Yee 1996)?

In the final unit (13:12–14:1 [Eng. 13:12–16]), Ephraim has to ask itself whether the line about rescue from Sheol is a promise, a rhetorical question, or an open question. And

222 JOHN GOLDINGAY

it has to face the possibility that its name, which Ephraim's father linked with fruitfulness (*pārâ*, Gen. 41:52), suggests that it is a wild donkey (*pere'*: the verb in v. 15 is the hapax *pārā'*). The subsequent threat pictures a fountain and spring failing and drying up; but the verb for failing (*yābēš*) is pointed as if from the verb for being shamed (*bûš*). Samaria, for its defiance of Yhwh, will bear guilt and therefore have to make restitution ('*āšam*; cf. 13:1); but bearing its guilt will imply desolation and devastation (*šāmēm*).[5]

15.3. RECOLLECTION

Francis Landy (2001: 265) asserts, "Metaphor is a form of memory" and "'YHWH, God of Hosts, YHWH is his memory' (Hos. 12.6)." He adds that metaphor "opens the possibility of continuity" and of retaining a sense of the past (p. 265). Hosea 12–13 makes multiple appeals to Israel's past story and Yhwh's past involvement with Israel. In the terms of current interpretive trends, these appeals invite consideration in the framework of intertextuality and the study of social memory; in the terms of an older framework, Hosea implies a typological relationship between Israel's past story (particularly the story of its ancestor Jacob) and its present life (so Fishbane 1985: 376–78; Blum 2009; Moon 2018: 192–95). Allusiveness and ambiguity continue in Hosea's appeal to Israel's memory and to its awareness of its story known to us from the Torah and the Former Prophets, as he pursues his aim to get Israel to turn from its faithlessness.

Hosea 12–13 refers to a number of scenes in the Torah and the Former Prophets: the exodus, Yhwh's giving prophets visions, Gilead and Gilgal, Jacob's flight to Aram, Moses's bringing the Israelites out of Egypt, the setting up of the state of Ephraim, the journey through the wilderness, and the appointment of kings. The sequence of references thus bears no relationship to the sequence within the biblical narrative. While there is no doubt about some of these references, some allusions are less certain. In general, Hosea's lexical connections with other texts are not numerous. The connections are thematically reworked, and they prize rhetoric over historical detail (Smith 2018: 256). But some verbal links with the Jacob story are noteworthy: examples are Jacob "fleeing," "serving" for a wife, and "keeping" sheep in that connection (e.g., Gen. 27:43; 28:2; 29:15; 30:31).

The allusions to Jacob in Hos. 12:4–5 (Eng. 12:3–4) are particularly intriguing. There are numerous ways of understanding the overlaps between Hos. 12–13 and people and events in the Torah and the Former Prophets, particularly Jacob in Genesis, and all have advocates: (1) Hosea knew Genesis in something like the form we know it (written or oral); (2) the author of Genesis knew Hosea in something like the form we know it; (3) Hosea knew the stories in Genesis in an earlier written or oral form; or (4) the references to the Jacob stories found their way into Hosea at a later stage in the development of the Hosea scroll. Consideration of the question is complex because of ongoing scholarly debate on the origins of Genesis and of Hosea.[6] Whereas some approaches to intertextuality depend on knowing which text came first, other approaches operate with the assumption that one can learn from comparing texts without knowing the answer to that question. My working assumption is that Hosea knew the Jacob story in something like the form we have it in Genesis, but nevertheless he is "making free use" of the traditions (Macintosh 1997: 476). "Hosea is not writing out a history of Jacob; he uses the Jacob narrative for his own rhetorical ends" (Moon 2018: 200). But most of the words in 12:4–5 (Eng. 12:3–4) parallel words in the Jacob story, and a number are unusual enough to confirm that it is no coincidence. Hosea is familiar with a version of the story that is not so different from the one in Genesis.

After the move within 12:1–3 (Eng. 11:12–12:2) from metaphor through ambiguity to explicitness and clarity, and from Ephraim and Judah to the Jacob of the present, v. 4 (Eng. v. 3) jumps back to long ago events involving ancestor Jacob, and returns to ambiguity. In some way, the action of Ephraim/Judah/Jacob in the present needs to be considered in light of the past story of Jacob, as a replay of his actions in the past (and perhaps of Judah's actions, for which see Gen. 38; Josh. 7, though Hosea does not pick up that possibility). Genesis does not explicitly critique Jacob, and neither does Hosea. In general, Genesis just tells the story of Jacob and Esau, without painting either character as a good guy or a bad guy, and Hosea does the same.

When Esau and Jacob were born, Jacob (*yaʿăqôb*) was holding into Esau's heel (*ʿāqēb*), which was why they named him Jacob (Gen. 25:26). The urgency with which Jacob was pursuing Esau foreshadows the story that will follow, without there being an implication that Jacob was at fault in the urgency of his pursuit. Genesis leaves open the possibility that he was simply pursuing the destiny he was to have within Yhwh's purpose; he was acting in fulfillment of Yhwh's word (Tg). In due course, not unreasonably, Esau criticizes Jacob (Gen. 27:36), turning the noun "heel" into the verb meaning "grasp by the heel" (*ʿāqab*). Hosea picks up this verb, leaving readers to work out whether it implies critique, or rather, to work out how it suggests they should think about themselves.

The parallel colon in 12:4b (Eng. 12:3b) not only fails to resolve that ambiguity, but deepens it. Like Genesis, Hosea leaps from birth to adulthood and thus to "manhood" or vigor. Or is it to trouble, sorrow, or impiety? In their absolute form, "manhood" (*ʾôn*) and "trouble" (*ʾāwen*) are distinguishable, but in their suffixed forms they are identical. In the narrow context of the parallelism in v. 4 (Eng. v. 3), manly vigor provides an apposite complement to the womb, but in the broader context of 12:1–7 (Eng. 11:12–12:6), impiety fits well (cf. LXX). The word occurs with this sense six times in Hosea, usually in pejorative references to Beth-El as Beth-Aven or Aven (contrast v. 5b [Eng. v. 4b]), but also shortly in v. 12 (Eng. v. 11). One could say that Jacob was indeed in trouble (though the word is not used) on the occasion to which this colon refers. But on that occasion "he exerted himself (*śārâ*) with God" (or a god or gods; Vg turns *ʾĕlōhîm* into an envoy). The verb corresponds with Gen. 32:29 (Eng. 32:28); it occurs only in these two passages, and there is doubt as to its identity. It looks like a back-formation from the name Israel with which Gen. 32:29 (Eng. 32:28) connects it, and possibly Hosea is assuming the name change in Genesis and the paronomasia.

In 12:5a (Eng. 12:4a) Hosea extends the reference to, or reworking of, the passages in Genesis (or of some alternative version of their story). "He exerted himself" has the same meaning as the verb in v. 4b (Eng. v. 3b), though it must come from a byform *śûr* rather than *śārâ*. But retrospectively, the colon underscores the ambiguity in that verse by speaking of Jacob exerting himself "towards an envoy (*mal'āk*)." Genesis 32 itself is systematically ambiguous regarding the identity of Jacob's wrestling opponent. It refers to him as an *'îš* and as *'ĕlōhîm*, but not as *mal'āk* (here, Aq and Theod turn the envoy into God), though there are *məlākîm* in v. 1 (Eng. v. 2) and Jacob referred to one in 31:11. Jacob's opponent "saw that he did not win in relation to him" and then acknowledged, "You have exerted yourself with God [or with a god or gods] and with human beings, and won" (Gen. 32:26, 29 [Eng. 32:25, 28]). Hosea agrees, at least on the verbs: "He exerted himself towards an envoy, and won." But there follows in the parallel colon the most strikingly independent note in Hosea: he "cried and sought grace with him." Is the envoy crying and seeking grace?[7] Syntax does not point in this direction, and it is not what envoys usually do. More likely, Hosea invites the current Jacob to see the ancestor Jacob as providing a model as he cries, seeks grace, and finds Yhwh at Beth-El (Hosea's only positive reference to Beth-El; cf. Sweeney 2000: 120). If it is Yhwh who finds Jacob at Beth-El (the third-person references in v. 5b [Eng. v. 4b] are unclear, as they are in Gen. 32:26 [Eng. 32:25]; see survey in Ben Zvi 2005: 249–51), that extends the invitation to reflection and the possible encouragement. Yhwh's finding Jacob was an election motif earlier (9:10) (Wolff 1974: 213; contrast Dozeman 2000: 65, 69).

Either way, much of v. 5 (Eng. v. 4) does not follow the story in Gen. 32; it either reflects another version or it constitutes a piece of creative midrash. And even if the Genesis story existed in Hosea's day in something like the form we know, Hosea's acquaintance with it may be an acquaintance with a story that he heard told, rather than a story he read in a scroll. His words resonate with other elements in the Jacob story in Genesis and reflect the way an intertextual relationship works by allusion to half-remembered phrases that come to be part of new combinations. Thus:

- Jacob cried; in Gen. 33:4, Jacob and Esau cried (they had cried earlier: 27:38; 29:11).
- Jacob sought grace with the envoy (*ḥānan* hitpael); in Gen. 32:6 (Eng. 32:5); 33:8, 10, 15, Jacob hoped to find grace with Esau.
- There is a finding; Gen. 32:6 (Eng. 32:5); 33:8, 10, 15 refer to finding grace.
- The finding happens at Beth-El; Gen. 28 and 35 refer to events at Beth-El.
- At Beth-El Yhwh speaks; in Gen. 35:15 Jacob refers to God speaking to him there.

For vv. 3–5 (Eng. vv. 2–4), the implications are as follows:

- Hosea's taking up the Jacob story can further Yhwh's confrontation of Ephraim by getting Ephraim to reflect on that story.
- Mixing references to the past, present, and future can encourage the audience to make the link; the function of appeal to memory is to enhance self-understanding in the present.
- The very last word in the verses makes that point most explicit: "he speaks with us."

- The result is to mollify the confrontation in 12:1–2 (Eng. 11:12–12:1), not reducing the challenge, but indicating that turning to Yhwh (exerting oneself, seeking grace) is open to Ephraim.
- The parallels making links with elements scattered through the Jacob story in Genesis yield a summary of the story that relates to Hosea's aims in speaking to Ephraim.
- The location of the links, scattered in this way, makes it more likely that Hosea is using the Genesis story in order to formulate his message.

In these verses Hosea thus continues to work with an ambiguity and allusiveness that is sometimes reducible but often not, because he wants Ephraim to keep thinking of different possibilities for itself.

NOTES

1. See Ibn Ezra and Qimchi in *Miqra'ot Gedolot*.
2. Cf. Rashi, Ibn Ezra, and Qimchi in *Miqra'ot Gedolot*.
3. I take *šiḥetkā* as a noun (Macintosh 1997: 535–36), though it looks more like a qatal verb; so understood, v. 9 would belong with what follows.
4. So Rashi, Ibn Ezra, and Qimchi in *Miqra'ot Gedolot*.
5. Rashi in *Miqra'ot Gedolot* assumes the first verb; Ibn Ezra and Qimchi in *Miqra'ot Gedolot* at least invite an association with the second.
6. See Blum 2000; 2009; 2015; Schott 2015; Whitt 1991; Na'aman 2014.
7. So Rashi, Ibn Ezra, and Qimchi in *Miqra'ot Gedolot*.

REFERENCES

Andersen, Francis I., and David Noel Freedman. 1980. *Hosea: A New Translation with Introduction and Commentary*. AB 24. Garden City, NY: Doubleday.

Ben Zvi, Ehud. 2005. *Hosea*. FOTL 21A/1. Grand Rapids: Eerdmans.

Blum, Erhard. 2000. "Noch einmal: Jakobs Traum in Bethel—Genesis 28,10–22." In Steven L. McKenzie and Thomas Römer, eds., *Rethinking the Foundations: Historiography in the Ancient World and in the Bible; Essays in Honor of John Van Seters*. BZAW 294. Berlin: de Gruyter, 33–54.

Blum, Erhard. 2009. "Hosea 12 und die Pentateuchüberlieferungen." In Anselm C. Hagedorn and Henrik Pfeiffer, eds., *Die Erzväter in der biblischen Tradition: Festschrift für Matthias Köckert*. BZAW 400. Berlin: de Gruyter, 291–321.

Blum, Erhard. 2015. "Once Again: Hosea and the Pentateuchal Traditions." In Cana Werman, ed., *From Author to Copyist: Composition, Redaction, and Transmission of the Hebrew Bible; Studies in Honor of Zipi Talshir*. Winona Lake, IN: Eisenbrauns, 81–94.

Dozeman, Thomas B. 2000. "Hosea and the Wilderness Wandering Tradition." In Steven L. McKenzie and Thomas Römer, eds., *Rethinking the Foundations: Historiography in the Ancient World and in the Bible; Essays in Honor of John Van Seters*. BZAW 294. Berlin: de Gruyter, 55–70.

Fishbane, Michael A. 1985. *Biblical Interpretation in Ancient Israel*. Oxford: Clarendon.

Goldingay, John. 2020. "Hosea 4 and 11, and the Structure of Hosea." *TynBul* 71: 181–90.

Goldingay, John. 2021. *Hosea—Micah*. Baker Commentary on the Old Testament. Grand Rapids: Baker.

Gruber, Mayer I. 2017. *Hosea: A Textual Commentary*. LHBOTS 653. London: T&T Clark.

Ibn Ezra, Abraham ben Meir. Commentary on Hosea in *Miqra'ot Gedolot*. www.Sefaria.org.

Lancaster, Mason. 2021. "Wounds and Healing, Dew and Lions: Hosea's Development of Divine Metaphors." *CBQ* 83: 407–24.

Landy, Francis. 2001. *Beauty and the Enigma and Other Essays on the Hebrew Bible*. JSOTSup 312. Sheffield: Sheffield Academic Press.

Landy, Francis. 2011. *Hosea*. Readings: A New Bible Commentary. 2nd ed. Sheffield: Sheffield Phoenix.

Macintosh, A. A. 1997. *A Critical and Exegetical Commentary on Hosea*. ICC. Edinburgh: T&T Clark.

Mays, James Luther. 1969. *Hosea: A Commentary*. OTL. London: SCM.

McKenzie, Steven L. 1986. "The Jacob Tradition in Hosea xii 4–5." *VT* 36: 311–22.

Moon, Joshua N. 2018. *Hosea*. Apollos Old Testament Commentary 21. London: Inter-Varsity Press.

Na'aman, Nadav. 2014. "The Jacob Story and the Formation of Biblical Israel." *Tel Aviv* 41: 95–125.

Na'aman, Nadav. 2015. "The Book of Hosea as a Source for the Last Days of the Kingdom of Israel." *BZ* 59: 232–56.

Na'aman, Nadav. 2021. "Harsh Criticism of Pekah's Rebellion in the Book of Hosea." *BN* 188: 43–49.

Qimchi, David. Commentary on Hosea in *Miqra'ot Gedolot*. www.Sefaria.org.

Rashi [Rabbi Shlomo Yitzhaqi]. Commentary on Hosea in *Miqra'ot Gedolot*. www.Sefaria.org.

Rudolph, Wilhelm. 1966. *Hosea*. KAT 13/1. Gütersloh: Mohn.

Schott, Martin. 2015. "Die Jakobpassagen in Hosea 12." *ZTK* 112: 1–26.

Smith, Cooper. 2018. "The 'Wilderness' in Hosea and Deuteronomy: A Case of Thematic Reappropriation." *BBR* 28: 240–60.

Sweeney, Marvin A. 2000. *The Twelve Prophets*. Vol. 1. Berit Olam. Collegeville, MN: Liturgical.

Van Ruiten, Jacques. 2012. "The Image of Jacob in the Targum of Hosea 12." *JSJ* 43: 595–612.

Whitt, William D. 1991. "The Jacob Traditions in Hosea and Their Relation to Genesis." *ZAW* 103: 18–43.

Wolff, Hans Walter. 1974. *Hosea: A Commentary on the Book of Hosea*. Hermeneia. Philadelphia: Fortress.

Yee, Gale A. 1996. "The Book of Hosea: Introduction, Commentary, and Reflections." In L. E. Keck et al., eds., *The New Interpreter's Bible Volume 7*. Nashville: Abingdon, 195–297.

PART III

THEOLOGICAL AND LITERARY ELEMENTS, THEMES, AND MOTIFS

CHAPTER 16

....

METAPHORS IN THE BOOK
OF HOSEA

....

MASON D. LANCASTER

THIS chapter offers a guided tour through the weird and wonderful metaphorical land-scape of Hosea, with tangential avenues for further exploration identified along the way. This tour will focus on networks of metaphors spanning larger sections of the scroll (book), rather than on a few specific metaphorical expressions, allowing a survey of the whole scroll—admittedly in broad strokes.

Appreciating Hosea's metaphors is important for the broader study of the scroll for two interrelated reasons. First, metaphors are ubiquitous in Hosea. Hosea is widely regarded as containing a greater density of metaphors than almost any other Hebrew Bible book, perhaps alongside Song of Songs and Psalms. Wolff (1974: xxiv) observes, "No other prophet—indeed, not one writer in the entire Old Testament—uses as many similes as Hosea does. He may take one metaphor and develop it in detail or, more frequently, he clothes the thought of each succeeding sentence in new imagery." The question is not whether one interprets metaphors when reading Hosea since they are unavoidable, but whether one does so in an informed and sensitive way.

Second, much of the message of the scroll is communicated primarily or exclusively through metaphors. Nwaoru (1999: xiii) concludes that the metaphors are "indispensable" for understanding Hosea's message, in that they "succinctly define YHWH's mood and Israel's behaviour." At the same time, the metaphors often function to obscure meaning; they frustrate understanding. Hartsfield (2009: 164) notes that this "dissonance created by polar messages is literarily represented by a variety of images derived from natural phenomena, agrarian realities, and familial structures that illustrate intriguing and oftentimes disturbing depictions of the strained divine–human relationship between Yahweh and ancient Israel." One must understand metaphors if one is to understand Hosea at all.

Hosea 5:10–6:6 is an example of the ubiquity and variety of metaphor in the book. Metaphoric density is evident in 6:1–3, where nine metaphors converge to highlight what YHWH has done and will assuredly do. Metaphoric vacillation is prominent a few verses earlier (5:10–15), where Yhwh is a wrath-flooder, a moth, rottenness, a king, and a lion, while Israel is a boundary-marker-mover, "crushed," incurably sick, and the lion's prey. Metaphoric tension is evident across these passages: Is Yhwh one who will certainly heal and revive Israel (6:2–3) or one who will hew them by the prophets and kill Israel with words (6:5)? As Mays (1969: 7) aptly summarizes, "Metaphors pour from [Hosea's] mouth."

A survey of Hosea's common metaphor source domains and their distribution also highlights the importance of metaphor in Hosea (see Lancaster 2023). Given that they dominate the opening chapters of the book, sexual and marital metaphors are the most common metaphor domain in Hosea. Numerically speaking, the farmer source domain (God as farmer, Israel as plant or animal) is a close second (agricultural imagery is interspersed with the sexual and marital metaphors of Hos. 1–3), followed by the domain of God as parent/father and Israel as son in third place. After the relatively homogeneous metaphorics of Hos. 1–3, God-as-farmer, God-as parent, and God-as-destructive-animal are all more common domains in Hos. 4–14 than God-as-husband. Thus, while "root metaphors" have been discredited on a theorical basis and should be avoided, Dearman (2010: 11, 44–50) may be on the right track that "head of household" is an "encompassing metaphor" in Hosea, a good starting point to account for the conceptual systematicity of Hosea's metaphors (Kövecses 2017: 19–23).

These more common metaphors are followed by (in order of decreasing prevalence) healing, judicial, leonine, shepherding, disciplinary, and political (i.e., suzerain-vassal) metaphors. We also find metaphors as diverse as Israel as moldy bread (or gray hair; 7:9), a useless vessel (8:9), and a ravaged plant (10:1); Samaria's king as a twig on the rapids (10:7); God as a moth (5:12), bereaved mother bear (13:8), and executioner (10:2 [עֹרֵף]); invading armies as whirlwinds (13:15) and birds of prey (8:1); and divine distance as death for Israel (5:4, 6; 9:1; 14:2 [Heb. 14:3]).

An appreciation of metaphor in Hosea is essential to virtually every other aspect of its study and understanding. It is not merely that grasping the metaphors helps us read Hosea, but that it is impossible to understand the book apart from them.

16.1. APPROACHES TO METAPHOR IN HOSEA STUDIES

Scholars' methodological choices have indelibly shaped the current state of Hosean metaphor studies. Since the beginning (see Lancaster 2021), study of metaphor has been mostly limited to what are now called "deliberate" metaphors (Steen 2017). These are metaphors that are knowingly constructed as literary or spoken metaphorical expressions, often for special rhetorical effect, such as "Juliet is the sun" or "God is a lion." To date, the vast majority of Hosean metaphor studies are interested in so-called deliberate metaphors. Metaphors for Yhwh and Israel will be an unavoidable focus of this chapter, given that the scroll is almost exclusively concerned with their relationship (with occasional reference to Yhwh's competitors for Israel's allegiance).

In the past forty years since the advent of cognitive theories of metaphor, however, interest has arisen in "unconscious" or "cognitive" metaphors (Kövecses 2017). These are the "everyday" metaphorical ways we speak (e.g., "After *coming all this way*, our relationship *hit a dead end*.") and the cognitive frameworks they reflect (LOVE IS A JOURNEY). Despite this being the focus of most non-biblical-metaphor research, very little work has been done on unconscious/cognitive metaphors in Hosea, as has been done elsewhere in the Hebrew Bible (Tilford 2017). Van Hecke (2005) is an exceptional example, using conceptual blending theory to illuminate Hos. 4:16.

Metaphors are a special, wild, kind of words (and conceptual frameworks) that do many things at once. Amid a proliferation of metaphor theories, metaphor researchers have recognized the limits of any particular theory and begun to emphasize the need for integrated and holistic theories. Examples include Raymond Gibbs Jr.'s (2017: 67) dynamic account of metaphor wherein "metaphorical behaviors are always emergent properties of a dynamical, self-organizing system such that no single force controls the process of metaphor production and understanding," or Steen's (2011; 2017) deliberate metaphor theory, which seeks to incorporate conceptual, linguistic, and communicative aspects of metaphor. Some scholars have adopted Steen's work to study biblical metaphors (van Loon 2018; van Wolde 2020), but interpreters have not often applied to Hosea any of the integrated approaches that account for the cognitive, emotional, volitional, social, historical, rhetorical, and literary functions of Hosea's metaphors (though see Lancaster 2023 for such an attempt).

Most Hosea studies have adopted a theory of metaphor to better understand historical dimensions and referents of the scroll's metaphors (Keefe 2001; Kelle 2005; Hong 2006; Yee 2012). Others have adopted sensitive literary readings of the book's metaphors (Fisch 1988: 136–57; Landy 1995). Almost all metaphor studies are based on the final form of Hosea, though Seifert (1996) omits certain metaphors as post-Hosean and Cruz (2016) offers an example of thoroughgoing diachronic metaphor study in Micah. This chapter, too, will be based on MT Hosea, since the final form is the only stable—indeed extant—literary context in which to study the metaphors.

Many scholars focus on particular metaphorical expressions or domains, whether as specific as an earthquake (Blair 2007) or as general as God (Seifert 1996). Certainly those of greatest interest have been the sexual and marital metaphors of Hos. 1–3 (addressed more fully below). Sharon Moughtin-Mumby (2008: 6–30) offers especially insightful reflections on the interpretive implications of one's theory of metaphor, arguing that "traditional" scholars who view Hos. 1–3 favorably often use an outdated substitutionary account of metaphor, while many feminist scholars critiquing Hos. 1–3 hold a more methodologically sound conceptual view of metaphor.

Four projects are noteworthy for attempting some measure of comprehensiveness beyond Hos. 1–3. Bridgette Seifert (1996) begins with the question, "How can humans speak about God?" and studies metaphors for God in several passages under four themes: betrayed love, imminent disaster, experienced care, and incomprehensible compassion. Göran Eidevall (1996) examines all metaphors in Hos. 4–14 drawing on Kittay's (1987) perspectival account of metaphor, and develops a new method, "metaphorical criticism," in the process. Both Seifert and Eidevall conclude with penetrating observations synthesizing the metaphorical worlds of Hosea. As the most exhaustive treatment on metaphors across most of the scroll, Eidevall's work has earned widespread use among scholars as an almost canonical reference work on this topic. Nwaoru (1999) provides a helpful categorization of metaphors, but comparatively little analytic depth or substantial engagement with metaphor theory. My previous work (Lancaster 2023) examines 103 metaphors for God among fifteen metaphor clusters in Hos. 4–14, analyzes their intra- and intercluster interactions, and gathers an aspectival character portrait of Yhwh.

The following discussion reflects an interest in networks or clusters of metaphors across Hosea (cf. Labahn and Verde 2020), a phenomenon recently emphasized by non-biblical-metaphor scholars. Ricoeour memorably observed more than four decades ago that a "metaphor never comes alone. One metaphor calls for another and all together they remain alive thanks to their mutual tension and the power of each to evoke the whole network" (1975: 94; for more recent empirical studies, see Cameron and Stelma 2004; Cameron and Maslen 2010; Low et al. 2010). Additionally, a fundamental aspect of metaphor is its function to change one's perception of the world. Ricoeur (1981: 7), for instance, explored metaphor's ability to "redescribe reality." Lakoff and Johnson, in their seminal work inaugurating conceptual metaphor theory (2003: 157), recognized that metaphor has "the power to define reality." This is certainly no less true when we come to Hosea. The net effect of the book's multifaceted metaphorical functions is to subvert and reinvent the various worldviews of Hosea's audience(s).[1] Brueggemann (2008: 7) summarizes this point:

> What the poetry of Hosea—poetry that characterizes God—does is to load us with a world that is not available to us—and surely did not exist—until this utterance. . . . The imagined poetic world of Hosea creates alternative space in which Israel can live, if and when it is willing to forego either the certitude of *quid pro quo* or the narcotic of entitlement.

I will attempt to substantiate this claim by identifying at least one way each metaphor network deconstructs and reinvents Israel's world.

16.2. Metaphor Networks in Hosea

Having finished with introductions, let us commence our tour through the labyrinth of Hosea's metaphorical landscape. Again, this tour will focus on unique and salient networks of metaphors for each of six broad swaths of the scroll.

16.2.1. Hosea 1–4

The scroll of Hosea begins with a sign-act which has long captivated readers, for good or for ill. In Hos. 1–3, the prophet takes on a promiscuous woman (אשת זנונים) as a prophetic sign-act comparing Israel to the promiscuous wife and Yhwh to a faithful and long-suffering husband: "Continue to love a woman who has a lover and is an adulteress—just like Yhwh loves the house of Israel, though they keep turning to other gods and loving sacred cakes of raisin" (3:1).[2] But some of the imagery is shocking and violent. Yhwh threatens: "I will strip her naked / and expose her as in the day she was born, / and make her like a wilderness, / and turn her into a parched land, / and kill her with thirst" (2:3 NRSV [Heb. 2:5]). And later: "Now I will uncover her shame / in the sight of her lovers, / and no one shall rescue her out of my hand" (2:10 NRSV [Heb. 2:12]). The marital and sexual metaphors of Hos. 1–3 are partially responsible for the revival of metaphor study within biblical scholarship (along with similar passages in Jer. 2–3; Ezek. 16; 23) through the work of feminist scholars over the past four decades (for recent examples with surveys of past work, see Moughtin-Mumby 2008; Wacker 2012; Macwilliam 2014). Though interpreters have tended to focus on the sexual and marital imagery of chs. 1–3, these metaphors also feature heavily in Hos. 4 (vv. 10–15). There, Yhwh declares that "a promiscuous spirit has led them astray, / and they were sexually unfaithful to their God (4:12) "(ויזנו מתחת אלהיהם; cf. 5:3–4, 7; 6:10; 9:1).

The scholarly consensus for generations has been that so-called cultic prostitution constituted the historical referent and source domain to these metaphors. This has been thoroughly disproven as a figment of scholarly imagination; no such institution can be shown to have existed in ancient West Asia (DeGrado 2018; Bird 2019). The antideity polemic of these chapters (see esp. 2:10, 15, 18, 19 [Heb. 2:12, 17, 20, 21]) has long been assumed, though recent interpreters have argued that "Baal(s)" functions metaphorically to refer to socioeconomic systems (Keefe 2001) or other political entities (Kelle 2005).

In keeping with a holistic approach to metaphor which attends to its textual function for readers, it is crucial to observe that these metaphors are directed at Israel's male leadership. The metaphors publicly shame Israel's leadership into behavioral conformity by likening these men to sexually promiscuous women (Haddox 2011). The marital and sexual metaphors of Hos. 1–4 reflect "Hosea's polemic against the oppressive, interlocking political, religious, and economic structures that supported the male elite, whom he characterizes as sexually promiscuous" (Yee 2012: 303). The interweaving of agricultural and sexual metaphors (see Stovell 2015) may suggest "issues of land use and exploitation by these elites, as well as Hosea's promises of a renewed land and agricultural prosperity" (Yee 2012: 303).

After the marital sign-act introduction of Hos. 1–3, the reader finds Hosea's message conceptualized in a second metaphorical category: the scroll of Hosea constitutes Yhwh's legal case against Israel, prosecuted by Hosea.[3] The scroll has three cycles (chs. 1–3; 4–11; 12–14), each consisting of three loosely organized legal stages: indictment, sentencing, and redemption. Alternatively, the three stages could be conceived of in terms of relational justice: responsibility, chastisement, and restoration (Laldinsuah 2015). The second cycle (Hos. 4–11) begins as Yhwh declares through the prophet:

> Hear the word of the Lord, O people of Israel;
>   for the Lord has an indictment (ריב) against the inhabitants of the land. (4:1 NRSV)

Hosea summarizes the indictment in "opening arguments" ("Swearing, lying, and murder, / and stealing and adultery break out" [4:2 NRSV]) reminiscent of the Decalogue (Exod. 20:13–16; Deut. 5:17–21), which itself summarizes the covenant Hosea prosecutes (Hos. 8:1). The third cycle (Hos. 12–14) similarly begins with

> The Lord has an indictment (ריב) against Judah,
> and will punish Jacob according to his ways,
> and repay him according to his deeds. (12:2 NRSV [Heb. 12:3])

That both cycles after the sign-act begin with the declaration of a legal case (ריב; the verb also occurs in 2:2 [twice; Heb. 2:4]; 4:4) suggests that the legal and judicial metaphors are essential conceptual structuring features of the scroll. These metaphors undermine the worldview of Israel's cultic and political leadership who were inclined to believe that Yhwh was a deity whom they could control and would remain on their side to do their bidding (cf. 6:1–3). These legal metaphors clarify, to the contrary, that Israel is accountable to Yhwh. The nation's relationship with their deity is bilateral (cf. Zehetgruber 2020), and Yhwh will not overlook Ephraim's transgressions.

16.2.2. Hosea 5–6

Hosea 5:8–6:6 has long been a locus of Hosea studies for historical reasons (Alt 1953), but the passage is especially interesting for a study of the metaphorics of the scroll. These verses constitute the highest density of metaphors in a book which already ranks among the highest in the Hebrew Bible for metaphorical density (Lancaster 2023: 57, 233). They also exemplify the book's diverse, tensive, and networked use of metaphor. Uniquely, however, they present an interesting case study of metaphor competition (cf. Hawley 2018).

The speaker(s) in 6:1–3 has long been contested. Is this God, Hosea, or Israel's leadership speaking? If Hosea or the nation's priesthood, do these words reflect genuine repentance or mere lip service? In my view, 6:1–3 are the words of Israel's cultic leadership who are "going through the motions" to get what they want from the nation's deity. Reflecting the imagery of Baal, they believe Yhwh too will "revive us" and bring "the spring rains that water the earth" (6:2, 3). The nation's leaders are certain of Yhwh's future benevolence, saying, "like the dawn, his coming forth is assured" (v. 3).

Bracketing their prayer is Hosea's rebuttal (5:8–15; 6:4–6). Hosea rejects their mostly positive construal of Yhwh as a storm god with a wholly negative construal. Hosea's response consists almost entirely of metaphors related to ancient West Asian storm gods, such as Yhwh's use of words as weapons and bringing a divine verdict with the sun (6:5; Lancaster and Miglio 2020). It is as if Hosea responds to the popular understanding of Yhwh as a storm god by saying, "You think that is what kind of storm god he is? Easily placated? No, Yhwh is the kind of storm god who will bring devastating judgment on your fickleness and religious vacuity."

This is but one example (for another, see Zimran 2018) of how the metaphors of Hos. 5–6 are part of worldview competition over the nature of Israel and their patron deity. "Metaphor, or something very much like it, is what renders possible and intelligible the acquisition of new knowledge" (Petrie and Oshlag 1993: 582), so metaphors are often involved in negotiating between disparate perspectives (e.g., Grady 2017; Musolff 2017). Indeed, metaphors tend to cluster most substantially at precisely those places most heavily involved in the rhetorical purpose of the discourse (Cameron and Stelma 2004: 134; Cameron 2008; Kimmel 2010: 98). It should not, therefore, be surprising that metaphor density reaches its peak around Hos. 6:1–3, as Hosea grasps at the limits of language to pile up diverse and shocking imagery to convince Israelite leadership of their mistaken metaphors—metaphors which Hosea thinks will cost Israel its national life.

16.2.3. Hosea 7–8

Hosea 7–8 is representative of Hosea's tendency to vacillate between seemingly unrelated metaphors, in this case to describe domestic politics, foreign policy, and cultic matters. Hosea 7 continues Israel's indictment, describing their "crimes" which prevent Yhwh healing Israel (6:11b–7:1). The imagery of the chapter revolves around "eating and being eaten" (Eidevall 2020: 122). The initial focus is on the "evil deeds" of the royal house (7:3, 5), which are depicted using multiple entailments of a complex of baking metaphors (7:3–9). As "adulterers," their passions are likened to the heat of an oven which is so hot it does not need to be stoked (7:4, 6). The baking domain then provides an opportunity for a smooth transition to international politics, as Ephraim's indecisive foreign policy ("mixing with the nations"; note the baking allusion) has resulted in Ephraim being an "unturned cake" (7:8; עגה בלי הפוכה)—that is, an inedible loaf: burned on one side, uncooked on the other.

The "unturned cake" metaphor then begins a series of diverse metaphors highlighting how things are not working as they should for Israel, and, by extension, for Yhwh. Israel's foreign policy has left them as an inedible cake (7:8; cf. 8:10); their indecision is like a thoughtless dove: normally good at navigation, but now utterly lost (7:11); Yhwh has trained them but their training has not paid off (7:15); they are a slack, and therefore worthless, bow (7:16) and a useless vessel that no one wants (8:8; ככלי אין חפץ בו); the harvest does not yield what it ought (8:7) and the normal sources of food cannot feed them (9:2); Ephraim's indecisive attempts at appeasement have left them like a wild ass (normally a communal animal) wandering alone (8:9). Even their religious practices fail: altars that should remove sin instead multiply it (8:11), God's own instructions are ignored (8:12), sacrifices no longer please the deity they are designed to appease (8:13), and Yhwh's wife prefers the wages of a prostitute over the commitment of marriage (9:1), all because Israel has forgotten the very One who made them (8:14). This network of apparently unrelated metaphors is therefore meant to conclude Yhwh's indictment of the Northern Kingdom by highlighting that their attempts to chart their own course are fruitless, and Yhwh is not getting what he wanted from Israel. As far as the deity is concerned, Israel is good for nothing.

16.2.4. Excursus on Pseudo-Metaphors

Another important metaphorical feature of this pericope is the use of more veiled metaphorical functions. The "Assyria-Egypt" motif is one such instance, and the pair occurs first in 7:11: "Ephraim has become like a gullible dove—thoughtless! Egypt they call; [then] Assyria they go!" The "Assyria-Egypt" pairing recurs four more times in Hosea (9:3; 11:5, 11; 12:1 [Heb. 12:2]). Zimran argues that Egypt and Assyria function in the book as a "correlative pair" that "consistently indicates distance from God and the forging of alternative relationships" (Zimran 2021: 20). While Assyria and Egypt are obviously meant as literal references to contemporary nations, their presence as a pair with a discrete motif takes on a metaphorical function as well. Assyria and Egypt individually are not metaphors, but the book uses their pairing as a figurative tool, a "motif with symbolic significance," to display distance from God (Zimran 2021: 10). The first instance in 7:11, for example, highlights not only "Israel's plea to the nations as useless, but also as incompatible with turning to the God of Israel" (Zimran 2021: 12). The motif's "assertion regarding the limitations of human power" is consistent with "the ideological focal points of the unit [7:8–12]" (Zimran 2021: 13).

There are other places where Hosea uses double-duty terms which intend a literal referent but also serve a figurative function in the discourse. We will see below that Jacob functions similarly in Hos. 12. Israel both "is" and "is not" the patriarch. This differs from a simple metaphor because in the case of Assyria, Egypt, and Jacob, the expressions do mean what they appear to mean—they literally refer to those entities—but they also carry more allusive (and elusive!) figurative meanings (i.e., those of divine distance, or of Israel's identification with the sins of Jacob). If this is true of the "Assyria-Egypt" motif and the patriarch, perhaps this pattern invites us to revisit Kelle's aforementioned claim (2005) that the "Baal(s)" references in the book serve, at least in part, a metaphorical function referring to foreign suzerains.

16.2.5. Hosea 9–11

Returning to our sequential tour through the metaphorical landscape of Hosea, the networks in Hos. 9–11 differ in one key respect from those preceding. While the various metaphor networks in chs. 5–6 and 7–8 are characterized by diversity and fluctuation, Hos. 9–11 is characterized by comparative metaphorical homogeneity. These three chapters are overwhelmingly dominated by two basic metaphor domains: (1) Yhwh as parent / Israel as child, and (2) Yhwh as farmer / Israel as plant or animal. Particularly beginning in 9:10, Israel is portrayed as wild grapes and the early fig which Yhwh was pleasantly surprised to find in the wilderness. "Ephraim's glory" is then immediately likened to a bird (9:12), before Ephraim is again compared to a plant (9:13). Next, Israel is conceptualized as a wayward son who is banished from the house (9:15, 17),[4] interspersed with images of female barrenness and infanticide (9:16) and Israel as a ravaged plant (10:1). Historically, interpreters have favored a negative rendering of גפן בוקק as "ravaged vine" (NJPS; cf. Isa. 24:1; Nah. 2:3), but recently a positive interpretation ("luxuriant vine" [NRSV]) has prevailed. The positive reading, however, relies on a conjectured *hapax* in light of an allegedly positive context. This is mistaken in my view (see Lancaster 2023: 104). Israel is languishing apart from the care of its proper farmer, Yhwh. Hosea 10:1 thus emphasizes the movement in 9:10–17 from surprising abundance to barrenness (Laldinsuah 2015: 224–27).

The vegetative imagery continues as Israel's legal system is awash in false oaths and lawsuits "like poisonous weeds in a plowed field" (10:4 NIV), Samaria's king is helplessly carried away like a twig on the rapids (10:7), and thorns and thistles overcome Israel's altars (10:8). In one of the more illuminating extended metaphors, Ephraim is figured as a cow who initially enjoyed and was well suited to farm work (the meaning of ואני עברתי על טוב צוארה in 10:11a). Alas, Ephraim has frustrated Farmer-Yhwh's plans and has not joyfully produced what Yhwh expected (10:11b). In a pointed inversion of this otherwise homogeneous metaphorical relationship, Israel then takes the role of farmer as Yhwh instructs them to "sow equity" and "reap the fruit of loyal love" (זרעו לכם לצדקה קצרו לפי חסד; 10:12), but instead Israel has planted wickedness and reaped evil (10:13).

The parent-child domain appears again in 11:1–3, as Yhwh declares his love for his "son" in the beginning—namely at the exodus (11:1). Yhwh even taught Ephraim to walk, but they have not recognized Yhwh's kindness (11:3) and have instead chased after other providers (11:2). In my view, v. 4 switches to a metaphor of a farmer easing the yoke off an animal, but some see there a maternal image of feeding a human child (Schüngel-Straumann 1987). The parental metaphor is often understood to continue in 11:8–9, as Yhwh vacillates over whether and to what extent to punish this rebellious child who is nonetheless the object of great compassion (Leung Lai 2004). The chapter closes with Israel in various wild animal forms and Yhwh no longer a farmer but a victorious lion (11:10–11).

What is one to make of the fact that Hos. 9:10–11:11 consists almost entirely of rapid switches between only two source domains? Definitive answers may elude us, but let me suggest one possibility. A conceptual metaphor may be defined as "understanding one domain of experience (that is typically abstract) in terms of another (that is typically concrete)" (Kövecses 2017: 13). The power of metaphor comes from the fact that metaphor arises from our embodied life experiences and draws on known realities to illuminate lesser-known realities (Kövecses 2015). In these sentencing (9:1–11:7) and redemption (11:8–11) sections of this second cycle (4:1–11:11), what better-known, more concrete, more visceral, more relatable, and therefore more compelling realities could one draw on for an agrarian community than those of plants, animals, and family? When the scroll is "closing its case" in this second cycle, so to speak, perhaps it dispenses with the less emotionally compelling metaphors (e.g., twigs and storm gods) and relies on those most likely to have an emotional effect on the audience—to "strike home." During sentencing, the hearers/readers are reminded of those frustrating times when their sons (9:15) and animals (10:11) do not obey, and they are told they are just that way with Yhwh. At the close of ch. 11, though, recipients are reminded of those times when disciplining their children is appropriate, but their compassions overwhelm their inclination to punish absolutely. Yhwh is just like that, Hosea claims (11:8–9).

16.2.6. Hosea 12

The third and final cycle (Heb. 12:1–14:9; 14:10 is an epilogue) begins the renewed indictment (12:3) with an extended analogy using the patriarch Jacob (12:4–5, 12–13; Hebrew versification used throughout the section below). Scholars have typically been divided between whether the analogy functions negatively (Jacob is an example of duplicity and betrayal to which Israel is likened) or positively (Jacob is a model of repentance to which Israel is invited). More likely, Hosea is using both elements of their ancestor's story. The deception and treachery that now characterize Israel (12:1–2, 8) find their genetic origin in the patriarch of the Northern Kingdom (12:4–5) (Fishbane 1985: 378). But Jacob did not stay estranged from the brother whom he betrayed. Just as Jacob made amends with his brother (Gen. 33:1–20) and restored a covenant at Gilead with Laban, whom he cheated (Gen. 31:22–55), so Israel is invited to return to Yhwh whom they have cheated and make amends (Hos. 12:5, 7, 12) (Holladay 1966).

Hosea thus makes two claims through the metaphorical functions of the Jacob allusions: (1) the audience is by nature (genetically) deceptive, adversarial, and prone to betrayal for personal gain yet also the object of divine election (vv. 1–2, 4, 6, 8–9), but (2) they can be reconciled to Yhwh by returning (v. 7) and seeking favor (as Jacob did with Esau [v. 5]) and reestablishing a covenant (as Jacob did with Laban [v. 12]) because "God speaks to us!" (v. 5).

Why use an analogy to make this point? How does Jacob operate metaphorically in service to the message of ch. 12? The metaphorical use of the patriarch makes both the indictment and the invitation more compelling. Israel has apparently taken great pride in their eponymous ancestor, yet the allusions draw attention to the patriarch's failures and identify them as the genetic origin of Israel's current issues. The constant vacillation

16.2.7. Hosea 13–14

Hosea's final two chapters depict Israel's metaphorical death and resurrection. After nine chapters of relentless accusations and forthcoming judgment, the central theme of ch. 13 is death. The chapter begins by noting that Israel incurred guilt through Baal and died (13:1] ויאשם בבעל וימת]). Israel continues in their idolatrous, fickle, and treacherous ways (13:2–3), and so the God who once shepherded them in the wilderness (13:4–5) will now fall upon them as a variety of terrifying wild animals (13:6–8). In the face of Yhwh's "raw power" and the inability of language to capture such realities, Hosea's "recourse is to multiply metaphors, even and especially in close proximity" (Strawn 2005: 272). The vacillation in 13:6–8 reflects a seminarrative progression. A simple divine lion then becomes leopard-Yhwh who will crouch (אשור; note the allusion to Assyria), ready to pounce, alongside the path. Yhwh is then an angry bear bereaved of her cubs who will confront Israel and rip open their chest cavity (ואקרע סגור לבם). The image of a furious mother bear suggests that "YHWH's aggression . . . is not simply the reflex action of a predator who kills to eat, but a rage over loss" (Dearman 2010: 324). Finally, lion-Yhwh will devour them (ואכלם) as a wild animal would tear them to shreds (תבקעם).

The chapter concludes with Yhwh's invitations to Death and Sheol to take Israel away. Some read Hos. 13:14a as positive affirmations, and נחם as prohibited vengeance, such as in the NJPS translation:

> "From Sheol itself I will save them,
> Redeem them from very Death.
> Where, O Death, are your plagues?
> Your pestilence where, O Sheol?
> Revenge shall be far from My thoughts." (see also 1 Cor. 15:55.)

But I understand v. 14 as questions expecting a negative response— functionally invitations for Death and Sheol to bring their plagues upon Israel—and נחם as prohibited compassion, as reflected in the NRSV translation:

> "Shall I ransom them from the power of Sheol?
> Shall I redeem them from Death? [Implied answers: no.]
> O Death, where are your plagues?
> O Sheol, where is your destruction? [Implication: I want them to come!]
> Compassion is hidden from my eyes."

The deity will not rescue them from death, because leniency will not factor into the verdict. Israel is pictured in this chapter also as a rebel who deserves all the aforementioned consequences, culminating in death:

> "Samaria shall bear her guilt,
> > because she has rebelled against her God;
> they shall fall by the sword,
> > their little ones shall be dashed in pieces,
> > and their pregnant women ripped open." (13:16 NRSV [Heb. 14:1])

As the death knell rings, Israel's prospects look quite dark. The transition to the final chapter, then, could not be starker, as death turns to vibrant life (Oestreich 1998). After an initial invitation for Israel to return to Yhwh (14:1–3 [Heb. 14:2–4]), the metaphor of healing—so far used to say that Israel cannot and will not be healed (5:13; 6:1; 7:1)—is inverted as Yhwh heals Israel's perpetual waywardness because Yhwh has chosen to love Israel "freely" (נדבה) and his anger has turned away (14:4 [Heb. 14:5]). Consequently, the nation that has so often been pictured as a dying plant (10:1), and most recently was the subject of an entire chapter of death (ch. 13), is now reimagined in its glorious floral resurrection. Up to nine metaphors depicting Israel as flourishing plants are packed into three verses (14:5–7 [Heb. 14:6–8]).

What was the cause of this rejuvenation? Sandwiched between the declaration of Yhwh's generous love (14:4 [Heb. 14:5]) and Israel's floral resurrection, we find a unique image of Yhwh as dew (טל). Dew has thus far been a figure for Israel's disloyalty (6:4) and their rapid exile (13:3), but now it becomes a figure for the divine self. In the arid regions of Palestine, dew is often the only source of water for many plant species for much of the year. While the dew of Israel's inconstancy led to the dew of their quick exiling, the dew of Yhwh's love will be their restoration.

Finally, it is worth noting how the metaphors of these last two chapters especially interact with imagery used for other deities and nation-states across ancient West Asia. The lion imagery of 13:7–8 is often associated with Israel's Assyrian overlords. Assyrian kings are not depicted as lions, but they often showcase their prowess and vigor through reliefs depicting their lion hunts. Hosea thus claims that the "Great King" (cf. 5:13; 10:6) who claims to defeat lions is not to be feared so much as Yhwh, the unbeatably fierce lion who will tear Israel to shreds. It is Yhwh, not Assyria or the horses and chariots of Israel (14:3 [Heb. 14:4]), who will provide their ultimate protection and rescue.

Other imagery is associated with Canaanite deities. In 13:1, Israel bore guilt through Baal and died (ויאשם בבעל וימת), thus juxtaposing two Canaanite deities (Ba'al/Ba'lu and Motu) in successive words. Israel has so wed herself to her other husband Baal that she shall suffer the same consequence Baal did (cf. 2:18; 13:1): death. Hosea 13:14 depicts the supreme God, Yhwh, summoning Motu to devour Yhwh's people. But whereas Ba'lu eventually defeated Motu in Ugarit, Hosea claims that Yhwh will become the God of Death to defeat Israel. The scorching east wind which comes as a "blast from Yhwh" (13:14) is widely associated with Motu in Canaan.

Not only are metaphors appropriated; they are also polemical. That Yhwh acts as dew to restore Israel undercuts the role of Baal, a storm god who brings precipitation and has a daughter named "Dew." It is Yhwh, not Baal, who will be the exclusive life-giving source of Israel's resurrection (14:5 [Heb. 14:6]). That Yhwh is depicted—for the only time in the entire Hebrew Bible—as a kind of tree in the book's penultimate verse undercuts the role of Asherah. It is as if Yhwh were claiming to be the only "tree of life" that Israel needs (Tångberg 1989: 92). In short, the vast majority of metaphors in ch. 14 are polemically appropriated (see Hundley 2013: 99–100), reflecting their function of overcoming alterity between different viewpoints (Cameron and Stelma 2004). Hosea does this by claiming that "in YHWH all aspects of the Canaanite gods are united" (Korpel 1990: 594) and therefore Israel needs no other deities but Yhwh (Seifert 1996: 259–62).

16.3. The Cumulative Effect of Hosea's Metaphors: Reshaping Israel's Reality

Hosea's metaphors seek to subvert and replace Israel's whole world. While not every metaphor is designed to revolutionize Israel's worldview, the quantity and nature of Hosea's metaphors suggest that the scroll seeks to undermine Israel's perceptions and replace them with an alternative and holistic worldview encompassing religion, self, national identity, politics, ethics, family relationships, economics, and more.

Before metaphor "'redescribes' reality," it must first create "rifts in an old order" (Ricoeur 1981: 22). We have seen how the metaphors of Hosea tear down Israel's perception of themselves as virtuous, faultless, and entitled; of Yhwh as perpetually benevolent and obliged to rescue; of Baal as provider of all that Israel enjoys; of Assyria as healer; of Samaria's king as unassailable; of fraud and empty sacrifice as acceptable economic and religious activities; and of political and religious fickleness as expedient. "The big house yields no real life, need not be feared, cannot be trusted, and must not be honored" (Brueggemann 2001: 74).

On the ashes of those deconstructed illusions, the metaphors reconstruct a world in which Yhwh is the sole provider, healer, and sovereign of Israel. In this "world of possible impossibility" (Brown 2002: 215), Israel's fidelity to Yhwh and to one another is both possible and desirable because all of Israel's needs and hopes can be found with, in, and through Yhwh's loyalty to Israel. In Hosea's imagined future, Yhwh's loyalty to Israel will one day be reciprocated, and changing metaphors might just be the way to get there.

Notes

1. By "worldview," I do not strictly refer to cognitive content. I include an individual's and community's emotional experiences, value systems, social systems, possibilities for action, etc.

2. Translations are my own unless otherwise stated.
3. Form-critical scholars have long debated whether the biblical prophets reflect a "covenant lawsuit" genre. While such a genre and its associated forms likely never existed, the extant book of Hosea reflects a framework of legal prosecution, as shown here. As Ben Zvi (2005: 111–12) observes, Hos. 4:1 "served to evoke or play with common images associated with legal proceedings that existed in the world of knowledge of the readership."
4. Some argue Israel is a divorced wife, but the parallels to disowned son are more convincing (compare Judg. 11:7; see Eidevall 1996: 154; Lancaster 2023: 99–102). Either way, Yhwh is conceived of as a patriarch disowning a member of his house.

REFERENCES

Alt, Albrecht. 1953. "Hosea 5,8–6,6: Ein Krieg und seine Folgen in prophetischer Beleuchtung." In *Kleine Schriften zur Geschichte des Volkes Israel*. Munich: Beck, 2:163–87.

Ben Zvi, Ehud. 2005. *Hosea*. FOTL. Grand Rapids: Eerdmans.

Bird, Phyllis A. 2019. *Harlot or Holy Woman? A Study of Hebrew Qedešah*. University Park, PA: Eisenbrauns.

Blair, Merryl. 2007. "God Is an Earthquake: Destabilising Metaphor in Hosea 11." *Australian Biblical Review* 55: 1–12.

Brown, William P. 2002. *Seeing the Psalms: A Theology of Metaphor*. Louisville, KY: Westminster John Knox.

Brueggemann, Walter. 2001. *The Prophetic Imagination*. 2nd ed. Minneapolis: Fortress.

Brueggemann, Walter. 2008. "The Recovering God of Hosea." *HBT* 30: 5–20.

Cameron, Lynne. 2008. "Metaphor and Talk." In Raymond W. Gibbs Jr., ed., *The Cambridge Handbook of Metaphor and Thought*. New York: Cambridge University Press, 197–211.

Cameron, Lynne, and Robert Maslen, eds. 2010. *Metaphor Analysis: Research Practice in Applied Linguistics, Social Sciences and the Humanities*. London: Equinox.

Cameron, Lynne, and Juurd H. Stelma. 2004. "Metaphor Clusters in Discourse." *Journal of Applied Linguistics* 1: 107–36.

Cruz, Juan. 2016. *Who Is like Yahweh? A Study of Divine Metaphors in the Book of Micah*. FRLANT 263. Göttingen: Vandenhoeck & Ruprecht.

Dearman, J. Andrew. 2010. *The Book of Hosea*. NICOT. Grand Rapids: Eerdmans.

DeGrado, Jessie. 2018. "The Qdesha in Hosea 4:14: Putting the (Myth of the) Sacred Prostitute to Bed." *VT* 68: 8–40.

Eidevall, Göran. 1996. *Grapes in the Desert: Metaphors, Models, and Themes in Hosea 4–14*. ConBOT 43. Stockholm: Almqvist & Wiksell.

Eidevall, Göran. 2020. "Of Burning Ovens, Half-Baked Cakes, and Helpless Birds: Exploring a Cluster of Metaphors in Hosea 7." In A. Labahn and D. Verde, eds., *Networks of Metaphors in the Hebrew Bible*. BETL 309. Leuven: Peeters, 111–22.

Fisch, Harold. 1988. *Poetry with a Purpose: Biblical Poetics and Interpretation*. Bloomington: Indiana University Press.

Fishbane, Michael. 1985. *Biblical Interpretation in Ancient Israel*. Oxford: Clarendon.

Gibbs, Raymond W., Jr. 2017. "Metaphor, Language, and Dynamic Systems." In Elena Semino and Zsófia Demjén, eds., *The Routledge Handbook of Metaphor and Language*. Abingdon: Routledge, 56–69.

Grady, Joseph E. 2017. "Using Metaphor to Influence Public Perceptions and Policy: How Metaphors Can Save the World." In Elena Semino and Zsófia Demjén, eds., *The Routledge Handbook of Metaphor and Language*. Abingdon: Routledge, 443–54.

Haddox, Susan E. 2011. *Metaphor and Masculinity in Hosea*. StBibLit 141. New York: Peter Lang.

Hartsfield, Wallace. 2009. "Hosea." In Hugh R. Page Jr., Randall C. Bailey, Valerie Bridgeman, Stacy Davis, Cheryl Kirk-Duggan, Madipoane Masenya, Nathaniel Samuel Murrell, and Rodney S. Sadler Jr., eds., *The Africana Bible: Reading Israel's Scriptures from Africa and the African Diaspora*. Minneapolis: Fortress, 164–68.

Hawley, Lance R. 2018. *Metaphor Competition in the Book of Job*. Journal of Ancient Judaism Supplements 26. Göttingen: Vandenhoeck & Ruprecht.

Hecke, Pierre van. 2005. "Conceptual Blending: A Recent Approach to Metaphor Illustrated with the Pastoral Metaphor in Hos 4,16." In Pierre van Hecke, ed., *Metaphor in the Hebrew Bible*. BETL 187. Leuven: Leuven University Press, 215–31.

Holladay, William Lee. 1966. "Chiasmus, the Key to Hosea 12:3–6." *VT* 16: 53–64.

Hong, Seong-Hyuk. 2006. *The Metaphor of Illness and Healing in Hosea and Its Significance in the Socio-Economic Context of Eighth-Century Israel and Judah*. StBibLit 95. New York: Peter Lang.

Hundley, Michael B. 2013. "Here a God, There a God: An Examination of the Divine in Ancient Mesopotamia." *Altorientalische Forschungen* 40: 68–107.

Keefe, Alice A. 2001. *Woman's Body and the Social Body in Hosea*. JSOTSup 338. Sheffield: Sheffield Academic.

Kelle, Brad E. 2005. *Hosea 2: Metaphor and Rhetoric in Historical Perspective*. SBLAB 20. Atlanta: SBL.

Kimmel, Michael. 2010. "Why We Mix Metaphors (and Mix Them Well): Discourse Coherence, Conceptual Metaphor, and Beyond." *Journal of Pragmatics* 42: 97–115.

Kittay, Eva F. 1987. *Metaphor: Its Cognitive Force and Linguistic Structure*. Oxford: Clarendon.

Korpel, Marjo Christina Annette. 1990. *A Rift in the Clouds: Ugaritic and Hebrew Descriptions of the Divine*. UBL 8. Münster: Ugarit-Verlag.

Kövecses, Zoltán. 2015. *Where Metaphors Come From: Reconsidering Context in Metaphor*. New York: Oxford University Press.

Kövecses, Zoltán. 2017. "Conceptual Metaphor Theory." In Elena Semino and Zsófia Demjén, eds., *The Routledge Handbook of Metaphor and Language*. Abingdon: Routledge, 13–27.

Labahn, A., and D. Verde, eds. 2020. *Networks of Metaphors in the Hebrew Bible*. BETL 309. Leuven: Peeters.

Lakoff, George, and Mark Johnson. 2003. *Metaphors We Live By*. 2nd ed. Chicago: University of Chicago Press.

Laldinsuah, Ronald. 2015. *Responsibility, Chastisement, and Restoration: Relational Justice in the Book of Hosea*. Carlisle: Langham Monographs.

Lancaster, Mason D. 2021. "Metaphor Research and the Hebrew Bible." *CBR* 19: 235–85.

Lancaster, Mason D. 2023. *Hosea's God: A Metaphorical Theology*. SBLAIL 48. Atlanta: SBL Press.

Lancaster, Mason D., and Adam E. Miglio. 2020. "Lord of the Storm and Oracular Decisions: Competing Construals of Storm God Imagery in Hosea 6:1–6." *VT* 70: 634–44.

Landy, Francis. 1995. "In the Wilderness of Speech: Problems of Metaphor in Hosea." *BibInt* 3: 35–59.

Leung Lai, Barbara M. 2004. "Hearing God's Bitter Cries (Hosea 11:1–9): Reading, Emotive-Experiencing, Appropriation." *HBT* 26: 24–49.

Loon, Hanneke van. 2018. *Metaphors in the Discussion on Suffering in Job 3–31: Visions of Hope and Consolation*. BIS 165. Leiden: Brill.

Low, Graham, Zazie Todd, Alice Deignan, and Lynne Cameron, eds. 2010. *Researching and Applying Metaphor in the Real World*. Human Cognitive Processing 26. Amsterdam: John Benjamins.

Macwilliam, Stuart. 2014. *Queer Theory and the Prophetic Marriage Metaphor in the Hebrew Bible*. BibleWorld. London: Routledge.

Mays, James Luther. 1969. *Hosea: A Commentary*. OTL. Philadelphia: Westminster John Knox.

Moughtin-Mumby, Sharon. 2008. *Sexual and Marital Metaphors in Hosea, Jeremiah, Isaiah and Ezekiel*. OTM. Oxford: Oxford University Press.

Musolff, Andreas. 2017. "Metaphor and Persuasion in Politics." In Elena Semino and Zsófia Demjén, eds., *The Routledge Handbook of Metaphor and Language*. Abingdon: Routledge, 309–22.

Nwaoru, Emmanuel O. 1999. *Imagery in the Prophecy of Hosea*. ÄAT 41. Wiesbaden: Harrassowitz.

Oestreich, Bernhard. 1998. *Metaphors and Similes for Yahweh in Hosea 14:2–9 (1–8)*. Friedensauer Schriftenreihe: Reihe A, Theologie 1. Frankfurt: Peter Lang.

Petrie, Hugh G., and Rebecca S. Oshlag. 1993. "Metaphor and Learning." In Andrew Ortony, ed., *Metaphor and Thought*. 2nd ed. Cambridge: Cambridge University Press, 579–609.

Ricoeur, Paul. 1975. "Biblical Hermeneutics." *Semeia* 4: 29–148.

Ricoeur, Paul. 1981. *The Rule of Metaphor: Multi-Disciplinary Studies of the Creation of Meaning in Language*. Translated by Robert Czerny. Toronto: University of Toronto Press.

Schüngel-Straumann, Helen. 1987. "God as Mother in Hosea 11." *Theology Digest* 34: 3–8.

Seifert, Brigitte. 1996. *Metaphorisches Reden von Gott im Hoseabuch*. FRLANT 166. Göttingen: Vandenhoeck & Ruprecht.

Steen, Gerard J. 2011. "The Contemporary Theory of Metaphor: Now New and Improved!" *Review of Cognitive Linguistics* 9: 26–64.

Steen, Gerard J. 2017. "Deliberate Metaphor Theory: Basic Assumptions, Main Tenets, Urgent Issues." *Intercultural Pragmatics* 14: 1–24.

Stovell, Beth M. 2015. "'I Will Make Her Like a Desert': Intertextual Allusion and Feminine and Agricultural Metaphors in the Book of the Twelve." In Mark J. Boda, Michael H. Floyd, and Colin M. Toffelmire, eds., *The Book of the Twelve and the New Form Criticism*. SBLANEM 10. Atlanta: SBL, 37–61.

Strawn, Brent A. 2005. *What Is Stronger Than a Lion? Leonine Image and Metaphor in the Hebrew Bible and the Ancient Near East*. OBO 212. Göttingen: Vandenhoeck & Ruprecht.

Tångberg, K. Arvid. 1989. "'I Am like an Evergreen Fir, from Me Comes Your Fruit': Notes on Meaning and Symbolism in Hosea 14:9b (MT)." *SJOT* 2: 81–93.

Tilford, Nicole L. 2017. *Sensing World, Sensing Wisdom: The Cognitive Foundation of Biblical Metaphors*. SBLAIL 31. Atlanta: SBL.

Tully, Eric J. 2018. *Hosea: A Handbook on the Hebrew Text*. Baylor Handbook on the Hebrew Bible. Waco, TX: Baylor University Press.

Wacker, Marie-Theres. 2012. "Hosea." In Luise Schottroff and Marie-Theres Wacker, eds., *Feminist Biblical Interpretation: A Compendium of Critical Commentary on the Books of the Bible and Related Literature*. Grand Rapids: Eerdmans, 371–85.

Wolde, Ellen van. 2020. "A Network of Conventional and Deliberate Metaphors in Psalm 22." *JSOT* 44: 642–66.

Wolff, Hans Walter. 1974. *Hosea*. Translated by Gary Stansell. Hermeneia. Philadelphia: Fortress.

Yee, Gale A. 2012. "Hosea." In Carol A. Newsom, Sharon H. Ringe, and Jacqueline E. Lapsley, eds., *Women's Bible Commentary*. 3rd, rev., updated ed. Louisville: Westminster John Knox, 299–308.

Zehetgruber, Katrin. 2020. *Zuwendung Und Abwendung: Studien Zur Reziprozität Des JHWH/Israel-Verhältnisses Im Hoseabuch*. WMANT 159. Göttingen: Vandenhoeck & Ruprecht.

Zimran, Yisca. 2018. "The Notion of God Reflected in the Lion Imagery of the Book of Hosea." *VT* 68: 149–67.

Zimran, Yisca . 2021. "The Prevalence and Purpose of the 'Assyria-Egypt' Motif in the Book of Hosea." *JSOT* 46: 3–23.

CHAPTER 17

INTERTEXTUALITY AND TRADITIONS IN THE BOOK OF HOSEA

GÖRAN EIDEVALL

17.1. INTRODUCTION

THE following essay is based on a systematic and extensive mapping of intertextual relations between Hosea and other biblical books. Verse by verse, I have gone through the book of Hosea, searching (with the aid of concordance as well as computer) for various types of links to passages in other parts of the Hebrew Bible, as well as to major biblical traditions.

The primary purpose of this mapping has not been to try to establish literary dependence (which text has influenced the other) or to gain support for specific hypotheses concerning the dating of the texts or traditions involved. My aim is instead to contribute to a refined understanding of the literary and theological profile of the book of Hosea.

17.2. INTERTEXTUALITY IN HOSEA

In this section an overview of intertextual connections between Hosea and other parts of the Hebrew Bible is followed by a number of cases studies.

17.2.1. Intertextual Connections: An Overview

The number of potential connections between Hosea and other biblical books, based on such factors as vocabulary, is immense. Hence, it is necessary to identify the most relevant cases. In order to avoid subjectivity in the process of selection, one should apply well-defined criteria. For the purposes of this survey, I have defined a significant case of intertextuality as a literary connection between two texts, which fulfills two or more of the following requirements:

(a) verbatim correspondence, comprising a sequence of more than three words (quotation)
(b) shared vocabulary, involving co-occurrence of one or several unusual words and/ or an unusual collocation of words
(c) shared motifs and/or metaphors
(d) shared topic and/or theological perspective
(e) shared frame of reference, indicated by the mention of names, toponyms, or events

In Hosea (as in any other literary composition), some types of intertextuality are more frequent than others. In actual practice, a combination of criteria (b) and (c), shared vocabulary and shared motifs/metaphors, proved to be applicable in many cases. By contrast, I was only able to identify one direct quotation, albeit unmarked, and one case of quotation-like reuse, both stemming from the book of Amos (see below).

Generally speaking, the results of this investigation tend to confirm the findings that have been presented in previous research, typically in the form of case studies. In his commentary on Hosea, for instance, Andrew Dearman (2010: 353–55, 361–62, 379–81) has included some excurses containing detailed accounts and discussions of intertextual relations between Hosea and other texts in the Hebrew Bible (Deut. 32; Ps. 106; and Exod. 34:6–7). As a rule, my results coincide with Dearman's. It is worth noting, however, that there seems to be a rather high degree of subjectivity involved in the process of defining and naming shared motifs or themes.

Studying intertextuality in a systematic way yields insights of different kinds. On the level of details, I have uncovered a number of possible links that might shed new light on the interpretation of certain passages. However, the most interesting outcome of my investigation is probably the resulting overall picture of relations between Hosea and other parts of the Hebrew Bible.

17.2.2. Patterns of Abundance and Absence

Arguably, negative results are equally as important as positive ones in an overview of this kind. I will therefore point out cases of abundant intertextuality as well as cases of (near) absence of significant connections.

First and foremost, the book of Hosea contains a large number connections to various motifs and themes in the Pentateuch. Frequently, however, a certain utterance in Hosea seems to refer, or allude, to a *tradition* about an event or an era in the past, such as the exodus from Egypt, rather than to a specific *text*. In such cases, I think it is somewhat misleading to use the label "intertextuality," since it presupposes a relationship between texts. In terms of intertextuality in a stricter sense, a poem placed toward the end of the Pentateuch, the Song of Moses (Deut. 32), stands out as one of Hosea's most prominent dialogue partners. I was able to detect twenty-five significant links between the Song of Moses and the book of Hosea (see below).

Rather unsurprisingly, the results of my mapping indicate that the book of Hosea is more closely connected to the corpus of prophetic writings than to any other part of the Hebrew Bible. The intertextual links to all three of the Major Prophets are relatively rich in number: Jeremiah shows the highest quantity (35), followed by Isaiah (22) and Ezekiel (19). In terms of shared motifs with passages in Hosea, two clearly defined units, Isa. 31 and Jer. 2, are particularly interesting. These two are included in the selection of "intertexts" that will be discussed below.

Among the Minor Prophets (the Twelve), Amos is clearly Hosea's primary dialogue partner. I have identified fourteen significant intertextual connections between Hosea and Amos, including one quotation and one case of near quotation. In the context of a prediction concerning massive destruction of cities and fortifications, Hos. 8:14 reuses a refrain from Amos 1–2: "I will send fire against . . . and it will consume . . ." (cf. Amos 1:4, 7, 10, 12; 2:2, 5). There can be no doubt that the book of Amos is the source. The same applies to the utterance in Hos. 4:15b, which modifies Amos 5:5 (as well as Amos 4:4?) in an admonition to avoid certain cultic sites (Gilgal and Bethel, the latter called Beth-Aven). I agree with Jörg Jeremias (1996: 176–77) that these formulations probably were borrowed from Amos in the course of a Judah-oriented redaction of Hosea. As regards the remaining connections, which primarily involve shared motifs, I prefer leaving the question of direction of influence unanswered.

In contrast to Amos, the remaining books among the Twelve display conspicuously few connections to Hosea, reaching a total of just twelve. This raises questions regarding a popular line of research that tends to treat the Twelve as a consciously edited book with twelve parts, rather than an anthology-like collection comprising twelve separate books.[1] In my opinion, this hypothesis fails to account for the fact that the book of Hosea has much more in common (especially in terms of motifs and themes) with Jeremiah and Isaiah than with such books as Micah or Zephaniah.

It is also remarkable that the intertextual connections between Hosea and the books belonging to the wisdom literature are relatively few. Several scholars have maintained that large parts of Hosea betray influence from the wisdom tradition, regarding both form and content.[2] If this is correct, one would expect more than eighteen cases of shared motifs (half of them relating to Proverbs), most of them without any significant correspondence as regards vocabulary or phraseology. Apparently, the extent of sapiential influence on Hosea has been modest. Instructive here is the contrast between the late addition in Hos. 14:10, which is replete with wisdom language, and virtually all the preceding utterances in Hosea.

The total amount of connections between Hosea and Psalms (twenty-five by my count) is far from impressive. Around a third of them concern Ps. 106.[3] In terms of both its genre, as a poetic retrospective on Israel's early history, and its theological perspective, Ps. 106 has much in common with a number of passages in Hosea (see 9:10; 11:1–4; 13:4–6), as well as with the Song of Moses (see discussion below).

One of the most unexpected results of my investigation concerns the Song of Songs. This relatively short collection of love poetry contains nearly as many significant intertextual links to Hosea as the entire Psalter (twenty-four according to my criteria). It should be noted, however, that most of these connections pertain to one specific passage, namely Hos. 14:6–8 (Heb. 14:7–9), which depicts a utopian future characterized by restored harmony in the relationship between Yhwh and his people (see below).

Finally, the fact that Hosea lacks clear connections to those books in the Hebrew Bible that are commonly dated to the postexilic era (such as 1–2 Chronicles, Ezra, Nehemiah, Haggai, Zechariah, and Daniel) would seem to pose a problem for scholars who claim that Hosea was composed in the Persian period.[4] There are, admittedly, some intriguing points of contact between Hos. 4 and Mal. 2. However, they are probably best explained in terms of redactional activity within the emerging collection of the Twelve.[5]

17.2.3. Selection of Intertexts

In the process of identifying intertexts of particular interest I have employed the criteria described above in a search for well-defined literary compositions (rather than isolated verses), displaying a large amount (and, ideally, a rather high concentration) of links to the book of Hosea. In addition to shared motifs and vocabulary, I have also been looking for similarities with regard to literary genre and/or theological perspective.

This resulted in a list comprising four texts: Deut. 32 ("The Song of Moses"), Isa. 31, Jer. 2, and the Song of Songs (entire book). They represent different parts of the Hebrew Bible, as well as different types of intertextuality. Broadly speaking, they represent two genres, poetry and prophecy. This accords well with the observation that large parts of Hosea can be characterized as "prophetic poetry."

A detailed discussion of the interpretative significance of each intertextual relation between these four texts and Hosea would probably require a monograph. I will treat the two prophetic texts (Jer. 2 and Isa. 31) rather briefly. Thereafter, I will display and discuss the connections between Hosea and the two poetic texts (the Song of Moses and the Song of Songs) in more detail.

17.2.4. Prophetic Parallels: Jeremiah 2 and Hosea

The second chapter in the book of Jeremiah provides a retrospective panorama on major events in (traditions about) Israel's early history, interspersed with accusations centering on (required) monolatry and (repeated) apostasy. In terms of topic and theological perspective, Jer. 2 belongs to the same group of texts as Ps. 106 and the Song of Moses. From the perspective of intertextual links to Hosea, Jer. 2:1–9 is the most interesting passage. The following motifs and metaphors are shared by Jer. 2:1–9 and various passages in Hosea:

(a) election taking place when personified Israel was young: Jer. 2:2; Hos. 2:17 (Eng. 2:15); 11:1
(b) the people pictured as choice fruits: Jer. 2:3; Hos. 9:10a
(c) Yhwh as the god who brought Israel out of Egypt: Jer. 2:4; Hos. 13:4
(d) divine guidance in the wilderness: Jer. 2:2, 6; Hos. 13:5
(e) apostasy as soon as the people entered the land: Jer. 2:7; Hos. 9:10b; 13:6
(f) priests rejecting Yhwh and his law/instruction (*tôrâ*): Jer. 2:8; Hos. 4:6
(g) Yhwh contending (*rîb*) with the people and its leaders: Jer. 2:9; Hos. 4:1, 4

One may add that typically Hoseanic expressions and metaphors are found also in subsequent parts of Jer. 2, such as the nation exchanging its "glory" (Jer. 2:11; Hos. 4:7), Israel being depicted as a vine (Jer. 2:21; Hos. 10:1), and the people being portrayed as a wild ass (Jer. 2:24; Hos. 8:9). Based on these observations, I find it likely that Jer. 2 is dependent on (some version of) the book of Hosea, although the possibility of influence in the opposite direction cannot be ruled out. On closer examination, the idea conveyed by or the emphasis of the utterance is sometimes notably different.[6] One may perhaps speak of a process of creative adaptation in a new historical context.

17.2.5. Similarity Regarding Imagery: Isaiah 31 and Hosea 11

In a previous study (Eidevall 1993), I have called attention to a number of striking similarities between Isa. 31 and Hos. 11, ranging from setting and genre to imagery and vocabulary. Arguably, the following are the most conspicuous parallels:

(a) references to Egypt (Isa. 31:1, 3; Hos. 11:1, 5, 11) as well as to Assyria (Isa. 31:8–9; Hos. 11:5, 11)
(b) the phrase "no(t) human" (*lō' 'îš*) used in order to emphasize exclusively divine dimensions of an event
(c) abrupt juxtaposition of leonine and avian metaphors within a depiction of divine agency in the context of a national crisis. In both texts (Isa. 31:4–5; Hos. 11:10–11), a somewhat ambiguous portrayal of Yhwh as a roaring or rapacious lion is immediately followed by a simile involving flying birds, which conveys an unambiguously hopeful message.

These intertextual connections are best explained by two factors in combination: shared setting and editorial activity. To begin with, both texts are based on oracles that most likely originated during the last decades of the eighth century BCE. It is reasonable to assume that prophetic circles operating within the same historical setting (albeit on different sides of the border between Israel and Judah) would have had access to a common repertoire of images and phrases. At a later stage, possibly, the existing parallels between these two passages, in terms of shared motifs and themes, sparked the creation of further parallels. For instance, an editor of Isa. 31 may have used Hos. 11 as a source of inspiration.

17.2.6. Closely Related Compositions: The Song of Moses and Hosea

In terms of both quantity (the number of significant connections) and quality (the degree of shared theological perspective), the poem in Deut. 32, known as the Song of Moses, must be regarded as the textual composition in the Hebrew Bible that is most closely connected to Hosea. Links to this poem can be found in almost every chapter in Hosea. Conversely, as shown by this table, every part of the Song of Moses contains one or several links to Hosea:

Deut. 32: Motifs and Metaphors	*Occurrences in Hosea*
v. 2 words of teaching are like rain	10:12 righteousness like rain
v. 2 life-giving dew	14:6 (Eng. 14:5)
v. 5 (and v. 20) a perverse generation	5:7 alien children
v. 6 the people are foolish and senseless	4:14; 7:11; 13:13
v. 6 Yhwh as the people's father	11:1 (implicitly)
v. 10 Yhwh found Jacob/Israel in a desert	9:10a
v. 10 divine care in the wilderness	13:5 (cf. 2:16 [Eng. 2:14]; 11:3)
v. 12 (and v. 39) Yhwh and no other god	13:4
vv. 13–14 Yhwh feeding the people	13:6 (cf. 11:4)
v. 15 the people growing sated and fat	13:6
v. 17 performing sacrifices to other gods	11:2
v. 18 the people have forgotten their creator	2:15 (Eng. 2:13); 8:14; 13:6
v. 21 the people have provoked Yhwh	12:15 (Eng. 12:14)
v. 21 "not a people" (about another nation)	cf. 1:9 "not my people"
v. 25 sword bereaving in the street	9:12 11:6 sword in cities
v. 32 vine and grapes (of enemies)	9:10 grapes; 10:1 vine (Israel)
v. 39 "I, I . . ." (divine self-declaration)	5:14
v. 39 Yhwh kills and makes alive	6:1–2; cf. also 9:16; 13:7–8
v. 39 Yhwh wounds and heals	6:1–2; 7:1; 11:3; 14:5
v. 39 no one else can deliver	5:14

This enumeration of shared motifs and metaphors may seem impressive, although it is not exhaustive.[7] In itself, however, such a catalog of (alleged) parallels is of limited value for the interpretation of the texts involved. Its significance depends on whether it can be supplemented and supported by observations pertaining to other levels. As regards

Hosea and the Song of Moses, this is definitively the case. Most importantly, Deut. 32 represents a full-length version of a poetic retrospective on the history of Israel, a genre that surfaces in a series of miniatures in Hosea (see 9:10; 10:1, 9, 11; 11:1–4; 13:1, 4–6).[8]

One may add the observation that in these two compositions Israel's early history is described and evaluated from a similar theological point of view, centering on the principle of monolatry, and emphasizing the contrast between Yhwh's providential care and the people's proclivity for cultic transgressions. Interestingly, it is also possible to detect traces of a common story line in Deut. 32:7–18 and in some passages in Hosea (9:10; 11:1–2; 13:4–6), featuring the following stages:

(a) divine election of Israel (Deut. 32:7–9; Hos. 9:10a; 11:1; 13:4)
(b) a period in the desert, apparently characterized by a harmonious relationship between Yhwh and his people (Deut. 32:10–12; Hos. 9:10a; 13:4)
(c) a period of apostasy, beginning as soon as the Israelites approached the cultivated land (Deut. 32:15–18; Hos. 9:10b; 11:2; 13:6).

In both Deut. 32:15 and Hos. 13:6, the third and last stage (apostasy) is metaphorically described in terms of satisfaction and subsequent forgetfulness. More specifically, the Israelites are portrayed as sheep (an individual animal in Deut. 32:15; a herd in Hos. 13:6) that have been provided rich pasturage. When they have eaten their fill, however, they become ungrateful and arrogant, and turn away from their shepherd (Yhwh). Ola Wikander (2013) has called attention to some striking similarities between the role of this motif in Deut. 32:15 and in a Hurrian-Hittite narrative, the *Epic of Liberation*. This is a reminder that many passages in the Hebrew Bible, such as Deut. 32:15–18 and Hos. 13:4–6, are parts of wider networks involving extrabiblical texts and traditions.

In the case of Hosea and the Song of Moses, it is hardly possible to determine the direction of influence, partly because the dating of Deut. 32 is a contested issue. To this comes the observation that the parallels between the texts pertain mainly to the level of content and ideas. In a case of direct literary dependence, one would expect a higher degree of shared vocabulary and phraseology. Therefore, I tend to agree with Dearman (2010: 354), who has suggested that the authors of both compositions had "access to a common matrix of traditions and similar points of view."

17.2.7. Linked to Love Poetry: Hosea 14:6–8 and the Song of Songs

All chapters in the Song of Songs contain motifs that occur in one or several instances in Hosea. This would seem to indicate that the language of love poetry permeates this prophetic book. In the text of Hosea, however, these links are far from evenly distributed. The most compelling similarities with passages in the Song are concentrated in the

INTERTEXTUALITY AND TRADITIONS IN THE BOOK OF HOSEA   253

utopian vision that concludes the book, and particularly in 14:6–8 (Eng. 14:5–7). Hence, the following discussion will take its point of departure there:

> 6 I will be like the dew to Israel.
> He will blossom like the lily. He will strike root, like Lebanon.
>
> 7 His shoots will spread, his splendor will be like the olive tree,
> and his fragrance will be like Lebanon.
>
> 8 They will return and dwell in its/his shade; they will grow (or: revive) grain.
> They will blossom like the vine, and its fame will be like the wine of Lebanon.
> (Hos. 14:6–8 [Eng. 14:5–7])

Several motifs in this passage are quite common in biblical poetry. Some of them, such as the dew and the vine, have occurred previously in Hosea (dew: 6:4; 13:3; vine: 2:14 [Eng. 2:12]; 10:1). Hence, they can be understood as intratextual echoes, variations, or reversals. Nonetheless, it is evident that this passage, with its use of garden-related language in a depiction of a restored relationship, is closely related to the Song of Songs.

Arguably, the expression "like Lebanon" (*kallĕbānôn*), which is repeated at the end of each strophe in vv. 6–8 (with a slight variation in v. 8), serves as an intertextual marker. Nothing in the preceding text in Hosea has prepared the reader for such an extended comparison with the landscapes and gardens of Lebanon. Among early readers of Hos. 14, this refrain-like phrase, "like Lebanon," would therefore probably have evoked associations to the Song of Songs, where such references to Lebanon are used as a rhetorical device in order to enhance someone's beauty or splendor (see Song. 4:11; 5:15; 7:5).

Once this intertextual connection between Hos. 14:6–8 and the Song of Songs has been recognized, it is possible to discover a large number of additional shared motifs and metaphors:[9]

> v. 6: dew (Song. 5:2); to blossom or bud (*prḥ*; Song. 6:11; 7:13); "like the lily" (Song. 2:1–2)
>
> v. 7: like a tree (Song. 2:3); fragrance (Song. 1:3, 12; 2:13; 4:10–11; 7:9, 14); "fragrance . . . like Lebanon" (Song. 4:11)
>
> v. 8: "in its/his shade" (Song. 2:3); vineyard (Song. 2:13; 6:11; 7:9, 13); to blossom or bud like a vineyard (cf. Song. 6:11; 7:13); like wine (cf. "more than wine" in Song. 1:2, 4; 4:10)

Echoes of the Song of Songs (or, perhaps, of an earlier collection of love songs with similar contents) also appear elsewhere in Hosea. Motifs that might be related to this kind of poetry are found in almost every chapter. In most cases, however, the link is rather vague. The most striking example of a connection to the Song, besides those found in Hos. 14:6–8, is the theme of seeking and (not) finding. This thematic thread runs through Hosea in its entirety (see Hos 2:8–9 [Eng. 2:6–7]; 5:6, 15; 7:10; 9:10; 10:12; 12:5; 14:9 [Eng. 14:8]).[10] In the Song of Songs, it surfaces in a couple of passages (Song. 5:6–8;

6:1). One phrase in the depiction of the (metaphorical) wife's futile search for her lovers ("she will seek them, but not find them," Hos. 2:9 [Eng. 2:7]) has a close counterpart in a dreamlike sequence in the Song, which is narrated by the female voice: "I sought him, but did not find him" (Song. 5:6 NRSV).

One may add that the adaptation of motifs from the Song of Songs in Hos. 14 (and elsewhere in Hosea) involves elements of transformation. The dynamic dialogue between two lovers, one male and one female, who describe each other, has been replaced by a monologue where an implicitly male divine/prophetic voice describes the personified nation in predominantly male grammatical terms. As Landy (2011: 202) observes, "The elimination of the feminine persona has the effect of desexing the Song." At the same time, it is worth noting that masculine pronouns are sometimes attached to motifs that are associated with the woman (the bride) in the Song of Songs, such as the lily (Hos. 14:6 [Eng. 14:5]; cf. Song. 2:1–2).

From a theological point of view, finally, it is evident that the authors/editors of Hosea borrowed motifs and metaphors from poetic depictions of human lovers, but then applied them on a different level, as a means to describe the interactions between Yhwh and his people, Ephraim/Israel. This kind of theological reuse of motifs from the realm of love poetry might have contributed to the development of an allegorical reading of the Song of Songs.

17.3. THE USE OF TRADITIONS IN HOSEA

Focusing primarily on references to traditions linked to the Pentateuch in Hosea, this section provides an overview, a case study, and a discussion of a rhetorical device typical of Hosea, namely reversals of traditions.

17.3.1. References to Traditions: An Overview

The book of Hosea contains numerous references to theological traditions associated with the Pentateuch, such as the exodus from Egypt and the period of wilderness wanderings. Several monographs have been dedicated to questions arising from such observations: When and why were these allusions created? Which version of a certain tradition was known to the author or editor responsible for a certain passage in Hosea?[11] Instead of attempting to answer such questions concerning origins, I will focus on how these traditions are used in various passages in Hosea. In many cases, all we have is a brief allusion. As shown in the ensuing section, there is one notable exception from that rule—namely, the treatment of the Jacob traditions in Hos. 12. In the final section, I will demonstrate how Hosea uses other pentateuchal traditions, such as those relating to the covenant and the exodus, in a highly creative way, as theological themes that can be varied or even reversed.

Something should also be said about those traditions known from other parts of the Hebrew Bible that are not mentioned in Hosea. Most remarkably, all traditions relating to Zion theology are absent. Although the book of Hosea contains many references to Judah as a geographical and political entity, the city of Jerusalem is never mentioned. One looks in vain for formulations conveying the idea that Yhwh has chosen the temple in Jerusalem, on Mount Zion, as his abode on earth. This can, to some extent, be explained as a result of Hosea's focus on the Northern Kingdom. It is, however, illuminating to make a comparison with the book of Amos, which denounces the Northern Kingdom within a decidedly pro-Judean framework, consisting of a reference to Zion as Yhwh's residence (Amos 1:2) and a promise to "restore David's fallen hut" (Amos 9:11).[12] Note that Hos. 3:5 (probably of postexilic origin) envisions that the Israelites in the future will turn to "David their king." Nonetheless, Hosea's silence concerning the special status of Jerusalem makes this book unique among the prophetic writings in the Hebrew Bible.

17.3.2. A Portrait with Two Faces: Jacob Traditions in Hosea 12

Hosea 12 contains clear references to traditions about the patriarch Jacob. According to a broad scholarly consensus, the relevant texts (vv. 3–7 and 13 [Eng. vv. 2–6 and 12]), presuppose a version of the Jacob story that is similar to (if not identical with) the one preserved in Genesis.[13] As shown by Weyde (1994: 329–50), these few verses in Hosea manage to allude, in a condensed way, to almost all important episodes within Gen. 25–35, and roughly in the same order. This can be illustrated by a list of the intertextual links in Hos. 12:4–5 (Eng. 12:3–4):

> v. 4a: the birth of the twins (Gen. 25:21–26) and Jacob's deceitful behavior toward Esau (Gen. 25:27–34; 27:1–40)
>
> vv. 4b–5aα: the nocturnal struggle at Jabbok (Gen. 32:22–33)
>
> v. 5aβ: the reunion of Jacob and Esau (Gen. 33:1–11)
>
> v. 5b: Encounters between Yhwh and Jacob at Bethel (Gen. 28:10–22; 35:1–15)

It is difficult to assess the rhetorical function of the references to the Jacob tradition in Hos. 12 because they are terse in style and replete with puns and ambiguities. Opinions differ widely when it comes to the characterization of the patriarch in this text. Whereas several scholars maintain that Hos. 12 portrays Jacob negatively, as a deceitful trickster without faith (Blum 2009: 302–3; McKenzie 1986: 320; Vollmer 1971: 114–15), others aver that the patriarch here is pictured as a positive example for the addressees. In my opinion, it is a mistake to presuppose that the image must be either that of a villain or that of a hero. I agree with those who detect an ambivalent attitude to Jacob in Hos. 12 (e.g., Daniels 1990: 50). He appears to have been deliberately depicted as a figure with both positive and negative traits. On one hand, he is inclined to deceive others; on the other, he is eager to walk with Yhwh. Arguably, it is precisely in this way that he can, in the words of Else Holt (1995: 39), "serve as an example of a conversion that is to be imitated." If one recognizes the complexity of Jacob's character in Hos. 12, as both sinner and penitent, and at the same time as both patriarch in the past and personification of the nation, it becomes possible to make sense of the exhortation in v. 7 (Eng. v. 6) (so Weyde 1994: 348–49). Further, the enigmatic formulations in v. 5b (Eng. v. 4b) take on a profound meaning. This translation aims at capturing the inherent ambiguities in the Hebrew text: "At Bethel he found/finds (or: met/meets) him/us, and there he spoke/speaks to us."[14]

In more than one respect, the use of the Jacob tradition in Hos. 12 is atypical for the book of Hosea. As shown in the next section, references to traditions usually take the form of brief allusions. As a rule, no details relating to narratives known from the Pentateuch are mentioned. Rather than being brought together into a larger unit, as is the case in 12:3–7 (Eng. 12:2–6), such allusions to various traditions tend to be scattered throughout the book of Hosea.

17.3.3. Traditions and Transformations: Reversals of Creation and Exodus

In a previous study focused on metaphorical utterances and themes (Eidevall 1996: 240–42), I coined the expression "rhetoric of reversal" as a way of describing a characteristic feature that contributes to making the textual world of Hosea unique. As a stylistic device in literature, a "reversal" can be defined as an instance of recognizable reuse or recurrence involving a strong element of contrast and transformation. This phenomenon can be observed on different levels, ranging from recontextualized words and phrases to reinterpreted motifs and themes. In the following, I will focus on reversals of major biblical (and, mainly, pentateuchal) traditions in Hosea. This functions as a powerful rhetorical device with interesting theological implications. The examples of such reversals in Hosea are manifold. One passage (4:3) seems to describe a reversal of God's act of creation (see DeRoche 1981: 403–6). In the following, I will discuss two theological traditions that are subject to multiple variations and reversals: the covenant and the exodus.

In the case of the covenant tradition, a negated version precedes the first positive reference. In ch. 1, it is announced that the covenantal relationship between Yhwh and Israel has been annulled, by means of the symbolic name given to one of the prophet's children, "Not My People (lōʾʾammî)" (Hos. 1:9; cf. Exod. 6:7; Lev. 26:12; Jer. 24:7). This name may express the very opposite—namely, an affirmative statement ("My People")—once the prefixed negation is removed. It contains the potential for its own reversal, and thereby it seems to foreshadow a reversal of the initial reversal of the covenant tradition, something that is announced in 2:3 (Eng. 2:1). However, rather than marking a happy end, this prefigured change of a symbolic name merely serves as a prelude to the ensuing oscillations between affirming and denying the human–divine covenantal relationship (see 2:11–15, 20–25 [Eng. 2:9–13, 18–23]; 4:17; 7:1, 10; 8:1; 11:8–9; 13:1; 14:5, 9 [Eng. 14:4, 8]).

A similar pattern emerges with Hosea's allusions to the exodus from Egypt. The exodus theme surfaces for the first time in Hos. 2:17 (Eng. 2:15) in an expression of divine (or, prophetic) nostalgia. According to this vision, the only way to escape from the prevailing impasse, allegedly caused by the people's recalcitrance, is to start all over again, in a state of harmonious coexistence, "as in the days of her youth, as when she went up from the land of Egypt" (2:17b [Eng. 2:15b]). Later on, as this theme reappears, it takes on a more sinister tone. According to 8:13, Israel will be forced (implicitly, by Yhwh) to return to Egypt. The story of the foundational journey from Egypt will be, so to speak, rewound. This message, which is repeated in 9:3, entails a complete collapse of the exodus tradition. Instead of a fresh start, involving restored reciprocity, this reenactment appears to signify the end of all hopes for a better future. In actual practice, it is reasonable to assume that the utterances in 8:13 and 9:3 refer primarily to (imminent or past) deportations to Assyria, as indicated by 9:3b: "Ephraim shall return to Egypt, and they shall eat unclean food in Assyria." Quite possibly, the author/editor had exilic existence in Egypt in view, as well, at least for some groups (see 9:6).

One important aspect of the rhetoric of reversal is that it allows the author to introduce abrupt and unexpected changes. Thus, the sense of despair evoked by the announcements in 8:13 and 9:3, which appear to imply annulment of the entire tradition of salvation history, is temporarily alleviated in 11:1 by means of a relapse into divine nostalgia (cf. 2:17 [Eng. 2:15]). However, this positive reference to the exodus from Egypt is almost immediately followed by a renewed declaration, in 11:5, that the people must return to Egypt (cf. 9:3). Then, in 11:11, this circle of repeated variations is broken by a prophecy that reverses all previous reversals. It conveys a hopeful message concerning deported Israelites, in both Egypt and Assyria: "I will return them to their homes, says Yhwh" (11:11b).

In all the Hosea passages reviewed so far, the exodus from Egypt is used as a theological theme, serving to illustrate Yhwh's capacity to act against human expectations. None of the brief allusions has featured any details associated with the exodus as a story about an event in the nation's past. This changes at the end of ch. 12. Between two divine self-declarations that trace the relationship with Israel back to the time of Egypt (12:9 [Eng. 12:8] and 13:4), we find a statement of a different kind. It reminds the addressees of one vital aspect of the exodus drama—namely, the human leadership: "By a prophet Yhwh brought Israel from Egypt, and by a prophet he was guarded" (12:14 [Eng. 12:13]). The fact that Moses is not mentioned by name has puzzled many interpreters. I suggest that an open and inclusive formulation ("a prophet") was chosen in order to facilitate an associative link between Moses and the prophetic voice that speaks throughout the book of Hosea. It is implied, one may infer, that the mission remains the same: to guide and guard the people (see also Holt 1995: 48).

17.4. Conclusion

It is possible to detect a vast amount of intertextual links between the book of Hosea and other parts of the Hebrew Bible. Still, Hosea has its own distinct profile among the prophetic writings. Composed in a style that can be described as a fusion of prophecy and poetry, it turns out to be particularly closely connected to two intertexts outside the prophetic corpus: the Song of Moses and the Song of Songs. While focusing on the fate of Ephraim, the book of Hosea is silent regarding Zion. It contains numerous allusions to the major theological traditions that are associated with the Pentateuch, such as creation, covenant, and exodus. Frequently, however, these references take the form of reversals. This stylistic device contributes to the book's theological profile. According to Hosea, Yhwh is a God of reversals, always capable of overturning the prevailing state of affairs. Such a theology may induce anxiety in periods of security, but also hope in times of disaster and despair.

Notes

1. For this approach, see Redditt and Schart 2003. For critique, see Ben Zvi 1996.
2. See Wolff 1974: xxiv; Dell 2011; Krispenz 2020.
3. For a detailed account of connections between Ps. 106 and Hosea, see Dearman 2010: 361–62.
4. See, above all, Bos 2013.
5. With Leuchter 2014.
6. For further details, see Holt 1995: 127–30.
7. A similar yet somewhat different list is provided by Dearman 2010: 354–55.
8. Further examples of this genre, each of them with intertextual links to Hosea, are found in Jer. 2 (discussed above) and in Pss. 78; 80; 106.
9. Although most modern Hosea commentaries mention connections to the Song of Songs, these parallels tend to play a marginal role in the interpretation of Hos. 14. See, e.g., Ben Zvi 2005: 298 and Wolff 1974: 234. Francis Landy (2011: 201–3) is a notable exception to this rule.
10. See further, Eidevall 1996: 248–52.
11. See Daniels 1990; Holt 1995; Neef 1987; Vollmer 1971.
12. See further Eidevall 2017: 18–19, 24, 97, 239.
13. See Daniels 1990: 51; Neef 1987: 45–47; Schott 2015: 26.
14. On the ambiguities in Hos. 12:5b, and the multiple possibilities involved in translating and interpreting the Hebrew text, see Ben Zvi 2005: 249–51; Good 1966: 144–46; McKenzie 1986: 316–17.

References

Ackroyd, Peter R. 1963. "Hosea and Jacob." *VT* 13: 245–59.

Ben Zvi, Ehud. 1996. "Twelve Prophetic Books or 'the Twelve': A Few Preliminary Considerations." In James W. Watts and P. R. House, eds., *Forming Prophetic Literature:*

Essays on Isaiah and the Twelve in Honor of John D. W. Watts. JSOTSup 235. Sheffield: Sheffield Academic Press, 125–56.

Ben Zvi, Ehud. 2005. *Hosea.* FOTL 21A/1. Grand Rapids, MI: Eerdmans.

Blum, Erhard. 2009. "Hosea 12 und die Pentateuchüberlieferungen." In A C. Hagedorn and H. Pfeiffer, eds., *Die Erzväter in der biblischen Tradition.* BZAW 400. Berlin: de Gruyter, 291–321.

Bos, James M. 2013. *Reconsidering the Date and Provenance of the Book of Hosea: The Case for Persian-Period Yehud.* LHBOTS 580. London: Bloomsbury T&T Clark.

Daniels, Dwight R. 1990. *Hosea and Salvation History: The Early Traditions of Israel in the Prophecy of Hosea.* BZAW 191. Berlin: de Gruyter.

Day, John. 1986. "Pre-Deuteronomic Allusions to the Covenant in Hosea and Psalm lxxviii." *VT* 36: 1–12.

Dearman, J. Andrew. 2010. *The Book of Hosea.* NICOT. Grand Rapids, MI: Eerdmans.

Dell, Katharine J. 2011. "Hosea, Creation, and Wisdom: An Alternative Tradition." In James Aitken, K. J. Dell, and Brian Mastin, eds., *On Stone and Scroll: Essays in Honour of Graham Ivor Davies.* New York: de Gruyter, 409–24.

DeRoche, Michael. 1981. "The Reversal of Creation in Hosea." *VT* 31: 401–9.

Dozeman, Thomas B. 2000. "Hosea and the Wilderness Wandering Tradition." In Steven McKenzie and Thomas Römer, eds., *Rethinking the Foundations: Historiography in the Ancient World and the Bible.* BZAW 294 Berlin: de Gruyter, 55–70.

Eidevall, Göran. 1993. "Lions and Birds as Literature: Some Notes on Isaiah 31 and Hosea 11." *SJOT* 7: 78–87.

Eidevall, Göran. 1996. *Grapes in the Desert: Metaphors, Models, and Themes in Hosea 4–14.* ConBOTS 43. Stockholm: Almqvist & Wiksell International.

Eidevall, Göran. 2017. *Amos: A New Translation with Introduction and Commentary.* Anchor Yale Bible 24G. New Haven: Yale University Press.

Good, Edwin M. 1966. "Hosea and the Jacob Tradition." *VT* 16: 137–51.

Holt, Else Kragelund. 1995. *Prophesying the Past: The Use of Israel's History in the Book of Hosea.* JSOTSup 194. Sheffield: Sheffield Academic Press.

Jeremias, Jörg. 1996. "The Interrelationship between Amos and Hosea." In James W. Watts and Paul R. House, eds., *Forming Prophetic Literature: Essays on Isaiah and the Twelve in Honor of John D. W. Watts.* JSOTSup 235. Sheffield: Sheffield Academic Press, 171–86.

Krispenz, Jutta. 2020. "Hosea—the Wise Prophet?" In J. Krispenz, ed., *Scribes as Sages and Prophets: Scribal Traditions in Biblical Wisdom Literature and in the Book of the Twelve.* BZAW 496. Berlin: de Gruyter, 79–98.

Landy, Francis. 2011. *Hosea.* 2nd ed. Sheffield: Phoenix.

Leuchter, Mark. 2014. "Another Look at the Hosea/Malachi Framework in the Twelve." *VT* 64: 249–65.

Macintosh, A. A. 1995. "Hosea and the Wisdom Tradition." In John Day, Robert P. Gordon, and Hugh G. M. Williamson, eds., *Wisdom in Ancient Israel: Essays in Honour of J. A. Emerton.* Cambridge: Cambridge University Press, 124–32.

McKenzie, Steven L. 1986. "The Jacob Tradition in Hosea xii 4–5." *VT* 36: 311–22.

Neef, Heinz-Dieter. 1987. *Die Heilstraditionen Israels in der Verkündigung des Propheten Hosea.* BZAW 169. Berlin: de Gruyter.

Redditt, Paul R., and Aaron Schart, eds. 2003. *Thematic Threads in the Book of the Twelve.* BZAW 325. Berlin: de Gruyter.

Schott, Martin. 2015. "Die Jakobpassagen in Hosea 12." *ZTK* 112: 1–26.

260   GÖRAN EIDEVALL

Vollmer, Jochen. 1971. *Geschichtliche Rückblicke und Motive in der Prophetie des Amos, Hosea und Jesaja*. BZAW 119. Berlin: de Gruyter.

Weyde, Karl William. 1994. "The References to Jacob in Hos 12:4–5." In Arvid Tångberg, ed., *Text and Theology*. Oslo: Verbum, 336–58.

Wikander, Ola. 2013. "Ungrateful Grazers: A Parallel to Deut 32:15 from the Hurrian/Hittite *Epic of Liberation*." *SEÅ* 78: 137–46.

Wolff, Hans Walter. 1974. *Hosea*. Trans. G. Stansell. Hermeneia. Philadephia: Fortress.

CHAPTER 18

GOD'S CHARACTER IN THE BOOK OF HOSEA

BO H. LIM

18.1. METHODOLOGY FOR STUDYING THE CHARACTER OF GOD

WORKS on Hosea have described the character of God in starkly different ways from a God of long-suffering love to an abusive domestic partner. Given the range of interpretations regarding the character of God in the book, an examination of method and assumptions ought to be considered from the outset. When speaking of the character of God, theologians in the past typically meant God's essential attributes like love, holiness, justice, and so forth. More recently, following literary studies, biblical scholars have begun to characterize God in the Bible just as one would examine human literary characters.[1] Lee Humphreys, drawing on and modifying the work of Robert Alter, identifies the following textual indicators for the characterization of God in the Bible: (1) External description of physical appearance; (2) What other characters in the story say of a character; (3) Accounts of a character's actions; (4) Direct speech by the character; (5) Reports on the character's inner thoughts; (6) Direct statements about the character by the narrator (Humphreys 2001: 8–14; Alter 1981: 116–17). These textual indicators function on a scale from less to more reliable in their ability to describe the character of God.

As much as the literary study of the character of God in Hosea is a descriptive exercise (sometimes providing scholarship that serves people of various faith commitments), it is not entirely objective. Stuart Lasine identifies the dynamics of the reading process that occur when describing literary characters: (1) "Psychologizing" is common in human activity and therefore operative while reading. Readers inevitably construct judgments about characters in narratives based on the ethical categories they use in daily life. (2) People perceive others, including those in literature, typologically, so a bias exists toward thinking of oneself as a round character and judging others as flat. Social psychologists have observed that humans tend to characterize others in a reductive manner to resolve tensions they experience in their relationships. Based on these tendencies, Lasine observes, "When, as biblical interpreters, we evaluate (and thereby achieve closure on) a biblical character, we must ask ourselves whether we have chosen to explain their behavior in the way that is most comforting and familiar (including methodologically familiar) to *us*" (Lasine 2012, italics orig.). He finds that biblical scholars tend to reduce God to a flat character, particularly when dealing with portrayals of God's judgment or anger. He writes, "While scholars have increasingly called attention to the God's 'dark side,' to reduce Yahweh to a 'demonic,' 'capricious,' or 'amoral' deity is to flatten the complex manner of his presentation in biblical narrative (and poetry). As we have seen, God acts in a number of different ways in scripture and displays different traits in different situations" (Lasine 2016: 472–73). In Hosea, God is both loving and angry, and is described in various genres. Readers ought to heed Lasine's cautions and not oversimplify the character of a complex God.

Describing and evaluating any one literary character also occurs within the reader's understanding and judgments of other characters within the story. In a book like Hosea, where character is revealed through the course of interpersonal relationships, any understanding of God will be intertwined with one's view of Israel, God's covenant partner. Daniel Castelo offers the reminder, "Readers may not understand YHWH's character, but then again, they may not understand Israel's either," and goes on to caution, "Morally evaluating the covenant partnership is fraught with challenges that reflect very much the formation and limitations of contemporary cultural and societal conditions" (Lim and Castelo 2015: 94). In recent years, feminist interpreters have demonstrated how the marital metaphor has been inconsistently applied to God, Israel, and the nations, and much contemporary debate regarding the portrayal of the character of God in Hosea is determined by how far the metaphor ought to be applied (see O'Brien 2008: 29–48).

There are also unique challenges to describing the character of God in the Bible due to religious reasons. Preconceived notions about God often dictate the degree to which readers will allow a particular biblical text to inform their understanding of the divine. Meir Sternberg observes that for many religious readers, "God's character tends to constancy and man's to variability" (Sternberg 1985: 324). This tendency is affirmed in biblical writings (cf. Num. 23:19; 1 Sam. 15:29). Even though the Bible acknowledges mystery and partiality in any understanding of God, it presents God with greater consistency and transparency than human characters. Hosea will assert that God is categorically different from humans (11:9), yet any characterization of God will be accomplished by the means and standards employed to describe and evaluate human characters. Marianne Thompson sums up the challenges of describing the character of God when she writes, "The reader is always held in tension between the objective constraints of the text and the constraints of the knowledge, imagination, cultural location, religious convictions, and spirituality by which her or his reading of God is informed" (Thompson 1993: 186–87). In this essay, I cannot engage how all these factors affect the characterization of God by readers, but I will address some of the key factors in interpreting Hosea's presentation of God.

Since Hosea is a composite work, readers will have to determine which texts to prioritize in interpretation. Given that Hos. 1:2, "The beginning of the word to Hosea," serves as a natural start to the prophecy, it appears that 1:1, "The word of the LORD that came to Hosea son of Beeri, in the days of Kings Uzziah, Jotham, Ahaz, and Hezekiah of Judah, and in the days of King Jeroboam son of Joash of Israel" (NRSV), was added as a later superscription. Scholars have suggested this superscription functions not only as an introduction to Hosea but also to the collection of the Book of the Four (Hosea, Amos, Micah, Zephaniah), and eventually to the Book of the Twelve. This superscription identifies Hosea as a prophetic book, a genre in which the final form of Hosea serves as a theological norm for the community (Ben Zvi 2003). Understood this way, all texts within Hosea, whether spoken by the prophet himself or written by a later redactor, possess equal authority to its readers. What then is to be made of Alter and Humphrey's taxonomy of texts? Are some texts to be more reliable than others in describing the character of God? While all texts carry equal authority, texts are not uniform in kind, so certain texts may describe the character of God more clearly than others. For example, direct statements about God by the narrator more clearly describe the character of God than a single action of God. Whether one text is more important than another will depend on numerous factors, and opinions may vary. I will follow Humphrey's taxonomy of texts by first examining texts that are direct statements about God's character and then move to those that are more opaque.

18.2. DIRECT STATEMENTS ON GOD'S CHARACTER BY THE REDACTOR

Hosea lacks direct statements made about the character of God by a narrator, since Hosea is didactic rather than a story, yet the prophetic book does conclude with a direct statement describing God made by the final redactor to the book. Gerald Sheppard suggested that at a late stage in the development of Hebrew Bible literature, wisdom became a major theological and hermeneutical category for interpreting the Law and the Prophets, and sapiential introductions or conclusions were added to books such as Eccl. 12:13–14; Pss. 1–2; and Hos. 14:9 (Heb. 14:10) (Sheppard 1980). Viewed in this manner, the wisdom saying, "Those who are wise understand these things; those who are discerning know them. For the ways of the LORD are right, and the upright walk in them, but transgressors stumble in them" (Hos. 14:9 [Heb. 14:10]), serves as both a conclusion and a hermeneutical key to reading the book, since prophetic books were meant to be reread. Scholars have observed numerous intertextual links between Exod. 34:6–7 (and the surrounding narrative of 32:1–34:10) and Hosea and the Book of the Twelve. Raymond Van Leeuwen argues that Hos. 14:9 (Heb. 14:10) employs Exod. 34:6–7 as a base text for developing an overarching theodicy within the Twelve (Van Leeuwen 1993). If this is the case, then the final form of the book of Hosea assumes the character of God as self-disclosed by God in Exod. 34:6–7, "The LORD, the LORD, a God merciful and gracious, slow to anger, and abounding in steadfast love and faithfulness, keeping steadfast love for the thousandth generation, forgiving iniquity and transgression and sin, yet by no means clearing the guilty, but visiting the iniquity of the parents upon the children and the children's children, to the third and the fourth generation" (NRSV). This text is important due to its numerous appearances in quotations or allusions throughout the Hebrew Bible, and in Exodus it is spoken directly by God in a theophany at Sinai. The final redactor concludes the book of Hosea with the reminder that interpreting the prophecy requires readers to identify God in Hosea with the God of Sinai described in Exod. 32–34.

In addition to extolling wisdom and discernment, Hos. 14:9 (Heb. 14:10) claims, "The ways of Yhwh are straight, and the righteous will walk in them, but sinners will stumble in them." This editorial comment defends the integrity of God when God judges people for their sin. The word "stumble" occurs earlier in 14:1 (Heb. 14:2), "Return, O Israel, to the LORD your God, for you have stumbled because of your iniquity" (NRSV), suggesting 14:1–9 (Heb. 14:2–10) is a unity. Based on the parallelism of the clauses in 14:9 (Heb. 14:10) Gruber concludes, "The entire structure conveys the idea that astute individuals should understand on the basis of God's promises in Hos. 14.2–9 that God can be trusted to behave justly" (Gruber 2017: 596). To summarize, the final redactor to the book of Hosea views God as gracious in forgiveness but also just in punishment of sinners.

18.3. REPORTS ON THE INNER THOUGHTS OF GOD

Hosea 6:4 and 11:8–9 are both remarkable for containing direct speech revealing God's inner thoughts, a rare occurrence in the Hebrew Bible. In both texts, God's thoughts and emotions appear to be conflicted when dealing with the waywardness of God's elect people, Israel. Given the rarity of candid self-disclosures of God's inner life, it is difficult to determine how such expressions ought to be received, and unsurprisingly their interpretations are contested. For example, George Smith considers Hos. 11:8–9 "the greatest passage in Hosea—deepest if not highest of the book" (Smith 1928: 1:324). J. McKenzie views the same words as a moment of weakness, and the appeal to divinity contained in the passage as Hosea's attempt to cover up the emotional frailty of God (McKenzie 1955: 172).

God's self-disclosure appears in the form of questions: "What shall I do with you, O Ephraim? What shall I do with you, O Judah? Your love is like a morning cloud, like the dew that goes away early" (Hos. 6:6 NRSV). This passage occurs within the unit of

GOD'S CHARACTER IN THE BOOK OF HOSEA   265

Hos. 6:1–6 that serves as a discursive response between the people and God to actions described in the previous unit. In Hos. 5:8–15, God declares punishment will befall Ephraim and they will become a desolation because rather than seek Yhwh, they sought the Assyrian king to heal (*raphe'*, 5:13) the nation. In 5:14–15, God will be like a lion to Ephraim and Judah and tear (*taraph*, 5:14) them and go away until the people acknowledge their guilt and seek God. Given the numerous verbal links to the previous passages, Hos. 6:1–3 appears to be the people's response to God's judgment in 5:8–15, since the people acknowledge that God has "torn" (*taraph*, 6:1) them, express the need to be healed (*rapha'*, 6:1), and call for the people to repent and know the LORD (6:3). Although certainly theologically orthodox and liturgically appropriate in content, it appears the people's confession is insincere. God employs the people's precipitation metaphor in 6:3 to describe God's compassion: "He will come to us like the showers, like the spring rains that water the earth" (6:3 NRSV), and responds by characterizing the people as "like a morning cloud, like the dew that goes away early" (6:4 NRSV). God considers their promises vacuous and their loyalty evanescent. In Hos. 6:6, God declares that God desires covenant faithfulness and knowledge rather than sacrifice and burnt offerings, so it appears Israel intended merely to satisfy no more than its cultic obligations. In response to the people's empty words, God exclaims, "What shall I do with you, O Ephraim? What shall I do with you, O Judah?" (6:4 NRSV). These words describe God's exasperation and frustration in dealing with an unfaithful and disingenuous people. Similar speech and emotion appear in Mic. 6:3, "O my people, what have I done to you? In what have I wearied you? Answer me!" (NRSV). In Mic. 6, God speaks these words in a situation like that of Hos. 6, where God is unsatisfied with the people's cultic sacrifices (Mic. 6:6–7) and instead desires the people "to do justice, and to love kindness, and to walk humbly with [their] God" (v. 8).

In Hos. 11:8 God once again reveals God's inner thoughts in the form of questions, but in this case the mind of God appears to be less determined than in 6:4 and the emotion felt is not one of frustration but possibly of turmoil: "How can I give you up, Ephraim? How can I hand you over, O Israel? How can I make you like Admah? How can I treat you like Zeboiim? My heart recoils within me; my compassion grows warm and tender" (NRSV). With regard to the character of God, the issue most debated is whether these questions are merely rhetorical or genuinely existential. In contrast to a rhetorical question posed merely for dramatic effect with a preconceived answer, in an existential question, the outcome is yet to be determined and multiple possibilities exist. Gerald Janzen writes, "As I mean this term, an existential question has to do with the fact of being alive. And being alive is a matter of personal growth and becoming, understood as a temporal process through the power of decision exercised in active response to possibilities which stand before one" (Janzen 1982: 12). The nature of the question deals with one's existence, so the very character of the being is at stake in posing the question. Existential questions include dialogue partners, so in this case the outcome related to the nature of God will not be determined by God alone. Understood in this manner, Hos. 11 not only narrates a history of Israel, but also a history of God's own formation. While Janzen acknowledges his indebtedness to process theologians, he believes the exegesis of Hos. 11:8–9 demands this understanding of God and that the Hebrew Bible reads more naturally with a process theology perspective.

Janzen asserts that the last phrase of 11:8 ought to be translated, "My heart changes itself (*haphak ʿal*) upon me, my change of mind grows fervent altogether!" He concludes that this expression signifies a transformation in the existence of God. He believes wrath arises not from Godself, but rather from the world, and so in the passage an aboriginal form of God is transformed into a new being who can incorporate wrath into divine Eros. In a response to Janzen, James Mays concedes that the first cola can be translated, "my mind has changed," but goes on to object that no use of the Hebrew phrase *haphak ʿal* suggests a transformation in the existence of a person in the manner Janzen claims (Mays 1982: 47). Joy Kakkanattu translates the same phrase, "My heart recoils within me, my entrails become altogether warm" (Kakkanattu 2006: 12). He observes that the last two cola of the verse are parallel, so rather than recapitulating the entire first cola as suggested by Janzen, it is God's "entrails" or sense of compassion that is growing warm or fervent. Kakkanattu finds that the phrase "expresses more the intense inner tension, involving the will and feeling of Yahweh, *before reaching a fundamental decision, than the change of a decision....* What is highlighted is the struggle within Yahweh, a struggle between the sense of justice and love" (2006: 81, italics mine). He argues that the struggle that 11:8 describes is not a change of mind to spare Israel the fate of Admah and Zeboiim but rather the inner tension God experiences attempting to keep intact God's choice to elect Israel despite their infidelity. This conflict is resolved in God's own self; God is not obligated to any other force or being when making this decision. Kakkanattu finds that Hos. 11:8–9 ought to be understood similarly to Jer. 31:20, "Is Ephraim my dear son? Is he the child I delight in? As often as I speak against him, I still remember him. Therefore I am deeply moved for him; I will surely have mercy on him, says the LORD" (NRSV). Process theology may not provide the most natural reading of the Hebrew Bible as Janzen suggests. Mays (1982: 48) writes, "Certainly any approach which slights or de-emphasizes the status of divine wrath within the life of God does not do justice to the claims of the Old Testament." Readers may morally and religiously object to the notion of a God who exercises wrath, but it is another thing to claim that a God of wrath does not appear in the Hebrew Bible.

In other texts, the holiness of God (i.e., the distinction between divinity and humanity) serves as the basis for God's immutability (Num. 23:19; 1 Sam. 15:29). In Hos. 11:9 holiness serves as the basis for God to suspend anger toward Israel and instead prioritize compassion: "I will not execute my fierce anger; I will not again destroy Ephraim; for I am God and no mortal, the Holy One in your midst, and I will not come in wrath" (NRSV). The God described in Hos. 11:8–9 is not unemotional, since these verses describe God experiencing both anger and compassion. What these verses reveal about the character of God is that God, unlike humans, is not overcome by uncontrollable and unjustifiable rage that would jeopardize God's relationship to the covenant people.

18.4. Accounts of God's Actions

Since Hosea is a didactic work composed of prophetic speech and not a narrative, Humphrey's and Alter's prioritization of accounts of God's actions over God's direct speech may not apply in this case. Many of God's actions in Hosea are directly voiced by God. The only actions that are described by someone other than God occur in ch. 1 and ch. 3, and both texts describe God's commands to the prophet regarding his familial relationships. These relationships symbolize God's political and military actions toward Israel and Judah. Let us consider God's commands to Hosea and God's political actions toward Israel and Judah as depicted literarily in the book reveal about God's character.

Marital affairs attract the human gaze, so it is unsurprising that speculations on Hosea's marital and family life abound, especially given the terseness of the biblical accounts. Gomer's promiscuity has scandalized Jewish and Christian readers for centuries, and Yvonne Sherwood has cataloged the wide range of readings that attempt to absolve God of any wrongdoing for commanding Hosea to marry Gomer (Sherwood 1996: 40–82). While the biblical text is remarkably terse in describing Hosea's marriage and family life, entire novels, plays, and movies have attempted to portray it in elaborate detail. Biblical scholars have been unable to resist the temptation to reconstruct the events of Hosea's marriage(s) or speculate on Hosea's psychological state. For example, A. Macintosh (1997: 126) admits, "The fact remains, however, that we do not certainly know the answers to these questions and it is likely that we never will," yet he then goes on to offer an elaborate reconstruction of the events of Hosea's family life. Moughtin-Mumby (2008: 213) rightly declares, "It is time to abandon this 'quest for the historical Hosea'" given the paucity of historical data. The narratives in ch. 1 and ch. 3 ought to be understood according to their literary function within the ancient prophetic book.

Hosea 1–3 does not provide a continuous narrative of the marriage or family life of Hosea but includes two distinct prophetic sign-acts interrupted by a prophetic oracle. Hosea 2:2–23 (Heb. 2:4–25) functions as a discrete prophetic oracle that finds its basis in the first prophetic sign-act of 1:2–2:1 (Heb. 1:2–2:3) since they both culminate with the mention of Ammi/Lo-ammi and Ruhamah/Lo-ruhamah (2:1, 23 [Heb. 2:3, 25]). The basic narrative of ch. 1 is assumed by the author of ch. 2, yet the latter text is a theological and poetic parenesis that accompanies the prophetic sign-acts of ch. 1. It does not describe Hosea and Gomer's relationship. The oracles of 2:2–23 (Heb. 2:4–25) are related to the narrative of 1:2–2:1 (Heb. 1:2–2:3) at the level of a similar prophetic message but not as continuous literary or historical events. For this reason, I will not consider ch. 2 among the "Accounts of God's actions" since it is speech and not event.

The narratives in Hos. 1:2–2:1 (Heb. 1:2–2:3) and 3:1–5 describe prophetic sign-acts which typically do not possess a consistent symbolic function. For example, the numerous sign-acts performed by Jeremiah and Ezekiel have little to do with one another and in some cases the prophet plays competing roles. In Hosea, chs. 1 and 3 are to be read in conjunction given all their textual links and the unifying household and marital metaphor. Marvin Sweeney (1996: 19) categorizes Hos. 1 and 3 as a "Report of a Symbolic Action." This genre is defined as:

> A first or third person narrative that describes the prophet's performance of an act intended to symbolize YHWH's intentions or actions toward the people. The symbolic action frequently accompanies a prophetic word or vision, and it functions as a sign to confirm the efficacy of that word or vision . . . the form contains three elements: (1) an instruction to perform a symbolic act; (2) the report that the act was performed; and (3) a statement that interprets the significance of the act.

According to this definition, the actions are not to be interpreted beyond that of the accompanying word or vision. Just as readers ought to be cautious in interpreting the exact nature and details of the outrageous commands for Isaiah to walk naked and barefoot for three years (Isa. 20:2–4) or Ezekiel to lay on his left and right side for 430 days (Ezek. 4:4–6), so too they ought to reserve judgment as to the exact nature of Hosea's marriage.

Although Gomer has captured the attention of most readers, ch. 1 is primarily focused on the children of promiscuity, not the promiscuous woman. Gomer functions only as a vehicle to bear three children, and it is they who take center stage to serve as prophetic signs. Children are normally understood to be a blessing from Yhwh, but in Hos. 1 they are ominous signs of God's impending judgment on the people. The prophetic sign-acts collectively demonstrate a father's rejection of his children. Whereas the first child serves as a prophetic sign for the end of the Northern Kingdom, the latter two children signify the dissolution of Yhwh's covenant with Judah (1:6–9). All three names signify God's judgment and rejection of his people: Jezreel, "No Compassion," and "Not My People." If the statement, "call your brother, 'Ammi' and your sister, 'Compassion,'" conclude the first literary unit in 2:1 (Heb. 2:3), then the children are told early in the narrative that their names of judgment will be reversed. If they are the audience of the salvation oracle in 2:14–23 (Heb. 2:16–25), they will hear that their names will ultimately signify God's salvation rather than judgment.

How one evaluates God's decision to appoint Hosea's children as prophetic signs is difficult. Did they feel unloved and rejected? Did they grow up in shame as bastard children? If it is to the children of Gomer that God commands, "Plead with your mother, plead" (NRSV, 2:2 [Heb 2:4]), then it appears the children possess an adversarial relationship with their mother due to her multiple lovers. Chapter 1 describes a God who goes to great lengths to communicate to God's people that they need to repent from their sinful ways. In this case, God commands the prophet to perform morally questionable actions that likely cause him to experience heartache and his children to experience parental neglect.

The second prophetic sign-act in Hos. 3:1–5 contains two actions and consequently two distinct prophetic messages. While some commentators believe that first-person accounts ought to be prioritized and so place the events of ch. 3 before the events of ch. 1, the fact that the prophet acknowledges that "the LORD said to me *again*" (3:1 NRSV) suggests that these events occur later. The woman of ch. 3 is unnamed and referred to as an "adulteress," so it is possible, although unlikely, that this is a different woman than

Gomer. In this case, the prophet is explicitly instructed to love her even though she has another lover, and this act will come at significant financial expense for Hosea to secure marital rights. The second action is not explicitly commanded by God but nonetheless Hosea forces the woman to abstain from sex, whether with him or any other man, to symbolize Israel's experience of exile where they will be without king, prince, and cultic worship. In this second prophetic sign-act, God once again commands the prophet to perform a morally questionable action that will cause him heartache. Both he and the woman will experience the frustration of a lengthy abstinence from sex. Because of the woman's unfaithfulness and the husband's purchase of marital rights, the narrative assumes that the prophet possesses the right to control her body. God considers discipline in the form of sexual abstinence to symbolize the experience of exile for Israel, as an act of love. In summary, the prophetic sign-act narratives of Hos. 1 and 3 describe a God who commands individuals to perform unusual or extraordinary tasks at great personal cost to illustrate a divine message to people.

The sign-act of ch. 3 symbolizes the Babylonian exile, since mention of a Davidic king is made in 3:5. But the more immediate and prominent event that Hosea describes as God's act of discipline is the Assyrian conquest of Israel. The book of Hosea depicts this national catastrophe as an act of God that will eventuate in Israel's renewal and restoration. In Hos. 5:14 God states, "For I will be like a lion to Ephraim, and like a young lion to the house of Judah. I myself will tear and go away; I will carry off, and no one shall rescue" (NRSV). Hosea 11:5 declares, "They shall return to the land of Egypt, and Assyria shall be their king, because they have refused to return to me" (NRSV). Hosea employs a rich vocabulary for "lion" to signify the fierceness of God's judgment against Ephraim at the hands of the Assyrians (cf. 13:7–8). The degree of God's agency in the Assyrian conquest can be interpreted within a continuum of direct to indirect causation. Paul Fiddes claims, "While the Hebrew idiom is of direct causation, with God sending the Assyrian army to wreak havoc, we are to understand this theologically in a more indirect way; God consents to the self-destructive consequences of sin in Israelite society, which make it an easy prey to the invader. By no means should we suppose that God plans or approves the brutality of the Assyrian king and army, for which they, under due time, will be under the same judgement" (Fiddes 1993: 184). What is clear is that the God who is depicted as a lion views Assyrian conquest as a means of temporal discipline, not final judgment. The final form of Hosea proclaims a message of hope that Yhwh will summon Israel from exile, and they will return in repentance to Yhwh (Hos. 2:19–20 [Heb. 2:21–23]; 3:5; 5:15; 11:10–11). Yhwh in Hosea is one who sovereignly judges and disciplines Israel through Assyrian conquest, yet promises to restore the people to their land and to their devotion to Yhwh.

18.5. Reflections

The remainder of the essay will move away from Humphrey's and Alter's categories. Hosea does not contain descriptions of God's physical appearance nor reports of what other characters say of God. One might consider the entire prophetic book as God's direct speech, since its contents are introduced as "the word of the LORD" (1:1; 4:1). Rather than a tidy summary of the character of God in Hosea, what follows are hermeneutical and theological reflections on the issues involved when interpreting Hosea's portrayal of God.

Hosea assumes the right for a husband and father to discipline his family members out of love, and violence is portrayed as a legitimate means to do so. The metaphors employed to describe God and Israel assume social contexts where men possess the authority to discipline unfaithful women and disobedient children. The book of Hosea employs the metaphors of marital infidelity and rebellious children to symbolize Israel's sins of religious idolatry, political disloyalty, social injustice, and corrupt leadership. For centuries, readers of Hosea have questioned this character of God as portrayed within the literary world of the prophecy for commanding Hosea to marry a promiscuous woman, but more recently interpreters have objected to the religious use of a text that employs metaphors relying on social structures that are oppressive toward women and children. For some, this calls into question the character of the text as sacred scripture. Not only does God commit violence, but the text is considered oppressive by normalizing domestic abuse.

The reception history of Hosea demonstrates that possibilities for interpreting the metaphors in Hosea abound. Some view the God of Hosea as manipulative and abusive, others see Hosea's God as sympathetic and kind, and still others may be scandalized by God's seemingly immoral actions in the book. Some readers cannot fathom that the God they worship could be abusive, nor imagine that the book of Hosea would influence anyone to commit domestic violence. But others claim that the metaphors for God in Hosea support unjust social, cultural, religious, and political practices or systems. People experience different forms of injustice based on their social location. Women and children are far more often at risk of domestic violence, so it is not surprising gender plays an important role in interpreting Hosea since the prophecy features marriage and parental metaphors.

Since, as Steve Fowl (1995) has argued, "Texts Don't Have Ideologies,"[2] it ought to be acknowledged that reading involves a great deal of indeterminacy, due not simply to the diversity of texts but also to the varied interests of readers. Because of this indeterminacy all readers of Hosea ought to heed the caution of feminist interpreters concerning how the book may be used to perpetuate injustice. Hosea is not unique among the biblical books in this regard, and interpretive decisions on Hosea ought to be made in consideration of other texts. The Bible has been, and continues to be, used both to liberate and oppress, so judgments regarding the ongoing use of texts must acknowledge the Bible may contribute to both outcomes. Communities and individuals will possess varying opinions on what texts are deemed valuable and what associations are made and not made with biblical texts. People of faith have always selectively appropriated scripture, and at times their own survival depended on doing so, particularly when biblical texts had been weaponized against them.

Here I propose that it is possible to read Hosea as scripture without delegitimizing other readings. One does not need to ignore the depictions of anger and violence nor the possibility that the text may be abused. Yet the God of Hosea may be understood in a salutary manner. While texts do not have ideologies, "concepts have dates" (Doran 2005: 144). While there are limitations to determining the exact origins of Hosea, texts are written and received within human contexts, and the book of Hosea has been understood as sacred scripture for Jews and Christians. Those who view Hosea in this way today and seek the knowledge of Hosea's God in a salutary manner can learn from these religious communities. They understood that the people that produced and preserved the text of Hosea saw themselves as the elect people of the God portrayed in the text. While people of faith could openly question the justice of God, as demonstrated in the biblical texts' ongoing concern for theodicy, they did so with certain assumptions and boundaries. The readers of Hosea believed that they possessed a unique covenantal relationship to God that depended both on the sovereign grace of God, as well as the people's ongoing trust and obedience. They believed this God to be holy, so while communication and communion was possible between covenantal partners, God's people acknowledged human speech carried limitations for properly describing God. Castelo believes once these conditions are met, Hosea can be read in a salutary manner:

> Once one continually affirms the vast difference between YHWH and Israel as covenant partners, that admission itself creates the possibility, in covenant history and speech, for a more radical and daring depiction of the interstices of covenant interaction. In other words, as the difference between covenant partners is registered primarily and thoroughly throughout covenant thinking, so the language marking their interrelationship can be stretched to scandalizing proportions, because the language itself is vigilantly recognized as provisional throughout. (Lim and Castelo 2015: 94–95)

This understanding of covenantal relationship between readers and God allows for the speech of Hosea to be understood as mere analogy and metaphor. The community knew that should the Bible describe God as male, they ought not to equate male with God. Admittedly such a view of scripture does not eliminate tensions. Jews and Christians assume an understanding of God as they read scripture, yet the text also functions to inform their view of God. When the two are incongruent, people may choose to reject or revise their view of God and/or the scriptures.

Just as a greater elasticity to speech is granted in intimate human relationships, so too the range and depth of speech with God will depend upon the nature and strength of the bonds that tie humans and God together. Honest speech that exposes vulnerabilities and pain possesses the power to draw persons who are committed to each other into deeper intimacy, but it also carries the potential to offend, frighten, and sever fragile relationships. The book of Hosea is an exploration of divine desire through the metaphors of human desire, and human passions continue to mystify because they often involve opposing feelings of love and hate, attraction and loathing, acceptance and rejection, and forgiveness and anger. Through acknowledging that Hosea's God is holy and therefore vastly different from humans, the book of Hosea may be understood as speech from a loving God. Human desire is never without risk, and so it is unsurprising that a book on divine desire has scandalized its readers and continues to test whether humans will be devoted to its God.

NOTES

1. This essay is a literary-theological study of the character of God rather than a historical investigation into origins of Hosea's God in the manner of Lemche 1992.
2. Fowl (1995) concedes that it is impossible to determine whether texts do or do not possess ideologies. Given this hermeneutical impasse, he proposes a pragmatic approach where ideologies are critically acknowledged and examined at the level of readers rather than texts. David Janzen (2021: 60, italics mine) similarly adopts a pragmatic approach to reading texts and writes, "It is the meaningful text, not the physical one, that has meaning, and *the meaningful text is the reader's production.*"

REFERENCES

Alter, Robert. 1981. *The Art of Biblical Narrative.* London: George Allen & Unwin.

Ben Zvi, Ehud. 2003. "The Prophetic Book: A Key Form of Prophetic Literature." In Marvin A. Sweeney and Ehud Ben Zvi, eds., *The Changing Face of Form Criticism for the Twenty-First Century.* Grand Rapids, MI: Eerdmans, 276–97.

Dearman, J. Andrew. 2010. *The Book of Hosea.* NICOT. Grand Rapids, MI: Eerdmans.

Doran, Robert M. 2005. *What Is Systematic Theology?* Toronto, ON: University of Toronto Press.

Fiddes, Paul S. 1993. "The Cross of Hosea Revisited: The Meaning of Suffering in the Book of Hosea." *Review and Expositor* 90: 175–204.

Fowl, Stephen E. 1995. "Texts Don't Have Ideologies." *BibInt* 3: 15–34.

Gruber, Mayer I. 2017. *Hosea: A Textual Commentary.* LHBOTS 653. London: Bloomsbury T&T Clark.

Humphreys, W. Lee. 2001. *The Character of God in the Book of Genesis.* Louisville, KY: Westminster John Knox.

Janzen, J. Gerald. 1982. "Metaphor and Reality in Hosea 11." *Semeia* 24: 7–44.

Janzen, David. 2021. *The Liberation of Method: The Ethics of Emancipatory Biblical Interpretation.* Minneapolis, MN: Fortress.Kakkanattu, Joy Philip. 2006. *God's Enduring Love in the Book of Hosea: A Synchronic and Diachronic Analysis of Hosea 11,1–11.* FAT 2, 14. Tübingen: Mohr Siebeck.

Lasine, Stuart. 2012. *Weighing Hearts: Character, Judgment, and the Ethics of Reading the Bible.* LHBOTS 568. New York: Bloomsbury.

Lasine, Stuart. 2016. "Characterizing God in His/Our Own Image." In Danna Nolan Fewell, ed., *The Oxford Handbook of Biblical Narrative.* New York: Oxford University Press, 465–77.Lemche, Niels Peter. 1992. "The God of Hosea." In Eugene Ulrich, John W. Wright, Robert P. Carroll, and Philip R. Davies, eds., *Priests, Prophets, and Scribes: Essays on the Formation and Heritage of Second Temple Judaism in Honour of Joseph Blenkinsopp.* JSOTSup 149. Sheffield, UK: JSOT Press, 241–57.

Lim, Bo H., and Daniel Castelo. 2015. *Hosea.* THOTC. Grand Rapids, MI: Eerdmans.

Macintosh, A. A. 1997. *A Critical and Exegetical Commentary on Hosea.* ICC. Edinburgh, UK: T&T Clark.

Mays, James L. 1982. "Response to Janzen: 'Metaphor and Reality in Hosea 11.'" *Semeia* 24: 45–51.

McEntire, Mark. 2013. *Portraits of a Mature God: Choices in Old Testament Theology.* Minneapolis, MN: Fortress.

McKenzie, J. L. 1955. "Divine Passion in Osee." *CBQ* 17: 287–89.

Moughtin-Mumby, Sharon. 2008. *Sexual and Marital Metaphors in Hosea, Jeremiah, Isaiah, and Ezekiel.* Oxford: Oxford University Press.

O'Brien, Julia M. 2008. *Challenging Prophetic Metaphor: Theology and Ideology in the Prophets.* Louisville, KY: Westminster John Knox.

Pentiuc, Eugen J. 2002. *Long-Suffering Love: A Commentary on Hosea with Patristic Annotations.* Brookline, MA: Holy Cross Orthodox Press.

Sheppard, Gerald T. 1980. *Wisdom as a Hermeneutical Construct: A Study in the Sapientializing of the Old Testament.* BZAW 151. Berlin: Walter de Gruyter.

Sherwood, Yvonne. 1996. *The Prostitute and the Prophet: Hosea's Marriage in Literary-Theoretical Perspective.* JSOTSup 212. Sheffield: Sheffield Academic.

Smith, George Adam. 1928. *The Book of the Twelve Prophets.* Vol. 1. London: Hodder and Stoughton.

Sternberg, Meir. 1985. *The Poetics of Biblical Narrative: Ideological Literature and the Drama of Reading.* Bloomington: Indiana University Press.

Sweeney, Marvin A. 1996. *Isaiah 1–39 with an Introduction to Prophetic Literature.* FOTL 16. Grand Rapids, MI: Eerdmans.

Thompson, Marianne Meye. 1993. "'God's Voice You Have Never Heard, God's Form You Have Never Seen': The Characterization of God in the Gospel of John." *Semeia* 63: 177–204.

Van Leeuwen, Raymond C. 1993. "Scribal Wisdom and Theodicy in the Book of the Twelve." In Leo G. Perdue, Brandon Scott, and William Johnston Wiseman, eds., *In Search of Wisdom: Essays in Memory of John G. Gammie.* Louisville: Westminster John Knox, 31–49.

Yee, Gale A. 1996. "The Book of Hosea: Introduction, Commentary, and Reflections." In Leander E. Keck, ed., *The New Interpreter's Bible Volume 7.* Nashville: Abingdon, 95–297.

CHAPTER 19

....

KINGSHIP AND POLITICAL POWER IN THE BOOK OF HOSEA

....

HEATH D. DEWRELL

THE book of Hosea is fiercely critical of those who held positions of power in ancient Israel, includinztg the Israelite king. In this, Hosea is hardly unique among the biblical prophetic books, which tend to depict the ruling classes in a negative light more often than not. On the other hand, it is strikingly different from nearly contemporaneous Neo-Assyrian prophecies, which consistently depict the Assyrian king in glowing terms. For example, a prophecy attributed to a certain Issar-la-tashiyat, an Assyrian prophet from the city of Arbela (modern Erbil), declares[1]:

> Esarhaddon, king of the lands,
> do not fear!
> Which wind that has risen
> whose wing I have not broken?
> Your enemies
> like apples of Sivan
> will roll at your feet.
> The Great Lady am I;
> I am Ishtar of Arbela,
> who will throw at your feet
> your enemies.
> Which word
> that I have spoken
> could you not stand upon?
> I am Ishtar of Arbela.
> Your enemies will I flay.
> I will give you. I am
> Ishtar of Arbela.

Before you,
behind you
I walk. Do not fear.
You, in the midst of cramping,
I, in the midst of woe,
I will arise; I will sit down.

Compare Issar-la-tashiyat's prophecy above to a portion of a prophecy found in Hos. 7:3–7:

In their wickedness they make the king glad,
the officials in their lies.
All of them are adulterers
like an oven burning
from a baker,
he will cease stirring,
from kneading dough
until its leavening.
The day of our king!
The officials make sick the heat of wine.
He draws his hand with mockers.
For they bring like the oven their mind into their conspiracy.
All the night their baker sleeps.
At morning it burns like a blazing fire.
All of them are hot like the oven.
And they consume their judges.
All their kings fell.
None of them is calling me.

As the awkwardness of the translation above suggests, there is much about this passage that is unclear, a common feature of the Hosea's poetry. The prophecy here probably concerns a secret coup staged by the "officials" against the king, but it is unclear which king this is—several of the final kings of Israel fell victim to plots and usurpers—and unfortunately we have little information about any of these usurpations other than the names of the lead usurper and of the king who fell victim to each coup. What is clear enough, however, is that this oracle from Hosea is by no means a message of reassurance for the king or the officials. While Issar-la-tashiyat's prophecy and Hosea's are both structured in poetic lines and employ metaphorical language to describe the enemies of the king—wind and apples for the Assyrian king's foes and dough, a baker, and an oven for the enemies of the Israelite king—the Israelite conspirators are presented as having been successful in their treachery, unlike the Assyrian enemies who were thwarted by Ishtar's protection. Despite presenting the conspirators in a negative light, though, this oracle from Hosea does not appear to take the side of the king either. The kings failed to call on Yhwh for deliverance, and thus fell to their enemies. This major difference between biblical and Assyrian prophecy may be due to the groups who collected and compiled the oracles. The Assyrian prophecies were collected and housed in royal archives under royal sponsorship, so it makes sense that those selected for inclusion would contain good news for the king. We have frustratingly little information concerning who was responsible for preserving the prophecies collected in Hosea, but it seems very unlikely that the royal court at Samaria played any significant role in the process, given their content.

One should not misunderstand Hosea as entirely antimonarchic, however. Hosea's view of kingship is a nuanced one, as several previous treatments of the topic have demonstrated.[2] While Hosea's prophecies are clearly more negative from the king's perspective than the Assyrian prophecies, a close reading reveals these nuances. Rather than offering either a blanket condemnation or an unqualified endorsement of Israelite kings and kingship, in its present state the book of Hosea depicts a three-stage outline for the past, present, and future of the institution. Hosea begins with the corrupt and wicked kings of the past. This period is followed by a present or soon-to-come interim situation in which Yhwh punishes Israel by removing Israelite kingship altogether. No native Israelite king will rule and Israelite kingship will be taken up by the Assyrian king instead. Finally, after this interim period without a native king, Hosea envisions a future in which a Davidic king will rule a united Israel and Judah with Yhwh's full support, thereby restoring the presently corrupt institution. This three-stage process strikingly mirrors the three-stage process that Hosea presents concerning Israel's past unfaithfulness, imminent or present punishment, and future restoration and prosperity.

19.1. KINGSHIP CORRUPTED

While the book of Hosea nowhere attacks the institution of kingship in and of itself in the way that, for example, Judg. 9 or 1 Sam. 8 and 12 do, Hosea has nothing positive to say concerning the individuals who occupied the position of king in Samaria. Its opening chapter's invective begins by condemning the "House of Jehu" for "what happened at Jezreel," possibly a reference to the bloody coup described in 2 Kgs. 9–10. According to that account, beginning in Jezreel and ending in Samaria, Jehu either killed or ordered to be killed King Joram of Israel, King Ahaziah of Judah, the queen mother Jezebel, seventy sons of King Ahab, and an entire temple full of Baal worshipers. Then, according to the Kings account, he turned the Baal temple itself into a latrine. While the Kings account reports all of this slaughter and destruction in a primarily positive light, it would be no surprise if others described such violent acts in less approving terms than they are reported there. Perhaps Hos. 1 offers this more critical and negative assessment of those events, and Jehu's revolt is condemned here rather than praised as in Kings.

Somewhat problematically for this possibility, though, the date of Jehu's overthrow of the Omride dynasty and the beginning of the period during which Hosea's superscription (1:1) sets its oracles (the reign of King Jeroboam II of Israel) are separated by over sixty years. If the crime alluded to is indeed Jehu's coup, and if the superscription has any historical value (both potentially contestable claims), then this would be a case of delayed justice, comparable to the way in which the Deuteronomistic History blames the fall of Jerusalem in 586 BCE on sins that Judah's King Manasseh had committed a century earlier (2 Kgs. 23:26, 24:3). While Jehu, the actual perpetrator of the crimes, would have gone down to his grave in peace, Hosea would be declaring that his descendants are to be judged for their ancestor's actions. This is possible, but it could also be the case that Hosea is condemning a more recent scion of the house of Jehu for some misdeed that has been omitted from the Kings account of Israel's history. We simply may not have access to the details of the event that has drawn Hosea's ire here. Whatever happened in Jezreel, though, the penalty is that Yhwh will remove the "kingship" (*mamləkût*) of the "House of Israel" (Hos. 1:4) as a result.

Even if Jehu himself is the target of the prophecy contained in Hos. 1, more recent kings fare little better in the book. A prophecy contained in Hos. 5 lambasts the "house of the king," along with the "priests" and the "house of Israel." Together they constitute a "snare to Mizpah" and "a net spread out on Tabor" (v. 1). The prophecy goes on to accuse them all of "whoring" and "being unclean" (v. 3). Again, though, despite Hosea's harsh, colorful, and at times even obscene language, there is no indication here that the office of the king itself is at issue any more than the institution of the priesthood is. It is the individuals who occupy these offices that are the problem, and it is the removal of the offending parties from these offices, not the abolition of the offices themselves, that Hosea announces. Further, technically Hosea targets not the king himself here, but "the house of the king" (*bêt hammelek*), a phrase that elsewhere in the Hebrew Bible refers most often to the physical building where the king resided, but occasionally by extension to the members of the royal court,[3] as Hosea uses it here.

This is significant because in the book of Hosea Israel's kings have almost no agency of their own. They are almost always depicted as being acted upon rather than acting. The vast majority of the time, while kings may be illegitimate, they are presented as victims of conspiracy and intrigue rather than perpetrators of Israel's misdeeds. This picture stands in stark contrast to the depictions of the kings of both Israel and Judah in the Deuteronomic History or those of the kings of Judah in Chronicles. In both of those corpora, the kings' power over their subjects and their culpability for the nation's behavior is nearly complete. This is most clearly evidenced by the fact that when the Israelite kings "walk in the way/sins of Jeroboam" they "cause Israel to sin" ($\sqrt{ht}$ C-stem).[4] In the world of the Deuteronomic Historian or the Chronicler, the king is the primary agent, and nearly everyone else is merely following orders. Hosea's king, in sharp contrast, is almost entirely passive. In addition to the apparent coup described in Hos. 7 outlined above, in Hos. 8:4 it is Israel who "makes kings" ($\sqrt{mlk}$ C-stem) and "makes officials" ($\sqrt{śrr}$ C-stem). Likewise, in Hos. 10:3, the people say "we have no king" and ask that even if they did have one, "What will he do for us?" Similarly, in Hos. 13:10–11, Yhwh speaking in the first person states, "I gave you a king in my anger, I took [him] in my wrath." The king is installed, deposed, given, and taken, but rarely is the king depicted as an active agent in Hosea.

On the other hand, the "officials" (*śārîm*) do play an active role and bear a significant portion of the blame for Israel's woes. It is the "officials" who ambush the king in Hos. 7. They are "rebels" (*sōrərîm*; Hos. 9:15; note the wordplay). Even the "officials of Judah" (*śārê yəhûdâ*; Hos. 5:10) are subject to Hosea's censure, despite the book's general focus on the Northern Kingdom of Israel. While we lack detailed information about the finer points of the court structure of ancient Israel, it is likely that the "house of the king" addressed in Hos. 5 and the *śārîm* condemned elsewhere in the book are one and the same group, or that at the very least there was a significant degree of overlap between the two bodies. Whoever they were, the reason that these are the political leaders who receive the lion's share of Hosea's attention, rather than the king himself, is difficult to discern. It could be that this focus reflects the fact that the final years of the Israelite monarchy were a time during which royal authority was at an all-time low. Of the six Israelite kings who reigned in the second half of the eighth century BCE, four were assassinated and one was arrested and deported by the Assyrians. The fall of Samaria and the abolition of the monarchy would have left a power vacuum in which various officials would have played an even bigger role, without a king to check their authority (see Hos. 10:3).

Alternatively, the book of Hosea's focus on the "officials" may simply reflect its geographical remove from Samaria. The majority of Hosea's geographical referents—Bethel, Gilgal, Benjamin, etc.—cluster in the southern region of Israel, near the border of Judah. It may thus simply be the case that the people responsible for the composition and transmission of the book of Hosea had more interaction with various lower officials than with the king himself and for that reason focused their attention on the rulers with whom they most often came into contact. Whatever the cause for Hosea's focusing the blame for Israel's misdeeds on officials rather than the monarchy, though, the punishment for these misdeeds falls most immediately on the king himself.

19.2. Kingship Removed or Transferred

While the blame may lie primarily with Israel's "officials," it is the king himself who is swept away and deposed as a consequence of their actions. The punishment for Israel's unfaithfulness is most explicitly laid out in Hos. 10:8: "Samaria—its king is blotted out like foam upon water," and again a few verses later in Hos. 10:15b: "At the dawn, the king of Israel was utterly blotted out." According to Hosea, though, the agent responsible for Israel's king's fall is neither conspiring officials nor invading Assyrians; it is Yhwh himself who has taken kingship away from Israel: "Where[5] is your king then, that he may save you in all of your cities? Your judges, of whom you said, 'Give to me a king and officials?' I gave you a king in my anger, and I took [him] in my wrath" (Hos. 13:9–11). These two verses contain perhaps the most mixed and apparently negative assessment of kingship in the entire book. The prophecy assumes that the king is someone whom the people could reasonably expect to save them and someone specifically requested by the people for this purpose. Here, though, Yhwh claims to have given the people a king reluctantly, in his "anger."

This is the one place in the book of Hosea where the prophecies depict kingship itself as inherently undesirable, echoing the sentiments most clearly expressed in the Hebrew Bible in 1 Sam. 8. There, in response to the unscrupulous behavior of the prophet Samuel's sons, the people of Israel reject the institution of prophet/judge for their leadership and instead demand a king to rule over them "like all of the (other) nations." Yhwh takes this demand as a rejection not of Samuel and his sons, but of Yhwh himself (1 Sam. 8:6–7). Despite their rebellion, Yhwh gives the people what they have requested, but not without Samuel's lengthy warning concerning the ways in which the king would oppress his subjects. The situation described in Hos. 13:9–11 is strikingly similar to that in 1 Sam. 8. The king was given at the request of the people, and it is Yhwh himself who gave them their king, despite opposing the idea. The new idea in Hos. 13 is that Yhwh will take away Israel's king in the same angry manner in which he gave the king to them.

Nonetheless, this is the only instance in Hosea in which the institution of kingship as a whole is presented as undesirable. Generally speaking, Hosea assumes that kingship is a generally positive thing, and its removal is presented as a punishment. For example, elsewhere one finds the loss of kingship as the loss of a benefit akin to sacrifice and the ephod: "For many days the Israelites will dwell, and there will be no king, and there will be no official, and there will be no sacrifice, and there will be no pillar, and there will be no ephod or teraphim" (Hos. 3:4). Hos. 13's negative depiction of kingship with its "I gave you a king in my anger" (v. 11) follows on the question, "Where is your king then, that he may save you in all of your cities?" (v. 9). Even while suggesting that Yhwh may oppose the institution of kingship, the prophecy indicates that the people saw the king as a source of salvation. Whatever Yhwh's attitude toward the monarchy, the people are presented as approving of the institution. Although Yhwh had only given Israel a king in his "anger," removing Israel's king is an act of punishment not of deliverance.

This is not the only way in which the institution of kingship is described in somewhat contradictory terms. While Hos. 3:4, cited above, presents the throne of Israel as vacant, "there will be no king" ('ên mélek), elsewhere the removal of kingship is described more as a transfer of kingship from a native king to a foreign one. This idea is stated most clearly in Hos. 11:5: "[Israel] will return to the land of Egypt, and Assyria, he is its king. For they refused to return." Here in describing the end of the monarchy and the beginning of the exile in terms of a "return to the land of Egypt," Hosea depicts a sort of reversal of the exodus, from freedom into bondage. This time, though, Assyria will play the role of pharaoh. Rather than Israel having "no king," as in Hos. 3, here Israel's punishment is the replacement of native kingship with foreign rule.

This idea of Israelite kingship as transferred to the Assyrians may also help to interpret the pronouncement in Hos. 1:4b, "For yet a little while, and I will visit the blood of Jezreel on the house of Jehu, I will cause the kingship of the house of Israel to cease (wəhišbattî mamləkût bêt yiśrā'ēl)." At first glance, this language may seem to indicate that Yhwh is doing away with kingship altogether, but it is specifically the "kingship *of the house of Israel*" that will cease. The Hebrew word for kingship here, *mamləkût*, is an interesting one. Elsewhere in the Hebrew Bible, the word appears nine times, always in construct to another noun. In every case but two, this "kingship" is the "kingship of" an individual person—of Og, king of Bashan (Josh. 13:12, 30, 31), of Sihon, king of the Amorites (Josh. 13:21, 27), of "my father" (= Merib-baal/Mephibosheth's father Saul) (2 Sam. 16:3), or of Jehoiakim (Jer. 26:1). Even in this handful of cases, though, there is some variation in the sort of entity that is indicated by the term.

The "kingship of Og" and the "kingship of Sihon" refer to geographical regions. For this reason, "kingdom" is probably closer to its meaning in those cases than "kingship" is. The references to the *maml∂kût* of Og or of Sihon appear in the context of Joshua's division and allotment of the Transjordan, long after the Og and Sihon had been defeated and their people destroyed and dispossessed (Num. 21:21–35). Yet one could still speak of the *maml∂kût* of each in reference to the contemporary land that they once inhabited. The term refers not to the abstract idea of kingship, but to the land itself. If this were the meaning of the term in Hos. 1:4b, though, then to "cause the kingship of the house of Israel to cease" would refer to destroying the actual physical terrain of Israel, which does not appear to be what the prophecy has in view.

A better analog is probably to be found in the cases of Saul's and Jehoiakim's "kingship." In both of those cases, *maml∂kût* refers to the reign of the individual who possessed it—that is, their "kingship" more than their "kingdom." Second Samuel 16:3 is especially enlightening, as it refers to a "kingship" that has been taken away. Ziba claims that Merib-baal/Mephibosheth hopes that the "house of Israel" (*bêt yiśrā'ēl*) will "return" (√*šwb* C-stem) his father's "kingship" (*maml∂kût*) to him. This idea of a kingship that can be taken away jibes well with the terms use in Hos. 1. An even closer parallel to Hos. 1:4, though, is found in 1 Sam. 15:28. There, Samuel declares to Saul that Yhwh has rejected him as king with the words "Yhwh has torn the kingship of Israel from upon you today" (*qāra' YHWH 'et-maml∂kût yiśrā'ēl mē'ālêkā*).[6] Here, as in Hosea, "kingship" stands in construct with the people governed—here "Israel" and in Hosea the "house of Israel"—not to the individual who is governing them. As in Hosea, the context involves a loss of kingship, but contrary to Hosea, in Samuel the kingship of Israel is transferred to someone else. According to 1 Sam. 15:28, Israel will still have its kingship, but it will no longer belong to Saul.

Hosea goes even further than this, though. In Hosea, Yhwh promises to put an end to the kingship of the "House of Israel" altogether. Tearing away Saul's kingship does not mean that Israel will no longer have a king. Rather, it means that someone else will rule Israel instead of him. The declaration in Hos. 1:4b concerning putting an end to the kingship of the House of Israel could mean that Israel will have no king at all, as Hos. 3:4 asserts. It could also mean, however, that Israel will no longer have a native ruling house/dynasty and that the kingship will pass to someone who is not of the "House of Israel," i.e., the Assyrians, as Hos. 11:5 indicates. Whichever of the two ideas the verse is expressing, and without harmonizing the various prophecies collected together in the book of Hosea more than the texts will allow, one can say that the general picture painted in Hosea is that the punishment for the misdeeds of the Israelites and their leaders is the removal of native Israelite kingship. In some texts, the absence of native kingship is emphasized, while in other texts foreign rule is the focus.

In either case, both the demise of native kingship and the emergence of Assyrian rule is presented as an act of Yhwh. In the Assyrian prophecies, Ishtar of Arbela promised the Assyrian king that she stood with him against his enemies. According to Hosea, on the other hand, it is Yhwh who has used the Israelite kings' enemies against them and taken their side. It is interesting that both Ishtar and Yhwh take credit for the Assyrian king's success, albeit obviously in very different ways. Ishtar supports the Assyrian king because of her affection for and devotion to him. Yhwh supports the Assyrian king against the Israelites as a mechanism for punishing his faithless people, akin to Isaiah's depiction of Assyria as the "rod of [Yhwh's] anger" (Isa. 10:5). Whichever deity gets the credit, though, the end result is that Israel will fall and that its kingship will be taken away and handed over to the Assyrian king.

This dismal state of affairs is not the end of Hosea's historical narrative, though. Despite declaring an end to native Israelite kingship, this is not the final word in Yhwh's plan. Rather, this period during which kingship is taken away from Israel is only the second part in a three-part plan, an intermediate step in a process that will eventually lead to the restoration of Israel and Israelite kingship, this time united with Judah under Davidic rule.

19.3. DAVID AS THE ONCE AND FUTURE KING

If the most explicit renunciation of Israelite kingship is found in Hos. 3:4's "and there is no king," the clearest description of how Israelite kingship will look after this time of punishment has passed is found only a verse later in Hos. 3:5: "Afterward, the Israelites will dwell, and they will seek Yhwh their god and David their king, and they will fear Yhwh and his goodness in the latter days." While many scholars suspect that some or all of the more hopeful passages that look forward to restoration are secondary additions, in the form of Hosea as we presently have it, punishment and exile are neither the end of Israel nor of Israelite kingship. Not only will kingship return to Israel, but it will come in the form of Judahite Davidic rule, uniting the two kingdoms of Israel and Judah under a single king. The two united kingdoms will then worship Yhwh together and enjoy a state of restored prosperity.

Less explicit, but likely meaning essentially the same thing, is Hos. 2:2 (Eng. 1:11): "The Judahites and the Israelites will assemble together. They will set for themselves one head (*rō(')š 'eḥad*), and they will go up from the land, for great is the day of Jezreel." Here neither "David" nor a "king" is mentioned, so it is possible that this "one head" who will govern both Judah and Israel refers to someone other than a Davidic king, but there is good reason to suspect that a Davidic king is also in view here. Critical scholars almost unanimously take this verse to be part of an addition attributable to a Judahite redactor. Along with the preceding verse, it interrupts the conceptual flow of the prophecy, with Hos. 2:1 (Eng. 1:10) directly contradicting Hos. 1:9's "You are not my people," with its "In the place of which it was said of them, 'You are not my people,' it will be said of them, 'Children of a living god.'" These verses introduce Judah into a series of prophecies primarily directed at Israel in a way that detracts from the prophecy's rhetoric, much in the same way that Judah's jarring appearance in Hos. 1:7a does. While some of the references to Judah in Hosea may date to the earliest stages of the book, the mentions of Judah and David in the first three chapters in particular appear most likely to be secondary due to the fact that they run counter to the claims of the material that surrounds them, often undoing a judgment announced in the verse immediately prior, as in Hos. 1:9 and 2:1 (Eng. 1:10). Nonetheless, secondary or not, in the form of the book as we have it, Israel's promised restoration involves the reestablishment of local rule under a Davidic king. While "David" appears nowhere else in the book of Hosea, his appearance near the beginning of the book colors the way in which the reader encounters other more positive and hopeful passages in Hosea, such as Hos. 14, and invites reading these passages which lack a mention of David, or kingship at all, in light of the early restoration-focused passages that do. It is also significant that pointing back to David's reign in the past as the model for future restoration presents a tidy analog for Hosea's use of the exodus event at the beginning of Israel's history as its model for the restoration of the nation as a whole.

19.4. ISRAEL, THE EXODUS, KINGSHIP, AND DAVID

Drawing together the various references to kingship in the book of Hosea, one can trace a three-phase process surrounding Israelite kingship. Hosea has nothing good to say about the native Israelite kings of Hosea's present or recent past. They were installed without Yhwh's approval, and Yhwh is now moving to depose them. With these kings out of the picture, Israel will be ruled either by "no king" or by a foreign Assyrian king, probably two ways of saying essentially the same thing. Eventually, however, Israel will come to its senses, return to Yhwh, and unite with Judah under a single Davidic king. This overall picture is striking in that Hosea's depiction of the removal of and subsequent restoration of Israelite kingship closely parallels its vision of the restoration of Israel as a whole. Like its kings, Israel is also currently corrupt, will also undergo a time of privation, but will likewise then be restored in a pristine state as the people of Yhwh.

In tracing this general trajectory, Hosea's prophecies frequently allude to the exodus legend. In Hos. 11:1, Yhwh declares, "For Israel was a child, and I loved him. From Egypt I called my son." Likewise, Hos. 12:14 (Eng. 12:13) recollects, "By a prophet Yhwh brought Israel up from Egypt, and by a prophet he was kept." Even more directly, in Hos. 12:10a (Eng. 12:9a) Yhwh declares, "I am Yhwh your god from the land of Egypt." For Hosea, the time of the exodus was an idyllic time, when Yhwh first became Israel's god and Israel became Yhwh's people. Hosea also contains clear allusions to some version of the Jacob legends (Hos. 12:3–5, 13 [Eng. 12:2–4, 12]), but the exodus serves as the crucial event that brought Yhwh and Israel together.

Since then, though, Israel has broken faith with Yhwh. They have "sacrificed to the baals and offered incense to idols" (Hos. 11:1b). Israel "inquires by its wood, they proclaim by its rod for itself. For a spirit of whoredom led them astray, and they whored out from under their god" (Hos. 4:12). This accusation concerning Israel's "whoring," especially prominent in the first three chapters that present Hosea's marriage metaphor but which also appears, albeit less prominently, in subsequent chapters, represents one of the central themes of the book: Yhwh has been faithful to Israel, but at some point between the time of the exodus from Egypt and the present, Israel has rejected Yhwh and turned to other sources of support. As recompense for Israel's having abandoned Yhwh, Yhwh in turn will undo that original exodus event: "They will return to Egypt" (Hos. 8:13bβ). "They will not dwell in the land of Yhwh. Ephraim will return to Egypt, and in Assyria they will eat that which is unclean" (Hos. 9:3). "[Israel] will return[7] to the land of Egypt, and Assyria, he is its king" (Hos. 11:5). The Assyrian conquest of Israel is thus presented as a sort of undoing of the exodus, as a return to the bondage of Egypt.

Nonetheless, this reverse exodus back to Egypt is not merely punitive in nature. It is an opportunity for a fresh start, where Yhwh and Israel can begin again. At the end of Hos. 2, one of the most disturbing chapters in the Hebrew Bible—one in which Hosea's/Yhwh's "wife" is stripped naked, killed with thirst, and involuntarily confined—the tone shifts abruptly, "Therefore I [= Yhwh] will seduce her. I will cause her to walk in the wilderness, and I will speak upon her heart. I will give to her her vineyards from there and set the valley of Achor as a door of hope. She will respond there as in the days of her youth, like the day that she came up from the land of Egypt" (Hos. 2:17 [Eng. 2:15]). Similarly, Hos. 12:10 (Eng. 12:9) reads, "I am Yhwh your god from the land of Egypt. Yet again I will cause you to dwell in tents as in the days of the assembly." The words "tents" and "assembly" here (Hebrew *ʾōhālîm* and *môʿēd*) recall the "tent of assembly" (*ʾōhel môʿēd*) that plays a prominent role in the wilderness wandering stories of the Pentateuch. There, it is a place where Yhwh meets with the people of Israel. Israel's return to Egypt is thus also a return to the wilderness period that followed the exodus, the period during which Yhwh's and Israel's relationship began. This relationship, now broken, will be repaired by undoing the past and going back to the start, before things went off course. The narrative arc in Hosea's prophecies thus paints a picture in which things were once good, but they are now beyond repair without starting over from the beginning.

Kingship in Hosea follows a similar arc. Current and recent kings are worthless and illegitimate. The immediate solution to this state of affairs is the removal of Israelite kingship altogether. Israel will have no king of their own; the foreign king of Assyria will play this role. Kingship itself, however, is not entirely rejected. Indeed, in the book of Hosea as it currently stands, kingship will eventually be restored by going back to its beginnings. While Hosea draws on the exodus legend for its language and conception about sin, punishment, and restoration with regard to Israel as a people, when addressing the institution of the monarchy, it instead draws on the David legend. The reign of David was a time during which Israel and Judah were remembered as united as a single kingdom and under a single king. In the Deuteronomistic History, in spite of his numerous failings and misdeeds, David is repeatedly held up as the ideal king and the standard by which all subsequent kings are measured.[8] The present form of the book of Hosea appears to share this assessment and sees the most effective way of restoring the institution of Israelite kingship to be to go back to its beginning.[9] Whether the idyllic past of the exodus or the idyllic past of the United Monarchy under David, Hosea's solution to Israel's transgressions is to start anew, wipe away the past, and return to the days before Israel turned aside from following Yhwh.

19.5. CONCLUSION

While Hosea has very little positive to say about the recent kings of Israel, the book is not philosophically opposed to the monarchy or kingship as an institution. Rather, Hosea depicts kingship as a potential source of support and deliverance, but the institution has become so corrupt and ineffectual that it can no longer carry out this function. For this reason, Yhwh has decided to wipe away Israelite kingship and to leave Israel without its own king for a time. The only king that Israel will have for the foreseeable future is the foreign Assyrian king. In the present form of the book of Hosea, however, this period of foreign subjugation represents a temporary state of affairs. Israelite kingship is removed in order eventually to be remade and restored. Just as Hosea has Israel return to Egypt and the wilderness where it first met Yhwh in order to start their relationship anew, so also must Israel return to the halcyon days of the United Monarchy under King David to restore its kingship and kingdom to the state that Yhwh originally intended.

NOTES

1. All translations of ancient texts, including biblical texts, are the author's. For an edition of this prophecy, SAA 9.1.1, including the transliterated Akkadian text, see Parpola 1997: 4–5 and Nissinen 2019: 112–13.
2. See especially Gelston 1974: 71–85; Emmerson 1984: 56–116; Machinist 2005; Goswell 2017; Sweeney 2020: 489–506, esp. 490–93. The present study has benefited from each of these treatments of the topic. It primarily diverges from them in eschewing questions concerning both the redaction history and the specific historical contexts that gave rise to the various oracles in Hosea that center on kingship. Instead, I am primarily concerned with the way kingship is depicted in the book as we have it and how that depiction accords with the way in which Hosea's prophecies treat the people of Israel as a whole.
3. 2 Sam. 15:35; 16:2; 19:19; 2 Kgs. 7:9, 11.

4. 1 Kgs. 14:16; 15:30, 34; 16:2, 19, 26; 21:22; 22:53; 2 Kgs. 3:3; 10:29, 31; 13:2, 6, 11; 14:24; 15:9, 18, 24, 28; 17:21; 23:15.
5. Reading "where" with the versions against MT "I will be."
6. The parallel in 1 Samuel is somewhat problematic, though, as there is a textual variant at precisely this point in the Greek tradition, with Vaticanus reading, "The Lord has torn your kingship from Israel from your hand today." Other Greek witnesses, however, agree with MT. The redundancy of Vaticanus probably indicates a conflate text here. The Targum, Peshitta, and Vulgate all support MT, but it is possible nonetheless that the Greek tradition may point to an older reading, "The Lord has torn your kingship from Israel today," which would offer a less tight parallel to the word's usage in Hosea than the MT of 1 Samuel as it currently stands.
7. MT reads *lōʾ yāšûb ʾel-ereṣ miṣrayim* "he will *not* return to the land of Egypt," but this is almost certainly a scribal error. The sense of the passage requires Israel to go to Egypt so that they can "flutter like a bird from Egypt" a few verses later in Hos. 11:8. Most likely, *lô* "to him" originally concluded the previous line (so OG αὐτῷ) which at some point was mistaken for the homophone *lōʾ* "not" and misunderstood as the first word in this line rather than as the final word in the previous one.
8. 1 Kgs. 3:3, 6, 14; 9:4; 11:4, 6, 33–34, 38; 14:8; 15:3, 5, 11; 2 Kgs. 14:3; 16:2; 18:3; 22:2.
9. Or rather, one should say almost its beginning, excluding Saul, who makes no obvious appearance in the book. Some have seen the mention of "Gibeah" in Hos. 10:9 as an allusion to Gibeonite Saul and the initial misstep that constituted his reign. This is possible, but by no means certain.

REFERENCES

Emmerson, Grace I. 1984. *Hosea: An Israelite Prophet in Judean Perspective.* JSOTSup 28. Sheffield: JSOT Press.

Gelston, A. "Kingship in the Book of Hosea." 1974. In James Barr, ed., *Language and Meaning: Studies in Hebrew Language and Biblical Exegesis; Papers Read at the Joint British-Dutch Old Testament Conference Held at London, 1973.* OtSt 19. Leiden: Brill, 71–85.

Goswell, Gregory. 2017. "'David Their king': Kingship in the Prophecy of Hosea." *JSOT* 42: 213–31.

Machinist, Peter. 2005. "Hosea and the Ambiguity of Kingship in Ancient Israel." In John T. Strong and Steven S. Tuell, eds., *Constituting the Community: Studies on the Polity of Ancient Israel in Honor of S. Dean McBride, Jr.* Winona Lake, IN: Eisenbrauns, 153–81.

Nissinen, Martti. 2019. *Prophets and Prophecy in the Ancient Near East.* 2nd ed. WAW 41. Atlanta: SBL.

Parpola, Simo. 1997. *Assyrian Prophecies.* SAA 9. Helsinki: Helsinki University Press.

Sweeney, Marvin A. 2020. "Kingship in the Book of the Twelve." In Lena-Sofia Tiemeyer and Jakob Wöhrle, eds., *The Book of the Twelve: Composition, Reception, and Interpretation.* VtSup 184. Leiden: Brill, 489–506.

CHAPTER 20

SIN AND PUNISHMENT IN THE BOOK OF HOSEA

JOSHUA N. MOON

20.1. INTRODUCTION

IT is hard to find a more fitting theme for the bulk of Hosea (arguably the entirety of it) than the pairing of sin and punishment. On every page, and many times on every page, we find a portrait of Yhwh punishing sin through the sharp-tongued preaching of a prophet. In part for that reason, this present essay will be more concerned with a general imaginative frame. There is too much to delve into the details of every instance, so we will be content more with macrolevel questions of theological portrayal in the book. After all, for contemporary moral intuitions no concern puts Hosea more firmly in the category of the suspicious—if not outright dangerous—texts of the ancient (and especially because of the Christian Bible, the modern) world than its theological presentation of sin and punishment. Hosea is distrusted and even despised not for the book's teaching of sin and punishment, but for its portrayal of God as the one in whose hand sin and punishment are paired. It is a theological challenge to read Hosea on sin and punishment.

Readers need some way to grasp (not tame) the theological realities of sin and punishment, and in ways that honor the historical realities of the text as a work coming to us from the distance of the ancient Levant. Yet even in terms familiar to the world of biblical scholarship, the prominence of sin and punishment in Hosea has not meant an easy time describing the relationship between the two. There certainly is a relationship, betrayed both by the persistence and the tight patterns of wordplays. But the contours of that relationship have proven difficult and, at least much of the time, unsatisfying. I will argue below that a theological response is readily available in the political imaginations of the ancient Levant: that in Hosea we see Yhwh as a king who pursues justice in his land. While not escaping some contemporary (or ancient) opprobrium, this image allows us to do justice to the contours and shape of sin and punishment as theological realities in Hosea—that is, as realities that are consistently exposed (sin) and dealt with (punishment) by Yhwh.

To confront the main weakness with my proposal, I acknowledge at the outset that Hosea has numerous metaphors for Yhwh's relation to Israel, and only once is there what appears to be a direct citation of Yhwh's kingship (see below). Yet something like this metaphor must govern the book. What right does Yhwh have to enter into judgment? What right to require sole loyalty of this people? How do we describe Yhwh's devotion to care about justice in this particular land? To claim he is a betrayed lord? We could appeal simply to a covenant rooted in the exodus, and have good grounds for it. But, as will be developed below, this language moves us into the imagery of kingship. The key here is that the very act of entering into judgment, set in the context of the ancient Levant, entails the world of kingship. Theological imaginations work within the social worlds of those who do the imagining. And within the ancient Levant, the work of entering into and executing judgment was a kingly work. The deity (especially in Israel) was the King of kings to whom that work was most directly tied. That Hosea does not explicitly name the metaphor is only true if we have already divorced judgment from kingship. To name Yhwh as judge was to name him as king. And that ought to shape how we read and hear the relationship of sin and punishment in Hosea.

20.2. Punishment for Sin as Retributive Justice

In 1955 Klaus Koch published a famous essay arguing against retribution as a punitive act of God in the prophets (Koch 1955). For Koch, the relationship of sin to punishment comes through the already-established connection between a deed committed (good or bad) and the result of that deed. Yhwh, in the Hebrew Bible, plays the role of a midwife (*Hebammandiest*), who does not cause but merely serves the birth of a particular "inherent" consequence. Hosea played a major role in his argument, embodied in the classic statement:

> Because they have sown the wind,
> they will reap the whirlwind. (8:7)

A division developed in mid-twentieth-century scholarship, some of which can be seen in two of the monumental works spanning from one generation to the next. First, we have the declaration of Walther Eichrodt in 1933:

> [H]owever far ancient Israel may have been from limiting the divine wrath entirely to the exercise of *retributive justice*, the latter is without doubt its proper and principal sphere of operation.

288 JOSHUA N. MOON

Or more strongly, he claims that during Persian rule:

> The wrath of God is strictly limited to the sphere of retributive justice, which metes out reward and punishment to the individual. (Eichrodt 1961: 263, 287)

Yet within a generation we have another titan of the field, Gerhard von Rad, siding entirely with Koch:

> Like a stone thrown into water, every act initiates a movement for good or evil: a process gets under way which, especially in the case of a crime, only comes to rest when retribution has overtaken the perpetrator. But this retribution is not a new action which comes upon the person concerned from somewhere else; it is rather the last ripple of the act itself which attaches to its agent almost as something material. (von Rad 1962: I.384–85)

For von Rad, the connection to Yhwh comes in terms of Yhwh as the "universal cause," with the result that

> it is out of place to speak of a "doctrine of retribution," for the idea of retribution, in that it understands "punishment" as an additional forensic act, implies a legal way of thinking which is absolutely foreign. (von Rad 1962: I.386)

Koch has found a few other followers, even if less influential than von Rad (e.g., Tucker 1997). Yet on the whole the positive aspect of his proposal has rightly been seen as a failure. Not only in the prophets generally but in Hosea in particular retribution comes to the fore with such repetition and directness that we would have to strain hard not to see it. The patterns of sin and punishment throughout the prophets take form as some kind of retributive punishment that comes from outside the act itself—that is, from Yhwh (Miller 1982). But rather than throwing out the whole of Koch's argument, we must ask what we mean by retribution, and the kind of retribution that would be particularly fitting when reading Hosea.

To begin, consider the world of theology—for instance, a simple claim of something like Paul's declaration, "the wages of sin is death" (Rom. 6:23). Such a claim makes clear that the connection between a deed and its consequence need not rest solely in a claim of Yhwh as universal cause. We could use classic theology here, but for its graphic richness I will use Karl Barth's language of sin/evil as *das Nachtige* (Barth 2010: III/3, §50; Wüthrich 2021). When a deed participates in *das Nachtige*—he uses the term to mean an aggressive nothingness, an active reality whose being exists in negation (negative ontology)—then we have an inherent connection between a deed (sin) and its consequence (death/nothingness). Thus far we are in the field of Koch and von Rad, though in a different mold than they suggest. Fitting this motif, at a number of key points in Hosea, Yhwh's act toward the sin is the removal of his self-as-salvation. From the opening salvos we read of Yhwh "no longer" showing mercy (1:6), a withdrawal of his saving presence. We read later, "let him be" (4:17). Yhwh absents himself so that the people wander without finding him (5:6). In all this, we have the terror of punishment as Yhwh abandons the people to what the sin brings (*das Nachtige*).

And yet it would be disingenuous to ignore what is plain to Eichrodt and to the vast majority of scholars: the language of the prophets, Hosea among them, regularly returns to Yhwh's punishment not as a general universal cause but as a direct or efficient cause. It is not simply that Yhwh has ordained all things and has ordained that sin would bring death, but that Yhwh takes to himself the role of bringing the death that is sin's wage. "I will bring the blood of Jezreel upon the house of Jehu" (1:4). The compilations of retributive texts in the Levant are impressive and easy to find (French 2021: 75–104; Peels 1995). And in none of them do we find support for the deity's role as a helper of an already-effected consequence tied to the deed. Throughout Hosea, Yhwh personally brings retribution, not only handing over (as it were) to *das Nachtige* but executing the fitting judgment:

> I will visit his ways upon him,
> and his deeds I will return to him. (Hos. 4:9)

Yhwh takes it upon himself to bring about the punishment as an act of retributive justice according to something like the principle of a *lex talionis*: that which was put forth comes back upon the wrongdoer. But how does Yhwh cause it to come back?

Unfortunately, most conversations—certainly those of Koch/von Rad and Eichrodt—have failed to give much thought to the way in which we use language like "retribution." For Eichrodt, retribution lies purely in the realm of law and covenant: "the Israelite is certain that God in his turn will act toward him in accordance with those principles of law with which he himself is well acquainted" (Eichrodt 1961: I.243). More recent political philosophy sometimes broadens but often shares such a connection. John Rawls, for instance, defines retribution only in passing:

> What we may call the retributive view is that punishment is justified on the grounds that wrongdoing merits punishment. It is morally fitting that a person who does wrong should suffer in proportion to his wrongdoing. (Rawls 1999: 21–22)

Retribution in these senses refers to a calculated fit, that deed x performed by an individual deserves—and so receives—result y, on account of either a legally or a morally binding reality. Punishment comes to set the ledger to rights. I find myself having to agree with Koch and von Rad: retribution in this sense sits ill in Hosea.

Against Koch, however, that does not exhaust the debate. Retribution still exists on every page of Hosea, but need not mean a calculation of what suffering is morally proportionate to any given wrong (Rawls), nor as a declaration of the agreed upon legal consequences (Eichrodt). Rather, retribution comes as a direct answer and response to the wrong done. It is important, but insufficient, to speak of retribution as containing a "like-for-like" rhetorical punishment in the prophets that is tied to juridical concerns

(Wong 2001). Retribution involves the thing done coming back upon the doer, but it is not a mechanistic or "natural" coming-back. More helpful here is Oliver O'Donovan:

> The core of the retributive idea is the thought that in punishment something which the offender has put forth comes back. . . . [Yet:] What the offender gets back in being punished is different from what was put forth, not an echo but an answer. (O'Donovan 1999: 110)

Here we can fit the varieties of retributive principles explicit both in Hosea and the wider ancient Levant: retribution comes as an answer, a direct response elicited by the wrong done. It is not an echo, a tit-for-tat, much less is it a proportional calculus of suffering. Yhwh sees or hears the wrong, and answers it.

We could try to tie up the discussion at this point with a theological claim: Yhwh answers all that participates in *das Nachtige* by actively banishing it into *das Nachtige*. And that is, in some sense, where we are headed. But that moves us too far from the book of Hosea and the world of the ancient Levant to be much help. I want instead to move back into the historical realities at play in the political and theological imaginations of the ancient Levant, to frame and justify this kind of connection of sin and punishment in Yhwh's hand, as we find it in Hosea.

Our first step is to recognize that "retribution" in O'Donovan's sense works only within the conviction that there is a right ordering of the world. For Rawls, of course, justice lies entirely within the plane of social ordering with individual obligations arising from consent within the social body. But that puts us far from both the Hebrew Bible, where we find a keen (if unsystematic) sense of righteousness or justice arising as part of a proper *Weltordnung* (Schmid 1968; Brandenburger 1991; Müller 1994). The payoff here is that retribution in the sense I am proposing works not by constant referral to a legal or moral ledger to see what calculated punishment fits this particular crime; it works by reference to a rightly ordered world. We could speak here with ancient Greek philosophy's language of *eudaimonia*, but there is no reason to go so far afield; the same dynamics in evidence in the Hebrew Bible are evident as well in Egyptian and Assyrian thought (Groenweld 2002; Maul 1998).

The world of the ancient Levant offers the perfect way to imagine all of these dynamics at play—retribution as bringing an answer to the wrong put forth, and the pursuit of a rightly ordered world—and all in a way that fits the rhetoric of Hosea exactly: the role of Yhwh as King.

20.3. JUSTICE AS A KINGLY WORK

The notion that bringing justice is a kingly work appears as far back as legal texts ranging from Mari to Egypt to Assyria to Babylon. Lipit-Ishtar, for instance, is said to have been called by Numanmir "to establish justice in the land, to wipe away complaint from the mouth ... to promote the well-being of Sumar and Akad" (Kitchen and Lawrence 2012: no.10, §1). But most famous of all Levantine texts on this theme is the stela of Hammurabi, which opens:

> At that time (it was) me, Hammurabi, a devout prince, who fears the gods, to make justice appear in the land, to destroy the evil and the wicked, so that the mighty might not exploit the weak ... to improve the well-being of my people. (Kitchen and Lawrence 2012: no.14, §1.P3)

He claims later that he is "the perfect arbiter" (§2.P13), he is "the one who makes justice visible, who keeps the people straight" (§3.P19), or "king of justice" (§6b.E17). This work is tied to his role as king under the gods who appointed him. Throughout the ancient Levant, and not least in the Hebrew Bible, human kings ruled in a derivative sense, gaining authority and legitimacy—and their proper role in the world—as those under the deity/deities.

The same dynamics are clear if we move south to Egypt, noted particularly in texts of royal propaganda:

> I am a king who (both) speaks and acts:
>   what comes to pass through me is what I plan ...
> who takes thought for the poor and stands up for the meek,
>   (but) who is not mild to the enemy who attacks him. (Baines 2013: 35)

The authority to act on behalf of the poor and meek, bringing retribution on their enemy, is the pursuit of justice in the land. Another text is even more explicit:

> Re has placed King N
> on the earth of the living
> for ever and ever
> judging humanity and propitiating the gods,
> realizing order (*ma'at*) and destroying disorder (*izfet*). (Baines 2013: 42)

The king here brings judgment in order to set the world right. *Ma'at* is not merely an abstracted legal reality, but incorporates cosmic order that includes rightly ordered relationships between people, and between the people and the gods (Assmann 2001). The ideal Egyptian king brought justice and so realized this kind of order, and the whole of it came in service to the deity who desired *ma'at*.

We move closer to Hosea through a letter from a scribal scholar to Assurbanipal of Assyria, just a generation or so removed from the prophet:

> Aššur, [the king of the gods], called the name of [the king], my lord, to the kingship of Assyria, and Šamaš and Adad, through their reliable extispicy, confirmed the king, my lord, for the kingship of the world. A good reign—righteous days, years of justice; copious rains, huge floods, a fine rate of exchange! The gods are appeased, there

is much fear of god, the temples abound; the great gods of heaven and earth have become exalted in the time of the king, my lord. The old men dance, the young men sing, the women and girls are merry and rejoice; women are married and provided with earrings; boys and girls are brought forth, the births thrive. The king, my lord, has revived the one who was guilty and condemned to death; you have released the one who was imprisoned for many [ye]ars. Those who were sick for many days have got well, the hungry have been sated, the parched have been anointed with oil, the needy have been covered with garments. (Parpola 1993: no.226)

Unabashed flattery notwithstanding, we see here "a picture of what the good Mesopotamian king was expected to bring about: messianic bliss" (Lambert 2013: 70).

The Hebrew Bible evidences this same idea of the king as bringer of justice. The most straightforward summary comes in Jeremiah:

> Hear Yhwh's word, king of Judah, who sits on the throne of David . . . :
> Bring about justice and righteousness,
>   save the one robbed from the hand of the oppressor.
> As for the stranger, the fatherless, or the widow—do them no wrong; no violence.
>   And do not shed innocent blood in this place. (Jer. 22:2–3; cf. 21:12)

Or yet more succinctly in Micah:

> Hear now, you chiefs of Jacob and rulers of the house of Israel:
>   Is it not for you to acknowledge justice? (Mic. 3:1)

There are many more such citations. In the political imagination of the ancient Levant, the role of executing justice in the land lay in the hands of the king or ruler; it was rather uniformly imagined that to speak of a king was to speak of a judge, and to speak of one bringing justice to the land was to speak in kingly language.

Moreover, the human king's pursuit of justice came at the behest of, and as an obligation to, the deities—as seen above both from Assyria and Egypt (and, of course, the Hebrew Bible). Some have found a difference between Israel and the wider Levant, suggesting that in the Hebrew Bible Yhwh rather than the king acted as the sole guarantor of justice in the land (Artus 2004: 31). If such an argument holds, it would only emphasize the point at issue here: the human king lives under and serves Yhwh's Torah, with Yhwh as the proper King of kings who alone legislates and is responsible for justice and righteousness in the land (Vogt 2006). When the king is called on to pursue justice in the land, we are not to imagine the work divorced from Yhwh's own desire and role.

Hosea evidences these assumptions at a few points, though solely in the negative. We see them at play in the human king taking delight in "evil" (7:3; cf. 7:5), the opposite of the *Weltordnung* of righteousness/justice. We see them in the somewhat cryptic remark to the ruling structures that "the judgment (*mishpat*) is for you"—a declaration that the justice which should have been brought by the rulers will now be brought against them. But the more general point holds: that in the Levant, we have a uniform commitment to the king as a bringer of justice to his land. The divorce between kings and judges, almost intuitive to modern Western thought, had no role in the ancient Levant. In the world that produced Hosea, the great judge—the one chiefly responsible for justice in the land—was the king, acting under the call and direction of the deity. Even if all the people were called to "do justice," it was the king's work to make sure this was done.

20.4. YHWH AS A KING WHO BRINGS JUSTICE

Yhwh, God of Hosts
Yhwh is his memorial name (Hos. 12:6 [Eng. 12:5])

That Yhwh is king in Israel stands as a central pillar in the Hebrew Bible, repeated in various forms. It can be seen in the passing remark from Hosea quoted above. To speak of Yhwh or God "of hosts" arises from the insistence on Yhwh as king (Mettinger 1982). While older scholarship seemed unable to shake the appeal of a *Chaoskampf* mythology of a divine warrior when seeing such phrases, a better image is an ancient throne room, with the deity-king represented as the head of his armies. The context of Hos. 12:6 (Eng. 12:5) places us in very old traditions in Israel, and here at the center of the tradition is the claim of Yhwh in his kingly place. For all the importance of Yhwh as king in the Hebrew Bible (a point shared with distinctions in the wider ancient Levant), there has been rather little reflection on its place and development (one exception is Flynn 2014). Correspondingly, there has been almost no reflection on how such a widely attested notion might shape prophetic texts like Hosea, whether in their composition or their reception.

As stated above, while granting that Hosea has no other explicit reference to Yhwh as king, something like this role for Yhwh must be in place to make sense of the book. The other metaphors throughout Hosea, especially that of husband in the early chapters, only emphasize this fact. Such a relationship in the ancient world was not the modern sense of two equal parties entering a mutually beneficial arrangement in the pursuit of individual self-satisfaction. Power dynamics can be overstated, but there was an authority vested in the husband in the relationship. The expectation of fidelity (culturally so defined) went both ways (as Hos. 3:3), but from the start of Hosea, Yhwh claimed a particular kind of role over the people and the land. We could also cite the parent/child metaphor (2:1–2, 6 [Eng. 1:10–11; 2:4]; 3:1; 4:1; 11:1–10). These metaphors live as expressions or variations on a theme that fits handily with Yhwh-as-King and demand at least something of the sort to be in place. There is also a repeated interest of Yhwh in the land, not just a general people—and the land not simply as an ecological matter but as the place in which Yhwh's justice and righteousness are meant to be seen (e.g., 2:20, 25 [Eng. 2:15, 23]; 4:1). In other words, land here is understood in political terms, as overtly claimed at 9:3 ("They shall not remain in Yhwh's land"). Such language might fit the familial metaphors but sits far better in the political realm of kingly rule. Yhwh rules over a land and the people in the land; in short, a political kingdom.

Among the great sins in the early parts of Hosea is the repeated lack of "knowledge" of Yhwh (4:1–6; 5:4; 6:6), language that has regularly been connected to covenants in the ancient Levant (Huffman 1966). In Eichrodt, and widely in discussions of retribution, language of covenant is central. But less often pointed out is that the "knowledge/acknowledgment" in these covenants has to do with fidelity to a king, as Huffmon originally noted. Thus in one Hittite treaty:

> Now, you, Huqqanas, (shall) acknowledge only (me), the Sun-king, as your master; and (also) the son of mine whom, the Sun-king, denotes: "Him shall all acknowledge!" . . . Now you, Huqqanas—(it is) that one whom you must acknowledge. (Kitchen and Lawrence 2012: no.60.3)

It seems hard not to parallel what we find in Hosea:

> I am Yhwh your God from the land of Egypt, you shall acknowledge no other god but me, and no savior but me. (Hos 13:4)

Or we can move north to Assyria and find again the common (to the point of banal) insistence on absolute loyalty to the rightful king and his line:

> We will love [Assurbanipal], king of Assyria, and [hate his enemy]. [From] this [day] on for as long as we live, Assurbanipal, [king of Assyria], shall be [our king and lord. We will not install] nor seek another king or another lord for [ourselves]. (Parpola and Watanabe 1988: no.990.32)

Again, Hosea's language is close at hand, though largely in the negative:

> Your love is like a morning cloud, like dew that goes away. (Hos. 6:4)

The rulers "dearly love disgrace," when they ought to love Yhwh (4:18). And so Yhwh "hates" them and will "love them no more" (9:15; for the positive, cf. 11:4; 14:5 [Eng. 14:4]). In all of these instances, Israel's sin comes tied to the covenant language of treaties with kings. Insofar as covenants and treaties form a part of the background, it is Israel's betrayal and rejection of their rightful king that haunts Hosea's use of the language.

We could say this another way: Hosea confronts us with "sin" not simply (or primarily) as a juridical matter of legal principles, but as political treachery against their rightful king. We read of the political reality that they have "forsaken Yhwh" to pursue drink (4:10–11). And it may be, as Brad E. Kelle (2005) has argued, that the large amount of metaphors of infidelity in ch. 2 arises from political entities, which would, once more, bolster the present argument. The insistence throughout Hosea on Yhwh-alone is not a religiohistorical development toward monotheism as a philosophical idea (as Lang 1983). It is an exposing of political treachery against Israel's rightful king, to whom they were meant to give sole allegiance just as assumed and expressed in treaties and covenants with kings throughout the ancient Levant.

20.5. Yhwh's Kingly Pursuit of Justice

None of the above points are overly controversial, except that they have lived far removed from imaginative frames for reading sin and punishment in the prophets. It is apparent even on the surface that in Hosea Yhwh pursues justice in the land. And in the ancient Levant, that work is directly taken to be a king's responsibility. So putting these together, we find in Hosea exactly what the psalms of Yhwh's kingship would lead us to expect, even if in Hosea (given its focus) it takes more localized forms:

> Yhwh sits enthroned forever;
>> he has established his throne for justice,
> and he judges the world with righteousness;
>> he judges the peoples with integrity. (Ps. 9:7–8)

> Say among the nations, "Yhwh reigns!
>> Yes, the world is established; it shall never be moved;
>> he will judge the peoples with integrity." (Ps. 96:10)

> Make a joyful noise before Yhwh the King . . .
>> for he comes to judge the earth.
> He will judge the world with righteousness,
>> and the peoples with integrity. (Ps. 98:6, 9)

> Yhwh reigns! Let the peoples tremble;
>> He sits enthroned upon the cherubim . . .
> The King in his might loves justice . . .
>> you have executed justice and righteousness in Jacob. (Ps. 99:1, 4)

Such motifs are common enough to be almost banal in the Hebrew Bible, yet their application to reading the prophets remains minimal. For instance, Vannoy tiptoes toward the point when critiquing Koch's thesis as

> too sweeping to do justice to numerous OT texts that represent Yahweh as intervening in various situations to impose blessing or punishment in his role as divine warrior and judge. (Vannoy 1996: 1141)

I agree, except note that Vannoy speaks of "divine warrior" and "judge" without mentioning what it is that holds both roles together throughout the ancient Levant and especially the Hebrew Bible: the role of the king. Yhwh intervenes to impose blessing or punishment (as in Hosea) in his role as Israel's king, and King of her human kings.

Some have begun to notice and make these connections, though largely focused on Second Temple Jewish thought, following the leads of Egon Brandenburger (1993) and Karlheinz Müller (1994). So Christian Stettler, in his study of the Last Judgment, can say about the Hebrew Bible what fits perfectly the argument here:

> Already from the early monarchy Yhwh was seen as a kingly judge, who like an earthly king sets the entire order of the world right through judgment and war. (Stettler 2011: 57)

What else do we see in Hosea except Yhwh setting his kingdom to rights through judgment and war—that is, Yhwh in his kingly role? For instance, we can turn to the prominent salvo that opens the main part of the book:

> Hear Yhwh's word, O children of Israel,
> for Yhwh has an accusation against the inhabitants of the land:
> For there is no faithfulness,
> and there is no steadfast love,
> and there is no knowledge of God in the land. Swearing, and lying, and murder,
> and stealing, and adultery—
> they burst forth and shed blood and more blood!
> Therefore the land mourns, and all who live in it faint,
> with the beast of the field and the birds of the heavens;
> even the fish of the sea are swept away. (4:1–3)

The punishment here could fit Koch's arrangement: the result of the sins of omission (v. 1) and commission (v. 2) are a mournful and empty land (v. 3). We could plead a divine passive ("are swept away"), but for argument's sake we have a land reaping the consequences of wrongdoing, with Yhwh not even cited. But a better reading sees Yhwh's land failing: it has become a desperately improper *Weltordnung*—a direct counterpoint to the letter to Assurbanipal above. If we are imagining Yhwh as king in the land, this is a rather pitiful land to rule. And thus, immediately on the heels of this disordered world, Yhwh acts. And in the order given to the book, Yhwh acts initially by bringing retribution on the unfaithful priests in the image of a single representative—"Mr. Priest," as Mayer Gruber (2017: 192) designates him:

> You (O priest) will stumble in the day,
> and the prophet also will stumble with you at night.
> I will cut off your mother—
> my people are cut off for their lack of knowledge—
> because you have rejected knowledge;
> so I reject you as my priest.
> And because you have forgotten the instruction of your God,
> I myself will forget your children. (4:4–7)

None of this now fits Koch's scheme. Even with a number of textual uncertainties, the back-and-forth of wordplay and divine action foregrounds Yhwh's retribution. Yhwh answers the wrong, bringing that which they put forth back upon their heads. It is language of generational destruction, the complete ending of the priest's line through destruction of parent, priest, and children (Lohfink 1961). The priests reject knowledge, and Yhwh answers by rejecting them completely as priests.

Yhwh does not produce a simple echo of the wrong, nor does he calculate a suffering particularly fitting the moral or contractual ledger. Rather, Yhwh rises up and pursues justice against the priests for their failure relative to a rightly ordered world. He provides an answer to their wrongs, terrible as the answer is for them. This is the dynamic that holds throughout the book. The relationship of sin and punishment is a relationship of a world-out-of-order and Yhwh's answering that reality. Yhwh answers from his role as the one with responsibility to bring justice—that is, as Israel's rightful king.

20.6. JUSTICE AND THE
END OF PUNISHMENT

In discussing Yhwh's judgments on sin in the prophets, Bernd Janowski emphasized the image of kingship in a similar manner to what I have suggested, though with some differences. His emphasis falls on the positive reality Yhwh brings about through his kingly judgment:

> [Yhwh is a] merciful king who hears the cry of the poor and gives them justice—just as elsewhere in the ancient Near East the sun god, or his representative the king, rescues the oppressed and punishes injustice. (Janowski 2000: 734)

The goal of Yhwh's punishment is justice in the land. I mentioned above that retribution (in the sense used here) cannot be divorced from a *Weltordnung*, the right ordering of the world. If we take retribution as purely a juridical concern—a tit-for-tat calculation, or Rawls's morally fitting punishment—then the end or goal of punishment is found in the suffering of the wrongdoer; the punishment is its own end. One satisfies a ledger of legal or moral consequence. Yet in kingly metaphors, we are in a different world entirely. Here, the end of Yhwh's kingly judgment (including retributive punishment) is a world set right—a kingdom rightly ordered by its king. Punishment for sin does not carry its own end, but pushes toward the end of justice in the land. It looks beyond itself to the world that can be established when all causes of injustice are removed.

In negative terms, Yhwh's coming in judgment in Hosea leaves behind a land without injustice. I mentioned earlier the disordered world described early in the book:

> Swearing, and lying, and murder, and stealing, and adultery—
> they burst forth and shed blood and more blood! (4:2)

Yhwh's coming in judgment would set the land free from the evils and provide a life without the wrong. Otherwise put, even in the simple negative of wiping out such evils, there is a positive end or goal that is built around the king (Yhwh) desiring justice.

But the positive form appears explicitly at least a few times in the book, above all in 6:1–6: "He tore us that he might heal us; he struck us down that he might bind us up" (6:1). In the contextual imagery, Yhwh has come as a lion to tear the evildoer (5:14), which is the appropriate answer to the evils done (retributive justice). Yet he tears in order to heal—not to heal the lion's tearing, the tearing was to expose the wound. The retributive punishment is not its own end. The end is a land of justice and a people healed, as is then said directly:

> This is why I have hewn them by the prophets,
> slain them by the words of my mouth,
> and why my judgment goes forth as light:
> because I desire steadfast love, not sacrifice;
> and the knowledge of God rather than burnt offerings. (6:5–6)

Again, the textual uncertainties here do not impact the clear point: Yhwh's judgment comes as the expression of a desire for a world set right, in language of *ḥsd* and *ydʿ*, which again connects to the worlds of royal treaties/covenants.

Yet the most important evidence for this positive end of judgment comes in the form of the "oracles of salvation" that scholars have too often separated from those of judgment. That separation obscures their common end. Hosea takes a shameful wife and has shameful children whose names are the fitting embodiment of Israel's shamefulness (1:1–9). In the terms used here, Gomer and the children embody Yhwh's retribution. Yet the far side of retribution is the undoing of their disgrace: a people cleansed of the pollution of wrongdoing, and given honor in place of their shame (2:1–2, 16 [Eng. 1:10–11; 2:14]; 3:1–5; cf. Moon 2015).

Consider also the great poem of 11:1–11, where Yhwh's kindness—built around parent/child language common in royal treaties and covenants—is refused through idolatry and infidelity. And so Yhwh pronounces exile as the fitting answer to their rebellion (11:5–7), only then to express the longing of compassion that turns away from a complete destruction and establishes (again, on the far side of that retribution) a proper ordering of the world. The people go into exile to Egypt and Assyria, as the retribution declared, yet are then brought back in peace and safety (11:8–11).

One final illustration of this point comes at the conclusion of the book, which presents the readers with the moral and liturgical response to the whole of Hosea. And that response is precisely this world of justice and submission to Yhwh's kingship:

> Return, O Israel, to Yhwh your God,
> for you have stumbled in your iniquity.
> Take with you words, and return to Yhwh. Say to him:
> "Take away all iniquity, receive the good,
> and we shall pay the fruit of our lips.

Assyria will not save us,
we will not ride on horses,
and we will no longer say 'our God' to what our hands made,
for it is in you the orphan finds mercy." (14:2–4 [Eng. 14:1–3])
Yhwh, in turn, will act as the benevolent provider and protector (14:5–9 [Eng. 14:4–8]).

Retribution has an end, and the hope that the retribution declared and painted throughout Hosea might not come again entails the establishing of fidelity to Yhwh's sole rule over his people.

20.7. CONCLUSION

The God with whom we are confronted by the book of Hosea is a God of justice. Sin and punishment are bound together, though they are incessantly bound together under the hand of Yhwh as he seeks justice. Deeds in Hosea have consequences. Indeed, it may be as we see hinted a number of times, that Yhwh has only to withdraw to see the perpetrators of injustice and rebellion swallowed by death. The consequences are bound to their deeds; the wages of sin is a falling into *das Nachtige* entirely, apart from Yhwh's saving presence. But what we find is a God unwilling to sit and see the land and people live (and so die) in that reality. "Yhwh's goal is always salvation" (Stettler 2011: 269). The punishment of sin in the prophets comes as retribution, as has long been pointed out. That which was done is brought back upon the offender; we see that in the rhetoric, the wordplays, and the careful manner in which we have a "fittingness" between the crime and the punishment (at least in ancient Levantine terms). But it makes far better sense to imagine the deed "brought back" in O'Donovan's terms: as an answer for the wrong, not an echo. It may be that punishments for adultery come in terms of expected stripping of rights and rewards (cf. Huehnergard 1985) and so fit legal expectations. But even here we miss much if we assume retribution (even in other Levantine texts) to live apart from the pursuit of a rightly ordered world (*Weltordnung*). The punishment is not its own end, but justice—the world set right—is the end. Retribution answers rather than echoes. The punishment for the infidelity answers the infidelity, exposing its truth. Yhwh does not echo infidelity with infidelity, wrong with wrong; he answers the betrayal within his passionate pursuit of fidelity and justice in his land.

Kingship is the most relevant metaphor for holding all of these matters together as they come to expression in Hosea's rhetoric. Ancient Levantine kings were responsible for justice as the pursuit of a rightly ordered world, in terms of cultic, economic, and sociopolitical order. Kings were to bring about justice as representatives and the "right-hand" of the god(s), including through exercise of judgment against the wrongdoers and rebels. The image of Yhwh as true or absolute King of kings in Israel was widespread and offers the perfect format for understanding Hosea in terms of the ancient Levant. Hosea presents us with a king confronting the desperately disordered world of his kingdom.

Yhwh comes onto the scene as a king pursuing justice. Yhwh wants a kingdom where righteousness, justice, steadfast love, and mercy flourish (2:21 [Eng. 2:19]), and he wants loyalty so that he is the tree from which the people pluck their blessing (14:9 [Eng. 14:8]).

The theological portrait is not of a deity abstractly interested in moral concerns, nor one who punishes out of insistence that matters be handled "just so" lest he lose his temper. It is not even a portrait of a deity cold and unyielding in the dispensing of "justice" in terms of orderly legal or moral ledgers, dispensing whatever suffering might fit the particular wrong. The theological portrait is a deity who looks on his land, sees injustice spreading, and acts (with sword drawn) to end that injustice. As their king, Yhwh interposes himself between his people and their headlong pursuit of what ends in *das Nachtige*. Hosea, as we have it, was gathered and passed down for the sake of future generations within that theological-sociological reality called "Yhwh's people." Future generations were to imagine themselves under the eye and the care of a king above their own kings, who will not sit idly by unmoved and uncaring about rebellion and injustice. This king is jealous for justice and loyalty so that his land and people might flourish. Israel's king acts to set his kingdom right, to the harm of those who give themselves to death and to the hope of those who suffer.

REFERENCES

Artus, O. 2004. "'Droit et Justice' comme fondements de la Loi: Un lieu de 'discontinuité entre la théologie de la Torah et les textes du Proche-Orient Ancien." In *Le Jugement dans l'un et l'autre Testament I: Mèlanges offerts à Raymond Kuntzmann*. Paris: Cerf, 19–32.

Assmann, J. 2001. *Ma'at: Gerechtigkeit und Unsterblichkeit im Alten Ägypten*. 3rd ed. Munich: C.H. Beck.

Baines, J. 2013. "Ancient Egyptian Kingship: Official Forms, Rhetoric, Context." In John Day, ed., *King and Messiah in Israel and the Ancient Near East: Proceedings of the Oxford Old Testament Seminar*. London: Bloomsbury, 16–53.

Barth, K. 2010. *Church Dogmatics*. 14 vols. G.W. Bromiley and T. F. Torrance, trans. Grand Rapids, MI: Hendrickson.

Brandenburger, E. 1991. "Gerichtskonzeptionem im Urchristentum und ihre Voraussetzungen: Eine Problemstudie." *SNTU* 16: 5–54.

Brandenburger, E. 1993. *Studien zur Geschichte und Theologie des Urchristentums*. SBAB 15. Stuttgart: Verlag Katholik Bibelwerk.

Eichrodt, W. 1961 (orig. 1933). *Theology of the Old Testament: Volume One*. London: SCM.

French, N. 2021. *A Theocentric Interpretation of* ורע טוב הדעת: *The Knowledge of Good and Evil as the Knowledge for Administering Reward and Punishment*. Vandenhoeck & Ruprecht.

Flynn, S. W. 2014. *YHWH Is King: The Development of Divine Kingship in Ancient Israel*. VTSup 159. Leiden: Brill.

Groeneweld, A. 2002. "Psalm 69:23a–30b and Divine Retribution: A Question of *Ma'at*?" *OTE* 15.3: 657–74.

Gruber, M. I. 2017. *Hosea: A Textual Commentary*. London: Bloomsbury.

Huehnergard, J. 1985. "Biblical Notes on Some New Akkadian Texts from Emar (Syria)." *CBQ* 47: 428–34.

Huffmon, H. B. 1966. "The Treaty Background of Hebrew yāda." *BASOR* 181: 31–37.

Janowski, B. 2000. "Gericht Gottes. II. Altes Testament." *RGG 3.* Tübingen: Mohr Siebeck: 733–34.

Kelle, B. E. 2005. *Hosea 2: Metaphor and Rhetoric in Historical Perspective.* SBLAB 20. Atlanta: SBL.

Kitchen, K. A., and P. J. N. Lawrence. 2012. *Treaty, Law, and Covenant in the Ancient Near East.* 3 vols. Wiesbaden: Herrasowitz.

Koch, K. 1955. "Gibt es ein Vergeltugsdogma im Alten Testament?" *ZTK* 52: 1–42.

Lambert, W.G. 2013. "Kingship in Ancient Mesopotamia." In John Day, ed., *King and Messiah in Israel and the Ancient Near East: Proceedings of the Oxford Old Testament Seminar.* London: Bloomsbury, 54–70.

Lang, B. 1983. *Monotheism and the Prophetic Minority: An Essay in Biblical History and Sociology.* Sheffield: Almond.

Lohfink, N. 1961. "Zu Text und Form von Os 4:4–6." *Biblica* 42: 308–11.

Maul, S. M. 1998. "Der assyrische König: Hüter der Weltordnung." In Jan Assmann, Bernd Janowski, and Michael Welker, eds., *Gerechtigkeit: Richten und Retten in der abendländischen Tradition und ihren altorientalischen Ursprüngen.* Munich: Wilhelm Fink, 65–78.

Mettinger, T. 1982. "YHWH as Sabaoth, the Heavenly King on the Earthly Throne." In T. Ishida, ed., *Studies in the Period of David and Solomon and Other Essays.* Winona Lake, IN: Eisenbrauns, 109–38.

Miller, P. D., Jr. 1982. *Sin and Judgment in the Prophets: A Stylistic and Theological Analysis.* SBLMS 27. Chico, CA: Scholars.

Moon, J. N. 2015. "Honor and Shame in Hosea's Marriages." *JSOT* 39.3: 335–51.

Müller, K. 1994. "Gott als Richter und die Erscheinungsweisen seiner Gerichte in den Schriften des Frühjüdentums: Methodische und grundsätzliche Vorübergegangen zu einer sachgemäßeren Einschätzung." In H.-J. Klauck, ed., *Weltgericht und Welvolendung: Zukunftsbilder im Neuen Testament.* Freiburg-Basel-Wien: Herder: 23–53.

O'Donovan, O. 1999. *Desire of the Nations: Rediscovering the Roots of Political Theology.* Cambridge: Cambridge University Press.

Parpola, S., ed. 1993. *Letters from Assyrian and Babylonian Scholars.* SAA 10. Helsinki: Helsinki University Press.

Parpola, S., and K. Watanabe, eds. 1988. *Neo-Assyrian Treaties and Loyalty Oaths.* SAA 2. Helsinki: Helsinki University Press.

Peels, E. 1995. *The Vengeance of God: The Meaning of the Root NQM and the Function of the NQM-Texts in the Context of Divine Revelation in the Old Testament.* Leiden: Brill.

Rawls, J. 1999. "Two Concepts of Rules." In Samuel Freeman, ed., *John Rawls: Collected Papers.* Cambridge, MA: Harvard University Press, 20–46.

Schmid, H. H. 1968. *Gerechtigkeit als Weltordnung: Hintergrund und Geschichte des alttestamentlichen Gerechtigkeitsbegriffes.* BHT 40. Tübingen: Mohr Siebeck.

Stettler, C. 2011. *Das letzte Gericht: Studien zur Endgerichtserwartung von den Schriftpropheten bis Jesus.* WUNT 299. Tübingen: Mohr Siebeck.

Tucker, G. 1997. "Sin and 'Judgment" in the Prophets." In H. T. C. Sun and K. L. Eades, with J. M. Robinson and G. I. Moller, eds., *Problems in Biblical Theology: Essays in Honor of Rolf Knierim.* Grand Rapids: Eerdmans, 373–88.

Vannoy, R. J. 1996. "Retribution: Theology of." *NIDOTTE* 4: 1140–49.

Vogt, P. T. 2006. *Deuteronomic Theology and the Significance of Torah: A Reappraisal*. Grand Rapids: Eisenbrauns.

Von Rad, G. 1962. *Old Testament Theology*. Edinburgh: Oliver and Boyd.

Wong, K. L. 2001. *The Idea of Retribution in the Book of Ezekiel*. Leiden: Brill.

Wüthrich, M. 2021. "An Entirely Different 'Theodicy': Karl Barth's Interpretation of Human Suffering in the Context of His Doctrine of *das Nichtige*." *IJST* 23.4: 593–616.

CHAPTER 21

....

REPENTANCE IN THE BOOK OF HOSEA

....

MARK J. BODA

21.1. INTRODUCTION

THE theme of repentance refers to a dynamic evident throughout the Hebrew Bible in which there is relational estrangement or repair.[1] The language of "turning" is thus often employed, highlighting the shift that occurs in the relationship. This shift is frequently expressed using Hebrew verbs like הפך, סור/שׁור, שׁוב, and פנה and their cognate nouns. That relationship lies at the core of the theme is seen in the summary of the prophetic message in Zech. 1:3: "Return to me (Yhwh), so that I may return to you." Connected with this relational dynamic are certain behaviors, whether moral, ritual, or verbal, and there is concern for authenticity which involves the fullness of human engagement. Hosea is filled with this theme from beginning to end as the relationship between Yhwh and the nation of Israel (and, at times, Judah) is explored in great detail, often highlighting pain and estrangement in that relationship but also hope and restoration of that relationship.[2] As Marvin Sweeney writes, "The book of Hosea is formulated to call for Israel's return and the restoration of its relationship with YHWH" (Sweeney 2000: 7). The approach here considers the vocabulary and imagery associated with relational shifts in both human and divine partners and the strategies provided for restoration of relationship.[3]

21.2. VOCABULARY OF REPENTANCE IN HOSEA

Hosea uses the vocabulary that dominates the theme of repentance within the Hebrew Bible in general and the prophets in particular, employing the verb שׁוב (to return) and its related cognate מְשׁוּבָה (going back) throughout (Hos. 2:9 [Eng. 2:7], 11 [Eng. 2:9]; 3:5; 4:9; 5:4, 15; 6:1; 7:10, 16; 8:13; 9:3; 11:5, 9; 12:3 [Eng. 12:2], 7 [Eng. 12:6], 15 [Eng. 12:14]; 14:2 [Eng. 14:1], 3 [Eng. 14:2], 5 [Eng. 14:4], 8 [Eng. 14:7]), as well as the verbs סור/שׁור (to turn aside; Hos. 2:4 [Eng. 2:2], 19 [Eng. 2:17]; 7:14; 9:12), הפך (to turn/change; Hos. 11:8), and פנה (to return; Hos. 3:1). The use of this vocabulary is varied, highlighting the complicated nature of relational repair throughout Hosea.

This vocabulary is associated with both the deity and the people and in both negative and positive ways—that is, it can refer to either party turning away from or turning back to the other. At times, it is the people who are returning to the deity, whether that is depicted as a failure at present (שׁוב: 5:4; 7:10, 16), commanded as a response in the present (שׁוב: 6:1; 12:7 [Eng. 12:6]; 14:2 [Eng. 14:1], 3 [Eng. 14:2]), or envisioned as a hope in the future (שׁוב: 3:5). Hosea 2:9 (Eng. 2:7), however, shows that there are forms of returning (שׁוב) to relationship with the deity that are deemed insincere. Sometimes the people are depicted as turning away from Yhwh, usually to other deities (פנה: 3:1; סור: 7:14; מְשׁוּבָה: 11:7). But there is a turning away which can be positive for Israel's relationship with Yhwh, a turning away from inappropriate relationships (סור Hiph: 2:4 [Eng. 2:2]). There is a form of Israel's return in Hosea that expresses divine punishment for their sin—that is, a return to Egypt (שׁוב: 8:13; 9:3; 11:5). While this use of return is not repentance, the connection to repentance is made clear in 11:5 as the prophet ties such a return to Egypt to Israel's refusal to repent (שׁוב). The opposite is also true since Hos. 14:8 (Eng. 14:7) describes the people's return (שׁוב) to abundance at the end of a section calling Israel to repentance and depicting Yhwh's promise to heal their apostasy. The divine promise in the end is to heal the people's waywardness (מְשׁוּבָה) in Hos. 14:5 (Eng. 14:4), which assumes that such waywardness was the basic orientation of the community.

The vocabulary of repentance, however, is also linked to the deity, not surprisingly since this relationship involves two partners. In Hos. 9:12, Yhwh uses the vocabulary of turning as he warns of the judgment coming upon Ephraim: "Indeed also woe to them, when I turn away (שׁור[4] from them." In contrast, 11:8 expresses Yhwh's struggle with bringing judgment, declaring how his heart is changed (הפך Niphal) within him, which leads him not to carry out his fierce anger nor return (שׁוב) to devastating Ephraim (11:9). Similarly in 14:5 (Eng. 14:4), Yhwh speaks of his anger turning away (שׁוב Qal) from Israel. Yhwh promises to do a work among the people in 2:19 (Eng. 2:17), a divine initiative that will remove (סור Hiphil) the names of false gods from their lips.

This overview of vocabulary associated with the shift in relationship between Israel and Yhwh highlights the key tension within the book. Other vocabulary, however, is associated with these depictions of and calls to relational shifts. Love is key to understanding the restoration of relationship in the book of Hosea.[5] Initially, love is expressed by Yhwh through the semantic range of the verb רחם Piel (have compassion; 1:6, 7; 2:6 [Eng. 2:4], 25 [Eng. 2:23]; 14:5 [Eng. 14:4]) and its cognates (רֻחָמָה, loved one: 2:3 [Eng. 2:1]; רַחֲמִים, compassion: 2:21 [Eng. 2:19]), as well as the name of the second child born to Hosea and Gomer (לֹא רֻחָמָה, Lo-Ruhamah: 1:6, 8). These words are all associated with

Yhwh's love for or removal of love from Israel.[6] Beginning with Hos. 2, the verb אהב (Qal, Piel), along with one of its cognates (אַהֲבָה), is also used. These verbs and noun express the love of Yhwh toward Israel in terms of familial relationships: first, Israel as a wife (3:1) and later as a child (11:1, 4). In Hos. 9:15, Yhwh not only declares, "I will no longer love them" (Ephraim), based on their sinful deeds committed at Gilgal, but also that he "hated them" (שׂנא), the polar opposite. Hosea 13:14b speaks of hiding "compassion" (נחם) from Yhwh's eyes. But then in 14:5 (Eng. 14:4), Yhwh provides concluding hope by promising to love them even as he heals their apostasy and turns his anger away from them. This vocabulary of love signals the key shift in the relational dynamic between Yhwh and Israel, one that begins with the love of Yhwh for the people (3:1; 11:1, 4), leads to a removal of that love (1:6, 8; 2:6 [Eng. 2:4]; 9:15), and ends with a renewal of love (2:3 [Eng. 2:1], 21 [Eng. 2:19], 25 [Eng. 2:23];14:5 [Eng. 14:4]).

While the vocabulary related to the verb רחם (to have compassion) and its cognates is only connected with the love expressed by Yhwh, the vocabulary related to the verb אהב (to love) and its cognates is used to describe the love expressed by both Yhwh and Israel. In contrast to the deity, though, whose love is always directed toward Israel, Israel's love is always directed toward entities other than Yhwh (2:7 [Eng. 2:5], 9 [Eng. 2:7], 12 [Eng. 2:10], 14 [Eng. 2:12], 15 [Eng. 2:13]; 3:1; 4:18 [love shameful ways]; 9:1, 10; cf. 12:8 [Eng. 12:7]).[7] The vocabulary of love again helps the reader see the relational dynamic between the deity and the people and highlights the shifting orientation of both divine and human partners.

This study of the vocabulary associated with relational shifts between the deity and people in Hosea lays a foundation for more specific analysis of these relational shifts within the book. I turn now to specific activities and images associated with relational shifts—first, those connected with the people turning away and then turning back to Yhwh, and second, those connected with the deity turning away and then turning back to the community.

21.3. ISRAEL

The language of repentance is first of all associated with the nation of Israel, both in terms of turning away and turning back to Yhwh.

21.3.1. Activities and Images of Israel Turning Away from Yhwh

Hosea uses a breadth of lexical stock to typify the nation turning away from Yhwh. One finds the range of words related to sin in Hebrew, whether sin (חַטָּאת 4:8; 8:13; 9:9; 13:12;), 10:9 חטא), guilt/iniquity (עָוֹן 5:5; 8:13; 9:7, 9; 10:10; 13:12; 14:2 [Eng. 14:1]), guilt (אשׁם:

14:1; 5:15 [Eng. 13:16]), rebellion (14:10; 7:13 פשע [Eng. 14:9]), evil (7:2 רָעָה; 7:15 רַע; 9:15 רֹע; 10:15; 9:15; 3), wickedness (10:13 רֶשַׁע), injustice (10:9 עַוְלָה, 13), or evil deeds (9:15; 7:2 מַעֲלָל). Forgetfulness is key at various points throughout the book (2:15 שׁכח [Eng. 2:13]; 4:6; 13:6). The people reject knowledge (4:6 מאס), deal treacherously (בגד: 5:7), and stray away from Yhwh (11:12 רוד; 7:13 נדד). Ubiquitous in the opening three chapters of the book, the language of promiscuity is often employed in the rest of the book (זנה 4:10, 18; 5:3; 9:1; זְנוּת 4:11; 6:10; זְנוּנִים 5:3),[8] and connected with this is the language of adultery (7:4 נאף), betrayal (בגד: 5:7; 6:7), abandonment (עזב, 4:10), and covenant breaking (6:7).

While the language of relational shift away from Yhwh covered so far is more general in nature, at times specific acts of apostasy are mentioned in Hosea. Illicit religious activities top the list. In places, the activity focuses on the worship of Baal(s) (2:10 [Eng. 2:8], 18 [Eng. 2:16]; 9:10; 11:2; 13:1), and in others, calf idols (8:5, 6; 10:5; 13:2)[9] or idols in general (3:4; 4:12, 17; 5:11; 8:4; 11:2; 13:2; 14:8 [Eng. 14:7]).[10] There is concern over certain sacred rituals like sacrifice (3:4; 4:13, 14, 19; 6:6; 8:11; 10:1, 2; 12:12 [Eng. 12:11]; even human sacrifice: 13:2), burning incense (11:2), slashing oneself (7:14),[11] eating raisin cakes (3:1),[12] erecting sacred pillars (3:4; 10:1, 2; cf. Deut. 16:22), and consulting the ephod (3:4; cf. Exod. 25:7 with Judg. 8:27) or a diviner's staff (4:12). While these activities highlight the trust of the community in religious entities other than Yhwh, there are also indications that the community's trust was placed in nonreligious sources both internal and external to Israel. Internally, they looked to royal figures (3:4; 8:4; 13:10) or their own military prowess (10:13). Externally, they looked to foreign nations like Egypt (12:1 [Eng. 11:12]) and especially Assyria (5:13; 8:9; 10:6; 12:2 [Eng. 12:1]; 14:4 [Eng. 14:3]). But there are other dysfunctions evident in the community, involving injustice such as cursing, lying, murder, stealing, adultery, bloodshed, false charges, manipulation of boundaries, fraud, bribery (4:2, 4; 5:2, 5, 10; 6:8, 9; 7:1; 10:4; 12:1 [Eng. 11:12], 2 [Eng. 11:1], 8 [Eng. 11:7], 15 [Eng. 11:14]). In a couple of instances, the arrogance of the community is highlighted (7:10; 13:6).

Images are also important to the depiction of relational shifts in the book of Hosea. The initial imagery of the book appears in the opening three chapters that depict relational shifts in terms of the relationship between adult males and females. Children are employed as part of the imagery, but largely at this stage used to depict the shifts in relationship between their parents.[13] Hosea 1:2 identifies Gomer as a promiscuous woman and adulterous wife, and links her to the nation guilty of marital unfaithfulness to Yhwh. This depiction continues into ch. 2, which links the mother and wife to adultery (2:4 [Eng. 2:2], 7 [Eng. 2:5]), now depicted as pursuing and relying on "lovers" to provide her sustenance and related to other gods (see 2:10 [Eng. 2:8], 15 [Eng. 2:13], 19 [Eng. 2:17]). The activity of the metaphorical unfaithful woman in Hos. 3 can be implicitly discerned from 3:4 in the list provided: king, prince, sacrifice, sacred pillars, ephod, household gods. Whereas the earlier depiction in Hos. 2 focused on Israel's reliance on illegitimate deities or means of worship, Hos. 3 focuses on Israel's dependence on their own royal and priestly resources, whether legitimate or illegitimate, rather than Yhwh.

Other images also appear in Hosea for the relational shift of the community away from Yhwh. Hosea 4:16 uses the image of a stubborn cow to typify Israel's lack of fidelity to Yhwh, contrasting it with the much smaller lamb trained to feed in a meadow. This image appears within a text referring to illicit activities at various northern shrines. The comparison of the quickly dissipating morning fog/early dew with the "steadfast love" (חֶסֶד) of Ephraim and Judah in Hos. 6:4 highlights the fickle nature of Israel's relational connection with Yhwh. This contrasts with the people's expectation of Yhwh's faithful appearance using the images of dawn as well as autumn and spring rains in the previous verse (see below).

In 7:4–7 the image of a hot oven is used to describe the apostasy of the people. This image is related to wicked activity of leaders within the community, which includes injustice (v. 1) and adultery (v. 4, whether unfaithfulness to Yhwh or their partners) that at first delights the king (v. 3), but ultimately leads to his demise (v. 7). The language of a burning fire that grows in intensity throughout the night suggests enduring activity that is encouraged by the royal house. The key violation in view is expressed in the final phrase: "none of them calls on me" (7:7). The image of the baker mentioned in the oven metaphor of 7:4 is then applied to Ephraim as a whole, whose mixing with the nations is compared to a "flat loaf not turned over" (7:8). The mixing with the nations, indicating the nation's compromising political alliances, may introduce the image of the loaf, drawing on the process of mixing dough with oil and connected with the griddle described in the Torah (Exod. 29:2; Lev. 2:5; cf. Wolff 1974: 126). The loaf is in view in the second half of v. 8, describing an "unturned cake that burns left too long on the side of the oven" (Sweeney 2000: 80). The consequences are clear in what follows in v. 9 as foreigners consume the nation's strength since Israel is arrogant and refuses to return to Yhwh and seek him (v. 10).

The image of the dove follows immediately in 7:11, depicted as "clueless" and without any inner fortitude (heart) as it vacillates between reliance on Egypt and Assyria rather than Yhwh. In 7:16, the people's lack of repentance, here including lack of reliance on Yhwh, results in the comparison to a "slack bow," referring to a weapon that is not pulled taut and so is useless in the hand of a warrior for any protection against the foreign nations. The farming image of 8:7 is used to refer to receiving back a harvest of windy destruction that has grown beyond what they have sown, a reference to their apostasy.

In 9:1, Israel is depicted as a prostitute who receives wages on the threshing floor.[14] In 10:4, the people's abusive injustice in the courts is likened to poisonous plants sprouting on a furrowed field. In 10:11–13, the agricultural image continues as Ephraim is first compared to a cow trained to thresh, while Judah and Jacob are likened to a cow trained to harrow. This should lead to sowing righteousness, reaping steadfast love, breaking up unplowed ground through seeking Yhwh, who promises showers. Such positive behavior is not forthcoming, however, as instead the nation has planted wickedness, reaped evil, and eaten deceptive produce.

The image of Israel as the child of Yhwh in Hos. 11 makes clear the connection between the vocabulary of love and repentance reviewed above. It begins by highlighting the love expressed by Yhwh at the outset of Israel's history (11:1, 4). This love was not

308   MARK J. BODA

reciprocated by Israel, who "went away from me" (11:2),[15] which leads to Yhwh's concern that they will experience a reversal of the exodus due to their refusal to repent (11:5, 7). The passage goes on to expose the passionate turmoil within the deity, who has a change of heart and envisions a day when Israel will follow Yhwh and return to their homes (11:10–11). The emphasis in this passage is on the early pattern of Israel's apostasy (turning away) and yet Yhwh's consistent prioritizing of love and compassion for his people. The only hope for relational wholeness lies with Yhwh and his undeserving grace for a recalcitrant people.

Hosea 12 employs the image of Jacob, that patriarchal figure who represents Israel as a nation. The image begins with Jacob's birth (12:4 [Eng. 12:3]; cf. Gen. 25:26), then focuses on him wrestling with the heavenly figure at Bethel (12:4–5 [Eng. 12:3–4]; cf. Gen. 32:24–29; 35:15) before relating the tradition of Jacob fleeing to Paddan-Aram and acquiring a wife (12:13 [Eng. 12:12]; cf. Gen. 28:5; 29). The book of Hosea uses this image to highlight Israel's struggle with both Yhwh and humanity (12:4 [Eng. 12:3]), and this struggle is what justifies divine punishment (12:3 [Eng. 12:2]), even though it will become a pattern for renewal (see below). In Hos. 13:13, Ephraim is likened to a child within its mother's womb, but when the time for birth arrives, it does not enter into the birth canal.[16] The pain associated with this moment of childbirth may relate to the discipline Yhwh dispensed, which could have led to a new life but instead resulted in death (v. 14).

These passages provide a breadth of powerful language and images that capture the attention of the reader in order to fully grasp the condition of this apostate nation.

21.3.2. Activities and Images of Israel Turning Back to Yhwh

Depictions of the positive relational shift of the people back to Yhwh are more limited in the book of Hosea, but still significant. The ideal future picture of a penitential Israel will involve seeking (בקש Piel) Yhwh, as well as trembling (פחד) before him (3:5). The same verb for seeking (בקש Piel) appears alongside the failure to shift (שוב) in 7:10. Seeking Yhwh is key to the renewal envisioned after exile in 5:15 (בקש Piel, שחר Piel) and the ideal that Yhwh desired when choosing Israel (דרש, 10:12). There is a link between repentance and "knowing" (ידע) in 6:1–3. To "know" should be understood in a relational rather than cognitive sense, since it is often used in connection with the covenant between Yhwh and Israel (Boda 2009: 249–50, 289, 298). Knowing (ידע) and returning (שוב) to Yhwh are aligned also in 5:4. Hosea 7:14 refers to the ideal of Israel crying out (זעק) to Yhwh from their hearts (לב), while 10:3 mentions revering (ירא) Yhwh. The call to "return to your God" in 12:7 (Eng. 12:6) is linked to other actions in the clauses that follow. First, returning involves activities on the horizontal (fellow human) relational level with calls to maintain (שמר) steadfast love (חסד) and justice (משפט). Second, returning also involves the vertical (Yhwh) relational level with the call to wait (קוה Piel) for Yhwh. Returning (שוב) to Yhwh in 14:2–4 (Eng. 14:1–3) involves verbal expression ("take with you words"), and the words provided admit sin, request forgiveness, eschew reliance on Assyria and other gods, and express trust in Yhwh.

The book of Hosea also employs multiple images to depict this positive relational shift back to Yhwh. While 2:9 (Eng. 2:7) depicts Israel as a woman returning insincerely to her husband, in 2:16–18 (Eng. 2:14–16), Israel is a woman who responds to the advances of the male deity.[17] Hosea 3:3 speaks of a woman living in faithful relationship with a man, with emphasis on sexual exclusivity. The image of the trained cow in a yoke used in 10:11 for the ideal hope of Israel producing a crop aligned with Yhwh's priorities (righteousness, steadfast love) relates to seeking Yhwh. Hosea 11:10–11 compares the future returning exilic community to trembling birds, possibly describing their reverence for Yhwh (cf. 3:5). The final verse of Hosea (14:10 [Eng. 14:9]) contrasts the righteous and the rebellious in terms of their connection to the "straight ways of Yhwh," with the righteous walking on them while the rebellious stumble.

21.4. Yhwh

The language of repentance is secondly associated with Yhwh, again in terms of turning away and turning back to Israel.

21.4.1. Activities and Images of Yhwh Turning Away from Israel

The book of Hosea not only depicts the relational shifts displayed by Israel, but also describes Yhwh turning away from Israel. Descriptions often note various judgments that Yhwh will send upon the nation, especially with the language of punishment, discipline, repayment, or rejection (e.g., 2:15 [Eng. 2:13]; 4:6, 9; 5:1, 2, 6; 8:13; 9:7, 9, 17; 10:10; 12:3 [Eng. 12:2], 15 [Eng. 12:14]). The judgment will affect the land of Israel physically, ruining its produce (e.g., 2:11 [Eng. 2:9], 14 [Eng. 2:12]; 5:7) and rendering it useless for sustaining life (e.g., 2:5 [Eng. 2:3]; 4:3; 5:9). There will be defeat in war (1:5; 10:9–10, 14; 11:6; 13:16), including destruction of cities (8:14; 10:14), removal of leadership (10:7, 15; 11:6; 13:10), experiences of hunger (4:10) and bondage (10:10). Furthermore, Yhwh will destroy their religious infrastructure, including altars, sacred pillars, and high places (10:2, 8; 12:12 [Eng. 12:11]). At several points, the language of relational shift speaks of Yhwh's treatment of children, a shocking image. Hosea 9:11–16 depicts Yhwh bereaving the people of their children by slaying them, hindering mothers from conceiving or giving birth, and drying up their breasts (cf. 10:14; 13:16). At times, the emotion underlying these divine actions is revealed: Yhwh's anger burns against the rebellious people (5:10; 8:5; 12:15 [Eng. 12:14]; 13:11; cf. 11:9; 14:5 [Eng. 14:4]).

Some images serve to capture the imagination. In the midst of the marriage metaphor of chs. 1–3, Yhwh threatens to strip his spouse and expose her nakedness as if she was a new-born baby (2:5 [Eng. 2:3]; cf. 2:11 [Eng. 2:9]), an action which would have brought shame to this woman representing the nation.[18] Within the same metaphorical context, Yhwh speaks of rejecting the children of this woman because of their illegitimacy (2:6–7 [Eng. 2:4–5]; cf. 4:6). Hosea 5:10–15 provides a series of images for Yhwh's relational shift: "a flashflood of water" (5:10),[19] "moth" and "rot" (5:12),[20] and finally "a lion" describing "the stages of a lion's successful hunt: capture, killing, and dragging away" (5:14–15; cf. 6:1) (Dearman 2010: 186). In 7:12, Yhwh is a hunter who captures birds, fitting for Israel, which is likened to a senseless dove in 7:11. Hosea 13:7–8 returns to the images of land predators (lion, leopard, bear), all of whom violently attack their prey. And finally, 13:15 depicts Yhwh as the dry eastern winds from the desert devoid of life-giving water from the west and the Mediterranean.

21.4.2. Activities and Images of Yhwh Turning Back to Israel

The book of Hosea also presents Yhwh's relational shift toward Israel. The initial image is drawn from relational dynamics between a man and a woman. Yhwh speaks of his tender courting behavior in 2:16 (Eng. 2:14), leading his bride into the wilderness, a place associated with their first love after the Exodus. There he entices her (cf. Exod. 22:15; Judg. 14:15; 6:5, 29) and speaks tenderly to her (see below). This courtship is followed by betrothal leading to an enduring faithful relationship (2:21–22 [Eng. 2:19–20]). The wilderness image reappears in Hos. 13:5, which speaks of Yhwh caring for and feeding the people. Agricultural imagery is used in 2:25 (Eng. 2:23) as Yhwh sows Israel in the land. Hosea 6:3 uses the creation imagery of the sun and rain to typify Yhwh's relational stance toward his people, even if the failure of the nation will frustrate this hope. The imagery of rain also appears in 10:12, which speaks of Yhwh showering his righteous salvation on the people. Familial language reemerges in ch. 11, and there Yhwh's parental activity not only includes his love, training, and leading of the infant Israel (11:1–4), but also his consistent calling to Israel as a wandering child (11:1). While the lion image was used to depict Yhwh's relational shift away from Israel (see above), 11:10 employs it for Yhwh's rescue of his children from exile. Yhwh is depicted as a healer, first in 7:1 and then in 14:5 (Eng. 14:4). The closing section of Hosea likens Yhwh to the life-giving water of dew (14:6 [Eng. 14:5]), as well as to "a leafy juniper" (14:9 [Eng. 14:8]) from which Israel can draw its fruitfulness. Emotions connected with Yhwh's shift toward Israel are mentioned on a couple of occasions. In 11:8, the anger that had dominated his stance toward Israel is replaced by his compassion which has been aroused. Similarly, 14:5 (Eng. 14:4) speaks of Yhwh's anger being turned away as he now loves the nation.

21.5. STRATEGIES FOR REPAIRING THE RELATIONSHIP

One final issue to investigate is the way the book of Hosea envisions renewal of the relationship between Yhwh and Israel. The book describes strategies that remind the reader of the complicated nature of reconciliation.

Hosea 1 introduces the reader to the image world that will continue through ch. 3—namely, the relational dynamics between a man and a woman which involved the production of children.[21] In the initial chapter, the prophet is commanded to marry the woman Gomer and have children with her, something Hosea does. The first child, a son (Jezreel), is related to the prophet and becomes a sign of the coming judgment of the Jehu dynasty. The second and third children (a girl, Lo-Ruhamah; a boy, Lo-Ammi) are not specifically tied to the prophet,[22] and both spell disaster for Israel, emphasizing first the removal of Yhwh's tender love for Israel, while providing enduring hope for Judah, and then the loss of Israel's status as Yhwh's "people," a statement about covenant rupture (1:9: "for you are not my people and I am not your God"). The judgment against the Jehu dynasty expressed through the birth of the first child (Jezreel) is linked to "the massacre at Jezreel" (v. 4),[23] while the judgment against Israel expressed through the births of the two subsequent children is linked to as of yet unmentioned sinful acts implicitly expressed through the reference to forgiving them (v. 6). The conclusion of the passage 2:1–3 (Eng. 1:10–2:1) shifts to future promise, looking to an era when Israel will be renewed, return to the land, and both the "Lo-Ammi" (2:1 [Eng. 1:10]) and "Lo-Ruhamah" (2:3 [Eng. 2:1]) destinies will be reversed as Israel joins Judah under "one leader." The process depicted here provides no space for human response. It simply declares judgment and then looks to a day when the situation will be reversed.

Hosea 2 provides more details on Yhwh's strategy for restoring the relationship with his covenant partner Israel, again using the image world of a relationship between a man and a promiscuous woman. Having focused on the children of the woman in Hos. 1, Hos. 2 begins by addressing those children before speaking about them with the focus on their mother. The initial tactic for restoration of relationship in 2:4–6 (Eng. 2:2–4) is a warning relayed through Israel's children. This is followed in 2:7–10 (Eng. 2:5–8) by Yhwh restricting her movements (2:8 [Eng. 2:6]), frustrating her plans to connect with her illicit lovers (2:9 [Eng. 2:7]). This appears to have some success in light of the words attributed to the woman: "I will go back to my husband as at the beginning, for it was better for me then than now" (2:9 [Eng. 2:7]).[24] But 2:10 (Eng. 2:8) reveals that she does not recognize Yhwh as her provider. This lack of recognition is what prompts the third tactic of Yhwh (2:11–15 [Eng. 2:9–13]), which entails disciplining her by removing those provisions she attributed to her lovers, including grain, wine, and fabric for clothing, as well as the feasts associated with these provisions. The final tactic (2:16–25 [Eng. 2:14–23]) represents a significant shift from those which preceded. In contrast to earlier tactics, Yhwh promises to "court" Israel as he did once before in the wilderness, speaking tenderly to her (Gen. 34:3; Isa. 40:2) and restoring her fertile vineyards. Yhwh envisions a future positive response from Israel, one in which she will put away illicit worship and embrace Yhwh as her husband as they enter into an enduring relationship typified by the positive qualities of righteousness, justice, love, compassion, and faithfulness. Israel will then "know" (ידע) Yhwh. As noted earlier, this concluding focus on "knowing" is relational rather than merely cognitive, something made clear by the covenantal formula which concludes the chapter in 2:25 (Eng. 2:23): "I will say to the ones called 'Not my people': 'You are my people'; and he will say, 'You are my God.'" Overall, this chapter provides various tactics for relational repair: warning, restrictions, discipline, and courtship. Only the fourth tactic is seen as successful in this chapter, pointing to the need for a divine initiative that would surpass the earlier strategies.

Hosea 3 also provides a strategy for how Yhwh will restore relationship with Israel. The passage begins with a description of the unfaithfulness of the wife, identifying her as an adulteress who is loved by another man, which is connected with the Israelite worship of other gods and pagan practices (sacred raisin cakes).[25] The strategy involves the freeing of this unfaithful wife through payment and the invitation to a committed reciprocal relationship. This is then connected to a future period[26] when Israel will live without royal or religious impediments (v. 4) and afterward experience a renewal of the kingdom ruled by Yhwh and the Davidic king (v. 5). The final strategy in Hos. 2 is similar to that found in ch. 3, as both entail a divine initiative that involves a response of the people (cf. 2:17–18 [Eng. 2:15–16], 22 [Eng. 2:20], 25 [Eng. 2:23] with 3:3, 5).

Strategies seen in these opening chapters appear in the remainder of the book. Considerable emphasis is placed on divine judgment, as the nation turns away from Yhwh, which compels Yhwh to remove himself from them (5:6), and the day of rebuke is announced (5:8–9). At various points, opportunities or patterns for renewal can be discerned. Hosea 6:1–3 may contain a prophetic invitation to repentance in the wake of divine judgment, here employing cohortative forms ("let us return . . . let us know . . . let us pursue knowing") to invite a return to relationship, based on the trustworthy character of Yhwh compared to the patterns of sun and rain. However, what follows in 6:4–7:16 makes clear that while there is some form of response from the people that includes sacrifice (6:6) and wailing (7:14), it has no enduring (6:4) or authentic (7:14) character. Alongside this activity are continuing acts of injustice, misplaced trust in the nations, and idolatry (ch. 7).

An echo of the invitation to return to relationship also appears in Hos. 8:2: "Israel cries to me: 'Our God, we know you,'" but the prophet treats these as mere words, since on both sides of this citation the people's failure is rehearsed: "the people have broken my covenant; they have rebelled against my teaching" (8:1); "Israel has rejected that which is good" (8:3). In the wake of this failed return, the prophet consistently highlights the apostasy of the nation while declaring judgment (chs. 8–10).

Hosea 11 depicts the frustrating nature of divine strategies for relationship. Here Yhwh is depicted as loving Israel as a child, calling him forth from Egypt, teaching Ephraim to walk by holding his arms, healing him, leading him lovingly, caressing and feeding him (11:1–4). But this strategy backfires, as it only leads to the nation increasingly going astray (11:2) and not recognizing Yhwh as the source of this love (11:3). The only strategy appears to be judgment (11:5–7), but then a divine cry breaks in, expressing

Yhwh's overwhelming compassion for the nation which shows he will abandon plans for judgment (11:8–9). No details are provided on how this will be accomplished, but 11:10–11 provides an expectation that following such divine grace, the people will follow Yhwh and be released from captivity to return home.

The image of the patriarchal figure Jacob in Hos. 12 represents not only the apostasy of the nation but also the renewal of relationship. Through weeping (בכה) and seeking favor (חנן Hitpael), Jacob finds (מצא) Yhwh and speaks (דבר Piel) with him (12:5 [Eng. 12:4]). This appears to be a pattern for Israel's penitential response to Yhwh, suggested by the call in 12:7 (Eng. 12:6) to return (שוב) to God through acts of justice and the posture of trust. However, 12:8 (Eng. 12:7)–13:16 makes clear that the people do not embrace this model for repentance, and this leads to the experience of judgment (13:14b–16).

Hosea 14 concludes the book with a final strategy for renewal as Israel is called to return to Yhwh (14:2 [Eng. 14:1]) and to do so using words (14:3 [Eng. 14:2]). The words to be used ("say to him") in prayer begin in 14:3b (Eng. 14:2b) with the request, "Forgive all our guilt and bring goodness, so that we may repay with the sacrifices of our lips,"[27] before declaring their rejection of reliance on Assyria and manufactured gods (14:4 [Eng. 14:3]). This prompts a response from the deity, who promises healing of their apostasy, an abandonment of divine wrath, and a new era of flourishing in the land (14:5–9 [Eng. 14:4–8]). The concluding verse is a reminder of the need for actions that align with the ways of Yhwh (14:10 [Eng. 14:9]).

The book of Hosea presents various strategies for Israel to realize renewal of relationship with their God. Judgement dominates the book, but also various opportunities to repent and express repentance. At one point, the deity expresses discontent with judgment, gesturing to the ultimate need for divine grace to make the relationship possible. These strategies highlight the need for human responsibility to sustain the relational dynamics between the people and deity but also emphasize the need for divine intervention to "heal their waywardness and love them freely," as presented in the concluding section of the book (14:5 [Eng. 14:4]).

21.6. Hosea in the Twelve

Hosea functions in all ancient canonical traditions as the lead book among the Book of the Twelve (Minor Prophets).[28] Near the end of this collection, Zechariah underscores the importance of the theme of repentance to the prophetic tradition in the declaration: "Return to me, so that I may return to you" (Zech. 1:3; cf. Mal. 3:7).[29] In this summary of the message of the prophets, Zechariah emphasizes the relational dimension of repentance: it is a return first and foremost that involves relational partners. The follow-up summary of the earlier prophets in Zech. 1:4 is a reminder that the relational dimension cannot be divorced from the behavioral dimension ("Turn from your evil ways and from your evil deeds"), but the relational is prioritized. Hosea as the opening book of the Twelve powerfully depicts the message of penitence which will drive the agenda of the prophets. There will be moments of success, as we find in Joel (2:12–27) and Jonah (ch. 3), but generally the Twelve reveal the frustration with human ability to repent. As depicted so well in Hosea (see esp. chs. 11 and 14), hope lies ultimately with the divine partner, whose heart will be filled with compassion to forgive the community, lovingly care for them, and provide a healing touch to eliminate all waywardness.

NOTES

1. On the approach taken to repentance in this article, see further Boda 2015, as well as my initial foray in Boda 2009: 295–304.
2. The approach to Hosea taken in this article is one focused on the message of Hosea to its original audience and fits within the "cultic-religious interpretation" identified by Kelle (2009: 203), although without necessarily specific connections to sexual rituals. That there are socioeconomic and historical-political implications is also clear, but the focus in this article will be on the presentation of the relationship between deity and people (see further Nogalski 2011: 28–30). On the challenges of reading Hosea in our contemporary context, see Dempsey 2016: 40.
3. Noting especially Dempsey (2016: 37), who highlights Hosea's "vivid, metaphorical language"; see also Dearman (2010: 43) on how metaphor dominates Hosea's narrative theology.
4. This is a byform of the verb סור associated with penitence (see introduction above).
5. See the excellent discussion in Nogalski 2011: 28–29.
6. Nogalski (2011: 29) argues that "YHWH's fidelity to Israel is not in dispute, despite YHWH's threat to end the long-standing relationship with Israel." No matter how one handles this theological issue, the names of the children announce a clear shift in relationship.
7. In 3:1, this verb is used for the love of a person other than Yhwh for Israel.
8. On the connection between the language of prostitution and religion, see the helpful review in Kelle 2009: 204–6.
9. On the "calf" in Hosea, see Dearman 2010: 224–26. In view here is the Israelite cult established by Jeroboam I at Bethel (and Dan) as noted in 1–2 Kings (esp. 2 Kgs. 17:21–23; cf. Nogalski 2011: 119).
10. Whether this was related to the worship of other gods or worship of Yhwh through inappropriate means; see Kelle 2009: 206; 2010: 339–45. For a different interpretation of the references to Baal, see Kelle 2005.
11. Relying on some Hebrew manuscripts and the OG to read גדד Hitp (following Andersen and Freedman 1980: 475).
12. Relying on the OG for "raisin cakes"; see Macintosh 2014: 95. On their role in the cult, see below.
13. On the importance of the root metaphor of the "patrimonial household," see Dearman 2010: 10–13.
14. Possibly a reference to celebrations taking place in connection with the harvest season, see Gen. 38; Ruth 3. Dearman (2010: 236–37) notes, "Harvest season and threshing

activities provided a good setting for cultic practices associated with fertility," and also makes connections to ch. 2 (2:7 [Eng. 2:5], 14 [Eng. 2:12]).

15. Following the OG (ἐκ προσώπου μου αὐτοί) and redivision/repointing of the MT (מִפָּנַי הֵם); see BHS.

16. There is some debate over the meaning of these verses; here I follow Dearman 2010: 327–28; contra Macintosh 2014: 543–46.

17. See 2:22 (Eng. 2:20) for "knowing" Yhwh, which probably has sexual connotations; cf. Gen. 4:1; 19:8; Num. 31:17; Judg. 11:39; 21:12 (Macintosh 2014: 85).

18. On the debate over the social background of this image and its connection to divorce proceedings, see Kelle 2009: 194–95.

19. As Macintosh (2014: 202) states, "Yahweh will pour forth upon them, like the water of the flashfloods of Israel/Palestine, his fury (cf. Isa. 8.7; Jer. 14.16)."

20. This traditional translation has been challenged by Macintosh (2014: 207–8), who suggests these are words for diseases. But Job 13:28 treats these as similes and points to the moth as eating a garment. Sweeney (2000: 67) notes how such imagery "conveys the same slow and unseen deterioration" (cf. Dearman 2010: 185).

21. For the debate over the complicated portrayals in Hos. 1–3, see Kelle 2009 and Davies 1992: 105–9. For an approach that sees cohesion between the depictions in these chapters, see Routledge 2018.

22. Notice how v. 3 specifically uses the phrase "for him" (לוֹ), which is missing in vv. 6 and 8.

    Jezreel: "And she bore for him a son" (וַתַּהַר וַתֵּלֶד־לוֹ בֵּן, v. 3)
    Lo-Ruhamah: "And she conceived again and she bore a daughter" (וַתַּהַר עוֹד וַתֵּלֶד בַּת, v. 6)
    Lo-Ammi: "And she conceived and bore a son" (וַתַּהַר וַתֵּלֶד בֵּן)

    However, Macintosh (2014: 21) explains this as "natural economy of language in the report of the birth of a second and third child."

23. On the referent of "the massacre at Jezreel" see Dearman 2010: 92–94.

24. Wolff (1974: 36) notes that the language of "first husband" is the language of divorce initiated by the woman herself, and that Deut. 24:1–4 treats this as legally impossible. For the irony in this statement, see Sweeney 2000: 31.

25. For the connection between raisins and sexual love, see Song. 2:5, although they are related to more general gifts in 2 Sam. 6:19//1 Chr. 16:3. For the connection of cakes (using a different word) to religious rituals, see Jer. 7:18; 44:19 (cf. Macintosh 2014: 97–98).

26. Notice the use of "many days" in both vv. 3 and 4.

27. Here taking the MT "bulls" as referring to sacrifice; for debate, see Sweeney 2000: 138; cf. Dearman 2010: 338.

28. See the bibliography in Kelle 2010: 354. Dearman (2010: 100) notes how Hos. 1:2–9 introduces a problem that is resolved in the final verse of Malachi, which closes the Twelve.

29. On the importance of repentance to the Twelve as a whole, see House 2003, Boda 2011, and LeCureux 2012.

REFERENCES

Andersen, Francis I., and David Noel Freedman. 1980. *Hosea: A New Translation with Introduction and Commentary*. AB 24. New Haven, CT: Yale University. Press.

Boda, Mark J. 2009. *A Severe Mercy: Sin and Its Remedy in the Old Testament*. Siphrut 1. Winona Lake, IN: Eisenbrauns.

Boda, Mark J. 2011. "Penitential Innovations in the Book of the Twelve." In Brian A. Mastin, Katharine J. Dell, and James K. Aitken, eds., *On Stone and Scroll: A Festschrift for Graham Davies*. BZAW 420. Berlin: De Gruyter, 291–308.

Boda, Mark J. 2015. *"Return to Me": A Biblical Theology of Repentance*. New Studies in Biblical Theology. Leicester, UK: Apollos.Davies, Graham I. 1992. *Hosea*. New Century Bible. London, UK: Marshall Pickering.

Dearman, J. Andrew. 2010. *The Book of Hosea*. NICOT. Grand Rapids, MI; Cambridge, UK: Eerdmans.

Dempsey, Carol J. 2016. *Amos, Hosea, Micah, Nahum, Zephaniah, Habakkuk*. New Collegeville Bible Commentary. Old Testament 15. Collegeville, MN: Liturgical Press.

House, Paul R. 2003. "Endings as New Beginnings: Returning to the Lord, the Day of the Lord, and Renewal in the Book of the Twelve." In Aaron Schart and Paul Redditt, eds., *Thematic Threads in the Book of the Twelve*. BZAW 325. Berlin: de Gruyter, 313–38.

Kelle, Brad E. 2005. *Hosea 2: Metaphor and Rhetoric in Historical Perspective*. SBLAB 20. Atlanta: Society of Biblical Literature.

Kelle, Brad E. 2009. "Hosea 1–3 in Twentieth-Century Scholarship." *CBR* 7 (2): 179–216.Kelle, Brad E. 2010. "Hosea 4–14 in Twentieth-Century Scholarship." *CBR* 8 (3): 314–75.

LeCureux, Jason T. 2012. *The Thematic Unity of the Book of the Twelve*. Hebrew Bible Monographs 41. Sheffield: Sheffield Phoenix.

Macintosh, A. A. 2014. *Hosea*. ICC. New York: T. & T. Clark.

Nogalski, James. 2011. *The Book of the Twelve: Hosea-Jonah*. Smyth & Helwys Bible Commentary. Macon, GA: Smyth & Helwys.

Routledge, Robin. 2018. "Hosea's Marriage Reconsidered." *TynBul* 69: 25–42.

Sweeney, Marvin A. 2000. *The Twelve Prophets, Volume 1: Hosea, Joel, Amos, Obadiah, Jonah*. Berit Olam. Collegeville, MN: Liturgical Press.

Wolff, Hans Walter. 1974. *Hosea*. Hermeneia. Philadelphia, PA: Fortress.

CHAPTER 22

GENDER AND SEXUAL VIOLENCE IN HOSEA

KIRSI COBB

22.1. INTRODUCTION

"THAT her husband is angry enough to beat or mutilate her means that she has provoked him, that she deserves what she gets." In her comparison of the so-called marriage metaphor[1] in the Hebrew Bible to contemporary cases of domestic abuse, Garcia Fay Ellwood (1988: 88) has illustrated well the problematic portrayal of gender and sexual violence in the first three chapters of the book of Hosea. To illustrate Israel's fickle relationship with her God (1:2), the prophet is commanded to marry an *eshet zenunim*, "a promiscuous woman" (1:2), identified as Gomer (1:3). After the birth of three children, who are given ambiguous and ominous names (1:3–9), Hosea/God accuses Gomer/Israel of infidelity, resulting in a grisly mixture of violence, sex, and shame: the husband, among others, strips her naked, walls her in, and exposes her genitalia in public (2:2–13 [Heb. 2:4–15]). After these shocking events, Hosea/God lures his wife back, and they enter a blissful marital union (2:14–23 [Heb. 2:16–25]). In ch. 3, Hosea is told to take an "adulterous" woman as his wife, possibly Gomer or another woman, leaving the exact state of Hosea's marital affairs uncertain.

In an ancient version of "she deserved it," Hos. 1–3 presents Gomer/Israel as a hypersexualized female, who for her own good needs to be violated so that she will forsake her "lovers" and swear allegiance to her husband alone. Such a portrayal of the male is highly problematic and has resulted in various ways to interpret Hosea's message. Stretching from metaphor theory to trauma and memory studies, this essay will explore these and suggest ways Hos. 1–3 can be approached without accepting the husband's brutal treatment of his wife, or God's treatment of Israel, at face value.

22.2. Love, Metaphor, or an Unfortunate Choice?

According to Derek Kidner (1981: 26), in Hos. 2:2–23 (Heb. 2:4–25) "we see the divine Lover taking His time and using every art to win a response [from Israel] that will make the reconciliation genuine." The husband's (God's) initiative to win back his adulterous wife (Israel) with both judgment (vv. 2–13) and grace (vv. 14–17) should be understood as paving the way for the "*Perfect bliss*" of genuine loving affection as witnessed in Hos. 2:18–23 (Kidner 1981: 26–33; his italics). God is the "Lover" who will, quite literally, "try everything and anything" (Macintosh 1997: 69) to win back his bride, ultimately bringing the saga of "God's Love Story" (Anderson 1975: 425–36) to a rapturous conclusion.

The depiction of God/Hosea as committed albeit desperate men tugs the audience's heartstrings and garners understanding for their deeds; yet this effort comes at a high cost, as the very real issues of abuse, violence, and death are often sidelined or minimized. As Renita Weems (1995: 85) notes, "What effect does reading descriptions of women battered, mutilated, and raped as a poetic device for divine judgment have on audiences who have been raped and battered and who live daily with the imminent threat of being raped and battered?" We need better understanding of gender roles, violence, and their interaction both in the text and the lives of its recipients to truly appreciate the content and potential impact of Hosea's message.

A possible way to comprehend the violence is to study its metaphoric quality. Hosea's marriage to Gomer is in some way supposed to symbolize God's involvement with Israel (Hos. 1:2), which raises the question of how these relationships, and the violence that ensues, should best be understood. Richtsje Abma (1999: 7) has helpfully defined metaphor as "a literary device in which terms from two different areas of life are brought together in order to achieve a special meaning which goes beyond the ordinary meaning of words or concepts." In a metaphor, the term described (tenor) is presented with a figurative expression (vehicle) to bring new insights to the audience's awareness that may not have been otherwise achieved (Richards 1981: 52–55). In our case, Hosea's relationship with Gomer (the vehicle) helps the audience understand God's bond with Israel (the tenor).

If the various punishments meted out in Hos. 2 are therefore taken as metaphoric references of God's punishment of Israel, would this make the passage more understandable? As noted in conceptual theories of metaphor (Lakoff and Johnson 1980), metaphors form an essential part of our understanding of reality even to the extent that "our ordinary conceptual system, in terms of which we both think and act, is . . largely metaphorical" (p. 454). Metaphors are not "less" in their meaning by being "just metaphors." Rather, metaphors affect our very existence: they encourage us to think and act in appropriate ways in a particular cultural context (pp. 454–55, 465–67, 481–86). This means that even if we understand Hos. 2 as referring to God's treatment of Israel rather than Hosea's treatment of Gomer, it does not make the poem any less violent (Exum 1996: 101–2). The development of interactive theories of metaphor (Richards 1981; Black 1962) have successfully illustrated that the relationship between the respective parts of the metaphor is not a one-way street where, in our example, the national level of the metaphor can remain untouched by the individual. Rather, both parts of the metaphor function interactively and are modified by the other's existence (Black 1962: 35–47; Richards 1981: 51–55). Furthermore, both the vehicle and tenor will bring with themselves a *"system of associated commonplaces"* (Black 1962: 40; his italics)—that is, "the stock of common knowledge" that the author and audience would have shared about the terms (43). In our example, the metaphor can only function if the violence meted out against the woman on both individual and national levels is at least in some way comprehensible, even justifiable, within the wider cultural understanding of the community (see Baumann 2003: 97–98).

Furthermore, it is not at all clear that Hos. 2 should be understood on a purely national level. As noted by Katharine Doob Sakenfeld (2003: 105), if "the marriage as a prophetic acted sign was intended to show the people their own unfaithfulness . . . it might also have been used to show how God would respond." In other words, if the prophet's marriage was meant to be illustrative not just in word but in deed of God's response to the people, the possibility of Gomer having been harmed in the process becomes a likely possibility. Even the discourse in 2:2–13a (Heb. 2:4–15a) is ambiguous as the metaphoric nature of the speech is not emphasized and the identity of the speaker (YHWH, v. 13b) is only revealed much later (Connolly 1998: 58–59). Since Hosea (rather than God) has, in fact, married a promiscuous woman and the punishment in Hos. 2 "is expressed exclusively . . . as punishment of a real, human wife by a real, human husband" (Connolly 1998: 59), the lines between individual and national suffering remain ambivalent.

But exactly what kind of punishment is implied? Brad Kelle has convincingly argued that the metaphors in ch. 2 are borrowed from two image-bases: one that deals with actual marriage and divorce practices in ancient Near Eastern legal texts and the other, the ancient Near Eastern custom of personifying cities as female, which in the prophetic corpus is used to describe the destruction of a city via the metaphor of a woman subjected to violence (Kelle 2005: 49, 91–92; 2008: 98–101). If depicted as a woman, a city can "be desired, conquered, protected, and governed," with the male typically associated with the active role of conquest and the violent deeds that ensue (Maier 2021: 256; cf. Kelle 2008: 104). This depiction is especially fitting of siege warfare, where the taking of a city is both metaphorically comparable to the abuse of women in war and the likely result of enemy combatants entering a city (Kelle 2008: 104; Poser 2021: 341–45). The sexually violated female body thus acts as an appropriate metonym for the community shattered by war (Keefe 1993; cf. Claassens 2020: 136). Such texts, according to Kelle (2005: 81–109), belong to the latter image base and should be treated as metaphorical descriptions of a city's demise.

If the abuse of the female body is a metaphor for the destruction of a city, the identity of the wife could further help clarify the meaning of the passage. Several scholars have argued that the metaphorical wife in Hos. 2 stands for the Samarian male elite and leadership (Haddox 2011: 32, 88–90; Keefe 2001: 199; Kelle 2005: 90, 285–86; Yee 2012: 299–300).[2] As Hosea's intended audience would have consisted mostly of men, describing them as an adulterous woman would have been a shocking image aimed to disabuse the elite from their own notions of superiority via feminization and promote God as the ultimate alpha male (Haddox 2011: 88–90; Kelle 2005: 285–86). Although the metaphor is based on violence against a woman, the recipients of the punishment would have been male: no "real" women were envisaged in the process (see Carroll 1995: 283).

However, can the intended audience of the metaphor and its literary representation be so strictly divided? One of the most explicit passages depicting sexual violence in Hos. 2 is v. 10 (Heb. v. 12), which reads, "So now I will expose her lewdness before the eyes of her lovers; no-one will take her out of my hands" (NIV). That the stripping referred to here would be a punishment for adultery has been adequately disputed by Peggy Day (2000a; 2000b; Morse 2018: 148–49). Rather, the stripping could be a portrayal of Samaria's imminent destruction from which her "lovers" cannot save her (Kelle 2005: 255). The exposure of the woman's "lewdness" (*nablut*) is a curious term which Kelle (2005: 255–57) argues works on two levels. On the one hand, *nablut* (based on the Akkadian word *baltu/bastu*) refers to the woman's genitals (cf. nakedness in 2:3) and hence is a metaphoric description of the city's destruction; on the other, based on the Hebrew noun *nebalah* ("foolishness"), *nablut* can refer to the woman's adulterous conduct. Hosea 2:10 thus exposes the wife's sexual misdeeds and describes Samaria's predicted destruction.

Even so, could the description of the woman's sexual humiliation implicate something more? According to Kelle (2005: 255), stripping the woman naked in sight of her lovers does not work on an individual level; however, I wish to present an alternative possibility. Kelle rightly points out that *nebalah* ("foolishness") sometimes occurs in the Hebrew Bible in situations of sexual misconduct (Gen. 34:7; Deut. 22:21; Jer. 29:23). However, most of these references occur during (threatened) sexual acts committed by men such as the rapes of Dinah and Tamar (Gen. 34:7; 2 Sam. 13:12) or the threatened violation of the Levite and the eventual gang rape of his concubine (Judg. 19:23–24; 20:6, 10; cf. Jer. 29:23). As noted by Yvonne Sherwood (1996: 304), these allusions are chilling echoes to stories of male-initiated rape in a passage that never actually names the husband's action toward his wife as rape. However, since the woman cannot be "rescued" from her husband's hands, and the phrase "I will uncover her genitals" has semantic parallels in various passages that imply either offensive sexual conduct or sexual violence (Lev. 18:18–19; 20:11, 17–2; Isa. 47:3; Ezek. 16:37; Baumann 2003: 96; Magdalene 1995: 331–32; Gafney 2017: 53–54), it seems that the use of sexual force is also intended in Hos. 2:10.[3] Portrayals of God as the initiator of sexually violent encounters can also be found in Jer. 13:22–26 and Nah. 3:5–7, where degrading fates are depicted for the feminized cities of Jerusalem and Nineveh. Both passages are replete with sexually charged language implying the violation of the cities by God (Gafney 2017: 50–53; cf. O'Brien 2002: 68–69). As in Hos. 2:10, words commonly used in the Hebrew Bible for rape are absent, which "may reflect some limits in the poet's rhetoric about his own God," as noted by Wilda Gafney (2017: 51). Even if the text may wish to mask God's actions behind ambiguous language, the violation of women in warfare in both biblical (Num. 31:9, 25; Judg.

21; 1 Sam. 30:1–2; 2 Chr. 28:8–15; Isa. 13:16; Zech. 14. 2) and contemporary contexts would indicate that the sexual abuse of women is to be imagined in the sacking of these cities (Gafney 2017: 50–55, 57).

That the sexual violation of women in war is used as a symbol for the destiny of Samaria in Hos. 2:10 raises several issues. First, even if the main target of the metaphor was the male elite, sexual abuse and other degradations of women (and men) likely became a reality once Samaria was sacked by the Assyrians in 722 BCE; hence, the line between metaphor and reality becomes ambiguous or disappears altogether (cf. Poser 2021: 341–45; Kelle 2008: 105). Second, the depiction of the male elite as a raped woman appropriates women's suffering for men's political and theological ends. This is problematic, not least because it displaces the responsibility of the male leadership onto a female character and thus obscures if not eliminates male responsibility (Claassens 2020: 144; cf. Hos. 4:13–14). Finally, the metaphor stands on gendered assumptions about women and the use of their bodies in warfare. In biblical texts, rape of women is often understood more as the violation of property rights than abuse of a woman's sexual autonomy (e.g., Num. 31:17–18; Deut. 22:28–29; cf. Exod. 20:17; Deut. 5:21). This assumption undergirds a worldview where women's sexuality is to be regulated as the property of their fathers/husbands and can be violated by other men (Gafney 2017: 48–49, 55; Thistlethwaite 1993: 59–66; Magdalene 1995: 337–39; Yee 2012: 301–2). After all, the rape of another man's female dependents would be an attack on the man's masculinity and his ability to protect "his" women (Magdalene 1995: 338–39; Haddox 2011: 70–72). Patriarchy thus colors both the metaphor and its meaning. Portrayals of the rape and/or the unfaithfulness of wives, as well as the feminization of the king and soldiers, are also found in some ancient Near Eastern treaty curses, which may have provided some of the background for Hosea's imagery (Magdalene 1995: 341–46; Haddox 2011: 70–71, 88–89; Lim 2015: 63–67). These further illustrate the gendered assumptions, the vulnerable position, and the often-horrific fate of women in war. Even if no "real women" were the target audience of the metaphor, patriarchal assumptions about gender and rape provide a comprehensible background on which the metaphor securely rests.

That the husband would threaten sexual abuse on his wife "in the sight of her lovers" (2:10) rather than, for example, demand their punishment (Day 2000a: 239–41), may contradict the idea that the verse describes the punishment of an individual woman (Kelle 2005: 255). Certainly, there seems to be no legal reason for this behavior; however, another cause might be found in the world of androcentric pornographic fantasies (Brenner 1995, 1996, 2021; Exum 1996: 104–5; Scholz 2014: 93–99; Setel 1985). Emma Nagouse (2019; cf. Morse 2018) has suggested that the display of the adulterous wife's sexuality for all to see could be viewed through the contemporary phenomenon of revenge pornography or, according to Rhiannon Graybill (2017: 49–70), a possession movie—a subgenre of horror. In the first instance, the vengeful fantasy of raping an unfaithful wife before her lovers could help to establish the cuckolded husband's masculinity and dominance, even if only in his mind's eye. Akin to possession movies, the ravaged female form offers a space for male identities and anxieties to be negotiated by displacement. The woman thus becomes a battleground on which fantasies, vengefulness, and identities play out with only the male ever coming out on top. Hence, even if a husband attacking his wife before her lovers might seem unrealistic, the image itself plays directly into the hands of male dominance and ownership with which the text is more than familiar.

Is it, however, possible that in Hos. 2 we are simply dealing with an unfortunate choice of a metaphor? As Gale Yee argues (2012: 305), "When the metaphorical character of the biblical image is forgotten, a husband's physical abuse of his wife comes to be as justified as God's retribution against Israel." Likewise, Weems (1995: 112) warns against "risky deductions" that can arise from the use of "rigid correspondence" and "oversimplification" of the marriage metaphor. As she succinctly notes, "There is, as far as this writer is concerned, no similarity between battering husbands and avenging gods" (106; cf. Yee 2012: 304). What we have is a "risky" and even "dangerous" metaphor that needs to be handled with caution. In the interactive theories of metaphor discussed earlier, both the vehicle and tenor are modified by the other's presence. Admittedly, vehicles are both similar and dissimilar to their tenor and cannot simply be equated. Still to draw such a rigid line between these (non)correspondences as Yee and Weems do is problematic. Sherwood (1996: 284–85) observes that not only does this go against the principal that "the vehicle describes the tenor" (i.e., the actions of a human husband describe those of the divine), but in the book of Hosea the difference between the two husbands is also not so easily separated. Rather, the line between the divine and human husbands' actions in Hos. 2 is so ambiguous that it is unlikely that these descriptions should not in some way be understood as endorsed in both human and divine realms.

Another solution to this dilemma would be to claim that the metaphor is unfortunate and should be substituted for or rejected in favor of others, such as a friend or a lover (Baumann 2003: 237; cf. Maier 2021: 271–72). However, a different metaphor would simply bring a different set of problems and would not communicate the message that the book professes (O'Brien 2008: 45–46). In Hos. 2, the violent depictions and the supposed reconciliation are inextricably linked, and none of these elements can be removed without distorting the image of the human–divine relationship. Rather than being an unfortunate choice, the metaphor remains problematic on both human and divine levels and cannot be easily mediated by either restriction or replacement.

22.3. JUST PUNISHMENT OR DOMESTIC ABUSE?

The actions of the husband in Hos. 2 might seem somewhat unpalatable to contemporary readers. However, in its own cultural context, could Hosea's/God's deeds be justified? In 2:13 (Heb. 2:15), the husband threatens his wife with public sexual humiliation, which has been read by Francis Andersen and David Noel Freedman (1980: 248–49), as well as Renita Weems (1989: 98; cf. 1995: 48), as corresponding to her earlier actions: the former view the punishment as a reversal of the wife's sexual unfaithfulness in private, whereas Weems connects the wife's stripping to her display of vulgar apparel in vv. 4 and 13 (Heb. vv. 6, 15).[4] The principle of *lex talionis* can be observed in both interpretations and leads to the question of whether, at least within its ancient context, the punishments could have been warranted.

Hosea 2 describes a situation where a wife has refused to submit to her husband's authority and committed illicit acts, including adultery. Kelle (2005: 49, 58–79) argues that ancient Near Eastern legal texts dealing with marriage and divorce practices reveal several options for recourse available to the husband of which execution is merely one (cf. 2:3–4 [Heb. 2:5–6]). Others include imprisonment (2:6–7 [Heb. 2:8–9]) and divorce with severe financial repercussions for the wife (2:9–10 [Heb. 2:11–12]). That we are dealing with options and not actions is made clear by the Hebrew word *pen* ("lest") in 2:3, which introduces the first possibility (execution) as a threat (Kelle 2005: 233). Other options are presented by *laken* ("therefore") (2:6, 9, 14 [Heb. 2:8, 11, 16]). Of these, the first two present actions or threats that God will not commit, whereas the last describes reconciliation as the viable and even preferred course of action, covering the second half of the chapter (2:14–23 [Heb. 2:16–25]; Clines 1979; Kelle 2005: 239, 243, 247, 266).

Even though the text seemingly presents threats and not actions, research in domestic abuse has illustrated that the threat of violence can be as, or even more, effective than the actual deed (Herman 1992: 77; Stark 2007: 251). The fact that we are dealing with a list of threats might be of little comfort to the recipient, especially since during the fall of Samaria we can presume these became a reality. Additionally, threats still leave the issue of the justification of these acts. On the level of the text, the husband is entitled to take punitive measures against his wife just as God can presumably punish Samaria for her deeds. Yet, even if both husbands are entitled to these actions, it leaves open the question as to what a contemporary (or even an ancient) reader would make of the character of a husband that not only contemplates but graphically visualizes these options (Scholz 2014: 93–99). Furthermore, just because the passage relies on ancient Near Eastern legal texts and the realities of war to justify Hosea's/God's position, this does not make the content less problematic. In the United Kingdom, marital rape became illegal under the Sexual Offences Act in 2003. This does not mean that marital rape did not occur before, or that at least some of the victims did not feel distressed or violated. Likewise, the UN recognized rape as a war crime in 1993; however, women are still frequently raped in war, and its effects are not minimized by its illegality. The victims of either would be completely justified in wondering about the character of their assailants regardless of laws, and so would the audience of Hos. 2.

Several scholars have noted the similarities between the threatened acts in Hos. 2 and those found in situations of intimate partner violence (IPV) or domestic abuse (Blyth 2021: 51–57, 68–96; Ellwood 1988; Exum 1996: 101–28; Graetz 1995: 126–45; Weems 1995; Yee 2012). The marriage in Hos. 1–3 is not a union of equals, and in an abusive situation the power in the relationship rests predominantly with the perpetrator. To make the victim comply with the abuser's wishes, several tactics may be employed including coercive control, which is defined by Women's Aid (2022; cf. Stark 2007: 228–29; Collins 2019: 15) as "an act or a pattern of acts of assault, threats, humiliation and intimidation or other abuse that is used to harm, punish, or frighten their victim." Examples of these acts are not hard to find in our passage. Hosea 2:2–13 (Heb. 2:4–15) weaves a sinister web of intimidation and fear, where the woman is threatened with, among other things, death (v. 3), sexual violence (vv. 3, 10), entrapment (vv. 6–7), and destitution (vv. 9, 12). Even the imagined reconciliation in vv. 14–23 (Heb. vv. 16–25) is disturbing, as this could simply be described as a change in tactics: instead of threats, the abuser subdues his victim "by courtship" (Herman 1992: 82). Often referred to as love-bombing, the perpetrator retains an emotional bond with the victim by overwhelming them "with positive experiences" (Collins 2019: 30; cf. Blyth 2021: 81), which in Hos. 2 include a second honeymoon and renewal of vows (vv. 14–15, 19–20). However, the entire experience is narrated from the husband's point of view and ultimately leads to him re-establishing control over his wife (Scholz 2014: 96).

Such portrayals can be especially troubling to those who have experienced abuse in their relationships; however, listening to the stories of survivors might well be a way of bringing further depth and meaning to the text. In view of my own experience of domestic abuse, I have discussed Hos. 2 with Rachel Starr, a theologian and author on domestic violence (Cobb 2020: 112–33), whereas Nancy Nam Hoon Tan (2021: 93–116) reads Hos. 1–3 together with Hong Kong sex workers. Both publications challenge the power dynamics in the text and the way the passage continues to victimize women and normalize male violence. My article (Cobb 2020: 121) emphasizes the "toxic mix of love, shame and guilt" that resulted from my boyfriend's humiliating treatment of me coupled with the so-called honeymoon phase, which I describe as "imagined, temporary bliss." Likewise, the sex workers interviewed by Tan ardently resisted "the notion that violent male control can be justified or redemptive" (2021: 108), calling Hosea/God "'mad' and someone who could not comprehend what mutual love and respect in a relationship were" (2021: 107). Listening to the lived experience of these women can begin to unravel the depths of harm presented and perpetrated in and through these texts. Challenging the legitimization of male violence in ancient and contemporary contexts can transform our understanding of both human and divine relationships.

So, does Israel/Gomer deserve what is coming to her? On the level of the text, God's/ Hosea's actions are deemed legitimate and deserved. If Hosea was the first prophet to describe God's relationship with Israel as a marriage (Baumann 2003: 85; Kruger 1983: 107; Sakenfeld 2003: 99–100; Yee 2012: 299), then Hos. 2 offers an unprecedented view into the intensity of God's emotions toward the metaphorical wife and her crimes in a way that perhaps other images could not (Baumann 2003: 97–98; Fernández 2021: 282–85). However, contemporary (and ancient) audiences might question a view of Hosea/God where love is intimately tied with a man's ability to threaten and humiliate his partner. This depiction relies on patriarchal conceptions of gender, violence, and power from which at least some might wish to distance themselves.

22.4. Teaching Tool, Cultural Trauma, and Counterstories

Long after Samaria's fall in 722 BCE, Hos. 1–3 would have formed a valuable part of the social memory[5] of the postexilic community in Yehud and undoubtedly functioned as a teaching tool. As noted by Ehud Ben Zvi (2008: 54), as the literati read and reread the book, they "hoped to learn them [YHWH's words and teachings] and teach Israel to behave accordingly." The depiction of the fall of Samaria is most memorable with its use of pathos, familial imagery, and overtly sexualized language (Ben Zvi 2019: 290). The story would have served as a horrific warning not to reject God's ordinances; yet the narrative would have also created a sense of shared identity and hope. Although Israel had rejected God, as God's chosen people they were also destined for a utopian future as depicted in Hos. 2:14–23 (Heb. 2:16–25; Ben Zvi 2019: 303). Israel had suffered a horrific punishment due to its sins, but due to God's inexplicable love, the people would also be redeemed (Ben Zvi 2004: 380 n. 33, 382; 2022: 414).

As a depiction and an explanation of war, the book of Hosea could also be described as survival or trauma literature since, as noted by Louis Stulman (2014: 180), "the prophetic corpus is by and large a complex literary response to the massive collapse of social and symbolic structures." The Assyrian invasion of Samaria and the resultant violence would have raised questions about the status of Israel and the potency of her God. It would not have wounded just individual Israelites but also their corporate sense of "religious and national identity" (Eyerman 2013: 41). Such wounds have been described by Ron Eyerman (2013) and Jeffrey Alexander (2012) as cultural trauma—that is, "acute discomfort" in the collective's identity due to some form of (perceived) misfortune or disaster that is interpreted as harmful and needs "cultural construction," in the form of shared expression and explanation on the level of the community (Alexander 2012: 10, 13, 19). In the case of the postexilic literati, the fall of Samaria would have taken place over a hundred years ago, in which case the trauma could be most aptly referred to as a "chosen trauma" (Volkan 2001; cf. Ben Zvi 2019: 301–2). Vamik Volkan (2001: 87) illustrates how one generation's sense of collective loss can be "deposited" into the next generation, often due to the "past generation's inability to mourn losses of people, land or prestige." If this inability persists, these mental images or "representations of the shared traumatic event" are passed on through the generations and become part of the collective's identity (Volkan 2001: 87–88). Eventually, what is important about the chosen trauma is not historically accurate detail but how the trauma links the members of the group together and defines their self-image (88).

As a chosen trauma, the fall of Samaria would have echoed through the generations and required representation and even justification. To achieve this, "carrier groups" would have been needed—"collective agents" who in society were in a position and had the talent to create meaning and promote certain interpretations of the trauma (Alexander 2012: 20). Since in our example we are dealing with written rather than oral prophecy, such agents would have included the author(s) and editors of the book of Hosea during or most likely after Samaria's fall (Stulman and Kim 2010: 9–11; cf. Holt 2014: 169) such as the literati in postexilic Yehud (Ben Zvi 2008: 43–44, 53, 56–57). The fact that we are still reading the book of Hosea and that the pattern of sin-rejection-redemption operates in several prophetic books testifies to the persuasiveness of the story arc; yet we must acknowledge that this version would have come at the cost of suppressing the lived experience of at least some of the individual survivors and the views of others who may not have understood Samaria's fate in this way (Janzen 2019). Rather, what the book of Hosea achieved was the re-creation of the community's national and religious identity against the horrors of war.

For the explanation in the book of Hosea to be successful, this "new master narrative" needed to address four specific issues: "*the nature of the pain*," "*the nature of the victim*," "*relation of the trauma victim to the wider audience*," and "*attribution of responsibility*" (Alexander 2012: 20–22; his italics). In our narrative, the nature of the pain or "what actually happened" (Alexander 2012: 21) is the fall of Samaria; however, what is of particular interest here is the attribution of responsibility. According to Hos. 1–3, the Israelites, and especially their leadership, have caused their suffering by adulterous behavior (Hos. 1:2; 2:2, 4, 5, 7, 8, 12–13). Although the Israelites may well have contributed to their own downfall, this is not on its own an adequate explanation, as it completely ignores larger geopolitical concerns, such as the Assyrian leaders/armies who invaded Samaria (cf. O'Connor 2011: 56). For the individual victims of trauma, self-blame can function as a survival mechanism: acknowledging one's guilt establishes a form of control over the event and might make it more bearable than admitting "utter helplessness" (Herman 1992: 53–54; cf. Frechette 2015: 25; 2017: 245–46; Poser 2021: 345; Carr 2014: 32–33). On a cultural level, self-blame can also assist in re-creating communal identity. In the book of Hosea, blaming the Israelites has at least a twofold benefit: first, it releases God from culpability; and second, it gives the people, somewhat counterintuitively, agency (O'Connor 2011: 43–44; Stulman and Kim 2010: 14–15; Carr 2014: 32–33; Cobb 2020: 122–23). In the first instance, blaming the people establishes God as all-powerful: God has not been defeated by empires or their deities (Smith-Christopher 2004: 156–57). Rather, through the invasion God administered punishment in order to draw Israel back. In the second instance, self-blame enables the people to have agency: if their faithlessness caused the disaster (Hos. 2:1–13), their renewed faithfulness (especially if aided by God, 2:19–20; Ben Zvi 2019: 287, 289, 298–99) might have the opposite effect (2:14–23). Although such an explanation could seem unreasonable, Kathleen O'Connor (2011: 43–44) has noted that in order for trauma survivors to "resume life . . . they must have meaning, interpretation, explanation, even if the explanation is ephemeral, inadequate, partial, or outright wrong." Rather than risk the collapse of the collective's religious and national identity, a story that keeps these intact is, at least for the community, better than having no identity, and no meaning, at all.

Hosea 1–3 uses metaphoric language to depict the fall of Samaria. This is significant since, according to Ronald Granofsky (1995: 6), literary symbols facilitate "a removal from unpleasant actuality by use of distance and selection." Symbols afford a certain distance from the experience by not describing it directly and by selectivity evoke only some aspects. In this way, "literary symbolism" affords what Granofsky calls a " 'safe' confrontation with a traumatic experience" (p. 7). The use of symbols and metaphors has been shown to aid the recovery of individual experiences of trauma (Anker 2009; Claassens 2020: 9, 129), and in terms of cultural trauma, using indirect descriptions is also helpful. Rather than retraumatize the individual members of the collective, the use of symbols and metaphors allows the author(s) and the audience to view the trauma "at a distance, as if it were happening on a stage to someone else" (O'Connor 2014: 214). In the book of Hosea, the horrors of war are brought down to a more intimate and familial setting via the use of the marriage metaphor. In this way, the audience can view the fall of Samaria from a "safe" distance by imagining the marital troubles of Hosea/God, as well as by focusing only on some elements of the tragedy, such as the wife's/Israel's culpability. This kind of narrative has been helpfully named by Simeon Whiting (2020: 242), using a term from William Morrow (2011), as "a proxy memory," a trauma narrative that "helped the authors express and memorialise their own trauma without directly describing the experiences which traumatised them." By using metaphor, the authors/editors of Hosea were able to voice their chosen trauma in ways that facilitated the presentation and explanation of the adversity without directly evoking memories of war.

Such a "proxy memory" would have created a lasting and meaningful explanation for the fall of Samaria. For this purpose, the horrendous punishments in Hos. 2:1–13 might have been in some way a fitting description of the horrors the victims of war had experienced (O'Connor 2011: 54–55; Stulman and Kim 2010: 11). Furthermore, the hyperbolic language and the treatment of Gomer/Israel would have left the guilt of the Israelites in no doubt, functioning not only as a teaching tool but perhaps as a type of revenge fantasy—that is, "actual descriptive thoughts on how to get even with the perpetrator" (Goldner, Lev-Wiesel, and Simon 2019: 2). Punishing their ancestors in their minds' eye may have helped the postexilic generation to safely release some of the frustration caused by living under colonial power (cf. Holt 2014: 174; Smith-Christopher 2004). However, even if the narrative would have provided relief for pent-up anger, it remains problematic. As noted earlier, the story would have gone counter to the lived experience of some of the individual victims/survivors, especially that of women (and men) who may have experienced firsthand abuse of the kind described in Hos. 2:1–13 (Cobb 2020: 123–24). For them, the metaphor would not have provided a safe distance to describe the war or even necessarily to vent their anger; rather, it would have further underwritten the problematic script that the punishment was in some way deserved. For the community, Hos. 1–3 may have provided meaning, but this meaning is based on harmful gendered assumptions and paid for by the erasure of the experience of individual victims.

Trauma narratives such as these can indeed be troubling, and to find meaning in them can be problematic, especially for a contemporary audience. However, appreciating the traumatic character of these stories might offer a possibility. As noted by O'Connor (2011: 43–44), for trauma survivors to live again, they need interpretation of their trauma, even if this interpretation is "inadequate . . . or outright wrong." Likewise, Christopher Frechette (2017: 244) has noted that "it is not a function of the text's [trauma narrative's] capacity to express a complete or universal truth." Rather, the narrative is part of a meaning-making process that offers "momentary glimpses" in order to "stave off chaos for the moment" (O'Connor 2011: 56). Perhaps passages such as Hos. 1–3 should be seen as an attempt to create order out of chaos, even if this order is not perfect. Hosea 1–3 might offer a window not to universal truth, but to the meaning-making process of a community after a disaster.

Furthermore, as noted by Ben Zvi (2019: 77–79; 2022: 403–14), narratives such as Hos. 1–3 are not always straightforward; they portray a certain "fuzziness" and allow for complementary and even competing discourses to exist in tension. Stulman and Kim (2010: 189) find voices of quiet dissent in Hos. 2:3–4 (Heb. 2:5–6), where the graphic depiction of the woman's fate might not only be a description of the consequences of Israel's adultery, but a cryptic criticism of God and his "divine mistreatment of exiles who are brutally abandoned." In her intertextual reading of Daughter Zion (Lam. 1) with J. M. Coetzee's novel *Disgrace*, Juliana Claassens (2020: 145–50) seeks to find moments where the female characters might be breaking the veneer of the male narrative. Such efforts are limited, as we can only see the text through the eyes of the male author, but can help to establish a counterstory for the women by focusing on the restoration of their identity and agency (pp. 146–47). In Hosea, such a moment might be found in 2:12a and 15a (Heb 2:14a, 17a), where the ownership of provisions is in dispute: Gomer claims the vines and fig trees are payment from her lovers (v. 12a), whereas in v. 15a the vineyards are described as a gift from her husband. Although this might be a way for the author to display Gomer's arrogance, the juxtaposition of these competing claims raises the possibility that Gomer is, as noted famously by Sherwood (1996: 320), "a thoroughly modern miss." Gomer strikes her own contracts in a manner comparable to the "modern view of economics of prostitution"; rather than be subjugated, she provides a service (Sherwood 1996: 319–20; cf. Moughtin-Mumby 2008: 263–68). Some of the Hong Kong sex workers (Tan 2021: 111) stated that they had turned to the profession to provide for their families, and when considering Gomer, they suggested that her financial contribution to the household had been forgotten by Hosea/God. Furthermore, a couple of the sex workers admitted that they would rather "remain independent than entrust their future to a man who would control everything" (112). Such diverse voices, whether they arise out of intertextual readings, the life experience of readers, or other instances of "fuzziness" in the text, can open the narrative for new interpretations. Although these voices might not be quite as loud as we would like, they are enough to suggest alternative readings and in so doing, to entice us all to encounter the text anew.

22.5. CONCLUSION

Hosea 1–3 has been described in such differing ways as a love story, pornography, and domestic violence. Righteous punishment and pathos intermingle in a story that is wrought with sex and violence, with the feminine presented as the sinful and the masculine as the normative. The imagery in chs. 1–3 is certainly memorable, and as a teaching tool, would have provided a warning for the community in Yehud not to follow in Samaria's footsteps.

However, the book of Hosea also displays instances of "fuzziness." Whether this is Gomer's claim that her vineyard is a reward for her services (2:12a [Heb. 2:14a]) or a masked cry of the exiles against God's treatment (2:2–3 [Heb. 2:4–5]), the book presents a narrative where gender roles are at least questionable. One might inquire about the "loving" character of Hosea/God as he is unable to keep his wife happy at home or under his control, and instead broods over graphic punishments of his wanton wife (cf. Stone 2005: 126; Haddox 2011: 151–52, 155; Sherwood 1996: 222–23). Scholars have also pointed out the maternal image of God that appears in Hos. 11:1–4, 8–9, which could at least challenge if not counterbalance the portrayal of God as a despotic husband (Carden 2006: 453–54; Macwilliam 2011: 100–3; Schüngel-Straumann 1995; Stone 2005: 126). In its final form, the book of Hosea is ultimately a proxy memory, a chosen trauma passed on through subsequent generations. Although the narrative blamed the victims, it also secured the continued existence of the community's identity and of their God. With an ear to the voices of survivors and with an understanding of trauma literature, Hos. 1–3 offers the contemporary reader snippets of insight into communal meaning-making. Its picture of God is dark and threatening, yet unstable enough to let in the occasional glimmer of light.

NOTES

1. For the multiple uses of the "marriage metaphor" in prophetic texts, see Moughtin-Mumby 2008.
2. Interpretations regarding the nature of Israel's infractions range from religious transgressions (Macintosh 1997: 42, 48–50; Mays 1969: 25–26; Wolff 1974: 13–15, 34–35) to political and/or socioeconomic misalliances (Keefe 1995; 2001; Kelle 2005: 111–66, Haddox 2011: 1–7, 20–22), or a combination thereof (Yee 2003: 81–109; 2012: 299–300). For our purposes, the nature of Israel's offense is not as important as the recognition that her deeds are likened to a sexual transgression of a wife against her husband and met with equal severity.
3. Daniel Smith-Christopher (2004: 150–51) has argued that the stripping could be a reference to the actual treatment of prisoners of war "in Neo-Assyrian and Neo-Babylonian military practice." If so, the act of stripping could open the reference to other expressions of humiliation at the hands of the conquerors in addition to or apart from rape.
4. In her later monograph, Weems (1995: 90) notes that overall the woman's punishment is "brutal," "borders on the pornographic," and "in many respects exceeds the crime."
5. By "social memory," Ben Zvi refers to what is often described as collective or cultural memory (see Whiting 2020: 212–23). Social memory consists of memories of what the collective "imagine to have happened and which they are socialized to remember" (Ben Zvi 2019: 7). It is the past as the community remembers and does not require historical accuracy. Social memory has firm links to the community's identity formation and concerns

that they have in the present, of which the book of Hosea offers a good example (Ben Zvi 2008; 2019: 274–93).

REFERENCES

Abma, Richtsje. 1999. *Bonds of Love: Methodic Studies of Prophetic Texts with Marriage Imagery (Isaiah 50:1–3 and 54:1–10, Hosea 1–3, Jeremiah 2–3)*. Assen: Van Gorcum.

Alexander, Jeffrey C. 2012. *Trauma: A Social Theory*. Cambridge and Malden: Polity.

Andersen, Francis I., and David Noel Freedman. 1980. *Hosea*. AB 24. New York: Doubleday.

Anderson, G. W. 1975. "Hosea and Yahweh: God's Love Story (Hosea 1–3)." *RvwExp* 72/4: 425–36.

Anker, Johan. 2009. "Metaphors of Pain: The Use of Metaphors in Trauma Narrative with Reference to Fugitive Pieces." *Literator* 30/2: 49–68.

Baumann, Gerlinde. 2003. *Marriage as a Metaphor for the Relationship between YHWH and Israel in the Prophetic Books*. Trans. Linda M. Maloney. Collegeville: Liturgical.

Ben Zvi, Ehud. 2004. "Observations on the Marital Metaphor of YHWH and Israel in Its Ancient Israelite Context: General Considerations and Particular Images in Hosea 1.2." *JSOT* 28/3: 363–84.

Ben Zvi, Ehud. 2008. "Reading Hosea and Imagining YHWH." *HBT* 30: 43–57.

Ben Zvi, Ehud. 2019. *Social Memory among the Literati of Yehud*. Berlin; Boston: de Gruyter.

Ben Zvi, Ehud. 2022. "The Marital Metaphor of YHWH and Israel in Ancient Israel with a Focus in Its Occurrence in Hosea 1–3." In Emanuel Pfoh, ed., *Patronage in Ancient Palestine and in the Hebrew Bible: A Reader*. The Social World of Biblical Antiquity —Second Series 12. Sheffield: Sheffield Phoenix, 384–422.

Black, Max. 1962. *Models and Metaphors: Studies in Language and Philosophy*. Ithaca: Cornell University Press.

Blyth, Caroline. 2021. *Rape Culture, Purity Culture, and Coercive Control in Teen Girl Bibles*. London: Routledge.

Brenner, Athalya. 1995. "On Prophetic Propaganda and the Politics of 'Love': The Case of Jeremiah." In Athalya Brenner, ed., *A Feminist Companion to The Latter Prophets*. Sheffield: Sheffield Academic, 256–74.

Brenner, Athalya. 1996. "Pornoprophetics Revisited: Some Additional Reflections." *JSOT* 21/70: 63–86.

Brenner-Idan, Athalya. 2021. "Pornoprophetics Revisited, Decades Later." In L. Juliana Claassens and Irmtraud Fischer, eds., *Prophecy and Gender in the Hebrew Bible*. The Bible and Women 1.2. Atlanta: SBL, 359–71.

Carden, Michael. 2006. "The Book of the Twelve Minor Prophets." In Deryn Guest, Robert E. Goss, Mona West, and Thomas Bohache, eds., *The Queer Bible Commentary*. London: SCM, 432–84.

Carr, David M. 2014. *Holy Resilience: The Bible's Traumatic Origins*. New Haven and London: Yale University Press.

Carroll, Robert P. 1995. "Desire under the Terebinths: On Pornographic Representation in the Prophet—A Response." In Athalya Brenner ed., *A Feminist Companion to The Latter Prophets*. FCB 8. Sheffield: Sheffield Academic, 275–307.

Claassens, L. Juliana M. 2020. *Writing and Reading to Survive: Biblical and Contemporary Trauma Narratives in Conversation*. The Trauma Bible 1. Sheffield: Sheffield Phoenix.

Clines, D. J. A. 1979. "Hosea 2: Structure and Interpretation." In Elizabeth A. Livingstone, ed., *Studia Biblica 1978/ Sixth International Congress on Biblical Studies, Oxford 3–7 April 1978*. Sheffield: University of Sheffield Press, 83–103.

Cobb, Kirsi. 2020. "Reading Gomer with Questions: A Trauma-Informed Feminist Study of How the Experience of Intimate Partner Violence and the Presence of Religious Belief Shape the Reading of Hosea 2:2–23." In Karen O'Donnell and Katie Cross, eds., *Feminist Trauma Theologies: Body, Scripture and Church in Critical Perspective*. London: SCM, 112–33.

Collins, Natalie. 2019. *Out of Control: Couples, Conflict and the Capacity for Change*. London: SPCK.

Connolly, Tristanne J. 1998. "Metaphor and Abuse in Hosea." *Feminist Theology* 6/18: 55–66.

Day, Peggy L. 2000a. "The Bitch Had It Coming to Her: Rhetoric and Interpretation in Ezekiel 16." *BibInt* 8/3: 231–54.

Day, Peggy L. 2000b. "Jerusalem's Imagined Demise: Death of a Metaphor in Ezekiel XVI." *VT* 50/3: 285–309.

Ellwood, Gracia Fay. 1988. *Batter My Heart*. Pendle Hill Pamphlet 282. Wallingford: Pendle Hill.

Exum, J. Cheryl. 1996. *Plotted, Shot, and Painted: Cultural Representations of Biblical Women*. Sheffield: Sheffield Academic.

Eyerman, Ron. 2013. "Social Theory and Trauma." *Acta Sociologica* 56/1: 41–53.

Fernández, Marta García. 2021. "The Marriage Metaphor in the Prophets: Some Gender Issues." In L. Juliana Claassens and Irmtraud Fischer, eds., *Prophecy and Gender in the Hebrew Bible*. The Bible and Women 1.2. Atlanta: SBL, 277–91.

Frechette, Christopher G. 2015. "The Old Testament as Controlled Substance: How Insights from Trauma Studies Reveal Healing Capacities in Potentially Harmful Texts." *Interpretation* 69/1: 20–34.

Frechette, Christopher G. 2017. "Two Biblical Motifs of Divine Violence as Resources for Meaning-Making in Engaging Self-Blame and Rage after Traumatization." *Pastoral Psychology* 66/2: 239–49.

Gafney, Wilda C. M. 2017. *Nahum, Habakkuk, Zephaniah*. Wisdom Commentary. Collegeville: Liturgical.

Goldner, Limor, Rachel Lev-Wiesel, and Guy Simon. 2019. "Revenge Fantasies after Experiencing Traumatic Events: Sex Differences." *Frontiers in Psychology* 10/886: 1–9.

Graetz, Naomi. 1995. "God is to Israel as Husband Is to Wife: The Metaphoric Battering of Hosea's Wife." In Athalya Brenner, ed., *A Feminist Companion to the Latter Prophets*. Sheffield: Sheffield Academic, 126–45.

Granofsky, Ronald. 1995. *The Trauma Novel: Contemporary Symbolic Depictions of Collective Disaster*. New York: Peter Lang.

Graybill, Rhiannon. 2017. *Are We Not Men? Unstable Masculinity in the Hebrew Prophets*. New York: Oxford University Press.

Haddox, Susan E. 2011. *Metaphor and Masculinity in Hosea*. Studies in Biblical Literature 141. New York: Peter Lang.

Herman, Judith. 1992. *Trauma and Recovery: The Aftermath of Violence; From Domestic Abuse to Political Terror*. New York: Basic.

Holt, Else K. 2014. "Daughter Zion: Trauma, Cultural Memory and Gender in Old Testament Poetics." In Eve-Marie Becker, Jan Dochhorn, and Else K. Holt, eds., *Trauma and Traumatization in Individual and Collective Dimensions: Insights from Biblical Studies and Beyond*. Göttingen: Vandenhoeck & Ruprecht, 162–76.

Janzen, David. 2019. "Claimed and Unclaimed Experience: Problematic Readings of Trauma in the Hebrew Bible." *BiblInt* 27: 163–85.

Keefe, Alice A. 1993. "Rapes of Women/Wars of Men." *Semeia* 61: 79–97.

Keefe, Alice A. 1995. "The Female Body, the Body Politic and the Land: A Sociopolitical Reading of Hosea 1–2." In Athalya Brenner, ed., *A Feminist Companion to the Latter Prophets*. Sheffield: Sheffield Academic, 70–100.

Keefe, Alice A. 2001. *Woman's Body and the Social Body in Hosea*. JSOTSup 338; GCT 10. London; New York: Sheffield Academic.

Kelle, Brad E. 2005. *Hosea 2: Metaphor and Rhetoric in Historical Perspective*. SBLAB 20. Atlanta: SBL.

Kelle, Brad E. 2008. "Wartime Rhetoric: Prophetic Metaphorization of Cities as Female." In Brad E. Kelle and Frank Ritchel Ames, eds., *Writing and Reading War: Rhetoric, Gender, and Ethics in Biblical and Modern Contexts*. SBL Symposium Series 42. Atlanta: SBl, 95–111.

Kidner, Derek. 1981. *Love to the Loveless: The Story and Message of Hosea*. Leicester: IVP.

Kruger, Paul A. 1983. "Israel, the Harlot (Hos 2:4–9)." *JNSL* 11: 107–16.

Lakoff, George, and Mark Johnson. 1980. "Conceptual Metaphor in Everyday Language." *Journal of Philosophy* 77/8: 453–86.

Lim, Bo H. 2015. "Hosea 2:2–23 [2:4–25]." In Bo H. Lim and Daniel Castelo, *Hosea*. The Two Horizons Old Testament Commentary. Grand Rapids: Eerdmans, 63–78.

Macintosh, A. A. 1997. *A Critical and Exegetical Commentary on Hosea* International Critical Commentary. Edinburgh: T&T Clark.

Macwilliam, Stuart. 2011. *Queer Theory and the Prophetic Marriage Metaphor in the Hebrew Bible*. London: Equinox.

Magdalene, F. Rachel. 1995. "Ancient Near Eastern Treaty-Curses and the Ultimate Texts of Terror: A Study of the Language of Divine Sexual Abuse in the Prophetic Corpus." In Athalya Brenner, ed., *A Feminist Companion to the Latter Prophets*. Sheffield: Sheffield Academic, 326–52.

Maier, Christl M. 2021. "Daughter Zion and Babylon, the Whore: The Female Personification of Cities and Countries in the Prophets." In L. Juliana Claassens and Irmtraud Fischer, eds., *Prophecy and Gender in the Hebrew Bible*. The Bible and Women 1.2. Atlanta: SBL, 255–75.

Mays, James L. 1969. *Hosea*. London: SCM.

Morrow, William S. 2011. "Deuteronomy 7 in Postcolonial Perspective: Cultural Fragmentation and Renewal." In Brad E. Kelle, Frank Ritcher Ames, and Jacob L. Wright, eds., *Interpreting Exile: Displacement and Deportations in Biblical and Modern Contexts*. SBLAIL 10. Atlanta: SBL, 275–93.

Morse, Holly. 2018. "'Judgement Was Executed upon Her, and She Became a Byword among Women' (Ezek. 23.10): Divine Revenge Porn, Slut-Shaming, Ethnicity, and Exile in Ezekiel 16 and 23." In Katherine E. Southwood and Martien A. Halvorson-Taylor, eds., *Women and Exilic Identity in the Hebrew Bible*. LHBOTS 631. London: T&T Clark, 129–54.

Moughtin-Mumby, Sharon. 2008. *Sexual and Marital Metaphors in Hosea, Jeremiah, Isaiah, and Ezekiel*. Oxford: Oxford University Press.

Nagouse, Emma. 2019. "'I Will Strip Her Naked and Expose Her as in the Day She Was Born': Gomer, Blac Chyna, and Revenge Pornography." Paper presented at the Women and Gender in the Bible and the Ancient World Conference, Glasgow, 29 March.

O'Brien, Julia M. 2002. *Nahum: A New Biblical Commentary*. Sheffield: Sheffield Academic.

O'Brien, Julia M. 2008. *Challenging Prophetic Metaphor: Theology and Ideology in the Prophets*. Louisville: Westminster John Knox.

O'Connor, Kathleen M. 2011. *Jeremiah: Pain and Promise*. Minneapolis: Fortress.

O'Connor, Kathleen M. 2014. "How Trauma Studies Can Contribute to Old Testament Studies." In Eve-Marie Becker, Jan Dochhorn, and Else K. Holt, eds., *Trauma and Traumatization in Individual and Collective Dimensions: Insights from Biblical Studies and Beyond*. Göttingen: Vandenhoeck & Ruprecht, 210–22.

Poser, Ruth. 2021. "Embodied Memories: Gender-Specific Aspects of Prophecy as Trauma Literature." In L. Juliana Claassens and Irmtraud Fischer, eds., *Prophecy and Gender in the Hebrew Bible*. The Bible and Women 1.2. Atlanta: SBL, 333–57.

Richards, Ivor A. 1981. "The Philosophy of Rhetoric." In Mark Johnson, ed., *Philosophical Perspectives on Metaphor*. Minneapolis: University of Minnesota Press, 48–62.

Sakenfeld, Katharine Doob. 2003. *Just Wives? Stories of Power and Survival in the Old Testament and Today*. Louisville: Westminster John Knox.

Scholz, Susanne. 2014. *Sacred Witness: Rape in the Hebrew Bible*. Minneapolis: Fortress.

Schüngel-Straumann, Helen. 1995. "God as Mother in Hosea 11." In Athalya Brenner, ed., *A Feminist Companion to the Latter Prophets*. Sheffield: Sheffield Academic, 194–218.

Setel, T. Drorah. 1985. "Prophets and Pornography: Female Sexual Imagery in Hosea." In Letty M. Russell, ed., *Feminist Interpretation of the Bible*. Philadelphia: Westminster, 86–95.

Sherwood, Yvonne. 1996. *The Prostitute and the Prophet: Reading Hosea in the Late Twentieth Century*. Sheffield: Sheffield Academic.

Smith-Christopher, Daniel L. 2004. "Ezekiel in Abu Ghraib: Rereading Ezekiel 16:37–39 in the Context of Imperial Conquest." In Stephen L. Cook and Corrine L. Patton, eds., *Ezekiel's Hierarchical World: Wrestling with a Tiered Reality*. SBL Symposium Series 31. Atlanta: SBL, 141–57.

Stark, Evan. 2007. *Coercive Control: How Men Entrap Women in Personal Life*. Oxford: Oxford University Press.

Stone, Ken. 2005. *Practicing Safer Texts: Food, Sex and Bible in Queer Perspective*. London and New York: T&T Clark.

Stulman, Louis. 2014. "Reading the Bible through the Lens of Trauma and Art." In Eve-Marie Becker, Jan Dochhorn, and Else K. Holt, eds., *Trauma and Traumatization in Individual and Collective Dimensions: Insights from Biblical Studies and Beyond*. Göttingen: Vandenhoeck & Ruprecht, 177–92.

Stulman, Louis, and Hyun Chul Paul Kim. 2010. *You Are My People: An Introduction to Prophetic Literature*. Nashville: Abingdon.

Tan, Nancy Nam Hoon. 2021. *Resisting Rape Culture: The Hebrew Bible and Hong Kong Sex Workers*. London and New York: Routledge.

Thistlethwaite, Susan Brooks. 1993. "'You May Enjoy the Spoil of Your Enemies': Rape as a Biblical Metaphor for War." In Claudia V. Camp and Carole R. Fontaine, eds., *Women, War, and Metaphor: Language and Society in the Study of the Hebrew Bible*. Semeia 61. Atlanta: Scholars, 59–75.

Volkan, Vamik D. 2001. "Transgenerational Transmissions and Chosen Trauma: An Aspect of Large-Group Identity." *Group Analysis* 34/1: 79–97.

Weems, Renita J. 1989. "Gomer: Victim of Violence or Victim of Metaphor?" *Semeia* 47: 87–104.

Weems, Renita J. 1995. *Battered Love: Marriage, Sex, and Violence in the Hebrew Prophets*. Minneapolis: Fortress.

Whiting, Simeon. 2020. "The Cruel Sea: An Examination of Exodus 13.17–15.21 through the Lenses of Trauma Theory and Collective Memory Studies," PhD, diss., University of Birmingham.

Wolff, Hans Walter. 1974. *Hosea*. Hermeneia. Philadelphia: Fortress.

Women's Aid. 2022. "What Is Coercive Control?" https://www.womensaid.org.uk/information-support/what-is-domestic-abuse/coercive-control/, accessed May 27, 2022.

Yee, Gale A. 2003. *Poor, Banished Children of Eve: Woman as Evil in the Hebrew Bible*. Minneapolis: Fortress.

Yee, Gale A. 2012. "Hosea." In Carol A. Newsom, Sharon H. Ringe, and Jacqueline E. Lapsley, eds., *Women's Bible Commentary*. 20th anniversary ed. Louisville: Westminster John Knox, 299–308.

PART IV

INTERPRETIVE THEORIES AND APPROACHES

CHAPTER 23

HOSEA IN FEMINIST AND WOMANIST INTERPRETATION

VANESSA LOVELACE

23.1. INTRODUCTION

AN essay on feminist and womanist interpretation of the book of Hosea involves several expectations and assumptions. One assumption is that the reader is already aware of what feminist and womanist biblical scholarship looks like. Yet, the invitation to write about feminist and womanist interpretation of Hosea was met by this author with both interest and skepticism—interest because the subject is important for contemporary images of female sexuality, and skepticism because I recognized that the terms "feminist" and "womanist" could be contested ones. Just who is a feminist biblical critic, and must one be a woman to be a feminist? And what about a womanist? Is she just a black feminist? Thus, I find it necessary to offer a basic overview of the terms. By feminist biblical interpretation, I am referring to a shared set of assumptions about the texts and certain readers of the texts. The first assumption is that the biblical text is androcentric or male-centered and supports a male dominated, patriarchal worldview that subordinates women (and children) to men. Thus, feminist readers are suspicious that male interests are being served even when a female character is depicted in a favorable light (Exum 1995). Another assumption is that all interpreters bring their biases to their readings of the text and therefore no interpretation is free of a certain degree of subjectivity that comes with the reader's life experiences, despite claims by traditional, mainstream biblical scholars that an objective, value-neutral interpretation is possible with the "right" tools and skills.

Feminist biblical interpreters have been largely white because the first women to enter the academic field of biblical studies in the 1970s were all white. It would be another decade before the first black and Asian women would join their ranks. Although they shared some of the same assumptions as their white peers about the text, nonwhite women brought with them perspectives of race, gender, and class that were different. Moreover, the importance of biblical authority in interpretation also often differed from black women to white women. Both feminist and womanist scholarship on Hosea is possible. "Womanist" interpretations of Hosea in particular are open to challenges and opportunities along several fronts. For one, as indicated by Nyasha Junior (2015), not only are US-born black women (and other women of color) biblical scholars with terminal degrees in Hebrew Bible/Old Testament and New Testament/Early Christianity significantly underrepresented (less than .01% according to the Society of Biblical Literature), but also not all black women biblical scholars identify themselves or their scholarship as feminist and/or womanist.

Furthermore, Junior explains that the term "womanist" is often mistakenly regarded as synonymous with black or African American women scholars. As she notes, while biblical scholarship by *women* is not assumed to be feminist, "in biblical studies often the work of African American biblical scholars is assumed to be womanist" (Junior 2015: 96).[1] Nonetheless, most women who self-identify as womanist biblical scholars are black.[2] Still, despite the differences in hermeneutical approaches, both feminist and womanist interpreters share a general concern with gender and women's issues in the biblical texts. Given the small (but noteworthy) amount of womanist biblical scholarship in general and fewer works on the Latter or Minor Prophets in particular, I hope that readers' anticipation of womanist interpretations of Hosea in this volume are not raised only to fall short of expectations.

23.2. THE DEVELOPMENT OF FEMINIST AND WOMANIST BIBLICAL CRITICISM OF HOSEA

Feminist and womanist biblical scholarship on Hosea emerged in the 1980s. The appeal was largely due to the book's use of provocative sexual imagery to express God's relationship to Israel. While other prophetic texts used similar language, Hosea's was the oldest and the most developed in communicating Israel's apostasy as a woman's sexually illicit behavior. Women biblical scholars often found Hosea's gendered choice to communicate his message to Israel's male elites both intriguing and problematic. Early feminist approaches to reading Hosea focused on the text's androcentrism, which figures a male prophet (Hosea) as God, thus making God male, as well as on the troubling sexual imagery used to describe the relationship between God and Israel in gendered, asymmetrical terms with the woman subordinate to the man. The use of the marriage metaphor to depict Israel's deity as a wronged husband, the male elite members of Israel as his adulterous wife, and the land as exhibiting sexually illicit behavior also troubled women biblical critics. Traditionally, male critics often took Hosea's use of the marriage metaphor as a positive development in the history of Israel's religion over against Canaanite religious practices.

Another problem that feminist biblical critics have with Hosea is its scriptural authority that lends credence to gender imbalance in male-dominated societies. Some fear that modern readers will accept the image of God punishing Israel metaphorically as divine sanction for the husband threatening the wife with physical violence. The power of the book of Hosea to influence male–female relationships in contemporary society is central to the interpretations of Hosea by feminist and womanist critics. These concerns appear in the selections below. They do not constitute a comprehensive list of titles but rather an overview of feminist and womanist interpretation of Hosea. The contributions range from the 1980s to the present and include varied works from interpreters who are women and men, Jews and Christians, white, black, and Asian.

Before surveying these interpretations, a few words of orientation are in order. The book of Hosea is found in the division of the Jewish Tanakh called the Latter Prophets. The Latter Prophets consist of four books or scrolls: Isaiah, Jeremiah, Ezekiel, and the Book of the Twelve (Minor Prophets). In the Christian Old Testament, the final corpus is separated into twelve individual books. Hosea appears first in the Twelve, but the book of Amos is chronologically older. While the interrelationship between Hosea and Amos is widely known, the role of Hosea in relation to the Twelve is only recently beginning to receive the attention it deserves.

Hosea begins with a superscription that also serves as an introduction that alerts the reader to expect prophetic discourse to follow, indicated by the typical prophetic formula, "The word of the LORD." In this case, the recipient of that word is Hosea ben Beeri, an eighth-century prophet reported as active during the reigns of Kings Uzziah, Jotham, Ahaz, and Hezekiah of Judah, and the reign of King Jeroboam son of Joash of Israel. The mention of these rulers situates Hosea in the temporal setting of the mid-eighth century BCE. Although the kings of Judah ruling at the time are included, his ire is directed specifically at Israel's ruling class and priests. Hosea vituperates Israel on political and religious grounds.

Hosea's condemnation of Israel emanated from various dimensions of Israel's alliance with Assyria, first established during the reign of Jeroboam's great grandfather Jehu in 841 BCE. Second Kings credits Jeroboam II (786–746 BCE) with the restoration and expansion of the original borders of Israel, which brought a period of peace, stability, and economic prosperity to Israel. Some interpreters conclude that instead of seeing this alliance as successful, Hosea viewed it as a betrayal of Israel's covenant with Yhwh. He also blamed the priests for leading the people to abandon the covenant by engaging in Canaanite cultic practices. Thus, the book of Hosea is a polemic against the political and religious elites. But its ingenuity or notoriety, depending on your view, is its use of female sexual imagery to communicate the relationship between Yhwh and Israel.

23.3. Feminist and Womanist Readings of Hosea from the 1980s to 1990s

As previously mentioned, the 1980s and 1990s saw the development of feminist and womanist hermeneutical approaches to Hosea. However, to speak of feminist approaches to Hosea in their early stage is to assume that there were clearly defined criteria like some of their counterparts in nonreligious studies. Many of the authors may have viewed themselves as feminists in their political stances on women's equality or been sympathetic to feminist principles but may not have specifically named a feminist theoretical framework for their scholarship. Others may have inferred that their personal or professional feminist position is reflected in their hermeneutical approach, even if they did not name their exegetical analyses of Hosea as feminist. Many of the examples explored below frequently cite and critique other "feminist" perspectives on Hosea despite those scholars not having identified themselves or their methodology as feminist. Still, some contributors are explicit in their feminist hermeneutics.

Despite inconsistencies in its early development, there is some consensus on the themes explored in these initial feminist readings of Hosea. First, feminist biblical interpretations of Hosea are attentive to female sexual imagery in the book and its use by male and female characters, human and divine. Another theme is Hosea's depiction of female sexuality as symbolic of sin, especially in relation to forbidden religious activity related to hypothesized sacred prostitution and Canaanite fertility cults. A related theme is growing skepticism of the existence of sacred or temple prostitution in Israel or the ancient Near East. There is also the theme of the meaning of the term *eshet zenunim*, variously translated "wife of whoredom" (NRSV), "promiscuous woman" (NIV), and "woman of whoredom" (JPS), and how it has come under scrutiny by feminist and womanist interpreters as it relates to the condemnation by critics of the wife Gomer's sexual behavior. Most of the analyses featured below overwhelmingly focus on Hos. 1–3, where the prophetic marriage metaphor to symbolize God's relationship to Israel is depicted in sexual female imagery. The examples are presented in chronological order.

23.3.1. Feminist Interpretations in the 1980s and 1990s

The objectification of female sexuality as a symbol of evil in the book of Hosea is the subject of T. Drorah Setel's article, "Prophets and Pornography: Female Sexual Imagery in Hosea" (1985). Setel applies a feminist theoretical approach to exploring the relationship between the historical events in late eighth-century Israel and the prophet Hosea's depiction of these events through an objectified view of female sexuality. Setel describes the objectification of female sexuality as "pornographic" because it depicts female sexual experience as negative or sinful in relationship to a positive male standard, degrades and publicly humiliates women, and treats female sexuality as an object of male domination.

Her focus is primarily on Hosea's marriage in chs. 1–2 as metaphorically conveying the relationship between Israel and God in female sexual imagery.

Phyllis Byrd's article, "To Play the Harlot: An Inquiry into an Old Testament Metaphor" (1989), problematizes the translation and interpretation of the Hebrew root *znh* by commentators as "prostitution" in the Hebrew Bible, particularly its metaphorical or figurative use that relies on female behavior to symbolically figure the behavior of collective Israel. Bird begins by explaining that the verb can be used literally to indicate professional prostitution or figuratively to mean apostasy or illicit cultic activity, thus raising questions about Hosea's intended use. Another question she raises is whether there was a fertility cult or sacred prostitution in Canaanite religions as is commonly identified by interpreters of Hos. 4. Byrd maintains that the terms for "prostitutes" and "sacred/consecrated women," along with other classes of female cult functionaries, never overlap into sexual activity in the cultic sphere or cultic activity associated with prostitution, despite some traditional commentators making the connection in Hosea.

Mary Joan Winn Leith's "Verse and Reverse: The Transformation of the Woman, Israel in Hosea 1–3" (1989) speaks of the reversal of the creation myth of Israel in cosmic terms by the prophet Hosea's metaphorical language. She suggests that the prophet transforms Israel metaphorically into a woman who must suffer the punishment of her wrongdoing but is promised redemption and recreation. The woman's threatened return to the wilderness conjures the exodus, wilderness wandering, and possession of the promised land. According to Leith, the cosmic pattern of Israel's creation has three " 'movements': accusation, punishment, and restoration" described by the prophet in feminine imagery, which conform to a pattern of a rite of passage (96).

A Feminist Companion to the Latter Prophets, edited by Athalya Brenner (1995), is the eighth in the series A Feminist Companion to the Bible, published by Sheffield Academic Press. The publisher describes the volume as a combination of the Hebrew Bible and feminist hermeneutics by leading scholars that "offers a sharp confrontation between the voice of the prophetic male and the resistance of the feminist reader." The essays in the volume are arranged in three parts: (1) The Case of Hosea; (2) On the Pornoprophetics of Sexual Violence; and (3) Should We Trust the God of the Prophets? I will only highlight the essays on Hosea, which are the overall focus of the volume (eleven of eighteen essays).

Carole Fontaine's essay, "Hosea" (1995a), was originally published in a two-volume reference book on the Bible. Fontaine's article is a historical-critical approach that lacks a feminist hermeneutic. The theological and literary presuppositions of the historical accuracy of Hosea and Gomer's marriage and the existence of a Canaanite cult of sacred sexuality in ancient Israel reflect traditional perspectives. Fontaine explains that Hosea's "theological achievement" is its use of the marriage metaphor to mirror God's relationship to Israel to express God's disdain for Israel's participation in sacred sexuality (53). However, in her second essay in this collection, she acknowledges the lack of a feminist critique in her earlier article and provides a "Response to 'Hosea'" (Fontaine 1995b). There she expresses her frustration that she was required to disregard her own research and findings on Hosea for a historical-critical approach.

Alice A. Keefe challenges interpretations of Hosea that accept the view that the prophet's female sexual imagery inscribes a dualistic worldview in her essay, "The Female Body, the Body Politic, and the Land: A Sociopolitical Reading of Hosea 1–2" (1995). Rather than following the approach of analyzing the text from the perspective that Hosea's female sexual imagery is a denunciation of Israel's apostasy in a supposed Canaanite religious fertility cult over against Israel's religion, Keefe argues that Hosea's images of female sexual transgression "function rhetorically as a commentary upon the pressing sociopolitical conflicts of Hosea's time" (72). Thus, Keefe concludes that rather than a marriage metaphor, Hosea's trope is a family metaphor that reflects the shock to Israel's identity through disruption of land distribution and social organization.

Androcentric readings of Hosea that delimit the boundaries of Gomer are the focus of Yvonne Sherwood's essay, "Boxing Gomer: Controlling the Deviant Woman in Hosea 1–3" (1995). Sherwood first identifies the similarities between androcentric and feminist readings of Hosea as their "self-consciousness about their inventiveness" (102). She argues that androcentric and feminist interpreters are both inventive in their approaches to problematic texts. However, androcentric readings are usually described as objective by comparison and thus superior to feminist readings which are deemed subjective, or against the grain, and therefore less legitimate. Nevertheless, Sherwood surveys four ancient and four modern commentaries on Hosea to argue that, in their subjectivity, male commentators' reading strategies seek to tame or erase Gomer in the text. She claims, "Disturbed by Gomer, the text urges control of the deviant woman, and demands that she be boxed in, hemmed in by thorn bushes, and surrounded by walls" (105, in reference to Hos. 2:6 [Heb. 2:8]). Various strategies control her, rehabilitate her, or erase her from the text.

The troubling marriage metaphor that symbolizes the adulterous marriage between Hosea/God and Gomer/Israel is the subject of Naomi Graetz's essay, "God Is to Israel as Husband Is to Wife: The Metaphoric Battering of Hosea's Wife" (1995). Graetz takes on the prophets and rabbis for "enshrining the legal subordination of women in metaphor" (139). She finds troubling *Exodus Rabbah's* sympathetic overtures to Hosea/God as a long-suffering husband who punishes Gomer/Israel for straying from "her" husband but is willing to woo "her" back and restore "her" to "her" former state because "he" loves Gomer/Israel (128). She sees the husband–wife relationship in Hos. 2 as an explict case of a batterer and his battered wife. Graetz argues that the marriage figured metaphorically in Hosea is dangerous for its commentary on women. She insists that "the language of Hosea and the other prophets and rabbis who use objectified female sexuality as a symbol of evil has had damaging affects on women" (138). Nonetheless, she finds possibilities within Jewish tradition for reforming Hosea's problem of women's subordination in the ritual act of males donning the *tefillin* (phylacteries) every morning and in a midrash from *Parashat Ekeb* (Deut. 7:12).

Francis Landy, like Graetz, interrogates Hos. 2 in "Fantasy and the Displacement of Pleasure: Hosea 2:4–17" (1995). Landy notes that part of the feminist critique of Hosea is that the book silences the woman's voice and her point of view, as well as objectifies and degrades her. Landy explores the fantasy of desolation and sexual exposure in Hos.

2. He describes how the husband's/God's fantasy of exposing the metaphorical woman's nakedness both excites and disgusts the husband as her lovers look upon her but cannot possess her. By exposing her, the husband simultaneously abandons her and exerts control over her. The husband's jealousy is the motive for battering his wife. Landy reads 2:4–17 (Eng. 2:2–15) intertextually with Song. 5:2–7, where both women suffer humiliation for their sexual impropriety.

John Goldingay (1995) describes his hermeneutical approach in "Hosea 1–3, Genesis 1–4 and Masculist Interpretation" as "post-feminist." His interpretation of Hos. 1–3 builds on feminist readings from a complementary male perspective, not one meant to replace them. Goldingay emphasizes his position that women's insights of the Bible belong alongside male ones. He refers to his project as "masculist interpretation," one that draws on men's experience to illuminate Hosea. He interprets Gen. 1–4 alongside Hos. 1–3 as the relevant text for defining masculinity and informing male–female relationships. He identifies what he refers to as the "holy trinity" of masculinity in Gen. 1–4, which he contends also appears in Hos. 1–3: (1) men define themselves over against women; (2) men are meant to have power and authority; and (3) and men have physical strength or a propensity for violence. In reference to Hos. 1–3, Goldingay finds that the first feature of masculinity evident is that "Yahweh is incomplete without Israel as men are incomplete without women. It is he who seeks her, not she who seeks him" (165). He finds God's initiative in the relationship as the second feature, but he also notes the presence of the third feature in Hosea's portrayal of God as violent.

Mayer Gruber's (1995) article is a commentary on H. L. Ginsberg's translation of Hos. 4:10–19 in the *New Jewish Version of the Hebrew Scriptures*. Gruber defends as positive the view of sexuality and marriage offered by the biblical prophets over against the teenage sexuality represented by the goddess, Ishtar. He contends that 4:10–19 offers a more "noble and ennobling" view of marriage and sexuality (172). Gruber suggests that the problem in Hosea is that both men and woman abandoned true intimacy for physical intimacy, which from Hosea's perspective is apostasy. Thus, the prophet's contribution to marriage and sexuality in 4:10–19 is to castigate men who seek sexual intimacy outside their marriage and to defend women who respond in kind as a cry for help.

Margaret S. Odell searches for the identity of the priest's mother in Hos. 4:5 in "I Will Destroy Your Mother: The Obliteration of a Cultic Role in Hosea 4:4–6" (1995). Odell argues that woman in Hos. 4:5 is not the biological mother or wife of the priest as others have surmised but rather is a cultic official, a "mother" in the cult whose role is to "lead in the festal celebrations of the gifts of God" (181). Thus, she is a colleague of the priest and prophet. The mother's offense, as Odell identifies it, is that she praises Baal not Yhwh, not her involvement in cultic sexual activity, as some commentators find. Thus, her cultic role is erased from the text.

Helen Schüngel-Straumann (1995) examines the maternal image of God using historical perspectives in "God as Mother in Hosea 11." Her exegetical analysis yields feminine imagery for God as a mother taking her nursling to her breasts and giving suck to the child. She describes the imagery of the various historical stages Israel goes through (exodus, wilderness wandering, etc.) under Yhwh's guidance in 11:1–4 as "from the world of infants to show how God makes life possible, protects and shields it like a mother bringing up her child" (203).

Marie-Theres Wacker's (1995) article "Traces of the Goddess in the Book of Hosea" closes the section on Hosea in Brenner's volume. Wacker searches for evidence of a quarrel with the goddess tradition in the Hebrew Bible—a task she observes is fraught with anti-Jewish polemics by Christian feminists who blame Jews for the death of the goddess. Wacker identifies several references in Hosea that could hint at the presence of female deities, including possible references to Asherah in 4:17–19, wordplay on a goddess in 4:12c–13c, and hints of goddess iconography and motifs throughout chs. 2, 4, 11, and 14. Based on the evidence, Wacker maintains that there is a significant goddess theme in Hosea.

Yvonne Sherwood's (1996) monograph picks up on the consensus that the book of Hosea contains "problematic texts" (linguistically, emotionally, theologically) and explores the book's complexities with the same criteria as critics and reviewers of Shakespeare's problem plays. She focuses on Hos. 1–3 in four literary studies across four chapters. Chapter 1 uses ideological criticism, reader-response criticism, and Fredric Jameson's metacommentary theory to confront the discomfort of scholars with the text about Gomer-bat-Diblayim, or the "wife of prostitution." Despite their reading strategies used to "control her—restriction, humiliation, erasure and improvement," Sherwood attempts to reclaim Gomer from those who would vanquish her from the text. Chapter 2 is a semiotic analysis of the sign language in Hos. 1–3, particularly the marriage to Gomer as a signifier of idolatry and the symbolic names of the children. Chapter 3 is a deconstructive reading of Hos. 1–3 using Jacques Derrida's reading of texts to reveal conflicts that affirm and deny the same features. Chapter 4 is a feminist analysis of Hos. 1–3 drawing together the theoretical insights from the three previous studies. She rebuffs feminist readings of Gomer that reduce her role to serving the androcentric interests of the prophet, a "looking-glass for patriarchal ideology" (254). Rather, Sherwood asserts that the task of feminist criticism is to "step through the looking-glass, like Alice, and to retrieve the female character from her 'virtual' and reflective role" (255).

Gale Yee's (1998) commentary on Hosea in the *Women's Bible Commentary* focuses on hermeneutical matters such as gender and sexuality, class conflicts, and ecological struggles. Her treatment of gender and sexuality focuses on key areas in the text such as marriage and adultery, cultic prostitution, and sexuality. Yee describes the patrilineal, patrilocal kinship structure and its honor/shame value system as two key features of ancient Israel's institution of marriage that are important for the reader seeking to understand the use of the marriage metaphor in Hosea.[3]

Another matter of sexuality Yee confronts is what she terms the "phenomenon of so-called cultic prostitution" (208). Yee questions interpreters who maintain that Hos. 4:14–19 reflects a Canaanite practice of cultic prostitution. Allegedly, Canaanite men had ritual sex with cultic prostitutes in a re-enactment of the "sacred marriage" between the god Baal and the goddess Anat to produce rains that would quicken fecundity in humans, animals, and the land. Not only have some scholars assumed that Hosea was lashing out against this practice in his condemnation of Israel but also they have regarded Hosea's wife and the daughters of Israel as being guilty of cultic prostitution. Yee and others dispute the phenomenon of cultic prostitution in Canaanite ritual practices in the ancient Near East and the association of cultic sexual activity with the daughters of Israel in Hos. 4:14b.

23.3.2. Womanist Readings in the 1980s and 1990s

Womanist interpretations of Hosea are one of those contested topics that I mentioned at the beginning of this essay. For one, the term "womanist" is used interchangeably with "feminist" in the self-identification of the same black woman biblical scholar who wrote the two writings on Hosea explored below. Renita Weems, widely regarded as a pioneering womanist biblical scholar, published "Gomer: Victim of Violence or Victim of Metaphor?" in 1989. In a footnote, she describes her concerns as a "feminist biblical scholar" with the texts' use of sexual violence against a *woman* to convey the divine–human relationship, and her concerns as a "black and womanist biblical scholar" with "physical and sexual exploitation of *anyone*" to make a theological claim (90 n. 10; emphasis original). The second publication included in this category is Weems's *Battered Love: Marriage, Sex, and Violence in the Hebrew Bible* (1995). I chose to include it as a womanist reading of Hosea because Weems self-identifies as womanist in publications, lectures, and sermons and her stated interests in the metaphorical depictions of sexual violence in the book's introduction are related to her identity as a woman and an African American (see Cone and Wilmore 1993: 216–24).

Weems, along with many black women religious scholars of her generation, were still trying to find their voice and the language to express their perspectives as black women at a time when the term "womanist" was just becoming part of black women's vernacular, especially after the publication of Alice Walker's *In Search of Our Mothers' Gardens: Womanist Prose* (1983) made the term popular. Thus, while giving black women a new term to self-identify their commitments, Weems, as the first black woman to earn a terminal degree in Hebrew Bible/Old Testament in 1985, was still trying on the term for fit when she published her works on Hosea.

"Gomer: Victim of Violence or Victim of Metaphor?" is an exegetical analysis of the sexual imagery and violence in the judgment speeches in Hos. 2:4–25 (Eng. 2:2–23), which are framed by the prophet's obedience to God in chs. 1 and 3. Weems establishes the highly emotive impact of Hosea's literary characterization of the divine–human relationship as a marital union between a man and woman gone astray in the accusations, threats, punishment, and reconciliation in ch. 2. She does not emphasize the socioeconomic issues in the text as some feminist authors have. However, she does a superb job of helping the reader make the connection between the husband accusing the wife of falsely crediting her lovers with providing for her and showing them up by publicly exposing her while they stood by helpless with God's accusations against Israel for doing the same. She implores biblical theologians to consider the implications of such biblical imagery. The danger she raises is the risk of metaphor being taken for the thing it signifies. While the strength of the marriage metaphor may shed light on God's love, anger, and forgiveness, it leaves unresolved the question of divine retribution.

Weems's monograph *Battered Love: Marriage, Sex, and Violence in the Hebrew Bible* (1995) explores the propensity for biblical prophets to use popular notions of gender and sexuality of their time to persuade a male audience. Specifically, she interrogates the combination of marriage, sex, and violence against women rhetorically in prophetic texts to both fascinate and shock readers. She demonstrates that "the prophets' success or failure as orators depended in the end on their ability to convince their audiences that viable connections could be drawn between the norms governing the sexual behavior of women and God's demands on Israel" (3). She also raises the concern that the biblical prophets' depictions of women's sexuality contribute to the lasting impression of women's sexuality as sinful, evil, and dangerous. Weems traces the metaphorical use of marital and sexual imagery in the prophetic literature back to Hosea. She notes that not only is Hosea the first prophet to use the marriage metaphor to describe the relationship between Israel and God, but as the only eighth-century northern prophet whose oracles have survived, his influence on the preaching of later generations of prophets is notable. Hosea's metaphorical use of a dispute between a husband and wife to draw attention to the divine–human relationship includes accusations of adultery, threats, sexual violence, chastisement, and reconciliation. Weems notes that the metaphor goes to extremes to convey the "extent of Israel's theological and moral estrangement from God," but she also finds assurance in the metaphor's ability to "illustrate in tender, comforting, romantic language and imagery what Israel's existence would be like reconciled to the one God" (50).

23.4. FEMINIST READINGS IN THE 2000S

Alice Keefe's book, *Woman's Body and the Social Body in Hosea 1–2* (2001), is an expansion of her essay published in Brenner's collection (1995). Keefe challenges scholarly interpretations that insist that Hosea's marriage metaphor is a repudiation of the "false" Canaanite fertility religion in defense of the true religion, ethical Yahwism. In this interpretation, Hosea is exalted as a champion of Western monotheistic religions, but feminist scholars see the peril in Hosea's gendered and dualistic metaphor that pits Israelite and Canaanite religions against each other. Keefe contends, "Instead of lauding Hosea's attack on fertility religion as a theological accomplishment, feminist scholars have indicted Hosea for his role in advancing the patriarchal and misogynistic character of the Western religious traditions" (2001: 9). Yet, Keefe argues that this dualistic interpretation of Hosea by both traditional and feminist readers is a product of their dualistic assumptions regarding Canaanite religion and the feminine rather than of elements inherent in the text itself. The result, according to Keefe, is the association of Hosea's adulterous wife as guilty of engaging in the Canaanite fertility cult, a phenomenon whose existence is disputed. She attempts to redeem the text from this erroneous reading by offering an alternative framework for interpreting Hosea.

Marie-Theres Wacker's article "Hosea: The God-Identified Man and the Women of Israel/Israel as Woman" (2002) explores gender dynamics in the book of Hosea by engaging the final form of the text. Wacker describes the gender relations fundamental to the metaphor as the relationship among the prophet, God, and the woman in a threefold sense: God commands Hosea to take a woman of whoredom as a wife, to have children of whoredom, and the land represented the woman that has committed whoredom and departed from God. In this case, whoredom is characterized as female sexual behavior. Thus, Wacker shows that not only gender relations between a man and woman but also sexuality, specifically a woman's unrestrained sexual behavior, is a central component of the book's rhetorical strategy. She explains that this is problematic because the text affirms the message that men are the victims of women's illicit sexual activity and thus "legitimizes and authorizes all sorts of control over women, if not violence against them" as divinely sanctioned (151).

Rather than reject the message in Hosea, Wacker searches for "hermeneutical help" with redeeming the book's questionable gender relations. She finds help first in chs. 1, 3, and 9, where her exegetical analysis provides her with a gender balance based on the birth of the children and their names to counter the gender inequality of the relationship between the man and woman. She also notes the literary distinction between the women engaged in sexually illicit activities and the daughters and brides in ch. 9. Wacker finds enough support in the text to exonerate Hosea of accusations of misogyny "as someone who despises women" (2002: 155).

23.5. Womanist Readings in the 2000s

The Hosea commentary in the Wisdom Commentary series by Cheryl A. Kirk-Duggan and Valerie Bridgeman (2023) shares the goals of the series to provide a detailed feminist interpretation. This commentary constitutes the only explicit work of womanist interpretation on Hosea at the current time. I invited Kirk-Duggan and Bridgeman to share their reflections on the commentary. With regard to their womanist approach, they state the following[4]:

> Our Womanist biblical analysis provides a contextual, lived framework to focus on numerous components that affect how we see/hear/read the received story during the early part of the twenty-first century, from North America and specifically from the United States. Foundational to our work is to name the systemic, privileged heteronormativity inscribed within the text that commentators often reinscribe. As womanist scholars, we have been friends for over three decades and share mutual respect and intellectual curiosity. We live interreligious, intergenerational, interdisciplinary realities amid heightened global violence that intentionally targets

gender, race, sexualities, age, class, ability, and the socio-political, with the conflation of religion and state in overdrive. We name the incongruities and ugliness within an alleged sacred text, Hosea, ostensibly designed to call out abuse of power, lack of covenantal faithfulness, and the danger of humans destroying the cosmos that itself oppresses. Womanist analysis empowers and attends to how women and girls experience oppression, then and now, amid many hidden and explicit complexities of a white supremacist, patriarchal, capitalistic, misogynistic cosmology wrapped within a nationalistic theology that marries faith and state. The exegesis examines the cast of divine and human characters, including creation itself, who have complicated relationships that involve covenant, disobedience, and violence. As with all relationships, characters face challenges of major proportions. We call out the explicit and subtle divine and human explosive violence. While many read the book of Hosea metaphorically, we call God to account for the heinous, abusive actions in the book. Globally, such actions play out as one in three persons daily experience domestic violence and sexual assault—justified by sacred texts.

Kirk-Duggan and Bridgeman state that the "fire and passion of Womanist scholars who study, teach, write, interpret, preach, and minister" call for "new kinds of interpretation, accountability, and change as liberation." They give this approach a new label: "Womanist biblical emancipatory theory." They explain:

> Womanist biblical emancipatory theory embraces a message of hope and transformation towards engendering mutuality and community amid the responsibility and stewardship of freedom and honors the *Imago Dei*, the image of God, the essential goodness in all persons, regardless. We wrestle with the scriptures amid the absurdity of oppression and embrace an embodied relationality of thought, being, and existence. A Womanist emancipatory theory embraces a message of hope and transformation towards engendering mutuality and community amid the responsibility and stewardship of freedom. This embodied spirituality of relationality involves a process of working for justice, of human beings creating systems that are catalysts for change, rooted in an ultimate source of all reality. Every person is important and relational. Womanist biblical criticism and theology heighten awareness to exorcise oppressive evil, moving towards change, balance, promise, and healing. The interconnectedness of the divine with all creation is a vitality of empowerment. Looking to Hosea, this vitality presses our concerns that we prepare our ears, minds, and hearts to hear the text significantly, to note the crises and the ambiguities, as well as the conundrums which seem inexplicable.

23.6. CONCLUSION

This essay attempted to demonstrate the diversity, complexity, and challenges of defining feminist and womanist readings of Hosea since their development in the 1980s. As mentioned previously, all women biblical scholars are not feminists, and all black women biblical scholars are not womanists. Additionally, not all feminists are women, or at least there are male biblical critics who are sympathetic to feminist concerns. Several male contributors to *A Feminist Companion to the Latter Prophets* (Brenner 1995) engaged in conversations with feminist biblical critics at various meetings and chose to address feminist issues in analyses of Hosea. While they sought common ground with feminist interpreters on egalitarian views of men and women, they also tended to find the positive in the text despite the disgust and horror of the violent sexual imagery to convey the divine–human relationship in Hosea. However, efforts to find redeeming value in the text are not limited to male interpreters. Both feminist and womanist critics found the marriage metaphor's restoration of Israel after the jealousy, accusations, and punishment evidence of God's love for Israel. This reflects the wide spectrum of feminist and womanist approaches to metaphorical language in prophetic books in general and Hosea in particular—a spectrum likely to continue into the next generation of scholarship on Hosea.

NOTES

1. Still today, feminist biblical interpretations by white women scholars predominantly appear in religion databases and Internet searches for "feminist biblical interpretation," even though there are black women biblical scholars who identify as feminist.
2. Many black and other women of color were inspired by Alice Walker's (1983) four-part poetic definition of "womanist" in her widely acclaimed compilation of nonfiction essays, articles, reviews, and speeches that largely lay out her ideas of "womanist" theory.
3. Gale Yee published her dissertation on Hosea as *Composition and Tradition in the Book of Hosea: A Redactional Critical Investigation* (Atlanta: Scholars Press, 1987).
4. All subsequent quotations are email correspondence from Cheryl Kirk-Duggan to Valerie Bridgeman and Vanessa Lovelace, July 29, 2022.

REFERENCES

Brenner, Athalya, ed. 1995. *A Feminist Companion to the Latter Prophets*. Sheffield: Sheffield Academic.

Byrd, Phyllis. 1989. "To Play the Harlot: An Inquiry into an Old Testament Metaphor." In Peggy Day, ed., *Gender and Difference in Ancient Israel*. Philadelphia: Westminster, 75–94.

Cone, James H., and Gayraud S. Wilmore, eds. 1993. *Black Theology: A Documentary History, vol. 2, 1980–1992*. Maryknoll, NY: Orbis Books.

Exum, J. Cheryl. 1995. "Feminist Criticism: Whose Interests Are Being Served?" In Gale A. Yee, ed., *Judges and Method: New Approaches in Biblical Studies*. Minneapolis: Fortress, 65–90.

Fontaine, Carol. 1995a. "Hosea." In Athalya Brenner, ed., *A Feminist Companion to the Latter Prophets*. Sheffield: Sheffield Academic, 40–59.

Fontaine, Carol. 1995b. "A Response to 'Hosea.'" In Athalya Brenner, ed., *A Feminist Companion to the Latter Prophets*. Sheffield: Sheffield Academic, 60–69.

Goldingay, John. 1995. "Hosea 1–3, Genesis 1–4 and Masculist Interpretation." In Athalya Brenner, ed., *A Feminist Companion to the Latter Prophets*. Sheffield: Sheffield Academic, 161–68.

Graetz, Naomi. 1995. "God Is to Israel as Husband Is to Wife: The Metaphoric Battering of Hosea's Wife." In Athalya Brenner, ed., *A Feminist Companion to the Latter Prophets*. Sheffield: Sheffield Academic, 126–45.

Gruber, Mayer. 1995. "Marital Fidelity and Intimacy: A View from Hosea 4." In Athalya Brenner, ed., *A Feminist Companion to the Latter Prophets*. Sheffield: Sheffield Academic, 169–79.

Junior, Nyasha. 2015. *An Introduction to Womanist Biblical Interpretation*. Louisville: Westminster John Knox.

Keefe, Alice. 1995. "The Female Body, the Body Politic and the Land: A Sociopolitical Reading of Hosea 1–2." In Athalya Brenner, ed., *A Feminist Companion to the Latter Prophets*. Sheffield: Sheffield Academic, 70–100.

Keefe, Alice A. 2001. *Woman's Body and the Social Body in Hosea*. JSOTSup 338. GCT 10. London; New York: Sheffield Academic.

Kirk-Duggan, Cheryl A., and Valerie Bridgeman. 2023. *Hosea*. Wisdom Commentary. Collegeville: Liturgical, forthcoming.

Landy, Francis. 1995. "Fantasy and the Displacement of Pleasure: Hosea 2:4–17." In Athalya Brenner, ed., *A Feminist Companion to the Latter Prophets*. Sheffield: Sheffield Academic, 146–60.

Leith, Mary Joan Winn. 1989. "Verse and Reverse: The Transformation of the Woman, Israel, in Hosea 1–3." In Peggy L. Day, ed., *Gender and Difference in Ancient Israel*. Minneapolis: Fortress, 95–108.

Odell, Margaret S. 1995. "I Will Destroy Your Mother: The Obliteration of a Cultic Role in Hosea 4:4–6." In Athalya Brenner, ed., *A Feminist Companion to the Latter Prophets*. Sheffield: Sheffield Academic, 180–93.

Schüngel-Straumann, Helen. 1995. "God as Mother in Hosea 11." In Athalya Brenner, ed., *A Feminist Companion to the Latter Prophets*. Sheffield: Sheffield Academic, 194–218.

Setel, T. Drorah. 1985. "Prophets and Pornography: Female Sexual Imagery in Hosea." In Letty M. Russell, ed., *Feminist Interpretation of the Bible*. Philadelphia: Westminster, 86–95.

Sherwood, Yvonne. 1995. "Boxing Gomer: Controlling the Deviant Woman in Hosea 1–3." In Athalya Brenner, ed., *A Feminist Companion to the Latter Prophets*. Sheffield: Sheffield Academic, 101–25.

Sherwood, Yvonne. 1996. *The Prostitute and the Prophet: Hosea's Marriage in Literary-Theoretical Perspective*. JSOTSup 212. GCT 2. London; New York: Sheffield Academic.

Wacker, Marie-Theres. 1995. "Traces of the Goddess in the Book of Hosea." In Athalya Brenner, ed., *A Feminist Companion to the Latter Prophets*. Sheffield: Sheffield Academic, 219–41.

Wacker, Marie-Theres. 2002. "Hosea: The God-Identified Man and the Women of Israel/Israel as Woman." *Korean Journal of Old Testament Studies* 13 (2002): 147–66. Walker, Alice. 1983. *In Search of Our Mothers' Gardens: Womanist Prose*. San Diego, CA: Laura Media.

Weems, Renita J. 1989. "Gomer: Victim of Violence or Victim of Metaphor?" *Semeia* 47: 87–104.

Weems, Renita. 1995. *Battered Love: Marriage, Sex, and Violence in the Hebrew Bible*. Minneapolis: Fortress. Yee, Gale A. 1998. "Hosea." In Carol A. Newsom and Sharon H. Ringe, eds., *The Women's Bible Commentary*. Louisville: Westminister John Knox, 207–15.

CHAPTER 24

MASCULINITY STUDIES AND HOSEA

SUSAN E. HADDOX

MASCULINITY studies emerged in biblical studies in the 1990s and has made numerous contributions to the analysis of gender in the biblical texts. Masculinity studies or masculist interpretation, like feminist interpretation, places gender construction at the center of textual analysis. Masculist interpretation contributes to gender analysis because so many biblical texts are focused on men. As a central aspect of human identity, gender is significant not only for individuals but also for community status. A society's construction of gender and gender relationships often embeds underlying power structures, so that gender comes to symbolize power and prestige in different spheres of influence. Masculinity is especially associated with power in the fields of warfare and politics. Masculist interpretation reveals the ways that gender pervades the rhetoric and assumptions of the texts without assuming that the male is the unreflective norm.

Hosea was one of the earliest Hebrew Bible texts given a masculist interpretation and it has sustained the interest of interpreters. Like other prophetic texts, Hosea engages gendered imagery, as well as many other image fields. The types of approaches under the umbrella of masculinity studies are diverse. These include perspectives that draw from reader-response criticism, cultural anthropology, linguistics, psychoanalysis, cultural criticism, and queer theory. Interpreters have focused on masculinity as defined in terms of hegemonic masculinity, femininity, boyhood, and embodiment. These various approaches have found fertile ground in the image fields of Hosea. Much of the early interpretive attention to Hosea, especially from scholars interested in gender, focused on the marriage metaphor in Hos. 1–3. While feminist criticism has provided much insight into the problematic nature of the metaphor, focusing on the dynamics of the relationship and the abusive nature of the husband, the emphasis tends to be on the implications for the construction of women and femininity. Masculist interpretation focuses on the construction of masculinity and how the rhetoric of the text affects the male audience. In addition, masculist interpreters have examined many of the other images and rhetoric in the book.

24.1. Defining Masculinity

One of the questions that arises in masculist interpretation of Hosea is how to define masculinity. Much of contemporary masculinity studies depends heavily on the work of Raewyn W. Connell (2005) in the social sciences. Connell proposed a multiple masculinities model that has been taken up by many biblical masculinity scholars. Connell used the term "hegemonic masculinity" to refer to the dominant form of masculinity associated with social power. What characteristics define that power will vary from society to society. Thus hegemonic masculinity is culturally dependent and can change over time. Because it is associated with power, hegemonic masculinity tends to change relatively slowly. People who want to obtain power adopt characteristics associated with power, causing that form of masculinity to self-perpetuate, even though no one person embodies all of the hegemonic elements. Within any given society there are also other functional masculinities. Complicit masculinities are those that are not in power but support the hegemonic masculine structures. Subordinate masculinities are marginalized. These masculinities are not fixed entities but are negotiated within a dynamic cultural context.

Determining characteristics of hegemonic and other forms of masculinity in a historical society creates challenges. In the case of biblical scholarship, one challenge is that access to society is primarily through texts written for polemical purposes. These texts do not necessarily reflect the reality of gender conceptions and relationships between actual human beings. Instead, they represent constructions of gender that often serve multiple symbolic purposes. Such is especially true with Hosea. Hosea as a prophetic text employs gender in many symbolic ways and represents highly constructed figures used for polemical purposes. Scholars have taken different approaches to this challenge.

One approach is to use biblical texts in combination to elucidate characteristics of masculinity. This method still requires caution, as none of the biblical texts are ethnographies. The narrative texts often seem more straightforward than prophetic texts; however, the characters within are not necessarily any less a construction. One of the first attempts at a masculist reading of Hosea came from John Goldingay (1995), who compared Gen. 1–3 and Hos. 1–3, drawing characteristics of masculinity from the former and applying them to the portrayal of God in the latter. Goldingay specifically tied his approach to feminist criticism, in his attempt to bring conscious awareness to the construction of masculine gender in Hosea. The overall attempt, however, was mostly a reader-response reflection on the masculine gender dynamics in the text. The essay maintained an essentialist perspective, focusing on men's strength, sexuality, and aggressiveness. He also used the psychoanalytic idea from Sigmund Freud that since boys' relationships with their mothers are cross-gendered while girls' relationships are same-gendered, boys have a different need for relationship as adults. He then somewhat casually applied these insights to the portrayal of God as the male husband in the marriage metaphor. While there are many problematic elements in Goldingay's reading, it does make a first attempt at taking seriously the construction of masculinity, including the masculinity of God, in Hosea. Later interpreters have picked up the thread and provided a variety of more careful studies.

David Clines uses this technique in several studies, most influentially in his study of David (Clines 1995). He identifies several categories of traits comprising David's masculinity that have been used extensively by later scholars. These include David as a talented musician and a beautiful specimen of a man. He displays prowess both physically as an active warrior and verbally as a persuader. He bonds with other men, particularly with Jonathan, and does not have close relationships with women, despite marrying several of them. Clines (2002) has done the same kind of inventory with other texts, including from the prophets. While most prophets are not warriors, the texts do include strength and violence. They show concern with honor, holiness, and tradition. They show significant verbal skill, though the extent of their persuasiveness is undetermined. Clines argues that they are largely womanless, though that claim can be disputed as most of them appear to have been married.

Though influential, Clines's technique reveals the problems with using it. He looks at men whom he assumes to embody Israelite masculinity and draws characteristics from them. However, as even he notes, while David is considered ideal in many ways, he is not completely representative of masculine norms. It is even more doubtful that the prophets, especially the writing prophets, represent ideal Israelite masculinity. Assuming a man is an ideal representative and then drawing the characteristics of masculinity from that man is the height of circular reasoning.

To counter that problem, other scholars have incorporated different types of information into their construction of masculinity, including texts and iconography from surrounding cultures. Cynthia Chapman (2004) compiles images from Assyrian royal inscriptions and friezes and examines the portrayal of gender in warfare. Since warfare is a standard masculine realm, it is a fruitful area for investigating relevant images. She uses these Assyrian constructions in conjunction with biblical texts from the Assyrian period to create a fuller picture of gender symbolism.

Another way to gather data on masculinity is to look at cross-cultural studies in anthropology. While this also carries risks of generalizations and anachronism, when used carefully, such studies can provide helpful insights into ancient masculinities. Studies of Mediterranean and other pastoral cultures where honor plays an important role in social standing have been the most frequently used. Some scholars combine these different approaches to try to provide checks on the problems of each individual method. For example, I have combined the insights of cross-cultural studies in masculinity from anthropology and the representations of gender in Assyrian inscriptions and friezes with examples in the biblical texts (Haddox 2011). When there is agreement among the different sources, there is higher likelihood that a given characteristic is representative of masculinity in ancient Israel. When there are differences, further analysis about whether the differences reflect a cultural particularity or the portrayal of alternative masculinities is warranted. Rather than drawing characteristics of masculinity from individual characters, as does Clines, I note common characteristics across many

24.2. THE ROLE OF MASCULINITY IN HOSEA

In addition to the definition of masculinity, a central question is what role masculinity plays in the text. Masculinity is embedded in Hosea's use of metaphor. My monograph focuses on how masculinity functions rhetorically, as the prophet critiques the leaders of Israel (Haddox 2011). Using methods from cognitive anthropology, I look at how metaphor is used to move people around in social space. I consider how masculinity applies in the political and socio-religio-economic realms. I divide my study into two major sections: metaphors related to gender-based imagery and metaphors related to other images. These metaphors work to move people along axes of potency, activity, and goodness, characteristics drawn from James Fernandez's (1986) work in cognitive anthropology, looking at how metaphors function to create identity and social relationships in a culture. Hegemonic masculinity is associated with high scores along all three axes: potency in warfare, sexuality, and political power; activity and agency; and qualities of honor and morality. Israel's leaders seem to think they are fulfilling each of these areas of masculinity, but Hosea's rhetoric moves them down each of the axes, attacking the leader's masculinity.

The gendered imagery in Hosea includes both male and female sexual imagery. The marriage metaphor has gained by far the most scholarly attention. Hosea casts the elite male audience, normally in the position of a high-status husband, as an unfaithful wife. The wife exercises agency but with dishonorable actions, being unfaithful to her husband. As a result, her actions are constrained by her husband and she is subject to attack by her lovers. By placing the elite males into the role of the wife, Hosea undermines the masculinity of the leaders in at least two ways: first, they are moved into a subordinate social role; and second, they act dishonorably in that role.

The metaphor also has implications for the masculinity of God. While God is portrayed in the role of the husband, it is notable that this husband only partially fulfills the characteristics of masculinity because of his lack of ability to control the wife figure. The potency of the husband is brought into question because of the uncertain paternity of the children. The wife's misattribution of grain and wine raises questions about the husband's ability to provide. Although the husband takes action after the fact to constrain and punish the wife, the husband did not have the capacity to maintain the wife's loyalty. She took the action, and he did not. Finally, although in certain patriarchal contexts the husband's punitive actions may seem justified, their vengeful nature is not unambiguously good. Read with modern eyes, they are, in fact, abusive. Within the rhetorical setting, stripping honor and power from God may be an additional indictment of the Israelite leaders. As good Yahwists, they should reinforce the potency, action, and goodness of God, not undermine it.

The marriage metaphor is not the only source of gendered imagery in Hosea, though it has drawn the most attention. There are several types of male imagery used throughout the book. Many of these relate to illicit sexual relationships, such as fornication and adultery, and potency. Although the term *znh* ("fornication") is usually discussed with the female as subject, there are nine cases in Hosea where *znh* has a male subject or implied subject, including the personified nation of Israel gendered as male. Few commentators have considered the connotations that the males are engaging in illicit sex, either literally or metaphorically. One example occurs in Hos. 4:10, which reads, "They will eat but not be sated; they will fornicate but not break through/out." Though ambiguous, the phrase implies some lack of potency, whether a lack of progeny resulting from intercourse or the inability to complete the sexual act. Either is a challenge to the masculine status of the subject. A more clearly masculine form of sexual misconduct is indicated by the term *na'aph* ("adultery"). Adultery in the ancient Near Eastern context is defined as a crime against a man by his wife and the man with whom she sleeps. It is a theft of the sexual rights of one man by another. As a metaphor in political contexts, it often refers to treason, as is the case in Hosea. The term occurs in a significant cluster in Hos. 7, which describes a political coup. These terms for illicit sexual relationships undermine the goodness of the men, question their judgment and honor, and imply impotency—all ways to subvert their masculinity.

A variety of images directly undermine the potency of Israel's leaders. Many of these are euphemisms for erections or lack thereof and include references to sticks and staffs, as well as baking and bow imagery. Hosea 4:12 chastises the leaders that "my people asks his stick and his staff tells him." While many commentators have associated these with cultic items, a phallic interpretation links them with the preceding and following references to fornication in vv. 10–11 and 12b. In other words, the leaders are not thinking with their minds but another part of their anatomy. The language mocks the perceived potency of the male leaders, questioning other elements of their masculinity, especially honor and judgment. A second category of images relates to baking. The oven is used as a symbol in complexes with the adultery imagery, referring to the heat of illicit sex and treachery. The conspiracy in Hos. 7 is likened to a rising dough, symbolizing leaders imagining their power against the king increasing. Then Ephraim is compared to a cake unturned—burned on one side and doughy on the other (7:8). The bread is literally half-baked and useless, as is the state of Ephraim. Internal treachery leads to destruction by the Assyrians. Eventually, the bread, the leader's strength, molds (7:9). The leaders' perceived political power is a delusion.

Another potency image found in Assyrian friezes, texts, other biblical passages, and a few key places in Hosea is bow imagery. The bow functions as a symbol of military and sexual potency. In Assyrian treaties and other texts, the bow is a symbol of masculinity, as the loom is a symbol of femininity. In the Assyrian images, the king is often shown standing upright with a full beard, holding a drawn bow. The defeated enemies are small, often naked or half-clothed, and have slack bows. Sometimes they are forced to cut their bows in half. The slack bow represents their defeat and is often linked in the friezes with connotations of rape and sexual humiliation. In Hos. 1:5, Yhwh vows to break the bow of

Israel in the valley of Jezreel, threatening the masculine potency of the Israelite leaders in military and political terms. While difficult to translate, 7:16 states that the leaders "will return, not 'up'—they are like a slack bow!" The first part of the verse has puzzled many interpreters, creating speculation about whether it is a reference to worship in some form. Viewed as an impotency image, it critiques the leaders' self-delusion as powerful political actors in a chapter focused on a political coup framed with adultery imagery. All of the male imagery has the rhetorical effect of undermining, and often mocking, the masculinity of the male elite leaders of Israel. They think they are potent and powerful, but the prophet reveals that ultimately all their attempts at gaining power will come to naught.

In addition to gender-based imagery, Hosea employs many other types of metaphors. While these may not immediately alert the reader to their implications for masculinity, my examination (Haddox 2011) shows that the images work to move the leaders in the same direction in social space as do the gendered images—namely, down the axes of potency, activity, and goodness. In other words, they move the leaders to less masculine spaces. The non-gender-based images include parent-child, sickness and healing, and animals and plants, both domestic and wild. In the case of the parent-child imagery, Ephraim/Israel is usually portrayed as the child. As will be discussed below, masculinity relates not only to femininity but also to boyhood. Thus, just as portraying the leaders as a wife undermines their masculinity, so does portraying them as a boy. Just as the wife was unfaithful, so the child in Hos. 11 is disobedient, walking away from the good parent. In Hos. 2, the children are not agents, but objects of the actions of their parents, both the wayward mother and the punitive father. In Hos. 11, the child has more agency but no more sense. Ephraim is also compared to a foolish fetus in Hos. 13:13, refusing to recognize the signs of labor and be born.

The leaders are also displayed as parents, in both literal and figurative terms. As parents, they do not fulfill their responsibilities. The fathers in Hos. 4 are not able to control their daughters and daughters-in-law, who commit fornication and adultery. Instead, they set bad examples by engaging in such activities themselves. They display neither control of themselves or their dependents, nor honor. Later references portray Ephraim as the parent of alien or destroyed children in Hos. 5:7 and 9:11–16. Again, their inability to create progeny to carry on their name undermines their masculinity.

Another set of images involves sickness and healing. In this set, humans get sick and cause sickness, but never heal. When they get sick, their potency is reduced. When they cause sickness, their goodness is reduced. Thus, this imagery also reduces their masculine characteristics. Ephraim sees his sickness and sores in Hos. 5:13 and seeks healing from the wrong source, so is impotent even in his effort to restore potency. Ephraim makes the kings they are plotting to overthrow sick with wine (7:5), mixing ill-intent with their power to sicken.

In the animal imagery, Ephraim is sometimes the hunter and sometimes the prey. When hunting, Ephraim's efforts are often misdirected and fruitless (5:15) or passive but treacherous as snares and traps (5:1–2). More frequently, Ephraim is the prey hunted by God. In this case, Ephraim clearly lacks potency, brought down as birds in a net. Birds or herbivores, usually domestic animals, represent Ephraim. The birds flutter or are trapped; the herbivores are stubborn but under the control of the farmer. Yhwh, by contrast, is represented by predators, including lions, bears, and leopards—all of which tear their prey, as Yhwh will punish Ephraim. The animal imagery places Yhwh high on the potent and active axes, and Ephraim low on those axes, and thus less masculine.

Similar to the hunting imagery, Ephraim as a farmer proves inadequate. He herds and sows the wind, reaping the whirlwind (12:2 [Eng. 12:1]; 8:7). He plows wickedness and harvests injustice (10:13). Because of their misdirected actions, their crops will fail to feed them (9:2). This contrasts with the potency and success of Yhwh as a farmer who sows Jezreel into the earth (2:25 [Eng. 2:23]) along with the grain and new wine. Yhwh herds Ephraim, showing care and power, and occasionally antipathy, toward the flock (13:7). Ephraim appears several times as a plant. Plants are seldom associated with potency and activity, although they can be more or less good in purpose. The prophet lauds Ephraim as grapes in the wilderness or the first fruits of the fig in 9:10, like a special treat. Other times, Ephraim is an unfruitful vine (9:16; 10:1). Hosea 14 offers several positive images of Ephraim as a plant, producing proper fruit in a reconciled state with Yhwh. There is only one image of Yhwh as a plant—a cypress tree that produces fruit to sustain Ephraim (14:9 [Eng. 14:8]). The agricultural and plant imagery again places the leaders in a less potent, less active, less good social space, reducing their masculinity. A final set of images relates to natural phenomena, such as wind and water. In this imagery, Yhwh is portrayed as the powerful winds and rains, sometimes as the actual wind and sometimes controlling it. Humans are the transitory dew or fruitlessly pursue the wind, unable to control it, making a mockery of their self-deluded potency and action.

My previous study (Haddox 2011) examines how general characteristics of masculinity underlie Hosea's rhetorical strategy. These characteristics are present both in images that are clearly gendered and in those that are not. According to cognitive anthropology, a metaphoric predication serves to create identity and move a person in social space. Hosea's extensive use of metaphor moves the audience from a space of activity, potency, and goodness—all traits associated with a construction of masculinity in Israel—to lower positions in the social grid. Yhwh occupies the most masculine position in the space, although there is some variation in Yhwh's portrayal because of the variety of metaphors and the complex nature of the metaphorical relationships.

I employ an approach grounded in anthropology and rhetoric, but the instability concerning masculinity in the text lends itself to queer readings that further question the definition and role of masculinity for the audience, the prophet, and God. Scholars have explored both the queering of the prophet's and audiences' masculinities to various degrees. Stuart Macwilliam (2011) looks specifically at the marriage metaphor in Hos. 1–3. His approach is not explicitly masculist but does address issues of masculinity. In comparing the role of marriage in the prophets Jeremiah and Hosea, Macwilliam observes that God undermines Jeremiah's masculinity by prohibiting him from marrying. Hosea's masculinity is reduced by the command to marry a promiscuous woman. In both cases, God directly subverts the masculinity of the prophet. Macwilliam explains that the slipperiness of the metaphor in turn casts doubts on God's masculinity:

"One wonders about a Yhwh whose role as a masculine partner has been to some degree paralleled by a human husband whose masculinity is under question" (114). Macwilliam downplays the idea that there are feminine images of God present in Hosea, though noting the ambiguity in ch. 11, but his reading allows for cracks in the portrait of Yhwh as the ultimate hegemon.

Another of Macwilliam's contributions to a masculist reading of Hosea is his treatment of the conciliatory aspects of the marriage. In many feminist readings, Yhwh's speaking to the wife in the wilderness and restoring the relationship to better times are read in terms of cycles of abuse. A violent partner often apologizes and is forgiven, then later engages in further violence. Macwilliam argues that there is no "cycle" present in Hosea; the text provides a linear account of punishment and restoration. He further claims that reading the reconciliation in a positive light undermines certain heteronormative elements. The male audience is cast in the role of the wife, but not only for the purposes of shame and humiliation. Instead, there is a positive model for the men cast in a feminine position in relationship to Yhwh. It leaves the men in the position of subordination to Yhwh, one of receptiveness and intimacy. A positive interpretation of the reconciliation can thus challenge gender norms that cast a negative value on femininity. What appears on the surface as a heteronormative relationship actually queers the audience, and to some extent, Yhwh.

Several scholars have considered the implications of placing males in a female relationship to Yhwh. Howard Eilberg-Schwarz (1994) was one of the earliest scholars to observe that the receptiveness of the prophet places him in the position of the feminine in relation to a masculine God. If the man is placed in the position of the woman, then the woman has to be pushed out of the scene entirely. Rhiannon Graybill (2016) takes this analysis further, studying the queerness of the prophetic body in Hosea through the lens of horror. The horror genre frequently features the female body in a state of openness, either to possession or torture. The female body often acts as the site of masculine displacement. Graybill uses Carol Clover's (2015) work on the horror genre to explore this aspect. As Clover puts it, "For a space to be created in which men can weep without being labeled feminine, women must be relocated to a space where they will be made to wail uncontrollably; for men to be able to relinquish emotional rigidity, control, women must be relocated to a space in which they will undergo a flamboyant psychotic break, and so on" (105). Graybill argues that the violence of Hosea does not represent simple misogyny, but also masculine displacement. Prophecy is a disruptive act. The prophetic role by definition requires openness to God, threatening masculine bodily integrity.

The lens of horror highlights this problem of masculine openness. The disruptive, opening force of prophecy is displaced onto the feminine, so that the masculine can maintain the appearance of closedness while still experiencing the word of God. The wife in Hosea shows openness both to her lovers and to punishment. By displacing this threat onto the wife, the masculinity of the prophet is preserved. In the text, there are many levels of fluidity: between the woman's body and the land; between the prophet's body and God's body; between male and female bodies, as the predominantly male audience is cast as the wife. The excess of violence and openness of the woman in Hosea relativizes the openness of the prophet. Graybill focuses on the intensity and affect of the queer body as it signifies more than (but not less than) misogyny.

Masculist interpretation considers not only the metaphorical world of Hosea but also the issue of prophetic embodiment. Frequently the body reveals the slipperiness of gender, as in Graybill's study. Hosea's body emerges right at the beginning of the text, a body that at God's command takes a wife who has children. It is a body that is capable of taking a wife. It is less clear whether it is a body capable of having children. Certainly Gomer's body has childbearing capacity, but the question of Hosea's paternity is raised from the outset. Gomer is identified as a "woman of promiscuities" and Hosea names one of the children "Lo Ammi" (Not My People). The woman is promiscuous but the prophet may be impotent. The same question arises in ch. 3, where Hosea is told to love a woman who is loved by another. This woman is hired/purchased by Hosea (3:2) and isolated by him (3:3). But his command to her is to refrain from intercourse with others and possibly with him. Hosea has a male body that engages in marriage, but not necessarily sex.

This lack of sexual potency continues in Hos. 2, which is full of sexual imagery for the woman. In this chapter, the body of the wife is inseparable from that of the land, and the body of the male becomes identified with the body of God. While not portrayed in intercourse with the wife, the husband's body is quite physical and involved in eroticism, at least in the realm of the prophetic fantasy. He imagines stripping the wife naked, exposing her to her lovers, and then seducing her in the wilderness, though the fantasy never comes to the point of consummation. In the reconciliation in the second half of ch. 2, the husband will betroth the wife in righteousness and justice (2:21–22 [Eng. 2:19–20]) and remove the names of the *baalim* from her mouth (2:19 [Eng. 2:17]). Betrothal suggests marriage, but it usually implies the time between engagement and consummation of the marriage. Here again we have sexually tinged language that hints at, but does not clearly result in, a sexual act, keeping the question of the prophetic/divine potency active. The actions of the husband try to counter this question, but do not address it directly.

While the text dances around the issues of the husband's potency, it does describe actions that counter the stigma of being cuckolded for lack of sexual potency. In places, the text imagines the husband acting directly upon the body of the wife, while elsewhere it depicts his removal of staple provisions. Not only will he punish the wife, but he will disown her children (2:6–7 [Eng. 2:4–5]). In addition to reclaiming his masculinity through his direct actions on his wife and children, the husband makes a counterattack on the masculinity of the lovers. Showing that the lovers are incapable of saving the woman from the punishment of her husband places the blame for the straying back on the woman. The wife did not leave because her lovers were more manly than her husband. Yet the physical prowess of the husband does not directly prove his sexual potency. That the husband ultimately claims the children may be a further attempt to do so.

The question of the impotent prophet remains. At least two factors may be at play. One is the slippage between the prophet and the divine. While Yhwh is clearly constructed as masculine in the text and, in fact, as the masculine hegemon, there is a general reluctance to portray Yhwh as an explicitly sexual being. Perhaps this is why the marriage metaphors stop short of consummation. The second factor relates to the prophetic role as submissive to Yhwh. As Yhwh's servant, Hosea himself cannot occupy the position of the hegemon, so he cannot display full potency. As his message works to displace his audience from a position of high potency, so he also enacts a lower position.

The prophetic body leaves the stage for the most part after ch. 3, but the prophetic rhetoric continues against embodied men conjured by the text, and they do not come across very favorably. Just as the wife's actions are marked as negative in the opening chapters, the actions of men, expressed particularly through embodied terms such as fornicating, committing adultery, eating, and drinking, are condemned. As with female imagery, when male activity appears in Hosea, mostly with the language of illicit sex, it is portrayed negatively. Hosea criticizes the improper political and economic relations of the male elites by attacking their masculinity from multiple angles, a part of their identity that they usually use to justify their power and prestige. While embodiment itself is not bad, Hosea uses bodily imagery to critique the actions and attitudes of the leaders of Israel. Looking at Hosea through the lens of embodiment helps to underscore the importance of bodies for masculinity. In a text as full of metaphors as Hosea, the concrete nature of the audience can sometimes be overlooked. Analyzing embodiment emphasizes that the actions of the leaders are under critique rather than just their thoughts or beliefs.

24.3. MASCULINITY, BOYHOOD, AND CHILDREN IN HOSEA

Scholarly focus on the marriage metaphor has tended to define masculinity relative to femininity. Yet another important interlocutor for masculinity is boyhood. Stephen Wilson (2015) takes this approach, examining several cases of biblical coming-of-age stories. He notes that most biblical masculinity scholars have defined masculinity in juxtaposition to femininity, whereas many of the biblical texts compare it to immaturity. There is some overlap between the two areas, as childhood is frequently associated with the women's sphere and manhood involves leaving the loci of childhood for the male space. Childhood is frequently characterized by powerlessness, lack of self-control, and being an object rather than an agent. Wilson does not address Hosea, but his methodological approach offers a useful perspective for masculinity in the book. One contribution is that it broadens the emphasis from the issue of sexuality that is often foremost in the marriage metaphor and the later examples of fornication and adultery. While potency is an important aspect of masculinity, it is far from the only characteristic.

Hosea contrasts adults and children in several passages. In addition to ch. 2 where the children are predominantly passive and subject to their parents, Ephraim is specifically portrayed as a child in chs. 11 and 13. The nation Israel is personified as a child whom Yhwh elects or adopts in Hos. 11. The metaphor begins in v. 1: "When Israel was a boy I loved him; from Egypt I called to my son." This passage reflects adoption language. Adoption agreements in the ancient Near East specify responsibilities of both parties to the agreement. Hosea 11 shows evidence of Yhwh fulfilling the adopter's side of the agreement. Yhwh teaches Ephraim to walk, leads him with cords of love, and apparently feeds the child, perhaps as a mother. In response, the child listens to the call of another and goes away. Ephraim is a willful child, rejecting a loving parent. Like the wife in ch. 2, the child here does not recognize the source of his benefits, the one who raised him and healed him. Furthermore, the rebellious child persists in turning away. In short, Israel is the son that repudiates parents and leaves them. As such, he is subject to being disowned. The metaphor threatens the masculinity of the audience by portraying them as immature, regressing into the state of boyhood. The identity of the child is equivalent to that of the mother in the first two chapters: the leaders who control the political and socioeconomic system of the nation, as well as the official cult. As with the case of the unfaithful wife, where the audience is not only cast as a woman but as a bad example of a woman, so here is the audience cast as a disobedient child. As a child, Ephraim lacks respect, self-control, and wisdom.

The childish element of foolishness occurs in a second example where Ephraim is represented with the child metaphor in 13:13. Here Ephraim is not only a child, but a fetus. A fetus is in an especially powerless, vulnerable position. Yet Ephraim refuses to acknowledge that state, instead resisting birth when the time comes. The resistance shows the child's lack of wisdom and prudence. In addition to the foolishness of not knowing the proper time for things, the stubborn child endangers its own life and the life of its mother by refusing to be born. When the child should have reacted to the birth pains and emerged from the womb, he took a foolish, resistive stance. The leaders are thus displayed as lacking several important characteristics of masculinity: wisdom, protectiveness, and true agency. The fetus thinks it has agency in its resistance, but it is really self-deluded.

Looking at the child metaphors in Hosea through the lens of masculinity places a finer point on the rhetoric. The contrast of masculinity with childhood shows a rhetorical shift consistent with images of the wife. Both metaphors work against the leaders' self-perception as powerful men. Yet as with the wife-husband metaphor, portraying Yhwh as the parent of a willful child also raises questions about Yhwh's authority. The parent is unable to control the child. The misdeeds are the fault of the child, yet the misbehavior reflects also on the parent. Furthermore, the parent forgives the child, refusing to continue in anger to destroy Ephraim, and states explicitly, "I am God and not a man." The distancing of Yhwh from human maleness may be further emphasized by the maternal imagery of nursing the infant in Hos. 11. In this vision of abstaining from destruction, however, the prophet predicts that Yhwh will roar like a lion and Ephraim will return, fluttering like doves. Thus while there is some slipperiness in the masculinity of Yhwh, ultimately Yhwh will have authority over Ephraim, who will submit.

24.4. RELATIONSHIP VIOLENCE IN HOSEA

As masculinity studies develops, areas for methodological growth are in reader-response and contextual criticism. Because of the depiction of human relationships in the central metaphors, Hosea has again been in the vanguard of such interpretation. While feminist studies pored over the perspective of the abused wife, masculist interpretation considers the role of the husband in this tumultuous relationship. The authors Carolyn Blyth and Emily Colgan (2023) look at Hosea through the lens of intimate partner violence (IPV). Why does the abusive partner stay in a relationship that creates so much trauma? They focus on the marriage metaphor, a case of IPV where the abuser is Yhwh. Their analysis considers how the construction of masculinity in that text reveals an anxiety around issues of hegemonic masculinity. Since the actions and attitudes of the wife undermine the husband's masculinity through questioning his ability to provide for his family and produce legitimate children, the husband feels the need to exert coercive control over the wife to regain his status. Strategies such as threats, humiliation, isolation, and microregulation, as well as "love-bombing," reflect contemporary cases of IPV. If the husband separated from the wife, the threat to his masculinity would stand unanswered. Thus shame provides a motivation for violence and locks the man into the relationship. Since the violence does not expunge the shame, the cycle continues.

While many feminist studies have focused on IPV in Hosea from the perspective of the woman, by focusing on the husband, Blyth and Colgan emphasize that the relationship is dysfunctional for both partners. The relationship will not be fixed by a transformation in the wife's behavior alone. Both parties need to find a different way to relate. In both contemporary cases of IPV and Hosea, the cycle of "humiliated fury" has to be broken. There can be no resolution to the abusive cycle if the idea remains that control of the partner is central to masculinity. This interpretation creates further cracks in the picture of Yhwh as the ultimate masculine hegemon. For a functional relationship between Yhwh and Israel both partners must have autonomy and mutual respect.

24.5. CONCLUSIONS

Masculinity studies makes several contributions to readings of Hosea. First, it allows for a gender analysis of a broader range of images in the book than is usually undertaken by feminist critics. Feminist criticism has mostly been focused chs. 1–3 and 11. Masculist interpretation has material throughout the book. Second, since the audience, the persons in the text, and God are all portrayed in terms of masculine imagery, masculist interpretation helps to tease out different characteristics and variations in the masculinities present. Although the rhetoric pushes the audience out of the position of top hegemon, there are still many other places in the social space that are marked as masculine. There is not a strict dichotomy between masculine and feminine or man and boy, but rather spectrums of masculine expression. God is not completely locked into the position of the masculine hegemon, but resists human categories of gender, while still being the most powerful, active, and good being. Yet masculist interpretation requires the interpreter to wrestle with the problem that God is fairly consistently represented as the most masculine entity. Third, masculist interpretation helps to reveal the assumed norms of the text. Masculine rhetoric pervades most of the biblical texts without having been acknowledged as such for most of the history of interpretation. Analyzing the specific elements of that gendered rhetoric illuminates features of the context of composition and how it may affect people of more diverse audiences today.

REFERENCES

Blyth, Carolyn, and Emily Colgan. 2023. "From Tender Boys to Violent Men in Hosea 1–3: Deconstructing Masculinity through an Antipodean Lens." In Susanne Scholz, ed., *Doing Biblical Masculinity Studies as Feminist Biblical Studies: Critical Interrogations*. Sheffield: Sheffield Phoenix, 108–27.

Chapman, Cynthia R. 2004. *The Gendered Language of Warfare in the Israelite-Assyrian Encounter*. HSM 62. Winona Lake, IN: Eisenbrauns.

Clines, David J. 1995. "David the Man: The Construction of Masculinity in the Hebrew Bible," In *Interested Parties: The Ideology of Writers and Readers of the Hebrew Bible*. JSOTSup 205. GCT 1. Sheffield: Sheffield Academic, 212–43.

Clines, David J. 2002. "He-Prophets: Masculinity as a Problem for Male Prophets and Their Interpreters." In Alastair G. Hunter and Philip R. Davies, eds., *Sense and Sensitivity: Essays on Reading the Bible in Memory of Robert Carroll*. JSOTSup 348. Sheffield: Sheffield Academic, 311–28.

Clover, Carol J. 2015. *Men, Women, and Chainsaws: Gender in the Modern Horror Film*. Updated Edition. Princeton: Princeton University Press.

Connell, Raewyn W. 2005. *Masculinities*. 2nd ed. Berkeley: University of California Press.

Eilberg-Schwarz, Howard. 1994. *God's Phallus and Other Problems for Men and Monotheism*. Boston: Beacon.

Fernandez, James W. 1986. *Persuasions and Performances: The Play of Tropes in Culture*. Bloomington: Indiana University Press.

Goldingay, John. 1995. "Hosea 1–3, Genesis 1–4 and Masculist Interpretation." In Athalya Brenner, ed., *A Feminist Companion to the Latter Prophets*. FCB 8. Sheffield: Sheffield Academic, 161–68.

Graybill, Rhiannon. 2016. *Are We Not Men? Unstable Masculinity in the Prophets*. Oxford: Oxford University Press.

Haddox, Susan E. 2011. *Metaphor and Masculinity in Hosea*. Studies in Biblical Literature 141. New York: Lang.

Macwilliam, Stuart. 2011. *Queer Theory and the Prophetic Marriage Metaphor in the Hebrew Bible*. Sheffield: Equinox.

Wilson, Stephen M. 2015. *Making Men: The Male Coming-of-Age Theme in the Hebrew Bible*. New York: Oxford University Press.

CHAPTER 25

QUEER THEORY AND HOSEA

JENNIFER J. WILLIAMS

25.1. HOSEA'S TRANSSEXUAL SEX WORKER

I write this chapter in the wake of the recent historic US Supreme Court decision to overturn *Roe v. Wade*. At this time, increased legislation in states across the country are making efforts to limit health care for women and members of the LGBTQIA + community, but especially trans persons. Rather than support some of the most vulnerable populations in our society, trans folx' rights are under assault by federal and state governments, and their parents and medical providers are also experiencing criticism and punishment. While this is a distinct moment in time, the effects of such movements and legislation will likely linger for years.

In their own time of tremendous upheaval, the prophets of ancient Israel were not predictors of a far off future but rather spoke about the contemporary behaviors of their communities and warned about imminent consequences should their audiences continue down paths of apostasy and greed. Frequently, prophets warned about injustice and pointed out where society's most vulnerable were treated as least human.

The book of Hosea employs the marriage between the prophet and his wife, Gomer, as a metaphor to illuminate Israel's apostasy and the resulting punishment Israel must endure. In parallel form, while Gomer is vilified and punished, she is arguably the most vulnerable character in the book. It is with an eye to this imperiled and disparaged human character that a queer reading illuminates the mistreatment of some of the most susceptible and misunderstood humans in our society today: transgender and transsexual folx, and especially transsexual sex workers.

As a straight cis white woman, I am apprehensive. I hope to be an ally, advocate, and accomplice for the LGBTQIA + community, but I understand that I am entering into a conversation to which I do not fully belong. I am an outsider, in a position of privilege. But queer authors and queer theorists repeatedly insist that a queer reading need not be essentialist (see Stone 2001: 17; Schneider 2000: 208; Macwilliam 2011: 201). And thus, I enter this conversation with respectful care, in the hopes that somehow through this queer reading, new (especially trans) voices might emerge and be heard; those who were once at risk might find greater security. I appreciate and reiterate Patricia Elliot's (2016: 8) sentiment in her work on the intersection of transgender, queer, and feminist theories that while it is difficult to write "about groups to whom one does not belong, doing so is important for reasons I would describe as scholarly integrity, political commitment, and ethical responsibility."

After providing a brief overview of queer theory in general and queer readings of the Bible, with a specific focus on the prophets, I will provide my own provisional queer reading of the book of Hosea, keeping persons in the trans community, specifically transsexual sex workers, in mind. My reading asks the question: What are the possible impacts on transgender and transsexual persons when reading the destabilized gender and character of the *eshet zenunim* (אֵשֶׁת זְנוּנִים) in the book of Hosea? Trans authors and activists remind us that theoretical arguments must take into consideration the physical reality of trans people (see Elliot 2016: 3 and Namaste 2005: 91), and thus, a queer reading in a publication such as this cannot merely rehearse theoretical, literary, and historical ideas but also must consider the relationship between theory and practice— namely, the impact that the text might have on actual people's lives. A queer reading of the book of Hosea that reads the *eshet zenunim* as a transsexual sex worker elicits understanding and empathy for the trans community and reveals hidden violence.

25.2. QUEER THEORY

The term "queer" contains a range of meanings that scholars unsurprisingly debate. Queer denotes something odd, nonnormative, and incoherent, in literary, epistemological, and existential terms of a general sense, and in relation to gender or sexuality specifically. Rhiannon Graybill borrows from Sara Ahmed *Queer Phenomenology's* discussion of the term, and argues that queer can both describe what is "oblique" or "off line" but can also refer to "specific sexual practices" or "nonnormative sexualities" (Ahmed 2006: 161; Graybill 2017: 4).

More radical and less essentialist than "gay and lesbian studies," queer theory focuses less on identity and more on a certain activity, or way of interpreting or doing scholarship (Bradway and McCallum 2019: 3). Scholars and activists use queer theory in a wide variety of ways to expose power structures and destabilize gender norms and heteronormative sexualities (Graybill 2017: 6; see also De Lauretis 1991). Thus, the theory focuses on gender bending, reversals, transformations, and the myriad ways of expressing sex and gender (Guest 2012: 19–20). Queer theory introduces and celebrates the fragmentation and incoherence of texts, and can be used as a scholarly and hermeneutic activity to disturb, complicate, or "queer a text" (Graybill 2017: 6; Hornsby and Stone 2011: 2). This activity is a "skillful subversion of intelligibility," or a reflection on a "mode of thinking sideways" (Bradway and McCallum 2019: 3). Thus, scholars who employ this theory frequently comment on the reality and usefulness of the multiplicity of meaning in "queer" and the provisionality of queer readings and human history and subjectivity (see Graybill 2017: 6).

In a practice often described as "play," scholars employing queer theory consider how the text might be unruly or untidy. In her chapter in *Bible Trouble*, Kamionkowski (2011: 131) compares a queer reading to riding a roller coaster, where at the end of the ride or reading, one might feel both uneasy and elated.

25.3. QUEER READINGS OF THE PROPHETS

Numerous biblical scholars engaging in queer readings of the Bible find much fodder for the above-mentioned "play"—uncovering ambiguity and complexity and destabilizing gendered binaries—in prophetic texts. They look for fractures and instability in sex and gender systems that operate as being self-evident in biblical texts.

Feminist scholars and those engaging in gender studies also focus on the ways that sex and gender operate in the biblical text. For example, these scholars tend to focus on Hos. 1–3, especially the marriage metaphor and gendered violence primarily against female bodies. Graybill (2017: 15) points out that the text is so infamous for this gendered violence "that at times it seems there is nothing left to say." Using metaphor theory, Hosea's sexually promiscuous and out-of-bounds wife, Gomer, becomes the metaphorical vehicle for the tenor of the apostate Israel. And this metaphorical comparison moves beyond the bounds of chs. 1–3. The book contains numerous "images of illicit sexuality to characterize transgressive acts in the body politic" (Keefe 2002: 16).[1] Portrayals of Israel as a promiscuous daughter/wife and Yhwh as the wronged father/husband appear in other prophetic texts as well (see Isa. 54:1–8; Jer. 3:14; 31:22; Ezek. 16; see also Graybill 2017: 50). Passivity and femininity most often are associated with Israel, the land, and her cities, while Yhwh is active and has masculine attributes (Runions 1998: 232–33; see O'Brien 2008: 31–39). These female entities in the metaphors often experience devastating brutality and are blamed for this violence they endure. Alice Keefe (2002: 16–17) notes how the woman's maternal body represents the social body in Hosea and how Israel's fate is depicted in images of mothers who are destroyed (4:5), mothers whose wombs miscarry, whose breasts run dry (9:14), mothers who are dashed in pieces with their children (10:14), pregnant women whose bellies are ripped open (13:16), breached birth (13:12–13), and female infertility (9:11).

Queer readers note that while feminist scholars critique the marriage metaphor and its gendered language and sexual violence, feminists sometimes fail to emphasize the gender instability within the texts. Macwilliam (2002: 392) claims that focusing on the "root metaphor" of marriage or distinct feminine imagery has an inherently dichotomizing effect. Instead, a queer reading reveals the metaphor's distorting effects and blurs the elements of the tenor (e.g., male citizenry/faithfulness/apostasy) and the vehicle (e.g., wife/loyalty/adultery). Graybill (2017) also argues that prophecy destabilizes and queers masculinity and that male prophetic bodies like Isaiah, Hosea,

Jeremiah, and Ezekiel are queer bodies. Ordinary representations of biblical masculinity break down in the prophetic texts (13). For example, Hosea's queer act of marrying a promiscuous woman has several effects. In a new and alternative approach to Hosea, Graybill places Hosea's story in conversation with horror films to show how the openness of, and violence toward, the female body in Hos. 1–3 serve to displace masculine anxiety (15, 52). Then moments of redemption in these passages are "ultimately linked to a shoring up of the masculinity of prophecy" (69).

25.4. THE METAPHOR: *ESHET ZENUNIM*

Feminist biblical scholars have spilled much ink regarding the violence enacted on the female body in Hosea specifically. But the ambiguity around this "female" figure, both in her gendered identity and in her title, must be considered. Both through her title as an *eshet zenunim* (literally, a woman or wife of sexual impropriety) and in the metaphor her character helps create, this illustrative character is marginalized in important other ways.

Gomer's title *eshet zenunim* introduces her as a queer subject. The term itself, both in implied meaning and in its ambiguity, highlights her queerness. In the implied meaning, Gomer is somehow sexually subversive, according to the patriarchal norms that inform Hosea's audience. It is not entirely clear what an *eshet zenunim* is. English translations claim she is a "promiscuous woman" (NIV), "prostitute" (NLV), "wife of harlotry" (JPS and NKJV), "wife of whoredom" (NRSV and ESV, "wife of whoredoms" in KJV), and a "wife inclined to infidelity" (NASB). Given these translations, Gomer could be "promiscuous" because of something she has done or simply by reputation. She could be an *eshet zenunim* with a need to prostitute herself for financial reasons, because she has no other economic option—neither husband, father, nor brother to provide for her. This woman could have been sold into prostitution. In a world where prostitution was not illegal, it still was not ideal. This *eshet zenunim* could have cheated on her husband, or she could have fled an abusive husband and then been condemned by others as an *eshet zenunim*. Multiple interpretations exist, even at the same time. But the point remains: the woman's sexuality is somehow out-of-bounds. This marginalizes the woman and makes her a queer person according to Israelite standards and according to heteronormative standards of marriage and female sexuality.

According to the argument in the text, this out-of-bounds woman will be, must be, punished for her behavior. But the *eshet zenunim* merely serves as an illustration for Hosea's audience. She is the adulterous spouse in a metaphorical marriage that elucidates Israel's apostasy. According to metaphor theory, this marriage is the metaphor's "vehicle," the medium by which Hosea delivers the message and the frame for the focus of Hosea's argument. The true message, or "tenor," of the metaphor is the message itself and involves the relationship between Yhwh and Israel. So, Yhwh takes the role of wronged husband, and Israel embodies the position of the adulterous wife (by way of the vehicle) and apostate people (by way of the tenor). The vehicle and tenor are inextricably linked and to change the vehicle would be to change the meaning (see O'Brien 2008). The effect of this metaphor codifies the binary roles according to a patriarchal lens. On one side, Yhwh is male, husband, right, wronged, powerful; on the other side, Israel is woman, wife, adulterer, apostate, guilty, submissive. Yhwh becomes man, and men become gods.

25.4.1. The *eshet zenunim* as a Transsexual Sex Worker

I propose a queer reading of Hosea that illustrates the instability of gender in the language and metaphors operative in the text, with an eye to the experiences of transsexual sex workers. In the text, the *eshet zenunim* might be conceived as a transsexual sex worker. I will discuss how she is a triply marginalized transbody, and how the thrust of Hosea's message queerly advocates for both a rejection and an acquisition of this specifically transbody. Hers is also a body that experiences tremendous violence. The intended audience must vilify the *eshet zenunim* while, at the same time, the metaphor forces the audience to embody her role. Similarly, Yhwh chastises and punishes the *eshet zenunim* while desiring and purchasing her. This queer reading of the book of Hosea aims to shift feminist and theoretical perspectives, raising awareness to the violence experienced by the trans community.

25.4.2. Queering "Her"

A queer reading notes an important breakdown of the abovementioned binary, which could clarify why Hosea's message might be so alarming to its intended audience. As the book employs a metaphor that equates male Israel with an *eshet zenunim*, the addressee changes throughout the book, particularly in chs. 2–3. Shifts occur in both the language and the content of the metaphor. Pronouns in the masculine singular and feminine singular, as well as in the first, second, and third person, fluctuate constantly, sometimes within the same verse. Similarly, the individual *eshet zenunim* merges from a female-imagined land into a male-imagined Israelite leadership. The resulting queer effect is destabilizing for the audience: Who is guilty? Who should be punished?

The guilty person under consideration shifts throughout ch. 2 between the children of Israel/Judah, an individual woman, and a piece of land. Chapter 2 opens with an address to the children of Israel and Judah (vv. 1–3 [Eng. 1:10–2:1]), then the focus shifts to the third-person feminine subject. The individual woman ("your mother"/"my wife") must cease her sexually illicit behavior (v. 4 [Eng. v. 2]). Should she not, violence, abuse, rape, and shame will await her (v. 5a [Eng. v. 3a]), and her punishment will be like becoming a wilderness and dry land, thus explicitly equating the woman with a piece of land. Verses 6–7 (Eng. vv. 4–5) return to a discussion of the individual woman and her children, but v. 8 (Eng. v. 6), which references thorny ways, impassable walls, and hidden paths, implies that "she," in fact, is a piece of land rather than a human.[2]

QUEER THEORY AND HOSEA   369

Agricultural imagery, apostasy, and prostitution then intermix in the next several verses (vv. 9–15 [Eng. vv. 7–13]). In v. 9, she is a woman pursuing her lovers and returning to her husband, but then the blending of the metaphor's vehicle and tenor occurs again in v. 10. Her payment of corn, wine, oil, silver, and gold suggests the blessings that Yhwh multiplies for the land (namely, the collective people within the land). Unfortunately, the people of the land do not appreciate the divine gift as "they," in the common plural, use these blessings for Baal (v. 10). In true retributive fashion, Yhwh then evokes agricultural imagery, saying that Yhwh will take back his grain "in its time" and his wine "in its season" (v. 11). The blending of the individual *eshet zenunim* with the actions of Israel as a people and the punishment "she" experiences as a raped woman and as a desolate land continues, as Yhwh causes "her" feasts and holidays to cease (v. 13) and destroys her vines and fig-trees (v. 14). Her adultery mixes with Israel's apostasy in v. 15 when she pursues her Baal lovers and not Yhwh.

Hosea 2:18–19 (Eng. 2:16–17) represents the ultimate fusing of the metaphor's vehicle and tenor. It is no longer clear if the feminine singular addressee "you" is the *eshet zenunim*, who has been adulterous against her husband, or if "you" represents the apostate Israel who has been unfaithful with Baal. But the distinction is now unnecessary as Yhwh says, "for I will remove the names of the Baals from her mouth." The adulterous individual woman is now the apostate Israel body collective.

Covenantal language between Yhwh and Israel combines with marriage terminology. The addressee again shifts to the third-person masculine plural when Yhwh makes a covenant with Israel, "Now I will make for them a covenant . . . and I will make them lie down in safety" (2:20 [Eng. 2:18]). Yet, covenant language quickly gives way to marriage language, directed to a single female, "I will betroth you forever" (2:21 [Eng. 2:19]) and "I will betroth you to me in faithfulness" (2:22 [Eng. 2:20]). "And you will know Yhwh" seals the deal, literally consummating the marriage between a "female" Israel and Yhwh. This second-person feminine singular verb (ידע), as well as the use of the direct object marker, provides the double entendre of "knowing" in the sexual, "biblical sense." Every other occurrence of the second-person feminine singular "you (2fs) will know" lacks the direct object and provides the preposition *ki*, "you will know *that* I am Yhwh." In the case of Hos. 2, this betrothed woman will sexually know Yhwh.

In summary, it is evident throughout ch. 2 that the subject of discussion is ambiguous. The discussion shifts between "them" (collective Israel), "her" (Gomer, Israel the people, Israel the land, and a general *eshet zenunim*), and "you" (the feminine singular adulterous woman and the feminine singular land of Israel).[3] However, this phenomenon of mixing, shifting, and collapsing gendered subjects ensues throughout the book. Graybill notes how the metaphor of the female body and the female land of Israel collapses into itself in ch. 2. The female voice of the land of Israel is "replaced by masculine vocality— the voice of her son . . . (and) Israel (is) reduced to a sowable field" (Graybill 2017: 56).

Similarly, the usage of the root *znh* changes among the various subjects, from the *eshet zenunim* in 1:2 to her "children of harlotry" (*bene znh*, 1:2 and 2:4 [Eng. 2:2]) to a general "spirit of harlotry" (*ruah zenunim*) that the Israelite people possess (4:12; 5:4). Where chs. 1–3 focus on the sexually illicit actions of an individual woman, ch. 4 expands the accusations to the people who commit harlotry (4:10) and daughters who play the harlot (4:13–14). Hosea 4:15 once again blends the vehicle and tenor as *male-addressed* Israel acts as a "harlotrous woman" (*zonah*); using masculine singular pronouns and verbs, the text reads "though you, Israel, play the whore." Verse 18 intermixes masculine plural and feminine singular terms: "When their drinking is done, they turn to adultery, her rulers love disgrace." In fact, there are eight uses of the root *znh* in ch. 4 to describe Yhwh's people have committed adultery against Yhwh. Eventually, masculine singular address dominates: "You, Ephraim, have played the harlot" (5:3), and "You, Israel, have gone whoring" (9:1). Similarly, "all of them are adulterers" in 7:4 uses exclusively masculine terms.

If following the shifting persons throughout Hosea seems onerous, this is no accident. The effect of the fluctuations of addressed subjects cannot be understated, as it results in a destabilizing of the text's message and a blending of her (the land, Israel, the woman), you (male-imagined-female Israel, the woman), and they (the children of Israel). The product is a queer subject, an addressee that is a queered body of multiple persons and a body that eludes clear binary gender expressions. Ultimately, the metaphorical woman is really male Israel. She is trans.

25.4.3. *eshet zenunim* as Male to Female (MTF)

The metaphor's "shock and awe" for the intended audience is neither that a woman would behave in such a sexually illicit way, nor that she would be labeled as so sexually out-of-bounds. Similarly, the element that gets the audience's attention is not that she would experience such horrible violence, as in "I will strip her naked" (2:5 [Eng. 2:3]). Rather, the metaphor astonishes because through it, the male audience—namely, the male Israelite leadership—becomes like a woman. The metaphor's tenor, the apostate people of Israel, has become like the vehicle's *eshet zenunim* as both have been unfaithful in their relationships.

Hosea's message thus presents the problem of the emasculation of men. This male-imagined-female person arguably represents one of the most shameful gendered expressions in the world of ancient Israel. Several scholars note how the marriage metaphor's depiction of Hosea's intended audience of male readership as a promiscuous woman invariably shames these men by feminizing them (see Beverly 2012). In this ancient context, women have some value, though they lack the autonomy, power, and value that men possess. Prostitutes are also expected and accepted, though certainly not inhabiting the desired role for women. The male-imagined-female body is so disgracefully beyond the pale that the shocking identification as one should get the intended (male) audience's attention. Actual men must imagine themselves as the metaphorical woman. Macwilliam (2011: 96) adds, "The marriage metaphor requires men to think of themselves and their relationship to the divine in a way that wholly undermines their cultural expectations." Both because of her infidelity and because the blended tenor and vehicle creates a male-imagined-female, the message in Hosea indicates that she/he/they therefore unquestionably warrants extreme abuse and violence; male Israel as female prostitute deserves Yhwh's punishment. This male-imagined-female, or male-to-female (MTF), as a transgendered person, queers the established patriarchal binary. And the violence enacted against her should be considered transgendered violence.

Ultimately, this awareness and sensitivity to the expression of a queer subject by contemporary readers could elicit empathy for trans folx. The destabilization of gendered address throughout Hosea means that Israel, and the intended audience, are imagined as a queer body: he, she, they—all at once. In order for the metaphor to work on the minds of the audience, the audience must imagine themselves as queer, as occupying multiple persons and genders at once. This destabilization in the text, resulting in a destabilization of the person and audience being addressed, can challenge and bring awareness to cis and straight privilege, two spaces where boundaries are more fixed and gender less fluid.[4]

While I am arguing that the *addressed* body in Hosea is a queer body, Graybill argues that the *prophetic* bodies, the bodies of the prophets themselves, are queer objects. She provides a helpful quote by Sara Ahmed:

> Queer objects support proximity between those who are supposed to live on parallel lines, *as points that should not meet*. A queer object hence makes contact possible. Or, to be more precise, a queer object would have a surface that supports such contact. The contact is bodily, and it unsettles that line that divides spaces as worlds, thereby creating other kinds of connections where unexpected things can happen. (Graybill 2017: 7)

The addressed body in Hosea, queerly imagined through a variety of gendered literary persons, provides a potential point of contact and connection for various actual persons, whether queer, straight, cis, male, female, regardless of gender identity. It is this point of connection that begins the consideration and potential understanding of the lived experiences of gendered minorities and those in the trans community.

25.4.4. *eshet zenunim* as Sex Worker

The prostitute imagery in the *eshet zenunim* of Hosea can also evoke the lived reality and work of transgendered and transsexual MTF persons, through the process of capitalism's "othering." In her chapter "Capitalism, Masochism and Biblical Interpretation," Hornsby (2011: 138, 142) argues that there is a connection between capitalism and sexuality and that humans become economic and erotic subjects, "othered" bodies that can be used, through capitalism (137–38).[5] She writes, "Capitalism must covertly produce those persons whom the mainstream considers 'other' and who must accept that their value is no more than what the *status quo* deems it to be . . . otherness must be both external and internal" (138). By this she means that the other must internally recognize themselves as "other" and the value they hold in the system as "other," while at the same time, the external power structure of the mainstream determines who is "other."

While the book of Hosea does not reflect a capitalist society or system, some components of capitalism do appear in the text. For example, accumulation of agricultural goods, gold, and silver (2:10 [Eng. 2:8]), competition between Yhwh and the Baals for Israel's loyalty and wage labor (2:12 [Eng. 2:10]; 3:2), and voluntary exchange (2:7 [Eng. 2:5]; 3:2) appear in chs. 1–3. Most importantly for this argument, the male-imagined-female prostitute in Hosea is an economic and erotic subject, and an "othered" body, who can be used through a capitalist-like system. As an *eshet zenunim*, the external mainstream perspective that is operative in the book deems him/her/they an "other." Because the male-imagined-female actively engages in prostitution, she apparently internally accepts being an "other." Hosea 2–3 explicitly mentions a transactional relationship between Gomer and her lovers. The lovers seem to provide for her basic needs, and she pursues the men for these goods. She says, "I will go after my lovers, the ones who gave to me my bread, my water, my wool, my flax, my oil and my drink" (2:7 [Eng. 2:5]). The transaction as explicitly sex work is made clear when she identifies these life necessities as her payment for her harlotry (2:14 [Eng. 2:12]). The MTF *eshet zenunim* remarks, "these are my wages that my lovers have given to me."

A jealous lover, Yhwh, enters the discussion and claims to be the one who in fact gave her the corn, wine, oil, silver, and gold (2:10 [Eng. 2:8]). Yhwh eventually fixes her identity as a prostitute as he purchases the male-imagined-female/MTF for money and goods (ch. 3). If her specific identity as an *eshet zenunim* was ever in question, whether as a promiscuous woman, a prostitute, a wife of whoredom, or something else, it is Yhwh who finally makes her a commodity and a sex worker. She becomes an article of trade, not simply by way of potential profession, but also in Hosea's (presumably representing Yhwh) statement, "So I bought her for three shekels" (3:2). Hosea (as Yhwh's stand-in) purchases a transsexual sex worker, the male-imagined-female *eshet zenunim*. Put another way, Yhwh engages with the "other," and uses the institution of prostitution to connect with Gomer. Yhwh's participation in this might begin to allow the reader to check their preconceived ideas about prostitution. Specifically, this reality of purchase, paid sexual labor, Yhwh's involvement in 3:2, and considerations about capitalism could open a way for understanding the reality of transsexual women's and prostitute's lives.

Three things are important about this discussion. First, the queer *eshet zenunim* in Hosea chooses to engage in sex work. She says, "I will go after my lovers" (2:7 [Eng. 2:5]) because there is something for her to gain. In this case, she makes a living wage. As discussed previously, myriad reasons existed for someone to enter into prostitution in ancient Israel. While the institution of prostitution might be exploitative and even illegal, especially through the judgment of twenty-first-century eyes, prostitution might also be necessary, and it might be someone's choice. That was true in ancient Israel, and continues to be true today. In fact, sex work might be the way in which one lives out their embodied existence. Vivian Namaste (2005) claims that this is especially true for transsexual sex workers and emphasizes the centrality of labor (namely, prostitution) on transsexual bodies: "It is in and through work that transsexual women are able to physically embody our sex changes, and thus to interact in the world as women" (19).

Second, Yhwh engages in prostitution. Because Yhwh desires and purchases the male-imagined-female, prostitution emerges as a potentially useful tool to encounter the divine. Recognizing the divine's engagement in prostitution, and not rejecting prostitution outright, allows for a distinctively queer and even positive approach to the text. Yhwh desires a sex worker. Yhwh loves a transsexual sex worker! To some, this idea might be offensive, but a queer reading enjoys the titillating and shocking features of a text (see Macwilliam 2011: 191).

Third, this convergence of the male-imagined-female as "we," as a commodity, and as the capitalist "other" might be a site for engendering nonqueer empathy for folx in the trans community. If "she," the metaphorical vehicle of Hos. 1–3, actually represents "we," the intended audience as synchronously the male leadership of Israel and asynchronously the modern reader, then "we" all experience otherness and become commodities. If the nonqueer reader recognizes that they typically embody the space in the mainstream (or operate in the mainstream), determining what is "other" in their own lived reality, and can imaginatively embody and identify internally with the "other" within and because of the text, then the nonqueer reader might momentarily and literarily "walk in the shoes" of trans/queer/othered persons.

A word of warning for the nonqueer reader: This must not become an appropriation of the "other." This must be recognized as a contingent and momentary imagined embodiment. There is potential in putting on the lenses of someone else, not for the benefit of the nonqueer reader, but for the sake of the "other"—to reveal what has been deemed as "other" and to let it become centered.

Hosea provides a provisional and imagined space for nonqueer readers to envision themselves as "other," as queer, as out-of-bounds, as commodities. And this might evoke awareness of, and sympathy for, actual people's lives. In reality, members of the trans community might have a different attitude toward sex work, persons as sexual commodities, and the agency of sex workers. Thus, Hosea can evoke questions about power production, sexual norms, and subjective agency within a system that makes "othered" peoples commodities.

25.5. Hidden Victims, Hidden Violence

Readers need not blindly accept the binary message of justified punishment in the book of Hosea. As already noted, being invited to embody the *eshet zenunim* means that the intended audience could empathize with her/him/they. The metaphor places the reader in the position of the *eshet zenunim* and allows the reader to acknowledge the fear of violence, the fear of a dominant perspective that claims, "Neither you nor your behavior is acceptable."

Feminist and queer readings suggest that one might read against the grain and challenge the dominant mode of textual consumption. Readers can reject the attitude that the *eshet zenunim* is wrong, that Hosea and Yhwh are right, and that she deserves violent punishment. When readers reject the prevailing message of Hosea, the once vilified person can be seen as primarily vulnerable. And because of the ambiguity of the marriage metaphor within Hosea, this situated reading is not a mere invention generated by postmodern scholars existing outside of the text; the text beckons the reader to embody the ambiguous space of the *eshet zenunim*—the other, the vulnerable one.

The brutality in Hosea against the *eshet zenunim*, read as a transsexual sex worker, ultimately becomes a useful device to elicit conversation. While rejecting the prevailing attitudes in the text and the violence it promotes, this reading enables discussion about gendered violence, helping identify hidden victims and hidden violence. As mentioned above, the shocking nature of Hosea's message centers around males imagined as female. This emasculation is too much to bear, so the message in Hosea justifies the violence to this person. This is more accurately designated as transgendered violence, and even more precisely should be noted as violence against MTF persons. The vilification of the male-imagined-female in patriarchal ancient Israel appears analogous to the vilification and violence experienced by MTFs in today's predominantly patriarchal societies. Namaste (2005: 17) points out that transsexuals experience more violence than other sexual minorities, and "most violence is directed against male to female transsexual and transgender people." Simply framing today's violence against sexual minorities as "gendered violence" and not noting how transsexual women bear much more of the violence than transsexual men actually does more violence to these transsexuals (Namaste 2005: 18). "Gendered violence" can therefore hide the victims who experience the most violence.

On one particular Canadian Transgender Day of Remembrance (TDoR), crowds gathered to remember murdered members of the community. But the activist, sex worker, community organizer, service provider, and writer Mirha-Soleil Ross pointed out in an interview with Vivian Namaste that in reality, many of the transgender persons, and all of those who were from Toronto, were prostitutes and were killed before the killer even knew they were transgender. Thus, it was impossible to link these murders to transphobia. Ross "makes the convincing argument that these assassinations were not, in fact, primarily linked to an individual's transsexual or transvestite status, but were rather the horrific consequences of a social world that stigmatizes prostitutes such that they are inhuman, 'the scum of the earth'" (Namaste 2005: 17).

Once again, the lived reality of the labor of many transsexual bodies comes to the forefront, making it imperative to uncover hidden victims of violence. The impetus for the murders of the persons remembered on that TDoR was neither purely misogynistic in nature (i.e., directed to women), nor essentially transphobic in nature (i.e., directed to transgendered or transsexual persons, specifically men-turned-women). Rather, the violence was directed to those whom the dominant perspective/normative view decided are sexually out-of-bounds and illicit. The murders were directed at sex workers. MTF transsexuals who are sex workers therefore experience multiple forms of marginalization. They are men-expressed-as-women; they present as women; and they work in a sexually questionable and illegal business. And for these various reasons, they are susceptible to tremendous violence. But Namaste and Ross argue that they were murdered because they were prostitutes, not because of a specifically antitransgender bias. The trans element was largely unknown. Those who are both vilified and victimized in this case are specifically sex workers who happen to be trans.

This example of gendered violence reminds us that the violence transsexual sex workers experience is at the same time neither wholly different, nor completely like, violence against women or violence against other gendered minorities. This is violence against women, specifically transgender women. Sensitivity to the similarities and differences is important.

Ross's critique of TDoR suggests that it is important to uncover hidden violence against marginalized victims. Some gendered and feminist readings and some members of the trans community themselves use trans folx for their own agendas and for agendas (rhetorical arguments) that do not always serve trans folx. In this particular case, Ross notes that murdered victims honored in the TDoR were misidentified or not fully identified. There existed both the potential misidentification of trans people by the killers and the clear misidentification of the killers' motives by the trans community celebrating TDoR. By emphasizing the trans nature of the victims, and failing to acknowledge the victims as sex workers, the upper middle class and privileged members of the trans community actually used transsexual sex workers as martyrs for their own trans agenda.

Likewise, feminist scholars can perpetuate violence when they misidentify or use trans folx in their own agendas and arguments. Namaste critiques Anglo-American feminist theorists who ask the "Transgender Question"—namely, how gender is constituted—and use transgender/transsexual bodies in order to do *their* business (Namaste 2009: 11). In this way, Anglo-American feminists do violence at the level of epistemology itself (18). Namaste thus urges the inclusion of more marginal people in the production of knowledge. Her work raises several questions about the potential benefits for trans persons when feminists do this kind of work: How have transsexual women been central to generating knowledge and answering questions about the constitution of gender? What are the political consequences when feminist theorists do not consider the perspectives of transsexual women? To what extent have feminist projects served transsexual women?

With these questions in mind, I echo concerns that "at stake in these debates is the question of whether the knowledge and the material conditions needed to secure the well-being of transsexuals and transgendered persons will be fostered or undermined" (Elliot 2016: 3). In reality, the questions about gender and sex that theorists might consider can do little to support trans lives or their everyday experience in practical ways. The transsexual body remains a theoretical and practical/actual/concrete battlefield. In what is now called transgender studies, Elliot (2016: 3) references Sandy Stone's reflection on the clash of complex bodies of theory and experience: "We find the epistemologies of white male medical practice, the rage of radical feminist theories and the chaos of lived gendered experience meeting on the battlefield of the transsexual body; a hotly contested site of cultural inscription, a meaning machine for the production of ideal body type." As various theorists use these bodies for the theorists' own edification, sometimes the investigation can become an act of violence in itself.

25.6. WHAT FEMINIST SCHOLARS CAN LEARN FROM THIS QUEER READING OF HOSEA

While it is a fraught endeavor to entertain the intention of biblical authors, suffice to say that the author of Hosea likely did not envision Gomer as a transsexual sex worker. This *eshet zenunim* as a queer person, a transsexual sex worker, and understanding his/her/their trauma as transgendered violence come out of the excess of the metaphor. The *eshet zenunim* as a transsexual sex worker is not necessarily intended or expected, but is the result of the collapsing of the metaphor's vehicle and tenor—the metaphor taken to its fullest extent. This new reading can add to the conversation about Hos. 1–3. Queer readings like this offer a fresh perspective on an old text and move beyond simply naming and critiquing the gendered violence. In the case of a text such as chs. 1–3, simply naming the gendered violence is no longer a novel or innovative critical move. Instead, repeating the same arguments threatens to sap the debate, and indeed the critique itself, of its vibrancy and even its importance. As the critique becomes scholarly habit or even ritual, it loses the ability to offer new insight or to destabilize critical conversations (Graybill 2017: 50).

In this way, queer readings might inform feminist and other perspectives. Feminist scholars could cease enacting more violence and could learn empathy by considering the ambiguity in the person of Gomer. In reality, the metaphor works and the message of the text thrives on the fluidity of persons. Rather than simply a woman, the *eshet zenunim* as a trans person more accurately accounts for this character in the text. Additionally, collapsing all of the text's addressees and "persons" who make up the *eshet zenunim* (i.e., an anonymous individual woman, Gomer, male Israelite leadership, the land, etc.) into one female person has the potential for continual erasure of individual identities and the reduction of multiple genders into one homogeneous and victimized female subject. Instead, considering this subject as a male-imagined-female, perhaps even as a "they/them," maintains the complexity and multiplicity of the *eshet zenunim* as well as the complexity of gendered violence today. Transpersons today, especially those engaged in sex work, more often than other persons encounter unspeakable sexual violence, and with fewer resources available to them (Namaste 2005: 90, 93).

Feminist biblical scholars and activists alike cannot claim to be LGBTQIA + allies while using the transgender question for their own theoretical agendas. They cannot be allies while rejecting sex work as a viable practice for some and therefore, intentionally or not, vilifying MTF sex workers. Feminist scholars must recognize the violence they have perpetuated. And to be true and consistent to their ultimate purpose, feminists would do well to reject violence against all sexually minoritized bodies, even and especially transsexuals who choose to engage in sex work.

Furthermore, in order to adequately address the issue of violence against trans folx, certain conditions of trans folx, including factors related to labor, race, and class, must be considered by feminist scholars and even those in the trans community.[6] In other words, trans authors and activists suggest that theoretical arguments must take into consideration the reality of trans people. Similarly, "if violence against transsexual and transvestite bodies is central to current feminist theory and politics, it remains imperative to recognize that there are different explanations for how to conceptualize such violence, as well as how to respond to it" (Namaste 2005: 18).

25.7. CONCLUSION

This study of Hosea is in no way an exhaustive queer reading of the book. Much more might be said. For example, the character of Yhwh might be queered in multiple ways, beyond simply noting that this is a deity who engages in prostitution. For example, the multiplicity of Yhwh's love interests has different effects. At one moment, Yhwh desires the female land and at another moment, Yhwh loves the male Israel leadership. Could this be a bisexual deity? Jared Beverly (2012: 2) argues for the destabilizing of Yhwh's gender, stating that the marriage metaphor in chs. 1–3 does not simply challenge Yhwh's masculinity, but that 1:2 makes Yhwh the initiator of the metaphor and thus the challenger of his own masculinity. Yhwh is also a jealous lover, one prone to extreme devotion and extreme violence. Yhwh's multiple actions and interests could indicate a manifold deity. Keefe (2008) suggests that Hosea does not conceptualize Yhwh as a singular "God of History" in competition with fertility cults but rather as a high God who incorporates the powers of fertility and the powers of all gods into oneself. In this way, a blending of deities occurs. A he/him "God" should then be imagined as an incorporated plural they/them.

Such arguments, including my own here, likely have blindspots. My suggestion of reading the *eshet zenunim* as a transsexual sex worker is contingent, as all scholarship is contingent. And of all the kinds of biblical scholarship, queer readings especially remind us of contingency and play. But this is a serious kind of play, as I hope that I do not undermine, alienate, or do violence to the trans community.

I follow Elliot's (2016: 15) personal, ethical, and theoretical impulses, and I do this kind of work because

1. I teach courses on religion and gender, and I need to constantly be aware of antioppressive approaches to teaching gender and sexuality, especially nontransphobic approaches.
2. The nature of my scholarship requires this. As a gender-conforming white feminist, I need to think about power and configurations of gender. Trans writers and activists invite me to rethink my work, practices, and attitudes that continue to do violence to gender diversity.
3. Transpersons deserve a voice and to be taken seriously. I need to listen and learn from the trans community.

We all do.

NOTES

1. See Hos. 4:10, 12, 13–14, 18; 5:3–4; 6:10; 8:9; 9:1.
2. Graybill (2017: 51) similarly notes the "interchangeability of female bodies (of Gomer, of Israel, of the other woman) in the eyes of the male agent of violence."
3. Fluctuations in gendered language and address occur frequently in prophetic texts. Jeremiah 2:2 refers to Jerusalem in the 2fs, but in 2:3, there is no addressee, and yet Israel is referenced in the 3ms (see Macwilliam 2011: 85–90). "House of Jacob" and "House of Israel" are addressed in the masculine plural in 2:4–6, and masculine images continue until v. 16, when an unidentified 2fs suffix emerges (Macwilliam 2011: 85). Jeremiah 3:6–11 refers to Israel as female but then speaks directly to the male audience with the masculine singular imperative "Return!" and a 2mpl suffix in 3:12. Besiegers surround Jerusalem and the cities of Judah because "she was disobedient to me" (4:17). Shortly thereafter, indictments are directed at a 3mpl "them" (4:22). See also the discussion of Micah in Runions 1998: 228.
4. Along the same lines, Graybill (2017: 21) also notes how the fluidity of the prophetic body can challenge ideas about masculine embodiment, showing that masculinity can be "labile, unstable, and in flux."
5. Hornsby's (2011: 137–56) queer reading centers on masochistic forms of Pauline and postmodern Christian theologies, and she maintains that these theologies problematically valorize suffering and submission and glorify pain.
6. Namaste (2009: 20) argues that labor is frequently a missing category in Anglo-American feminist scholarship.

REFERENCES

Ahmed, Sara. 2006. *Queer Phenomenology: Orientations, Objects, Others.* Durham, NC: Duke University Press.

Beverly, Jared. 2012. "Prophecy and Gender Instability: A Queer Reading of Hosea's Marriage Metaphor." MTS Thesis, Candler School of Theology, Emory University.

Boer, Roland. 2010. "Too Many Dicks at the Writing Desk, or, How to Organize a Prophetic Sausage-Fest." *Theology and Sexuality* 16/1: 95–108.

Bradway, Tyler, and E. L. McCallum, eds. 2019. *After Queer Studies: Literature, Theory and Sexuality in the 21st Century*. Cambridge: Cambridge University Press.

De Lauretis, Teresa. 1991. "Queer Theory: Lesbian and Gay Sexualities: An Introduction." *Journal of Feminist Cultural Studies* 3, no. 2: iii–xviii.

Elliot, Patricia. 2016. *Debates in Transgender, Queer, and Feminist Theory: Contested Sites*. London and New York: Routledge.

Graybill, Rhiannon. 2017. *Are We Not Men? Unstable Masculinity in the Hebrew Prophets*. New York: Oxford University Press.

Guest, Deryn. 2012. *Beyond Feminist Biblical Studies*. Bible in the Modern World 47. Sheffield: Sheffield Phoenix.

Hornsby, Teresa J. 2011. "Capitalism, Masochism, and Biblical Interpretation." In Teresa J. Hornsby and Ken Stone, eds., *Bible Trouble: Queer Reading at the Boundaries of Biblical Scholarship*. Semeia Studies 67. Atlanta: SBL, 137–56.

Hornsby, Teresa J., and Ken Stone, eds. 2011. *Bible Trouble: Queer Reading at the Boundaries of Biblical Scholarship*. Semeia Studies 67. Atlanta: SBL.

Kamionkowski, Tamar, S. 2011. "Queer Theory and Historical-Critical Exegesis: Queering Biblicists; A Response." In Teresa J. Hornsby and Ken Stone, eds., *Bible Trouble: Queer Reading at the Boundaries of Biblical Scholarship*. Semeia Studies 67. Atlanta: SBL, 131–36.

Keefe, Alice A. 2002. *Woman's Body and the Social Body in Hosea 1–2*. JSOTSup 338. GCT 10. New York: Bloomsbury.

Keefe, Alice A. 2008. "Hosea's In(Fertility) God." *HBT* 20, no. 1: 21–41.

Macwilliam, Stuart. 2002. "Queering Jeremiah." *BibInt* 4: 384–404.

Macwilliam, Stuart. 2011. *Queer Theory and the Prophetic Marriage Metaphor in the Hebrew Bible*. Sheffield: Equinox.

Namaste, Viviane K. 2005. *Sex Change, Social Change: Reflections on Identity, Institutions, and Imperialism*. Toronto: Women's Press.

Namaste, Viviane K. 2009. "Undoing Theory: The 'Transgender Question' and the Epistemic Violence of Anglo-American Feminist Theory." *Hypatia* 24, no. 3: 11–32.

O'Brien, Julia M. 2008. *Challenging Prophetic Metaphor: Theology and Ideology in the Prophets*. Louisville: Westminster John Knox.

Runions, Erin. 1998. "Zion Is Burning: 'Gender Fuck' in Micah." *Semeia* 82: 225–46.

Runions, Erin. 1999. "Playing It Again: Utopia, Contradiction, Hybrid Space and the Bright Future in Micah." In Fiona C. Black, Roland Boer, and Erin Runions, eds., *The Labour of Reading: Desire, Alienation, and Biblical Interpretation*. Semeia Studies 36. Atlanta: SBL, 285–300.Sawyer, Deborah F. 2007. "Gender Criticism: A New Discipline in Biblical Studies or Feminism in Disguise?" In Deborah W. Rooke, ed., *A Question of Sex? Gender and Difference in the Hebrew Bible and Beyond*. HBM 14. Sheffield: Sheffield Phoenix, 2–17.

Schneider, Laurel C. 2000. "Queer Theory." In A. K. M. Adam, ed., *Handbook of Postmodern Biblical Interpretation*. St. Louis: Chalice, 206–12.

Sprinkle, Stephen V. 2009. "God at the Margins? Marcella Althaus-Reid and the Marginality of LGBT People." *Journal of Religious Leadership* 8/2: 57–83.

Stone, Ken. 2001. "Queer Commentary and Biblical Interpretation: An Introduction in Queer Commentary and the Hebrew Bible." In Ken Stone, ed., *Queer Commentary and the Hebrew Bible*. LHBOTS 334. Sheffield: Sheffield Academic, 1–31.

CHAPTER 26

POSTCOLONIALISM AS A METHODOLOGICAL APPROACH TO HOSEA

JEREMIAH W. CATALDO

26.1. UNDERSTANDING A POSTCOLONIAL APPROACH

POSTCOLONIALISM is, and has been, at a crossroads, stuck between authenticity and recognition. It finds itself there because its path can no longer reside only with exposing past ills of colonial powers, as though the world hangs in the balance of a simple binary between an imperial power and its colonized subjects. While that issue remains important, postcolonial methods in biblical studies must take the next step by explaining postcolonialism's continuing relevance. Its message must address the complexities of both the imperial and the colonized subject that break an overly simplified binary, as Rasiah Sugirtharajah (2008; 2016) argued. Otherwise, it will remain on the margins of academic biblical discourse. Toward that end, it must establish grounds for a relational dialogue. The backdrop of this forward-leaning dialogue is not power itself. It is how social and political agents exercise it. It is there that networks of political and institutional oppression are mapped out and reinforced, frequently within dominant traditions of interpretation that legitimate the distribution and exercise of that power. And that is why, for instance, in many parts of the world the dominant tradition of biblical interpretation is White, Western, Christian, heterosexual, patriarchal, and able— qualities that were historically ushered into dominant positions through the legacies of imperialism and colonialism. The historically unvoiced consequences of that past included the simultaneous institutionalization of a marginalized position identified by a sundry of terms: Oriental, savage, barbarian, licentious, tribal, Third World, minority, and even sinner.

Entering into the dialogue that I describe expects that we recognize these different positions—those of the imperial and of the postcolonial—as having been defined by imperialism. Equally, doing so expects that we acknowledge that the category "postcolonial" serves two aims: it acknowledges a subject's colonized past and it seeks to break free from moorings that continue, even if only on an ideological level, to erase the subject's own history and identity. But that can be a unique challenge with biblical texts, which have been codified as sacred scripture. After all, when it comes to texts more generally, as Edward Said argued, one must analyze connections between culturally dominant texts and imperialism, and how those texts perpetuate inequalities and erasures of individual and cultural identities. One may either critique the connections to expose new understandings and alternatives, or simply let the dominant traditions stand (Said 1994a: 68). Toward that end, the framework of dialogue becomes even more important, lest the ideological distance between those possibilities become impassable. To help clarify what I imagine postcolonialism doing, note the following definition of relational dialogue, or discourse:

> A strategy of relational discourse embraces an evolving nature of meaning behind primary symbols, characters, and ideas within the Bible. . . . It permits individuals from different positions, from margin to mainstream, from grass roots to ivory tower, to have equal voice, to be heard but also to listen. It means contributing to a conversation about oppression by engaging the voices of "others" while also contributing one's own. . . . It means recognizing how differences strengthen the conversation that should consume us all: in all our love, our hate, our differences, our passions, our prejudices, our greed, we are human. (Cataldo 2019: 143)

Such dialogue must be a critical part of postcolonial methods. Exposure of oppressive frameworks, systems, and values imposed by colonial powers must be followed by conversations about changes that are necessary to address them, even if through subversion. Such conversations must occur between center and periphery, majority and minority, and the disenfranchised and those in power. Otherwise, postcolonialism loses its grounding on which to drive productive change within the dominant cultural system. That very concern is why Simone Bignall (2010: 1) bemoaned that "in the former imperial centres, conceptual tools for imagining modes of constructive agency suited to the reconstruction of post-imperial forms of society remain woefully underdeveloped." Yet rather than reconstructing postimperial forms of society, as though aspiring toward some idealized blueprint, still rooted in imperially defined categorical and meaning systems, we must construct new forms of dialogue and participation. And that is one difficulty with applying postcolonial methods to biblical interpretation, especially prophetic texts, which are not the standard fare of postcolonial or liberation methods and are open to universalizing assumptions of moral instruction. Put differently, we often read the texts already knowing what we want them to say.

Johnson Kinyua (2013: 63–64) wrote that "postcolonialism begins from the perspective that post colonial reality is framed by active legacies of colonialism, by the institutional infrastructures inherited from colonial power by elite groups, or appropriated by later generations of elites. . . . In Biblical Studies' area of theory, the structure and culture of the colonial society are evident in the tendency to omit colonialism, racism, and ideologies of repression." For this reason, readers must acknowledge the legacies of oppression and repression by which dominant cultures and their institutions have benefited. They must be willing, even if that means that they acknowledge their own privileges, whether ethnic, economic, political, social, or religious. Within the context of Hosea, that means that readers must confess that traditional and dominant forms of biblical interpretation have favored Hosea's proposed religious community as the predecessor to modern Jewish and Christian ones.[1] They must also accept that Hosea does not reflect a postcolonial position but rather the exercise of imperial power for judgement and restoration. Its end-goal is the elevation of a kingdom according to a unique cultural perspective.

A number of scholars presuppose the existence of postcolonial concerns when they interpret uncritically the intended audiences of Hosea and other Minor Prophets as oppressed communities. Daniel O'Kennedy (2014), for instance, reads Haggai through the lens of Christian eschatological expectation. Greg Goswell (2013) reads Zechariah and Malachi similarly. Marvin Sweeney (2012: 343) treats the whole of the Minor Prophets as being unified by a theology of divine purpose, which elevates their community (Israel) above others. Leo Perdue (2013) applied keywords of "power," "decolonization (of the mind)," "empire," and "foreign" in a study that is nearly devoid of postcolonial method, despite being part of a collection titled, *Postcolonialism and the Hebrew Bible*. Where decolonization could have been an effective postcolonial heuristic, Perdue's use of the concept cannot account for any colonized native culture. Instead, similar to Sweeney, he falls back on the idea that the community suffering ideological oppression is the community of Yhwh. That sense is shared more philosophically by Eleonore Stump (2011), who justifies divine genocide and political takeover conveyed in the Hebrew Bible with the idea that God is lovingly grooming people through suffering—the very ideological ingredients justifying power enjoyed by empires. Bruce Birch (1997: 7) avoids colonialism altogether and focuses on the Christian ideal of divine love: "God's love speaks the final word." With relatively uninformed approaches, in terms of postcolonialism, as what these illustrate, the interpretive potential of Hosea's imagery becomes handicapped by theological expectations for testimonies about God's character, chosen community, and affirmation of believers' expectations about what those should be.

Moreover, these examples illustrate scholarly tendency to avoid long-term commitments of the type postcolonialism expects. The examples of Stump and Birch illustrate conservative tendencies among scholars to avoid challenging interpretations altogether by focusing on the more agreeable idea of divine love. These, I would posit, are some reasons postcolonialism remains on the margins, neglected in favor of universalizing and essentialist tendencies in interpretations that whitewash the oppressive and exclusivist elements of meanings and ideas advanced in the narratives of the biblical texts (see also Sugirtharajah 2008). And even when studies adopt it, its theoretical application is frequently shallow and does not challenge traditional, ideologically rooted understandings. Postcolonialism is, by nature, subversive and demands conviction. Its practitioners must allow it to aggressively pursue the space after colonialism in order to respond to the direct and collateral impact of a dominant, or dominating, culture on a subordinated one (Bignall 2010: 1–2). But how does one do that with Hosea?

It is easy to overlook the imperial position from which Hosea is frequently interpreted. J. A. Dearman's (2010) following comment, for example, reflects that position through its emphasis on an elect community by which the nation should be defined, according to Hosea: "The root metaphor is that of Israel as YHWH's household (with roles for marriage and children)" (31). To see the biblical community, whatever that may be, as ideal and the tendency to see ourselves reflected in it already sets up a hierarchy rooted in an insider-outsider, center-periphery binary. The binary is given universal status as the fundamental distinction between sinners and saints. It imagines that we are wrestling against adverse conditions, frequently deemed as "evil," to secure our own ways of life (I am borrowing in part from Sugirtharajah 2005: 90). It also creates the means by which indigenous or "other" cultures or communities may be recognized as different and negative (see Bignall 2010: 78–79). That issue resides at the heart of the Hebrew Bible's prejudice against foreigners. Much of the Hebrew Bible's focus, after all, is on the formation of an idealized community, or nation. Modern theological justification of divine genocide, infanticide, and oppression as inevitable consequences of sin owe their livelihoods to a simplistic us-them binary bolstering the imperialist aspirations of monotheism.

For certain, there are breadcrumbs enough in Hosea to tickle postcolonial ideas without challenging or subverting the power structures and hierarchies on which the work depends. The book deals with the aftermath of imperial conquest and tries to explain why the national symbol and pride failed. For example, "They appointed kings without me. They set up princes, and I didn't know. They made idols of silver and gold—as if they wanted to be cut down!" (Hos. 8:4).[2] That methodological approach, however, is not entirely postcolonial. Recognizing and identifying power structures rooted in empires is one thing. Understanding what happened to cultures and identities whose stories were not preserved is another. For instance, "They will not remain in Yhwh's land" (Hos. 9:3), draws inescapable boundaries around which community has the right to rule should it be restored in the land. Unpacking such verses benefits from Musa Dube's (2000: 57) argument, on which I expand slightly, that confirmation of imperializing tendencies expects a clear stance regarding political imperialism: does it construct difference and a condemnation of what is foreign, and does it employ gender and ethnic representations to construct relations of subordination and domination? Those questions, Dube opines, present a good litmus test. Hosea tends to betray conservative and exclusivist tendencies. Did its audience embrace such imperializing tendencies? Or did it suffer under the expression of them? The relatively obvious answers to those questions exposes some of the difficulties postcolonialism has with works such as Hosea.

Aware of that, we can finally put to rest the lazy assumption that imperial power structures are evidence enough of imperializing. That is a simplistic understanding that when shouldered with the work of postcolonial theory handicaps its subversive

384 JEREMIAH W. CATALDO

potential. Instead, subversive challenges or readings might, for example, adopt Hos. 6:9–10, with its accusation of marauding priests, as a condemnation of modern religious leaders and clergy, like Robert Jeffress and Joel Osteen in the United States, who benefit from the impact of colonialism on institutional structures, as well as its facilitation of control over dominant traditions of interpretation. We might read the following verse as an accusation of the status quo: "In Israel's house, I have seen horrible things. Ephraim behaves as a prostitute, and Israel/Judah sexually defiles itself" (6:10).

That is why postcolonialism must approach Hosea similar to what Ben Zvi (2005: 149–62) states, "[It's] not about mimesis or historicity, but about learning about YHWH, Israel's past and future, and the relations between the two." I would add that Yhwh in Hosea embodies a political symbol of a myopic past (the "past" of Hosea and most biblical texts is the historical portrayals of a particular aristocratic perspective) and an idealized future. In that imagined future of the literati, Yhwh looks increasingly like an emperor, only to be eagerly ushered on by later monotheistic traditions into the status of "one and only deity."

In Hosea, and other texts, the event of Israel's defeat (722 B.C.E.; note also 597, 586 B.C.E. [Judah]) needed explanation, and prophets largely did so by explaining it as divine punishment (frequently for failure to uphold national ideals). And while that holds strong nationalist overtones, it continues to be misinterpreted by modern readers assuming that Yhwh was teaching a unified theology to a chosen community. Yet the biblical prophets, as the literati portrayed them, were foremost nationalists not vanguards of monotheistic fidelity.[3] Their calls to return to Yhwh were not calls to return to a monotheistic faith but to a nationalist conviction of what it meant to be Israelite, which was defined through the meaning and experiential frameworks of a particular political community (cf. Hos. 2:6–7 [Heb. 2:8–9]).[4]

Certainly, Hosea referred to the historical Assyrian Empire (cf. 5:13; 7:11; 8:9; 11:5, 11; 14:3 [Heb. 14:4]). And it is possible to read Hosea strictly through that lens, as though Hosea was responding to the defeat of the Northern Kingdom by the Assyrian Empire in the eighth century BCE. It is also possible the text itself was written during the sixth century and interpreted historical Israel's experience with the Assyrian Empire as a foreshadowing of what could happen to Judah. Regardless of when it was written, however, we must deal with the final form of Hosea, and likely one that was redacted in the sixth century or later (see Ben Zvi 2008: 43–44). Ultimately, a postcolonial approach to Hosea must step outside any dogged desire to cling to the historical context (contra Bass 2021). Its focus is not on the historicity of the text but on whether the text has the rhetorical function "to empower its subjects to colonize or overcome colonialism" (Dube 2000: 58). Postcolonialism cares less about the historicity of Hosea's comments about the Assyrian (or Babylonian!) Empire and more about how those ideas as metaphors challenge the imperialist position that continues to bear down culturally on marginalized communities.

Even so, instead of the author's push for an established and stable nation, or kingdom, celebrating the universal nature of a monotheistic God, modern readers emphasize an obsession with religious fidelity on the part of the prophets: a stable political reality must be ensured through religious faith. For instance, Perdue argued that a cultural imperialism engulfed the people in exile (Perdue and Carter 2015: 81–82). The prophets, he argued, led the way in navigating the crises of Judean/Israelite identity that were brought on by imperial defeat. Consequently, his argument reinforces the conventionally celebrated idea that the exiles represented the remnant of Yhwh's people from which the ruling aristocracy for a reimagined kingdom would be chosen. Because of that, while it is tempting to see what Perdue described as "cultural imperialism" as evidence of a postcolonial position, Hosea does not focus on a colonized people. That Judean captives, for example, were not colonized in the more modern sense of the term is further suggested by extrabiblical evidence that Judeans existed in Babylonia in communities in which they preserved their own cultures (cf. Pearce 2006; Joannès and Lemaire 1999).

Hosea held a different understanding of Yhwh than what Jews and Christians attribute to God. Hosea's understanding was rooted in a clear association between geopolitical space and the divine (cf. the nuance of Jezreel in Hos. 2:21–23 [Heb. 2:23–25]; see also the reference to the land in 4:1–3). That emphasis on space is an assumption behind passages such as 2:6–7 (Heb. 2:8–9), which describe woman-Israel being fenced in so that she cannot leave and consort with other providers. With later developments of religious traditions, as the religions became more removed from any distinctive geographic space, concepts of God became those that were attached to the identity of the community rather than the space itself. In other words, the domain of its god would become the interrelationship of the people, or community, and not the land—a development that benefited from ideologies of empire and set the tone for later monotheisms.[5]

26.2. PURPOSE AND STRATEGY IN POSTCOLONIALISM

Postcolonialism deconstructs, identifies, and challenges the legacies of colonialism that have been preserved in meaning, interpretation, values, and concepts of truths. It does that by "invoking ideas of social justice, emancipation and democracy in order to oppose oppressive structures of racism, discrimination and exploitation" (Nayar 2010: 4). Simultaneously, it has moved beyond the effects of historical and political colonization and moved into the "more onerous task" of extending its scope into the present and future, often with a concentration on ideological colonialism (see Mishra and Hodges 2005: 376). Yet it also respects the colonial past by engaging it, even if its intent is to challenge the assumptions rooted in that past (see Ma'ilo 2015: 66). That respect, however, is not without its expectations. It expects reciprocating respect and recognition from those who have benefited from dominant traditions developed and reinforced with the colonial past. Colonizers must give ear to the colonized.

As its iteration in the concept of the "Global South" shows, postcolonialism has challenged the heritage of claimed material and political power over others as ideological colonialism throughout the world, which manifests in part through racism, discrimination, and exploitation, whether religious, social, political, or economic (Segovia 2018). Engaging Hosea through a postcolonial lens means reading it in a way that challenges dominant traditions of interpretation, as well as the cultures that preserve them. It means, sometimes, reading it against traditions that assume an understanding of monotheistic conviction as something that existed apart from imperialist ideologies. When Yhwh roars like a lion, for example, and his "children" return from Egypt and Assyria, a postcolonial reading might interpret "children" as colonized and minoritized peoples and Egypt and Assyria, the imperial and colonial powers, as the status quo of a dominant culture that oppressed them (Hos. 11:10–11). Perhaps more specifically, Egypt and Assyria may symbolize the dominant traditions that minority communities today must negotiate—perhaps even those of white, Western Christianity—as they seek to understand their own identities as displaced peoples on the margins of society.

Put differently, this strategy means "rereading" the conceptual and ideological domains enjoyed by dominant interpretive traditions (see Ben Zvi 2008: 43–46). But we must do so by moving beyond the simplified binary I described earlier:

> While postcolonialism does foreground questions of race and ethnicity it has increasingly turned away from the traditional "master race/victim race" binary of the early postcolonials of the 1980s. Indeed, postcolonialism does see empowerment in racial difference now. This agenda of postcolonialism as a form of thinking that helps emancipation, empowerment and enlightened engagement is best summarized by Henry Louis Gates, Jr.'s evocative comment: "We must now look beyond the I-got-mine parochialism of a desperate ear. We must look beyond that over-worked master-plot of victims and victimizers." (Cited in Nayar 2010: 34)

Simply put, postcolonialism must be subversive. In doing that, it must become a protest that opens dialogue. It is not meant to sit passively, bound by the traditions of any dominant interpretation. It demands justice for voices who have been silenced and whose histories have been overwritten. It challenges assumptions of power that dominant traditions or the institutional hierarchies of dominant cultures claim for themselves. Those, it cries, are who blaze like an oven and devour their rulers (Hos. 7:7). But its goal is not that alone; it carves out and protects spaces for the histories and traditions of minority communities. In such spaces exist also the opportunity to write new traditions, even in angered response to colonialism (Bignall 2010: 2). Doing so recognizes, "History is not some contingent, endlessly deferred, and nonfoundational language game; it has real, foundational value in the lives of the recently emancipated" (Mishra and Hodges 2005: 375–76). All told, the imperial position need not be one of a physical empire. It can reflect an individual or culture that benefits from the legacies (i.e., social and political institutions, hierarchies, and concomitant values) of empire or imperialism.

26.3. More Problems with Imperial and Postcolonial Positions in Hosea

We are finally at the fundamental issue: Who is the colonizer and who is the colonized in Hosea? Can that answer be found in Hosea's metaphors? "I will seduce her, and I will lead her to the wilderness and speak to her heart" (2:16 [Eng. 2:14]). Was Hosea's message one of postcolonial struggle or social-political critique? Was any justification of seduction—and we should note that the root *patah* ("seduce") can also mean "deceive"—rooted in the concern for the woman or in concern for the reestablished authority of the male figure? Perdue (2013: 188) argues Hosea sought to "decolonize the mind" of the Northern Kingdom, Israel, by delegitimating its rulers. Thus, the work's focus was on masculine authority. That argument, however, is a weak appeal to the problematic colonial binary. It assumes a dominant ideology by which the collective mind of the critiqued people should comport themselves. In that sense, it is the very opposite of postcolonialism. Not only that, but it loses the intent of the text.

As noted above, Hosea's audience could, from one perspective, be read as being in a postcolonial position in relation to either the Assyrian or Babylonian Empire. But that is a limited argument. Hosea's target audience was members of the aristocracy, not an actively colonized collective body. An additional limitation is that it is too easy for modern readers from a majority community to associate with Hosea's audience by spiritualizing the Israelites and Judeans as the elect community of God and the predecessor to the symbolic embodiment of what would later become the body of Christ for Christians or *qahal*, community, for modern Judaism. E. R. Jones, for example, did just that when he used Hos. 14:1 (Eng. 13:16) to explain British loss of control and physical, sometimes violent, responses to Brits in India (cited in Sugirtharajah 2005: 70). Jones cited bad management of native landholders and magistrates, British encouragement of heathen festivals, affirming caste, and discouraging missionaries and native converts as reasons for Britain's sin. Likewise, "Daniel Wilson," as Sugirtharajah writes, "the Bishop of Calcutta, saw the current rebels and traitors as God's rod of anger, as was the Assyrian monarch of old who was sent against a hypocritical nation" (70). Israel, in those interpretations, symbolized a mismanaged British Empire. Certainly, it is a possible interpretation, but one focused on the perspective of a dominant, imperial, and colonizing culture (an imperial position), which continues to reside with dominant traditions of Western monotheism. That we might see the previous interpretation as a possibility only emphasizes colonialism's legacy on biblical interpretation.

With more tempered theological justification, Peter Ackroyd (1968: 58–59) saw Hosea as part of an assumed uniform prophetic emphasis on restoration. This somewhat uncritical acceptance is more common than not among scholars. Concerning that tendency, note Mays (1969: 11), who comments on what needed to change preceding restoration: "The reproaches of Hosea were aimed at two primary targets; in his eyes the failure of Israel was manifested in its cultic and political life." Moreover, while Hosea mentions Assyria and Egypt, among other kingdoms, the work's focus is less on them as political powers and more on the failure of Hosea's national community to live up to the ideals the author saw as necessary. And therein lies part of the interpretive problem. What readers interpret as the (and for some, universal) community of Yhwh is a manifestation of the literati's imagination. To enumerate, Hosea's audience was not all of Israel or Judah. Women and children cannot find themselves in its metaphors except as symbols of promiscuity and profanity. Likewise, the economically disenfranchised were not the subjects of Hosea's merciful gaze. Can a text so seemingly unaware of the marginalized be sensitive to postcolonial concerns?

Hosea criticizes the actions of Israel's (and Judah's) leaders using sexualized metaphors that favor a masculine perspective (contra Perdue 2013: 174–75). As Hos. 2 conveys, the "woman" sees the imperial powers as "lovers." Clearly, that correlation shows the socially conditioned nature of metaphors in Hosea (Yee 1998: 207). That means our reading strategies must address the author's conditions and those of our own cultural traditions or positions. What does it mean, for instance, to read Yhwh as a husband, if Yhwh, the predecessor to the modern concept of God, is defined largely from the perspective of a dominant cultural institution or meaning framework (see Yee 1998: 207)? To answer that in the remaining discussion, consider the woman as a metaphor for the colonized subject.

Mays (1969: 48) argues that the switch from *baal* to *ish* as a term for Yhwh in relationship to the woman, both of which he translates as "husband," conveys a more intimate relationship between husband-Yhwh and wife-Israel. However, *ish* can also just mean "man." While one can translate it as "husband," there is no clear sign that a marriage ever takes place. Nevertheless, scholars often assume that because many of the prophets speak of a covenant relationship between Yhwh and Israel that at points appears modeled on marriage, Hosea must mean that. But it is equally possible, and here is where a postcolonial reading can issue one challenge, that the passage is not speaking of a more intimate relationship. Instead, it may be referring to one devoid of care, like the naked woman being led into the wilderness, stripped of all civilized relationships and objects of sensual pleasure (3:3–4), comprehending only rudimentary intellect, "me man, you woman." The tendency to read marital intimacy into the passage (but with or without sex?) reflects modern assumptions about marriage, which have been conditioned within an imperial West. The argument that *ishi* ("my man/husband"), in contrast to *baali*, which can mean "my husband," "my master," and "my lord," is more intimate is not strong. Such wishful, intimate interpretations are expressions of later ideological agendas. Nearly the entire context of Hos. 2 borders on misogyny. Hosea 3:1 does not help counter that point, either. "And Yahweh said to me again, 'Go! Love a woman who fucks friends and fornicates.'"[6] While some translations offer "a woman" as "wife," the word is *ishah*—see the previous discussion of *ish*—and the context does not clearly state that the woman is Hosea's wife. Instead, the text of Hosea presents the woman as a colonized body reinforcing the values and hierarchy of her patriarchal "lord."

From the perspective of traditional interpretation, these sorts of metaphors or symbols might be read in the sense that Yhwh loves the people in the same way that a husband should love his wife (so Hubler 2020). And within Christian tradition, that symbolizes how Christ loves the church. That tradition gives us a lot of theological nuance that can express a familial relationship, one rooted in emotion and love. But those are modern theological perspectives, and it is too easy to emphasize love while overlooking who gets left out in such symbols and metaphors. For instance, even an emphasis on a loving relationship overshadows the patriarchal nuance and values that have gone into the metaphor, in that the woman is subordinate to the husband. Readers also often overlook the fact that Yhwh's/God's punishment of the woman is the type of physical violence we would today identify as abuse in *any other* circumstance (see Yee 1998: 207).[7]

Another reason Hosea cannot be foisted from the colonial closet: the woman is treated as a problem for masculine honor and authority. "And Yhwh said to Hosea, 'Go! Take a fornicating woman and children born of harlotry'" (1:2).[8] She is a sexual problem: deviant, strong-willed, adulterous, and everything that is outside the ideal form of what a woman or a wife should be (see 1:2; 2:2–3, 5 [Heb. 2:4–5, 7]). So much so that some modern readers may see the book as an embarrassing example in which a prophet married a prostitute (see Birch 1997: 7). But again, there is no unequivocal evidence that the woman was a prostitute, nor that she and Hosea were married. (And is not taking women for sexual purposes an imperial activity?)

Hosea's sexual metaphors expose "postcolonial sexualities," wherein colonial discourse portrays (pre)colonized bodies as sexually insatiable, permissive, and immoral (Meghani and Saeed 2019: 297). That is the perspective that Edward Said's *Orientalism* (1994b; see also Schick 1999), for instance, discussed. The portrayal of the woman in Hosea as sexually licentious plays in an inverted fashion on the normative patriarchal fantasy of a woman who wants sex. In Hosea, the woman wants sex with other providers (or *baalim*), or other political leaders, and not Yhwh or Hosea. This speaks to the strategy of understanding how the portrayals of men and women reinforced the dominant position, that is, the imperialist position. It does not even matter if the woman was sexually active in terms of the metaphor. The weight of its condemnation needs only the assumption.

The biblical text portrays sexuality as something that must be controlled for the benefit of the man, or the dominant position. And if sexuality is more than just sex, if it speaks to how we understand and relate to each other, then it potentially exposes broader interpersonal and political relationships (Butler 2006; Foucault 1978; Sedgwick 2003). Thus, in Hos. 3:3–4, woman-Israel must live in the wilderness without sex, king, prince, sacrifice, sacred pillar, ephod, or idols.[9] She will be stripped of those relationships (religious, political, economic, social) before she will be allowed her own identity—but one still dependent on that of her masculine provider, or "man."

Assumptions about the woman, therefore, are rooted in normative presuppositions by the author and interpreter conceiving what a woman is and how she should behave in relation to a man, who is also symbolized by God, or Yhwh, who is always in a position of power. The binary is rooted in the perceived power structure. Hosea is never described, for instance, as being a problem. Likewise, Yhwh is never described as being a problem. Such assumptions are rooted in the idea that those two masculine figures, the positions they represent, are the ideal. And that those outside of the positions must conform to the framework defined from the vantage point of Yhwh and Hosea, or the masculine imperialist position, to use vocabulary from a postcolonial reading strategy (see Mishra and Hodges 2005: 338). Therefore, like the colonized subject, the woman who is acting outside of the expected norms is a problem and simply reinforces the need for a created framework with which to control her (see Hos. 2:6 [Heb. 2:8]).

Consider also the children of Hosea, who are named and then renamed, and who may represent colonized subjects because of their circumstances. For instance, the children are named "not my people," "no pity," and "Jezreel." The last designation alludes to the bloodshed that happened in the Jezreel Valley area (cf. 2 Kgs. 9–10). Without further context, they are simply children who are not themselves guilty of any action. And here we see a very clear colonial symbolism or metaphor in which colonial or imperial bodies will take over and treat colonized cultures as essentially children who lack sophisticated awareness of morality, ethics, civilization, and law. Dearman (2010: 80), for example, claims that the actions of the children and their mother symbolize Israel in "flagrant rebellion against the Lord." But that reduces the text once again to a monotheistic treatise of faith, and to one exclusive to a specific community. While Dearman's assessment is based on Hosea's near misogynist description of the woman, which could be interpreted as a symbolic description of actions that deviate from expected norms, the children in ch. 1 are never described as acting in one way or another (but cf. 2:4 [Heb. 2:6]). They are simply guilty based on the actions of their mother.

The children are named in a negative sense and are rejected because of what they do not represent (cf. Hos. 1:4–9)—namely, uniformity to the national ideal, as Hosea perceives it. They symbolize the development of a community, or communities, outside the position of the dominant one. In other words, they have not been enculturated properly. "Not my people," for instance, emphasizes a status that has been withheld from the community (Andersen and Freedman 1980: 205). Contrast that with the title "my people," which was a sacred designation that bolstered the exodus tradition—certainly an imperializing position (Andersen and Freedman 1980: 197)! This comparison assumes that religious conviction and identity were the basis for collective, national identity. But any religious sentiment Hosea expresses would not have been shared by all people across the social, economic, and political spectrum—much less shared by anyone who did not ethnically identify with the author's community. The sentiments were those of the literati and at least some of the social and political aristocracy. Assuming the alternative, however, only reinforces the imperialist position of biblical interpretation by identifying a specific community through which God, as an invisible emperor, exercises authority.

The renaming of the children also implies, on some level, an inculturation in which they are taught "proper" behavior. The ambivalence that is part of the children's symbolic names leans on the perspective of the interpreting community, whether they are negatively or positively named. The values attributed to the children are determined from the imperialist perspective, which is symbolized by Yhwh and Hosea. Or as Mays (1969: 190), with imperial fanfare proclaimed, "In Yahweh alone Israel may find life!"

26.4. POSTCOLONIALISM, PROPHETS, AND HOSEA

Postcolonial readings may benefit the most from seeing the prophets as social and political critics, not theological vanguards or champions. To assume that religion existed in the same sense in Israel and Judah that it does today is naïve. The prophets talked about Yhwh. They talked about fidelity to some sort of law or commandments attributed to Yhwh. But those conversations were rooted in concerns for the stability and the identity of their kingdoms. Theirs were nationalist concerns.[10] In a concern for community, one may adopt prophetic critique, a tool of postcolonialism and its subversive strategy, not as a relic of the past but as a strategy for challenging conventional, normative biblical meaning and interpretation.

Postcolonialism seeks subversive strategies for elevating the voice of the marginalized apart from imperialistic and colonial perspective. Subversion, however, does not have to be aggressive. It looks at the same relations, positions, frameworks, symbols, and metaphors within a text and translates them in a way that criticizes what is conventionally assumed about the dominant traditions, interpretive strategies, meanings, and values that reinforce the position of the dominant community. My essay has not been overt or aggressive as much as it has explored what it would look like to read Hosea from the inverted perspective. This reading challenges presumptions about truth or morality, seeking instead a reading strategy focused on human dignity. It pursues the value of human life across the spectrum of the world, oppressed by no community. In brief, it highlights the ethical responsibility of listening to others.

We listen. And we incorporate the concerns and the needs of others in ways that may demand that we challenge or change something about ourselves or the cultural assumptions, values, and frameworks of meaning that we use, or have traditionally used, to bolster biblical meaning and interpretation. Postcolonialism demands that we recognize that much of biblical interpretation has been a colonial enterprise, or has been conducted from an imperial position. It expects that if the Bible, as a sacred text, is to keep its importance and relevance, our reading strategies must be more globalized and aware of diversity. Postcolonial reading strategies, as they are evolving to accommodate experiences of the Global South and liberation theologies, may be better positioned to reinforce concerns for human dignity necessary within biblical interpretation. Hosea offers a good starting point for critiquing the very social and political institutions that we have relied on, without question, for generations.

Few good postcolonial interpretations of Hosea, or the prophets more generally, exist.[11] Hosea does not provide an easy model for postcolonial theory beyond a very loose colonial binary. Postcolonial methods do not help us understand much about the historical context of Hosea, which resists accurate historical reconstruction. Instead, postcolonial methods find their strength in critiquing the symbols and metaphors of Hosea that reinforce oppressive centers of power, and in challenging the dominant traditions of interpretation dependent on a colonial dichotomy to identify a particular community as Yhwh's chosen people ("my people"). Those very traditions have been and remain part of the problem.

> [T]he filthy truth is that the God of the Hebrew Bible plays favorites. Not so bad if there are many gods, so that every people has one, and thus *some* fighting chance in a conflict with Yahweh's tribe. But if the God of the Hebrew Bible is supposed to be the *only* God, the universalist God of the philosophers, then his favoring of Israelites over other peoples is unforgivable. (Antony 2011: 261–62)

Notes

1. Gunther Wittenberg (2013) attempts to challenge dominant traditions by putting Hos. 5:8–6:6 into dialogue with Milton Friedman, who advances neoliberal capitalism, and George Ritzer, who analyzes the "globalization of nothing." It is a rather ambitious attempt that ultimately fails. Still, it reflects the direction in which postcolonial studies should be going.
2. Unless otherwise stated, translations of Hosea are my own.
3. Contra Hubler (2020), who argues that Hosea saw covenantal worship as the "glue" of Israelite identity. Such reductive arguments are part of the reason postcolonialism's obligation entails challenging the imposition of modern monotheistic ideologies, which owe their origins to imperialism, as motivations for authors of ancient texts (contra Willis 2019).
4. Sometimes, this identity was not one rooted in the past as much as it was a reimagined identity that provided a corrective to the past, from the perspective of the prophets as nationalist critics. On the persistence of the name "Israel," see also Davies 2015: 64–66.
5. Even in the modern world, there is still a desire to see God linked to geographic space, as policies and opinions on the conflicts in the Middle East show. For example, Bass (2021: 58) states, "Hosea proclaims YHWH's word to YHWH's people," understanding that Yhwh is the universal God of Jewish and Christian monotheisms. He maintains that Hosea correlates Israel with Canaan, the people of which are vomited from the land because of sinful behavior (cf. Lev. 18:1–5, 24–30; p. 63). His argument is based on the traditional belief that Hosea's emphasis on judgment and its reversal reinforces the idea that the land was "given" by God to the community. And because Yhwh is God, the recipient of that gift remains until God decides differently.
6. What I have translated as "fuck" is the Hebrew root, *ahab*. In the context, however, "love" does not convey the attitude of the sentence. The woman is involved in adulterous relationships, behavior unlikely to be described as a positive expression of love and relationship.
7. How frequently do Western Christian audiences, for example, show themselves appalled by Middle Eastern Islamic cultures that practice stoning as a punishment for women?

8. Based on Hebrew text, it is not clear that the children were actually Hosea's or were the ones referred to in the following verses. It is possible that the children had already been born and were part of the acquisition. In that case, they would not be those mentioned in vv. 4–9. At any rate, we can assume that the children belonged to the woman.

9. Perdue's (2013: 176) argument that Hosea invokes the "sacred traditions," including the exodus out of Egypt and the conquest of Canaan, is not compelling. Certainly, it is possible, but it assumes, without strong evidence, that all individuals within society actively shared those traditions. Otherwise, the traditions to which he refers can only be said to be those of the literati, and possibly portions of the aristocracy, who would have had some invested interest in what the literati wrote.

10. Arguments that Hosea's focus was on an idealized image of the cult oversimplify the matter (e.g., De Andrado 2016). They also impose modern sentiments about religious fidelity, as separate from social and political matters, on an ancient context. More to the point for postcolonialism, such arguments benefit from interpretive traditions that burgeoned within colonial cultures.

11. For example, Dube (2000) only refers to Isaiah, Daniel, Zechariah, and Malachi on three different pages and roughly six references. The majority of those are references to a summary of Dickson's work (1991). In contrast, the typical references from Genesis, Exodus, Deuteronomy, and Joshua, and including Matthew from the New Testament, enjoy pride of place.

References

Ackroyd, Peter R. 1968. *Exile and Restoration: A Study of Hebrew Thought of the Sixth Century B.C.* Philadelphia: Westminster.

Andersen, Francis I., and David N. Freedman. 1980. *Hosea*. AB 24. New Haven: Yale University Press.

Antony, Louise. 2011. "Comments on 'Reading Joshua.'" In Michael Bergmann, Michael J. Murray, and Michael C. Rea, eds., *Divine Evil? The Moral Character of the God of Abraham*. Oxford; New York: Oxford University Press, 257–62.

Bass, Derek. 2021. "Hosea's Hermeneutics: Reading Scripture with the Prophet." *Presbyterion* 47 (1): 58–76.

Ben Zvi, Ehud. 2005. *Hosea*. FOTL 31a. Grand Rapids: Eerdmans.

Ben Zvi, Ehud. 2008. "Reading Hosea and Imagining YHWH." *HBT* 30: 43–57.

Bignall, Simone. 2010. *Postcolonial Agency: Critique and Constructivism*. Edinburgh: Edinburgh University Press.

Birch, Bruce C. 1997. *Hosea, Joel, and Amos*. Westminster Bible Companion. Louisville: Westminster John Knox.

Butler, Judith. 2006. *Gender Trouble: Feminism and the Subversion of Identity*. New York: Routledge.

Cataldo, Jeremiah. 2019. "Biblical Strategies for Reinterpreting Crises with 'Outsiders.'" In Jeremiah W. Cataldo, ed., *Imagined Worlds and Constructed Differences in the Hebrew Bible*. LHBOTS 677. London: T&T Clark/Bloomsbury, 127–43.

Davies, Philip R. 2015. *In Search of "Ancient Israel": A Study in Biblical Origins*. 2nd ed. London: T&T Clark.

De Andrado, Paba Nidhani. 2016. "Ḥesed and Sacrifice: The Prophetic Critique in Hosea." *CBQ* 78: 47–67.

Dearman, J. Andrew. 2010. *The Book of Hosea.* NICOT. Grand Rapids: Eerdmans.

Dickson, Kwesi. 1991. *Uncompleted Mission: Christianity and Exclusivism.* Maryknoll, NY: Orbis.

Dube, Musa W. 2000. *Postcolonial Feminist Interpretation of the Bible.* Atlanta: Chalice.

Foucault, Michel. 1978. *The History of Sexuality, Volume 1.* New York: Pantheon.

Goswell, Greg. 2013. "The Eschatology of Malachi after Zechariah 14." *JBL* 132 (3): 625–38.

Hubler, Caitlin. 2020. "No Longer Will You Call Me 'My Ba'al': Hosea's Polemic and the Semantics of 'Ba'al' in 8th Century B.C.E. Israel." *JSOT* 44 (4): 610–23.

Joannès, F., and André Lemaire. 1999. "Trois Tablettes Cunéiformes à l'onomastique Ouest-Sémitique." *Transeuphratene* 17: 17–33.

Kinyua, Johnson Kiriaku. 2013. "A Postcolonial Analysis of Bible Translation and Its Effectiveness in Shaping and Enhancing the Discourse of Colonialism and the Discourse of Resistance: The Gikuyu New Testament—A Case Study." *Black Theology* 11 (1): 58–95.

Ma'ilo, Mosese. 2015. "Celebrating Hybridity in Island Bibles: Jesus, the *Tamaalepō* (Child of the Dark) in Matatio 1:18–26." In Jione Havea, Margaret Aymer, and Steed Vernyl Davidson, eds., *Islands, Islanders, and the Bible: RumInations.* Semeia Studies 77. Atlanta: SBL, 65–76.

Mays, James Luther. 1969. *Hosea.* OTL. Philadelphia: Westminster.

Meghani, Shamira A., and Humaira Saeed. 2019. "Postcolonial/Sexuality, or Sexuality in 'Other' Contexts: Introduction." *Journal of Postcolonial Writing* 55 (3): 293–307.

Mishra, Vijay, and Bob Hodges. 2005. "What Was Postcolonialism?" *New Literary History* 36: 375–402.

Nayar, Pramod K. 2010. *Postcolonialism: A Guide for the Perplexed.* London: Continuum.

O'Kennedy, Daniel F. 2014. "Haggai 2:20–23: Call to Rebellion or Eschatological Expectation?" *OTE* 27 (2): 520–40.

Pearce, Laurie. 2006. "New Evidence for Jews in Babylonia." In Oded Lipschits and Manfred Oeming, eds., *Judah and the Judeans in the Neo-Babylonian Period.* Winona Lake, IN: Eisenbrauns, 399–411.

Perdue, Leo G. 2013. "Hosea and the Empire." In Roland Boer, ed., *Postcolonialism and the Hebrew Bible: The Next Step.* Semeia Studies 70. Atlanta: SBL, 169–92.

Perdue, Leo G., and Warren Carter. 2015. *Israel and Empire: A Postcolonial History of Israel and Early Judaism.* New York: Bloomsbury/T&T Clark.

Said, Edward W. 1994a. *Culture and Imperialism.* New York: Vintage.

Said, Edward W. 1994b. *Orientalism.* New York: Vintage.

Schick, Irvin Cemil. 1999. *The Erotic Margin: Sexuality and Spatiality in Alteritist Discourse.* London: Verso.

Sedgwick, Eve Kosofsky. 2003. *Touching Feeling: Affect, Pedagogy, Performativity (Series Q).* Durham, NC: Duke University Press.

Segovia, Fernando F. 2018. "Introduction." In Tat-Siong Benny Liew and Fernando F. Segovia, eds., *Colonialism and the Bible: Contemporary Reflections from the Global South.* Lanham, MD: Lexington, ix–xxxi.

Stump, Eleonore. 2011. "Reply to Draper." In Michael Bergmann, Michael J. Murray, and Michael C. Rea, eds., *Divine Evil? The Moral Character of the God of Abraham.* Oxford; New York: Oxford University Press, 204–8.

Sugirtharajah, R. S. 2005. *The Bible and Empire: Postcolonial Explorations.* Cambridge: Cambridge University Press.

Sugirtharajah, R. S., ed. 2008. *Still at the Margins: Biblical Scholarship Fifteen Years after "Voices from the Margin."* New York: T&T Clark.

Sugirtharajah, R. S., ed. 2016. *Voices from the Margin: Interpreting the Bible in the Third World.* 25th anniv. Maryknoll, NY: Orbis.

Sweeney, Marvin A. 2012. *Tanak: A Theological and Critical Introduction to the Jewish Bible.* Minneapolis: Fortress.

Willis, John T. 2019. "Hosea's Unique Figures of Yahweh." *Restoration Quarterly* 61 (3): 167–80.

Wittenberg, Gunther. 2013. "Prophecy for a Time of Global Crisis: Hosea 5:8–6:6." *Journal of Theology for Southern Africa* 146: 139–69.

Yee, Gale. 1998. "Hosea." In Carol A. Newsom and Sharon H. Ringe, eds., *Women's Bible Commentary: Expanded Edition with Apocrypha.* Louisville: Westminster John Knox, 207–15.

CHAPTER 27

PROLEGOMENA TO THE ECOLOGICAL INTERPRETATION OF HOSEA

PETER TRUDINGER

THE book of Hosea abounds in references to nonhuman elements of creation. They appear in every chapter, even the decidedly anthropocentric chs. 1, 3, and 11. Yet, for most of the modern period, their study was subordinated to the dominant interests in the relationship between the divine and the human, and Hosea's enigmatic marriage. The situation began to change late last century, with the rise of socioeconomic interpretations of Hosea and the development of an interest in ecology and the Bible.[1] Nevertheless, Hosea remains underrepresented in ecologically oriented biblical studies.

Interest in the study of the environment in all disciplines has developed over the last fifty or so years, somewhat in step with the realization of the accelerating capability of humanity to impact ecology. Our terminology has not kept pace with this growth. The word "creation" may be broad and refer to the universe (i.e., everything resulting from the Big Bang/initial divine activity), or it may be limited to our planet, or living things on the planet, or animals, or a category of life forms distinct from humans but excluding geographical features such as mountains or sky, or effects such as winds. In this essay, the somewhat clumsy terms "nonhuman elements of creation" or "nonhuman members of creation" will be used when necessary.

In Biblical Hebrew there is no term for creation. The closest may be the merism *hašāmayîm vāʾāreṣ* "the sky and the land," but this does not appear in Hosea. The land, *hāʾāreṣ*, has a wide semantic range so the interpreter must decide what is referred to in any particular instance—earth as a cosmological entity, land, land inhabited by humans and/or animals, or a specific region. Sky is hardly mentioned in Hosea and then mostly as the natural location of birds (2:18, 21 [Heb. 2:20, 23]; 4:3; 7:12). An expression such as "the beasts of the field and the birds of the sky and the fish of the sea" (4:3; cf. 2:18 [Heb. 2:20]) may be a merism encompassing nonhuman life.[2]

27.1. HOSEA AND NONHUMAN ELEMENTS OF CREATION

References to nonhuman elements of creation are the foundations and building blocks for any ecological interpretation of Hosea. I start by focusing on them, before moving to the question of the design of an interpretation. The task, however, is not as simple as it sounds.

A preliminary listing and categorization of the nonhuman elements in the book of Hosea includes the following:

A. Metaphors or images for God or humans[3]

1. God is like . . .
wild animals: lion (5:14; 13:7, 8; 11:10), bear (13:8), leopard (13:7), a generic wild animal (13:8); vulture (8:1)
    other life forms: a tree (14:8 [Heb. 14:9]), insect and/or rotting agent (5:12)
    natural phenomena: showers or rain (6:3), dew (14:5 [Heb. 14:6])

2. Humans (members of Israel, Ephraim, Judah, etc.) are like . . .
animals: heifer (4:16; 10:11), lamb (4:16), wild ass (8:9), dove or other bird (7:11, 12; 10:11)
plants: tree (9:16; 14:5, 6 [Heb. 14:6, 7]), palm (9:13), vine (10:1; 14:7 [Heb. 14:8]), lily (14:5 [Heb. 14:6]), weeds (10:4), a garden (14:5 [Heb. 14:6])
produce: grapes, fig (9:10), burned cake (7:8), chaff (13:3)
natural phenomena: mist and dew (6:4; 13:3), foam on a wave (10:7), smoke (13:3)

B. Items possessed or controlled by another, either God or human
The distinction here is between active and passive—that is, elements of creation that are described as having agency and doing something, albeit under the control of another, versus those that exist as possessions to be used (such as gifts).

1. Instrumental (active) agents under the control of God
thorns (2:6 [Heb. 2:8]), wild animals (2:12 [Heb. 2:14]), bow, sword, war (2:18 [Heb. 2:20]), new moon (5:7), harvest (6:11), fire (8:14), wind (13:15)

2. Instrumental (active) agents under the control of humans
wind (8:7; 12:1 [Heb. 12:2]), birds (9:8, 11), fruit and crops (10:13), idols (13:2), calves (13:2), springs (13:15), horses (14:3 [Heb. 14:4])

3. Objects possessed by God for utilitarian use
grain, wine, oil, wool, flax, gold, silver (2:8, 9 [Heb. 2:10, 11]), vineyards (2:12 [Heb. 2:14])
Valley of Achor (2:15 [Heb. 2:17])

4. Objects possessed by humans for utilitarian use
agricultural products: bread, water, wool, flax, oil, drink (2:5 [Heb. 2:7]; 7:14), barley, wine (3:2; 9:2), standing grain (8:7), vines, fig trees (2:12 [Heb. 2:14])

silver (3:2)
items for sacrifice (5:6; 8:13; 9:4)
calf of Samaria (8:6?)
spring (13:15), wind (12:1 [Heb. 12:2])
stones and fields (12:11 [Heb. 12:12]), threshing floor and wine vat (9:2)

C. Geographical references
named places: Jezreel (1:4–5, 11; 2:22 [Heb. 2:24]); Achor (2:15 [Heb. 2:17]); Mizpah,
    Tabor, Shittim (5:1–2); Gibeah, Ramah, Beth-Aven, Benjamin (5:8); Aven (10:8);
    Gilead, Gilgal (12:11 [Heb. 12:12]); Samaria (8:5–6); Lebanon (14:5–7 [Heb. 14:6–
    8]); Memphis (9:6accept); Aram (12:12 [Heb. 12:13]); Assyria (9:3; 11:11; 10:6);
    Egypt (2:15 [Heb. 2:17]; 9:3); Ephraim, Judah, Israel (*passim*)
mountains (4:13)
land (1:2, 11 [Heb. 2:2]; 2:3, 15, 18, 21–23 [Heb. 2:5, 17, 20, 23–25]; 4:1, 3; 6:3; 7:16; 9:3; 11:5,
    11; 13:4, 5)
sky (2:18, 21 [Heb. 2:20, 23]; 4:3; 7:10)
wilderness (2:3, 14 [Heb. 2:5, 16]; 9:10, 13:5, 15)

D. As agents who have their own initiative[4]
The land, in Hos. 4:3, mourns, and various creatures languish and perish. Other non-
    human elements that may exercise independent action include wine (4:12), the
    new moon (5:7), the calf of Samaria (8:5, 6), nettles (9:6), hills and mountains
    (10:8). However, these may also be examples of category *B*.
E. The treaty partners of Hosea 2:18, 19 (Heb. 2:20, 21)
wild animals, birds, creeping things, and humans.

This categorization offers a starting point, illustrative but not exhaustive. Some of the
decisions implicit in the listing may be open to question. For example, does a human
possess the wind, or is this a trope for futility? Should a dried-up spring be considered
a metaphor for lack of vitality? Is a threshing floor or a sword a legitimate nonhuman
element of creation? The distinction between nonhuman elements as passive objects or
active instruments is often blurred.

The geographical references raise more issues. Traditionally "land" is often translated
"earth," and "Sky" as "heavens." However, the semantic range of these words in English
is large. The NRSV of Hos 2:18–23 (Heb. 2:20–25) is an example of questionable shifts in
the translation of "land." "Wilderness," *hāmidbār*, is also an ambiguous term, as it has
been argued that Hosea (along with Deuteronomy) has a perspective on the term which
is not shared by other material, such as Numbers (Marlow 2009: 174–77; Smith 2018:
42–51).

With regard to geographical place names assigned by humans (e.g., Jezreel, Memphis,
Samaria), the question arises as to whether these should be interpreted as nonhuman
elements of creation or as a group of people and so a human element. Does Israel/
Ephraim refer to the human residents of a place or does it encompass nonhuman
elements? Does the calf of Samaria belong to the city, perhaps as a distillation of the
natural spirituality of the area, or is Samaria a convenient code word for the inhabitants

or leadership of the city? Does the city represent the nation (Trudinger 2008)? Some of these questions may seem straightforward, even nit-picking. However, ecological interpretation requires clarification of the scope of the nonhuman elements in a text.

The majority of the items in the list appear in Hos. 4–14. However, some recent interpretations find ecology behind the text in the interpretation of Hos. 1–3. The female figure in chs. 1–3 may be a metaphor for the land. Braaten (2022: 151), for instance, suggests, "In Hosea 1–2, Land is Yhwh's wife and Israel's mother." In this case, the nonhuman is not symbolic of the human. Quite the opposite, the human symbolizes a nonhuman element of creation.

Although the categorization above is imperfect, the exercise of creating it forms the starting point of an ecological interpretation of the book of Hosea. It draws attention to how the words of Hosea extend beyond the human realm, as well as to the inherent complexities of interpretation. Naïve questions can give rise to insights. A fully fledged ecological interpretation attempts to give weight to the nonhuman elements and confront the complexities.

27.2. Ecological Interpretation and Hosea

In general, ecological interpretation requires a shift in thinking about a text. Traditional biblical interpretation has focused on God, humans, and the relationship between these two, with other elements forming the background to this great drama. An ecological interpretation disrupts the set; the background enters the foreground, and is given a role equal to those of the main characters. If taxonomy is the starting point for interpretation, methodology goes hand in hand with it. How does interpretation balance the divine, human, and nonhuman elements?

The opening chapters of Hosea contain a notorious example of an interpretive balancing act, not in relation to ecology, but to gender equality. The female figure (and children) in these chapters is characterized as someone possessed and controlled by a male. Hosea, in chs. 1 and 3, procures a wife, controls her and her children (the latter through naming), and limits the activities of the female, before some restoration takes place. In ch. 2, the speaker (male) abuses the female, before "speaking to her heart" and apparently restoring the relationship. The traditional interpretation of these chapters operated with an androcentric reading that did not question the implicit behavioral and value judgments in the text, which was interpreted as expressing the tension between divine love and human sin. Since the second half of the twentieth century, feminist studies have called this reading into question. Among other things, their methodology has called out androcentric assumptions and centered the female characters in interpretation, rather than reading solely from the perspective of the male characters.[5] The text becomes a story of abuse and domination.

One of the outcomes of this second line of interpretation has been increased weight given to the socioeconomic context of Hosea. A superficial reading of Hosea's attack on the cult, which links the errors of Israel to idolatry and aberrant sexual activity, does not adequately account for the intensity of his critique, the message of contemporary prophets like Amos, or other contemporaneous evidence. Hosea's time was one when the rich elite exploited others in society along with the land, thus violating the requirements for justice and equity. The image of marriage and the sexually charged language are not to be taken at face value, but illustrate this perversion of righteousness. The abused woman in Hos. 1–3 is the land. This socioeconomic background forms the context for ecological readings of Hosea, especially as part of the Book of the Twelve (see Marlow and Harris 2022). The land suffers degradation from this exploitation, along with anguish for its nonhuman inhabitants. Braaten's (2022) essay is a valuable contribution to the study of Hosea in this context.

In general terms, ecological interpretations of Hosea face a methodological choice similar to that faced by feminist interpretation. Should ecological interpretation consider the nonhuman elements as subordinate to the human (and divine)? Or can the nonhuman elements be centered in the interpretation? The latter approach of centering has been developed and vigorously pursued by the Earth Bible Project.[6] This is not the only methodology, but will be the one outlined here. It provides a useful place to start building an ecological interpretation of Hosea.

The Earth Bible approach has two key features. First, it adopts a methodology borrowed from feminist critiques with three stages: suspicion, identification, and retrieval. Second, it centers the nonhuman elements contained in the text. To assist in this shift in perspective, it refers to a set of six ecojustice principles.

First, the three stages in the methodology:

1. Suspicion
   Ecological interpretation reads with a suspicion that the text is anthropocentric and/or the tradition of interpretation has been anthropocentric, in that either or both of these has centered and privileged the interests of the human subject. Part of the interpretive exercise is to suss out the ways in which the anthropocentric focus has been embedded in the text and tradition. The next step is to free the interpreter from this focus.

2. Identification
   When a reader encounters a text, the natural reflex is to identify with the human characters in the text, empathizing with or rejecting their emotions and actions. An ecological reading actively counters such a reflex by uncovering, as best as possible, and isolating any assumptions based on our humanity. Instead, empathy and identification are placed with the nonhuman elements, in effect making them characters in the text. A first step is for the reader to create their own list of nonhuman elements present in a text.

3. Retrieval
   Once the reader has identified with a nonhuman character in a text, it is possible to recast the text from the perspective of the nonhuman. This is a process akin to

"reading against the grain." A useful tool here is to imagine that one is speaking into the situation with the voice of the particular nonhuman character (Card 1986).

For example, a hermeneutic of suspicion questions the naïve, literal reading of the opening chapters of Hosea as reflecting an actual marriage. Here is another, somewhat playful, example. In Hos. 4:16, Israel is compared with a "stubborn heifer." One may ask about the perspective from which "stubborn" is defined. From a human perspective, "stubborn" refers to an attitude that does not acquiesce to the wishes of the master. A "stubborn heifer" is one that does not do what its human master wishes. It is a negative slur on the beast. From another perspective, however, stubbornness may be a positive quality, such as an indicator of standing up for one's values or of passive resistance. Elsewhere in the Bible, the story of Tamar and Judah (Gen. 38) might be seen as an example of positive stubbornness resisting hegemonic power. Among nonhumans, Balaam's donkey also showed stubborn resistance (Num. 22:22–30), although in this case it was encouraged by the vision of an angel. Tamar only had a vision of what was just. What would prompt stubbornness in a nonhuman? I will return to this below.

I now turn to ecological interpretation's six ecojustice principles:

1. *The Principle of Intrinsic Worth:* The universe, Earth, and all its components have intrinsic worth/value.
2. *The Principle of Interconnectedness:* Earth is a community of interconnected living things that are mutually dependent on each other for life and survival.
3. *The Principle of Voice:* Earth is a subject capable of raising its voice in celebration and against injustice.
4. *The Principle of Purpose:* The universe, Earth, and all its components are part of a dynamic, cosmic design, and each piece has a place in the overall goal of that design.
5. *The Principle of Mutual Custodianship:* Earth is a balanced and diverse domain where responsible custodians can function as partners with, rather than rulers over, Earth to sustain its balance and a diverse Earth community.
6. *The Principle of Resistance:* Earth and its components not only suffer from human injustices but actively resist them in the struggle for justice.

The principles are deliberately worded to be applicable within many faith traditions, or no tradition, as they make no reference to a deity. Within Christianity or Judaism, they do not presuppose a particular theological stance, such as progressive or conservative. Some of the principles are nowadays easily accepted, such as the principles of interconnectedness or resistance (e.g., seen as the negative impact human lifestyle has had on the global climate). Others may be questioned (such as the references to design). Some raise philosophical questions about agency and identity applied to nonhuman entities. Do, for instance, the principles of voice or resistance require imposition of unwarranted anthropomorphic concepts on the non-anthropic? What might (moral) agency mean for the nonhuman?

Pragmatically, a reader may employ the principles as heuristic guidelines, rather than normative rules. They provide entry points into the textual maze. They do not require the acceptance of a hermeneutic of suspicion-identification-retrieval; however, the two approaches complement each other.

Turning to the book of Hosea, the principle that stands out first is that of interconnectedness. Commentators have long noted that one of the themes in Hosea is the relationship between Yhwh and humans, usually Israel. Israel is the object of Yhwh's love, but also the source of distress and punishment. Both these poles are connected with the nonhuman world. Punishment is often characterized by impairment of the nonhuman world—for example by the failure of crops, bad weather, or "languishing" (e.g., 2:9, 12 [Heb. 2:11, 14]; 4:3; 8:7; 9:2–3). On the other hand, a restored relationship with Yhwh will reverse these disasters. Yhwh is moving unilaterally to restore this relationship (Hos. 11). The family/marriage metaphor in Hos. 1–3 and elsewhere is also inherently relational.

To what extent do these relationships provide an entry point to interconnectedness? The relationships primarily operate on a vertical axis. They are hierarchical. The principle of interconnectedness is more complex. It addresses the question of horizontal relationships between all members of the earth community. What is often omitted in analyses of the relationship between Yhwh and humans in Hosea is the explicit recognition that this relationship extends to nonhuman creation. In Hosea, relation is not a dipole but a triangle. For example, Marlow (2009: 109–11) eschews the Earth Bible approach to focus her study on the triad of God–humans–nonhuman creation. Braaten (2022) also emphasizes the interconnectedness of the land (exploited by rich elite) leading to degradation and suffering for the poor, animals, and crops. Weather sits behind much of the imagery in Hos. 2, as both the signified and signifier of metaphors for the relationship with Yhwh (Kato 2021: 6). Using a different approach altogether, Josiah (2014) has investigated the interconnectedness of humans, corruption, and environmental health by means of a survey. Interconnectedness is also present in Hosea among the nonhuman elements of creation (e.g., showers and the land in Hos. 6:3, and negatively with weeds in a field in Hos. 10:4, or predators feeding on other animals; see further below).

On the other hand, the extent to which Hosea provides support for the intrinsic worth of creation is problematic. As the list at the start of this essay shows, a large number of the references to the nonhuman elements of creation fall under the rubric of "utilitarian." These elements are used as gifts or are under the control of another party. The good and beautiful things of the world are valued as rewards or payments for services rendered (2:8 [Heb. 2:10]). Yhwh may proclaim, "When Ephraim was a child I loved him" (11:1), but where does Yhwh proclaim the intrinsic worth of a nonhuman element (cf. Jon. 4:11)? The cultural worldview of Hosea's time was hierarchical: God, male humans, female humans, others. The lack of intrinsic worth given to those below ruling elite males may be explicable by reference to culture, even though this ancient worldview may not be acceptable in modern culture. Is there anything in the text that subverts this worldview?

One possible subversive element may lie behind the covenant created in Hos. 2:18 (Heb. 2:20) (Braaten 2022: 153; 2001: 195–98; Huiser and Barton 2014). A covenant recognizes that both parties have some value. In this case, since the animals, birds, and fish were negatively affected by human behavior, the covenant shows that Yhwh regards them as worthy (see widows, orphans, and foreigners as worthy of protection in Exod. 22:21–22). It also highlights a relationship between humans and other living things (interconnectedness).

Two other observations also suggest that the intrinsic worth of nonhuman members of creation may be implicit in their literary functions. In literary theory, there is a distinction between flat and round characters. Flat characters are consistently two-dimensional and undergo very little or no development in the work. Round characters are more complex and can change, sometimes in unexpected ways. In the book of Hosea, most of the nonhuman characters, or elements of creation, are flat. Some, however, show complexity. Water (dew, rain) is portrayed both as ephemeral and life-giving (6:3, 4; 13:3; 14:5 [Heb. 14:6]). The image of a lion is both life-threatening as a beast that tears apart its prey (5:14; 13:7, 8) and a model of parenthood for its children (11:10). In the case of water, the characterizations are linked to different subjects, either Yhwh or humans. In the case of the lion, however, both metaphors refer to Yhwh. Nwaoru (2004) has also argued that the nonhuman elements of Hosea provide structural markers in the book.

The mention of the characterization of nonhuman members of creation in Hosea leads to another observation related to the first section of the listing above of nonhuman references. For Yhwh, the nonhuman references fall broadly into two classes: destructive and life-giving (Brueggemann 2008: 10–12). The destructive references dominate. Yhwh is a beast that rips apart its prey (5:14; 8:1; 13:7, 8). Yhwh is like a bodily illness that destroys its host (5:11–12, perhaps of gangrene from an agricultural wound, or some sexually transmitted disease or infection from an elite lifestyle, or a crop disease; Willis 2019: 168–69). The life-giving metaphors are usually set into the future as a result of change in human behavior (e.g., Hos. 14). For humans, the predominate class of nonhuman elements symbolizes misguidedness. For instance, humans are foolish, like birds (7:11, 12).[7] They only find completeness when they follow Yhwh.

In other words, the predominate characteristics of the nonhuman life in Hosea are overwhelmingly negative: violent, ferocious, fearsome (modeling Yhwh), and foolish (modeling humans). This observation is consistent with feminist studies of the portrayal of Yhwh in Hosea. How does one negotiate the disparity between Yhwh as abusive and Yhwh as nurturing? Certainly, Hos. 11 is a beautiful expression of Yhwh's love for Israel. But this sentiment is offset by many verses that are negative. To borrow an image, Yhwh may be "in recovery" (Brueggemann 2008), but still seems to fall off the wagon regularly in the book. There is a conflict between love and violence which may not be able to be resolved and may render Hosea in sum a "gray" text (Habel 2009). Only two of the ecojustice principles have been examined, and potentially Hosea has already been written off as a gray text!

Remember the heifer. What would prompt its stubbornness? Perhaps the portrayal of the nonhuman elements of creation as violent and destructive. Very many of the similes and metaphors for Yhwh portray destructive divine behavior, like an animal that tears apart its prey, or a human that strips a person naked and makes her/him a "wilderness." Would a heifer in its stubbornness be protesting against this violent portrayal of the natural world? The heifer resists the master, in community with the rest of creation, as if to say that this portrayal is unfair.

What are the implications of the wealth of negative metaphors for an ecological interpretation of Hosea? It is customary to say that a metaphor attributes a characteristic to its subject (tenor) by means of its object (vehicle). In other words, the flow of meaning in a metaphor is usually taken to be one way, in this case from the nonhuman to the divine or human subject. This represents a theocentric or anthropocentric interpretive strategy. However, a reverse flow of meaning also is present. A metaphor may attribute the status of its subject (tenor) to its vehicle. In the case of Hosea, some metaphors attribute violence to Yhwh and as a consequence endorse violence as a divine characteristic. In turn, violence is legitimated as a characteristic for true followers, if the faithful believe in imitating the deity, or potentially reified into one of the underlying laws of the universe. If Yhwh is like a ferocious lion, should not Yhwh's followers be ferocious in some way? In Hosea, this would apply for violence against women and equally for violence against other elements of creation.

The statements about the heifer above are observations based on the principles of resistance, custodianship (on the part of the heifer), and voice. The interpretation assumes that the heifer has some agency. But what agency do the nonhuman members of creation have in the book of Hosea? The only place in Hosea where agency is clearly linked to nonhuman elements is Hos. 4:3, where it is stated that "therefore the land mourns." This has been examined by Loya (2008), who concludes that "creation actively mourns the subversion of the created order, and this results in the languishing and perishing of all who live on it: the animals of the field, the birds of the air, and the fish of the sea" (p. 62; see also Braaten 2022: 155, and more generally, Hayes 2002). Mourning is a response to God's moral order. "As the necessary result of Israel's crimes, Earth *must* mourn" (Loya 2008: 61, italics original). Does this necessity remove the element of free choice inherent in agency or does land choose to accept the moral order, while humans sin with a high hand? The mourning of the land results in the destruction of other nonhuman life, a sad example of interconnectedness.

Another possible example of agency is associated with the covenant of Hos. 2:18 (Heb. 2:20). The NRSV has Yhwh saying, "I will make a covenant," which suggests that Yhwh dictates the covenant, much as a superpower might influence agreements between client states under its umbrella. However, the sense might be better rendered to portray Yhwh as the broker of such an agreement (Whitekettle 2012: 232–33). This would allow more agency to the covenant parties. In response to this covenant, there is a chain using the verb *'anah*, usually translated as "answer": "On that day, I will answer, saying of Yhwh, I will answer the sky and it will answer the land and the land will answer the grain and the wine and the oil and they will answer Jezreel" (2:21–22 [Heb. 2:23–24]). The nature of the "answer" is opaque. However, the verb can also have the meaning of "sing" (Martens 1991: 327). In this case, the verses may suggest a diverse chorus spanning creation and creator, all together joining in antiphonal praise (cf. Ps. 148). Are the members of this chorus agents or mere echoes of a divine exclamation? In sum, agency of the nonhuman elements in Hosea seems, for the most part, to lie in alternatives within the text which require study to unearth them.

There remains the principle of purpose. What questions does it prompt for Hosea? The description in Hos. 4:3 appears to be an undoing of the sequence of creation in Gen. 1 (Loya 2008: 54; Keefe 2008: 38–39). Human behavior causes the unraveling of the design of the universe (see the principles of interconnectedness, design, and custodianship). On the other hand, several verses in Hosea refer to a resolution of the relationship between Yhwh, humans, and nonhumans in the future, though it is not clear from the text whether this takes place at some unspecified point in historical time, or is an eschatological resolution. Is this then a source of hope for environmental preservation? Perhaps, or perhaps not. Historically, Hosea's words to the Northern Kingdom came to nought. The people were obliterated by Assyria with its policy of forced resettlement. Hosea's prophecies were preserved in the Southern Kingdom of Judah. However, the prophecy of restoration by a loving, recovered Yhwh was not fulfilled there either.

Today, we read Hosea in the context of an accelerating environmental crisis, where the nonhuman elements of creation appear to be spiraling toward extinction or on a trajectory toward tipping points that will render the earth uninhabitable by humans and other members of creation. Ironically, one might consider this as part of the design of the cosmos. Against this background, this essay has considered the references to the nonhuman in Hosea. Negative images prevail, and there is an emphasis on violence. All in all, regard for the natural world in the book of Hosea appears to be shallow. We live in a time when there is a desperate need for hope for the future of the environment and action to stave off disaster. So the questions remain: Is it possible to frame a positive ecological interpretation of Hosea? What hope do the words of Hosea communicate to us today?[8]

NOTES

1. For an overview of the history of interpretation of Hosea, see Kelle 2009 and 2010. Examples of the shift to interpretations that included ecology in a significant way include Keefe 1995 (socioeconomic) and Martens 1991 (ecological). A comprehensive and up-to-date account of the intersection of socioeconomic and ecological analyses of Hosea is given in Braaten 2022. This work also provides copious bibliographies for ecological interpretations of Hosea and other biblical material.
2. For the ways different English translations have interpreted ecological terms in a variety of passages, see Greenspoon 2008.
3. For metaphor in Hosea, see Kelle 2010: 355–60 and Lancaster in this volume. Most studies have focused on the relationship between God and humans. See also Ben Zvi 2008; Willis 2019.

4. Whether nonhuman elements can exhibit agency, particularly moral agency, is contested. Buss (2013) presents a case for their personhood. In relation to Hosea, the possession of agency is also dubious for some humans, in particular, Gomer.
5. For a summary of the two interpretations and the fundamental issues of meaning for an interpretive community, see Jacobson 1996. More recently, see Kelle 2009. Jacobson captures the dilemma of interpretation. For the educated elite of the academy, one interpretation may be quite acceptable. For another reading community, it fails. Since the backbone of ecological interpretation is the practical issue of the environmental crisis, faced by all communities, it is legitimate to ask of any interpretation, "Does it preach?"
6. The Earth Bible Team edited several volumes. The first series was simply called The Earth Bible. (The first volume was Habel 2000). These volumes contain useful explanations of the methodology including answering critiques. See also the introductions to Habel and Trudinger 2008 and Habel 2011. The latter is the first volume of the Earth Bible commentary series. As yet, there is no commentary on Hosea. Marlow (2009) offers a critique of the Earth Bible methodology and adopts a different approach (see Southgate 2008).
7. The implicit assumption here, that birds are intrinsically foolish, is questionable (see Kaplan 2015).
8. I acknowledge the gracious support and editorial suggestions of Brad E. Kelle.

REFERENCES

Ben Zvi, Ehud. 2008. "Reading Hosea and Imagining Yahweh." *HBT* 30: 43–57.

Braaten, Laurie J. 2001. "Earth Community in Hosea 2." In Norman C. Habel, ed., *The Earth Story in the Psalms and Prophets*. Sheffield: Sheffield Academic Press, 185–203.

Braaten, Laurie J. 2022. "God's Good Land: The Agrarian Perspective of the Book of the Twelve." In Hilary Marlow and Mark Harris, eds., *The Oxford Handbook of the Bible and Ecology*. Oxford: Oxford University Press, 148–65.

Brueggemann, Walter. 2008. "The Recovering God of Hosea." *HBT* 30: 5–20.

Buss, Martin. 2013. "Personhood and Ethical Regard." In Allan H. Cadwallader with Peter Trudinger, eds., *Where the Wild Ox Roams: Biblical Essays in Honour of Norman C. Habel*. HBM 59. Sheffield: Sheffield Phoenix, 76–86.

Card, Orson Scott. 1986. *Speaker for the Dead*. London: Century.

Greenspoon, Leonard J. 2008. "From Dominion to Stewardship? The Ecology of Biblical Translation." *JRS Supplement Series* 3: 159–83.

Habel, Norman C. 2000. *Readings from the Perspective of Earth*. Earth Bible. Sheffield: Sheffield Academic Press.

Habel, Norman C. 2009. *An Inconvenient Text: Is a Green Reading of the Bible Possible?* Adelaide: ATF.

Habel, Norman C. 2011. *The Birth, the Curse and the Greening of Earth: An Ecological Reading of Genesis 1–11*. Earth Bible Commentary Series 1. Sheffield: Sheffield Phoenix. Habel, Norman C., and Peter Trudinger. 2008. *Exploring Ecological Hermeneutics*. SBLSymS 46. Atlanta: SBL.

Hayes, Katherine M. 2002. *"The Earth Mourns": Prophetic Metaphor and Oral Aesthetic*. SBLAB 8. Atlanta: SBL.

Hiuser, Kris, and Matthew Barton. 2014. "A Promise Is a Promise: God's Covenantal Relationship with Animals." *SJT* 67: 340–356.

Jacobson, Diane. 1996. "Hosea 2: A Case Study on Biblical Authority." *CTM* 23: 165–72.

Josiah, UcheAwaji G. 2014. "Exploring the Ecological Implications of the Imagery of Hosea 5:4 for Nigeria." *Valley View University Journal of Theology* 3:33–45.

Kaplan, Gisela. 2015. *Bird Minds: Cognition and Behaviour of Australian Native Birds*. Clayton South: CSIRO.

Keefe, Alice A. 1995. "The Female Body, the Body Politic and the Land: A Sociopolitical Reading of Hosea 1–2." In Athalya Brenner, ed., *A Feminist Companion to the Latter Prophets*. FCB 8. Sheffield: Sheffield Academic, 70–100.

Keefe, Alice A. 2008. "Hosea's (In)Fertility God." *HBT* 30: 21–41.

Kelle, Brad E. 2009. "Hosea 1–3 in Twentieth Century Scholarship." *CBR* 7: 179–216.

Kelle, Brad E. 2010. "Hosea 4–14 in Twentieth Century Scholarship." *CBR* 8: 314–75.

Loya, Melissa Tubbs. 2008. "'Therefore the Earth Mourns': The Grievance of Earth in Hosea 4:1–3." In Norman C. Habel and Peter Trudinger, eds., *Exploring Ecological Hermeneutics*. SBLSymS 46. Atlanta: SBL, 53–63.

Marlow, Hilary. 2009. *Biblical Prophets and Contemporary Environmental Ethic: Re-Reading Amos, Hosea, and First Isaiah*. Oxford: Oxford University Press.

Marlow, Hilary, and Mark Harris, eds. 2022 *The Oxford Handbook of the Bible and Ecology*. Oxford: Oxford University Press.

Martens, E. A. 1991. "Spirituality and Environment in Hosea." *ACTS Theological Journal* 4: 317–39.

Nwaoru, Emmanuel O. 2004. "The Role of Images in the Literary Structure of Hosea VII 8–VIII 14." *VT* 54: 216–22.

Smith, Cooper. 2018. "The 'Wilderness' in Hosea and Deuteronomy: A Case of Thematic Reappropriation." *BRB* 28: 240–60.

Southgate, Christopher. 2008. *The Groaning of Creation: God, Evolution, and the Problem of Evil*. Louisville: Westminster John Knox.

Trudinger, Peter. 2008. "How Lonely Sits the City: Reading Lamentations as City and Land." In Norman C. Habel and Peter Trudinger, eds., *Exploring Ecological Hermeneutics*. SBLSymS 46. Atlanta: SBL, 41–52.

Whitekettle, Richard. 2012. "Freedom from Fear and Bloodshed: Hosea 2.20 (Eng. 18) and the End of Human/Animal Conflict." *JSOT* 37: 219–36.

Willis, John T. 2019. "Hosea's Unique Figures of Yahweh." *ResQ* 61: 167–80.

PART V

RECEPTION

CHAPTER 28

·······

HOSEA IN RABBINIC LITERATURE

·······

DEVORAH SCHOENFELD

HOSEA is a troubling book that begins with an unclear narrative of a troubled relationship and goes on to a lengthy vituperation of Israel that leaves little room or possibility for hope. In it the prophet is asked to put himself in a morally compromising position by marrying a sexually promiscuous woman (perhaps a prostitute) and then cruelly renouncing her and their children. There follows a highly disturbing passage in which Israel, or Gomer, is subjected to sexualized violence by God, or Hosea. After this, ch. 2 pivots to a passage describing a new covenant that God makes with Israel, as well as with all the animals, in which Israel will call God "my man" and not "my master," both Hebrew words for husband but with different implications for the power dynamics, and Israel and God will be married in righteousness and justice.

Yvonne Sherwood (1996: 11–17) calls the book of Hosea a problem text by analogy with Shakespeare's problem plays. God and the prophet, by acting in ethically questionable ways, do not fulfill the expectations of the reader, and leave the reader unsatisfied by what purports on the surface to be a happy ending. In Hos. 2, God (or the prophet) is violent toward Gomer (or Israel) in ways that are described in terms that are highly graphic:

> Else will I strip her naked
> And leave her as on the day she was born:
> And I will make her like a wilderness,
> Render her like desert land,
> And let her die of thirst. (Hos. 2:5 NJPS)[1]

This description of Divine behavior is so violent that Francis Landy (1995: 148) describes it as a pornographic fantasy. Hosea 2, on the other hand, concludes with a description of blissful union between human and Divine:

And I will espouse you forever: I will espouse you—with righteousness
and justice, And with goodness and mercy,
And I will espouse you with faithfulness;
Then you shall be devoted to the LORD. (2:21–22 NJPS)

But after everything that has happened, how can the dream of reconciliation be trusted?

Some scholars have gone so far as to suggest that the sharp break between the beginning and end of Hos. 2 suggests multiple authors, with dramatically different views of the Divine–human relationship (see overview in Kelle 2005: 8–13). But whatever its origins, by the Rabbinic period it would have been fully redacted into a single text, with no clear transition or explanation of the movement between the violence of the beginning of the chapter and the reconciliation at the end. One way to get from a troubling reality to a better one is through repentance. But is there repentance in the book of Hosea? It is unclear. In ch. 6, there is an attempt at repentance that appears to be rejected or unsuccessful. In ch. 11, God states that there will be an end to punishment even though Israel continues to refuse to repent because, as God states, "I am God, not man" (11:9 NJPS). In ch. 14, there is a call for a future repentance that might be successful at some future time. Twentieth- and twenty-first-century biblical scholarship has come to different conclusions about whether or not the book of Hosea moves from judgment to hope, and if so how this movement works (see Kelle 2010: 348). In any case, it seems not to happen in Hos. 1–3, at least not explicitly. As a result, Rabbinic attempts to find repentance narratives in the book involve creative readings that are dramatically different both from each other and from the most straightforward meaning of the biblical text.

This essay will argue that Rabbinic interpretation found a wide range of characters repenting in their retellings of the book of Hosea, from Israel to God to Hosea to Hosea's ancestor Reuben. Rabbinic exegesis does not attempt to reconcile these possibilities. These various stories of repentance are different attempts to work through some of the book's problems. How do we get from violence to reconciliation? How is change possible? What does it look like, and who needs to change?

28.1. Genesis Rabbah: Reuben Looks into the Pit

In Genesis Rabbah, Rabbi Eliezer identifies Hosea as the one who opens the way for repentance. His ability to do so is connected to the repentance of his ancestor Reuben, who repents for the sin of selling Joseph into slavery:

And Reuven returned to the pit (Genesis 37:29). Where was he? . . . Rabbi Eliezer said he was wearing sackcloth and fasting and when he finished he went and looked into the pit. This is what is written, "And Reuven returned to the pit." The Holy Blessed One said, "Never before has a person sinned before me and repented. You were the first one to repent, by your life your descendent will begin opening a path to repentance." Who is this? Hosea, as it is said, "Return, O Israel, to the Lord your God" (Hos. 14:2 NJPS). (Genesis Rabbah 84.19, author's translation; see Neusner 2007: 54–55)[2]

The idea that Reuben was the first person to ever repent is a surprising statement by the Midrash here that requires some unpacking. Reuben's story appears very late in the book of Genesis after many stories that could be thought of as stories of sin and repentance. What Rabbi Eliezer seems to be identifying as repentance, and as the first instance of it, is the word יָשֻׁב (returned), which is from the root *shin-vav-bet*, as is *teshuvah* (repentance).[3] Beyond the use of the root, Rabbi Eliezer also identifies as repentance Reuben's physical action in that he returns to the pit and looks at it. This is an action that in no way helps Joseph. It also is not an action of taking accountability, since after this Reuben participates with his brothers in lying to his father about what happened to Joseph. Rather than either of those things, what Rabbi Eliezer identifies as key to repentance, and what has not happened before in connection with the Hebrew root, is self-reflection—looking into the pit. That is what Reuben does and what Hosea helps Reuben's descendants accomplish through his problem story.

Selling Joseph into slavery was not Reuben's only sin that the Bible records. Reuben was also involved in sexual impropriety, and possibly sexual assault, when he lay with his father's concubine, Bilhah (Gen. 35:12). Reuben does not reflect on this act, and it is not brought up again until Jacob's "blessing" of Reuben in Gen. 49:4:

Unstable as water, you shall excel no longer; For when you mounted your father's bed, You brought disgrace—my couch he mounted! (NJPS)

Reuben is, like his descendant Hosea, morally compromised, unstable, and arguably sexually abusive. But he was, once, able to look into the pit, and that gave Hosea the ability to do the same.

28.2. Targum: Israel Repents

Targum Jonathan on the book of Hosea is an interpretive translation of the book into Aramaic that, while translating, edits and explains the texts in accordance with its own understanding of the nature of the Divine–human relationship (overall, see Cathcart and Gordon 1989: 1–20). The story of Hosea in the Targum is about the repentance of Israel. In it, Gomer does not exist at all. The Targum "translates" the words in Hos. 1:3, "So he went and married Gomer daughter of Dibalim" as "So he went and prophecied concerning them that if they repented, they would be forgiven; but if not, they would fall as the leaves of a fig-tree fall" (Cathcart and Gordon 1989: 29). The Targumist here makes two moves: he removes Gomer, and he introduces the concept of repentance, which is completely absent in Hos. 1. In v. 6, when Hosea is told to name one of his children Lo-Ruchama/Not-given-mercy, the Targumist translates this as a name that will be given to Israel, but only if they do not repent, since if they repent they will surely be forgiven. Thus, the Targum also introduces forgiveness and repentance here alongside allegory.

The Targumist continues to insert the concepts of return and repentance, both to weaken Divine rejection and to explain Divine benevolence. On 2:1 (Eng. 1:10), the Targumist writes, "And from the land where they were exiled among the nations, when they transgressed the law, and was said to them, 'You are not my people,' they shall return and be made great" (Cathcart and Gordon 1989: 31). Here Israel's repentance explains the sudden pivot from their rejection at the end of ch. 1 to their praise at the beginning of ch. 2. On Hos. 2:3 (Eng. 2:1), before introducing what the Targumist understands as a prophecy of Israel's exile (and not as sexualized violence toward a woman, since the allegory erases the woman character), the Targumist prefaces the speech with a call to prophets to bring Israel to repentance, so that the prophesied exile and destruction will not happen. Verse 4 states that this destruction is intended to be only temporary, until Israel repents (Cathcart and Gordon 1989: 11). In comments on 3:1, the Targumist emphasizes that once Israel repents they will be forgiven easily, "like a man who made a mistake and said something while intoxicated with wine," even for sins as severe as idolatry (35). So the Targumist presents a worldview in which destruction is not inevitable, repentance is always possible, and, once it happens, forgiveness is easy. This is dramatically different from the most straightforward reading of Hosea, in which it seems that Gomer is punished severely and it is not clear that repentance is even possible.

Later in the book of Hosea, the Targum returns to the idea that repentance is what will bring Israel to prosperity, and again inserts the concept of repentance even when it is not present in the biblical text (Cathcart and Gordon 1989: 8). For example, Hos. 13:9, "You are undone, O Israel! You had no help but me!" (NJPS)[4] is translated in the Targum as "When you corrupt your deeds, O house of Israel, the nations rule over you, but when you return to my law, my Memra [Word] is your support" (59). The context in ch. 13 is God destroying Israel without mercy; the Targum adds to it the concept of repentance to make clear that the destruction described here is neither inevitable nor permanent.

Israel's repentance does not imply that it was always sinful. As Jacques van Ruiten (2012) has pointed out, the Targum rewrites Hosea's description of Jacob in ch. 12 to turn him from a morally suspect figure into a role model. Hosea 12:4 (Eng. 12:3) describes Jacob as violent from the beginning: "In the womb he tried to supplant his brother; Grown to manhood, he strove with a divine being" (NJPS). The first part of the verse refers to Gen. 25:23–26, in which Jacob and Esau fight in Rebecca's womb and then Jacob is born holding on to Esau's heel. The second part refers to Gen. 32:25–29, in which Jacob fights with a man who later blesses him and renames him Israel, the one who fights with God, because he fought with God and prevailed. By connecting these two stories and describing them in the harshest possible terms, this verse builds a picture of Jacob as consistently violent throughout his life.[5] These accusations against Jacob are part of what van Ruiten (2012: 601) describes as a lawsuit against Israel and its ancestors, in which Israel's and Jacob's conduct is described as unworthy of their relationship with

God. In the Targum's rewriting, however, Jacob never did anything wrong. The Targum translates Hos. 12:4 as

> O prophet say to them: "Was it not said of Jacob even before he was born, that he would be greater than his brother? And by his might he contended with the angel." (Cathcart and Gordon 1989: 56)

The Targum adds and changes a few words to dramatically shift the significance of this verse. Jacob is not violent and did not strive with Esau but rather was born into prophesied greatness, which he later fulfilled when he contended with the angel. While in Hosea, Israel's bad behavior can be traced back to their ancestor Jacob, in the Targum, Jacob provides Israel with a model for how righteous they can be if they serve God properly (van Ruiten 2012: 602). This fits with the Targum's approach in which Israel's repentance is what is going to bridge the gap between the horrors described at the beginning of the book of Hosea and the descriptions of redemption and return to paradise in the second half of Hos. 2. Israel once was good and can be good again, as long as they emulate their ancestor Jacob.

Although in this approach Israel repents, Gomer does not repent in the Targum's version of the story because Gomer does not exist. Nor is Israel depicted as contemptible using the sexualized language of revulsion with which the woman is described in the biblical text. Israel is fundamentally good and has agency that makes repentance always possible. This means that nothing terrible described in the text is necessary or permanent. This hopeful reading is at the cost of the nearly total erasure of Gomer and her troubling presence in the text (for critique, see Sherwood 1995).

28.3. PESACHIM 87A–88: HOSEA REPENTS

The book of Hosea is quoted in many places in the Babylonian Talmud, but the most in-depth discussion of the book and its themes is in Pesachim 87a–88. In this discussion, it is Hosea who needs to repent and whose repentance drives the story. He sins by not doing his job advocating for Israel, and his repentance is to learn to intercede with God and to understand that his job as a prophet is to support God's love for Israel.

This Talmudic discussion is apropos of a halachic question regarding whether a married woman should eat the Passover offering, which is typically eaten with one's family, with her parents or her in-laws. It concludes that she has some autonomy in deciding this, and that it may depend on how warmly she is received by her husband's family. The Talmudic discussion connects this halachic debate about the Passover offering to the relationship between Hosea and Song of Songs:

> There is a homiletic interpretation of verses that conveys a similar idea, as it is written: "I am a wall, and my breasts are like towers; then I was in his eyes as one who

finds peace" (Song of Songs 8:10). And Rabbi Yoḥanan said: She is like a bride who was found perfect. She was warmly received in her father-in-law's house. And she eagerly hurries, as one pursued, to go to tell of her praise, i.e., her warm welcome, in her father's house. As it is written: "And it shall be at that day, says the Lord, that you shall call Me: My Husband, and shall call Me no more: My Master" (Hosea 2:18), of which Rabbi Yoḥanan said: She shall be like a bride in her father-in-law's house, where she experiences a close relationship with her husband. And she shall not be like a bride still in the betrothal period and living in her father's house, during which time her relationship with her husband has still not developed. (Pesachim 87a, Steinsaltz trans., Koren Noé Talmud)

Song of Songs 8:10 describes a young woman who insists that her brothers recognize her maturity and autonomy. The Talmudic discussion here applies it to describe a woman who is happily married because she is welcomed in her husband's family and wants that to be recognized. It then compares this imagined situation with another that it constructs from a verse in Hosea, in which woman has a close relationship with her husband. These are two different situations in which a woman might choose to celebrate the holiday with her husband's family. She might be a newlywed excited about her new and welcoming relatives, or it might be a mature, developed relationship.

After some discussion of Song of Songs, the passage returns to Hosea and begins a lengthy discussion focusing on the character of Hosea, whom it identifies as the first prophet of his time period. In this discussion, Hosea is the protagonist and the character who needs to repent:

> The Holy One, Blessed be He, said to Hosea: Your sons, the Jewish people, have sinned. Hosea should have said to God in response: But they are Your sons; they are the sons of Your beloved ones, the sons of Abraham, Isaac, and Jacob. Extend Your mercy over them. Not only did he fail to say that, but instead he said before Him: Master of the Universe, the entire world is Yours; since Israel has sinned, exchange them for another nation. The Holy One, Blessed be He, said: What shall I do to this Elder who does not know how to defend Israel? I will say to him: Go and take a prostitute and bear for yourself children of prostitution. And after that I will say to him: Send her away from before you. If he is able to send her away, I will also send away the Jewish people.[6]

This interpretation dramatically changes the story of Hosea and Gomer. In this reading, Hosea is the one who sinned, not Gomer. Further, all the harsh language of Hos. 2 was a setup. God told Hosea to say and do cruel things to his wife in order to show him that he would not be able to bring himself to do it. When God tells Hosea to cast Gomer away, God intends not that Hosea actually send Gomer away but that Hosea recognize that it would be impossible to do what God asks, and for Hosea to recognize that neither he nor God is able to see relationships as disposable.

This rereading takes the positive message of the end of Hos. 2 as primary and reads the beginning of the chapter through that lens. If the husband and wife at the end of ch.

2 are so comfortable and confident in each other that must mean that the events of the beginning of the chapter never have happened. Not only did they not happen, but Hosea explicitly refused to do them.

Pesachim 87b goes on to explain that this is the case even though Hosea is not sure whether Gomer's children are his:

> After two sons and one daughter had been born to him, the Holy One, Blessed be He, said to Hosea: Shouldn't you have learned from the example of your master Moses, who, once I spoke with him, separated from his wife? You too, separate yourself from your wife. He said to Him: Master of the Universe, I have sons from her and I am unable to dismiss her or to divorce her. In response to Hosea's show of loyalty to his family, the Holy One, Blessed be He, rebuked him and said to him: Just as you, whose wife is a prostitute and your children from her are children of prostitution, and you do not even know if they are yours or if they are children of other men, despite this, you are still attached to them and will not forsake them, so too, I am still attached to the Jewish people, who are My sons, the sons of My faithful who withstood ordeals, the sons of Abraham, Isaac, and Jacob. They are so special that they are one of the four acquisitions that I acquired in My world. (Pesachim 87b; Steinsaltz trans.)

Even though Pesachim reads Gomer as a prostitute who is indeed unfaithful to Hosea and may have given birth to children that are not his, it is Hosea who needs to recognize that he loves his wife and children and will not leave or harm them. As Sherwood (1996: 44–47) points out, this text solves the problem of the book of Hosea by leading Hosea, not Gomer, through the process of change and repentance.[7] Although the discussion describes her as promiscuous and adulterous, she is never expected to repent, nor is she blamed for any part of this story.

After Hosea repents and prays to God for forgiveness, God instructs Hosea that he must first pray for the Jewish people:

> Hosea stood and requested compassion upon the Jewish people and nullified the decree. God responded and began to bless them, as it is stated: "Yet the number of the children of Israel shall be as the sand of the sea, which cannot be measured nor numbered. And it will be that instead of that which was said to them: You are not My people, it shall be said to them: You are the children of the living God. And the children of Judea and the children of Israel shall be gathered together" (Hosea 2:1). "And I will sow her to Me in the land; and I will have compassion upon her that had not received compassion; and I will say to them that were not My people: You are My people" (Hosea 2:25). (Pesachim 87b, Steinsaltz trans.)

In this reading, the positive statements at the end of Hos. 2 are God's actual words to Israel. All the harsh words of the beginning of the chapter, in contrast, were never actually intended to be spoken to Israel, but rather were a way of bringing Hosea to repent.

In this interpretation, all the terrible things that God tells Hosea to say and do to Gomer were based on the assumption that Hosea would not do them, and that his refusal to do them would be the lesson that God intended to teach. God gave these commandments to Hosea with the intention that by refusing those commandments Hosea would repent and stop his anger at Israel. This rewritten Hosea becomes more similar to Jonah, who goes through a long character arc before he is willing to deliver God's prophecy.

Just as this Talmudic discussion changes the meaning of the harsh language toward Gomer, it also changes the meaning of God's intent to exile Israel by suggesting that it was not a punishment. In Pesachim 87b, Rabbi Elazar and Rabbi Yochanan both derive from different verses in Hos. 2 the idea that God exiled Israel only so that converts will join them.[8] This is followed by other suggestions based on different biblical verses that give other positive meanings to the exile—for example, that God may have exiled them to different places so that it is impossible to destroy all of them at once, or to enable them to be safe in Babylonia from the Romans (Pesachim 87b–88a). Just as Gomer was not punished, even though the language of the book of Hosea seems to imply that she was, so too Israel was not punished, even though both history and the language of the book seem to imply that they were.

The approach of this Talmudic discussion, in which Hosea is the one who changes his ways, parallels texts like Pesikta Rabbati, a ninth-century aggadic midrash collection, which presents Hosea as a model for how prophets are expected to change after castigating Israel:

> Indeed you cannot name a single prophet who after chastising Israel did not retract his words and provide Israel with a poultice to heal the words he had inflicted. Each and every wound there was, the prophet came back and sought to heal it. Hosea said, *I will no more have compassion upon Israel* (Hos. 1:6), but then, retracting, said, *And I will have compassion upon her that had not obtained compassion* (Hos. 2:25). The very mouth that uttered the words *For ye are not my people* (Hos. 1:9), withdrew them even as it brought healing with the words *I will say to them that were not my people: "Thou art my people"* (Hos. 2:25). (Pesikta Rabbati 44; see Braude 1968: 771–72).[9]

The passage goes on to cite five more examples where Hosea states harsh things and then retracts them, and describes this as a model for how prophets should behave. In Pesikta Rabbati 44, Hosea does exactly what Pesachim rebukes him for not doing and intercedes for Israel, and as a result the threats that Hosea makes to Israel are negotiated down from those that God asks him to make (see Braude 1968: 773).

There are other sources that indicate that change like this is expected of a prophet. Sifrei Deuteronomy 342 on Deut. 33:1 similarly explains that every time a prophet castigates Israel and tells them that repentance is impossible, the prophet later repents and changes (Gottleib, Ben-Hashar, and Penkower 2003: 64, 100, 224; Neusner 2007: 15). Sifrei presents Hosea as an example of this, describing the change from Hosea's harsh threats toward Israel to Hosea's kind words in ch. 14 as a result of the prophet's own development. In Pirkei de Rav Kahana 16.8, when Hosea finally changes his mind to speak comfortingly to Israel, they refuse to believe him and he needs God's help to convince them that he is sincere (Neusner 2007: 76; Sherwood 1996: 239–40).

In this approach, then, the story of Hosea is of a prophet who initially refused to fulfill his obligation to love and defend Israel. The cruelty that Hosea is asked to show to Gomer is read as explicitly wrong and not God's intent. By parallel, the harsh prophecies in the book are to be read largely as Hosea's failures, from which he only learns toward the end of the book in ch. 14.

28.4. NUMBERS RABBAH: GOD REPENTS

If in Pesachim 87a–88 Hosea repents, in Numbers Rabbah (approximately eleventh–twelfth century) God repents, with the help of prophets like Moses and Hosea. The story of Hosea and Gomer is paralleled with the story of the Golden Calf through a parable about a king and his wife:

> A king saw his wife kissing a eunuch. "I will divorce her," he said to her *shoshbin*. "I will cast her out. Let her go home to her father!" "But why?" asked the other of him. "Because I found her kissing a eunuch." "But," rejoined the other, "she will now rear up for you fine sturdy sons who will follow you in battle!" "There is no such hope from him," replied the king, "he can beget no children!" "Are you then wroth about a thing from which no benefit can be derived?" asked the other. . . . Moses suggested, "This calf which Israel have made can now be of assistance to Thee. He can send down rain while Thou will produce the dew!" "But," replied the Holy One, blessed be He, "is there any such hope from him?" "Then," came Moses's retort, "if there is no substance in him, why art thou wroth?" (Numbers Rabbah 2.15; see Slotki 1983: 49)

In this parable God initially fully rejects Israel, and it is only through the intercession of Moses that God takes back the rejection. God takes it back because Moses convinces God that it is entirely irrational, there was never any need for God to be angry and rejecting. But in doing so Moses also undermines and mocks the logic of male jealousy. If a woman is committing adultery, why be angry, she will bear you strong sons. And if it is a relationship that is unable to lead to children, why are you angry at all?

This parable is a direct rejoinder to other Rabbinic texts that draw explicit parallels between idolatry and adultery, between the jealousy of a husband and the jealousy of God. For example, Tanchuma Tzav 14.1:

> One who leaves all of these, the forgiveness, and the merit, and the blessing, and the life, and goes and worships idolatry, His great fire burns him, as it is said, "For the Lord your God is a consuming fire, a jealous God" (Deuteronomy 4:24). How is God jealous? As it is stated, "And I will betroth you in faith" (Hosea 2:22). Just as a husband is jealous regarding his wife, thus is the Holy One jealous. (author's trans.)

Here God is compared to a jealous husband, specifically using the language of Hosea, in order to justify punishment. The parallel is that God will be jealous of and punish a straying Israel just as a husband will be jealous of and punish a straying wife.

The Mechilta of Rabbi Ishmael 20.14.1 on Exod. 20 similarly connects Divine love and husbandly jealousy, deriving the comparison from the organization of the Ten Commandments:

> How were the Ten Commandments given? Five on one tablet and five on another. It is written "I am the Lord your God" and opposite it is written "Do not murder," in order for the text to teach us that one who murders us diminishes the image of the King. . . . It is written "There shall not be for you [other gods]" and opposite it is written "Do not commit adultery." The text teaches us that anyone who worships idolatry is committing adultery against God. As it is written: "the adulterous wife who welcomes strangers instead of her husband" (Ezekiel 16:32 NJPS), and "Go befriend a woman who while befriended by a companion consorts with others" (Hosea 3:1 NJPS). (author's trans. For discussion, see Gottleib, Ben-Hashar, and Penkower 2003: 152, 175)

This passage takes as its starting point the organization of the Ten Commandments into two tablets to show how the first five are parallel to the second five, which makes idolatry and adultery parallel. Hosea here is a key example as a text that brings this parallel to life.

Neither the passage in the Mechila nor the passage in Midrash Tanchuma tells a story of repentance. In each of them, the sins of adultery and idolatry are present and parallel, but there is no movement out of them. They take the imagery from Hosea, but not the dynamic movement of the tension between the beginning and end of Hos. 2. Numbers Rabbah dramatically reworks this narrative to undermine the logic of jealousy and in doing so allows for repentance. But contrary to expectations, the repentance is not the wife's and Israel's but the husband's and God's.

Numbers Rabbah 2.15 continues with a series of parables in which God progressively acts less and less angry. In the first one, God is compared to a king who threatened to divorce his wife and then immediately went and bought her jewelry, indicating that he did not mean anything that he said (Slotki 1983: 50). This parable reads the prophecies of Hosea as God saying things that God does not, in fact, mean, although they are still cruel things to say. The following parable compares God to a king who scolds his son for playing instead of going to school, and then immediately sits down with him for a nice dinner (Slotki 1983: 51). In this parable, the scolding is brief, temporary, and does not include any threats. This parable takes us much farther from the cruel language of the book of Hosea, with all its language of separation and divorce. In this parable, both the father and the son know that the father does not intend to end the relationship, and there is no threat of it, only scolding when the son does not do what is best for him. In the fourth parable, a king marries a woman whom he loves and cannot stop praising her, saying, "There is none more beautiful, none more excellent, none more steady than she!" (Slotki 1983: 51). His friends are surprised that he praises her so much, since her bed is unmade and the house is untidy, and conclude that he must truly love her, whether she cleans the house or not. In this parable, God does not reject Israel at all, even when Israel sins, and never says anything negative about Israel. All the negative things are said by someone else, and though they are descriptions of an objective fault, it is the fairly trivial negligence of an unmade bed.

In this series of parables, we see God moving from attempting to reject Israel (with only Moses preventing God from doing so) to fully accepting and going around praising Israel even though they sin. The series begins with Moses calling on God to change and stop rejecting Israel and then is followed by a series of parables in which God does exactly that, moving from rejection to affirmation and acceptance. Following this series of parables, the subsequent discourse in Numbers Rabbah 2.16 explains God's repentance in a different way, by comparing God to a parent who loses their temper at a small child (Slotki 1983: 53). In this passage, the lengthy railing at Israel in the first half of Hos. 2 is a "brief utterance" from which God immediately repents. This discussion provides an alternative for those who do not want to imagine God rejecting Israel even for a moment, and that is to reinterpret the words "you are not my people" to mean "you are my people whether you like it or not" (Slotki 1983: 55; Gottleib, Ben-Hashar, and Penkower 2003: 65). Here God's repentance looks more like that of a parent who is taking a breath after being impatient.

Numbers Rabbah 23.8 explicitly makes God's repentance part of a general principle—that when God promises to do something good that promise will endure, but when God promises to do harm that promise is invalid and God will repent of it. It derives this from an intensely literal reading of Num. 23:19: "God is not man to be capricious, Or mortal to change His mind. Would He speak and not act, Promise and not fulfill?" (NJPS). Instead of translating the last phrase as a rhetorical question, this midrash interprets it as a statement: yes, there are times that God promises and does not fulfill. This is something for which God should be praised, and one example of this is Hos. 2 in which God promises to reject Israel and then does not keep that promise (Gottleib, Ben-Hashar, and Penkower 2003: 66; see parallel in Midrash Tanchuma Massei 7).

Numbers Rabbah's main theme in the discussion of Hosea, however, is not repentance at all, but rather praise of Israel and hope for Israel's future. The verse that connects Hosea to Numbers is the discussion of the census in Num. 32:12, which Numbers Rabbah 2.12 connects to Hos. 2:1 "The number of the people of Israel shall be like that of the sands of the sea, which cannot be measured or counted" (NJPS). The discourses of Numbers Rabbah 2.13 and 2.14 build on this verse by describing the greatness and resilience of Israel, a theme to which it returns in discourse 2.17. So Numbers Rabbah's approach, in which God is the one who needs to repent, is consistent with a broader narrative in which Israel is consistently resilient and beloved.

Interpretations of Hosea that understand it to depict God's own repentance also appear elsewhere in Rabbinic texts. Sifrei Numbers 131 sees the change in Hosea as coming about because of changes in God, not changes in people:

422   DEVORAH SCHOENFELD

> Similarly, you say "You are not my people" (Hosea 1:9) and you say "The number of the people of Israel shall be like that of the sands of the sea, which cannot be measured or counted; and instead of being told, 'You are Not-My-People'..." (Hosea 2:1). How can one thing be related to the other? It can be compared to a king who got angry with his wife; he sent a certain scribe to write a divorce decree for her but before the scribe arrived the king became pleased with his wife again. The king said, "Should the scribe leave with nothing?" Rather he said, "Come write for her that I will double her marriage contract." (author's trans.)

This passage is part of a longer disagreement between Rabbi Akiva and Rabbi (Yehuda Ha-nasi), in which Rabbi Akiva argues that two sections of the Torah that are juxtaposed have a relationship with each other, and Rabbi argues that there are many places where two passages that are juxtaposed are "as far from each other as east from west." The passage points out the lack of relationship between Hos. 1:9, in which God rejects Israel, and Hos. 2:1 (Eng. 1:10) and other verses in that chapter, where God expresses great love for Israel. The obvious way to move from sin to acceptance would be for Israel to repent, but since no repentance is described as having happened in Hos. 1–2, the passage from Sifrei does not give that as a solution. Rather, God changes. First, God is angry at Israel, and then God is reconciled with Israel and gives Israel something more than before. It is not clear how or why God reconciles with Israel, but the action is entirely on the part of the king, not his wife (for parallels, see Gottlieb, Ben-Hashar, and Penkower 2003: 70).

The same passage in Sifrei Numbers 131 sees a similar dynamic at the end of the book of Hosea:

> Similarly you say, "Samaria must bear her guilt, For she has defied her God" (Hosea 14:1 NJPS), and you say, "Return, O Israel, to the Lord your God" (Hosea 14:2 NJPS). How can one thing be related to the other? It can be compared to a province that rebels against a king. He sends for a general and orders him to destroy it. This general was knowledgeable and thoughtful and said, "Take water for yourselves. If you do not, I will do to you what I did to a certain province and a certain other province." This is why it says, "Samaria must bear her guilt, For she has defied her God" and "Return, O Israel." (author's trans.)

In this passage, God intends to destroy Israel, but the prophet changes God's words to turn them into a call for repentance. It is the general (Hosea) and not the king (God) who is "wise and seasoned." God is willing to destroy Israel, but the prophet, and not God, understands what is necessary. The prophet understands that people need to be called to repentance, not destroyed, like the general understands that the province in rebellion could benefit from an offer of water.

Although Numbers Rabbah is a relatively late midrash, there are many other examples of this approach in Rabbinic texts. For example, Exodus Rabbah 46.4 describes the role of the prophet as calling God—not people—to repent. It compares God to a man who, when his children are behaving badly, says that they are not his children. But people say to him, they are obviously his children and look like him. Similarly, when God denies that Israel is God's child, it is the prophet's role to call on God to repent (Gottleib, Ben-Hashar, and Penkower 2003: 101). In Lamentations Rabbah Prologue 2, it states that when the Northern Kingdom of Israel was exiled God blamed them, but when the Southern Kingdom of Judah was exiled God accepted blame, in a way similar to a parent who raises two children; when the first one goes the wrong way, they blame the child, but when the second one does as well, they blame their parenting (Cohen 1983: 4–5; Neusner 2007: 99). In this interpretation, Hosea represents the first stage ("Woe to them for straying from Me," 7:13 NJPS) in which God does not even understand the role of parental responsibility, while Jeremiah represents the second ("Woe unto Me for My hurt," Jer. 10:19 NJPS). In Lamentations Rabbah 14.2, commenting on Hos. 5:15, God says, "I will go and return to my place until they acknowledge my guilt and seek my face," and then immediately regrets it, saying, "Woe is me! What have I done! I have brought my Presence to dwell below on account of the Israelites, and now that they have sinned, I have gone back to my earlier dwelling. Heaven forfend that I now become a joke to the nations and a source of ridicule among people" (Neusner 2007: 103). God refuses to accept consolation from the angel Metatron and ends the story weeping. In Berachot 32a, Hosea's is one of a long series of examples in which God bears some responsibility for Israel's sins. The particular verse from Hosea is 2:10 (Eng. 2:8), which states that God gave Israel the silver and gold that they used for Baal.

Reading God as the morally problematic actor in the book of Hosea may be, for the Rabbis, a way of taking seriously an internal critique expressed in the book itself. As Sherwood (1996: 223) points out, the very fact of the woman/Israel leaving God for Baal implies that she finds something inadequate in God. God's behavior in response to Israel's abandonment shows God in control, in the sense that God is able to punish, but also in an out-of-control rampage of violence, which speaks of insecurity. There is perhaps also a hint, as Francis Landy (1995: 156–57) suggests, in the abrupt transition from the first part of ch. 2 to the second, that God wishes to forget the violence that was inflicted, and this may suggest some Divine regret. In any case, Midrash Rabbah builds on these hints to construct a reading of Hosea in which God is flawed, and jealousy is not a virtue.

28.5. CONCLUSION

Does Gomer need to repent for adultery? Does God need to repent for doubting Israel? Does Hosea need to repent for not doing his job and advocating for Israel properly? Is there another story of repentance lurking in the background, that of Reuben weeping for Joseph before lying to his father about him? The differences between these possibilities suggest that the Rabbis are reading the book of Hosea as a story without an easy or obvious moral. No character is unequivocally heroic in this story, not even God.

Through the different retellings and reworkings of the story of Hosea, these Rabbinic readings allow multiple ways of grappling with Hosea as a story of repentance and change. An approach like the Targum's in which Israel repents (and Gomer is absent) can reduce some of the violence of the text and increase its hopefulness, at the cost of asking the reader to ignore the cruelty that is present in the biblical book. It allows the reader to read the story of a less-cruel God who always welcomes penitents. An approach which reads Hosea as an antihero protagonist, like that in Pesachim, allows the reader to engage with the story as a challenge never to desist from love and defense of one's fellow, since Hosea's sin is in not loving his neighbors enough or defending them from God. In a reading in which God is the one who repents or changes, it becomes a story about grace, and about how sometimes reconciliation is brought about through actions of the Divine. If Hosea is a problem story today, it seems that it was no less so for the Rabbis. This troubling text, like the pit that Reuben looked into, provided them an opportunity for reflection on sin and forgiveness, but not necessarily clarity or straightforward answers.

NOTES

1. The NJPS translation follows the Hebrew text verse numbers.
2. There is a parallel to this source in Pesikta de Rav Kahana 14.9 (Neusner 2007: 79).
3. This is not the first instance in which a word derived from that root appears in Genesis. It appears forty-two times prior to this in the book. In some cases, it clearly refers to physical return in a way that is difficult to connect to repentance (e.g., Gen. 8:9). Other places there are connotations of repentance, or it is connected to repentance by Rabbinic exegesis, but the repentance is incomplete. For example, in its comments on Gen. 3:19, Midrash Tanchuma Tazria 9:1 interprets the language about return as an invitation for Adam and Eve to repent for their sin, but also implies that they did not.
4. The meaning of the Hebrew is unclear but does not include the concept of repentance.
5. Hosea's strong critique of Jacob may be why Shabbat 55a concludes that *zhut avot*, the idea that Israel benefits from the merit of its ancestors, ended at the time of Hosea. The discussion in Shabbat bases itself on a different passage: "Now will I uncover her shame in the very sight of her lovers, And none shall save her from Me," (Hos. 2:12 NJPS) which, according to Rav, means that the merit of the ancestors will no longer save Israel.
6. Pesachim 87a, Steinsaltz trans. There is a parallel in Eliyahu Zuta 9, which also adopts the narrative of Hosea as sinful and repenting.
7. As Sherwood also points out, this frees the Rabbis to indulge in exaggerations of her sexuality that go far beyond what is present in the text. She observes that this is one of the few commentaries that holds Hosea morally culpable, and that by reading him as a fool, the Rabbis make him into a good match for the prostitute that he marries.
8. The implication here is that in Hos. 1:9 and 2:1 (Eng. 1:10) the people who are being called "not my people" are not Israel but rather people of the other nations who are not yet part of God's people but will be in the future (Gottleib, Ben-Hashar, and Penkower 2003: 144).
9. This passage is part of a lengthy discussion on repentance in which there are also examples of Israel and God repenting, some of which are from Hosea.

References

Braude, William G., trans. 1968. *Pesikta Rabbati: Discourses for Feasts, Fasts, and Special Sabbaths*. Yale Judaica Series 18. New Haven: Yale University Press.

Cathcart, Kevin J., and R. P. Gordon. 1989. *The Targum of the Minor Prophets*. The Aramaic Bible 14. Wilmington: M. Glazier.

Cohen, A. trans. 1983. *Midrash Rabbah: Lamentations*, vol. 1. London: Soncino.

Gottlieb, Isaac B., Menahem Ben-Hashar, and Jordan S Penkower, eds. 2003. *The Bible in Rabbinic Interpretation: Rabbinic Derashot on Prophets and Writings in Talmudic and Midrashic Literature*. [Hebrew] Ramat-Gan: Bar-Ilan University Press.

Kelle, Brad E. 2005. *Hosea 2: Metaphor and Rhetoric in Historical Perspective*. SBLAB 20. Brill: Leiden.

Kelle, Brad E. 2010. "Hosea 4–14 in Twentieth-Century Scholarship." *CBR* 8: 314–75.

Landy, Francis. 1995. "Fantasy and the Displacement of Pleasure: Hosea 2.4–17." In Athalya Brenner, ed. *A Feminist Companion to the Latter Prophets*. FCB 8. Sheffield: Sheffield Academic Press, 146–60.

Neusner, Jacob. 2007. *Hosea in Talmud and Midrash*. Studies in Judaism. Lanham, MD: University Press of America.

Sherwood, Yvonne. 1995. "Boxing Gomer: Controlling the Deviant Woman of Hosea 1–3." In Athalya Brenner, ed. *A Feminist Companion to the Latter Prophets*. FCB 8. Sheffield: Sheffield Academic Press, 101–25.

Sherwood, Yvonne. 1996. *The Prostitute and the Prophet: Hosea's Marriage in Literary-Theoretical Perspective*. JSOTSup 212. Sheffield: Sheffield Academic Press.

Slotki, Judah J., trans. 1983. *Midrash Rabbah: Numbers*, vol. 1. London: Soncino.

van Ruiten, Jacques. 2012. "The Image of Jacob in the Targum of Hosea 12." *Journal for the Study of Judaism in the Persian, Hellenistic and Roman Period* 43, no. 4–5: 595–612.

CHAPTER 29

HOSEA IN THE NEW TESTAMENT

STEVE MOYISE

29.1. Introduction

HOSEA was a popular prophet for the New Testament (NT) authors. There are six explicit quotations (Hos. 1:10 [Heb. 2:1]; 2:23 [Heb. 2:25]; 6:6; 10:8; 11:1; 13:14) cited in *The Greek New Testament* (UBS[5]: 859), two of which occur more than once (2:23; 6:6). This is more than any other Hebrew Bible (HB) prophet, with the exception of Isaiah. The prophet is specifically cited by name in Rom. 9:25 (ἐν τῷ Ὡσηὲ λέγει), using the form found in the Old Greek (OG) for the Hebrew הושע. There are also a number of significant allusions to Hosea in the NT (UBS[5]: 880), such as Jesus's resurrection "on the third day" (Hos. 6:2) and Paul's command, "Sow for yourselves righteousness" (Hos. 10:12). In addition, the divine marriage imagery of Hos. 1–3 lies behind the idea that Jesus is the bridegroom of the church, as well as referring to idolatry as prostitution. In the discussions that follow, I will proceed in the order of the texts in Hosea.

29.2. Hosea 1–3

As well as demonstrating that Jesus was the promised Messiah, the early church was particularly concerned to show that the scriptures foresaw the entrance of the Gentiles into the people of God. This naturally involved texts that use ἔθνη ("nations"), such as Gen. 18:18 (Gal. 3:8), Deut. 32:43 (Rom. 15:10), Ps. 116:19 (Rom. 15:11), and Isa. 9:1 (Matt. 4:15). But they were also attracted to Hos. 2:23 (Heb. 2:25) that predicted that those who were not God's people would become God's people, and those who had not received mercy would receive mercy.

Hosea 2:23 (Heb. 2:25)	1 Peter 2:10	Romans 9:25
And I will have mercy (ἐλεήσω) on "no-mercy" (οὐκ-ἠλεημένην), and I will say to "not my people" (οὐ λαῷ μου), "You are my people" (λαός μου εἶ σύ).	Once you were not a people (οὐ λαός), but now you are God's people (λαὸς θεοῦ); once you had not received mercy (οὐκ ἠλεημένοι), but now you have received mercy (ἐλεηθέντες).	Those who were not my people (οὐ λαόν μου) I will call "my people" (λαόν μου) and her who was not beloved (οὐκ ἠγαπημένην) I will call "beloved" (ἠγαπημένην).

It is interesting that both Peter and Paul swap the order of the clauses, perhaps indicating that they are drawing on a source rather than directly from Hosea (literary dependence between Peter and Paul is thought to be unlikely). Indeed, Paul further deviates from Hosea by using the verb ἀγαπάω ("love") rather than ἐλεήσω ("show mercy") for the second clause. This reading is found in some OG manuscripts of Hosea (Vaticanus, Venetus), but most scholars think that this derives from Romans (Wagner 2002: 82). It is possible that Paul has the underlying Hebrew (רחם) in mind or that he is continuing the "love" language from his previous quotation of Mal. 1:2–3 ("I have loved Jacob but I have hated Esau") in Rom. 9:13. In the next verse (Rom. 9:26), he cites Hos. 1:10 (Heb. 2:1).

Hosea 1:10 (Heb. 2:1)	Romans 9:26
And it shall be, in the place (במקום/ἐν τῷ τόπῳ) where (οὗ) it was said to them, "You are not my people," they too shall be called, (κληθήσονται καὶ αὐτοί) "children of the living God."	And it shall be, in the place (ἐν τῷ τόπῳ) where (οὗ/οὗ ἐάν – p46 FG) it was said to them, "You are not my people," there they shall be called (ἐκεῖ κληθήσονται) "children of the living God."

The phrase "children of the living God" is unique to Hosea and according to Macintosh (1997: 36) "suggests that, restored to the covenant relationship, Israel will be infused with life by the author of life." Perhaps this is what attracted Paul to the verse, since he states elsewhere that believers in Christ have become "children of God" (Rom. 8:14; Gal. 3:26). On the other hand, it is surprising that Paul not only includes the reference to "place" (ἐν τῷ τόπῳ) but seems to emphasize it by adding the word ἐκεῖ ("there"). His readers would not require a detailed knowledge of Hosea to know that he was addressing unfaithful Israelites in the Northern Kingdom, not Gentiles. Of course, some have argued that the reference to "place" makes no sense in Hosea either and should be taken to mean "in place of" (Gruber 2017: 102). Douglas Stuart (1987: 35) denies this possibility, but in any case, it would be difficult to argue this for the Greek phrase ἐν τῷ τόπῳ, despite Cranfield (1979: 501) finding an example in the third-century historian, Herodian. Thus, the major debate among NT scholars is how Paul thinks he can apply these verses from Hosea to Gentiles. James Dunn (1988: 575) says that it is

> hardly likely that Paul means to imply that the Gentiles who have responded to God's call have shown themselves thereby to be the lost and dispersed ten northern tribes. It is simply that scripture proves that those who were not God's people can by God's gracious act become his people.

This is not necessarily a case of Paul arbitrarily substituting Gentiles for Jews, for it is clear from Rom. 11 that Paul thinks the "hardened Israel" of his own day will be restored, and that this is in accord with scripture. It is more that Paul agrees with the thought of Hosea but also applies it, by analogy, to the Gentiles.

Mark Seifrid (2007: 647–48) does not think the word "analogy" goes far enough. When Hosea says that "my people" have become "not my people," he is effectively saying that they have become like the other nations. Hence, when Hosea promises that "not my people" will become "children of the living God," Gentiles are included within that promise. Ross Wagner (2002) is more tentative, noting that Paul consistently seizes on negative appellations in scripture in order to find references to Gentiles. Thus, Paul identifies Gentiles as the reference to the "nation without understanding" in Deut. 32:21 (Rom. 10:19), those "not seeking God" in Isa. 65:1 (Rom. 10:20), and "those who have not heard" in Isa. 52:15 (Rom. 15:21). He prefers the reading found in P[46] FG (οὖ ἐάν) to the text printed in NA[28] (οὖ), which he takes to mean, "*Wherever* people are estranged from God, there God is now actively calling out a people for himself" (Wagner 2002: 85).

Paul cites Isa. 65:1–2 in Rom. 10:20–21, but takes the first verse as a reference to Gentiles ("I have been found by those who did not seek me") and the second verse to Israel ("All day long I have held out my hands to a disobedient and contrary people"). Robert Foster (2016: 190–204) thinks that is precisely what he has done with Hos. 1:10 (Heb. 2:1). The initial reference is clearly to Jews ("And the number of the people of *Israel*"), but it is not clear that the antecedent of "in the place where it was said to *them*" is the same. Foster argues that Paul supplies the antecedent τὰ ἔθνη, and that there is nothing in Hos. 1:10–12 (Heb. 2:1–3) that rules this out. Paul is aided in this interpretation by a peculiarity of the OG, which offers different translations of והיה in the two clauses. In the first clause, it is rendered with an imperfect ("And the number of the people of Israel *was* like the sand of the sea"), but in the second clause, it is rendered by the usual future ("it *shall be* said to them, 'children of the living God' "). Thus, Paul finds in the OG translation a contrast between a decimated people, who were once like the sand of the sea, and an unspecified group who will be called "children of the living God." Foster (2016) extends this to how he thinks Paul would have read Hos. 2:1 (Heb. 2:3): "Say to your brothers, 'You are my people,' and to your sisters, 'You have received mercy.' " This is most naturally taken with the promise of the previous verse, that Israel and Judah will be reunited under one head (ראש/ἀρχὴν) and thus enjoy such familial relationships. However, Foster thinks the extending of familial relationships in 2:1 is in contrast to the subject of Hos 1:11 (Heb.

2:2)—namely, the unified Israel/Judah. It must therefore apply to a group of people different from the unified Israel/Judah—namely, the Gentiles.

More generally, the idea of God as husband to Israel in Hos. 1–3 is ultimately the source of the bridegroom language in the Gospels (Mark 2:19–20; John 3:29), the wedding imagery in some of Jesus's parables (Matt. 22:1–14; 25:1–13) and in the teaching of Paul (2 Cor. 11:2; Eph. 5:31–32), and the marriage of the Lamb in the book of Revelation (Rev. 19:7–8; 21:2). In keeping with the Christological perspective of the NT, it is Jesus, the embodiment of God, who is the groom and the church is the bride (Tait 2010). Thus, in Mark 2:19–20, Jesus utters an aphorism about the inappropriateness of fasting at a wedding and then adds: "The days will come when the bridegroom is taken away from them, and then they will fast on that day." If these words (or something similar) go back to Jesus, as for example Cranfield argues (1959: 107), it would help explain the developments that we find in Paul and Revelation.

In Matt. 22:1–14, Jesus compares the "kingdom of heaven" with a king who gives a wedding feast. The background is primarily the eschatological banquet in texts like Isa. 25, but the particular mention that it is a wedding feast (γάμος), and the fact that those originally invited are replaced by those who were not, suggests that Hosea is also in mind (Smolarz 2011: 152–62). In the parable of the Ten Virgins (Matt. 25:1–13), the emphasis is on being ready for the arrival of the bridegroom, for when he comes, "those who were ready went with him into the wedding banquet" (v. 10). The fact that Matthew understands this as an allegorical reference to Jesus is confirmed by the plea of those who miss out: "Lord, lord, open to us" (v. 11).

In 2 Cor. 11:2, Paul tells the Corinthians that he has "betrothed you to one husband, to present you as a pure virgin to Christ" (ESV). The aim of this betrothal is "a sincere and pure devotion to Christ" (v. 3), but Paul fears that, like Eve, they will be led astray. Paul appears to be casting himself as the bride's father, whose duty it is to keep his daughter pure until the marriage (Thrall 2000: 661). There are no specific verbal correspondences with Hosea, but Sebastian Smolarz (2011: 195) cites Hos. 2:19 (Heb. 2:21), Jer. 31:4, and Isa. 62:3–5 for the background of the saying.

A different rhetorical situation is envisaged in Eph. 5, where the author is seeking to regulate relationships within the household. In particular, the relationship between husband and wife is compared to the relationship between Christ and the church (v. 32). Christ loved and died for the church (v. 25) so that he might "present the church to himself in splendor, without a spot or wrinkle . . . holy and without blemish" (v. 27). The fact that it is now Christ who presents the church to himself rather than Paul is one of the reasons why some scholars think that Ephesians was written by a disciple of Paul rather than Paul himself (Muddiman 2001: 2–46).

In the book of Revelation, the announcement in Rev. 19:7–8 ("the marriage of the Lamb has come, and his bride has made herself ready; to her it has been granted to be clothed with fine linen, bright and pure") is followed by a vision of the New Jerusalem "prepared as a bride adorned for her husband" (Rev. 21:2). Commentators think that Isa. 61:10 ("adorned me with ornaments like a bride" NETS) and Ezek. 16:13 ("your clothing was of fine linen, rich fabric, and embroidered cloth") are the more immediate sources of the imagery, but Hos. 2:16–20 (Heb. 2:18–22) is also mentioned, where v. 19 says: "I will betroth you to me in righteousness and in justice, in steadfast love and in mercy" (ESV).

As in Hosea, the divine marriage imagery also allows the author of Revelation to describe the unfaithfulness of the people as prostitution. This begins with a warning against "Jezebel" and "her children," who according to John, are "beguiling my servants to practice fornication (πορνεῦσαι) and to eat food sacrificed to idols" (Rev. 2:20). Many scholars think the context for this accusation is participation in the local trade guilds, where "guild members would be expected to pay homage to pagan gods" (Beale 1999: 261). It is possible that such meetings descended into immorality (Osborne 2002: 157) and so the reference to πορνεῦσαι could be literal, but Aune (1998: 204) thinks John's epithet "Jezebel" suggests idolatry/apostasy rather than sexual immorality.

In Rev. 17–18, the accusation is broadened: "Come, I will show you the judgment of the great whore (πόρνης) . . . with whom the kings of the earth have committed fornication" (Rev. 17:1–2). Most scholars have taken "kings of the earth" literally and think that John's target is Rome or Roman power (Murphy 1988: 353). However, a minority of scholars have suggested that the biblical background of "whoredom" suggests a prior relationship to God and therefore Jerusalem is the focus, as it was in Jesus's teaching (Luke 19:41–44). Thus, Smolarz (2011: 273) takes "kings of the earth" to mean "rulers of the land of Israel." There are a number of specific allusions to Ezekiel (e.g., Rev. 17:16/Ezek. 23:29; Rev. 18:19/Ezek. 27:30) and Jeremiah (e.g., Rev. 17:4/Jer. 28:7; Rev. 18:3/Jer. 28:7), but the origin of the imagery lies in Hosea.

29.3. Hosea 6

There do not seem to be any references to Hos. 4–5 in the NT, but there are quotations and allusions to Hos. 6. First, the expression "on the third day" (ἐν τῇ ἡμέρᾳ τῇ τρίτῃ) occurs a number of times in the NT. According to the Gospels, Jesus used it to assert that after his crucifixion, he will be raised *on the third day* (Matt. 16:21; 17:23; 20:19). It is used in the apostolic preaching, when Peter says to Cornelius, "But God raised him from the dead *on the third day*" (Acts 10:40). And it is used by Paul as he summarizes the message that he received: "Christ died for our sins in accordance with the scriptures, and that he was buried, and that he was raised *on the third day* in accordance with the scriptures" (1 Cor. 15:3–4). The question is whether any of these sayings have been influenced by Hos. 6:2 ("After two days he will revive us; on the third day he will raise us up, that we may live before him"). The best candidates are those that use ἀνίστημι for resurrection (Luke 18:33; 24:7, 46), as in the OG of Hos. 6:2, though ἐγείρω/ἀνίστημι are close synonyms. Brian Lidbeck (2020: 108) is one scholar who thinks it likely that Hos. 6:2 is in mind. The evidence of the Targum could be used to support this, as even Jewish interpreters took the verse to be about resurrection, though the specific mention of "on the third day" has dropped out, perhaps to avoid the Christian interpretation (Pentiuc 2006: 182). On the other hand, it is not until Tertullian that Jesus's resurrection is explicitly linked to Hos.

6:2, and most scholars take "according to the scriptures" in 1 Cor. 15:4 as referring to "he was raised" rather than its timing ("on the third day").

In the story of Matt. 9:11–13, the Pharisees ask Jesus's disciples why he eats with tax collectors and sinners. Jesus replies, "Those who are well have no need (οὐ χρείαν) of a physician, but those who are sick" (v. 12). He then says: "Go and learn what this means, 'I desire mercy (ἔλεος θέλω), not sacrifice (οὐ θυσίαν).' For I have come to call not (οὐ) the righteous but sinners" (v. 13). In a later incident, the Pharisees spot the disciples plucking grain on the sabbath. This time, they respond with an accusation rather than a question: "Look, your disciples are doing what is not lawful to do on the sabbath" (Matt. 12:2). Jesus first responds by citing the example of David when he "entered the house of God and ate the bread of the Presence" (Matt. 12:3–4, referring to 1 Sam. 21:6). He then points them to the law, which recognizes that priests break the sabbath as they go about their duties but are nevertheless regarded as "guiltless" (Num. 28:9–10). This leads to the quotation from Hos. 6:6a: "But if you had known what this means, 'I desire mercy (ἔλεος θέλω) and not sacrifice (οὐ θυσίαν),' you would not have condemned the guiltless."

In the book of Hosea, the negative clause (6:6a) is followed by a comparative clause (6:6b: "the knowledge of God *rather* than burnt offerings"), leading to two opposing interpretations. Andersen and Freedman (1980: 430) read the first clause in light of the second and claim that "sacrifice is not denigrated; it is simply put in second place." On the other hand, Macintosh (1997: 234) reads the second clause in light of the first, insisting that "Hosea repudiates radically the whole sacrificial cult with its licentious feasting." Does the use of Hos 6:6a in Matthew's Gospel shed any light on this debate?

First, it is to be noted that both interpretations are present in the LXX tradition. Codex A has καὶ οὐ θυσίαν ("and not sacrifice"), while Codex B has καὶ ἢ θυσίαν ("rather than sacrifice"). Rahlfs (1979) and Ziegler (1967) both think that καὶ οὐ θυσίαν is original, in which case Matthew simply followed it and καὶ ἢ θυσίαν is a copyist error. However, Menken (2004: 229) thinks it is far more likely that the harder reading (καὶ ἢ θυσίαν) is original, and a later revisionist brought it into line with the Hebrew text. He thinks this happened prior to Matthew, but Gundry (1967: 111) thinks it is due to cross-contamination. Be that as it may, many scholars think that Matthew is in fact translating from the Hebrew (Davies and Allison 1988: 104; Kubiś 2020: 308).

Although it would be intriguing to know what Jesus thought about the matter, it is generally recognized that Matthew is responsible for the quotation in both stories. The reasons for this are: (1) it is absent from his Markan source (Mark 2:15–18; 23–28); (2) it is absent from the versions in Luke (Luke 5:27–32; 6:1–5); and (3) neither story is about sacrifice. Despite the triple use of οὐ ("not") in the first story, it seems that Matthew was attracted to the verse not because of its negation of sacrifice but its emphasis on mercy (ἔλεος). Jesus has already pronounced a blessing on the "merciful" (Matt. 5:7), and as Ulrich Luz (2001: 34) points out, "It is not by accident that from this point on the sick will address Jesus with ἐλέησον ("have mercy"; 9:27; 15:22; 17:15; 20:30–31)." Although it would be understandable that someone writing after the fall of Jerusalem would be attracted to a text that denies the value of sacrifices, that does not appear to be Matthew's meaning. For example, after Jesus heals a man suffering from leprosy, he instructs him to "go, show yourself to the priest, and offer the gift that Moses commanded" (Matt. 8:4). When stressing the importance of reconciliation, action should be taken even "when you are offering your gift at the altar" (Matt. 5:23). Even those who cite Hos. 6:6 in the later church (Tertullian, Clement, Ambrose, Chrysostom) focus on the mercy of God rather than the termination of sacrifices.

29.4. HOSEA 9:7

According to Luke 21:20–22, Jesus predicts the fall of Jerusalem and warns those in Judea to flee to the mountains, "for these are days of vengeance, as a fulfillment of all that is written" (v. 22). The "all that is written" no doubt refers to a range of judgment texts but the particular reference to "days of vengeance" (ἡμέραι ἐκδικήσεως) seems to point to the OG of Hos. 9:7 (αἱ ἡμέραι τῆς ἐκδικήσεως), although Jer. 51:6 (καιρὸς ἐκδικήσεως) is also a possibility.

29.5. HOSEA 10:8

The wish expressed in Hos. 10:8 ("They shall say to the mountains, Cover us, and to the hills, Fall on us") is cited twice in the NT:

> A great number of the people followed him, and among them were women who were beating their breasts and wailing for him. But Jesus turned to them and said, "Daughters of Jerusalem, do not weep for me, but weep for yourselves and for your children. For the days are surely coming when they will say, 'Blessed are the barren, and the wombs that never bore, and the breasts that never nursed.' *Then they will begin to say to the mountains, 'Fall on us'; and to the hills, 'Cover us.'* For if they do this when the wood is green, what will happen when it is dry?" (Luke 23:27–31)

Then the kings of the earth and the magnates and the generals and the rich and the powerful, and everyone, slave and free, hid in the caves and among the rocks of the mountains, *calling to the mountains and rocks,* "Fall on us and hide us from the face of the one seated on the throne and from the wrath of the Lamb; for the great day of their wrath has come, and who is able to stand?" (Rev. 6:15–17).

In both cases, the order of cover/fall has been reversed, which may indicate that the OG represented by Codex A was better known at this time than the order found in Codex B and MT. Luke follows the OG's καλύπτω ("cover, conceal, hide"), whereas Revelation uses the close synonym, κρύπτω. John Nolland (1993: 1137) thinks the meaning in Luke is "relief through death from the time of terrible suffering," but Revelation is different. John begins by saying that they "hid in the caves and among the rocks of the mountains"

(6:15). This suggests that the subsequent call to the mountains and rocks (πέτρα rather than OG βουνός) to fall/cover is for further protection, perhaps sealing the entrance of the caves. John explicitly adds to the fall/cover clause the words, "from the face of the one seated on the throne and from the wrath of the Lamb." The meaning is close to Isa. 2:10 ("Enter into the rock, and hide in the dust from the terror of the LORD, and from the glory of his majesty") and Isa. 2:21 ("enter the caverns of the rocks and the clefts in the crags, from the terror of the LORD, and from the glory of his majesty, when he rises to terrify the earth"). Indeed, the twin reference to God and his glory might have facilitated John's daring inclusion of the Lamb with the "one seated on the throne."

Most scholars think the meaning of Hos. 10:8 is about seeking death. Stuart (1987: 163) says that the "miseries endured will be so great that people will cry desperately for relief—in effect for sudden death and burial under the land's hills." On the other hand, as Mayer Gruber (2017: 423) notes, the most obvious antecedent of "They shall say to the mountains" is the shrines, personified as feeling "so disgusted with what has taken place on them and in their vicinity that they will ask to be obliterated through the agency of natural forces such as earthquakes and avalanches."

29.6. HOSEA 10:12

In 2 Cor. 9:10, Paul exhorts the Corinthians with the words: "He who supplies seed to the sower and bread for food will supply and multiply your seed for sowing and increase the harvest of your righteousness." Paul appears to have the OG of Hos. 10:12 in mind, which also uses σπείρω ("sow") and καρπός ("fruit"), as well as the particular combination γενήματα δικαιοσύνης ("harvest of righteousness"), which only occurs here (MT has וירה צדק לכם "rain righteousness upon you").

29.7. HOSEA 11:1

In Matthew's nativity story, Joseph is warned in a dream to "Get up, take the child and his mother, and flee to Egypt, and remain there until I tell you; for Herod is about to search for the child, to destroy him" (Matt. 2:13). This he does ("Then Joseph got up, took the child and his mother by night, and went to Egypt"), to which Matthew comments: "This was to fulfill what had been spoken by the Lord through the prophet, 'Out of Egypt I have called my son (υἱόν)'" (Matt. 2:15). Scholars are agreed that this is a quotation from Hos. 11:1b but not from the OG, which reads "his children" (τὰ τέκνα αὐτοῦ) rather than "my son" (לבני). It is the collective singular that allows the application to Jesus, who is called God's son eight times in Matthew's Gospel (3:17; 4:3, 6; 8:29; 14:33; 16:16; 26:63; 27:40). Bearing in mind that Matthew will go on to relate stories where Jesus was tested in the wilderness (Matt. 4:1–11) and ascended a mountain to deliver his teaching (Matt.

5:1), Richard France (2007: 81) says, "When Jesus 'came out of Egypt,' that was to be the signal for a new exodus in which Jesus would fill the role not only of the God-sent deliverer but also of God's 'son' Israel himself." Craig Evans (2012: 58) is similar, adding that the exodus which Jesus will inaugurate "will save God's people in an even greater way than they were saved long ago."

However, there are several problems with this explanation. First, one would have expected the quotation to come after Jesus's departure from Egypt (Matt. 2:21) rather than his journey to Egypt. Indeed, Robert Gundry (1994: 34) thinks that Matthew's point concerns "God's preservation of Jesus in Egypt as a sign of his divine sonship" rather than his departure. This makes good sense of the narrative and offers a parallel with the "earlier Joseph" who found sanctuary in Egypt. But it does not explain why Matthew quoted words about leaving Egypt if his purpose was to support a sojourn in Egypt.

Second, if Matthew wanted a quotation to support a "new exodus" theology, why not choose a text that actually looks forward to a new exodus, such as Hos. 11:11 ("They shall come trembling like birds from Egypt")? In response, many scholars argue that the meaning of a quotation is not restricted to the actual words quoted but evokes something of the surrounding context. Thus, the backward reference to the exodus in Hos. 11:1b is followed by a return to Egypt in 11:5 (if that is the correct meaning) and a departure from Egypt in 11:11. The citation of Hos. 11:1b acts as a pointer to the whole chapter. Some would go further, suggesting that the "surrounding context" extends to the whole book (Beale 2012: 60–64) or even the whole of the Minor Prophets (Shepherd 2011).

29.8. Hosea 13:14

[1]Shall I (I shall) ransom them from the hand of Sheol (?)
[2]Shall I (I shall) redeem them from Death (?)
[3]Where are (I shall be) your plagues, O Death (?)
[4]Where is (I shall be) your destruction, O Sheol (?)
[5]Compassion is hidden from my eyes.

There are numerous exegetical difficulties with this verse, but the context of v. 12 ("Ephraim's iniquity is bound up; his sin is kept in store") and v. 16 ("they shall fall by the sword, their little ones shall be dashed in pieces, and their pregnant women ripped open") suggests the theme is judgment. This is most obviously so if the first two clauses are understood as rhetorical questions (NRSV; NJB; REB; Macintosh 1997; Stuart 1987; Wolff 1974), which receive a negative answer in clause five. Clauses three and four then become either invitations for Death and Sheol to come and do their worst (Stuart 1987: 207) or derisory comments that would have been said had God redeemed Ephraim (Macintosh 1997: 546). The early versions and medieval exegetes took the first two clauses as statements but the meaning of clause five negated this becoming a reality. Thus

Rashi and Ibn Ezra both understood the verse in the sense of "in the past, I redeemed them but now I will be the agent of their destruction" (Macintosh 1997: 546).

In 1 Cor. 15, Paul is explaining and reinforcing the Christian doctrine of resurrection and cites clauses three and four in the following context:

> When this perishable body puts on imperishability, and this mortal body puts on immortality, then the saying that is written will be fulfilled: "Death has been swallowed up in victory (νῖκος)." *"Where, O death, is your victory (νῖκος)? Where, O death, is your sting (κέντρον)?"* The sting of death is sin, and the power of sin is the law. But thanks be to God, who gives us the victory through our Lord Jesus Christ. (1 Cor. 15:54–57)

If the final clause of Hos. 13:14 points strongly to a negative interpretation, the first clause of Paul's quotation ("Death has been swallowed up in victory") points strongly to a positive one. The words are most likely from Isa. 25:8 (בלע המות לנצח), though not from the OG text that has come down to us (κατέπιεν ὁ θάνατος ἰσχύσας), which strangely hails death as the conqueror. It may be that Paul is translating for himself (Hays 1997: 275) or using a revised version of the OG (Stanley 1992: 211), such as the one that came to be included in Theodotion (identical to Paul but hardly copied from Paul). If the latter, it seems that he has interpolated νῖκος ("victory") into his quotation/paraphrase of Hos. 13:14, since the MT has "your plagues" (דבריך) and the OG "your sentence" (ἡ δίκη σου).

Much of the debate in NT circles concerns the validity of such an exegetical move by Paul. After all, we are talking about the doctrine of resurrection, which is clearly a matter of dispute in Corinth (1 Cor. 15:12). Are opponents of the doctrine likely to be won over by a citation that manipulates the wording of the original and reverses its meaning? Hays (1997: 275) thinks so because Isa. 25:8 "does envision God's ultimate destruction of the power of death, and the reader who follows the allusion to its source will find a richly evocative portrayal of God's universal salvation for 'all peoples.'" Hosea 13:14 is not cited as a stand-alone text that supports resurrection but adds color to the main assertion of Isa. 25:8. In a collection of studies on "Composite Citations in Antiquity," Roy Ciampa (2018: 176) says:

> Paul takes two poetic texts addressing death's role in God's redemptive plans and creates a new three-line piece of poetry which celebrates death's defeat in light of the resurrection. In the new piece of poetry we perceive that death has been caught up in a narrative of conflict in which it has finally lost its battle and victory has gone to its opponents.

Although it is clear that Hosea's words on their own cannot support resurrection, it is worth asking whether Paul's assertion that they are a taunt has any merit. Macintosh (1997: 537–42) believes that the use of אהי in Hos. 13:10 is clearly derisory ("Where now is your king, that he may save you?") and suggests the same is likely to be true for 13:14 ("Where are your plagues, O Death?"). Since he thinks the first two clauses of 13:14 are most likely rhetorical questions, he understands the verse in the following way: "Shall I redeem them from the hand of Sheol? Shall I ransom them from death, [so that they should say] 'So much for your ravages, O Death! So much for your destruction, Sheol!'? No, relief is excluded from my view." The cited words are a taunt but only in the hypothetical sense of what Ephraim would say had God decided to redeem them. The final clause makes it clear that this is not going to happen.

A different connection with Paul arises from Mayer Gruber's (2017: 546) interpretation. He thinks that Hos. 13:14 has a positive meaning, and he arrives at that by taking אהי not as a form of the interrogative איה (OG: ποῦ "where?") but from the verb היה (as do Aquila and Symmachus, using ἔσομαι). The resulting interpretation is that God is in opposition to Death and Sheol. Thus, Gruber renders the verse: "I shall ransom them from Sheol. I shall redeem them from Death. I shall be your Pestilence, Death. I shall be your Scourge, Sheol. Pity will be hidden from my eyes." The "pity" (נחם) that is hidden from God's eyes is not aimed at Ephraim but at Death and Sheol. If Gruber is correct, then Paul has combined two texts which refer to the defeat of death (Isa. 25:8; Hos. 13:14) and drawn the (not unreasonable) implication that this implies resurrection.

29.9. CONCLUSION

The NT authors have drawn on both the salvation and judgment oracles in Hosea. For the former, the spectacular transformation of those designated as "not my people" to "my people" in Hos. 2:23 (Heb. 2:25) is quoted in 1 Pet. 2:10 and Rom. 9:25 and extended to the Gentiles. Paul further cites Hos. 1:10 (Heb. 2:1) that "not my people" (understood as Gentiles) have been transformed into "children of the living God" (Rom. 9:26). The revival of Israel promised in Hos. 6:2 seems to have provided the phraseology for Jesus's resurrection "on the third day" (Matt. 16:21; Acts 10:40; 1 Cor. 15:4). And the love shown to Israel when he was a child (Hos. 11:1) is applied typologically to the infant Jesus during his sojourn and departure from Egypt (Matt. 2:15). Finally, conceiving of the covenant in terms of "divine marriage" (Hos. 1–3) lies behind the conception of Jesus as the bridegroom (2 Cor. 11:2) and the church as his bride (Rev. 19:7–8).

From the judgment oracles, Matthew twice has Jesus cite Hos. 6:6—that God requires mercy not sacrifice. The plea to the hills to cover us and the mountains to hide us in Hos. 10:8 is cited in Luke 23:30 and Rev. 6:16, probably with the different meaning of "protect us" but still in the context of impending judgment. And the imagery of idolatry as prostitution in Hos. 1–3 lies behind the Babylon oracles in Rev. 17–18 (via Ezekiel). The citation of Hos. 13:14 is somewhat different, in that the judgment oracle is given a wholly positive interpretation in 1 Cor. 15:55 by eliding it with Isa. 25:8 and announcing that death has been defeated. In conclusion, Hosea was a significant prophet for the NT authors and allowed them to make key points about christology, salvation, judgment, and ecclesiology.

References

Andersen, F. I., and D. N. Freedman. 1980. *Hosea*. AB 24. Garden City, NY: Doubleday.

Aune, David E. 1998. *Revelation 17–22*. WBC 52C. Grand Rapids: Zondervan.

Beale, Gregory K. 1999. *The Book of Revelation*. NIGTC. Grand Rapids: Eerdmans.

Beale, Gregory K. 2012. *Handbook on the New Testament Use of the Old Testament*. Grand Rapids: Baker Academic.

Ciampa, Roy E. 2018. "Composite Citations in 1–2 Corinthians and Galatians." In Sean A. Adams and Seth M. Ehorn, ed., *Composite Citations in Antiquity Vol 2*. LNTS 593. London: T&T Clark, 159–89.

Cranfield, Charles E. B. 1959. *The Gospel According to St Mark*. Cambridge: Cambridge University Press.

Cranfield, Charles E.B. 1979. *A Critical and Exegetical Commentary on the Epistle to the Romans: Vol 2. Commentary on Romans IX–XVI*. ICC. Edinburgh: T&T Clark.Davies, W. D., and Dale C. Allison. 1988. *The Gospel According to Saint Matthew: Introduction and Commentary on Matthew I–VII*. ICC. Edinburgh: T&T Clark.

Dunn, James D. G. 1988. *Romans 9–16*. WBC 38b. Grand Rapids: Zondervan.

Evans, Craig A. 2012. *Matthew*. New Cambridge Bible Commentary. Cambridge: Cambridge University Press.

Foster, Robert B. 2016. *Renaming Abraham's Children: Election, Ethnicity, and the Interpretation of Scripture in Romans 9*. WUNT 2.421. Tübingen: Mohr Siebeck.

France, Richard T. 2007. *The Gospel of Matthew*. NICNT. Grand Rapids: Eerdmans.

Gruber, Mayer I. 2017. *Hosea: A Textual Commentary*. LHBOTS 653. London: T&T Clark.

Gundry, Robert H. 1967. *The Use of the Old Testament in St. Matthew's Gospel with Special Reference to the Messianic Hope*. NovTSup 18. Leiden: Brill.

Gundry, Robert H. 1994. *Matthew: A Commentary on His Handbook for a Mixed Church under Persecution*. Grand Rapids: Eerdmans.Hays, Richard B. 1997. *First Corinthians*. Interpretation. Louisville: John Knox.

Kubiś, Adam. 2020. "'I Delight in Love, Not in Sacrifice': Hosea 6:6 and Its Rereading in the Gospel of Matthew." *Collectanea Theologica* 90: 295–320.

Lidbeck, Brian W. 2020. *Resurrection and Spirit: From the Pentateuch to Luke-Acts*. Eugene, Or: Wipf & Stock.

Luz, Ulrich. 2001. *Matthew 8–20: A Commentary*. Hermeneia. Minneapolis: Fortress.

Macintosh, A. A. 1997. *A Critical and Exegetical Commentary on Hosea*. ICC. Edinburgh: T & T Clark.

Menken, Maarten J. J. 2004. *Matthew's Bible: The Old Testament Text of the Evangelist*. Leuven: Leuven University Press/Peters.

Muddiman, John. 2001. *The Epistle to the Ephesians*. London: Continuum.

Murphy, Frederick J. 1998. *Fallen Is Babylon: The Revelation to John*. Harrisburg, PA: Trinity Press.

Nolland, John. 1993. *Luke 18:35–24:53*. WBC 35C. Grand Rapids: Zondervan.

Osborne, Grant R. 2002. *Revelation*. Baker Exegetical Commentary on the New Testament. Grand Rapids: Baker Academic.

Pentiuc, Eugen J. 2006. *Jesus the Messiah in the Hebrew Bible*. New York: Paulist.

Rahlfs, Alfred. 1979. *Septuaginta: Id est vetus testamentum graece iuxta LXX interpretes*. Stuttgart: Deutsche Bibelgesellschaft.

Seifrid, Mark A. 2007. "Romans." In Gregory K. Beale and Donald A. Carson, ed., *Commentary on the New Testament Use of the Old Testament*. Grand Rapids: Baker Academic, 607–94.

Shepherd, Michael B. 2011. *The Twelve Prophets in the New Testament*. New York: Peter Lang.

Smolarz, Sebastian R. 2011. *Covenant and the Metaphor of Divine Marriage in Biblical Thought*. Eugene, OR: Wipf and Stock.

Stanley, Christopher D. 1992. *Paul and the Language of Scripture: Citation Technique in the Pauline Epistles and Contemporary Literature*. Cambridge: Cambridge University Press.

Stuart, Douglas. 1987. *Hosea-Jonah*. WBC 31. Waco, TX: Word.

Tait, Michael. 2010. *Jesus, the Divine Bridegroom in Mark 2:18–22: Mark's Christology Upgraded*. Rome: Gregorian & Biblical Press.

Thrall, Margaret E. 2000. *II Corinthians*. ICC. Edinburgh: T & T Clark.

Wagner, J. Ross. 2002. *Heralds of the Good News: Israel and Paul "In Concert" in the Letter to the Romans*. Leiden: Brill.

Wolff, Hans W. 1974. *Hosea*. Trans. G. Stansell. Hermeneia. Philadelphia: Fortress.

Ziegler, Joseph. 1967. *Septuaginta: Vetus Testamentum Graecum: DuodecimProphetae*. Göttingen: Vandenhoeck & Ruprecht.

CHAPTER 30

··

HOSEA IN POPULAR CULTURE

··

EMILY O. GRAVETT

MANY books of the Bible have inspired an abundance of later, popular, postbiblical material (though, really, where do we draw the line? see Breed 2014). Think of the flood from Genesis, which appears, adorably if not heteronormatively (Corse 2017), in animals going two by two into Noah's ark in children's picture books, or the gospels from the New Testament, which have shown up in music for millennia, as in, more recently, the rock opera *Jesus Christ Superstar* and Tupac's hip hop song "Black Jesuz." The book of Hosea's influence on later works is modest by comparison. But Hosea and his life, especially his commanded marriage to his wife of whoredom/harlotry, Gomer-bat-Diblaim, make a surprising number of appearances in contemporary popular ("pop") culture, especially by and for Christians.

There are many different ways to understand "popular culture" (see Storey 2006). Is it made by and for the people? Is it mass produced? Is it quantifiably the most popular? (And, if so, what is the minimum number or cut-off?) Is it whatever simply isn't high or elite culture, defined more by what it isn't than what it is? There are no easy answers. Complicating matters, too, is that our understanding of what's "popular" can and does change over time and depending on context. Sleeper hits, like the film *The Rocky Horror Picture Show* (1975), which initially flop in the box office, can take on new life, and cult classic status, later on. For the purposes of this essay, I will be considering recent works—media like movies—usually included in the realm of pop culture that engage with the biblical book of Hosea in some way, even if the particular examples I discuss below haven't necessarily risen (yet?) to the status of "popular."

30.1. ENGAGING HOSEA IN POPULAR CULTURE

On the Internet, there are a lot of straightforward appearances of the book of Hosea, as in video explanations (for instance, the Bible Project's overview of "Hosea"), asynchronous courses or study guides (e.g., "Knowing the Bible: Hosea," 2016), and online commentaries (e.g., "5 Powerful Lessons from the Book of Hosea," 2021). Of course, we can now use the power of the Internet to read the biblical text itself in a variety of translations and languages.

Some scholars have found profit in analyzing universal themes of infidelity, waywardness, devotion, heartbreak, suffering, and forgiveness in pop culture through the lens of or in conjunction with the biblical story of Hosea. For example, Donald Polaski's entry in *Teaching the Bible* (2005) is titled "Hosea Meets Hank Williams" and the song "You Win Again," whose lyrics include: "The news is out all over town / That you've been seen out runnin' around / I know that I should leave, but then / I just can't go / You win again / This heart of mine could never see / What everybody knows but me / Just trusting in you was my great sin." With such broad parameters, though, almost any love song or romcom could be brought into the Hosea fold.

Allusions to the book of Hosea in pop culture may be similarly widespread, especially in music. Bob Dylan seems to make some reference to the biblical story in his "Key West" song (2020): "Twelve years old, they put me in a suit / Forced me to marry a prostitute / There were gold fringes on her wedding dress / That's my story, but not where it ends / She's still cute, and we're still friends." Jenna Parr's song "The Runaway" (2020) was inspired by the biblical book of Hosea, but we only know it because of a social media post: "One day while reading the book of Hosea, I was inspired to write the song 'The Runaway.' I realized how much we can relate to that story, even in today's time." Similar is the song "Hosea," originally written by Catholic Gregory Nobert, as well as its later covers, most popularly John Michael Talbot's (2005), as well as Shane & Shane's "Hosea" (2002). It would not be obvious they were intending to riff on the biblical book without that single word "Hosea" in their titles. There is a mention of "our preacher, old mister Hosea" in *The Green Pastures*, a 1936 Hollywood film that tells a series of biblical stories with an all-Black cast; a brief synopsis of the biblical story, where Hosea "fell in love with Gomer," in *Walk on the Wild Side* (1962); and bookends mentioning the prostitution plot of Hosea in the movie *The Milky Way* (1969). For further details on these three, see Chattaway (2022). There is also—because why not?—a #hosea Twitter hashtag. Such subtle, circumscribed, or irregular engagements with the biblical book are too widespread and random to comprehensively catalogue—and do not lend themselves to deep analysis.

The most compelling examples of the book of Hosea in pop culture are the ones that appear in a few select mediums—notably, literature, movies, and songs—and that offer sustained, creative attempts at reimagining or retelling the biblical tale. Novels of this ilk include *Redeeming Love* by Francine Rivers (1997); *The Prophet's Wife*, an unfinished novel posthumously published, by Milton Steinberg (2010); *Love in a Broken Vessel* by Mesu Andrews (2013); and *Hosea* by Larry Christenson (2013). There is even an Amish interpretation (Emma 2021), autobiographical exegeses (Davies 2002), and a one-woman play (Campbell 2014). Films include *Amazing Love: The Story of Hosea* (2012, directed by Kevin Downes), *Hosea* (2019, directed by Ryan Daniel Dobson), and *Redeeming Love* (2022, directed by D.J. Caruso, a version of the novel with the screenplay coauthored by Rivers), along with a film ostensibly in production called *Hosea: An Undying Love*. There was apparently an episode of NBC's *Matinee Theater* (1958) devoted to "The Prophet Hosea," but nobody seems to be able to find it. And, finally, songs with sustained commentary include "Hosea's Wife" by Brooke Fraser (2006) and "Hosea" by Andrew Peterson (2008). In what follows, I offer selective analyses in the hopes of giving readers a sense of the major themes and consistent questions generated by Hosea in pop culture.

30.2. Analyzing Hosea in Popular Culture

Some of the pieces of pop culture hew close to the biblical one and make those connections quite clear. In his Foreword, Christenson claims he is writing a "historical novel" whose "background" is found in the biblical book of Hosea (2013: xi). Andrews calls her novel "biblical fiction," which "[pieces] together Scripture's truths with historical supposition" (2013: 10); she sets it in biblical times and focuses on the marriage of Gomer and Hosea in the context of the larger political and military upheavals. The allegory (Hosea's marriage with an unfaithful woman is meant to represent God's relationship with an unfaithful Israel) is there, too. Andrews mentions that Gomer loved as Israel loved, that Hosea's love for Gomer tells a story/serves a purpose, and that, in the end, Gomer returns to love Hosea and accept God into her heart. In Christenson's novel too, we are told, Hosea's "call to prophesy was intertwined with his life" (2013: 207); Hosea reveals that God's command "likened our marriage to the Lord's 'marriage' with Israel, a marriage of harlotry" (375). His whole book, like Andrews's, is a retelling of the biblical story. For its part, the movie *Amazing Love* literally shows a Bible on screen at the beginning, with its page turned to the start of the book of Hosea. Church youth group leader Stuart recounts the biblical story one night around the campfire. The teens in his care initially want to hear a ghost story, but, by the end, they are moved and motivated by what they just heard. At the conclusion, Stuart explains, "The story of Hosea is a picture, a picture of God's amazing love for us." Even the stories that are not set in biblical times, like the novel and movie *Redeeming Love* (California gold rush of 1850) or the movie *Hosea* (modern-day Oklahoma, 2001), retain enough connections to their biblical counterpart for us to recognize the link—and to fill in the blanks. This is often done through the name "Hosea" (as in main character Michael Hosea's last name in *Redeeming Love* or the title of the film *Hosea* itself) or similar plot points.

The quality of the pop-culture iterations varies, and the stories that aren't "faith-based" generally make for better works in their own right. Inspiration by a biblical book, even one compelling as a piece of literature on its own (and not all biblical books are; here's looking at you, Leviticus), is no guarantee that its successors will be good. The camping trip in *Amazing Love* takes place on an obvious sound stage—the trees in the forest are all lit up, at night, somehow—and actor Sean Astin (who starred in *Rudy* and *Lord of the Rings*, and who plays Stuart) looks tired, like he can't quite believe how low his career has sunk. Conversely, the director of *Hosea*, Ryan Daniel Dobson, is "a committed Christian who studied to be a minister, but he does not see his film as a 'Christian film,' at least not in the sense of those who make 'faith based' films. He does not preach. He wants to tell a compelling story that will leave the viewers with 'space' in their minds to think about the story and its implications for their own lives" (McNulty 2020). The opening scenes of Dobson's movie make for great cinematography—shots of worn-down churches, beaten-up trucks, shoes up on electrical lines—and they set the stage for the depressing tale of sex, drugs, alcohol, and abuse that follows. The evangelical agenda in the more overtly Christian works, like *Love in a Broken Vessel* or *Amazing Love*, sometimes proves too heavy of a yoke—and the works that get produced are compromised, if considered by any standards beyond their inspirational or devotional value. (Obviously readers may disagree; one reviewer's endorsement of *Redeeming Love* claims it is "the most powerful work of fiction you will ever read.")

Given that Hosea is such a short biblical book, with such a minor status, it is remarkable how voluminous some of the material is that was inspired by it. Andrews's and Rivers's novels are both over 400 pages. Christenson's tops them both at 533 pages. (It takes over 100 pages in his novel to even get to the betrothal.) This is a lot of space devoted essentially to a familiar-sounding plot: man loves woman, woman strays, heartbreak ensues. There is much, of course, that's missing in the original book, and these kinds of gaps have fascinated those who sought to engage with any of the stories from the Bible. One of the teen campers in the film *Amazing Love* notes this dissonance, interrupting Stuart to say, "Wait a minute, I've read this book and I don't remember any of what you're saying." Stuart admits that the book of Hosea doesn't go into detail regarding how Gomer and Hosea met or the circumstances of their marriage, even though he's telling about it all. Instead, as he says, he's just "coming up with a way that it might have happened, so you get a little more appreciation for the facts"—facts, presumably, being what the biblical text says verbatim.

So the creators of pop culture amend and embellish. Andrews interweaves stories from other biblical books, like Kings and Chronicles, into her story, which she admits exceeds historical data. Christenson similarly expands his scope and scale, describing the rise of, for instance, Assyrian leader Tiglath-Pileser III, the prophesying of Amos, the idolatrous worship of a golden calf from Egypt, the gory details of battle, life in captivity, and even a face-to-face encounter between Hosea and God. Steinberg creates a family for Hosea—a father (who is only implied by the "ben Beeri" of the biblical text, 1:1), a mother, and several siblings, including a "comely" brother (2010: 32) named Iddo who later consorts with Gomer. Rivers adds totally new characters too, like Michael Hosea's grieving and drunken brother-in-law Paul, or the sinister Duke, who first introduces the Gomer character Angel to her life of whoredom by sexually abusing her at a heart-breakingly young age. Rivers also starts each of her chapters with quotations from other pieces of literature, including Keats and Shakespeare, in addition to Proverbs, Matthew, and, of course, Hosea. The movie *Amazing Love* adds the camping trip as a frame, and a teenage girl from a broken home with a biblically sized attitude, to provide an excuse for the telling of the Hosea story.

The pop-culture engagements are especially interested in the characters' backstories. This is one way the creators add to and amplify the bare-bones biblical text. Angel, in *Redeeming Love*, has a pitiable prologue (which is interwoven into the film as flashbacks): her father is married and didn't want her; her mother lives only for her lover and is depressed; eventually the mother dies and she is sold into prostitution at age seven. The book tells us: "You didn't just walk away and say things had never happened. They *had*, and they left deep, raw, gaping wounds. Even when the wounds healed, there were scars" (1997: 254). Gomer in *Broken Vessel* has a similarly difficult childhood. Cate in *Hosea* was abused by one of her dad's friends, which, the movie implies, totally derails her life. It is telling that the novels and films feel the need to explain Gomer's (bad) behavior in some way, blaming it on a broken childhood or abuse. We don't get the same attention to the Hosea characters in the pop-culture depictions (or when we do, it's simply more good behavior—standing up to bullies in Christenson's novel or to a slave-owning father in *Redeeming Love*); apparently his behavior needs no explanation. But a woman having an affair, while married to a prophet of God? This requires some kind of explanation! (Personally, I think the goodness of Hosea is incomprehensible; how on earth did someone turn out so perfect?)

There is room to develop, in these examples of pop culture, the main characters' hobbies, passions, and interests; obviously, these moments of characterization make them seem like real people, not simply flat symbols. Cate, in *Hosea*, likes to take photos; her friend, a gallery owner, encourages her to make a living out of it. Her Hosea (a man named Henry) is an entrepreneur; he is trying to convert an old church into a restaurant called Sanctum. Steinberg's Hosea sings; this is when he comes alive. Hosea in Christenson's novel takes up carpentry to distract himself from the pain of Gomer's betrayal. Hosea of *Amazing Love* makes pottery; the jars are their only means of survival. Gomer of *Love in a Broken Vessel* shows a knack for pottery too. The women, especially, are rounded out, imagined as creative, as having passions and preferences of their own. The biblical text is silent on this score. As *Redeeming Love* (both the novel and the film) goes on, Angel begins to acquire marketable skills, no easy feat. In the beginning of the movie, her (later) husband Michael asks God to send him someone to share life with, specifying that "maybe she likes fishing." There is a scene in the middle of the film of him trying to teach Angel how to fish, which results in her obvious frustration. And then there is a sweet scene at the end, with the two of them together, plus their toddler son, fishing and laughing by the lake.

Yet, at times, the changes can make the stories feel unnecessarily long or repetitive. Hosea, in Christenson's novel, even says so directly (and, hilariously, only halfway through the novel): "Was this to be the endless cycle of our life? Sin, rebuke, tears and promises, reawakening love, another wandering from home and marriage bed, reproach, more tears, more broken promises?" (2013: 226). In Andrews's novel, Hosea leaves on a prophecy mission, Gomer feels angry and abandoned, and Hosea wishes she could just learn to trust him and his God; these plot points play out many times (which, to be fair, they do in the Bible too). Her characters are full of histrionics: Gomer stomps her foot, Hosea throws her over his shoulder, their faces drain of blood. There is a lot of weeping, shouting, grabbing. At one point, a newborn's features are called "rugged and chiseled." Christenson's own characters leap to their feet, gulp down their food, stare, seize, shout, shriek. Perhaps this is what happens when trying to take a relatively short biblical book, whose primary reading is metaphorical, and transform it into a much longer genre or a different medium. Novels are hundreds of pages. Movies are visual and aural. More details, more creative choices, are required to round out the story, to help it stand on its own: physical descriptions of people, additional locales, new characters, plot twists—all not found in the original. As one Amazon reviewer for the movie *Hosea* writes, "It is hard to watch in some places, but it puts meat on the bones of the Biblical story."

Yet, sometimes, even the pop culture remains elliptical. In the film *Hosea*, for instance, as one Amazon reviewer notes, "This is one of those films in which a good amount of meaningful action takes place out of sight of the viewer." We don't, for instance, see the Gomer figure in *Hosea*, Cate, having sex with any of her johns, even though she makes her living as a prostitute. Such moments are simply implied by shots of her stockinged legs, clothing on the floor, money in a purse. The most we get is her climbing onto the lap of a man in his car and unbuttoning her blouse. The relationship these works have to sex is worth considering, since the book of Hosea is, in some ways, a lot about sex, though, of course, it's not explicitly detailed there either. Gomer is presented as a harlot, and we know she had sex with someone because she bears multiple children throughout the course of the short book. Yet many of the instances of pop culture don't want to touch it. (Christenson is an exception; he describes Gomer cavorting with an Egyptian, for instance.) Much is left up to the imagination—much, actually, like the biblical text itself. The Christian "romance" novels (*Redeeming Love* and *Love in a Broken Vessel*) struggle the most here because they have all the markers of a regular romance novel—attraction, conflict, protection, and, ultimately, a happy ending—without any of the explicit sex stuff. The movies *Hosea* and *Redeeming Love* go the furthest, but only in the marital context. *Hosea* implies oral sex between Cate and Henry, but all we see are Cate's reactions; the camera stays on her face and torso. *Redeeming Love* (which is much more graphic than the novel) shows us a few sex scenes between Michael Hosea and Angel (his Gomer). The illicit sex is not portrayed graphically—understandable if one underlying (Christian) message is supposed to be that extramarital sex is verboten.

It is worth paying attention to patterns across these works—when the ways that the pop culture engages and reimagines the biblical texts are consonant. I've argued elsewhere (Gravett 2012) that when pop culture reimagines its source material similarly, we might return to the biblical text to query if there was something in the original that provoked it. These similar ways of filling in gaps can then teach us something of the Bible, as we move back and forth between the old and the new. One striking similarity is that the pop-culture creators imagine their harlot, Gomer, to be incredibly beautiful—though often ugly in personality (fitting, I suppose, since her main personality trait in the Bible is her moral indiscretion). When Christenson's Hosea sees Gomer for the first time, he thinks that "he had never seen someone so utterly a woman. . . . Her beauty struck him as strangely imperfect, yet perfect still" (2013: 34). He notices her eyes, cheeks, hair, breasts, hips, waist. Cate, in the movie *Hosea*, is told that she is "too pretty to be a hooker." Gomer in *Love in a Broken Vessel* is shown to be alluring to men, including Hosea, with her copper curls and sweet smell. Angel, a quintessential blonde, blue-eyed "American" in *Redeeming Love*, is so beautiful that men in the mining town wait outside just to watch her take walks; when she is introduced on stage at the end of the film, the crowd rises to its feet, whooping and applauding. Steinberg develops his Gomer character primarily through lingering physical descriptions and Hosea's intense attraction to her (see also Gravett 2019). The Gomer of *Amazing Love*, we are told by a shopkeeper, is "very beautiful," but she has "a wandering eye." Gomer in *Love in a Broken Vessel* is, like the red-headed cliche, hot-tempered, as well as impatient, self-absorbed, narrow-minded, materialistic, and mercurial. So too is Steinberg's Gomer. Christenson's Gomer can even trace her lineage back to Jezebel, that wicked temptress. She is "given to harsh words and moods that came on suddenly and vanished as quickly" (2013: 84). We are told that Angel, in *Redeeming Love*, feels that "the foulness was inside her, running in her blood" (Rivers 1997: 132). At one point in the movie, we watch a scene where she violently scrubs her naked body with stones in the middle of a river because of how unclean she feels.

Hosea, conversely, as one might expect from the biblical template, is generally rendered steady, strong, and devout. (The more interesting Hoseas are the ones, like Christenson's and Steinberg's, who have insecurities and hot tempers—you know, human traits, like their wives. Christenson's Hosea even strikes Gomer at one point, after calling her a whore.) In the *Redeeming Love* film, Hosea goes to church, he prays, he helps his neighbors, he pats his dog. He is a simple, kind man. Hosea is also routinely depicted (with the exception of Steinberg's Hosea who is "not beautiful" [2013: 31] and insecure about his looks) as handsome, muscular, bearded. Hosea in Christenson's novel is said to be "fine looking" (2013: 14); Gomer deems him "the most handsome man in all Israel!" (57). He uses his "strength and skill in fighting" (p. 16) to protect others against bullies and intruders. (It is a sign of his fall and heartbreak when, later in the novel, "his face had grown the stubble of a beard and his hair hung matted about his ears and neck," 387). Hosea in pop culture is a dreamy hunk from whom it seems preposterous that Gomer would stray.

Of course, nowhere does the biblical book of Hosea comment on Hosea's appearance, or Gomer's—though other important biblical characters are often marked by their physical beauty. The closest we get is Gomer decked out in jewelry in Hos. 2. And nowhere does it condemn her personality—beyond her life of whoredom. But, of course, just as today, I imagine the ancient Near East had its fair share of ugly prostitutes, and personable ones too. Now, some of this may be the pressures and constraints of working in different mediums: Hollywood actors, for instance, tend to be attractive and there is pressure to look a certain way to be in the business. (Even when Angel's mother Mae dies early on of an illness in *Redeeming Love*, the movie's makeup department can't quite disguise how lovely actress Nina Dobrev is.) But in the context of the Bible in pop culture, it's provocative. Why don't we ever get an ugly Gomer? Is it so unfathomable Hosea would or could love someone unattractive? Does this seem just a little *too* unkind of God, to saddle his prophet not only with an unfaithful wife, but a hideous one too? Of course, we might remember who Gomer is supposed to represent in this story, which is not just a tale of marital vicissitudes. Gomer is supposed to be God's people . . . and this story is written by the same.

Love in a Broken Vessel and *Redeeming Love*, perhaps against their authors' intentions, both call attention to how poorly the original biblical book works for anything beyond allegory. In the biblical book, for example, God decides that Hosea should give his children names that are reflective of God's relationship with Israel (e.g., "Lo-Ruhamah," or "not loved"). This works well as a plot device, if part of a metaphorical message, yet less well if it's supposed to be part of a story about a realistic family. The children receive these names in *Love in a Broken Vessel*, but Gomer, and even Hosea, can't bear to call them such terrible things, so they each get palatable nicknames (e.g., Rummy). In fact, pop culture doesn't seem to know what to do with the children in the biblical book at all, even though they are introduced in the very first chapter. In the film *Hosea*, there is only one child, Lucy, and her parentage isn't questioned; she is not meant to represent anything, except how inconvenient a baby's crying is at an important dinner party. A toddler and a pregnant belly only show up at the very end of the two-hour film version of *Redeeming Love*. In Rivers's book, the growing family is part of the epilogue; the children's names are Stephen, Luke, Lydia, and Esther (not the names from the book of Hosea). There are no children shown on screen at all in *Amazing Love*. The children work fine symbolically, in the biblical text, but become difficult to integrate into some of the more "realistic" stories found in pop culture.

These works also provoke some bigger, and more difficult, questions—questions that it turns out the biblical text may also provoke, if we pay attention. One facet that's particularly striking is the representation of how difficult it is to be a woman. The Bible depicts how difficult it is to be a prophet, which the pop culture picks up too: "Prophets lived an uncertain life in Israel. A prophet might be killed or imprisoned or shunned or shouted to silence when he spoke dread words of judgment" (Christenson 2013: 58). But the biblical text remains silent about Gomer's difficulties. These are presented as, at best, a learning opportunity for Hosea. Not so in the pop culture. Gomer of *Love in a Broken Vessel* is consigned to being a mother, but she doesn't feel cut out for the job. Who among mothers hasn't felt this way, not wanting to deal with midnight feeds, incessant crying, and projectile vomit? Gomer reminds us repeatedly that she has no reputable way to earn money. She is entirely at the mercy of men. "Why was she born a woman?" she wonders despairingly (Andrews 2013: 222). She feels stuck married to a man who believes in a god that, for 300 pages, she isn't even convinced exists, and he goes away on prophetic missions for months at a time, leaving her alone, sometimes directly after the birth of a child. As Christenson's Gomer says, "What kind of life could she have with such a man? Never would she know at night if he would return, or if she would receive word that he had been seized by authorities or stoned by the crowd! No woman could live with such uncertainty hanging over every day of her life" (2013: 72). The Gomers are beaten and raped repeatedly. At one point, Andrews (2013: 366) tells us that Gomer "emptied herself of all that was human" in order to survive. This is tough material.

And the difficulties for women don't stop the further from biblical times we get. Angel of *Redeeming Love* has nobody to turn to once her mother dies. She has no means to live on her own. What is there left for her to do but sell her body? At one point, she reflects, "I learned how cruel life can treat a woman alone" (Rivers 1997: 301). Cate, in the *Hosea* film, turns to cutting and prostitution, at the mercy of a volatile, abusive pimp, after a traumatic childhood experience. And this is modern-day Oklahoma, not the Judean desert. How does childhood trauma affect women as they grow up? What dangers, still, lurk for women—at night, in bars, at the hands of men? How are our bodies still not our own? These questions, nascent in the biblical text, unfortunately remain salient today. Readers may gain a newfound sympathy for Gomer by engaging with the pop-culture representations, a sympathy we realize the biblical story is coldly lacking, once returning to it.

Many of the works also call attention to the other women in the lives of Gomer and Hosea. In Christenson's novel, Hosea is especially close with his mother as a child; she is the first one he tells when he hears the words—"the notable Voice" (2013: 4)— of God; she was the one who encouraged him to study the scrolls with his father; she was the one who taught him the stories, songs, and laws of their people; she was the one who "felt God's love for Israel deeply" (28). In Andrews's novel, there are important mentors, notably a midwife named Merav of the brothel Gomer works in early on and, later, the kindly wife of Amos, Yuval, who teaches her to cook and tends to her children. In the movie *Hosea*, we are shown a scene of Cate braiding her friend/fellow prostitute Cristi's hair while they talk about shopping and yoga. When taking a photo of her, Cate tells Cristi, "Hold that smile, my darling." We are shown many interactions between Angel and other women throughout both the *Redeeming Love* novel and movie: fellow prostitutes, new friends, students at a school she opens called House of Magdalena! Like Christenson's Gomer, Angel has a mother in the book and the movie, and, though she dies early on, she is still a significant presence in her life, with memories and stories about her woven throughout.

Where are the other women in the biblical book of Hosea? Does Gomer have a mother? Who is helping her to birth and raise children? Who is watching all the children when she goes a'whoring? Where is the village? These omissions, unnoticeable to me when reading the biblical book on its own, seem glaringly obvious once I go back and reread.

Another difficult question, especially for *Redeeming Love* and *Hosea*, which don't fully commit to being an allegorical commentary on the relationship between God and Israel, is the rationale for saddling the Hosea character with such a difficult marriage at all. In *Redeeming Love*, Michael, when realizing Angel (at the time, the best-looking and highest-paid prostitute in the town) will be the one for him, chuckles: "Next time I pray to God for a woman to share my life, I'm gonna be a lot more specific." It grows less funny as the movie progresses and she continues to thwart and betray his love. We read, "He wept: he cursed her. He had loved her, and she betrayed him. She might as well have stuck a knife in his guts and twisted it" (Rivers 1997: 196). There is a sad scene in the film of him crying into his arms in the barn. Angel even asks, "Do you ever get the feeling God is playing some horrible joke on you?" (283). It does seem like God's hands are in this marital arrangement—Michael certainly thinks so—but we might wonder, as Michael did, "Why are you doing this to me, Lord?" (146). Without the analogy of God and Israel, why is this happening to him? Even encouraged or ordained by God, why should *he* have to suffer so, all to prove a point to . . . whom exactly? In Andrews's novel, God comes off as capricious and cruel. At one point, a character even asks, "Is Yahweh for us or against us?" (2013: 351). It's not always clear in these pop-culture reimaginings.

The biggest preoccupation, of both the biblical text and pop culture, is love. In the foreword to his novel, Christenson calls Hosea's marriage to Gomer "one of the most profound and moving portrayals of marriage in the entire Bible":

> Successful marriage is not a business of perfect people living perfectly by perfect principles. Rather, marriage is a place in which very imperfect people often hurt and humiliate one another, yet find the grace to extend forgiveness to one another, and so allow the redemptive power of God to transform their marriage. (2013: xi)

This is an interesting take, by a male author, but somewhat unnerving to me as a woman reader. The biblical account does involve perfection, but only on the side of Hosea, who never errs, despite his trials and suffering, and, of course, on the side of the (male) God. Gomer is the one who hurts; Gomer is the one who needs forgiveness. In Fraser's song, we hear, "We are Hosea's wife / We are squandering this Life," and in Peterson's, he sings, as Gomer, "Hosea, my heart is a stone." God is the teacher in these instances, Hosea the husband is the student, Gomer the wife is the subject, the lesson. Is this what we want from love? There is a total imbalance here—not to mention an instrumentalization of the woman—which may work for a Christian audience who thinks the husband should be the head of the marriage, like Christ is the head of the church, but is hard to swallow for anyone interested in domestic or marital parity.

The pop-culture iterations cause us to ponder: What is love? At the start of the film *Hosea*, the main characters, as kids, describe love as feeling like pop rocks in your chest or like you've been running super fast, but you never get tired. This is good writing, even though the child actors deliver the lines a bit woodenly, but it doesn't tell us much about love's content, basis, or behaviors. In Christenson's novel, we read that "from the moment [Hosea] set eyes on Gomer, she became more to him than just another woman"

(2013: 46). Why? (Later, they share many in-depth, intimate conversations—Gomer says, for instance, "I know more about you than friends I have known all my life. . . . And I want to know more" [56]—but these conversations haven't yet occurred when he first sees her.) When Michael assures Angel he loves her, as he often does throughout the film *Redeeming Love*, she replies: "You don't have any idea who and what I am other than what you've created in your own mind" (Rivers 1997: 150). What is the foundation or justification of this love?

Of course, the physical beauty I mentioned above plays a role here; it is mostly "love" at first sight for the Hoseas and Gomers. Michael Hosea is drawn to Angel when he sees her walking on the street. As in Steinberg, Hosea in *Love in a Broken Vessel* claims to love his Gomer, but the only time he seems stirred is when he remembers her as an innocent girl and when her physicality (curls, smell, figure) arouses him. He clearly doesn't appreciate her temper, her moods, or her impatience with the children. Of course, the inexplicability is part of the point, especially when it represents Jesus's unearned love for his people to a Christian audience.

The Hoseas display a constancy and a commitment, which represents their love; eventually Gomer returns (to her husband, to God) too. Despite the mistreatment, despite the heartbreak, the Hoseas can't quite give up on the Gomers. Christenson's Hosea still pines for Gomer, even after he puts her out of the house; he does not want to remarry and feels foolish for it. The songs, in particular, emphasize the steadfastness of love. Shane & Shane open theirs with the lyrics, "Come let us return" and, later, "Come let us return to the Lord." And Peterson's Gomer sings, "You set me free with that ball and chain / Hosea, I threw away the key / I'll never leave / Hosea, Hosea." Of course, this unwavering commitment makes perfect sense in the biblical metaphor of God's love for Israel (God never falters, but Israel does), but it is not always sensical in the pop-culture representations. In the film *Hosea*, Henry loves Cate from the time they are kids; it is the same with the Hosea in Andrews's novel. Nowadays, if someone still loved a person they knew when they were ten, after a decade of not seeing one another, I'm not sure we would view it positively, as a symbol of mature love and a healthy relationship.

The inclusion of a pimp character in the film *Hosea* (or, for that matter, the various brothel owners in the novel *Redeeming Love*) is masterful along these lines. We must ask, what role does he play from the biblical text? Where's the inspiration or justification? He didn't need to be included, but he is. Why? While God in the metaphorical reading of the biblical book is a loving, reliable husband who is heartbroken by his bride Israel's infidelity, to Gomer, in this same story, God is basically a pimp—setting her up with multiple men she pursues for material gain. In Andrews's book, surely against her own intentions, God seems as abusive and unpredictable as the pimp in *Hosea* (e.g., showering her with gifts, expressing love and affection, withdrawing it, threatening or even enacting physical violence). In all the reimaginings, Hosea is a kind man and a good husband to Gomer; God is not. I am hardly the first to have noticed the problems with the marriage metaphor in relation to domestic violence (e.g., Weems 1995). I am also, obviously, not the first to comment on the patriarchal construction of marriage, more generally, in the Hebrew Bible. Readers can decide for themselves to what extent

450 EMILY O. GRAVETT

we've moved away from this construction today (e.g., men still ask fathers for permission to marry their daughters, fathers still give women away at weddings, women still take their husbands' last names after marriage, etc.). How much distance is there, really, from the biblical text? The presence of a pimp in pop culture provokes these questions, to fruitful—though perhaps disturbing—ends.

30.3. CONCLUSION

Pop culture has steadily returned to the biblical book of Hosea, just as Hosea and Gomer returned to one another . . . and to God. In many cases, the pop culture that engages Hosea seems less to represent the grappling of its creators with the biblical story (as we see in so much other biblical reception, such as the book of Job) than the story simply being used as a springboard to tell the tale (e.g., Jesus's love for us all, ideal marriage, redemption of those who are broken) that the creators want to tell. Yet there are many instances in which movies and novels, in particular, provide commentary on and illumination of the biblical story through the way they reimagine and retell the biblical text. Aspects of the biblical story may go unnoticed on their own, but pop culture can shed new light on them, homing in on omissions, questions, or fissures, and laying them bare in their new ways of handling them. In particular, Gomer gets further or redeveloped in contemporary mediums—with a backstory, a family, friends, a personality, beauty. Interestingly enough, we may gain newfound understanding, even sympathy, for her character after interacting with the pop culture. By making their inspiration clear and by creating links to the biblical text, these various instances of pop culture open the possibility of comparison—and of a dynamic dialogue between the two worlds.

REFERENCES

Andrews, Mesu. 2013. *Love in a Broken Vessel: A Novel*. Grand Rapids, MI: Revell.
Breed, Brennan. 2014. *Nomadic Text: A Theory of Biblical Reception History*. Bloomington: Indiana University Press.
Campbell, Geri. 2014. *The Story of Gomer from the Book of Hosea*. Self-published.
Chattaway, Peter T. 2022. "Hosea at the Movies: Three Films and a TV Episode from the 20th Century," *Patheos*. Online: https://www.patheos.com/blogs/filmchat/2022/01/hosea-at-the-movies-three-films-and-a-tv-episode-from-the-20th-century.html
Christenson, Larry. 2013. *Hosea: A Novel*. Bloomington, MN: Bethany.
Corse, Sarah. 2017. "Two by Two: Heteronormativity and the Noah Story for Children." *Sociological Studies of Youth and Children* 23: 225–41.
Davies, Philip R. 2002. *First Person: Essays in Biblical Autobiography*. The Biblical Seminar 81. New York: Sheffield Academic.
Emma, Ashley. 2021. *Hosea and Gomer's Amish Secret*. The Amish Bible Story Series Book 2. Self-published.

Gravett, Emily O. 2012. "Biblical Responses: Past and Present Retellings of the Enigmatic Mrs. Job." *BibInt* 20: 97–125.

Gravett, Emily O. 2019. "The Risk of Retelling: Gomer-bat-Diblaim, Biblical Retrieval, and the Male Gaze in The Prophet's Wife." *BibInt* 27: 436–61.

McNulty, Ed. 2020. "Hosea (2019)." *Visual Parables*. Online: https://readthespirit.com/visual-parables/hosea-2019/. Accessed June 27, 2022.

Polaski, Donald. 2005. "Hosea Meets Hank Williams." In Mark Roncace and Patrick Gray, eds., *Teaching the Bible: Practical Strategies for Classroom Instruction*. Atlanta: SBL, 181–82.

Rivers, Francine. 1997. *Redeeming Love: A Novel*. Sisters, OR: Multnomah.

Steinberg, Milton. 2010. *The Prophet's Wife*. Springfield, NJ: Behrman House.

Storey, John. 2006. *Cultural Theory and Popular Culture: An Introduction*. 4th ed. Athens: University of Georgia Press.

Weems, Renita J. 1995. *Battered Love: Marriage, Sex, and Violence in the Hebrew Prophets*. Minneapolis: Fortress.

CHAPTER 31

THE GHOST OF HOSEA IN AFRICAN AMERICAN INTERPRETATION

AARON D. DORSEY

AFRICAN American interpretations of the book of Hosea are as wide-ranging and diverse as the book itself. Just as Hosea captures both the violence of judgment and the hope for redemption so has African American interpretation turned to Hosea both as a source for constructing identity after devastation and as a text that requires theological suspicion, if not ethical rejection. African American interpretation of Hosea focuses its attention on several themes: identity, the marriage metaphor, and ecology. This essay will give considerable attention to the work of Renita Weems, as her study of the marriage metaphors in Hosea, Jeremiah, and Ezekiel provides the most substantial examination of Hosea from an African American/womanist perspective. The marriage metaphor then also prompts direct discussion of hermeneutical ethics by womanist scholars. I will also follow a literary allusion to the book of Hosea by the African American novelist Toni Morrison. The allusion to Hosea creates the opportunity for new reflections on the book concerning appropriation, traumatic memory, and redemption.

The diversity of African American interpretation is related to the differing hermeneutical priorities of its interpreters. The term "African American interpretation" will be used here as an umbrella term for a variety of hermeneutical projects. The two most discernable trends are African American liberation hermeneutics and black feminist/womanist hermeneutics. These two trends, while discernably different, overlap and intersect in complex ways. Interpreters in the African American liberation tradition first prioritized race as a critical lens for biblical interpretation. These interpreters understand liberation as the dominant thread of the Hebrew Bible and the New Testament. As such, liberation is also the lens through which the Bible should be interpreted by asking the question, "How does a particular text contribute to the liberation of African Americans particularly, and of African descendants both in Africa and in the diaspora generally?" Black feminist and womanist interpretation is likewise concerned with racial liberation, but by centering the lives of black women it also considers how texts relate to gender, class, and sexuality. Renita Weems understands womanist interpretation as a response to the universalizing tendencies of white Western women, who sometimes write as if their experience is definitive for all women, and black male liberationists, who may speak as if the experience of black men is definitive for all people of color (Weems 2015: 46–47). Neither captures the unique class and gender experience of black women. However, these are not strict distinctions, but trends that continue to evolve in dialogue with one another and with other interpretive traditions. Generally, while the relevance of historical-critical methods has been debated, African American interpretation is not committed to any particular methodology. Rather, interpreters avail themselves of any method or theoretical approach that helps to either elucidate the liberatory potential of a biblical text (Bridgeman 2016: 483) or uncover oppressive ideologies. Black feminist/womanist interpreters emphasize the ethics of interpretation, first by seeking to expose hidden ideologies in biblical texts and then reserving the right to creatively interact with and even reject theologies and ideologies that they discern as harmful to the well-being of black women and other vulnerable communities.

The priorities of African American interpretation not only guide the interpretive act but also influence the texts that interpreters select for study. To a degree, this seems to have contributed to greater focus on the Hebrew prophets who more explicitly critique social injustice, such as Amos, Micah, Zephaniah, and Isaiah (Hobson 2012: 21–22). In contrast, it may seem that the book of Hosea focuses more on religious malpractice than social justice, though Alice Keefe (2001) and Gale Yee (2001) have troubled the idea of a religious/material-social dichotomy in the Hebrew prophets and have argued that Hosea's religious concerns are also critiques of unjust social and economic practices by the Israelite elite. African American liberationist interpreters have been drawn to Hosea's rhetoric concerning Egypt and made some comments on the sexual politics of Hosea. Here, Hosea tends to be interpreted in relation to a wide variety of other biblical texts in the context of each author's broader argument. The most significant attention to Hosea has been made by black feminist and womanist scholars whose concern for black women has guided their efforts to the marriage metaphor of Hos. 1–3. For similar reasons, they have also focused on Hosea's parent-child metaphor and Hosea's ecological vision.

31.1. African American Identity

Hosea occupies a critical role in the African American self-understanding as a people who once were not a people. Since the Maafa, a Swahili term that is used to designate the death and enslavement of African peoples during and since the Atlantic slave trade, African Americans have experienced a violent rupture of identity. White slave traders and owners deliberately disrupted African identities, making it either practically impossible or illegal for enslaved Africans to maintain a full connection to their cultural pasts.

Enslaved Africans and their African American descendants, while maintaining some characteristics of African cultural traditions and syncretizing them with Euro-American culture in unique and varied ways, have generally related to Gomer's third child, "Not-my-people" and Paul's quotation of Hosea in Rom. 9:25, "Those who were not my people I will call my people." Lo-Ammi (Not-my-people) resonates with an African American sense of having lost peoplehood, of having been violently displaced from the sources of our African identities. In "The Ethiopian Manifesto," Robert Alexander Young quotes Rom. 9:25 to affirm for African Americans that "God will make them into a people" again (Smith 2000: 86–87). Likewise, in her analysis of Toni Morrison's *Beloved*, Danille Taylor-Guthrie writes that Rom. 9:25 is often seen by African Americans as the route to their inclusion in Paul's promise (Taylor-Guthrie 1995: 120). Lo-Ammi's transformation from "Not-my-people" to "my-people" in Hos. 2:25 (Eng. 2:23) captures the hope of African Americans to be restored to a new peoplehood after devastation.

Hosea's references to Egypt provide a different source for African American identity. White supremacist biblical scholarship had diminished the presence of Africans in the Bible by refusing to read Egypt and Ethiopia/Cush as African or by reading African peoples in the Bible pejoratively. In *Stony the Road We Trod*, Charles B. Copher responded to the first issue by arguing for the presence of black peoples in the biblical texts during each era of biblical history. Copher includes Hosea's references to Egypt in 7:11ff, 9:3ff, 11:1, 12:10, and 14 (Eng. 12:9 and 13) as examples of African presence and Israelite interaction with African nations (Copher 1991: 159). In the same volume, Randall C. Bailey argues that, opposed to views that African nations were negatively imagined in ancient Israel, the ancient Israelites considered African nations and peoples as militarily strong, wealthy, wise, and as a norm for valuation. Israelites desired to be strong, wealthy, and wise like the nations of Africa. Bailey quotes Hos. 7:11 along with portions of Isaiah and Ezekiel to argue that the prophets had to consistently warn the Israelites against relying on Egypt precisely because they revered the Egyptians (Bailey 1991: 173).

However, the relationship between African Americans and Egypt remains complex. Black feminist/womanist scholar Wilda C. Gafney has troubled the association between African Americans, the Israelites, Judahites, and Egypt, noting the tendency to "lift up Egypt as the prototypical African (and wider world) civilization and culture . . . and then read ourselves as Israel in the Exodus narrative relinquishing the burden of blackness" (Gafney 2007: 61). Gafney does not necessarily oppose the association between African Americans and Egypt, or African American identification with the enslaved Israelites, but uses this as an example of how blackness must account for its position as both oppressor and oppressed. African American association with Egypt cannot disown Egypt as an enslaving and imperial power. An allusion to Hosea in "Prison, Where Is Thy Victory" by Huey P. Newton, one of the cofounders of the Black Panther Party, may make a similar caution. Brian P. Sowers (2020: 43) provides an intertextual reading of Newton, Paul, and Hosea by tracing the allusion to Hos. 13:14b, "O Death, where are your plagues? O Sheol, where is your destruction?" through Paul in 1 Cor. 15:55, "Where, O death, is your victory? Where, O death, is your sting?" He argues that Hosea's general warning against becoming like Egypt is similar to Newton's concern that Americans, including African Americans, may be hegemonically motivated to adopt the capitalistic and carceral logic of the United States. Sower's reading of Hosea overly blends Hosea's particular concerns with that of the Hebrew prophets generally. Hosea is not the source for the warning against becoming like Egypt, but rather the book discourages Israelite reliance on Egypt's military and economy. However, the potential allusion to a complicated relationship with Egypt and its imperialism remains intriguing and does further illustrate some of the challenges Hosea presents in respect to African American identity.

In a chapter of *The Africana Bible*, Wallace Hartsfield (2010) takes a different approach to the relationship between Hosea and African American identity. Hartsfield questions Hosea's vision of a pure Yahwistic faith in ancient Israel, noting that this was likely more an idealized history. In actuality, the faith of ancient Israel was always syncretistic. Similarly, Hartsfield writes that the Black Church is a syncretistic environment, the "unplanned offspring of African traditional religions and Christianity." The idea of a singular, unitary, and purely Christian Black Church is a myth not unlike Hosea's imagination of Israel's past. Additionally, Hartsfield relates the desire to worship Baal to the desire for prosperity in African American churches. He recognizes that the ancient Israelites were likely motivated to worship Baal, a rain and fertility deity, for very practical reasons—to survive in a harsh environment. Similarly, the African American desire for prosperity is not frivolous, but a natural consequence of the desire to survive in the United States (Hartsfield 2010: 167). Hartsfield does not draw an ethical lesson from these comparisons such as advocating for the Black Church to become more pure or for Black Christians to forsake prosperity, but merely notes these connections. He highlights the parallels between the conversations happening within the African American community and in ancient Israel, though we only have direct access to Hosea's side of the dialogue.

Hosea, then, has been appealed to as a theological ground for the creation of African American peoplehood, referred to as an example of African presence in the Bible, and engaged as a critical lens through which to view the debates concerning African American religious identity.

31.2. HOSEA'S METAPHORS

The marriage metaphor in Hos. 1–3 has been a major focus for African American, and almost exclusively black feminist/ womanist, interpreters. In these chapters, Hosea and Gomer's marriage is metaphorically related to Yhwh and Israel's marriage. This constitutes one of the metaphorical relations in these chapters, as the marriage of Yhwh and Israel may also function as a metaphor itself for the covenantal relationship established at Sinai/ Horeb. Hosea is instructed by Yhwh to marry a woman of prostitution (זנה) as a metaphorical parallel for how Israel had prostituted away from Yhwh (Hos. 1:2). The Hebrew root, z- n- h (זנה) is variously translated, but James Nogalski (2011: 39) has suggested that "the Hebrew root znh originally referred to any 'unregulated, illicit sexual behavior between man and woman.'" Hosea and Gomer then have three children, Jezreel, Lo-Ruhamah (Not-shown-compassion), and Lo-Ammi (Not-my-people), whose names are also metaphorical prophetic signs. Hosea 2:4–15 (Eng. 2:2–13) continues with the metaphor of Yhwh and Israel, in which Yhwh/the prophet accuse the woman of prostitution, threaten to strip her, kill her with thirst, hedge her in, recall sustaining physical goods, and expose her nakedness to her lovers, which should be understood as making her vulnerable to rape. Then, in a sudden change, Yhwh/the prophet promise to woo her, betroth her, and restore her children (Hos. 2:16–25 [Eng. 2:14–23]). Hosea 3 narrates another metaphorical marriage and reconciliation, either repeating/reinterpreting the prior verses or referencing a different marriage altogether.

In African American interpretation, this collection of metaphors, often termed the "marriage metaphor," has been analyzed most comprehensively by womanist biblical scholar Renita Weems. Beginning with her dissertation, Weems has written extensively on the marriage metaphor in Hosea, Jeremiah, and Ezekiel. Her first publication on the topic, "Gomer: Victim of Violence or Victim of Metaphor" (1989) recognizes that the metaphor describes Israel and God's relationship in a way that other metaphors cannot, but questions whether the metaphor is beneficial given its embedded patriarchy. The metaphor does portray the relationship between Yhwh as Israel as one of intimacy and it is able to narrativize Israel's history from "covenant (marriage) to apostasy (adultery) to punishment/judgment (sexual violence) to covenant renewal (reconciliation)," but in justifying God's abusive behavior the metaphor risks justifying a husband's abuse of his wife (Weems 1989: 99–100). Drawing on metaphor theory, she responds that readers must emphasize the dissimilarity embedded in the metaphor by questioning a one-to-one correlation with God and maintain multiple metaphors for God's relationship to God's people.

In a more personal and reflective book, *I Asked for Intimacy*, Weems (1993) returns again to the marriage metaphor. This book provides a unique view into how Weems struggled with Hosea, not first as a scholar, but as a fully invested African American woman and minister who knew and supported women in abusive relationships with their husbands. She recounts how battered women would lie to her about the abuse until it all came spilling out, but then how these women painfully pulled away from her when they returned to their abusers. Weems acknowledges that the challenge of interpreting Hosea is theological, worrying that "to lambaste Hosea was to lambaste God" (Weems 1993: 75). However, even if Gomer was only a victim of metaphorical violence, Weems concludes that "metaphors can be as harmful as violence itself . . . language from the pulpit that ignores women and silences the feminine cripples" (p. 78).

In her final work on the marriage metaphor, *Battered Love*, Weems (1995) offers what has remained a foundational interpretation of the marriage metaphor for African American interpreters and a classic in womanist interpretation generally. Attentive to literary criticism, Weems writes that all language about God is metaphorical, meaning it gestures and points toward God rather than describing God in literal terms. However, successful metaphors become incredibly challenging to disentangle once they have taken hold. She argues that Hosea's metaphor may have been particularly successful for many reasons: it is emotive, it makes Israelite history legible, and it may have been reinforced when Hosea's prophetic perspective was proven true by the Assyrian destruction of Israel in 722 BCE. The pathos of the metaphor plays on both male fantasy and fear, while also absolving men of any guilt for battering their wives. As such, it justifies violence and naturalizes the patriarchal ideological framework for readers. While the metaphor functions to make Israel's history coherent, it is also successful because it allows the Israelites to address God's incoherency. It explains God's silence and the "unpredictably abusing side of God" as the Israelites experienced it (Weems 1995: 71). She writes that while contemporary readers struggle with the image of an abusing God, but "to Israel it was a portrait that was too honest and consistent with reality as they knew to deny it" (83). Although Weems relates the metaphor to Israelite history and the Israelite exile, she takes a literary approach to read all of Hos. 2 synchronically, as if both the judgment and the reconciliation oracles were composed prior to the exile of Israel. This limits some of her reflections on how the metaphor functioned historically. For example, she considers the salvation portions to be motivation for idolatrous Israelite men to repent. Her literary approach also resulted in the argument that the salvation offered in Hosea makes Hosea/Yhwh's threats seem hollow and like the emotional overreactions of a hurt husband (51, 77, 92). It is difficult to reconcile the punishments both as hollow threats and as an actual depiction of Israel's suffering, which Weems argues likely cemented the metaphor in Israelite tradition, when one takes a synchronic approach in this manner.

After interpreting the place of the metaphor in Israel's history, Weems turns to consider how metaphors affect contemporary readers. She acknowledges that, at least while reading, audiences pretend agreement with authors. In this way, the metaphor affects even those who reject it. Until the argument is completed, readers must make the writing sensible by pretending to agree, even if the argument is absurd. Additionally, metaphors educate audiences and train their imaginations. Bailey (1995) has also written on the use of sex in the Hebrew Bible to train the imagination, particularly the use of sexual deviance to create stereotypes of foreigners. In the case of Hosea, the marriage metaphor teaches audiences that violence against women is not only acceptable, but "theologically defensible" (Weems 1995: 110). Hartsfield (2010: 167) echoes this concern, writing that because God's pathos becomes a pathology of abuse, the metaphor is risky. It can potentially interact with patriarchy in black communities, worsening the occurrences of black men seeking to remedy the shame they feel in broader society by reasserting their honor through dominating black women. Honor is exactly what Weems defines as the central issue in the marriage metaphor. While the metaphor may seem to reflect Hosea/ God's wounded emotion, it is more likely that it is Hosea/God's wounded pride that they attempt to reassert through violence. Ultimately, Weems rejects the metaphor insofar as it is used to conceptualize punishment and judgment, declaring it useless for such a theological question and that for her, "there is no similarity between battering husbands and avenging gods" (Weems 1995: 106).

Drawing and developing on Weem's interpretation, womanist biblical scholar Valerie Bridgeman expands on the themes of motherhood and the use of children in Hosea and the prophets. While women are presented in multiple ways by the Hebrew prophets—as virtuous mothers, adulterous women, and sometimes as daughters needing protection—Bridgeman argues that even the virtuous mother is defined by the needs of patriarchy (Bridgeman 2016: 485). The prophets' definition of the virtuous mother relates to a mother's ability to maintain a household and produce male heirs for the male head of household. It follows that even when the prophets present mothers in positive terms, such as Yhwh being a mother to Israel (Weems 1995: 22), this positive image still requires ideological interrogation. Considering the effect of Hosea's metaphors on children, Bridgeman argues that children in Hosea are used in a similar manner as women: they are meant "metaphorically to denigrate and berate men in power and accuse said men of being fickle or erratic" (Bridgeman 2016: 487). In Hosea and in the prophets generally, Bridgeman finds that the death and suffering of women and children are both considered collateral to male warfare, perhaps an indication of the immediate consequences of the ideologies that sustain the marriage and parent-child metaphor.

Despite the patriarchy-inflected nature of Hosea's vision for motherhood, black feminist/womanist scholars still find resources to encourage readers. Weems (1995: 30 n.126) interprets the parent of Hos. 11 as a mother, metaphorically linking Yhwh to femininity and motherhood. As an example of maintaining and making clear the presence of the feminine in the Hebrew Bible, Gafney reads the Hebrew verb r-ch-m as "mother-love" because the verb is related to the Hebrew noun for womb. Rather than translating Lo-Ruhamah as "Not-shown-compassion," Gafney translates her name, "No Mother-Love" (2010: 50). She translates Yhwh's reconciling betrothal with Israel in 2:21 (Eng. 2:19) as "I will betroth you . . . in mother-love." Gafney (2007: 64) also suggests that Hosea can speak to the one who "feel[s] like a motherless child" as Hos. 14:4b (Eng. 14:3b) says that in God "the orphan finds mother-love." Gafney's translations trouble an easy association between Yhwh and masculinity that is often dominant in the book of Hosea and the Hebrew Bible.

Hosea's metaphors are critically approached by black feminist and womanist scholars. Their harmful ideologies are directly confronted, but there remains a desire to find a healing and liberatory word for readers, especially for black women.

31.3. ECOLOGY

While the ecological implications of Hosea have yet to be fully developed in African American biblical interpretation, it has been mentioned in ways that deserve attention. Weems (1995: 51, 105) emphasizes that in Hos. 2, the restored marriage of Yhwh and Israel includes creation as an audience and beneficiary. The metaphor extends to the entire ecological order and ties together morality/sexuality, politics, and ecology. Weems bases her interpretation on the betrothal in Hos. 2:21–22 (Eng. 2:19–20) but does not consider the preceding verse. In Hos. 2:20 (Eng. 2:18), Yhwh makes a covenant, but not between Yhwh's self and the Israelites. Yhwh makes a covenant between Israel and "the wild animals, the birds of the air, and the creeping things of the ground." Yhwh goes on to declare, "I will answer the heavens, and they shall answer the earth, and the earth shall answer the grain, the wine, and the oil, and they shall answer Jezreel" (Hos. 2:23b–24 [Eng. 2:21b–22]). The full vision of Israelite restoration includes the establishment of a covenant among people, land, and animals in reciprocal relationships defined by answering and attending to one another.

This vision of covenant with the ecological order is pertinent in multiple manners. In the current context of global climate change and a mass extinction crisis, readers of Hosea must ask themselves about the nature of their covenant with the land and all of the creatures that live in relationship with the land. Further, African American interpreters, and any displaced or diasporic people, might consider how their respective identities can be reconstituted in relationship to the land. After surveying the Christian theological motivations involved in colonization and the violent identity-rupturing displacement of Africans and indigenous people, Willie Jennings (2010, 2018) offers a practice for the cultivation of new forms of identity and belonging. Jennings suggests that people find dirt, and dig their hands into it, finding and realizing again their relationship to the earth. He shows how racial identity is the product of white racial imagination and displacement—in the colonial era, whiteness itself replaced the ground on which identity was built. People were no longer defined by the rivers, mountains, valleys, plant and animal life that they knew, but by their relation to whiteness. Jennings roots the practice in his mother's garden as an inherited legacy from his enslaved-African ancestors who learned to live closely with and to love foreign land. Such a practice, digging one's hands into the dirt, is also resonant with Hosea's covenant between Israel and the land. To reconnect with the land, to locate one's identity in relationship to the land, is not to be understood as idealistic. I would argue that this also means feeling the tortured history realized upon it. For African Americans, this means that the land we now call home also bears the history of indigenous genocide, displacement, and subjugation, as well as the histories of other racialized, minoritized, and oppressed people groups who have left their homelands, willingly or otherwise. The land itself binds together the life and histories of all who live with it. And yet, the covenant in Hos. 2 may gesture to the realization that the restoration of a people includes and relies on the restoration of reciprocal loving relationships with one another and with the whole ecology of creation.

31.4. HERMENEUTICS AND ETHICS

African American scholarship on the book of Hosea has contributed directly to the development and articulation of African American biblical hermeneutics. In African

American biblical scholarship, hermeneutics is considered holistically, as a theory about how interpretation occurs as well as a set of practices and dispositions that facilitate reading. As mentioned above, African American hermeneutics tends to evade identifying itself with a singular theoretical approach, and this is true in terms of the hermeneutical theoretical frameworks that African Americans use. They show a nimble dexterity in their use of multiple classical theoretical approaches, and one can easily find the works of Schleiermacher, Dilthey, Gadamer, Ricoeur, Derrida, and so on in their bibliographies. The guide for using differing theoretical frameworks, as well as differing biblical methodologies, is a set of evolving hermeneutical priorities and practices. African American interpreters prioritize relevance to black communities and seek readings that contribute to the flourishing of black peoples (Smith 2017: 16–20). This priority requires African American interpreters to develop liberation-oriented practices of reading alongside a vision of biblical authority that permits dialogue with the text rather than strict submission (Parker 2021).

Weems (1995: 99–101) describes her reading practice as a "dual-hermeneutic." Her reading of the marriage metaphors in Hosea, Jeremiah, and Ezekiel both required and developed this approach. A dual-hermeneutic approaches biblical texts with reverence, but also with suspicion and a willingness to reject harmful ideologies. The structure of *Battered Love* mirrors her hermeneutical approach, as it first considers what can be learned from these metaphors, but then analyzes the violent effects the metaphors have on audiences, ancient and modern. However, her approach differs slightly from what is understood as a hermeneutics of suspicion. It is more so a hermeneutics of defense. Weems writes that "to read is to be prepared in many respects to fight defensively" (104). A reader must develop a posture that notices and reacts to a text's ability to pull the reader into its logics, affects, and ideologies. Weems refers to this as the way readers are "tempted by writers to read against their own interest" (104).

Any text can "tempt" readers against themselves, but assumptions of the Bible's authority and ability to reveal the nature of God increase the likelihood that a reader would not approach it defensively. The tendency of readers to approach biblical texts without suspicion is precisely what makes Hosea a critical book in African American hermeneutics. Weems later argues it is essential to introduce biblical readers to texts that are more obviously troubling or problematic in order to jump start the reader's critical interaction with the Bible (Weems 2015: 54). The recoil, perhaps even disgust, that a reader may experience in response to the image of a sexually abusive God is actually a foundation for womanist and African American interpretation. It begins the process whereby a reader can consider how a text functions in community and moves the reader to claim power and authority to make ethical decisions in relation to the Bible (Bridgeman 2016: 186–87). Guided by love for their communities, interpreters ask what promotes the well-being of their community, or what threatens to harm the community if it is unaddressed and tacitly accepted. By beginning with a wounding text and building an approach from there, African American biblical scholars construct a hermeneutic that is resilient, critical, and loving.

31.5. Appropriation and Memory

There are two epigraphs at the beginning of Toni Morrison's (2004) novel, *Beloved*: "Sixty Million and more" and "I will call them my people, which were not my people; and her beloved, which was not beloved. Romans 9:25." The first is a reference to the over sixty million enslaved Africans who died during the middle passage between Africa, North America, South America, and the Caribbean Islands. The second refers to Paul's quotation of Hos. 2:25 (Eng. 2:23). *Beloved* follows Sethe, a free African American woman. Traumatized by white slavery and frightened by the white people entering her African American community, Sethe attempts to kill her children to save them from white violence and does kill her daughter, Beloved, by drowning her in a river. Years later Beloved returns from the river in which she was drowned. She returns not only as Sethe's deceased daughter, but as an embodiment of the sixty million who drowned during the middle passage (Broad 1994: 191). *Beloved* explores questions of traumatic memory, identity, redemption, and imagining a future for African Americans without resolving many of the conflicts and incoherencies within and between these topics. Due to the epigraph, these topics are intertextually related to the book of Hosea. Intertextual readings of the main narrative of *Beloved* and these epigraphs have created new directions for considering the relationship between Hosea and African Americans. The allusion to Hosea particularly prompts questions of appropriation and questions concerning traumatic memory and identity.

In his writing on *Beloved*, Robert L. Broad (1994) believes that the Rom. 9:25 epigraph contributes to the theme of appropriation in the novel. Broad writes that Paul de-historicizes Hosea in order to use Hosea for his own purposes, the inclusion of the Gentiles. He interprets Paul's quote of Hosea and his following quote of Isaiah in Rom. 9:27 as supersessionistic, replacing the Jewish people with Gentiles as the new chosen people. He writes, "What we see is a writer working to oppress people by using their own writers and historians against them" (Broad 1994: 194–95). Whether one agrees with Broad's interpretation of Rom. 9 or not, though even those who contend against such a reading do so realizing the prominent history of supersessionistic interpretation of Rom. 9–11 (Ticciati 2017: 501–8), it is agreeable that Paul is using the text of Hosea in an unpredictable way. Rather than Hosea's restoration referring to Israelites who have suffered destruction and exile, Paul uses Hosea to advocate for the inclusion of Gentiles, perhaps even the figurative enemies of the Israelites. Broad then compares Paul's appropriation of Hosea to the appropriation of black stories by white people in *Beloved*. He argues that just as Paul used Hosea against Hosea's own, so do the white characters in *Beloved* and white persons outside of the novel (mis)appropriate black stories for their own benefit and often against the benefit of the African American originators. Danille Taylor-Guthrie (1995: 121–22) also regards the distortion of black stories by white institutions and characters as a prominent feature of *Beloved*. She does, however, interpret Paul more positively as expanding Jewish identity to included Gentiles, and by implication African

Americans, rather than believing Paul replaces the Jewish people with Christians. Both Broad and Taylor-Guthrie agree, however, that Morrison is concerned with the ways that black life and cultural production are misappropriated by white people against the interest of African American well-being.

The history of Hosea's appropriation may extend farther than Broad and other interpreters have suggested. Before Hosea is appropriated by Paul for Paul's purposes, Hosea's oracles were appropriated by Judahites for Judahite purposes. Many texts in the Hebrew Bible may have Northern Israelite origins (Fleming 2012), but Hosea's prophetic oracles are the only texts which claim to have originated from a Northern Israelite that are included in the Judahite scriptures. For two centuries prior to the destruction of the Northern Kingdom, Israel and Judah existed as separate kingdoms. Although history, common culture, and religious practices related the kingdoms, the degree of separation was such that Assyrian records understood Israel and Judah as belonging to two different geopolitical coalitions (Schneider 2002: 11). Shortly before the destruction of Northern Israel, Israel and Judah had fought against one another in the Syro-Ephraimitic War. Even though these kingdoms seemed to be related to one another, the nature of the relationship near 722 BCE certainly includes antagonism, hostility, and violence. Following the destruction of Israel, there is evidence for a large migration of Israelite refugees into Judah. The number of Israelite refugees who fled into Judah is still a matter of debate (Finkelstein 2015; Na'aman 2014), but some estimate that Jerusalem's population was over 50% Israelite following the Assyrian campaign against Samaria (Burke 2011: 49). Perhaps it is in this context, when a large number of refugees from a recently hostile kingdom entered Judah, that the Israelite prophet's words were appropriated by Judah. Even if the integration of Hosea's oracles into Judahite literature occurred later, perhaps in a hypothetical "Book of the Four" (Wöhrle 2020), they are still appropriated into a corpus of Judahite literature which serves Judahite purposes and has a markedly anti–Northern Israel disposition.

The appropriation of Hosea's oracles into Judahite literature is an earlier example of appropriation than that of Paul. I do not mean to suggest or guess at the intention of the Judahite compilers, only to acknowledge that the decision to appropriate Hosea's critiques shapes the Judahite imagination of the Israelites, including those who reside in Judah as refugees. Prophetic texts such as Jer. 3 and Ezek. 16 are only two of many examples of how Northern Israel came to be viewed as a standard of wrongdoing, a standard those prophets thought that Judah had come to surpass. While Hosea was an Israelite critiquing his own kingdom and people, Hosea's oracles were appropriated by Judah as an additional testimony to Israel's wrongdoing and as a justification for their traumatic punishment. Just as they do today, Hosea's oracles would have had an educational effect, training the affective responses of Judahites as they responded to the sufferings of the Israelites, prompting Judahites to perceive vulnerable Israelites, including Israelite women and children, not as people fleeing a random tragedy, but as people who deserved their current circumstances. In fact, in Hosea Yhwh had already announced the divine desire to kill the Israelites, to remove compassion from Israelite women and children, to send them fleeing, to dash the little ones to pieces, and to rip open their pregnant women (2:5–6 [Eng. 2:3–4]; 4:6; 9:12–13, 16–17; 13:16). We cannot know how Judahites responded to Israelite women and children, but we can see how Hosea's oracles would tempt the Judahites to view Israelite suffering as just. Hosea's prophecies render the vulnerable Israelites ungrievable; having been literarily raped, abused, and killed, they become even more vulnerable to harm by the readers of such texts (Dorsey 2022). Toni Morrison shows in *Beloved* that African Americans are aware of a similar pattern of appropriation when white supremacists use discourse of African Americans for their own purposes. This causes fear that an internal critique, such as the critique of African American patriarchy by African American feminists and womanists, will be appropriated by others who will use the critique to further stereotype, denigrate, and justify violence against African American people. Toni Morrison's allusion to Hosea through Paul mirrors the dual histories of (mis)appropriation and gestures toward its harmful consequences.

An additional parallel between *Beloved* and Hosea concerns how both texts struggle with traumatic history. Sethe's daughter, Beloved, returns carrying the memories of the Africans who died during the middle passage. As Sethe interacts with Beloved, she is confronting her own personal history of infanticide, but also the traumatic history of African American people. On the one hand, this interaction seems to be healing— traumatic pasts need to be told and retold to heal. But, as George Shulman (2008: 207) notes, Morrison complicates this picture. Interacting with Beloved, the traumatic past, is both healing and wounding, freeing and imprisoning. Trauma theorists have realized this vexed relationship with traumatic memory. Traumatic memories resist being narrativized. Sometimes, they intrude on the traumatized person in sleeping and waking dreams, at other times they disappear from memory altogether but still haunt the traumatized person and affect psychological health. Judith Herman (1997) argues that incorporating traumatic memories into narratives is necessary and healing, but that it can also stall the healing process if survivors come to identify so strongly with their trauma that their traumatic pasts become defining. Healing will eventually lead survivors to understand their trauma as less defining and possibly even as uninteresting. Morrison's novel replicates this process. The community is confronted by the past in Beloved, it is both healing and harmful, eventually the women gather and sing until Beloved is exorcised from the community, and finally they forget. Morrison (2004: 323–24) writes, "It was not a story to pass on . . . it was not a story to pass on . . . this is not a story to pass on." She tells the reader that the characters did not pass on the story: "So they forgot her [Beloved]. Like an unpleasant dream during a troubling sleep." Beloved haunted the community, both before and during her presence. Like a traumatic memory, the community could not imagine a new future until they first met her, and then let her go. Shulman (2008: 182, 196) suggests that in the process, Morrison questions the idea of being redeemed "*from* a traumatic past," and instead offers an image of redeeming the traumatic past itself, transforming demonic ghosts into ancestors.

Resonating with Toni Morrison's insight, and following her allusion to Hosea through Paul, I would offer that a redactional approach to Hosea offers African American communities a similar lesson. The redaction of Hosea is an ongoing debate, but it is accepted by at least some that if there was an eighth-century version of Hosea, it likely did not include the salvation oracles. The salvation oracles would more likely have been written not in response to Northern Israel's exile, but in response to Judah's exile in Babylon. The African American context—following slavery, emancipation, a failed reconstruction, the civil rights movement, and the current conditions of continued anti-Black racism—can be creatively related to the position of the exilic and postexilic redactors of Hosea. Without accepting the theological implications, African Americans can look at the prophecies of doom from Hosea, with all their graphic and tragic violence, and locate such violence in our own history. The history that Hosea describes, in fact, pales in comparison to the trauma the Israelites likely experienced, and the trauma African Americans have experienced since the Maafa. Hosea's poetic violence only metaphorically points toward the actual horrors that have occurred. The interpreter can imaginatively stand with the exilic redactor, no longer asking the question of whether or not rape and violence should happen, or whether it is God who performs those acts. But, standing with the redactor, African Americans can simply acknowledge, they did happen. We have been brutalized, cut-off from life, from the land. What now?

Then, the beautiful theological creativity of the redactor comes into sight. It is not over for the Israelite people. Read synchronically, the salvation oracles in Hos. 1–3 sound like a cycle of abuse; but read on the far side of traumatic history, they sound like healing. The desert, which was meant to kill her (Hos. 2:5 [Eng. 2:3]), will now be the place where Israel and God meet again (2:16 [Eng. 2:14]). Yhwh will betroth Israel, reconcile Israel with the earth, and rename and reclaim her children as Yhwh's own (2:16–25 [Eng. 2:14–23]). Here, the Judahite redactor is expressing hope for the Judahite exiles. However, in doing so, the redactor also expresses hope for the forgotten Israelite exiles as well. It was the Judahites' own experience of trauma and exile which aligned their interests with the interests of the exiled Israelites, which sensitized them to impossibility of living endlessly rejected by Yhwh and separated from home. In Hos. 2, Yhwh's turn to restoration is not even predicated on repentance, which is unique in the book. Yhwh simply decides to forgive and restore. The redactor not only writes a future for those who were deemed to have no future but also redeems history. The dead are redeemed. The ungrievable are made grievable again (Dorsey 2022). In concert with Toni Morrison, Hosea's later redactions point toward the possibility of healing from traumatic pasts and the redeeming of the dead.

31.6. Conclusion

The ghost of Hosea, even through Pauline allusions and literary epigraphs, presses its influence on African American life directly and indirectly, shaping the nature of African American discourse. Hosea is at once a source for constructing African American identity and a text that requires defensive reading to avoid the patriarchal ideologies embedded in its marriage metaphor. African Americans understand Hosea as a powerful book both in its hopeful promises, and its potential to harm, especially to harm women and children. African American interpretation of Hosea epitomizes the dual-hermeneutic. The ethical vision of African American hermeneutics often blurs the line between biblical studies and theology, as African American biblical scholars make themselves accountable to the theological effects of their interpretation. The scholars noted above account for the questions, "Who is God?, Who are we in relation to God?, and Who are we in relation to creation?," as these questions have a direct relationship to the ethics of biblical interpretation. Further study may continue to develop the ecological themes of Hosea as they relate to the climate crisis and to the development of identity in relation to the earth and animal life (see Trudinger in this volume). A redaction-critical examination of Hosea in relation to African American life requires further exploration to consider the potential of Hosea to address the complex issues of appropriation as well as reconciling with a traumatic past. The focus of African American interpretation of Hosea, regardless of method, is to discern how the biblical text can contribute to the freedom and flourishing of African American communities, other African and African diasporic communities, as well as the oppressed of every people in every place.

REFERENCES

Bailey, Randall C. 1991. "Beyond Identification: The Use of Africans in the Old Testament Poetry and Narratives." In Cain Hope Felder, ed., *Stony the Road We Trod: African American Biblical Interpretation*. Minneapolis: Fortress, 165–86.

Bailey, Randall C. 1995. "They're Nothing but Incestuous Bastards: The Polemical Use of Sex and Sexuality in the Hebrew Canon Narratives." In Fernando F. Segovia and Mary Ann Tolbert, eds., *Reading from This Place, Volume 1: Social Location and Biblical Interpretation in the United States*. Minneapolis: Fortress, 121–38.

Bridgeman, Valerie. 2016. "Womanist Approaches to the Prophets." In Carolyn J. Sharp., ed., *The Oxford Handbook of the Prophets*. Oxford: Oxford University Press, 483–90.

Broad, Robert L. 1994. "Giving Blood to the Scraps: Haints, History, and Hosea in Beloved." *African American Review* 28 (2): 189–96.

Burke, Adam A. 2011. "An Anthropological Model for the Investigation of the Archaeology of Refugees in Iron Age Judah and Its Environs." In Brad E. Kelle, Frank Ritchel Ames, and Jacob L. Wright, eds., *Interpreting Exile: Displacement and Deportation in Biblical and Modern Contexts*. SBLAIL 10. Atlanta: SBL, 41–56.

Copher, Charles B. 1991. "The Black Presence in the Old Testament." In Cain Hope Felder, ed., *Stony the Road We Trod: African American Biblical Interpretation*. Minneapolis: Fortress, 146–64.

Dorsey, Aaron. 2022. "Does Judah Weep for Israel? Hosea 1–2 and the Grievability of the Israelites." Paper presented at Annual Meeting of the Society of Biblical Literature. Denver, CO, November.

Finkelstein, Israel. 2015. "Migration of Israelites into Judah after 720 BCE: An Answer and an Update." *ZAW* 127 (2): 188–206.

Fleming, Daniel E. 2012. *The Legacy of Israel in Judah's Bible: History, Politics, and the Reinscribing of Tradition*. New York: Cambridge University Press.

Gafney, Wilda C. 2007. "Hearing the Word, Translation Matters: A Fem/Womanist Exploration of Translation Theory and Practice for Proclamation in Worship." In J. Harold Ellens, ed., *Text and Community: Essays in Memory of Bruce M. Metzger, Volume 1.* New Testament Monographs 19. Sheffield: Sheffield Phoenix, 55–66.

Gafney, Wilda C. 2010. "Reading the Hebrew Bible Responsibly." In Hugh R. Page and Randall C. Bailey, eds., *The Africana Bible: Reading Israel's Scriptures from Africa and the African Diaspora.* Minneapolis: Fortress, 45–51.

Hartsfield, Wallace. 2010. "Hosea." In Hugh R. Page and Randall C. Bailey, eds., *The Africana Bible: Reading Israel's Scriptures from Africa and the African Diaspora.* Minneapolis: Fortress, 164–68.

Herman, Judith Lewis. 1997. *Trauma and Recovery.* Rev. ed. New York: Basic.

Hobson, Christopher Z. 2012. *The Mount of Vision: African American Prophetic Tradition, 1800–1950.* New York: Oxford University Press.

Jennings, Willie James. 2018. "Can White People Be Saved? Reflections on the Relationship of Missions and Whiteness." In Love L. Sechrest, Johnny Ramírez-Johnson, and Amos Yong, eds., *Can "White" People Be Saved? Triangulating Race, Theology, and Mission.* Missiological Engagements. Downers Grove: IVP Academic, 27–43.

Jennings, Willie James. 2010. *The Christian Imagination: Theology and the Origins of Race.* New Haven: Yale University Press.

Keefe, Alice A. 2001. *Woman's Body and the Social Body in Hosea.* GCT 10. JSOTSup 338. New York: Sheffield Academic.

Morrison, Toni. 2004. *Beloved.* New York: Vintage International (orig. 1987).

Na'aman, Nadav. 2014. "Dismissing the Myth of a Flood of Israelite Refugees in the Late Eighth Century BCE." *ZAW* 126 (1): 1–14.

Nogalski, James D. 2011. *The Book of the Twelve: Hosea-Jonah.* Smyth and Helwys Bible Commentary 18. Macon, GA: Smyth and Helwys.

Parker, Angela N. 2021. *If God Still Breathes, Why Can't I? Black Lives Matter and Biblical Authority.* Grand Rapids: Eerdmans.

Schneider, Tammi J. 2002. "Through Assyria's Eyes: Israel's Relationship with Judah." *Expedition* 44 (3): 9–15.

Shulman, George M. 2008. *American Prophecy: Race and Redemption in American Political Culture.* Minneapolis: University of Minnesota Press.

Smith, Mitzi J. 2017. *Insights from African American Interpretation.* Insights: Reading the Bible in the Twenty-First Century. Minneapolis: Fortress.

Smith, Theophus. 2000. "'I Don't Read Such Small Stuff as Letters': Phenomenology of African American Engagement with the Bible." In Vincent L. Wimbush, ed., *African Americans and the Bible: Sacred Texts and Social Textures.* New York: Continuum, 83–91.

Sowers, Brian P. 2020. "Prison, Where Is Thy Victory? A Black Panther Theology of Mass Incarceration." *HTR* 113 (1): 24–44.

Taylor-Guthrie, Danille. 1995. "Who Are the Beloved? Old and New Testaments, Old and New Communities of Faith." *Religion & Literature* 27 (1): 119–29.

Ticciati, Susannah. 2017. "The Future of Biblical Israel: How Should Christians Read Romans 9–11 Today?" *BibInt* 25 (4–5): 497–518.Weems, Renita J. 1989. "Gomer: Victim of Violence or Victim of Metaphor?" *Semeia* 47: 87–104.

Weems, Renita J. 1993. *I Asked for Intimacy: Stories of Blessings, Betrayals, and Birthings.* San Diego: LuraMedia.

Weems, Renita J. 1995. *Battered Love: Marriage, Sex, and Violence in the Hebrew Prophets.* Minneapolis: Fortress.

Weems, Renita J. 2015. "Re-Reading for Liberation: African American Women and the Bible." In Mitzi J. Smith, ed., *I Found God in Me: A Womanist Biblical Hermeneutics Reader.* Eugene, OR: Cascade, 42–55.

Wöhrle, Jakob. 2020. "The Book of the Four." In Lena-Sofia Tiemeyer and Jakob Wöhrle, eds., *The Book of the Twelve: Composition, Reception, and Interpretation.* VTSup 184. Boston: Brill, 15–37.

Yee, Gale A. 2001. "'She Is Not My Wife and I Am Not Her Husband': A Materialist Analysis of Hosea 1–2." *BibInt* 9 (4): 345–83.

CHAPTER 32

HOSEA IN ASIA-CENTRIC INTERPRETATION

BARBARA M. LEUNG LAI

32.1. INTRODUCTORY REMARKS

A focus on the reception of Hosea places the discussion in this essay at the juxtaposition of two interconnected areas: (1) the interpreting community; and (2) the receiving community. The dynamics between interpreters' intent and audience's reception have been vibrantly examined under the rubrics of reading theories in the past three decades. Attending to Hosea within Asia-centric interpretation presents yet several layers of complexity that call for more refinement of definitions, as well as sociocultural, confessional, and contextual (re)considerations. Significant issues include how to define "Asia," how the social location of the interpreter may impact the reception of the audience, and how to identify the global Asia-"centric" communities.

32.1.1. Defining Asia-Centric

Asia, the East, or the Global South are very vague constructions. "What is Asia?" is the first question posted by R. S. Sugirtharajah in his monograph, *The Bible and Asia: From the Pre-Christian Era to the Postcolonial Age* (2013: 1–5). The multiple religions, languages, traditions, and sociocultural and political contexts represented by the ethnic groups that (originally) inhabited the continent of Asia do not form a collective whole. The lively discourse about Asian immigration and diaspora experience in North America has generated a renewed awareness of the intricacy of Asian identities. For example, in one recent volume (Chan, Daniel, de Leon, and Thao f.c.) four authors consciously represent their respective Asian backgrounds as East Asian, Southeast Asian, and South Asian, with one explicit commonality: telling their diaspora stories "in America." Note that there is no commonly recognized framework to sketch a pan-Asian identity, and particularity in defining one's Asian background is very much in demand. Additionally, to speak of "Asia-centric" requires more geographical and community-based specifications to bind the two concepts ("Asia" and "centric") together. This applies to both the interpreting and receiving communities.

This essay focuses on Asian interpreters of East, Southeast, and South Asia descents, writing primarily from the social locations of North America (i.e., Asian Americans and Asian Canadians) and, secondarily, from their respective homeland (e.g., Hong Kong, Singapore, India). On the receiving end, "Asia-centric" correspondingly refers to Asian faith communities in East, Southeast, and South Asia, as well as the diasporic Asian communities in North America, the United Kingdom, Australia, New Zealand, and elsewhere. This geographical mapping is changing rapidly in the twenty-first century. Due to the political situation in the Chinese-centric city of Hong Kong since 2019, mass exodus is happening with families leaving the now communist ruled police state of Hong Kong for places like the United Kingdom, Taiwan, Australia, Canada, and the United States The collective identity of "HongKongers" (versus Chinese) in diaspora is slowly but steadily taking shape in major cities worldwide. Conservatively speaking, this evolving identity of Asia-/Chinese-/HongKonger-centric community will be expanding more globally both in nature and scope.

32.1.2. Interpreting and Receiving Communities

Toward the end of the last century, biblical scholarship began to foreground the interconnection between the social location of the interpreters and the receiving communities (see Massey 1994; Segovia and Tolbert 1995). This work has flourished in the past three decades, moving toward global perspectives in biblical interpretation (e.g., see Keener and Carroll 2013; Roncace and Weaver 2014). Asian American and African American readings have been prominent (see Sun 2019; Kim and Yang 2019; Oduyoye 2003), but an emerging trend has focused on how minoritized cultural communities and Indigenous and Settler people interpret the Bible from the social location of Canada (see Medina, Hari-Singh, and Kim-Cragg 2019; Heinrichs 2018). Because Canada is a counterpart of the United States in North America and primarily an immigrant country, enunciating the social location of Asian-Canadian interpreters and an Asia-centric audience in Canada demands more internationally, culturally, and politically sensitive considerations. These include the cultural dissonance between first- and second-generation Korean/Japanese/Chinese/Filipino Canadians; the complex cultural mix of the second generation of Asian immigrant families; the conscious resistance of the dominant yet ambivalent labels of "model minority" and "perpetual foreigner" among Asians in North America in general (see Sun 2019); and the newly emerged "HongKonger" communities. The same criteria for consideration could be applied to diasporic Asia-centric communities in places outside of Asia and North America (e.g., in the United Kingdom, Australia, and New Zealand).

32.1.3. Limitation

The objective of this essay is to examine how different Asia-centric communities have received, appropriated, and used the book of Hosea. Given the complexities involved, delimitation is necessary to avoid overstatements and generalizations.

First, this essay relies primarily on works written in English. Singapore is the only country in East, Southeast, and South Asia where English is used by the public. English readers from non-English-speaking social locations are typically more privileged, elite groups in their respective societies. It is entirely up to the interpreter to pass on the interpretation in the representative language (e.g., Chinese, Korean, Malay) to impact the ordinary people at the receiving end.

Second, besides an exceptional few, many Asian interpreters in the academy cannot write and read competently in Asian languages, perhaps other than the language of their homeland. This reality imposes on Asian interpreters the question of both the legitimacy and adequacy of their representation and the effectiveness of their interpretation on their target audience at the receiving end (even if the social location of the interpreter and audience is the same). Explorations on the reception of Hosea have tended to be, more or less, academic endeavors within the guild of biblical scholars.

Third, relative to Euro-centric biblical interpretation, Asian and Asian American hermeneutics is a relatively new phenomenon. Asian scholarship on Hosea emerged toward the end of the last century and is flourishing now in the 2020s. Any sketch of Hosea's reception in Asia-centric interpretation operates with more of a recent and current timeframe for the scholarship and its impact.

32.2. Reading Hosea Contextually

The call for the contextualization of biblical interpretation has been heard, implemented, and is now flourishing among Asian interpreters worldwide, across different confessional stances and cultures (e.g., Kato 2012; Ro and Eshenaur 1984). Under the rubrics of reception and with a focus on the dynamics between the interpreter's task and the audience's reception, I have identified four areas of contextual considerations: (1) sociocultural context; (2) literary context; (3) political context; and (4) religious and ecclesiastical context. These are the pivotal criteria shaping an analysis and composite picture of Asia-centric reception of the book of Hosea. As noted previously, notwithstanding the limitations we face, Asia-centric interpretation on Hosea is more of a description of current work than a chronological sketch of historical eras and trends. My discussion will draw on resources written by Asian (East, Southeast, and South), and Asian-American/Canadian interpreters. They include commentaries on Hosea; essays of perspectival readings; literary analyses on the book; Chinese Bible translations; articles on the Book of the Twelve and Hosea's position within it; and Asian Bible commentary series (particularly, the Tien Dao Bible

Commentary, the South Asian Bible Commentary; and the Pastoral and Contextual Commentary).

Broadly speaking, the development of Asian interpretation on Hosea can be outlined in three stages: (1) the historical-critical period of investigation; (2) the literary engagements with the book including metaphorical and perspectival readings; and (3) the prominence of evangelical voices and the sharply focused pastoral and contextual interpretations. In terms of critical methods employed, this development could be articulated as moving from redactional and compositional inquiries to literary, theological, political, and contextual approaches.

32.2.1. Sociocultural Context

Singaporean American C. L. Seow and third-generation Chinese American, Gale A. Yee were the first Asian Americans to contribute to Hosea scholarship toward the end of the last century (see Seow 1992; Yee 1989; 1996). With the dominance of the historical-critical methods, both publications reflected then-current mainstream approaches (especially form-critical, compositional, and redactional investigations) to the texts of the Hebrew Bible. As reflected in the intellectual climate at that time, the interpretations of Hosea were divorced from any contemporary contextual considerations. There existed a distance between the interpreter's interpretation and the reader's reception in terms of appropriation. The impact of their works to the Asia-centric communities in North America and beyond was limited to the few minority Asian students in theology as an encouragement to go mainstream in establishing one's scholarship. This was significant considering that Asian biblical scholarship at that time was still in its infancy.

As Asian and Asian American scholars gradually increased within contemporary biblical scholarship, Y. K. Lee (2006: 60) commented on the current state of their sociocultural contexts. He observed that even though the social location of Asian Americans is North America, their interpretation reflects neither a purely western nor a purely Asian cultural orientation. It is an integrated mode of thinking. However, when it comes to the interpretation of Hosea, the need to consider Asian sociocultural contexts looms large.

There are few disputes as to the importance of the first three chapters of Hosea for the proposed interpretations of the prophet's marriage and family life and how they shape approaches to the whole book. Applicable to the more conservative societies of Southeast Asia (e.g., China, Taiwan, Korea, Japan, and Singapore) is a metaphorical interpretation. Many traditional Asian/Asian American/Canadian societies still hold to the Confucian thoughts—the Asian values explicated in the *Ren* (benevolence), *Yi* (righteousness), *Dao* (morality), and *De* (virtue). The uncompromised demands for fidelity within marriage, and the deep-rooted concepts of shame and honor within the family and clan (particularly for South Asians) make it difficult for the patriarchal Asia-centric communities to accept a historical and biographical reading of chs. 1–3. Moreover, it would be incomprehensible for the interpreter/translator/audience to conceive of God's commands in 1:2–3 and 3:1–3 as literal acts for the prophet. Adultery happening in a prophet's own family is inconceivable to the Asian mind and against all moral standards. Most Asian/Asian American interpreters will resort to a metaphorical reading of the chapters instead. Against such background, Gomer's unfaithfulness symbolizes Israel's infidelity toward God and the covenant relationship.

This metaphorical approach appears in the works of Asian/Asian American commentators. Devoid of any historical examination of the biographical data in Hos. 1–3, South Asian Santosh Varghese (2015: 115–28) affirms that a metaphorical meaning is intended. Hosea uses the metaphor of marriage to introduce something new to Israel's thinking, analogous to the covenant relationship between God and Israel. Regarding the act of "buying back" (3:2), Varghese comments that it would be thought provoking to the society of South Asia, where few men would be willing to take back an unfaithful wife.

Jerry Hwang's (2021) commentary on Hosea focuses on discourse analysis. While remaining exegetical and utterly contextual, this volume attends to the canonical and theological significance of Hosea, particularly within the development of the Book of the Twelve. Reading chs. 1–3 as Hosea's personal experiences, Hwang foregrounds the key message that Yhwh's covenant with the people is a family affair rather than a legal proceeding. The prophet's life mirrors the agony of Yhwh, who takes the initiative for reconciliation with an estranged household, Israel. Hwang sees a narrative of three sign-acts of Hosea's marriage and children. Hosea 1:2–2:3 (Eng. 1:2–11; 2:1) is the first sign-act; followed by the second sign-act in 2:4–25 (Eng. 2:2–23) as a quarrel speech in which Yhwh accuses Israel of apostasy. The third sign-act (3:1–5) points to Yhwh's reconciliation with his estranged wife. This approach leaves a dissonance between taking the chapters as the prophet's personal experiences and as sign-acts performed under divine command. There is quite a conceptual difference between the sign-acts of Isaiah (e.g., Isa. 8:1; 20:1–3) and the three sign-acts proposed by Hwang in chs. 1–3. If these are the firsthand experiences of Hosea, he did not simply perform them as a sign of Yhwh's unfailing love and reconciliation with Israel; he had to endure the agony and pain through his marriage and family life.

Affirming a metaphorical reading of Hos. 1–3 should take into consideration that the macrogenre of these chapters is metaphor. There is a marked disjunction between a narrative reading (historical events happened to Hosea's marriage and family) and a metaphorical reading. Korean American Bo H. Lim and Jeremiah W. Cataldo (2015) coauthored the commentary on Hosea in the Two Horizons Old Testament Commentary series. In keeping with the main objective of the series, they focus on the core theological message of the book and how it addresses today's Christian church. Lim notes that Hosea displays a considerable literary artistry, so the ambiguity regarding the historical events in chs. 1–3 may be intentional. Further, adopting the Bakhtinian notion of dialogic truth, any actual events of chs. 1–3 remain inconclusive (Bakhtin 1986). Lim calls for the abandonment of the quest for the historical Hosea. Rather than seeking to reconstruct the events of chs. 1 and 3, he says that the focus of commentary should be on "understanding the instructive value of the events and oracles" (Lim and Cataldo 2015: 36). Lim thus assigns 1:2–9 as the prophet's sign-act. The commentary offers a remarkable contribution to the Asia-centric communities in North America and elsewhere, both in its theological value and pastoral concerns. However, it gives one the impression that undertaking a theological-pastoral-contextual reading can easily avoid the interpretive issues associated with the events recorded in Hos. 1–3. For a more conservative Asian culture, a sign-act approach to the beginning chapters offers a better, more readily accepted interpretation.

Chinese commentators have taken up Hosea in the Tien Dao Commentary series. Samuel Y. C. Tang (1990) and Sow-Pheng Liew (2010) represent interpreters from two different periods. Tang surveys the arguments of four approaches to the first three chapters: (1) metaphorical; (2) historical; (3) a combination of both historical and metaphorical; and (4) narrative (in his own word, "*Zheng yi de*," i.e., "true to the original meaning"). He opts for the last interpretive path, with a focus on the actual personal experience of Hosea (Tang 1990: 13–19). Acknowledging the absence of historical data regarding Hosea's marriage and family life, Liew (2010: 12–20) ambiguously undertakes the metaphorical path and offers a contextual appropriation to the service of the servants of God through the symbolized prophetic acts. Readers find no resolution to the apparent conflicts between a narrative and a metaphorical reading of Hos. 1–3.

It is an undeniable fact that all translations involve interpretations, and thus translations matter. At the receiving end, a majority in the community of readers have no knowledge of Hebrew and rely solely on Bible translations, which are the translators' interpretations. In essence, the translator's interpretation is their Bible. Hwang (2022) notes this sentiment among early Chinese biblical translators such as Lamin Sanneh, who emphasized that translating the Bible is always a seminal act of doing contextual theology/interpretation. This observation can be illustrated through a survey of four Chinese versions of Hosea.[1] They belong to different periods and represent varied confessional stances. As the most used Bible in Chinese faith communities worldwide, the *Holy Bible: New Chinese Version* (Shen edition 2001) is the only one among the four that demonstrates a clear resistance to translating God's command to Hosea in 1:2 as "Go, take to yourself a wife of harlotry and children of harlotry." Instead, the translation goes, "*Ni qu qu yige xiang changji yiyang de nuren, shengyang xiang changji yi xiang de Ernu*" (i.e., literally, "Go take a woman *like* a harlot, and have adulterous children with her"). This version also gives the subtitle of ch. 1 as "Symbolic Marriage between Hosea and Gomer."

Interpreting the Bible is an arduous task, and helping readers understand within their sociocultural contexts is immensely challenging. On the receiving end, Sugirtharajah (2013: 5) has summed up the state of the matter precisely. He notes that Asian readers' culturally shaped perception of the Bible is complicated: "It has been at times stimulating, at times seditious, and at times synthetic."

32.2.2. Literary Context

Hosea represents an extensive use of metaphorical thinking and language. In his comparison of the Jeremiah scroll with Hosea, John Goldingay commented on the importance of metaphor in speaking of human relationship with God. Prophets do much of their thinking in imagery and there are few things we can say literally about God and the divine–human relationship without the use of metaphor. "Metaphor makes it possible to speak about things that we could not otherwise speak of" (Goldingay 2021: 57).

Metaphorical thinking has a significant impact on the Asian mind in general, and literary studies have attracted the attention of Asian/Asian North American interpreters. With the popularity of interdisciplinary approaches, synchronic reading of the biblical texts, and extended applications of metaphor theories to the field of biblical studies, there is now a plethora of Asian and Asian North American contributions on Hosea. They take two identifiable paths: (1) from "descriptive" to "normative"; and (2) the extension of metaphorical studies to previously unexplored lines of inquiry. The impact on the diverse Asia-centric audiences could be summarized in three areas: (1) theological; (2) canonical (the role of Hosea within the Book of the Twelve); and (3) appropriation to the Asian faith communities in respective contexts.

Not only does Hwang's (2021) discourse analysis commentary offer new angles of perception for the message of Hosea but also it contributes to understanding Hosea's canonical and theological significance within the Book of the Twelve. He concludes that Hosea has been placed at the head of the collection with chs. 1–3 as a comprehensive prologue. The themes introduced in Hos. 1–3, and further developed in the Book of the Twelve, characterize the Twelve as a coherent theological unity. Chinese Canadian Grace Ko's (2021) careful synchronic reading of the Book of the Twelve with the focus on theodicy and hope likewise provides a new dimension to the theology of the Twelve. Korean American Brittany Kim's (2021) focused exposition on Hos. 11:8a is another contribution on the rich literary artistry of Hosea that moves from descriptive elements to normative claims.

As a Chinese Canadian, I have offered an analysis of Hos. 11 (a masterpiece of Hebrew poetry) that attempted to break new ground toward literary studies and the act of reading (Leung Lai 2004). First, I appeal to the readers' (particularly Asian readers') noncognitive realm of understanding by proposing the combined act of "reading and emotive-experiencing." At the same time, I demonstrate what Abraham Heschel (1962: 1–11) has referred to as the "transitive character" of the divine pathos (i.e., from divine pathos to prophetic pathos, and then to readers' emotive experiencing). Second, I introduce the "Hermeneutics of Hearing" (see Nogalski and Sweeney 2000). Readers are encouraged to "hear the text" ("hearing God's bitter cries"). Third, my reading strategy provides a window to look into the emotion of God through God's self-lamenting "I"-voice. To a certain degree, Varghese's (2015) reading of Hosea also exhibits a forceful appeal to the Asian readers on the pain felt within God's own heart.

Against the background of the Confucius thought on *ḥesed* (not just a relational term that binds two parties together but one having to do with the Confucius teaching on *Li* [ritual] and *Ren* [benevolence, human goodness]), Tang's (1990: 13–98) commentary contains a substantial discussion of divine pathos. Reading between the lines, he has successfully demonstrated that contrary to the Confucius perspective, the *ḥesed* of God explicated in Hosea is a *ḥesed* of heart-broken pain. There is no "human goodness" that can generate that kind of "loving kindness" toward humankind.

The representative examples mentioned above attest to the fact that synchronic readings of Hosea open new windows of perception which appeal to both the cognitive and non-cognitive realms of Asian readers' understanding at the receiving end. Moreover, these contributions collectively, in a small way, demonstrate the proper way of constructing Hebrew Bible theology on the character and pathos of God, the idea of *ḥesed*, and the multi-faceted portrayal of the God-human relationship through metaphorical descriptions. In terms of the dynamics of interpreting and receiving, Asian and Asian North Americans are bringing biblical theology from the act of interpretation to the pulpit, then to the context of Asia-centric faith communities.

32.2.3. Political Context

Francis Landy (2011: 10) has firmly stated, "Hosea is undoubtedly patriarchal literature: Its God is male, its world is governed by male authorities and conventions, and the prophet is male." As many have noted, women function prominently in metaphoric contexts in the Hebrew Bible. For example, the adulterous wife of Hosea and the "strange woman" and "harlot" in Prov. 5 and 7 symbolize evil. Although these metaphoric figures stem from the literary conventions of the ancient Near East, they project harmful stereotypes about women. My discussion here will focus on the use of metaphors from the perspective of political, socioeconomic, and gender studies. The exotic, sadistic imagery for Gomer in Hosea has become fertile ground for feminist engagements.

Gale Yee has been among the most prominent scholars working on feminist studies of Hosea.[2] To define feminism in general terms, Yee states, "Feminism is political activism by women on behalf of women" (Yee 2018: 1). Concerning Hosea, she has identified three central metaphors in the major sections of the book depicting the relationship between Yhwh and Israel: (1) husband and wife (chs. 1–3); (2) parent and child (chs. 4–11); and (3) a combination of husband-wife and parent-rebellious son (chs. 12–14) (Yee 1996). However, the boundaries between history and metaphor in chs. 1–3 are blurred. On the one hand, in the form of a narrative, the text gives a brief biography of Gomer as Hosea's wife. Yet, the text is also explicit about the metaphorical function of Gomer within the book. The author includes the images of Gomer not for the sake of historical accuracy but to enhance the prophetic accusation of Israel's sin as adultery.

Yee (2003) has also extended the analysis to include the sexual and gendered metaphors in Hos. 4–14. The results demonstrate that Hosea intentionally used the abundance of metaphorical language to feminize and shame the male ruling elite in their commitment to unjust foreign and domestic policies (see also Carvalho 2018: 108–11). Along a similar path, Korean S. H. Hong (2006) attempts to incorporate a theoretical analysis of metaphor into a sociological discussion about the social reality of eighth-century Israel and Judah, using a comparative study of the concept of illness and healing in the ancient Near East and traditional East Asia. He broadens the scope of the socio-economic interpretation of the metaphors in Hos. 4–11 beyond the sexual and marital imageries to the explicit and implicit language of illness and healing (e.g., 5:13; 6:1, 7; 14:5 [Eng. 14:4]). Illness and healing used together is a metaphor figuring socioeconomic changes that are destructive to the society of the eighth-century Israel. With his detailed treatment of the representative passages (5:8–6:3 and 7:1–7), Hong concludes that the imagery of illness indicates the unjust policies of Israel's elite rulers, and the language of healing points to the prophet's yearning for the people of Israel to be restored in the cov-enantal relationship with God.

Most Asian (particularly South Asian) societies are patriarchal in nature and in social practice. Equality of life is often absent in Asian social orders where there are systematic segregations between the rich and the poor, the elite and the underprivileged. Patriarchal societies in Asia often put women in a subordinate role under male leadership. Asian and Asian American/Canadian women who belong to evangelical faith communities will most likely find themselves under the leadership of males. Against these varied con-textual make-ups, the results of feminist and socioeconomic approaches to metaphors in Hosea have had a significant impact on Asian readers. Asian women readers and un-privileged members of respective Asian societies are given not only a voice, but more importantly, a prescribed path and a welcoming window of opportunity to discover the book's messages and appropriate them to their own contextual situatedness. It is not through top-down interpretation, but the tactful analysis of literary conventions in-grained in the book—to ridicule those who are in positions of leadership and patriarchs of the ancient communities. These approaches open new horizons of reading Hosea and show global Asian readers the relevance of the biblical text to an individual's life-text. These impacts are both liberating and transforming.

32.2.4. Religious and Ecclesiastical Context

Against the diverse and complicated multi-faith religious context of the Asian societies, the interpreter's social location and/or the ability to understand the target audience play a crucial role. Unpacking the complex make-up of the religious context of the Asia-centric communities worldwide is challenging for all interpreters. Moreover, denomi-national affiliations at times would determine or even dictate how a message is received or what kind of message is to be rejected (e.g., the narrative reading of Hos. 1–3 as the personal experiences of the prophet). Evangelical congregations tend to be patriarchal and conservative. This is especially true among the Korean, Japanese, Chinese, Filipino, and Vietnamese churches in the United States and Canada. The interpreter's reading strategy of Hos. 1–3 often determines the level of receptivity among the audience.

Sun (2019: 256) has stated that the locus of Asian/Asian North American interpre-tation is the world in front of the text. This is only partially correct. Instead, in the contributions among Asians and Asian North Americans surveyed in this essay, it is evident that most of them have devoted due attention to the world of the text.

Notwithstanding their own ethnic and contextual background and the social location of their interpretation, they all seek to move from textual meaning to the contextual relevance of the readers. This dynamic of interpreting and receiving comes through textual analysis, exercising the power of imagination (or several cycles of dialoguing with the text), and appropriation (reliving and re-expressing, as all biblical interpretation is an act of re-expression).

As early as 1984, the contributors of the collection *The Bible and Theology in Asian Contexts: An Evangelical Perspective on Asian Theology* issued the call for the necessity of contextualizing the Bible within the diverse Asian religious contexts (Ro and Eshenaur 1984). With the emergence of the Society of Asian Biblical Studies (and its sponsored journal, *International Journal of Asian Christianity*), a space has been created to examine the dense and sophisticated linkage of religion and culture both in their distinctiveness as well as in a cross-cultural and cross-disciplinary perspective. This momentum allows broader generalizations and theorizations to emerge.

For example, Lim and Cataldo's (2015) commentary on Hosea states its goal as the interpretation of the prophecy of Hosea afresh considering both current research on the book and contemporary challenges facing the church today. The thrust of their arguments and conclusions is highly theological and pastoral. Varghese's (2015) treatment of the book likewise devotes a large discussion to the relevance of its message to the South Asia–specific religious context. Special attention is placed on the character, pain, and anger of God over the unfaithfulness of Israel and calls for people's repentance and return to God. Particularly, Varghese's appropriation of the departure of Israel from God as adultery is unique in the context of the South and West Asian religion which worships multiple gods. God forbids a syncretistic form of religion. Varghese calls for taking sin seriously, not compromising the major truths of scripture, especially regarding purity and separated lifestyle. Against their contextual background, the faith communities in Asia and South Asia (in particular) will find Varghese's interpretation of Hosea speaking directly to their contextual situatedness. There is no gap between interpretation and reception, shaping how the message of Hosea should be received and reappropriated.

The audience of Hwang's (2021) commentary on Hosea is "pastors and teachers." It is pastoral in orientation and pays due attention to the ecclesiastical context of its readers. Other than using discourse analysis as a reading strategy, Hwang's contribution to Hosea scholarship can be summarized in three areas: (1) the theology of Hosea, (2) Hosea's strategic position in the Book of the Twelve as its theological prologue binding the Twelve together as a theological unity, and (3) the appropriated message to pastors and the church. Hwang constructs a biblical theology of Hosea from text to pulpit, and then from pulpit to the ecclesiastical contexts of his readers.

Tang's (1990) and Liew's (2010) commentaries on Hosea in the Tien Dao Bible Commentary series are "exegetical" in nature. Exegesis is perceived as something belonging to the academy, and the Hebrew language is foreign to an average Chinese reader of Hong Kong and elsewhere in Asia. Reading between the lines, both authors demonstrate a great deal of effort to explicate something that is exegetical to the sociocultural-ecclesiastical context of their Chinese readers.

With a newly launched commentary series, the Asia Bible Commentary: A Pastoral and Contextual Commentary, the gap between Asian interpreters and the Asia-centric audiences in Asia will likely be removed. In keeping with the objective of the series, the first volume (on Joel, Nahum, and Malachi; Too Shao and Ching Shao 2021) is utterly pastoral in orientation, providing clear pointers and directives to the ecclesiastical and contextual situatedness of its readers.

32.3. Prospect

Several future trajectories present themselves for work on Hosea.

32.3.1. Reception

Reception history has been projected as one of the three future trajectories in Asian and Asian American biblical scholarship (Sun 2019: 255–56). As elucidated previously, the analysis in this essay is, more or less, a depiction of the newly emerged phenomena of reception study on the book of Hosea in Asian contexts. In the next decade of Asian and Asian American/Canadian engagements in biblical scholarship, interpreters should always have an eye to addressing the need at the receiving end of our scholarship, the readers. For example, perspectival readings as applied to Hosea could further expand readers' horizon in grasping the significant message of the book and be appropriated to the contextual situatedness in Asia-centric communities. We should persistently resist the status of being labeled as a minoritized or marginalized interpreter. Bringing the contextual considerations and integrated interdisciplinary studies to the foreground of interpretation is very much in demand. Perhaps decades from now, Asian interpreters worldwide will be able to speak of the "reception history" on Hosea in Asia-centric interpretation.

32.3.2. Toward New Paradigms of Reading

Within ideological-critical readings of any given text, there are two conventional reading strategies—namely, reading "with the grain" and reading "against the grain." Sun (2019: 239) has observed that traditional Eurocentric interpretation tends to read "with the grain," but Asian interpreters tend to read "against the grain." I have advocated another way of reading, reading "cross the grains," and have applied this new reading strategy to Ecclesiastes (Leung Lai 2013, 2019). Using the analogy of the production of plywood by gluing together veneers of adjacent piles having the woodgrain at right angle to each other, a high-quality, good-strength wood panel is formed. Specifically, plywood is bonded with grain running against one another and perpendicular to the grain direction. Applying a "cross-graining" reading to indeterminate texts like Hos. 1–3, with historical and metaphorical meanings apparently yielding different interpretations, has the potential of producing a richer and multilayered message.

On another front, Y. L. Hertig (2010) has proposed a Yinist paradigm as an alternative to Asian American feminist interpretations. Based on the ancient Asian conceptual framework of Yin and Yang in Taoism, she strives to affirm the existence of a "chaotic harmony" in biblical feminist interpretation. Incorporating the "cross-graining" and "harmonious chaos" reading strategies together into the reading of Hosea, the textual tensions associated with the historical reading of the marriage and family of Hosea are resolvable to the Asian mind. Hosea 11:9 reads, "For I am God and not man, the Holy One of Israel." God is the author of all Israelite laws and regulations, and has so decided to make an exception in the case of the command to the prophet. Using a "cross-graining" reading may further strengthen the interpretation, yielding a richer, multilayered meaning-significance of the text. The concept of "chaotic harmony" is also at home in Southeast Asian minds.

As the Chinese idiom goes, this essay "offers ideas that are of 'brick' quality, with the hope that it may generate something that is of 'jade' extravagance."

Notes

1. *The Chinese Union Version* (1919; the work of Western missionaries); *The Holy Bible: A New Translation by Lu Chen-Chung* (1970); *Holy Bible: New Chinese Version*, Shen Edition (2001); and *The Holy Bible*, Recovery Version (2007).
2. See the comprehensive survey of Yee's contributions in Kelle 2009 and 2010.

References

Bakhtin, Mikhail. 1986. *The Dialogic Imagination: Four Essays*. Edited by Michael Holquist. Translated by Caryl Emerson and Michael Holquist. Austin: University of Texas Press.

Carvalho, Corrine L. 2018. "Prophecy: The Challenge of Violence and Gender under Colonization." In Gale Yee, ed., *The Hebrew Bible: Feminist and Intersectional Perspectives*. Minneapolis: Fortress, 108–11.

Chan, Sabrina S., Linson Daniel, David de Leon, and La Thao. Forthcoming. *Learning Our Names: Asian American Christians on Identity, Relationships, and Vocation*. Downers Grove, IL: IVP Academic.

Foskett, Mary F., and Jeffrey K. Kuan., eds. 2006. *Ways of Being, Ways of Reading: Asian American Biblical Interpretation*. St. Louis: Chalice Press.

Goldingay, John. 2021. *The Book of Jeremiah*. NICOT. Grand Rapids: Eerdmans.

Heinrichs, Steve, ed. 2018. *Unsettling the Word: Biblical Experiments in Decolonization*. Maryknoll, NY: Orbis.

Hertig, Y. L. 2010. "Asian American Alternative to Feminism: A Yinist Paradigm." In Y. L. Hertig and Chloe Sun, eds., *Mirrored Reflection: Reframing Biblical Characters*. Eugene, OR: Wipf and Stock, 3–14.

Heschel, Abraham J. 1962. *The Prophets*, vol. 2. New York: Harper and Row.

Hong, S. H. 2006. *The Metaphor of Illness and Healing in Hosea and Its Significance in the Socio-Economic Context of the Eighth-Century Israel and Judah*. Studies in Biblical Literature 95. New York: Peter Lang.

Hwang, Jerry. 2021. *Hosea: God's Reconciliation with His Estranged Household*. Zondervan Exegetical Commentary on the Old Testament. Grand Rapids: Zondervan Academic.

Hwang, Jerry. 2022. "Bible Translation as Contextual Theology: The Case of the Chinese Union Version Bible of 1919." *International Journal of Asian Christianity* 5, no. 1: 89–114. Kato, Juliuskei. 2012. *How Immigrant Christians Living in Mixed Culture Interpret Their Religion: Asian-American Diasporic Hybridity and Its Implications for Hermeneutics*. Lewiston, NY: Edwin Mellen.

Keener, Craig, and M. Daniel Carroll R., eds. 2013. *Global Voices: Reading the Bible in the Majority World*. Peabody: Hendrickson.

Kelle, Brad E. 2009. "Hosea 1–3 in Twentieth-Century Scholarship." *CBR* 7, no. 2: 177–218.

Kelle, Brad E. 2010. "Hosea 4–11 in Twentieth-Century Scholarship." *CBR* 8, no. 3: 314–75.

Kim, Brittany. 2021. "How Can I Give You Up, Ephraim? (Hos 11: 8a): Theodicy in Hosea." In George Athas, Beth M. Stovell, Daniel Timmer, and Colin M. Toffelmire, eds., *Theodicy and Hope in the Book of the Twelve*. LHBOTS 705. London, New York, Oxford, New Delhi, Sydney: T&T Clark, 66–87.

Kim, Uriah Y. 2019. "More Than an Interpretation from a Different Perspective: A Postcolonial Reading from a Different Epistemological (Back)Ground." In Uriah Y. Kim and Seung Ai Yang, eds., *T&T Clark Handbook of Asian American Biblical Hermeneutics*. London, New York, Oxford, New Delhi, Sydney: T&T Clark, 186–95.

Kim, Uriah Y., and Seung Ai Yang, eds. 2019. *T&T Clark Handbook of Asian American Biblical Hermeneutics*. London, New York, Oxford, New Delhi, Sydney: T&T Clark.

Ko, Grace. 2013. "The Ordering of the Twelve as Israel's Historiography." In Mark J. Boda and Lissa M. Wray Beal, eds., *Prophets, Prophecy, and Ancient Israelite Historiography*. Winona Lake, IN: Eisenbrauns, 315–32.

Ko, Grace. 2021. "Theodicy and Hope in the Book of the Twelve." In George Athas, Beth M. Stovell, Daniel Timmer, and Colin M. Toffelmire, eds., *Theology and Hope in the Book of the Twelve*. London, New York, Oxford, New Delhi, Sydney: T&T Clark, 22–39.

Lai, Alan Ka Lun. 2019. "Chinese Canadian Identities and the Reading of the Bible." In Néstor Medina, Alison Hari-Singh, and Hyeran Kim-Cragg, eds., *Reading In-Between: How Minoritized Cultural Communities Interpret the Bible in Canada*. Eugene, OR: Wipf and Stock, 17–35.

Landy, Francis. 2011. *Hosea*. 2nd ed. Readings: A New Biblical Commentary. Sheffield: Sheffield Phoenix.

Lee, Y. K. 2006. "Reading the Bible as an Asian American: Issues in Asian American Biblical Interpretation." In Mary F. Foskett and Jeffrey K. Kuan, eds., *Ways of Being, Ways of Reading: Asian American Biblical Interpretation*. St. Louis: Chalice, 60–69.

Leung Lai, Barbara M. 2004. "Hearing God's Bitter Cries (Hosea 11:1–9): Reading, Emotive-experiencing, Appropriation." *HBT* 26, no. 1: 24–49.

Leung Lai, Barbara M. 2013. "Voice and Ideology in Ecclesiastes: Reading 'Cross the Grains.'" In James K. Aitken, Jeremy M. S. Clines, and Christl M. Maier, eds., *Interested Readers: Essays on the Hebrew Bible in Honor of David J. A. Clines*. Atlanta: SBL, 265–96.

Leung Lai, Barbara M. 2019. "Toward a Version of 'Narratival Hermeneutics'—Reading Ecclesiastes Ethno-Culturally with a Chinese Lens: Selfhood, Diaspora Experience, and the Search for Meaning." In Néstor Medina, Alison Hari-Singh, and Hyeran Kim-Cragg, eds., *Reading In-Between: How Minoritized Cultural Communities Interpret the Bible in Canada*. Eugene, OR: Wipf and Stock, 36–51.Liew, Sow-pheng. 2010. *Hosea*. Tien Dao Bible Commentary. Hong Kong, China: Tien Dao Publishing House. (Chinese)

Lim, Bo H. 2019. "Critical Methods and Critique: Theological Interpretation." In Uriah Y. Kim and Seung Ai Yang, eds., *T&T Clark Handbook of Asian American Biblical Hermeneutics*. London, New York, Oxford, New Delhi, Sydney: T&T Clark, 141–59.

Lim, Bo H., and Jeremiah W. Cataldo. 2015. *Hosea*. Two Horizons Old Testament Commentary. Grand Rapids: Eerdmans.

Massey, James E. 1994. "Reading the Bible from Particular Social Locations: An Introduction." In Leander E. Keck et al., eds., *The New Interpreter's Bible Volume 1: General and Old Testament Articles, Genesis, Exodus, Leviticus*. The New Interpreter's Bible. 12 vols. Nashville: Abingdon, 150–53.

Medina, Néstor, Alison Hari-Singh, and Hyeran Kim-Cragg, eds. 2019. *Reading In-Between: How Minoritized Cultural Communities Interpret the Bible in Canada*. Eugene, OR: Wipf and Stock.

Ng, Greer Anne Wenh-In. 2019. "As One Minoritized Reader to Another: Engaging Biblical Hermeneutics in Canada in the Twenty-First Century—A Critical Response." In Nèstor Medina, Alison Hari-Singh, and Hyeran Kim-Cragg, eds., *Reading In-Between: How Minoritized Cultural Communities Interpret the Bible in Canada*. Eugene, OR: Wipf and Stock, 122–34.

Nogalski, James D., and Marvin A. Sweeney, eds. 2000. *Reading and Hearing the Book of the Twelve*. SBLSymS 15. Atlanta: SBL.

Oduyoye, Amba. 2003. "Biblical Interpretation and the Social Location of the Interpreter: African Women's Reading of the Bible." In Susanne Scholz, ed., *Biblical Studies Alternatively: An Introductory Reader*. Upper Saddle River, NJ: Prentice Hall, 30–46.

Ro, Bong Rin, and Ruth Eshenaur, eds. 1984. *The Bible and Theology in Asian Contexts: An Evangelical Perspective on Asian Theology*. Taichung, Taiwan: Asia Theological Association.

Roncace, Mark, and Joseph Weaver, eds. 2014. *Global Perspectives on the Old Testament*. Upper Saddle River, NJ: Pearson.

Scholz, Susanne, ed. 2003. *Biblical Studies Alternatively: An Introductory Reader*. Upper Saddle River, NJ: Prentice Hall.

Segovia, Fernando F., and Mary Ann Tolbert, eds. 1995. *Reading from This Place: Social Location and Biblical Interpretation in the United States*, vol.1; and *Reading from This Place: Social Location and Biblical Interpretation in Global Perspective*, vol. 2. Minneapolis: Fortress.

Seow, C. L. 1992. "Hosea, Book of." *ABD* 3: 291–97.

Sugirtharajah, Rasiah S. 2013. *The Bible and Asia: From the Pre-Christian Era to the Postcolonial Age*. Cambridge, MA: Harvard University Press.

Sun, Chloe. 2019. "Recent Research on Asian and Asian American Hermeneutics Related to the Hebrew Bible." *CBR* 17, no. 3: 238–65.

Tang, Samuel Y. C. 1990. *A Commentary on the Twelve Prophets, 2—Hosea*. 2nd ed. Bible Commentary Series. Hong Kong: Tien Dao Publishing House. (Chinese).

Too Shao, Joseph, and Rosa Ching Shao. 2021. *Joel, Nahum, and Malachi: A Pastoral and Contextual Commentary*. Asia Bible Commentary Series. Carlisle, Cumbria: Langham Global Library.

Varghese, Santosh. 2015. "Hosea." In Brian Wintle, ed., *South Asia Bible Commentary: A One-Volume Commentary on the Whole Bible*. Grand Rapids: Zondervan, 1115–28.

Wintle, Brain C. ed. 2015. *South Asia Bible Commentary: A One-Volume Commentary on the Whole Bible*. Grand Rapids: Zondervan.

Yee, Gale A. 1989. *Composition and Tradition in the Book of Hosea: A Redactional Critical Investigation*. SBLDS 102. Atlanta: Scholars.

Yee, Gale A. 1996. "The Book of Hosea." In Leander E. Keck et al., eds., *The New Interpreter's Bible Volume 7: Introduction to Apocalyptic Literature, Daniel, the Twelve Prophets*. The New Interpreter's Bible. 12 vols. Nashville: Abingdon, 197–297.Yee, Gale A. 2018. "Introduction: Definitions, Explorations, and Intersections." In Gale A. Yee, ed., *The Hebrew Bible: Feminist and Intersectional Perspectives*. Baltimore: Project Muse; Minneapolis: Fortress, 1–38.

Yee, Gale A. 2019. "Of Foreigners and Eunuchs: An Asian American Reading of Isaiah 56:1–6." In Uriah Y. Kim and Seung Ai Yang, eds., *T&T Clark Handbook of Asian American Biblical Hermeneutics*. London, New York, Oxford, New Delhi, Sydney: T&T Clark, 261–72.

Yee, Gale A. 2003. *Poor Banished Children of Eve: Woman as Evil in the Hebrew Bible*. Minneapolis: Fortress.

Yee, Gale A. 2021. *Towards an Asian American Biblical Hermeneutics: An Intersectional Anthology*. Eugene, OR: Cascade.

ANCIENT SOURCES INDEX

For the benefit of digital users, indexed terms that span two pages (e.g., 52–53) may, on occasion, appear on only one of those pages.

Genesis

1: 405
1-3: 352–53
1-4: 343
10, 19: 32–33
12, 4b: 223
14, 2: 32–33, 204
14, 8: 32–33
14, 18-24: 56–57
17, 1: 56–57
18, 16: 32–33
18, 18: 426
19, 21-28: 204
19, 29: 32–33
20, 3: 67–68
25-35: 182, 255
25, 21-26: 255
25, 23-26: 414–15
25, 26: 223, 308
26, 3: 221
27, 36: 223
27, 40: 220
27, 43: 222
28: 74–75
28-29: 182
28, 2: 222
28, 5: 308
28, 10-22: 182, 255
28, 11-19: 74–75
28, 29: 308
29, 15: 222
30, 31: 222
31: 182
31, 13: 56–57
32: 74–75

32, 6: 224
32, 22-32: 74–75
32, 22-33: 255
32, 24-29: 308
32, 25-29: 414–15
32, 26: 223–24
32, 29: 223–24
33, 1-11: 255
33, 1-20: 238
33, 1-22-55: 238
33, 4: 224
34, 3: 311–12
34, 7: 320–21
35: 74–75
35, 1-15: 74–75, 255
35, 11: 56–57
35, 12: 413
35, 15: 224, 308
37, 29: 412–13
38: 223, 401
41, 52: 221–22
48, 11: 114–15
49: 125
49, 4: 413
49, 25: 56–57

Exodus

3, 14-16: 67
4-14: 190
4, 22-23: 199–200
5, 2: 190
5, 14: 403
6, 1-3: 67
6, 3: 73, 403
6, 4: 403

ANCIENT SOURCES INDEX

Exodus (*cont.*)
6, 7: 190, 256–57
7, 5: 190
7, 11: 403
7, 12: 403
8, 1: 403
11, 10: 403
13, 3: 403
13, 7: 403
13, 8: 403
14: 205
14, 4: 190
14, 5: 403
15, 13: 148–49
15, 17: 117
16-18: 182
19, 3-6: 202–3
20: 420
20, 13-16: 234
20, 17: 321
20, 20: 114–15
22, 15: 310
22, 21-22: 403
24, 4: 77
29, 2: 307
32: 73–74
32-34: 182, 263–64
32, 1-4: 74
32, 1-34, 10: 263–64
34, 6-7: 247, 263–64
34, 23: 47

Leviticus
2, 5: 307
18, 18-19: 320–21
20, 10: 164
20, 11: 320–21
20, 17-2: 320–21
25, 1-46: 187
26, 12: 256–57

Numbers
11-25: 182
21, 21-35: 280
22, 22-30: 401
23, 19: 262–63, 266, 421
25, 1-5: 72

28, 9-10: 431
31, 9: 320–21
31, 17-18: 321
31, 25: 320–21
32, 12: 421

Deuteronomy
1, 26-33: 203–4
2, 10: 321–22
4, 24: 419
5, 17-21: 234
5, 21: 321
7, 2: 220
7, 8: 190
7, 12: 342
9, 26: 190
13, 6: 252
15, 15-18: 148
19, 6: 44
19, 14: 85
22, 21: 320–21
22, 25-27: 164
22, 28-29: 321
27: 150
27, 17: 85
28, 68: 46–47
29, 22: 32–33
29, 23: 204
31, 22-30: 149
32: 247–48, 249, 251–52
32-33: 125
32, 7-9: 252
32, 7-18: 251–52
32, 8-9: 67
32, 10-12: 252
32, 15: 252
32, 15-18: 252
32, 21: 428
32, 27: 117
32, 43: 426
33, 1: 418–19
33, 26: 67–68
34, 10-12: 149

Joshua
3, 16: 30
4, 1-9: 77

Ancient Sources Index — continued

4, 19-5, 12: 75
7: 223
13, 12: 115, 279–80
13, 21: 279–80
13, 27: 279–80
13, 30: 279–80
13, 31: 279–80

Judges
5: 111–12, 125
6, 5: 310
6, 25-32: 68
6, 29: 310
9: 276
14, 15: 310
18, 4: 114
19, 23-24: 320–21
20, 6: 320–21
20, 10: 320–21
21: 320–21

Ruth
1, 1: 46
3, 8: 205

1 Samuel
1: 111–12
3, 1: 148
4, 4: 72
5: 111–12
7: 75
7, 3-4: 68
8: 276, 279
8, 4-8a: 191
8, 5-6: 190–91
8, 6-7: 279
8, 6-11: 191
8, 7: 191
8, 7-8: 190–91
8, 8a: 191
8, 8b-c: 191
8, 9a-b: 191
8, 9c-10a: 191
8, 11: 191
8, 11-18: 190–91
8, 12: 191
8, 14: 191

9, 12: 72
11: 75
11, 15: 216
12: 276
15: 75
15, 28: 280
15, 29: 262–63, 266
30, 1-2: 320–21
30, 2: 320–21

2 Samuel
11, 25: 114
13, 12: 320–21
16, 3: 115, 279–80
22, 11: 67–68

1 Kings
1, 1-2: 44
4, 7: 187
4, 27-28: 187
8, 28-29: 179
10, 26: 187
12: 73–74, 186–87
12, 21-24: 178–79
12, 28-30: 73–74
12, 28-32: 31
13: 143
14, 5: 114
14, 25: 186–87
14, 28: 186–87
15, 37: 28
16, 32: 68
18, 19: 68
18, 22: 102–3
21: 91–92
22: 179
22, 39: 83–84
22, 40: 68

2 Kings
1, 17: 68
2: 75
6, 8-7, 20: 25–26
6, 19: 114
8, 18: 68
8, 25: 68
8, 28-10, 27: 24

486   ANCIENT SOURCES INDEX

2 Kings (*cont.*)
9-10: 390
9, 14-36: 29
9, 21-26: 24
9, 27: 29
9, 30-37: 24
10, 1-12: 24
10, 7: 29
10, 11: 29
10, 14: 29
10, 18-28: 187–88
10, 28: 68
10, 31: 29
10, 32-33: 24–25
10, 32-34: 179–80
11, 1: 68
11, 1-20: 178–79
12, 18: 24–25
12, 18-19: 38
12, 18-20: 179–80
13, 1-8: 179–80
13, 1-9: 38
13, 2: 29
13, 5: 38
13, 11: 29
13, 12: 26
13, 25: 25–26
14: 178–79
14, 7: 25–26
14, 8-14: 25–26
14, 11-15: 26
14, 24: 29
14, 25: 26, 27, 39, 82–83, 105
15, 8-12: 180–81
15, 9: 29
15, 10: 27, 29, 31
15, 10-11: 31
15, 13: 27
15, 14: 28, 31
15, 19-20: 28, 87–88, 176, 177, 179
15, 23-26: 180–81
15, 25: 30, 31, 216
15, 29: 28, 32, 87–88, 178
15, 30: 28, 31, 87–88
16: 174–75
16, 5: 28
16, 5-9: 87–88, 177

16, 9: 178
17, 1-6: 87–88, 177
17, 3: 31, 32
19, 9: 119
19, 19-25: 193
20, 18: 116
22, 1-23, 30: 178–79
23, 17-18: 143
23, 26: 276–77
24, 3: 276–77

1 Chronicles
5, 6: 178
5, 26: 178
8, 34: 72
9, 40: 72

2 Chronicles
2, 17-18: 187
11, 1-12: 178–79
11, 2: 436
21, 12-15: 58–59
28, 8-15: 320–21
28, 16-21: 177
36, 23: 193

Ezra
1, 2-4: 193

Nehemiah
6, 7: 144–45
6, 14: 144–45
9, 32: 152

Job
4, 11: 116
28, 28: 208
34, 8: 30–31
34, 22: 30–31
37, 1: 205
37, 1-5: 73
41, 9: 116

Psalms
1-2: 263–64
5, 5: 73
5, 6: 30–31

ANCIENT SOURCES INDEX   487

6, 9: 30–31
7, 12: 73
7, 14: 117
9, 7-8: 295
14, 4: 30–31
18, 3: 73
18, 10: 67–68
18, 33: 73
18, 48: 73
22, 15: 116
28, 3: 30–31
29: 56–57
36, 13: 30–31
37, 15: 29
46, 10: 29
53, 1: 114
53, 5: 30–31
55, 3: 220
64, 3: 30–31
68, 32-35: 67–68
76, 4: 29
82, 1-2: 67
89, 8-9: 220–21
92, 8: 30–31
92, 10: 30–31, 116
94, 4: 30–31
94, 16: 30–31
96, 10: 295
98, 6: 295
98, 9: 295
99, 1: 295
99, 4: 295
101, 8: 30–31
103, 25: 73
104, 3: 67–68
106: 247, 248–50
116, 19: 426
141, 4: 30–31
141, 9: 30–31

Proverbs
9, 10: 208
22, 28: 85
23, 10: 85

Ecclesiastes
12, 13-14: 208, 263–64

Song of Solomon
1, 2: 253
1, 3: 253
1, 4: 253
1, 12: 253
2, 1-2: 254
2, 3: 253
2, 13: 253
4, 10: 253
4, 10-11: 253
5, 2: 253
5, 2-7: 342–43
5, 6: 253–54
5, 6-8: 253–54
6, 1: 253–54
6, 11: 253
7, 9: 253
7, 13: 253
7, 14: 253
8, 10: 415–16

Isaiah
1-39: 37
1, 1: 104–5, 185–86
2, 10: 432–33
2, 17-18: 312
2, 21: 432–33
2, 22: 312
2, 25: 312
3, 3: 312
3, 5: 312
5, 8: 85, 175
7: 28
7, 1-2: 87–88
7, 1-9: 174–75
8, 1: 472
8, 1-4: 105
8, 1-10: 28
8, 23: 28
9, 1: 426
9, 5-7: 57
10, 5: 281
11, 1-9: 57
13, 16: 320–21
17, 1-3: 28
19, 1: 67–68
20, 1-3: 472

488 ANCIENT SOURCES INDEX

Isaiah (*cont.*)
20, 2-4: 268
22: 248
22, 13: 114–15
23, 13: 116
24, 1: 237
25, 8: 435, 436
28, 1-3: 103–4
31: 249
31, 1: 250
31, 2: 30–31
31, 4-5: 250
31, 8-9: 250
39, 8: 98
40-55: 73
40-66: 57
40, 2: 311–12
40, 6: 98
40, 18: 73
43, 12: 73
44, 9-17: 77
45, 14: 73
45, 22: 73
46, 9: 73
47, 3: 320–21
52, 15: 428
54, 1-8: 366
62, 3-5: 429
65, 1-2: 428–29
66, 15: 67–68

Jeremiah
1: 98
1, 9: 148
2: 249
2, 1: 98
2, 1-9: 249–50
2, 2: 159, 162, 250
2, 3: 250
2, 5: 159–60
2, 7: 250
2, 8: 250
2, 9: 250
2, 21: 250
2, 24: 250
2, 31: 220
3: 462–63

3, 1: 143
3, 14: 366
4, 4: 207, 250
6: 207
6, 11: 207
6, 15: 116
7, 20: 207
7, 26: 102–3
10, 25: 207
13: 98, 207–8
13, 22-26: 320–21
15, 1: 148
16: 105
16, 1: 98
18, 20: 207
19: 166
21, 1: 98
21, 5: 207
21, 12: 207
22, 2-3: 292
24, 1: 98
24, 7: 256–57
25, 1: 98
25, 15: 207
26: 98
26, 1: 115, 279–80
27: 166
28, 7: 430
29, 23: 320–21
30, 23: 207
31, 4: 429
31, 20: 266
31, 22: 366
32, 31-32: 207
32, 37: 207
40, 11-12: 46
49, 35: 29
50, 4-5: 57
50, 19-20: 57
51, 6: 432

Ezekiel
1-3: 98
4: 98
4, 2: 152
7, 1: 98
8: 102–3

8, 1: 98
12: 98
12, 1: 98
16: 70, 101, 233, 366, 462–63
16, 1-13: 162
16, 13: 429–30
16, 18-19: 159–60
16, 37: 320–21
19: 248
23: 70, 233
23, 9-10: 159–60
23, 29: 430
24: 105
27, 30: 430

Hosea
1-2: 56
1-3: 14–15, 18, 50, 56–57, 92, 97, 101–3, 144,
    200–1, 230, 231–32, 233–34, 317, 323–24,
    326–29, 344, 351, 352–53, 357–58, 366, 373,
    376, 399, 400, 402, 412, 426–30, 436, 453,
    455–56, 464, 471–73, 474, 476, 478–79
1-4: 233–34
1, 1: 23, 37, 58–59, 69, 98, 119, 143, 185–86,
    269–70, 276–77
1, 1-9: 298
1, 1-14, 6: 132–33
1, 2: 29, 70, 91, 98, 131, 187–88, 263, 306, 317,
    326, 369–70, 389, 398
1, 2-2, 1: 267
1, 2-2, 3: 472
1, 2-5: 29–30
1, 2-9: 472–73
1, 3: 317, 413–14
1, 3-9: 317
1, 4: 50, 91, 113, 276–77, 280, 289
1, 4-5: 398
1, 4-9: 390
1, 4b: 279–81
1, 5: 50, 309, 355–56
1, 6: 304–5
1, 6-2, 5: 127
1, 6-9: 268
1, 7: 132, 304–5
1, 8: 91, 304–5
1, 8-9: 105
1, 9: 96, 221, 256–57, 281–82, 422

1, 10: 426, 428–29, 436
1, 10-12: 428–29
1, 11: 398
2: 70–72, 73
2, 1: 91, 131, 267, 281–82, 414, 421,
    422, 428–29
2, 1-2: 293–94, 298
2, 1-3: 56–57, 101–2, 161–62, 167,
    311–12, 368
2, 1-5: 127
2, 1-13: 327
2, 2: 29, 50, 117, 281–82, 326
2, 2-3: 329, 389
2, 2-13: 317, 323–24
2, 2-23: 267, 318
2, 3: 96, 98, 233, 256–57, 304–5, 311–12, 320,
    323, 398, 414
2, 3-4: 323, 328
2, 4: 306, 326, 368, 390
2, 4-5: 368
2, 4-6: 311–12
2, 4-15: 29, 455–56
2, 4-17: 342–43
2, 4-25: 14, 98, 105, 207–8, 345–46, 472
2, 4a: 101
2, 4aαb: 100
2, 4b-5: 101–2
2, 5: 186–87, 309, 310, 326, 370, 389, 397,
    411, 464
2, 5-6: 462–63
2, 5a: 368
2, 6: 293–94, 304–5, 323, 342, 368, 389–
    90, 397
2, 6-7: 310, 323, 359, 384, 385
2, 7: 96–97, 114, 162, 305, 306, 326, 372–73
2, 7b: 100, 101
2, 8: 69, 186–87, 311–12, 326, 397, 402
2, 8-9: 100, 105, 253–54
2, 9: 50, 96–97, 253–54, 303–4, 305, 309, 311–
    12, 323, 397, 402
2, 9-15: 369
2, 10: 50, 159–60, 162, 187–88, 233, 306, 320–
    21, 369, 372, 422–23
2, 10a: 101–2
2, 10a-11: 100
2, 11: 101–2, 113, 135, 303–4, 309, 310, 369
2, 11-15: 256–57, 311–12

ANCIENT SOURCES INDEX

Hosea (*cont.*)
2, 12: 100, 101, 187–88, 233, 305, 372, 397, 402
2, 12-13: 326
2, 12-15: 105
2, 12a: 329
2, 13: 69, 187–88, 369
2, 13-15: 126
2, 13-15a: 100
2, 14: 50, 115, 117, 305, 309, 323, 369, 372, 398
2, 14-19: 127
2, 14-23: 92, 268, 317, 323, 325
2, 15: 96–97, 101–2, 113, 117, 251, 305, 306, 309, 322–23, 397, 398
2, 16: 69, 135, 163–64, 187–88, 298, 310, 464
2, 16-17: 100
2, 16-18: 309
2, 16-20: 429–30
2, 16-22: 49–50, 162
2, 16-25: 56–57, 101–2, 167, 311–12, 325, 455–56, 464
2, 17: 69, 72, 159, 162, 250, 257, 283
2, 18: 163–64, 167, 306, 396, 397, 398, 403, 404–5, 415–16
2, 18-19: 369
2, 18-20: 92
2, 18-22: 57
2, 18-23: 318, 398, 399
2, 19: 50, 304, 306, 359, 398, 429
2, 19-20: 269
2, 19-22: 50
2, 20: 293–94, 369
2, 20-22: 458–59
2, 20-25: 256–57
2, 21: 299–300, 304–5, 369, 398
2, 21-22: 310, 359, 404–5, 412
2, 21-23: 385, 398
2, 22: 369, 398, 419
2, 22-4, 1: 127
2, 23: 114, 267, 426, 427, 436
2, 24: 50
2, 25: 293–94, 304–5, 310, 357, 418, 453–54, 461
3, 1: 233, 303–5, 420
3, 1-4: 98, 105–6
3, 1-5: 267–69
3, 2: 113, 359, 372, 397, 398, 472

3, 2-4: 126
3, 3: 293–94, 309, 359
3, 3-4: 388, 389
3, 4: 77, 134, 187–88, 279, 280–81, 306
3, 4-5: 88–89
3, 5: 56–57, 58–59, 105–6, 189, 255, 269, 281, 303–4, 308–9
4-11: 234, 475–76
4-14: 37–38, 50, 57–58, 96–97, 98–99, 230, 231–32
4, 1-3: 215–16
4, 1: 234, 250, 269–70, 293–94, 398
4, 1-2: 101, 200–1
4, 1-3: 385
4, 1-5, 1: 126
4, 1-5, 7: 189
4, 1-6: 294
4, 1-11, 11: 237–38
4, 1a: 102–3
4, 1b: 103
4, 1b-2a: 103
4, 2: 43, 234, 297, 306
4, 2b: 102–3
4, 3: 15, 256, 396, 398, 404, 405
4, 4: 100, 103, 306
4, 4-7: 296
4, 4-10: 101
4, 4b: 104–5
4, 5: 44, 221, 343, 366
4, 6: 100, 132, 221, 250, 305–6, 309, 310, 462–63
4, 7-8: 104–5
4, 7-14: 29
4, 8: 305–6
4, 9: 289, 303–4, 309
4, 10: 221, 305–6, 355, 369–70
4, 10-11: 127
4, 10-15: 44
4, 10-19: 89, 343
4, 10a: 104–5
4, 11: 44
4, 11-14: 101
4, 12: 77, 187–88, 283, 306, 355, 369–70, 398
4, 12-14: 77
4, 12b: 101–2
4, 12c-13c: 344
4, 13: 187–88, 306, 398

ANCIENT SOURCES INDEX 491

4, 13-14: 127, 187–88, 321, 369–70
4, 13a: 104–5
4, 14: 44, 113, 116, 251, 306
4, 14-19: 344–45
4, 14a: 104–5
4, 14b: 344–45
4, 15: 75–76, 216, 221
4, 16: 231, 307, 397, 401
4, 16-19: 101–2
4, 17: 256–57, 288–89, 306
4, 17-19: 344
4, 18: 113, 134, 294, 305
4, 19: 306
5-6: 234–35
5-7: 96–97
5, 1: 104–5, 116, 129, 309
5, 1-2: 101, 356–57, 398
5, 1-6, 3: 102–3
5, 1b-2a: 129
5, 2: 113, 306, 309
5, 3: 44, 105–6, 305–6, 369–70
5, 3-4: 89, 101–2
5, 4: 230, 294, 303–4
5, 5: 305–6
5, 6: 78, 96–97, 230, 253–54, 288–89, 309,
    312, 398
5, 6-7: 100, 101
5, 7: 77–78, 113, 251, 305–6, 309, 356, 397, 398
5, 8: 75–76, 177–78, 398
5, 8-6, 3: 475–76
5, 8-6, 6: 173, 176, 177, 181, 234
5, 8-9: 174–75, 312
5, 8-11: 99, 100–1
5, 8-14: 30, 101
5, 8-15: 82–83, 188, 235, 264–65
5, 10: 104–5, 175, 306, 309, 310
5, 10-6, 6: 229–30
5, 11: 70, 176, 306
5, 11-6, 3: 37, 40–42, 44, 45
5, 12: 129, 310, 397
5, 12-6, 3: 105–6
5, 12-13: 40
5, 12-14: 96–97, 99, 101, 102, 103–4, 176
5, 13: 42, 88–89, 96–97, 113, 191–92, 240, 306,
    356, 384, 475–76
5, 13-6, 1: 40, 42, 43, 47–48
5, 13b: 40

5, 14: 96–97, 251, 298, 397
5, 14-15: 41, 264–65, 310
5, 15: 41, 96–97, 303–4, 305–6, 308–9, 356–
    57, 422–23
5, 15-6, 3: 100
5, 15-6, 6: 99, 101, 176–77
6: 430–32
6, 1: 41–42, 43, 240, 298, 303–4, 475–76
6, 1-2: 251
6, 1-3: 78, 96–97, 105, 229–30, 234, 235, 264–
    65, 312
6, 1-6: 298
6, 1-11a: 188
6, 2: 41–42, 426, 430–31
6, 3: 397, 398
6, 3-4: 127
6, 4: 264, 294, 307, 312, 397
6, 4-6: 235
6, 4b: 104–5
6, 5: 96–97, 150, 152, 221, 235
6, 5-6: 298
6, 5a: 96
6, 5b: 96
6, 6: 78, 100, 264–65, 294, 306, 312, 426, 436
6, 6a: 431
6, 6b: 103
6, 7: 30, 96, 305–6, 475–76
6, 7-7, 2: 103
6, 7-7, 12: 101
6, 7-9: 30–31, 100–1
6, 7ff: 103
6, 8: 96, 103, 113, 306
6, 8-7, 1: 127
6, 8-9: 216
6, 9: 96, 103–5, 113, 114–15, 306
6, 9-10: 383–84
6, 9a: 103
6, 10: 44, 96, 383–84
6, 10a: 104–5
6, 10b: 101–2
6, 11: 397
6, 11a: 105–6
6, 11b: 42
6, 11b-7, 1: 43, 235
6, 11b-7, 1b: 188
7-8: 187–95, 235–36
7, 1: 43, 85, 86, 113, 189, 240, 256–57, 306, 310

ANCIENT SOURCES INDEX

Hosea (*cont.*)

7, 1-2: 43
7, 1-3: 37, 44, 47, 100
7, 1-7: 42-45, 475-76
7, 1-7, 7: 45
7, 1-10: 45
7, 1-13: 82-83
7, 1b: 103
7, 1C-7: 188
7, 2: 104-5, 113, 115, 189, 193, 305-6
7, 3: 42, 43, 104-5, 189, 235, 292-93
7, 3-7: 31, 189, 190, 275
7, 3-9: 235
7, 4: 44, 89, 101-2, 103-4, 113, 189, 235, 305-6
7, 4-7: 44-45, 307
7, 4aα: 104-5
7, 4b: 104
7, 5: 45, 113, 114, 235, 356
7, 5-6: 100-1, 189
7, 5-9: 100
7, 5a: 104-5
7, 5b: 104
7, 6: 44, 189, 235
7, 7: 189, 307, 386
7, 7-3: 103-4
7, 7a-b: 189
7, 7aβ: 104-5
7, 7b: 45, 104-5
7, 7c-d: 189
7, 8: 235, 307, 355, 397
7, 8-9: 102-3
7, 8-10: 45
7, 8-12: 103-4, 188, 190, 236
7, 8b: 103-4
7, 8b-9: 100-1
7, 9: 230, 355
7, 10: 253-54, 256-57, 303-4, 306, 398
7, 10a: 104
7, 11: 46, 49, 70, 185-86, 235-36, 251, 307, 310, 384, 397, 454
7, 11-12: 88-89, 205
7, 11b: 96-97
7, 11f: 454
7, 12: 310, 396, 397
7, 12-13: 126, 127
7, 13: 305-6
7, 13-8, 1: 127

7, 13-16: 101, 105-6, 188, 190
7, 13a-c: 190
7, 14: 113, 114, 303-4, 306, 312
7, 15: 46, 235-36
7, 16: 113, 134, 235-36, 303-4, 355-56, 398
8: 31-32
8-9: 329
8, 1: 185-86, 230, 234, 256-57, 312-13, 397
8, 1-3: 101
8, 1-4: 82-83
8, 1a-b: 190
8, 1b: 103
8, 1c-d: 190
8, 2: 190, 312-13
8, 3: 312-13
8, 4: 103, 277, 306, 383
8, 4-8a: 188
8, 4a-b: 190-91
8, 4b-6: 101-2
8, 5: 306, 309, 398
8, 5-6: 73, 74, 78, 185-86, 187-88, 398
8, 6: 74, 306, 398
8, 7: 195, 235-36, 287, 307, 397
8, 7-10: 101
8, 8-14: 188
8, 9: 70, 88-89, 113, 116, 230, 235-36, 250, 306, 384, 397
8, 10: 88-89, 113, 116, 130
8, 11-12: 101, 306
8, 12: 235-36
8, 13: 185-86, 235-36, 257, 303-4, 305-6, 309, 398
8, 13aβ: 74
8, 13bβ: 283
8, 14: 116, 193, 235-36, 309, 397
8, 14aα: 74
9-11: 237-38
9, 1: 46-47, 89, 230, 235-36, 305-6, 369-70
9, 1-2: 101-2
9, 1-3: 46-48
9, 1-4: 127
9, 1-11, 7: 237-38
9, 2: 114, 235-36, 357, 397, 398
9, 3: 46-47, 49, 236, 257, 283, 293-94, 303-4, 305-6, 398
9, 3-4a: 101
9, 3b: 104-5

ANCIENT SOURCES INDEX

9, 3ff: 454
9, 4: 113, 398
9, 4-6: 47
9, 4a: 104–5
9, 5: 101–2
9, 6: 101, 398
9, 7: 134, 305–6, 309, 432
9, 7-9: 101
9, 8: 104–5
9, 9: 305–6, 309
9, 9-10, 14: 127
9, 10: 72–73, 78, 104–5, 113, 248–49, 251–52,
  253–54, 306, 357, 397, 398
9, 10-11, 11: 237–38
9, 10-17: 101–2
9, 10a: 250, 251, 252
9, 10b: 252
9, 11: 366
9, 11-16: 356
9, 12: 237, 303–4
9, 12-13: 462–63
9, 13: 237, 397
9, 14: 366
9, 15: 75–76, 237, 278, 294, 304–6
9, 15-17: 82–83
9, 15aα: 75–76
9, 16: 237, 357, 397
9, 16-17: 462–63
9, 16Q: 115
9, 17: 237, 309
9, 27: 431–32
10: 31–32
10, 1: 113, 230, 250, 251–52, 306, 357, 397
10, 1-2: 77, 101–2, 187–88
10, 2: 306
10, 3: 277
10, 4: 114–15, 306, 397, 402
10, 5: 75, 187–88, 306
10, 5-6: 31, 88–89
10, 5-6a: 101–2
10, 6: 46, 49, 306, 398
10, 7: 237, 309, 397
10, 8: 187–88, 237, 278–79, 398, 426,
  432–33, 436
10, 9: 113, 251–52, 305–6
10, 9-10: 309
10, 9-15: 101–2

10, 10: 305–6, 309
10, 11: 251–52, 397
10, 11-13: 307
10, 11b: 237
10, 12: 214–15, 251, 253–54, 308–9, 426, 433
10, 13: 237, 305–6, 357, 397
10, 13-15: 82–83
10, 14: 309, 366
10, 15: 75, 305–6, 309
10, 15b: 278–79
11: 13–14, 265–66, 474
11, 1: 102–3, 105–6, 130, 199, 204, 207–8, 250,
  251, 252, 304–5, 307–8, 402, 426, 433–34,
  436, 454
11, 1-2: 74, 199, 252
11, 1-3: 237
11, 1-4: 199, 248–49, 251–52, 310, 313,
  329, 343–44
11, 1-6: 49–50
11, 1-11: 298
11, 1b: 283, 433–34
11, 2: 69, 72–73, 78, 103, 200, 204, 251, 252,
  306, 307–8, 313
11, 2-5: 127
11, 2b: 72
11, 3: 113, 134, 204, 313
11, 3-4: 200, 201, 202
11, 3a: 102–3, 105–6
11, 3aα: 102–3
11, 3b: 103, 105–6
11, 4: 136, 204, 304–5, 307–8
11, 4aα: 105–6
11, 4b: 102–3
11, 5: 49, 88–89, 198–99, 203, 236, 250, 283,
  303–4, 307–8, 384, 398
11, 5-7: 298, 313
11, 5-9: 203
11, 5a: 102–3
11, 6: 134, 309
11, 6-13, 1: 127
11, 7: 113, 204, 307–8
11, 8: 32–33, 207–8, 265–66
11, 8-9: 103, 208, 237–38, 256–57, 264, 265–66
11, 8-11: 237–38, 298
11, 8a: 105–6
11, 9: 74, 199, 207–8, 262–63, 303–4, 309
11, 10: 397

494 ANCIENT SOURCES INDEX

Hosea (*cont.*)

11, 10-11: 199, 204, 250, 307–8, 313, 386
11, 11: 98, 198–99, 208, 236, 250, 384, 398, 434
11, 11b: 257
11, 12-12, 6: 214–15
12: 238–39, 255–56
12, 1: 70, 186–87, 214, 236, 306, 397, 398
12, 1-2: 43, 46–48, 220, 238
12, 1-3: 103, 212–13, 214, 223
12, 1-7: 212–15, 223
12, 1-14, 9: 238
12, 2: 46, 47–48, 49, 114, 306, 357
12, 2-3: 220
12, 2b: 47–48
12, 3: 103, 303–4, 309
12, 3-4: 75
12, 3-5: 282–83
12, 3-7: 182, 256
12, 4: 308, 414–15
12, 4-5: 212–13, 222–23, 238, 255, 308
12, 5: 253–54, 313
12, 5-6: 105
12, 5a: 223–24
12, 6: 222, 293, 308–9, 313
12, 6-7: 212–13
12, 7: 214–15, 303–4, 313
12, 8: 238, 306
12, 8-12: 182
12, 8-14: 215–16, 221
12, 9: 29, 190, 257
12, 10: 74, 454
12, 11: 75–76, 398
12, 12: 129, 217, 306, 398
12, 12-13: 238
12, 13: 147–49, 282–83
12, 14: 257, 282–83, 454
12, 15: 217, 251, 303–4, 306, 309
12, 15-13, 15: 216–17
12, 100: 283
13-14: 239–41
13, 1: 72–73, 113, 217, 239, 251–52, 256–57, 306
13, 1-2: 73, 76, 78
13, 2: 133, 187–88, 306, 397
13, 2-3: 103
13, 3: 128, 397
13, 3-10: 126
13, 4: 126, 190, 251, 252, 257, 294, 398

13, 4-5: 239
13, 4-6: 248–49, 251–52
13, 5: 250, 251, 310, 398
13, 6: 250, 251, 252, 305–6
13, 6-8: 239
13, 6-11: 217, 221
13, 7: 113, 357, 397
13, 7-8: 269, 310
13, 8: 230, 397
13, 9: 414
13, 9-11: 82–83, 88–89, 189, 190–91, 278–79
13, 10: 306, 309
13, 11: 309
13, 12: 305–6
13, 12-13: 366
13, 12-14: 103
13, 12-14, 1: 218–19, 221–22
13, 13: 251, 308, 356, 361
13, 13-14, 1: 218
13, 14: 240, 426, 434–36
13, 14a: 239
13, 14b: 454–55
13, 14b-16: 313
13, 15: 310, 397, 398
13, 15-14, 1: 100
13, 15-14, 6: 126
13, 16: 240, 309, 366, 462–63
14, 1: 264, 305–6, 387
14, 1-3: 240
14, 2: 132, 230, 303–4, 305–6, 313,
    412–13, 422
14, 2-4: 105, 214–15, 218–19, 299, 308–9
14, 2-5: 37, 43
14, 2-9: 48–49, 100
14, 3: 303–4, 313, 384, 397
14, 4: 240, 294, 306, 313
14, 4-8: 313
14, 4b: 458
14, 5: 105–6, 241, 256–57, 304–5, 309, 310,
    313, 397, 475–76
14, 5-7: 240, 398
14, 5-9: 103, 299, 313
14, 6: 251, 254, 397
14, 6-8: 249, 252–54
14, 6-9: 57
14, 7: 397
14, 8: 304, 306, 397

ANCIENT SOURCES INDEX

14, 9: 253–54, 256–57, 263–64, 299–300, 310, 357
14, 9-10: 127
14, 10: 100, 219, 238, 248, 263–64, 305–6, 309, 313
14, 19: 303–4

Joel
1, 1: 104–5
2, 12-27: 313

Amos
1, 1: 98, 104–5, 185–86
1, 1-2: 143
1, 2: 255
1, 3-3, 2: 215–16
1, 4: 248
1, 7: 248
1, 10: 248
1, 12: 248
2, 2: 248
2, 5: 248
2, 8: 148–49, 186–87
2, 15: 116
4, 1: 186–87
5, 11: 186–87
6, 4: 83–84
6, 6: 186–87
7-9: 98
7, 10-17: 98
9, 11: 255

Jonah
1, 1: 105
3: 313
4, 11: 402

Micah
1, 1: 104–5, 185–86
2, 2: 85, 175
3, 1: 292
6, 4: 147
6, 6-7: 264–65

Nehemiah
1, 9: 131
2, 3: 237

3, 5-7: 320–21

Habakkuk
3, 8: 67–68
3, 15: 67–68

Zephaniah
1, 1: 104–5
3: 57

Haggai
2, 20: 98

Zechariah
1, 2-6a: 58–59
1, 3: 303, 313
7, 1: 98
14: 320–21

Malachi
1, 2-3: 427
3, 7: 313
3, 16-18: 151–52
3, 22: 147

New Testament
Matthew
2, 13: 433–34
2, 15: 130, 433–34, 436
2, 21: 434
2, 21-14: 429
3, 17: 433–34
4, 1-11: 433–34
4, 3: 433–34
4, 6: 433–34
4, 15: 426
5, 1: 433–34
5, 7: 431–32
5, 23: 431–32
6, 6: 431–32
8, 4: 431–32
8, 29: 433–34
9, 11-13: 431
12, 2: 431
12, 3-4: 431
14, 33: 433–34
16, 16: 433–34

ANCIENT SOURCES INDEX

Matthew (*cont.*)
16, 21: 430–31, 436
17, 23: 430–31
20, 19: 430–31
22, 1-14: 429
25, 1-13: 429
26, 63: 433–34
27, 40: 433–34

Mark
2, 15-18: 431–32
2, 19-20: 429
2, 23-28: 431–32

Luke
5, 27-32: 431–32
6, 1-5: 431–32
18, 33: 430–31
19, 41-44: 430
21, 20-22: 432
23, 27-31: 432
23, 30: 436
24, 7: 430–31
24, 46: 430–31

John
3, 29: 429

Acts
10, 40: 430–31, 436

Romans
1, 10: 427
6, 23: 288–89
8, 14: 427–28
9, 25: 426, 427, 436, 453–54, 461–62
9, 26: 427
10, 19: 428
10, 20-21: 428–29
15, 10: 426
15, 11: 426
15, 21: 428

1 Corinthians
15: 435
15, 3-4: 430–31
15, 4: 430–31, 436

15, 12: 435
15, 55: 436, 454–55

2 Corinthians
9, 10: 433
11, 2: 429

Galatians
3, 8: 426
3, 26: 427–28

Ephesians
5, 31-32: 429

1 Peter
2, 10: 427, 436

Revelation
6, 15-17: 432–33
6, 16: 436
17, 1-2: 430
17, 4: 430
17, 16: 430
18, 3: 430
18, 19: 430
19, 7-8: 429–30, 436
21, 2: 429–30
21, 12: 429

Ancient Near Eastern Texts and Inscriptions
ANET
284: 87–88

Annals
18, 3′–7′ 178
23, 1′-17′ 178
24, 3′–11: 178

Baal Cycle
KTU 1, 2 IV: 67–68

Calnah Summaries
4, 5′–8′ 178
4, 15′–17′ 178
9:r3–4: 178
9:r9: 178
13, 17′–18′ 178

ANCIENT SOURCES INDEX

COS
2, 295– 96: 87–88

DUL
233: 116

KTU
1, 1 IV, lines 2-4: 56–57
1, 1 V, line 22: 73
1, 2 IV: 67–68
1, 6.i.48: 115

Rabbinic and Other Jewish Literature
Exodus Rabbah
46, 4: 422–23

Genesis Rabbah
84, 19: 412–13

Lamentations Rabbah
14, 2: 422–23
Prologue 2: 422–23

Midrash Tanchuma
Massei 7: 421

Numbers Rabbah
2, 15: 419, 420–21
2, 16: 421
2, 12: 421
2, 13: 421
2, 14: 421
2, 15: 420–21
2, 16: 421
2, 17: 421
23, 8: 421

Pesachim (Babylonian Talmud)
87a-88: 415–19

Pirkei de Rav Kahana
16, 8: 418–19

Sifrei Deuteronomy
342: 418–19

Sifrei Numbers
131: 421–22

Tanchuma Tzav
14, 1: 419

Author Index

For the benefit of digital users, indexed terms that span two pages (e.g., 52–53) may, on occasion, appear on only one of those pages.

Abma, R., 318
Ackroyd, P., 387–88
Alexander, J., 325
Alt, A., 173–81
Alter, R., 261, 263, 267
Andersen, F., 1, 37, 116, 118, 125, 431
Andrews, M., 440–43, 444, 446–47, 449–50
Aune, D., 430

Bailey, R., 454, 457
Barr, J., 125–26
Barth, K., 288–89
Ben Zvi, E., 9–10, 37–38, 165, 201–2, 325, 328, 384
Beverly, J., 377
Bignall, S., 381
Birch, B., 382
Blyth, C., 362
Boda, M., 144
Boer, R., 86–87
Bos, J. M., 37–38
Braaten, L., 15, 399, 400
Brandenburger, E., 296
Bratten, L., 11
Brenner, A., 341
Bridgeman, V., 347–48, 457–58
Broad, R., 461–62
Brueggemann, W., 232
Buber, M., 193
Byrd, P., 341

Castelo, D., 262
Cataldo, J., 59, 472–73, 477
Cathcart, K., 131
Chaney, M., 86, 90

Chapman, C., 353
Christenson, L., 440, 444–45, 448
Ciampa, R., 435
Claassens, J., 328
Clines, D., 353–54
Clover, C., 358
Colgan, E., 362
Connell, R., 352
Cook, S., 9, 142, 145–46
Cranfield, C., 427–29
Cross, F. M., 100
Curtis, B., 144

Dahood, M. J., 114
Dar, S., 84–85
David, C., 132–33
Davis, E., 86–87, 90
Day, J., 37–38
Day, L., 160–61
Day, P., 320
Dearman, J. A., 9, 42–43, 44, 230, 252, 383, 390
Derrida, J., 344
Dewrell, H., 119
Dines, J., 127–28
Dobson, R., 440, 442
Dube, M., 383
Dunn, J., 427–28
Dylan, B., 440

Eichrodt, W., 287
Eidevall, G., 1, 231–32
Eilberg-Schwarz, H., 358
Elliot, P., 375–76, 378
Ellwood, G., 317
Elvey, A., 15

AUTHOR INDEX

Evans, C., 433–34
Eyerman, R., 325

Fales, F. M., 44–45, 46–47
Fernandez, J., 354
Fiorenza, S., 17
Fontaine, C., 341
Foster, R., 428–29
Fowl, S., 270
France, R., 433–34
Fraser, B., 440
Frechette, C., 327–28
Fredericks, D. C., 114
Freedman, D., 1, 37, 116, 118, 125, 322–23, 431
Fuchs, E., 12
Fuller, R., 126

Gafney, W., 320–21, 454–55, 458
Gelston, A., 124–25, 132–33
Gibbs, R., 231
Glenny, W., 128
Goldingay, J., 14–15, 343, 352–53, 473–74
Gordon, R., 131
Goswell, G., 382
Graetz, N., 342
Granosky, R., 326–27
Graybill, R., 164, 321–22, 358, 365, 366–67, 371
Gruber, M., 10, 13–14, 46, 50, 296, 343, 433, 436
Gundry, R., 431, 434

Habel, N., 15
Haddox, S., 14–15, 166–67
Halpern, B., 192
Harper, W., 125
Harrison, C., 128
Hartsfield, W., 229, 455, 457
Hayes, J., 83
Hays, R., 435
Herman, J., 463
Hertig, Y. L., 479
Holt, E., 255–56
Hong, S. H., 475–76
Hornsby, T., 167, 371–72
Humphreys, L., 261, 263, 267
Hurvitz, A., 112
Hutton, J., 115
Hwang, J., 199, 202, 207–8, 472, 473, 477

Jameson, F., 344
Janzen, G., 265–66
Jennings, W., 459
Jeremias, J., 1, 97, 99–101, 106–7, 248
Jones, E., 387
Junior, N., 337–38

Kakkanattu, J., 266
Kaminka, A., 128
Keefe, A., 13–14, 163, 200, 342, 346–47, 366, 377, 453
Kelle, B., 91–92, 294–95, 320–21, 323
Kidner, D., 318
Kim, B., 474
Kim, S., 127
King, P., 9–10
Kinyua, J., 381–82
Kirk-Duggan, C., 347–48
Kittay, E., 231–32
Ko, G., 474
Koch, K., 295, 296, 297
Kock, K., 287–90
Kuhnigk, W., 117

Landy, F., 200–1, 205, 222, 254, 342–43, 411, 423, 475
Langton, S., 213
Lee, Y. K., 471
Leith, M., 341
Levin, A., 117
Lidbeck, B., 430–31
Liew, S.-P., 473, 477
Lim, Bo H., 472–73, 477
Limburg, J., 1
Loya, M., 15
Lust, J., 130
Luz, U., 431–32

Macintosh, A., 118, 119, 267, 427–28, 431, 435–36
Macwilliam, S., 13–14, 357–58, 366–67, 370–71
Marlow, H., 201, 402
Marzouk, S., 115
Mays, J., 37, 229–30, 266, 387–88
McKenzie, J., 264
Menken, M., 431
Miller, J., 83
Morag, S., 115, 116, 118

Morris, G., 11, 199
Morrison, T., 461, 462–64
Morrow, W., 326–27
Moughtin-Mumby, S., 267
Müller, K., 296

Na'aman, N., 59–60
Nagouse, E., 321–22
Namaste, V., 372–73, 374
Neef, H.-D., 125
Newton, H., 454–55
Nissinen, M., 102–6
Nobert, G., 440
Nogalski, J., 146, 200–1, 207–8, 455–56
Nolland, J., 432–33
Nwaoru, E., 11, 229, 403
Nyberg, H. S., 110, 114

O'Connor, K., 206, 326, 327–28
Odell, M, 343
O'Donovan, O., 289–90, 299

Parr, J., 440
Past Regt, L., de., 11
Patterson, G., 125–26, 129
Perdue, L., 382
Peterson, A., 440
Polaski, D., 440
Premnath, D. L., 86–87

Rabin, H., 118
Rad, G. von 288
Rahlfs, A., 431
Rendsburg, G., 112–13, 114, 115, 116, 118, 119
Ricoeur, P., 232
Rivers, F., 440
Rollston, C. A., 118
Ross, M.-S., 374–75
Routledge, R., 202
Rudnig-Zelt, S., 9–10, 102–6
Rudolph, W., 114

Said, E., 90, 389
Sakenfeld, K., 319
Schart, A., 150
Schenker, A., 124–25
Schneiders, S., 12–13, 17

Schniedewind, W., 116, 118, 125
Scholz, S., 9, 13–14
Schüngel-Straumann, H., 13–14, 200–1, 202, 343–44
Schütte, W., 97
Seifert, B., 231–32
Seifrid, M., 428
Setel, T., 340–41
Sherwood, Y., 161–62, 165–66, 267, 320–21, 322, 328, 342, 344, 411, 417, 423
Shulman, G., 463
Sinclair, L., 10
Sivan, D., 116, 118
Smolarz, S., 430
Sowers, B., 454–55
Speiser, E., 116
Sperber, A., 131
Spiegel, S., 150
Starr, R., 324
Steinberg, M., 440, 442–43, 445
Strawn, B., 204, 208
Stuart, D., 1, 427–28, 433
Stulman, L., 325
Stump, E., 382
Sugirtharajah, R., 380, 468–69
Sun, C., 476–77, 478–79
Sweeney, M., 267–68, 303, 382

Talbot, M., 440
Tan, N., 324
Tang, S., 473, 474–75, 477
Taylor-Guthrie, D., 461–62
Tov, E., 126; 131
Tully, E., 114, 118

Ulrich, E., 127

Van der Woude, G., 130
Van Ruiten, J., 414–15
Vannoy, R. J., 295
Varghese, S., 472, 477
Vielhauer, R., 100–2
Volkan, V., 325

Wacker, M.-T., 13–14, 97, 102–6, 200–1, 344, 347
Wagner, R., 428

Walter, D., 132–33
Watts, J., 150
Weber, M., 194
Weems, R. J., 160, 163–64, 165, 318, 322, 345–46, 452–53, 456–57, 458, 460
Weinfeld, M., 149
Weitzman, M., 133
Weyde, K., 255
Wieder, A., 116
Wikander, O., 252

Wilson, S., 360
Wolff, H., 1, 9–10, 145–46, 188–89, 229
Wyatt, N., 73–74

Yee, G., 13–14, 86–87, 91–92, 100–2, 163, 164, 165, 200–1, 322, 344–45, 453, 475–76
Yoo, Y., 115, 116–17, 119

Ziegler, J., 127, 128, 431
Zimran, Y., 236